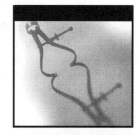

Effective Methods for Software Testing, Second Edition

William E. Perry

WILEY COMPUTER PUBLISHING

John Wiley & Sons, Inc.

NEW YORK • CHICHESTER • WEINHEIM • BRISBANE • SINGAPORE • TORONTO

This book is dedicated to my wife Cynthia, who for many years has been "testing" my ability to live in accordance with our marriage vows. She taught me that testing is a lifelong process, that testing is necessary to assure that you are meeting your objectives, and that testing can be fun if it is performed correctly. Thank you, Cynthia. What you have taught me is incorporated into many of the concepts presented in this book.

Publisher: Robert Ipsen
Editor: Robert M. Elliott
Managing Editor: Angela Smith
Test Design & Composition: PD & PS, Inc.

Published by John Wiley & Sons, Inc.

Published simultaneously in Canada.

This publication is designed to provide accurate and authoritative information in regard to the subject matter covered. It is sold with the understanding that the publisher is not engaged in professional services. If professional advice or other expert assistance is required, the services of a compenent professional person should be sought.

Library of Congress Cataloging-in-Publication Data:
Perry, William E.
    Effective methods for software testing / William Perry.—2nd ed.
        p.   cm.
    Includes bibliographical references.
    ISBN 0-471-35418-X (cl. : alk. paper)
    1. Computer software—Testing.   I. Title.
QA76.76.T48P46   1999
0005.1'421—dc21   99-044927

Printed in the United States of America

10   9   8   7   6   5   4   3

Contents

Acknowledgments

Special thanks go to Randall Rice and Larry Creel, whose creative materials have been incorporated into this book. anyone who has worked on a manuscript of this size knows it cannot be done without the assistance of a superhuman person to convert a rough document into a completed book. My super woman was Sabrina Leon. Thank you Sabrina.

How to Use This Book

This book offers two testing strategies designed to improve deficient capabilities and competencies. The first involves assessment of your organization's software testing capabilities. The second is based on evaluation of an individual software tester's competencies.

Strategy 1: Improving Deficient Software Testing Capabilities

There are eight software testing capabilities that drive the test process. The book can be used to improve deficiency in any of these eight capabilities (see Table I.1):

1. **User satisfaction test capability.** The key to improving user satisfaction with software testing is to involve the user at key points in the software testing process. Chapter 2 explains how to involve the user in developing the test strategy that will provide the framework for testing; Chapter 8 involves the user in defining the test objectives that will be the basis for building a test plan; and Chapter 13 involves the user in defining and executing the acceptance testing of software. User satisfaction can also be improved by regular reporting of the status and results of testing in a manner that makes it easy for the user to understand and take appropriate actions.

2. **Management supports test capability.** Effective testing requires strong management support. Support is needed so that the test strategy meets the needs of

the business, and appropriate time and resources are available to accomplish that strategy. Chapter 1 helps establish the need for management's support by providing a baseline of the current software testing capabilities and competencies. Chapter 2 involves obtaining management's support and concurrence in the test strategy that will be used to drive testing. Chapters 3 through 6 help define the resources that management must provide in order to create a proper environment for software testing. The resources will be used to build and operate a test lab complete with the necessary tools and techniques.

3. **Planning.** If you fail to plan, plan to fail. Chapter 8 explains how to plan a test, together with the components of a test plan.

4. **Training test capability.** Effective software testing begins and ends with education. Chapter 2 defines the test strategy that must include training; and Chapter 6 explains the 11-step testing process in which software testers must be trained.

5. **Use of processes test capability.** Without processing, testing is an art that is subject to significant variation in execution. Processes bring stability and consistency to software testing. Chapter 2 explains the importance of incorporating the use of processes into the test strategy. Chapters 6 through 26 are the generic software testing processes, explained step-by-step which are needed by most software testing organizations.

6. **Tools test capability.** Tools are necessary to provide effective and efficient software testing. Chapter 5 explains the processes for selecting and installing testing tools.

7. **Efficiency test capability.** Efficiency involves planning and performing software testing in a manner that provides the greatest coverage and the maximum assessment of business risks for the resources allocated. Chapters 3 through 5 explain the creation of the test environment that will provide for the greatest efficiency in software testing. Chapter 17 is designed to evaluate test effectiveness and efficiency so that the principles of continuous improvement can be applied to the testing processes.

8. **Quality control test capability.** Experience of leading organizations shows that software testers make as many or more errors in testing than developers make in the building of software systems. It raises the question, "Who tests the testers?" The answer is that quality control within the test process evaluates whether the process has been performed correctly. The test processes included in Chapter 6 through 26 incorporate quality control as a part of the process. Chapter 1 is a high-level quality control that can be used to evaluate software testing organization's capabilities and competencies. This assessment should be conducted on at least an annual basis to determine current status and movement from the previous assessment. Chapter 17 is an overall assessment of the effectiveness of the test processes. This, like the Chapter 1 assessment, establishes a baseline that can be used to determine movement from the previous assessment of test effectiveness.

Strategy 2: Improving Deficient Competencies of Software Testers

Assessing the skills of software testers requires evaluating competencies in five areas:

1. **General Skills.** General skills include such things as communication, professional development, quality principles, and concepts, as well as some methods for software development and maintenance. Information about and insight into these general skills are incorporated in all twenty-six chapters of the book.

2. **Test Skills/Approaches.** These skills involve the principles and concepts of testing, verification and validation methods, as well as test management, standards, and test environment. Chapters 2 through 6 of this book explain these skills and relate them to the strategic and tactical test approaches, techniques, and tools.

3. **Test Planning.** Test planning is a critical component of effective testing. An old axiom states, "If you fail to plan—plan to fail!" Chapter 7 is devoted to developing a software system test plan, and Chapter 13 explains how to build an acceptance test plan.

4. **Test Execution Competencies.** Execution of the test plan involves decomposition from the plan to test design, to performing tests, and through to defect tracking and management. Chapters 8 through 16 and 18 through 26 provide step-by-step processes for test execution. Chapters 8 through 16 incorporate executing a test plan; or Chapters 18 through 26 involve specialized technology testing challenges.

5. **Test Analysis, Reporting, and Improvement Competencies.** This category of competencies includes quantitative measurement, test reporting, and improving the testing process. Chapter 14 provides processes for test analysis and reporting, and Chapter 17 provides the process for improving testing.

Road Map Through This Book

The software testing capability assessment found in Chapter 1 can be used to establish goals for your organization. For example, if the Kiviatt Chart for your software testing capabilities is at Level 1 or 2, you might establish a goal of achieving Level 3 capabilities within two years.

You can establish goals for improving your tester's competencies by using the Quality Assurance Institute's developed common body of knowledge, found on the companion Web site for this book. Also, you might establish a goal to have all of your software testers certified as "Certified Software Test Engineers" within two years.

Once these goals are established, a plan needs to be put into place to accomplish those goals. Much of the insight and materials you'll need to do this can be found in this book. However, it is highly recommended that your testers and test managers attend testing seminars and conferences on a regular basis.

Part Two focuses on building an environment in which effective testing can occur. The environment begins with a test strategy. An important component of that strategy is establishing a software testing methodology, defining your testing techniques, and selecting, installing, and using testing tools.

Part Three provides an 11-step testing process for software testing. It leads testers from establishing test objectives through writing a test report. While this 11-step process needs to be customized for your organization, and perhaps customized for a specific test assignment, it contains all of the components that provide for effective testing.

The 11-step testing process is a generic test process. When that process is used for specialized processes and/or new technologies it needs to be supplemented. Part Four provides those supplements. This section is not intended to be complete, but rather to address the more common technological challenges facing testers. As new technologies are introduced in your organization, for example, voice recognition technology, additional supplements will be needed for the 11-step testing process for those technologies.

Part Five summarizes the types of documentation the testers should develop during the test process.

Table I.1   Using This Book to Improve Software Testing Capabilities and the Competencies of Testers

DEFICIENT CAPABILITY OR COMPETENCY	REFER TO CHAPTER(S)	ACTION ITEMS FOR IMPROVEMENT
Capabilities		
User Satisfaction	2	Involve user in developing test strategy
	7	Involve user in defining test objectives
	8	Report results of testing to user
	13	Involve user in acceptance testing
Management Support	1	Assess current capabilities and competencies
	2	Obtain management concurrence on test strategy
	3–6	Obtain resources to build test environment and processes
Training	2, 6	Obtain strategy and resources for training
Planning	7	Build and use a test plan
Use of Process	2	Incorporate use of processes into test strategy
	6–25	Use step-by-step processes
Tools	5	Select and install needed tools
Efficiency	3–5	Build efficient test environment
	17	Evaluate test effectiveness

(Continues)

Table I.1   *(Continued)*

DEFICIENT CAPABILITY OR COMPETENCY	REFER TO CHAPTER(S)	ACTION ITEMS FOR IMPROVEMENT
Quality Control	1, 17	Conduct regular assessments
	6–25	Incorporate quality control into every process Competencies
General Skills	1–26	Incorporated into all chapters
Test Skills/Test Approaches	2–26	Teaches strategic and tactical test approaches, techniques tools
Test Planning plan	7, 13	Explains how to build and use a test
Test Execution	8–16 18–25	Provides step-by-step test process
Test Analysis, Reporting, and Improvement	14, 17	Process for test analysis, reporting, and improvement

What's New in the Second Edition

This second edition of *Effective Methods for Software Testing* adds both structure and programs to the testing process. Chapter 1 in the new edition begins with new self-assessments on:

1. The adequacy of your testing function
2. The competency of your testers

The assessments results will help determine how to use the book most effectively. The test activities in the previous edition have been reworked into an effective 11-step test process. Each step is presented in a new workbench format. While all 11 steps contain new material, most notable are:

- In Chapter 8, the inspection process is presented in a more detailed format.
- In Chapter 12, guidance on developing scripts and processes for developing test data based on a user's view.
- In Chapter 13, a formal user acceptance test process with work papers.
- In Chapter 14, more guidance on developing test reports.

A major change is the addition of detailed test programs for special testing challenges in Part Four of the book. These include new programs for testing:

- Web-based applications
- Off-the-shelf software

- Multiplatform environments
- System security
- Data warehouse applications

In addition, the test program for client/server systems has been greatly expanded. New appendices, found both in the book and on the companion Web site, include an assessment of the status of software testing and the common body of knowledge for software testing.

What's on the Web Site

To access the companion Web site to this book, point your Web browser to www.wiley.com/compbooks/perry. There you will find:

- Current software testing survey results
- An extensive list of software testing techniques, presented in "how-to" format
- Lists of testing tools
- A case study on how one organization turned the material in this book into an in-house testing manual

Assessing Testing Capabilities and Competencies

Assessing Software Testing Capabilities and Staff Competencies

Software testing is an integral part of the software development process. The software development process is comprised of the following four components (see Figure 1.1):

1. **Plan (P): Devise a plan.** Define your objective and determine the strategy and supporting methods required to achieve that objective. The plan should be based on an assessment of your current situation, and the strategy should clearly focus upon the strategic initiatives/key units that will drive your improvement plan. Express a specific objective numerically. Determine the procedures and conditions for the means and methods you will use to achieve the objective.

2. **Do (D): Execute the plan.** Create the conditions and perform the necessary training to execute the plan. Make sure everyone thoroughly understands the objectives and the plan. Teach workers the procedures and skills they need to fulfill the plan and thoroughly understand the job. Then perform the work according to these procedures.

3. **Check (C): Check the results.** Check to determine whether work is progressing according to the plan and whether the expected results are obtained. Check for performance of the set procedures, changes in conditions, or abnormalities that may appear. As often as possible, compare the results of the work with the objectives.

4. **Act (A): Take the necessary action.** If your checkup reveals that the work is not being performed according to plan or that results are not what was anticipated, devise measures for appropriate action.

Testing only involves the check component of the plan-do-check-act (PDCA) cycle. The software development team is responsible for the three remaining components. The development team plans the project and builds the software (i.e., do component); the testers check to determine that the software meets the needs of the customers and users. If it does not, the testers report defects to the development team. It is the development team that makes the determination as to whether the uncovered defects are to be corrected.

The role of testing is to fulfill the check responsibilities assigned to the testers; it is not to determine whether software can be placed into production. That is the responsibility of the customers, users, and development team.

Who Is Associated with Testing?

The following parties have a vested interest in software testing:

Software customer. The party or department that contracts for the software to be developed.

Software user. The individual or group that will use the software once it is placed into production. (Note: This may be the customer or it may be parties other than the customer.)

Software developer. The individual or group that receives or assists in writing requirements, designing the software, building the software, and changing and maintaining the software as needed.

Software tester. The individual or group that performs the check function on the software. (Note: These may be a subset of the developers, an independent group, or a combination of the two.)

Information technology management. The individual or group with responsibility for fulfilling the information technology mission. Testing supports fulfilling that mission.

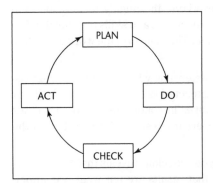

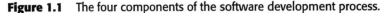

Figure 1.1   The four components of the software development process.

Senior organization management. The CEO of the organization and other senior executives who have the responsibility of fulfilling the organization mission. Information technology is an activity that supports fulfilling that mission.

Auditor. One or more individuals having the responsibility to evaluate the effectiveness, efficiency, and the adequacy of controls in the information technology area. Testing is considered a control by the audit function.

The Multiple Roles of Testing

Testing is an activity associated with any process that produces a product. It is used to determine the status of the product during and after the build or do component of the process. The role of testing changes as the type of process used to build the product changes. There is a continuum of build processes that can be divided into three categories.

Manufacturing

Manufacturing is a process that produces many similar products. In information technology, this is most synonymous with data center operations. In manufacturing processes, the products tend to be well defined. Testing is normally a binary activity that validates the presence or absence of product attributes. For example, in computer operations, testing would validate that the right data files have been mounted.

Job Shop

This is a process that builds products that, while different, possess many of the same characteristics. This building process would most commonly be associated with creating software. Since these products are customized, the specificity of the requirements is less than that associated with the manufacturing process. Thus, the testers cannot be assured that the requirements are, in fact, what the customer/user really needs. Testing of job shop products normally involves verifying that the requirements are correct, and then validating that the end product meets the true needs of the customer/user.

Testing in a job shop environment is a value-added activity. Since the do process cannot logically be expected to work, the check activity is used in conjunction with the do activity to assure that a high-quality product is produced.

The role of the user also changes in a job shop environment. The user becomes a part of the product, in that the skill sets of the user and the instructions provided by the user impact the effectiveness and efficiency of the software system. For example, the system depends on the user entering the correct data and properly interpreting the output and decision making. Thus, testing in a job shop environment also involves validating that the user, in fact, can use the system properly.

Professional Process

With this process, the products created are unique and may not resemble any other product. An example of professional products would be working with customers to determine how computer technology can assist them in solving their business problems. Using a professional product, the customer is generally the one who validates whether the product is satisfactory. However, testing of a sort can occur in a professional process by using peers to assess the reasonableness of the product. For example, in determining whether technology has been used effectively, a group of senior analysts may evaluate the recommended solution, or independent consultants can be brought in to perform the evaluation.

In any of these processes, any variation noted by the tester is a defect.

What Is a Defect?

A defect is a variance from a desired product attribute. Testers look for defects. There are two categories of defects:

1. **Defect from product specifications.** The product built varies from the product specified. For example, the specifications may say that a is to be added to b to produce c. If the algorithm in the built product varies from that specification, it is considered to be defective.

2. **Variance from customer/user expectation.** This variance is something that the user wanted that is not in the built product, but also was not specified to be included in the built product. The missing piece may be a specification or requirement, or the method by which the requirement was implemented may be unsatisfactory.

Defects generally fall into one of the following three categories:

1. **Wrong.** The specifications have been implemented incorrectly. This defect is a variance from customer/user specification.

2. **Missing.** A specified or wanted requirement is not in the built product. This can be a variance from specification, an indication that the specification was not implemented, or a requirement of the customer identified during or after the product was built.

3. **Extra.** A requirement incorporated into the product that was not specified. This is always a variance from specifications, but may be an attribute desired by the user of the product. However, it is considered a defect.

Defects versus Failures

A defect is incorporated into the software system. It can be classified as wrong, missing, or extra. It can be found within the software itself or in the supporting manuals and documentation. While the defect is a flaw in the software system, it has no impact until it affects the user/customer and the operational system.

A defect that causes an error in operation or negatively impacts a user/customer is called a failure. The main concern with defects is that they will turn into failures. It is the failure that damages the organization.

Some defects never turn into failures. On the other hand, a single defect can cause millions of failures. For example, a software defect that disrupts one million phone calls is one that causes one thousand failures.

Process Problems and Defect Rates

Most defects are caused by processes that do not work properly. For example, if the requirements process is flawed, the user of that process will not gather the proper information. If the training process taught a programmer that the ADD command would cause subtraction to occur, the programmer would write a defective line of code every time the ADD command was used. Quality experts, such as the late Dr. W. Edwards Deming, have frequently stated that at least 90 percent of all defects are caused by process problems.

Evidence from leading corporations has proved Dr. Deming to be correct. This is significant to the tester, because it makes the tester aware that any time a process is used, defects of approximately the same type and frequency will occur. For example, experience has shown that approximately 60 percent of all defects in the requirements phase are due to missing requirements. This is because the process was not effective in gathering all of the customer needs during that phase of software development. The implication is that testers should focus the majority of their efforts on looking for missing requirements, as opposed to wrong requirements.

Developers of sophisticated commercial software have used this premise in defining defect expectations. Through experience they determined, for example, that there should be 30 defects per thousand lines of code uncovered during testing. If testing does not uncover the 30 defects, a logical conclusion is that the test process was not effective. Thus, in some commercial software development organizations the software will be retested because of the very high probability that the first test effort did not uncover all of the defects. In most instances, the extra tests validate the assumption that more defects were present.

The number of defects produced in building software will depend on the maturity of the process—maturity meaning how much variability is permitted in the process. For example, the more that systems developers can deviate from the defined process, the greater the variability.

Using the software development process that exists in approximately 90 percent of all information technology groups (i.e., those generally considered to be immature processes or processes with great variability), one can expect approximately 60 defects per thousand lines of source code to be created during development. As the processes mature, these defect rates decrease.

In production, for immature processes, defect rates of six defects per thousand lines of source code are not unusual. Until recently, leading commercial software developers were producing software with production defect rates of one defect per thousand lines of source code, with the leading software developers now producing production code with defect rates of approximately one defect per 30,000 lines of source code.

The Business Perspective for Testing

Senior organization executives use the PDCA cycle thinking in developing their corporate strategy. Strategic plans are converted into business initiatives. The plan-do components of the PDCA cycle are easy to understand. From a senior executive's perspective, the check component is one that must address business risk.

Risk is the probability that undesirable events will occur. These undesirable events will prevent the organization from successfully implementing its business initiatives. For example, there is the risk that the information used in making business decisions will be incorrect or late. If the risk turns into reality and the information is late or incorrect, an erroneous business decision may cause a failed business initiative.

Controls are the means used by organizations to minimize risk. Software testing is a control. It can assist in eliminating or minimizing risks such as information arriving late or being produced in an incorrect manner. Thus, senior executives rely on controls such as software testing to assist them in fulfilling their business objectives.

The purpose of controls such as software testing is to provide information to management so they can better react to risk situations. For example, testing may indicate that the system will be late, or there is a low probability that the information produced will be correct. Knowing this information, management can then make decisions to minimize that risk: Knowing that the project may be late, they could assign additional personnel to speed up the software development effort.

Testers must understand that their business role is to evaluate business risk and to report those results to management. Viewed from this perspective, testers must first ensure they understand the business risk, and then develop test strategies focused on those risks. The highest business risk should receive the most test resources, while the lowest business risk should receive the least amount of resources. This way, the testers are assured that they are focusing on what is important to their management.

How Good Are Your Existing Test Process and Your Testers?

Improvement effort in software testing is a three-step process that is described as follows:

Step 1. Determine the current status of your testing capabilities. This involves understanding the capabilities of your testing process as well as the capabilities of your individual testers.

Step 2. Establish improvement goals. Determine and define the type of testing organization you would like to have in your organization, as well as the skill sets needed by your testers.

Step 3. Develop a plan to achieve your testing goals. The plan should be a well-defined series of tests that will take you from where you are to where you want to be.

The beginning step is one of self-assessment. Most testing organizations, as well as testers, believe they are doing a good job. However, there is no basis for making that determination. In order to make that determination, an assessment must be made against a "model" of a world-class testing organization, and a "model" of a fully competent tester.

During the past 20 years the Quality Assurance Institute has studied many organizations and has developed a model of a world-class testing organization. In addition, the certification board of the Quality Assurance Institute has established a common body of knowledge for a software tester. You can assess your organization against the Quality Assurance Institute's world-class model, and your individual testers' skill sets against the common body of knowledge for software testers.

These two assessments follow.

Assessing the Quality of Your Existing Test Process

During the past 20 years, the Quality Assurance Institute (QAI) has been studying what makes software testing organizations successful. The results are that QAI has identified eight criteria that are normally associated with world-class testing organizations. These eight criteria are test planning, training of testers, management support for testing, user satisfaction with testing, use of testing processes, efficient testing practices, use of test tools, and quality control over the testing process. When these eight criteria are in place and working the result is a world-class testing organization.

The assessment process developed by QAI has five areas to address within each of the eight criteria. The more of those areas that are in place and working the more likely that category will contribute to world-class testing. Figure 1.2 shows a cause-effect diagram indicating the areas to address, called *drivers*, that result in a world-class testing organization.

Software testing organizations can use the results of this assessment in any one of three ways:

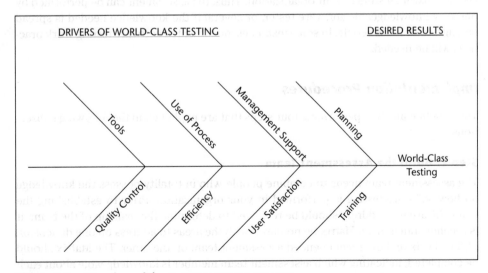

Figure 1.2   Overview of the test assessment process.

1. Determine your current software testing status versus a world-class testing organization. The responses in the area to address will indicate your strengths and weaknesses compared to a world-class testing organization.

2. Develop a software testing goal/object to become a world-class testing organization. QAI's world-class model indicates a profile of a world-class testing organization. Achieving that profile can become a goal/objective for your software testing organization.

3. Develop an improvement plan.

By doing the assessment, you will develop a Kiviatt Chart that shows where improvement is needed. Those areas in which you are deficient become the means for improving your software testing organization.

Practice Workbench

This workbench (see Figure 1.3) is designed to lead you through an assessment of your software testing function. The workbench begins with knowledge of your software testing function. A four-step process is designed to lead you from building an assessment team to analyzing the results of the assessment process. Because it is difficult for any organization to make significant improvements until they know where they are and where they want to be, the assessment process becomes a key component in any effective improvement plan.

Input Products

The only input needed to perform this assessment is a knowledge of your organization's software testing activities. The knowledge is usually possessed by one or more of the senior software testers in your organization. Thus, the assessment can be performed by one very knowledgeable software tester, or several if the knowledge needed is spread among two or more people. In some instances, documented software testing work practices will be needed.

Implementation Procedures

This practice involves performing four steps that are explained in the following subsections.

Step 1: Build the Assessment Team

The assessment team needs to combine people who in totality possess the knowledge on how software testing is performed in your organization. Prior to establishing the team, the areas to address should be reviewed to determine the makeup of the team. It is recommended that a Matrix be prepared with the areas to address on one dimension of the Matrix and the recommended assessment team on the other. The Matrix should be completed, indicating which assessment team member is knowledgeable about each of the areas to address.

If all areas to address have been associated with an assessment team member, it can be concluded that the assessment team is adequate to perform the assessment.

Step 2: Complete Assessment Questionnaires

The assessment questionnaire is comprised of eight categories and five areas to address for each category (a total of 40 areas to address). (See Work Papers 1.1 to 1.8)

For each area to address a Yes or No response should be made. The meaning of a Yes or No response follows:

A Yes response means all of the following:

- Criteria are formal and in place.
- Criteria are understood by testers.
- Criteria are widely used, where applicable.
- Criteria have produced some possible results.

A No response means any of the following:

- No formal item in place.
- Criteria are applied differently for different test situations.
- No consistency as to when used or used very seldom.
- No tangible results were produced.

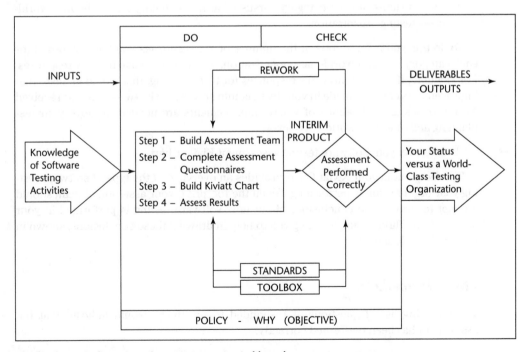

Figure 1.3   Software testing assessment workbench.

The assessment team should read aloud each area to address. The team should then discuss how that area is addressed in their software testing organization. Using the Yes/No response criteria, the assessment team needs to come to a consensus on whether a Yes or No response should be indicated for that area to address. The results of that consensus should be recorded on Work Papers 1.1 through 1.8. The assessment team may also wish to record comments that clarify the response and/or to provide insight in how that area may be improved.

Step 3: Build Kiviat Chart

Using Work Paper 1.9 (Kiviat Work Paper for Recording Software Testing Assessment Results), transcribe the results of completing Questionnaire 1. For each category the number of Yes responses should be totaled. A dot should be placed on the Kiviat Chart on the line representing the number of Yes responses. For example, if there were three Yes responses for test planning a dot would be placed on the test planning line at the intersection of the line representing three Yes responses. A dot should be put on the line representing all eight categories for the number of Yes responses. The dots are then connected by a line resulting in what is called a "footprint" of the status of your software testing organization versus a world-class testing organization.

Step 4: Assess Results

Two assessments should be made regarding the footprint developed on the Work Paper 1.9 Kiviat Chart as follows:

1. Assess status of each category versus what that category should be in a world-class testing organization.

To do this you need to look at the number of Yes responses you have recorded for each category versus a world-class organization, which would have five Yes responses. For example, if you had three Yes responses for test planning, that would indicate that improvements could be made in your test planning process. The two areas that received No responses are indications of where improvements are needed to move your test planning activities to a world-class level.

2. Interpret your software testing assessment Kiviat Chart.

The footprint in your Kiviat Chart provides an overview of the type of software testing your organization is performing. Given the footprint, your assessment team should attempt to draw some conclusions about how software testing is performed in your organization. Three examples are given to help in drawing these conclusions, shown in Figures 1.4, 1.5, and 1.6.

Check Procedures

The following list of questions, if responded to positively, would indicate that the assessment has been performed correctly:

1. Does the assessment team comprise the knowledge needed to answer all of the areas to address within the eight categories?

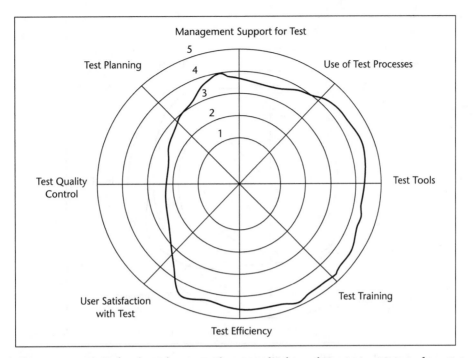

Figure 1.4   Example of a software testing organization using a test as a part of development.

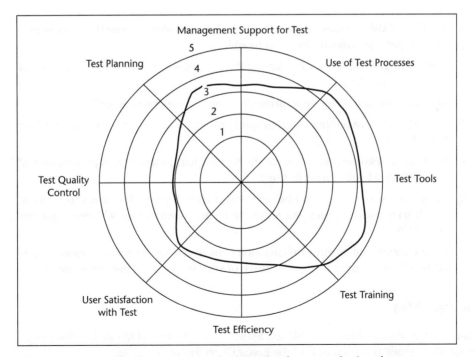

Figure 1.5   Example of a testing organization using, but not enforcing, the test process.

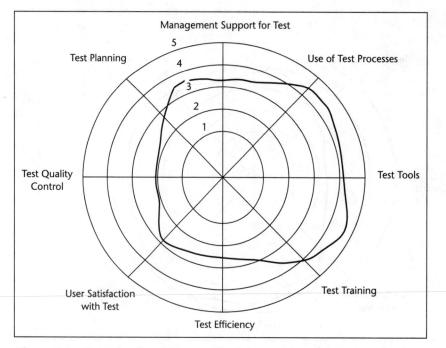

Figure 1.6 Example of a testing organization practicing testing as an art.

2. Are the individual assessors free from any bias that would cause them not to provide proper responses to the areas to address?

3. Was there general consensus among the assessment team to the response for each area to address?

4. Are the areas to address appropriate for your testing organization?

5. Have the areas to address been properly totaled and posted to the Kiviat Chart Work Paper?

6. Does the assessment team believe the Kiviat Chart footprint is representative of your software testing organization?

7. Does your assessment team believe that if they improve the areas to address, which have No responses, the software testing organization will become more effective?

8. Does your software testing organization believe that the overall assessment made of the Kiviat footprint is representative of your software testing organization?

Deliverables

There are two deliverables from this self-assessment. The first is the Kiviat Chart Work Paper. The second is the analysis of the Kiviat Chart footprint.

NOTE If your assessment team is having difficulty in drawing conclusions, send the results of your assessments to QAI, Managing Director, at www.QAIUSA.com and QAI will provide you with an interpretation of your Kiviat Chart.

Assessing the Quality of Your Testers

This practice will enable you to assess your individual testing competencies against the five skill categories in QAI's Common Body of Knowledge (CBOK) for the Certified Software Test Engineer (CSTE) certificate. At the conclusion of the assessment, you will develop a Kiviat Chart that shows your competencies against the skill categories needed to become a CSTE. You can use the results for designing a program to improve your personal test competencies.

The certification board of the Quality Assurance Institute established a common body of knowledge in 1998 for software testers. The objective of the common body of knowledge was to build the software testing profession, and establish a base for evaluating testers to become certified software test engineers. The building of the common body of knowledge was a two-year effort and it involved 100 experienced software testers.

The common body of knowledge for software testers involves five categories and 16 knowledge domains. The five categories are General Skills, Test Skills/Approaches, Test Planning, Executing the Test Plan, and Test Analysis Reporting and Improvement.

Using the CSTE CBOK, QAI has developed an assessment process for use by an individual tester. Note that this is significantly different from the examination software testers take to become certified. The assessment process provides a quick overview and a good indicator of the current status of an individual tester's competency.

Figure 1.7 shows a cause-effect diagram indicating the areas of competency assessment. In the diagram these are called the *drivers* that result in becoming a fully competent software tester. The drivers are in fact the five CBOK skill categories.

Practice Workbench

This workbench (see Figure 1.8) is designed to lead you through an assessment of your individual software testing competencies. The workbench begins with the CSTE CBOK. The three-step process is designed to lead you from understanding the CSTE CBOK to analyzing and using the results of the assessment process. Knowing the current status of your software testing competencies will enable you to develop an effective plan for improving your competencies.

Input Products

The only input needed to perform this assessment is the CSTE CBOK. Assessment is based on the five CBOK skill categories. The questions within the skill categories are based on the knowledge domains within those skill categories.

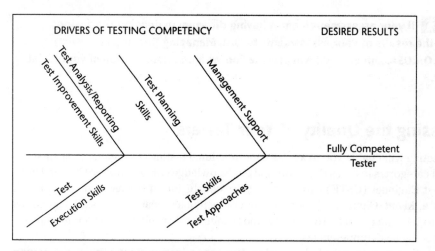

Figure 1.7   Test competency cause effect diagram.

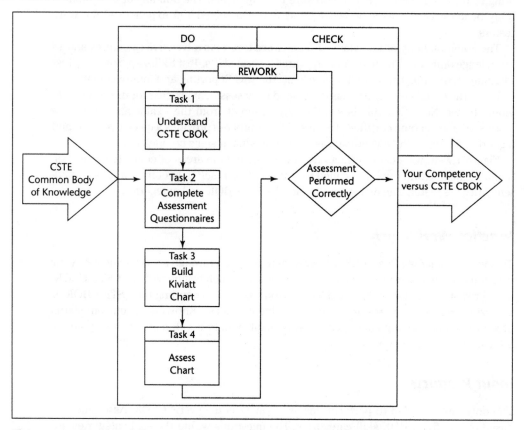

Figure 1.8   Workbench for conducting a test competency self-assessment.

Implementation Procedures

This practice involves performing three steps that are explained in the following sub-sections.

Step 1: Understand CSTE CBOK

Before you can effectively evaluate your software test competencies, you need to understand the common body of knowledge for software testing. The CSTE CBOK is available through the Quality Assurance Institute. This step requires you to read through the CBOK and to obtain clarifications of the material as necessary. The best source for these clarifications is the CSTE CBOK study guide, which is also available from the Quality Assurance Institute. (Note: The study guide can be obtained by applying for the CSTE certificate.)

Step 2: Complete Assessment Questionnaires

The assessment questionnaire in Work Paper 1.10 is comprised of five categories and 10 items in each category. There is a total of 50 items to assess. For each item to assess, a Yes or No response should be made. The meanings of the Yes and No responses follows:

- A Yes response means all of the following:
    - You have had formal training, experience, or self-study supporting this skill item.
    - You have actively used the skill in your personal or work life.
    - You have accomplished some positive result using this skill item.
- A No response means any of the following:
    - You do not understand the theory and concepts supporting the skill item.
    - You have never used the skill item in a personal or work situation.
    - You have used the skill item but you have never achieved any positive results.

Prior to answering each question, you should think through the meaning of the question. This may require referring back to the CSTE study guide. Using the Yes/No response criteria, you need to come to a consensus on whether a Yes/No response should be indicated for the skill item. The result of your assessment should be recorded on the appropriate questionnaire.

You need to progress sequentially through questionnaires 1 through 5. Note that you may wish to make notes on the questionnaire to clarify your response, or to indicate ideas on how you could improve your competency in that skill item.

Step 3: Build Kiviat Chart

For each of the five questionnaires completed in Step 2, total the number of Yes responses. Convert the number of Yes responses to a percentage by multiplying the number of Yes responses by 10 (e.g., 3 Yes responses $\times$ 10 = 30%).

Using Work Paper 1.11 (Kiviat Work Paper for Recording Software Testing Competency Assessment Results), transcribe the percentage for each of the five questionnaires. For the lines corresponding to the questionnaire name, put a dot on the Kiviat Chart for the percentage of Yes responses for that assessment competency category. For example, if there were three Yes responses for the test planning category, a dot would be placed on the test planning line at the intersection of the line representing 30 percent of responses. When all five dots have been placed on the Kiviat Chart, a line should be drawn connecting the five dots. This line is called a *footprint* that represents the status of your software testing competencies versus the competency specified in the CSTE CBOK.

Step 4: Assess Chart

Two assessments should be made regarding the footprint developed on Work Paper 1.11 as follows:

1. Assess the status of each category versus what the category should be as indicated in the CSTE CBOK. Any rating less than 100 percent indicates a potential area of improvement in that skill category. An analysis of the CBOK domains within the category will be helpful in determining where to focus improvement, as will studying the CSTE guide to identify areas for potential improvement.

2. Interpret your software testing competencies against your current job responsibilities. The footprint in your Kiviatt Chart provides an overview of your current test competencies. Using your current job description, develop another footprint, which you believe is needed to achieve your current job responsibilities. Any deficiencies should be your first objective for improvement; your second for improvement would be to achieve the skill competencies needed to become a CSTE.

Check Procedures

The following list of questions, if responded to positively, would indicate that the competency assessment has been performed correctly.

1. Do you have enough knowledge of the CBOK for CSTEs to correctly understand the assessment questions?

2. Do you understand the skill implications for each of the 50 assessment items in the questionnaires?

3. Do you understand the Yes and No response criteria, and have you used them in developing the competency assessment?

4. Do you believe the 50 assessment items fairly represent the competencies needed to be fully effective in software testing?

5. Do you believe that the Kiviat Chart footprint developed from this assessment is representative of your personal testing competencies?

Deliverables

There are two deliverables from this self-assessment. The first is the Kiviat Chart (Work Paper 1.11) with the recorded footprint. The second is the analysis of the Kiviat

Chart footprint. The analysis of the Kiviatt chart should follow the guidelines provided in Step 4.

Summary

This chapter provides a general introduction to software testing, the roles of testers, the concepts of defects and failures, as well as the business perspective for testing. It also provides a self-assessment document for your testing capabilities and your testing competencies. From this baseline the chapter proposes establishing improvement goals based on the Quality Assurance Institute's world-class testing model, and the common body of knowledge for a certified software test engineer. The results of those self-assessments will provide you with a baseline of your current capabilities and competencies as a software tester.

WORK PAPER 1.1 Criteria Category—Test Planning

ITEM NUMBER	AREAS TO ADDRESS	RESPONSE		COMMENTS
		YES	NO	
1	Do the testers identify the business and technical risks associated with implementing and operating software, *and* are those risks addressed in the test plan?			
2	Is a test plan created for each software system? Does the plan identify the test requirements/objectives *and* does it establish success criteria for each requirement?			
3	Are the users actively involved in the development of the test plan, *and* does the plan include user involvement in testing?			
4	Are test plans followed? Is approval required to deviate from the plan, *and* are the plans changed to reflect changing test approaches and changing software requirements?			
5	Does the test plan contain the criteria that the software must meet in order to be placed into production *and* do the users agree with that criteria?			

WORK PAPER 1.2   Criteria Category—Management Support for Test

ITEM NUMBER	AREAS TO ADDRESS	RESPONSE		COMMENTS
		YES	NO	
1	Does management provide the resources necessary (including calendar time) to adequately train, plan, conduct, and evaluate results for software testing assignments?			
2	Are testers involved from the inception through termination of software projects to ensure that testing concerns are continuously addressed?			
3	Does management allocate as many resources to the test processes and tools as it does to the development process and tools?			
4	Does management spend as much personal time on test planning and test execution as it does on development planning and development execution?			
5	Is management knowledgeable and sufficiently trained in test theory, processes and tools to effectively manage test planning and execution, and understand and effectively act on test results?			

WORK PAPER 1.3   Criteria Category—Test Processes

ITEM NUMBER	AREAS TO ADDRESS	RESPONSE		COMMENTS
		YES	NO	
1	Do testers follow processes to plan tests, prepare test data, execute tests, and develop and report test results?			
2	Can documented test processes be correctly interpreted by testers so that the test procedures can be followed as intended during use?			
3	Do the processes provided for testing cover all the activities that are needed to perform effective testing?			
4	Has a plan been developed *and* put in place to mature the test processes so they become more effective, efficient, and on time?			
5	Do the owners/users of the test processes (i.e., testers) build the processes used for testing?			

WORK PAPER 1.4   Criteria Category—Test Tools

ITEM NUMBER	AREAS TO ADDRESS	RESPONSE		COMMENTS
		YES	NO	
1	Do testers use an automated tool to generate and reuse test data?			
2	Are test tools selected in a logical manner? Meaning, test needs drive the search for/acquisition of test tools.			
3	Can testers only use test tools after they have received adequate training in how to use the test tools?			
4	Is test tool usage specified in the test plan? Meaning, usage of the tools is mandatory, not optional, or by the sole discretion of a tester.			
5	Has a process for obtaining assistance in using test tools been established, *and* does it provide testers with the needed instructional information?			

WORK PAPER 1.5 Criteria Category—Test Training

ITEM NUMBER	AREAS TO ADDRESS	RESPONSE		COMMENTS
		YES	NO	
1	Does a career training plan for testers exist, *and* is it in use to develop a tester from an unskilled state to a master tester state?			
2	Are testers adequately trained in test processes before using those processes for testing?			
3	Are testers trained in the theory of testing, risk analysis, the various approaches to testing, etc., so that they understand "why" they perform certain test tasks?			
4	Are testers trained in statistics so they understand the level of confidence they can provide a user by different test approaches and how to interpret test results?			
5	Are testers trained in how to measure process performance, *and* do they use the results of that measurement to improve the test processes?			

WORK PAPER 1.6 Criteria Category—User Satisfaction

ITEM NUMBER	AREAS TO ADDRESS	RESPONSE		COMMENTS
		YES	NO	
1	Do users get the information they need to track test progress and assess results prior to placing software into production?			
2	Are user surveys conducted to determine user satisfaction with test planning, test execution, test results, communications, etc.?			
3	Do users participate in tests that determine whether or not the software is acceptable for use?			
4	Are users presented with a plan for testing, *and* do they "approve" (i.e., agree) that if that plan is followed, they will consider testing to be satisfactory?			
5	Are the user support activities such as data entry, output usage, terminal usage, manual usage, etc., validated as part of testing?			

WORK PAPER 1.7   Criteria Category—Test Efficiency

ITEM NUMBER	AREAS TO ADDRESS	RESPONSE		COMMENTS
		YES	NO	
1	Has the test planned been developed so that the test resources will be allocated to validate that the major risks are addressed prior to minor risks?			
2	Has a measurement process been installed to measure the efficiency of the test processes?			
3	Is compliance to the budget and schedule measured and variances addressed effectively?			
4	Is tool usage measured to assess the contribution received from automated testing?			
5	Is the percentage of defects removed versus the total defects eventually attributable to a development phase measured?			

WORK PAPER 1.8   Criteria Category—Test Quality Control

ITEM NUMBER	AREAS TO ADDRESS	RESPONSE		COMMENTS
		YES	NO	
1	Are defects made by testers during testing recorded and effectively addressed?			
2	Is the test plan reviewed/inspected during/after completion by peers for adequacy and compliance to test standards?			
3	Does the test plan include the procedures that will be used to verify that the plan is executed in accordance with the plan?			
4	Are regular reports prepared that show the full status of testing individual software systems?			
5	Periodically, are the individual quality control reports summarized to show the efficiency and effectiveness of testing in the entire information services organization?			

WORK PAPER 1.9   Assessment Kiviat Chart

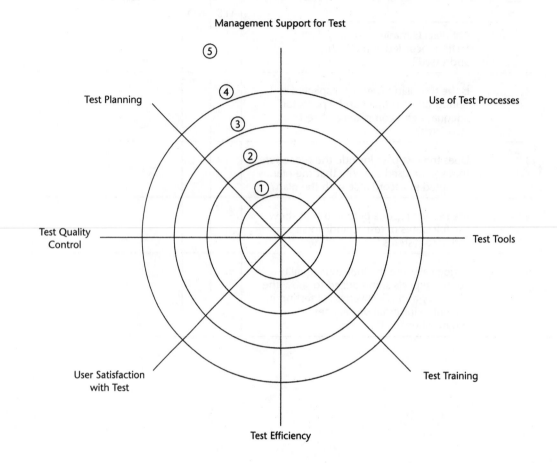

WORK PAPER 1.10   Tester Competency Self-Assessment

#	ITEM	RESPONSE YES	NO
	General Skills		
1	Do you have a process for preparing written presentations?		
2	Do you have a process for making oral presentations?		
3	Do you have a process for effective listening, which involves asking for clarification and providing feedback?		
4	Do you have a process for developing proposals and recommendations that include motivation and conflict resolution?		
5	Do you average a minimum of 40 hours of continuing professional education each year?		
6	Do you have the capability for building a team and leading that team as chairperson?		
7	Are you trained and effective in the role of a facilitator?		
8	Do you understand and practice quality principles in your day-to-day activities?		
9	Are you trained on how to develop, document, and improve work processes?		
10	Do you know the theory, concept, and practices for software development, operation, and maintenance?		
	Test Skills/Approaches		
1	Do you understand and use a testing vocabulary in your day-to-day activities?		
2	Do you understand and use in the proper sequence the levels of testing including unit, strain, integration, systems, regression, and acceptance?		
3	Do you understand the concepts, and use, a testing life cycle as part of your testing activities?		
4	Do you understand and use verification concepts, such as reviews and inspections, during the project life cycle?		
5	Do you understand the concepts and have you been involved in establishing a test environment, which involves implementing test processes, tools, and developing a test bed?		
6	Do you have a knowledge of and understand the professional testing standards, such as those issued by IEEE, NIST, and ISO?		
7	Do you have a process for monitoring and measuring test performance?		
8	Do you have a process for acquiring test tools?		
9	Do you have a process for implementing test tools?		
10	Do you have a unique process for testing software changes?		
	Test Planning		
1	Are you knowledgeable about the most common risks associated with software development in the platform you are working with?		
2	Are you knowledgeable about the most common risks associated with business applications?		
3	Do you understand and use a method for determining the magnitude and/or ranking the risks for both software and business risks?		
4	Can you develop contingency plans to reduce the magnitude of a known risk should the risk even occur?		
5	Can you develop test approaches that are effective for both structural and functional testing?		

(Continues)

WORK PAPER 1.10   *(Continued)*

#	ITEM	RESPONSE	
		YES	NO
6	Is tool usage specified in your test plan (i.e., tool usage is *not* optional)?		
7	Do you have the knowledge and can you work with users and customers, to develop success criteria/acceptance criteria for software prior to test?		
8	Do you have a process for developing a test plan?		
9	Do you have a process for establishing check procedures (i.e., quality control procedures) for a test plan, test design, building test cases, and ensuring that tests are performed correctly and completely?		
10	Do you have a process for writing test objectives?		
Executing the Test Plan			
1	Do you understand the concepts and can you develop the approach to be used for test design and test execution?		
2	Do you have the knowledge for, and can you develop, test data that will provide the coverage objectives specified in the test plan?		
3	Do you have a knowledge of the concepts involved in developing test scripts?		
4	When you develop test cases do you document the test objective, the techniques and approaches, as well as the expected result for each test case?		
5	Do you have a process for comparing and determining actual versus expected test results?		
6	Do you have a process for recording discrepancies/defects that occur in testing?		
7	Do you have process for tracking/monitoring defects from the time of identification to the satisfactory resolution of the defect?		
8	Do you understand the concepts of, and have a process for, regression testing?		
9	Do you have a process for updating the test plan during execution?		
10	Are you always trained in the use of a test tool prior to using that tool?		
Test Analysis Reporting and Improvement			
1	Do you understand code coverage, and have a process for determining the degree of coverage at the statement, branch, or path level?		
2	Do you understand the concepts of, and have a process for, requirements coverage that includes monitoring and reporting on the number of requirements exercised during tests?		
3	Are you skilled in the theories and concept of measurement?		
4	Can you use the metrics unique to test, for example, defect removal efficiency, defect density, and mean time to failure?		
5	Can you calculate the complexity of a software product?		
6	Do you have a process for preparing test reports?		
7	Do you have adequate statistical skills that you can draw a statistically valid conclusion from quantitative test results?		
8	Do you have a process for verifying that the test process has been performed correctly?		
9	Do you have a process for use in analyzing the effectiveness of a test process?		
10	Do you understand the concepts, and can you practice continuous process improvement?		

WORK PAPER 1.11   Tester Competency Kiviat Chart

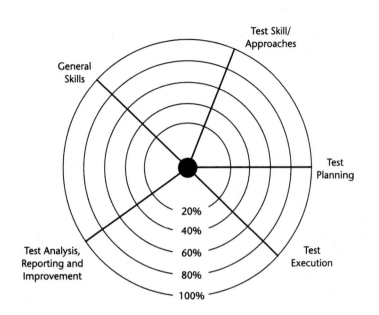

Building a Software
Testing Environment

# CHAPTER 2

Building a Software Testing Strategy

The biggest problem with testing is boredom. Information system development is an exercise in problem solving. As with any problem-solving activity, determining the validity of the solution is part of the process. Testing is the technique used to determine that the solution solves the problem.

Testing as used in this book encompasses the following three concepts:

1. The demonstration of the validity of the software at each stage in the system development life cycle

2. Determination of the validity of the final system with respect to user needs and requirements

3. Examination of the behavior of a system by executing the system on sample test data

The criticality of the problem determines the effort required to validate the solution. A computer system to control airplane landings or to direct substantial money transfers requires higher confidence in its proper functioning than does a carpool locator program, since the consequences of malfunction are more severe. For each computer system project, not only the product requirements but also the validation requirements should be determined and specified at the initiation of the project. Project size, uniqueness, criticality, the cost of malfunction, and project budget all influence the validation needs. Once the testing requirements are clearly stated, specific techniques for testing can be chosen.

Computer System Strategic Risks

A risk is a condition that can result in a loss. The concern about a risk is related to the probability that a loss will occur. The risk situation always exists, although the loss may not occur. For example, fire is a risk that is always present, but fires occur infrequently. However, because the risk of fire is always present, we must take countermeasures such as installing fire alarms, fire extinguishers, and buying fire insurance so that we can reduce the probability that the risk will occur.

We cannot eliminate risks, but we can reduce their occurrence and/or the impact of the loss. In our fire example, we can reduce the occurrence of the fire by building fire-walls, using fireproof material, and isolating potential causes of fire, such as electrical circuitry and smoking, from the area we wish to protect. We can reduce the impact of the loss due to the risk of fire by building two or more small buildings instead of one large one, installing fire-fighting equipment, and buying insurance to reimburse us for any loss.

The development and installation of a computer system introduces risk into the organization. These risks are ever present and need to be addressed in the development process in order to reduce the probability of loss associated with these risks to an acceptable level. One of the most effective methods to reduce computer system strategic risk is testing.

Types of strategic risk associated with the development and installation of a computer system can be:

- Incorrect results will be produced.
- Unauthorized transactions will be accepted by the system.
- Computer file integrity will be lost.
- Processing cannot be reconstructed.
- Continuity of processing will be lost.
- Service provided to the user will degrade to an unacceptable level.
- Security of the system will be compromised.
- Processing will not comply with organizational policy or governmental regulation.
- Results of the system will be unreliable.
- System will be difficult to use.
- Programs will be unmaintainable.
- System will not be portable to other hardware and software.
- System will not be able to interconnect with other computer systems.
- Performance level will be unacceptable.
- System will be difficult to operate.

Each of these risks can affect the proper functioning of a computer system. If any of these risks should occur, the result may be a substantial loss to the organization. For example, the risk of loss of continuity of processing may result in the inability to accept and process user transactions. The risk of the system being difficult to use may result in features not being used. In this case, the loss is the cost and effort expended to prepare capabilities that are not used.

An effective approach to testing is to identify and evaluate the risks in a computer system. Those risks deemed important to reduce become the areas for testing. A decision can be made as to how much risk is acceptable and then a test plan designed to achieve that goal. For example, if there is a risk that the service level will not provide a three-second response, then tests must be designed to validate whether the desired response can be achieved.

The risk concept makes a determination of how much or what type of testing is needed to perform an economic consideration. The economic decision determines whether defects in the system are acceptable, and if acceptable, how many. The determination of what is good or bad testing is shifted from a systems analyst/programmer decision to a logical business decision based on economics.

Economics of Testing

One information services manager described testing in the following manner: "Too little testing is a crime—too much testing is a sin." When control is viewed as a risk situation, this can result in over- and undertesting. The risk of undertesting is directly translated into system defects present in the production environment. The risk of overtesting is the unnecessary use of valuable resources in testing computer systems that have no flaws, or so few flaws that the cost of testing far exceeds the value of detecting the system defects.

Most of the problems associated with testing occur from one of the following causes:

- Failure to define testing objectives
- Testing at the wrong phase in the life cycle
- Use of ineffective test techniques

The cost-effectiveness of testing is illustrated in Figure 2.1 as a testing cost curve: As the cost of testing increases, the number of undetected defects decreases. The left side of the illustration represents an undertest situation in which the cost of testing is less than the resultant loss from undetected defects. At some point, the two lines cross and an overtest condition begins. In this situation, the cost of testing to uncover defects exceeds the losses from those defects. A cost-effective perspective means testing until the optimum point is reached, which is the point where the cost of testing no longer exceeds the value received from the defects uncovered.

Few organizations have established a basis to measure the effectiveness of testing. This makes it difficult for the individual systems analyst/programmer to determine the cost-effectiveness of testing. Without testing standards, the effectiveness of the process cannot be evaluated in sufficient detail to enable the process to be measured and improved.

The use of a standardized testing methodology provides the opportunity for a cause and effect relationship to be determined. In other words, the effect of a change in the methodology can be evaluated to determine whether that effect resulted in a smaller or

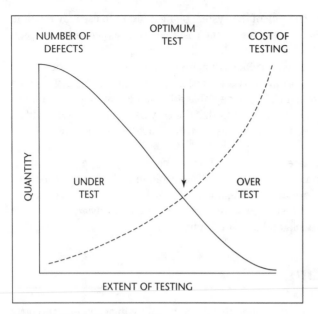

Figure 2.1 Testing cost curve.

larger number of defects. The establishment of this relationship is an essential step in improving the test process.

The objective of this book is to explain how to develop a testing methodology that enables an optimum cost-effective process to be used. The cost-effectiveness of a testing process can only be determined when the effect of that process can be measured. When the process can be measured, it can be adjusted to improve the cost-effectiveness of the test process for the organization.

Common Computer Problems

The U.S. General Accounting Office summarized the errors detected in computerized applications they reviewed in a report entitled *Improvements Needed in Managing Automated Decision-making by Computer Throughout the Federal Government* (FGMSD-76-5). It is reasonable to assume that these problems are typical of most computer systems, and thus those problems should be included in any test program. These problems, resulting in the applications automatically initiating uneconomical or otherwise incorrect actions, can be broadly categorized as software problems and data problems.

Software Problems

The identified software problems that most commonly cause bad decisions by automated decision-making applications include:

- Designing software with incomplete or erroneous decision-making criteria. Actions have been incorrect because the decision-making logic omitted factors that should have been included. In other cases decision-making criteria included in the software were inappropriate, either at the time of design or later, because of changed circumstances.

- Failing to program the software as intended by the customer (user) or designer, resulting in logic errors often referred to as programming errors.

- Omitting needed edit checks for determining completeness of output data. Critical data elements have been left blank on many input documents, and because no checks were included, the applications processed the transactions with incomplete data.

Data Problems

Input data is frequently a problem. Since much of this data is an integral part of the decision-making process, its poor quality can adversely affect the computer-directed actions. Common problems are:

- Incomplete data used by automated decision-making applications. Some input documents prepared by people omitted entries in data elements that were critical to the application but were processed anyway. The documents were not rejected when incomplete data was being used. In other instances, data needed by the application that should have become part of information services (IS) files was not put into the system.

- Incorrect data used in automated decision-making application processing. People have often unintentionally introduced incorrect data into the IS system.

- Obsolete data used in automated decision-making application processing. Data in the IS files became obsolete due to new circumstances. The new data may have been available but was not put into the computer.

Economics of System Development Life Cycle (SDLC) Testing

Studies at IBM demonstrated that an application system during the system development life cycle (SDLC) will produce 60 errors (defects). These studies also showed that testing prior to coding is 50 percent effective in detecting errors, and after coding, 80 percent effective. This study and others show that it is at least 10 times as costly to correct an error after coding as before, and 100 times as costly to correct a production error. Chemical Bank showed that two-thirds of the errors occur prior to coding.

These facts are illustrated in Figure 2.2 for a hypothetical system with 1,000 lines of source code. A normal SDLC test process is shown on the left in which testing occurs only after coding. In this example, all 60 errors remain after coding for testing, which detects 48 errors (60 times 80 percent equals 48) at an average cost 10 times as great as those detected prior to coding, resulting in a cost of 480 units. To that, we must add

1,200 units of cost representing the 12 remaining errors to be detected during production at a cost of 100 units each. The net test cost is 1,680 units. Using life-cycle testing, this can be reduced to 582 units or only one-third of the normal SDLC test concept cost (illustrated on the right side of Figure 2.2).

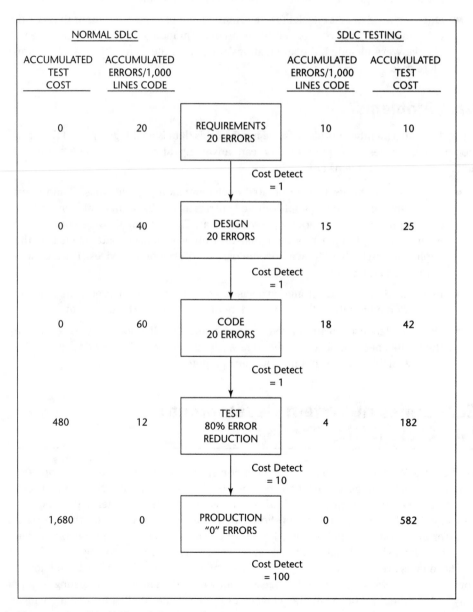

Figure 2.2 Economics of SDLC testing.

Testing—An Organizational Issue

Testing information services systems is not just an IT issue, but rather is an organizational issue. The IT department can verify that the system structure functions correctly, and can verify that the executable system performs the requirements as IT understands those requirements; but the IT department cannot test to determine that the executable system satisfies the needs of the organization.

Effective testing must be done by a team comprised of information services professionals and users. In corporations where the users are not readily available—in other words they are in a remote location—the users can be represented by a professional test group. Also, vendors of software may not be able, or may not want, to have users testing their systems during the developmental process. Again, in these instances, a professional test group can represent the users. The test group is known by different names, including IT testing, quality control, quality assurance, and inspectors.

The following technological developments are causing organizations to revise their approach to testing:

Integration. Technology is being more closely integrated into the day-to-day business, such that the business cannot operate without computer technology. For example, the airlines can only take reservations when their computer systems are operational.

System chains. Computer systems are interconnected into cycles of chains such that problems in one can cascade into and affect others.

The domino effect. One problem condition, such as a wrong price or a program defect, can cause hundreds or even thousands of similar errors within a few minutes.

Reliance on electronic evidence. With hard-copy documents being removed from processing, the validity of the transactions is dependent upon the adequacy of controls, and thus a control error may result in extensive losses.

Multiple users. Systems no longer belong to single users, but rather to multiple users, making it difficult to identify a single organizational unit responsible for a system.

The organizational approach to testing commences with a policy on testing computer systems. The policy should be developed under the direction of the IT department, but should represent the philosophy of the entire organization. Once the policy has been established, then the procedures and the methods of testing can be developed based upon the desires of management as expressed in the testing policy.

Establishing a Testing Policy

A testing policy (Figure 2.3) is management's definition of testing for a department. A testing policy involves the following four criteria:

TESTING POLICY
ABC INFORMATION TECHNOLOGY DEPARTMENT

TESTING DEFINITION

Determination of the validity of the computer solution to a business problem.

TESTING SYSTEM

Development and execution of a test plan in accordance with departmental procedures and user requirements.

MEASUREMENT OF TESTING

Cost of undetected defects.

TESTING STANDARDS

One defect per 250 executable program statements.

Philip Jones
George Wilson
Elizabeth Charney
Max Hartman

Figure 2.3   Testing policy.

1. **Definition of testing.** A clear, brief, and unambiguous definition of testing.
2. **Testing system.** The method through which testing will be achieved and enforced.
3. **Evaluation.** How information services management will measure and evaluate testing.
4. **Standards.** The standards against which testing will be measured.

Good testing does not just happen, it must be planned; and a testing policy should be the cornerstone of that plan. Figure 2.3 is a simplistic testing policy that an IT department could adopt. A good practice is for management to establish the testing policy for the IT department, then have all members of IT management sign that policy as their endorsement and intention to enforce that testing policy, and then prominently display that endorsed policy where it can be seen by everyone in the IT department.

Information services management normally assumes that their staff understand the testing function and what they, management, want from testing. Exactly the opposite is normally true. Testing is not clearly defined, nor is management's intent made known regarding their desire for the type and extent of testing.

Information services departments frequently adopt testing tools such as a test data generator, make the system programmer/analyst aware of those testing tools, and then leave it to the discretion of the staff how testing is to occur and to what extent. In fact, many "antitesting" messages may be indirectly transmitted from management to staff. For example, pressure to get projects done on time and within budget is an antitesting message from management. The message says, "I don't care how you get the system done, but get it done on time and within budget," which translates to the average systems analyst/programmer as "Get it in on time even if it isn't tested."

Methods

The establishment of a testing policy is an IT management responsibility. Three methods can be used to establish a testing policy:

1. **Management directive.** One or more senior IT managers write the policy. They determine what they want from testing, document that into a policy, and issue it to the department. This is an economical and effective method to write a testing policy; the potential disadvantage is that it is not an organizational policy, but rather the policy of IT management.

2. **Information services consensus policy.** IT management convenes a group of the more senior and respected individuals in the department to jointly develop a policy. While senior management must have the responsibility for accepting and issuing the policy, the development of the policy is representative of the thinking of all the IT department, rather than just senior management. The advantage of this approach is that it involves the key members of the IT department. Because of this participation staff is encouraged to follow the policy. The disadvantage is that it is an IT policy and not an organizational policy.

3. **Users' meeting.** Key members of user management meet in conjunction with the IT department to jointly develop a testing policy. Again, IT management has the final responsibility for the policy, but the actual policy is developed using people from all major areas of the organization. The advantage of this approach is that it is a true organizational policy and involves all of those areas with an interest in testing. The disadvantage is that it takes time to follow this approach, and a policy might be developed that the IT department is obligated to accept because it is a consensus policy and not the type of policy that IT itself would have written.

Testing is an organizational responsibility. It is the recommendation of the author that a user committee be convened to develop a testing policy. This meeting serves the following purposes:

- It permits all involved parties to participate in the development of a testing policy.

- It is an educational process where users understand the options and costs associated with testing.

- It clearly establishes for all involved departments that testing is an organizational responsibility and not just an IS responsibility.

Structured Approach to Testing

The traditional view of the development life cycle places testing immediately prior to operation and maintenance (see Figure 2.4). All too often, testing after coding is the only verification technique used to determine the adequacy of the system. When testing is constrained to a single phase and confined to the later stages of development, severe consequences can develop. It is not unusual to hear of testing consuming 50 percent of the development budget. All errors are costly, but the later in the life cycle that the error discovery is made, the more costly the error. An error discovered in the latter parts of the life cycle must be paid for four different times. The first cost is developing the program erroneously, which may include writing the wrong specifications, coding the system wrong, and documenting the system improperly. Second, the system must be tested to detect the error. Third, the wrong specifications and coding must be removed and the proper specifications, coding, and documentation added. Fourth, the system must be retested to determine that it is now correct.

If lower cost and higher quality systems are the information services goals, verification must not be isolated to a single phase in the development process, but rather, incorporated into each phase of development. One of the most prevalent and costly mistakes on systems development projects today is to defer the activity of detecting and correcting problems until late in the project. A major justification for an early verification activity is that many costly errors are made before coding begins.

Studies have shown that the majority of system errors occur in the design phase. Figure 2.5 represents the results of numerous studies that show that approximately two-thirds of all detected system errors can be attributed to errors made during the design phase. This means that almost two-thirds of the errors must be specified and coded into programs before they can be detected.

The recommended testing process is presented in Figure 2.6 as a life cycle chart showing the verification activities for each phase. The success of conducting verification throughout the development cycle depends upon the existence of clearly defined and stated products at each development stage. The more formal and precise the statement of the development product, the more amenable it is to the analysis required to support verification. Many of the new system development methodologies encourage firm products even in the early development stages.

The recommended test process involves testing in every phase of the life cycle. During the requirements phase, the emphasis is upon validation to determine that the defined requirements meet the needs of the organization. During the design and program phases, the emphasis is on verification to ensure that the design and programs

REQUIRE-MENTS	DESIGN	CODE (BUILD/ CONSTRUCTION)	TEST	OPERATION & MAINTENANCE

Figure 2.4   Traditional software development life cycle.

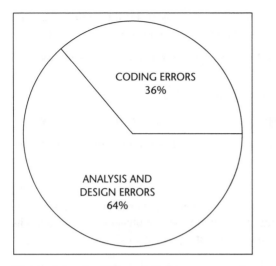

Figure 2.5 Analysis and design errors are the most numerous.

accomplish the defined requirements. During the test and installation phases, the emphasis is on inspection to determine that the implemented system meets the system specification. During the maintenance phases, the system will be retested to determine that the changes work and that the unchanged portion continues to work.

LIFE CYCLE PHASE	VERIFICATION ACTIVITIES
Requirements	• Determine verification approach
	• Determine adequacy of requirements
	• Generate functional test data
	• Determine consistency of design with requirements
Design	• Determine adequacy of design
	• Generate structural and functional test data
	• Determine consistency with design
Program (build/construction)	• Determine adequacy of implementation
	• Generate structural and functional test data for programs
Test	• Test application system
Installation	• Place tested system into production
Maintenance	• Modify and retest

Figure 2.6 Life cycle verification activities.

This book examines each phase of the life cycle and discusses the testing activities appropriate to that phase. The following activities should be performed at each phase:

1. Analyze the structures produced at this phase for internal testability and adequacy.

2. Generate test sets based on the structure at this phase.

In addition, the following should be performed during design and programming:

1. Determine that the structures are consistent with structures produced during previous phases.

2. Refine or redefine test sets generated earlier.

Throughout the entire life cycle, neither development nor verification is a straight-line activity. Modifications or corrections to a structure at one phase will require modifications or reverification of structures produced during previous phases.

Requirements

The verification activities that accompany the problem definition and requirements analysis phase of software development are extremely significant. The adequacy of the requirements must be thoroughly analyzed and initial test cases generated with the expected (correct) responses. Developing scenarios of expected system use may help to determine the test data and anticipated results. These tests will form the core of the final test set. Generating these tests and the expected behavior of the system clarifies the requirements and helps guarantee that they are testable. Vague or untestable requirements will leave the validity of the delivered product in doubt. Late discovery of requirements inadequacy can be very costly. A determination of the criticality of software quality attributes and the importance of validation should be made at this stage. Both product requirements and validation requirements should be established.

Design

Organization of the verification effort and test management activities should be closely integrated with preliminary design. The general testing strategy—including test methods and test evaluation criteria—is formulated, and a test plan is produced. If the project size or criticality warrants, an independent test team is organized. In addition, a test schedule with observable milestones is constructed. At this same time, the framework for quality assurance and test documentation should be established.

During detailed design, validation support tools should be acquired or developed and the test procedures themselves should be produced. Test data to exercise the functions introduced during the design process, as well as test cases based upon the structure of the system, should be generated. Thus, as the software development proceeds, a more effective set of test cases is built.

In addition to test organization and the generation of test cases, the design itself should be analyzed and examined for errors. Simulation can be used to verify properties of the system structures and subsystem interaction, design walkthroughs should be used by the developers to verify the flow and logical structure of the system, while design inspection should be performed by the test team. Missing cases, faulty logic, module interface mismatches, data structure inconsistencies, erroneous I/O assumptions, and user interface inadequacies are items of concern. The detailed design must prove to be internally coherent, complete, and consistent with the preliminary design and requirements.

Program (Build/Construction)

Actual testing occurs during the construction stage of development. Many testing tools and techniques exist for this stage of system development. Code walkthrough and code inspection are effective manual techniques. Static analysis techniques detect errors by analyzing program characteristics such as data flow and language construct usage. For programs of significant size, automated tools are required to perform this analysis. Dynamic analysis, performed as the code actually executes, is used to determine test coverage through various instrumentation techniques. Formal verification or proof techniques are used to provide further quality assurance.

Test Process

During the test process, careful control and management of test information is critical. Test sets, test results, and test reports should be catalogued and stored in a database. For all but very small systems, automated tools are required to do an adequate job—the bookkeeping chores alone become too large to be handled manually. A test driver, test data generation aids, test coverage tools, test results management aids, and report generators are usually required.

Installation

The process of placing tested programs into production is an important phase normally executed within a narrow time span. Testing during this phase must ensure that the correct versions of the program are placed into production; that data if changed or added is correct; and that all involved parties know their new duties and can perform them correctly.

Maintenance

Over 50 percent of the life cycle costs of a software system are spent on maintenance. As the system is used, it is modified either to correct errors or to augment the original system. After each modification the system must be retested. Such retesting activity is termed regression testing. The goal of regression testing is to minimize the cost of system revalidation. Usually only those portions of the system impacted by the modifications are retested. However, changes at any level may necessitate retesting, reverifying, and updating documentation at all levels below it. For example, a design change requires design reverification, unit retesting, and subsystem retesting. Test cases generated during system development are reused or used after appropriate modifications. The quality of the test documentation generated during system development and modified during maintenance will affect the cost of regression testing. If test data cases have been catalogued and preserved, duplication of effort will be minimized.

Test Strategy

The objective of testing is to reduce the risks inherent in computer systems. The strategy must address the risks and present a process that can reduce those risks. The system concerns or risks then establish the objectives for the test process. The two components of the testing strategy are the test factors and the test phase, defined as follows:

1. **Test factor.** The risk or issue that needs to be addressed as part of the test strategy. The strategy will select those factors that need to be addressed in the testing of a specific application system.

2. **Test phase.** The phase of the systems development life cycle in which testing will occur.

Not all test factors will be applicable to all software systems. The development team will need to select and rank the test factors for the specific software system being developed. Once selected and ranked, the strategy for testing will be partially defined.

The test phase will vary based on the testing methodology used. For example, the test phases in a traditional waterfall life cycle methodology will be much different from the phases in a Rapid Application Development methodology.

Test Factors

In designing a test strategy, the risk factors become the basis or objective of testing. The risks associated with testing will be called "test factors" in this book. While the test factors themselves are not risks, they are attributes of the software that, if they are wanted and not present, pose a risk to the success of the software, and thus constitute a business risk. For example, if the software is not easy to use, the resulting processing may be incorrect. The test process should reduce those test factors to a prespecified level. The definition of the test factors enables the test process to be logically constructed like other parts of information services.

When stated in a positive manner, the test risks become the factors that need to be considered in the development of the test strategy. See Figure 2.7 for factors and examples. The following list briefly describes the test factors:

Correctness. Assurance that the data entered, processed, and outputted by the application system is accurate and complete. Accuracy and completeness are achieved through controls over transactions and data elements, which should commence when a transaction is originated and conclude when the transaction data has been used for its intended purpose.

File integrity. Assurance that the data entered into the application system will be returned unaltered. The file integrity procedures ensure that the right file is used and that the data on the file and the sequence in which the data is stored and retrieved is correct.

Authorization. Assurance that data is processed in accordance with the intents of management. In an application system, there is both general and specific authorization for the processing of transactions. General authorization governs the authority to conduct different types of business, while specific authorization provides the authority to perform a specific act.

Audit trail. The capability to substantiate the processing that has occurred. The processing of data can be supported through the retention of sufficient evidential matter to substantiate the accuracy, completeness, timeliness, and authorization of data. The process of saving the supporting evidential matter is frequently called an audit trail.

Continuity of processing. The ability to sustain processing in the event problems occur. Continuity of processing assures that the necessary procedures and backup information are available to recover operations should integrity be lost due to problems. Continuity of processing includes the timeliness of recovery operations and the ability to maintain processing periods when the computer is inoperable.

Service levels. Assurance that the desired results will be available within a time frame acceptable to the user. To achieve the desired service level, it is necessary to match user requirements with available resources. Resources include input/output capabilities, communication facilities, processing, and systems software capabilities.

Access control. Assurance that the application system resources will be protected against accidental and intentional modification, destruction, misuse, and disclosure. The security procedure is the totality of the steps taken to ensure the integrity of application data and programs from unintentional and unauthorized acts.

Compliance. Assurance that the system is designed in accordance with organizational strategy, policies, procedures, and standards. These requirements need to be identified, implemented, and maintained in conjunction with other application requirements.

Reliability. Assurance that the application will perform its intended function with the required precision over an extended period of time. The correctness of processing deals with the ability of the system to process valid transactions correctly, while reliability relates to the system's being able to perform correctly over an extended period of time when placed into production.

Ease of use. The extent of effort required to learn, operate, prepare input for, and interpret output from the system. This test factor deals with the usability of the system to the people interfacing with the application system.

Maintainability. The effort required to locate and fix an error in an operational system. Error is used in the broad context to mean both a defect in the system and a misinterpretation of user requirements.

Portability. The effort required to transfer a program from one hardware configuration and/or software system environment to another. The effort includes data conversion, program changes, operating system, and documentation changes.

Coupling. The effort required to interconnect components within an application system and with all other application systems in their processing environment.

Performance. The amount of computing resources and code required by a system to perform its stated functions. Performance includes both the manual and automated segments involved in fulfilling system functions.

Ease of operation. The amount of effort required to integrate the system into the operating environment and then to operate the application system. The procedures can be both manual and automated.

TEST FACTOR	EXAMPLE
Correctness	Assurance that: • Products are priced correctly on invoices • Gross pay is properly calculated • Inventory-on-hand balances are correctly accumulated
Authorization	Assurance that: • Price overrides are authorized by management • Credits for product returns have been approved by management • Employee overtime pay is authorized by the employee's supervisor
File integrity	Assurance that: • The amounts in the detail records of a file support the control totals • Customer addresses are correct • Employee pay rates are correct
Audit trail	Assurance that: • Employee gross pay can be substantiated by supporting documentation • Sales tax paid to a specific state can be substantiated by the supporting invoices • Payments made to vendors can be substantiated should the vendor disavow receiving the payment
Continuity of processing	Assurance that: • Banking transactions can continue if computer becomes inoperational • Recovery of an on-line system can occur within the predetermined tolerances
Service levels	Assurance that: • Response time in an on-line system is within the time span tolerance • Application workload can be completed in accordance with the application schedule • Changes to the system can be incorporated within the agreed upon schedule

Figure 2.7 Test factor examples.

TEST FACTOR	EXAMPLE
Access control	Assurance that: • Programmers will not be given access to data • Access will be restricted to predetermined system resources • Automated access mechanisms will be current
Compliance	Assurance that: • Information services standards are complied with • System development strategy is followed • System is developed in accordance with budgets and schedules
Reliability	Assurance that: • Users can enter the correct information on a day-to-day basis • Errors can be correctly reprocessed • Appropriate action will be taken on system reports
Ease of use	Assurance that: • Input forms minimize input errors • Flow of work will be optimized in order to process work quickly • Reporting procedures will be written in easy-to-understand terminology
Maintainable	Assurance that: • Program documentation will be up-to-date • Program segments will point to other segments that need to be changed concurrently with that segment • Segments of programs will be identified with appropriate identifiers
Portable	Assurance that: • Computer program will only use common language features • System will be hardware independent • System will be independent of system software special features
Coupling	Assurance that: • Segments in one application requiring concurrent changes in other applications will be properly identified • Common documentation will be up-to-date • Changes will be coordinated
Performance	Assurance that: • System is completed within time and budget constraints • System achieves performance acceptance criteria • Hardware and software usage is optimized
Ease of operations	Assurance that: • Operation documentation is up-to-date • Operators are trained in any special application operating procedures • Correct version of programs run in production

Figure 2.7   *(Continued)*

Developing a Test Strategy

The test strategy is illustrated in Figure 2.8. This is a generic strategy, and will be the one presented in this book. However, this strategy will need to be customized for any specific software system. The applicable test factors would be listed and ranked, and the phases of development would be listed as the phases in which testing must occur.

Four steps must be followed to develop a customized test strategy. The completed customized strategy will be the test factor/test phase matrix as illustrated in Figure 2.8. The four steps are:

1. **Select and rank test factors.** The customers/key users of the system in conjunction with the test team should select and rank the test factors. In most instances, only three to seven factors will be needed. Statistically, if the key factors are selected and ranked, the other factors will normally be addressed in a manner consistent with supporting the key factors. These should be listed in the matrix in sequence from the most significant test factor to the least significant. Rank your factors in sequence from the most to least significant with Work Paper 2.1. Specific test risks can be substituted for factors, or you can expand the factors to describe risks in more detail.

2. **Identify the system development phases.** The project development team should identify the phases of their development process. This is normally obtained from the system development methodology. These phases should be recorded in the test phase component of the matrix. Record these phases in the test phase component of Work Paper 2.2, then copy the test factor appropriately from Work Paper 2.1 to Work Paper 2.2.

3. **Identify the business risks associated with the system under development.** The developers, key users, customers, and test personnel should brainstorm the risks associated with the software system. Most organizations have a brainstorming technique, and it is appropriate for individuals to use the technique in which they have had training and prior use. Using this technique, the risks should be identified and agreed upon by the group. The risks should then be ranked into high, medium, and low. This is a relational severity indicator, meaning that one-third of all risks should be indicated as high; one-third, medium; and one-third, low.

4. **Place risks in the matrix.** The risk team should determine the test phase in which the risk needs to be addressed by the test team, and the test factor to which the risk is associated. Take the example of a payroll system: If there was a concern about compliance to federal and state payroll laws, the risk would be the penalties associated with noncompliance. Assuming compliance was picked as one of the significant test factors, the risk would be most prevalent during the requirements phase. Thus, in the matrix, at the intersection between the compliance test factor and the requirements phase, the risk of "penalties associated with noncompliance to federal and state payroll laws" should be inserted. Note that this may be done by a reference number, cross-referencing the risk. The risk would then have associated with it an H, M, or L, for high, medium, or low risk.

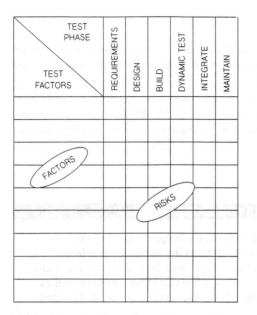

Figure 2.8   Test factor/test phase matrix.

Use Work Paper 2.1

Work Paper 2.1 allows you to make the most important factors your test specifications. The Work Paper should be completed jointly by the project and test teams. Rank the 15 factors from 1 to 15, with 1 as the most and 15 the least important factor. (You can also rank them as high, medium, or low. To use this tool correctly, five factors should be high, five medium, and five low.)

Field Requirements

FIELD	INSTRUCTIONS FOR ENTERING DATA
Number	A sequential number identifying the 15 test factors described in this chapter.
Test Factor	The 15 test factors described in this chapter.
Factor Rank	Rank the most important test factors, ideally 1 through 15; but in practice, this has proven difficult. As an alternative, pick the top five without ranking them; for example, just indicate a check in the Factor Ranked column. Or rank five of them high, five medium, and five low in importance.
Ranking Rationale	Explain why a particular test factor was ranked as indicated. For example, if correctness was ranked as the number 1 factor, the ranking rationale might explain that outputs would be sent to governmental agencies which have viewed incorrect reports negatively.

Use Work Paper 2.2

Copy the test factors from Work Paper 2.1 to Work Paper 2.2 listing the most important factor at the top and the least important factor at the bottom in the Test Factors column. Do not list any inconsequential test factors. Next, list the matching concerns in the appropriate test phase column. In the Figure 2.9 example, if accuracy was your highest test factor, the concern you'd list would be incomplete identification of all software requiring Year 2000 date corrections. A detailed example of how to complete and use this Work Paper follows.

Field Requirements

FIELD	INSTRUCTIONS FOR ENTERING DATA
Test Factors	Contains the factors ranked in importance. If the testers ranked the factors 1–15, then the number 1 test factor would be first in this column and the number 15 test factor would be last. However, if five test factors were ranked as important, then just those five test factors would be listed in this column.
Test Phase	The six most common test phases, as described in the text.
Test Concerns	In the horizontal column under each of the six test phases, list the test concern together with the strategy used to address that test concern. Figure 2.9 further describes documenting the test concerns and test strategy.

Example of Creating a Sample Test Strategy

The objective of the test strategy in Work Paper 2.2 is to identify concerns that will become the focus of test planning and execution. Express the concerns as questions so that the test strategy becomes a high-level focus for testers when they reach the phase where it's most appropriate to address a concern.

Let's look at a payroll system for a corporation that must transmit tax information to the appropriate government agency after January 1, 2000. For the purpose of this example, we will look only at the concern of transmitting tax information although there are other payroll concerns. We'll use the four-step process just described.

Step 1: Select and Rank Test Factors

Test factors for this kind of testing situation would include accuracy, authorization, audit trail, and reliability: accuracy, because your system must calculate taxes correctly; authorization because staff can pass inappropriately approved documents through the system; audit trail because your organization must be able to support the tax calculations; and compliance because your system must adhere to the laws governing deductions and reportings.

In our example we'll address only compliance, but all four would be listed and ranked. In Figure 2.9, in the Test Factor column, compliance is listed as the highest-ranked factor, along with a more specific description of how compliance relates to our example.

Step 2: Identify the Affected Phases

The objective of this step is to assess how many phases are affected by concerns, whether it be a single phase or all phases. In this example, compliance affects all Year 2000 phases.

Step 3: Identify the Test Concerns Associated with Each Phase and Factor

The objective of this step is to identify which concerns to address in which phase, with the concern expressed as a question. For compliance, we'd express our concerns as, "Has the tax transmission risk for our company and government been identified?" The following is a list of compliance concerns for three of the four Year 2000 phases and for dynamic testing:

Assessment. "Are all risks identified for both our company and governmental agencies?"

Plan. "Is there a plan in place to address transmitting tax data after January 1, 2000?"

Implementation. "Was the plan implemented?"

Dynamic test. "Will the transmission be tested between our company and governmental agencies?"

Step 4: Define the Test Strategy

You'll need to develop a test strategy for each concern to determine how the testers will test the implementation of the Year 2000 compliance solution. You will incorporate these strategies into the test plan and thus form the basis for your testing.

Testing Methodology

The testing methodology proposed in this book incorporates both testing strategy and testing tactics. The tactics add the test plans, test criteria, testing techniques, and testing tools used in validating and verifying the software system under development.

The testing methodology cube represents a detailed work program for testing application systems (see Figure 2.10). A detailed testing work program is important to ensure that the test factors have been adequately addressed at each phase of the systems development life cycle. This book provides a detailed description of the work program represented by the testing methodology cube.

TEST FACTORS (RANKED HIGH TO LOW)	SOFTWARE DEVELOPMENT PHASE			
	ASSESSMENT	PLAN	IMPLEMENT	DYNAMIC TEST
Compliance (Can tax information be transmitted after 1/1/2000?)	**Concern** Has tax transmission risk for our company and government been identified? **Test Strategy** Examine the assessment document to determine that a risk regarding transmission of tax data has been identified.	**Concern** Is there a tax transmission Y2K plan? **Test Strategy** Review the Y2K plan to determine how, and which, systems will be modified to ensure that tax data can be transmitted to the appropriate governmental agencies.	**Concern** Was the plan implemented? **Test Strategy** Inspect the programs that govern transmission of tax information to determine whether they were appropriately modified.	**Concern** Was the inplementation tested? **Test Strategy** Create a test, which will transmit to appropriate government agencies with a Year 2000 date.

Figure 2.9 Example of a complete test strategy matrix.

The cube is a three-dimensional work program. The first and most important dimensions are the test factors that are selected for a specific application system test strategy. If the testing process can show that the selected test factors have been adequately handled by the application system, the test process can be considered satisfactorily completed. In designing the test work program, there are concerns in each phase of the life cycle that the test factors will not be achieved. While the factors are common to the entire life cycle, the concerns vary according to the phase of the life cycle. These concerns represent the second dimension of the cube. The third dimension of the cube is the test tactics. There are criteria that, if satisfied, would assure the tester that the application system has adequately addressed the risks. Once the test tactics have assured that the risks are addressed, then the factors can also be considered satisfied and the test tactics are complete.

The three dimensions of the cube will be explained in detail in later chapters, together with the tools and techniques needed for the testing of the application system. The test factors have been previously explained. The test tactics outline the steps to be followed in conducting the tests, together with the tools and techniques needed for each aspect of testing. The test phases are representative of the more commonly accepted system development life cycles. Chapters 9 through 13 will be devoted to testing in each

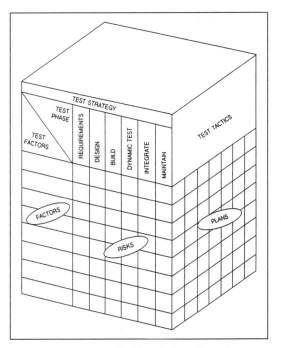

Figure 2.10   Strategical/tactical testing cube.

phase of the life cycle, and in that chapter the phase and test tactics for that phase will be explained in detail.

Status of Software Testing

Organizations spend billions of dollars on software development, yet fail to adequately test the software when completed. Thus, software is placed into production with embedded defects. Quality Assurance Institute surveys conducted over the past several years show that most production software contains three to six defects per thousand lines of source code.

The companion Web site shows the results of a survey conducted by the Quality Assurance Institute at one of its annual software testing conferences. This document will provide a good overview of the current status of software testing.

Summary

This chapter presents a guide for developing your test strategy: identifying risks, translating them into test factors, matching test factors with the concepts of concerns and test phases from Chapter 1, and readying you to create test tactics. The testing methodology cube presents an easy way to structure your strategy. In Chapter 3, we'll overview test tactics—the actual physical tests you'll use to alleviate your concerns and risks.

WORK PAPER 2.1   Test Factor/Risk Ranking

Field Requirements

FIELD	INSTRUCTIONS FOR ENTERING DATA
Number	A sequential number identifying the 15 test factors described in this chapter.
Test Factor	The 15 test factors described in this chapter.
Factor Rank	Rank the most important test factors, ideally 1 through 15; but in practice, this has proven difficult. As an alternative, pick the top five without ranking them; for example, just indicate a check in the Factor Ranked column. Or rank five of them high, five medium, and five low in importance.
Ranking Rationale	Explain why a particular test factor was ranked as indicated. For example, if correctness was ranked as the number 1 factor, the ranking rationale might explain that outputs would be sent to governmental agencies which have viewed incorrect reports negatively.

NUMBER	TEST FACTOR	FACTOR RANK	RANKING RATIONALE
1	Accuracy		
2	File Integrity		
3	Authorization		
4	Audit Trail		
5	Processing Continuity		
6	Service Levels		
7	Access Control		
8	Compliance		
9	Reliability		
10	Ease of Use		
11	Ease of Maintenance		
12	Portability		
13	Coupling		
14	Performance		
15	Ease of Operation		

WORK PAPER 2.2   Test Factors/Test Phase/Test Concerns

TEST FACTORS (RANKED HIGH TO LOW) \ TEST PHASE	REQUIREMENTS	DESIGN	BUILD	DYNAMIC TEST	INTEGRATE	MAINTAIN
Factor or Risks				*Test Concerns*		

Establishing a Software Testing Methodology

The testing methodology is the means by which the test strategy is achieved. The team that develops the testing methodology will use the test strategy matrix as requirements. It will be their task to determine the tests and the methods of performance needed to address the risks identified in the test strategy.

This chapter will describe the construction of a workbench for building software. The workbench will illustrate both the "do" and the "check" procedures. The check procedures are the test procedures. The chapter will then identify the eight considerations in developing a tactical work plan (i.e., test plan) for testing. A section defining terms common to testing is included in this chapter. Part Three of this book details the 11 steps proposed as a generic test methodology.

What Are You Testing For?

All testing focuses on discovering and eliminating defects or variances from what is expected. There are two types of defects:

1. **Variance from specifications.** A defect from the perspective of the builder of the product.

2. **Variance from what is desired.** A defect from a user (or customer) perspective.

Testers need to identify both types of defects.

Consider the example of a missile guidance system that is not Year 2000 compliant. Though the builder of the software can correct the problem so that the missile guidance system can now recognize Year 2000 dates, the date correction method increases the number of processing cycles, meaning that it now takes longer to perform the navigation routine than it did before. The extra cycle time causes the missile to veer from its projected path, detonating within the area in which it was launched. This is an obvious defect from the user perspective! We may have corrected the *producer* Year 2000 defect, but not the *customer* Year 2000 defect.

Why Are Defects Hard to Find?

Finding defects in a system is not easy. Some are easy to spot, others are more subtle. There are at least two reasons defects go undetected:

1. **Not looking.** Tests often are not performed because a particular test condition was unknown. Also, some parts of a system go untested because developers assume software changes don't affect them.

2. **Looking, but not seeing.** This is like losing your car keys, only to discover they were in plain sight the entire time. Sometimes developers become so familiar with their system that they overlook details, which is why independent verification and validation is used to provide a fresh viewpoint.

Defects typically found in software systems are the results of these circumstances:

IT improperly interprets requirements. Information technology (IT) staff misinterpret what the user wants, but correctly implement what the IT people believe is wanted.

The users specify the wrong requirements. The specifications given to IT are erroneous.

The requirements are incorrectly recorded. Information technology fails to record the specifications properly.

The design specifications are incorrect. The application system design does not achieve the system requirements, but the design as specified is implemented correctly.

The program specifications are incorrect. The design specifications are incorrectly interpreted, making the program specifications inaccurate; however, it is possible to properly code the program to achieve the specifications.

There are errors in program coding. The program is not coded according to the program specifications.

There are data entry errors. Data entry staff incorrectly enter information into your computers.

There are testing errors. Tests either falsely detect an error or fail to detect one.

There are mistakes in error correction. Your implementation team makes errors in implementing your solutions.

The corrected condition causes another defect. In the process of correcting a defect, the correction process itself institutes additional defects into the application system.

Usually, you can identify the test tactics for any test process easily; it's estimating the costs of the tests that's difficult. Testing costs depend heavily on when in the project life cycle testing occurs. As noted in Chapter 2, the later in the life cycle testing occurs, the higher the cost. The cost of a defect is twofold; you pay to identify a defect and to correct it.

Reduce the Cost of Testing

The cost of defect identification and correction increases exponentially as the project progresses. Figure 3.1 illustrates the accepted industry standard for estimating costs, and shows how costs dramatically increase the later you find a defect. A defect encountered during requirement and design is the cheapest to fix, so let's say it costs x. Based on this, a defect corrected during the system test phase costs $10x$ to fix. A defect corrected after the system goes into production? $100x$. Clearly, identifying and correcting defects early is the most cost-effective way to develop an error-free system.

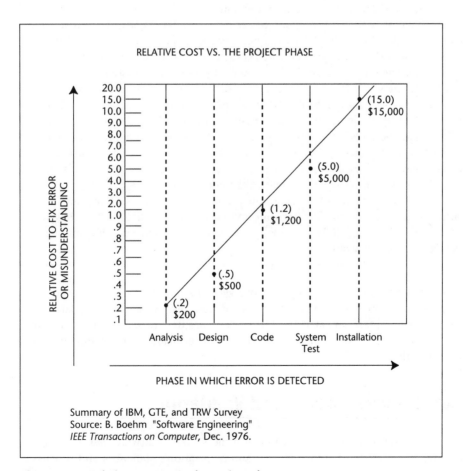

Figure 3.1 Relative cost versus the project phase.

Testing should begin during the first phase of the life cycle and continue throughout the life cycle. Although this book is centered around V-concept testing (which we'll detail in Chapter 6), it's important to recognize that life cycle testing is essential to reducing the cost of testing. The sidebar provides a brief outline of life cycle testing.

LIFE CYCLE TESTING

Life cycle testing involves continuous testing of the solution even after software plans are complete and the tested system is implemented. At several points during the development process, the test team should test the system in order to identify defects at the earliest possible point.

Life cycle testing cannot occur until you formally develop your process. Information technology must provide and agree to a strict schedule for completing various phases of the process for proper life cycle testing to occur. If IT does not determine the order in which they deliver completed pieces of software, it's impossible to schedule and conduct appropriate tests.

Life cycle testing is best accomplished by forming a test team. The team is composed of project members responsible for testing the system. They *must* use structured methodologies when testing; they should not use the same methodology for testing that they used for developing the system. The effectiveness of the test team depends on developing the system under one methodology and testing it under another. The life cycle testing concept is illustrated in Figure 3.2. It shows that when the project starts, both the development process and system test process also begin. Thus, the testing and implementation teams begin their work at the same time and with the same information. The development team defines and documents the requirements for implementation purposes, and the test team uses those requirements for the purpose of testing the system. At appropriate points during the development process, the test team runs the compliance process to uncover defects. The test team should use the structured testing techniques outlined in this book as a basis of evaluating the corrections.

As you're testing the implementation, prepare a series of tests that your IT department can run periodically after your revised system goes live. Testing does not stop once you've completely implemented your system; it must continue until you replace or update it again!

Now that we've identified generally what we're looking for, we're ready to break down the process into specific testing tactics. The four testing tactics of validation, verification, functional test, and structural test, which are the bread and butter of testing, can be separated into two groups: (1) validation and verification and (2) functional and structural testing.

What Are Verification and Validation?

A tester uses *verification* methods to ensure the system (software, hardware, documentation, and personnel) complies with an organization's standards and processes,

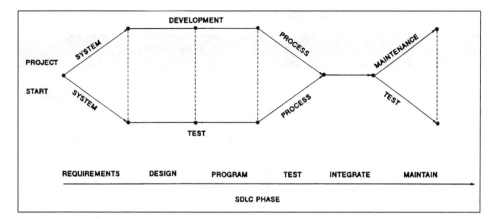

Figure 3.2   Life cycle testing concepts.

relying on review or nonexecutable methods. *Validation* physically ensures that the system operates according to plan by executing the system functions through a series of tests that can be observed and evaluated. Verification answers the question, "Did we build the right system?" while validation addresses, "Did we build the system right?"

Although this book will emphasize computer software, keep in mind that verification and validation techniques can be applied to every element of the computerized system. You'll find these techniques in publications dealing with the design and implementation of user manuals and training courses, as well as in industry publications.

Computer System Verification and Validation Examples

Verification requires several types of reviews, including requirement reviews, code walkthroughs, code inspections, design reviews, and review reviews. The system user should be involved in these reviews to find defects before they are built into the system. In the case of purchased systems, user input is needed to assure that the supplier makes the appropriate tests to eliminate defects. Table 3.1 shows examples of verification. The list is not exhaustive, but it does show who performs the task and what the deliverables are. For purchased systems, the term "developers" will apply to the supplier's development staff.

Validation is accomplished simply by executing a real-life function (if you wanted to check to see if your mechanic had fixed the starter on your car, you'd try to start the car). Examples of validation are shown in Table 3.2. As in Table 3.1, the list is not exhaustive.

Determining when to perform verification and validation relates to the development, acquisition, and maintenance of software. For software testing, this relationship is especially critical because:

- **The corrections will probably be made using the same process for developing the software.** If the software was developed internally using a waterfall

Table 3.1   Computer System Verification Examples

VERIFICATION EXAMPLE	PERFORMED BY	EXPLANATION	DELIVERABLE
Requirements reviews	Developers, Users	The study and discussion of the computer system requirements to ensure they meet stated user needs and are feasible.	Reviewed statement of requirements, ready to be translated into system design.
Design Reviews	Developers	The study and discussion of the computer system design to ensure it will support the system requirements.	System design, ready to be translated into computer programs, hardware configurations, documentation, and training.
Code Walkthroughs	Developers	An informal analysis of the program source code to find defects and verify coding techniques.	Computer software ready for testing or more detailed inspections by the developer.
Code Inspections	Developers	A formal analysis of the program source code to find defects as defigned by meeting computer system design specifications. Usually performed by a team composed of developers and subject matter experts.	Computer software ready for testing by the developer.

methodology, that methodology will probably be followed in making the corrections; on the other hand, if the software was purchased or contracted, the supplier will likely make the correction. You'll need to prepare tests for either eventuality.

■ **Year testers can probably use the test plans and test data prepared for testing the original software.** If testers prepared effective test plans and created extensive test data, those plans and test data can probably be used in the testing effort, thereby reducing the time and cost of testing.

Table 3.2   Computer System Validation Examples

VERIFICATION EXAMPLE	PERFORMED BY	EXPLANATION	DELIVERABLE
Unit Testing	Developers	The testing of a single program, module, or unit of code. Usually performed by the developer of the unit. Validates that the software performs as designed.	Software unit ready for testing with other system component, such as other software units, hardware, documentation, or users.
Integrated Testing	Developers	The testing of related programs, modules, or units of code. Validates that multiple parts of the system interact according to the system design.	Portions of the system ready for testing with other portions of the system.
System Testing	Developers, users	The testing of an entire computer system. This kind of testing can include functional and structural testing, such as stress testing. Validates the system requirements.	A tested computer system, based on what was specified to be developed or purchased.
User Acceptance Testing	Users	The testing of a computer system or parts of a computer system to make sure it will work in the system regardless of what the system requirements indicate.	A tested computer system, based on user needs.

Functional and Structural Testing

When your testers test your project team's solution, they'll perform functional or structural tests with the verification and validation techniques just described. Functional testing is sometimes called *black box testing* because no knowledge of the internal logic of the system is used to develop test cases. For example, if a certain function key should produce a specific result when pressed, a functional test would be to validate this expectation by pressing the function key and observing the result. When conducting functional tests, you'll be using validation techniques almost exclusively.

Conversely, structural testing is sometimes called *white box testing* because knowledge of the internal logic of the system is used to develop hypothetical test cases. Structural tests use verification predominantly. If a software development team creates a block of code that will allow a system to process information in a certain way, a test team would verify this structurally by reading the code, and given the system's structure, see if the code could work reasonably. If they felt it could, they would plug the code into the system and run an application to structurally validate the code. Each method has its pros and cons:

- Functional Testing Advantages:
  - Simulates actual system usage.
  - Makes no system structure assumptions.
- Functional Testing Disadvantages:
  - Potential of missing logical errors in software.
  - Possibility of redundant testing.
- Structural Testing Advantages:
  - You can test the software's structure logic.
  - You'd test where you wouldn't think to if you performed only functional testing.
- Structural Testing Disadvantages:
  - Does not ensure that you've met user requirements.
  - Its tests may not mimic real-world situations.

Why Use Both Testing Methods?

Both methods together validate the entire system. For example, a functional test case might be taken from the documentation description of how to perform a certain function, such as accepting bar code input. A structural test case might be taken from a technical documentation manual. To effectively test systems, you need to use both methods.

Structural and Functional Tests Using Verification and Validation Techniques

As stated, testers use verification techniques to confirm the reasonableness of a system by reviewing its structure and logic. Validation, on the other hand, strictly applies to physical testing, to determine whether expected results occur. You'll conduct structural tests primarily using verification techniques, and conduct functional tests with validation techniques.

Using verification to conduct structural tests would include:

Feasibility reviews. Tests for this structural element would verify the logic flow of a unit of software.

Requirements reviews. These reviews verify software relationships; for example, in any particular system, the structural limits of how much load (e.g., transactions or number of concurrent users) a system can handle.

Functional tests are virtually all validation tests, and inspect how the system performs. Examples of this are:

Unit testing. These tests verify that the system functions properly; for example, pressing a function key to complete an action.

Integrated testing. The system runs tasks that involve more than one application or database to verify that it performed the tasks accurately.

System testing. These tests simulate operation of the entire system, and verify that it ran correctly.

User acceptance. This real-world test means the most to your business; and, unfortunately, there's no way to conduct it in isolation. Once your organization staff, customers, or vendors begin to interact with your system, they'll verify that it functions properly for you.

Verification and validation are not mutually exclusive, so you will conduct functional tests with verification and structural tests with validation during your project. Table 3.3 shows the relationships just explained, listing each of the six test activities, who performs them, and whether the activity is an example of verification or validation. For example, when conducting a feasibility review, developers and users verify that the software could conceivably perform after the solution is implemented the way the developers expect.

Now that you've seen how you must verify and validate your system structurally and functionally, the last tool to introduce is a process template for employing these tactics, called the *testers' workbench*.

Table 3.3 Functional Testing

TEST PHASE	PERFORMED BY	VERIFICATION	VALIDATION
Feasibility Review	Developers, users	x	
Requirements Review	Developers, users	x	
Unit Testing	Developers		x
Integrated Testing	Developers, users		x
System Testing	Developers with user assistance		x
Acceptance	Users		x

Workbench Concept

To understand testing methodology, it is necessary to understand the workbench concept. In information technology workbenches are more frequently referred to as phases, steps, or tasks. The workbench is a way of illustrating and documenting how a specific activity is to be performed. Defining workbenches is normally the responsibility of a process management committee, which in the past has been more frequently referred to as a standards committee. There are four components to each workbench:

1. **Input.** The entrance criteria or deliverables needed to perform work.

2. **Procedures to do.** The work tasks or processes that will transform the input into the output.

3. **Procedures to check.** The processes that determine that the output meets the standards.

4. **Output.** The exit criteria or deliverables produced from the workbench.

NOTE The tools are not considered a part of the workbench because they are incorporated into either the procedures to do or procedures to check. The workbench is illustrated in Figure 3.3 and the software development life cycle, which is comprised of many workbenches, is illustrated in Figure 3.4.

The workbench concept can be used to illustrate one of the steps involved in building systems. The programmer's workbench consists of these steps:

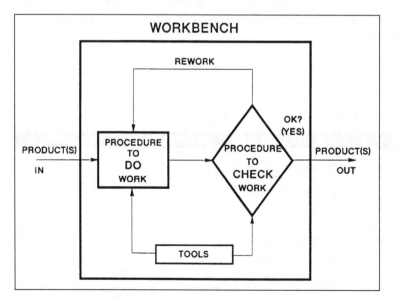

Figure 3.3   Workbench.

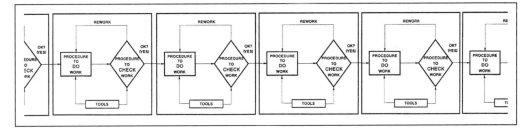

Figure 3.4   Software life cycle.

1. Input *products* (program specs) are given to the producer (programmer).

2. Work is *performed* (e.g., coding/debugging); a procedure is followed; a product or interim deliverable (e.g., a program/module/unit) is produced.

3. Work is *checked* to ensure product meets specs and standards, and that the procedure was followed.

4. If check finds no problems, product is released to the next workbench.

5. If check finds problems, product is sent back for rework.

As an example of how a project team would use the workbench to guide them through a project phase, we'll describe a sample validation of computer code. The programmer's unit test consists of these steps:

1. Give input products (e.g., program code) to the tester.

2. Perform work (e.g., coding and debugging); follow a procedure; produce a product or interim deliverable (e.g., the test results).

3. Check work to ensure test results meet test specs and standards and that the test procedure was followed.

4. If the check process finds no problems, release the product (i.e., test results) to the next workbench.

5. If the check process finds problems, send the product back for rework.

Chapters 6 through 17, which walk you through testing your software development project, describe each step in workbench format. Each chapter begins with a workbench description for that step.

Eight Considerations in Developing Testing Methodologies

This chapter explains eight considerations to convert the test strategy developed using the process in Chapter 2 into the test tactics or test plan that will be followed in executing the day-to-day testing.

The details on how to develop the specifics for the test tactics (test plan) are covered in Chapter 8. The objective of this chapter, and the eight considerations, is to provide the framework for developing the testing tactics. The eight considerations are listed below and then individually described:

1. Acquire and study the test strategy.
2. Determine the type of development project.
3. Determine the type of software system.
4. Determine the project scope.
5. Identify the tactical risks.
6. Determine when testing should occur.
7. Build the system test plan.
8. Build the unit test plan.

1. Acquire and Study the Test Strategy

Test strategy is normally developed by a team very familiar with the business risks associated with the software; tactics are developed by the test team. Thus, the test team needs to acquire and study the test strategy. In this study, the test team should be asking:

- What is the relationship of importance among the test factors?
- Which of the high-level risks are the most significant?
- What damage can be done to the business if the software fails to perform correctly?
- What damage can be done to the business if the software is not completed on time?
- Who are the individuals most knowledgeable in understanding the impact of the identified business risks?

2. Determine the Type of Development Project

The type of project refers to the environment/methodology in which the software will be developed. As the environment changes, so does the testing risk. For example, the risks associated with the traditional development effort are different from the risks associated with off-the-shelf purchased software. Different testing approaches must be used for different types of projects, just as different development approaches are used (see Figure 3.5).

3. Determine the Type of Software System

The type of software system refers to the processing that will be performed by that system. This step contains sixteen different software system types. However, a single soft-

TYPE	CHARACTERISTICS	TEST TACTICS
Traditional system development (and most perfective maintenance)	- Uses a system development methodology - User knows requirements - Development determines structure	- Test at end of each task/step/phase - Verify that specs match need - Test function and structure
Iterative development/prototyping/CASE	- Requirements unknown - Structure predefined	- Verify that CASE tools are used properly - Test functionality
System maintenance	- Modify structure	- Test structure - Works best with release methods - Requires regression testing
Purchased/contracted software	- Structure unknown - May contain defects - Functionality defined in user documentation - Documentation may vary from software	- Verify that functionality matches need - Test functionality - Test fit into environment

Figure 3.5 Project types.

ware system may incorporate more than one of these types. Identifying the specific combinations of software making up the project can help analyze lessons learned on past projects with similar types of software.

Batch (general). Can be run as a normal batch job and makes no unusual hardware or input-output actions (e.g., payroll program and wind tunnel data analysis program).

Event control. Does real-time processing of data resulting from external events. An example might be a computer program that processes telemetry data.

Process control. Receives data from an external source and issues commands to that source to control its actions based on the received data.

Procedure control. Controls other software; for example, an operating system that controls execution of time-shared and batch computer programs.

Advanced mathematical models. Resembles simulation and business strategy software, but has the additional complexity of heavy use of mathematics.

Message processing. Handles input and output messages, processing the text, or information contained therein.

Diagnostic software. Detects and isolates hardware errors in the computer where it resides, or in other hardware that can communicate with that computer.

Sensor and signal processing. Similar to that of message processing, but requires greater processing to analyze and transform the input into a usable data processing format.

Simulation. Simulates an environment, mission situation, other hardware; inputs from these to enable a more realistic evaluation of a computer program or a piece of hardware.

Database management. Manages the storage and access of (typically large) groups of data. Such software can also prepare reports in user-defined formats based on the contents of the database.

Data acquisition. Receives information in real time and stores it in some form suitable for later processing; for example, software that receives data from a space probe and files it for later analysis.

Data presentation. Formats and transforms data, as necessary, for convenient and understandable displays for humans. Typically, such displays would be for some screen presentation.

Decision and planning aids. Uses artificial intelligence techniques to provide an expert system to evaluate data and provide additional information and consideration for decision and policy makers.

Pattern and image processing. Generates and processes computer images. Such software may analyze terrain data and generate images based on stored data.

Computer system software. Provides services to operational computer programs (i.e., coordinates processing of components needed to meet need).

Software development tools. Provides services to aid in the development of software (e.g., compilers, assemblers, static and dynamic analyzers).

4. Determine the Project Scope

The project scope refers to the totality of activities to be incorporated into the software system being tested—the range of system requirements/specifications to be understood. The scope of new system development is different from the scope of changes to an existing system. This step describes some of the necessary characteristics, but this list must be expanded to encompass the requirements of the specific software system being tested. The scope of the project usually delimits the scope of the testing effort. Consider the following issues:

- **New systems development:**

  Automating manual business process?

  Which business processes will/won't be affected?

  Which business areas will/won't be affected?

  Interfacing to existing systems?

  Existing systems will/won't be affected?

- **Changes to existing systems:**

  Corrective only?

  Maintenance reengineering standards?

  Correction to known latent defects in addition to enhancements?

  Other systems affected?

  Risk of regression?

5. Identify the Tactical Risks

Strategic risks are the high-level business risks faced by the software system; tactical risks are subsets at a lower level of the strategic risks. The purpose of decomposing the strategic risks into tactical risks is to assist in creating the test scenarios that will address those risks. It is difficult to create test scenarios for high-level risks.

Tactical risks are divided into three categories:

1. **Structural risks.** The risks associated with the application and the methods used to build the application.

2. **Technical risks.** The risks associated with the technology used in building and operating the application.

3. **Size risks.** The risks associated with bigness in all aspects of the software.

Work Papers 3.1, 3.2, and 3.3 provide the method for assessing the structural, technical, and size risks. These Work Papers are to be completed by the test team interacting with the development team and selected end users/customers. Each of the three Work Papers identifies a risk, a rating for the risk, and a weight associated with the risk. The identification of the risk and its associated weight are supplied as part of the tactical risk assessment process. Weight is an indication of the relative importance of each risk in relationship to the other risks.

To complete Work Papers 3.1, 3.2, and 3.3 perform the following steps:

1. **Understand the risk and the ratings provided for that risk.** In most instances, ratings will be scores of 1 through 4, with the explanation of that rating in the rating column of the risk work paper.

2. **Determine the applicable rating for the software system being tested.** Select one of the listed ratings for each risk and place it in the rating column of the work paper. For example, on the structural risk assessment, if you deter-

mined that the amount of time since the last major change to the existing area of business was more than two years, you would note that a low rating was indicated, and put a 1 in the rating column.

3. **Calculate and accumulate the risk score.** The ratings you provided in the rating column should be multiplied by the weight to get a score. The score for each work paper should then be accumulated and the total score posted to Work Paper 3.4 (Risk Score Analysis Work Paper). When the three work papers have been completed, you will have posted three scores to the Risk Score Analysis Work Paper.

To complete Work Paper 3.4, the Risk Score Analysis Work Paper, follow these steps:

Step 1. Calculate average risk score by risk area. To do this, total the number of risks on the three work papers and divide that into the total score on Work Paper 3.4 to obtain an average score for the three risk areas. Do the same for the total risk score for the software.

Step 2. Post comparative ratings. After you have used these risk work papers a number of times, you will develop average scores for your application systems. Take the score totals for your application systems and rank them from high to low for each of the three risk areas. Then determine an average for the high third of the scores, the middle third of the scores, and the low third of the scores. This average is the cumulative rating for your company's applications, and can be permanently recorded on Work Paper 3.4. This will enable you to compare the score of the system you are testing against comparative ratings so you can determine whether the system you are working on is high, medium, or low risk in each of the three risk areas and overall.

Step 3. List at the bottom of Work Paper 3.4 all of the risk attributes from the three worksheets that received a high-risk rating. Identify the area (for example, structure) and list the specific risk that was given a high rating. Then, for each of those risks, determine the specific test concern and list it on Work Paper 3.4.

When you have completed this assessment process, the tactical risks will be well defined, enabling the insight gained from this step to be embedded into the test plan. Obviously, areas of high risk may need special attention; for example, if size puts the project in a high-risk rating, then extra test effort may be needed, focused on ensuring that the system can handle the volume or size of transactions specified for the software. Test concerns can be addressed by specific tests designed to evaluate the magnitude of the risk and the adequacy of controls in the system to address that risk.

6. Determine When Testing Should Occur

The previous steps have identified the type of development project, the type of software system, the project scope, and the technical risks. Using that information, the point in the development process when testing should occur must be determined. The previous steps have identified what type of testing needs to occur, and this step will tell when it should occur.

Testing can and should occur throughout the phases of a project. Examples of test activities to be performed during these phases are (see Figure 3.2):

A. Requirements phase activities
 - Determine test strategy
 - Determine adequacy of requirements
 - Generate functional test conditions

B. Design phase activities
 - Determine consistency of design with requirements
 - Determine adequacy of design
 - Generate structural and functional test conditions

C. Program (build) phase activities
 - Determine consistency with design
 - Determine adequacy of implementation
 - Generate structural and functional test conditions for programs/units

D. Test phase activities
 - Determine adequacy of the test plan
 - Test application system

E. Installation phase activities
 - Place tested system into production

F. Maintenance phase activities
 - Modify and retest

7. Build the System Test Plan

A tactical test plan must be developed to describe when and how testing will occur. This test plan will provide background information on the software being tested, on the test objectives and risks, as well as on the business functions to be tested and the specific tests to be performed.

Information on the test environment part of the test plan is described in Part Two of this book. Reference other parts of the book for development methodologies other than the waterfall methodology; for example, Chapter 18 addresses client/server systems.

The test plan is the road map that will be followed in conducting testing. The plan is then decomposed into specific tests and lower-level plans. After execution, the results are rolled up to produce a test report. The test reports included in Chapter 14 are designed around standardized test plans. A recommended test plan standard is illustrated in Figure 3.6; it is consistent with most of the widely accepted published test plan standards.

1. **GENERAL INFORMATION**

    1.1   Summary. Summarize the functions of the software and the tests to be performed.

    1.2   Environment and Pretest Background. Summarize the history of the project. Identify the user organization and computer center where the testing will be performed. Describe any prior testing and note results that may affect this testing.

    1.3   Test Objectives. State the objectives to be accomplished by testing.

    1.4   Expected Defect Rates. State the estimated number of defects for software of this type.

    1.5   References. List applicable references, such as:

    a)   Project request authorization.
    b)   Previously published documents on the project.
    c)   Documentation concerning related projects.

2. **PLAN**

    2.1   Software Description. Provide a chart and briefly describe the inputs, outputs, and functions of the software being tested as a frame of reference for the test descriptions.

    2.2   Test Team. State who is on the test team and their test assignment(s).

    2.3   Milestones. List the locations, milestone events, and dates for the testing.

    2.4   Budgets. List the funds allocated to test by task and checkpoint.

    2.5   Testing (systems checkpoint). Identify the participating organizations and the system checkpoint where the software will be tested.

    2.5.1   Schedule (and budget). Show the detailed schedule of dates and events for the testing at this location. Such events may include familiarization, training, data, as well as the volume and frequency of the input. Resources allocated for test should be shown.

    2.5.2   Requirements. State the resource requirement, including:

    a)   Equipment. Show the expected period of use, types, and quantities of the equipment needed.
    b)   Software. List other software that will be needed to support the testing that is not part of the software to be tested.
    c)   Personnel. List the numbers and skill types of personnel that are expected to be available during the test from both the user and development groups. Include any special requirements such as multishift operation or key personnel.

Figure 3.6   System test plan standard.

2. PLAN

    2.5.3   Testing Materials. List the materials needed for the test, such as:

        a)   System documentation
        b)   Software to be tested and its medium
        c)   Test inputs
        d)   Test documentation
        e)   Test tools

    2.5.4   Test Training. Describe or reference the plan for providing training in the use of the software being tested. Specify the types of training, personnel to be trained, and the training staff.

    2.5.5   Test to be Conducted. Reference specific tests to be conducted at this checkpoint.

  2.6   Testing (system checkpoint). Describe the plan for the second and subsequent system checkpoint where the software will be tested in a manner similar to paragraph 2.5.

3. SPECIFICATIONS AND EVALUATION

  3.1   Specifications

    3.1.1   Business Functions. List the business functional requirement established by earlier documentation, or Task 1 of Step 2.

    3.1.2   Structural Functions. List the detailed structural functions to be exercised during the overall test.

    3.1.3   Test/Function Relationships. List the tests to be performed on the software and relate them to the functions in paragraph 3.1.2.

    3.1.4   Test Progression. Describe the manner in which progression is made from one test to another so that the entire test cycle is completed.

  3.2   Methods and Constraints.

    3.2.1   Methodology. Describe the general method or strategy of the testing.

    3.2.2   Test Tools. Specify the type of test tools to be used.

    3.2.3   Extent. Indicate the extent of the testing, such as total or partial. Include any rationale for partial testing.

    3.2.4   Data Recording. Discuss the method to be used for recording the test results and other information about the testing.

    3.2.5   Constraints. Indicate anticipated limitations on the test due to test conditions, such as interfaces, equipment, personnel, databases.

Figure 3.6   *(Continued)*   *(Continues)*

---

3. SPECIFICATIONS AND EVALUATION

    3.3   Evaluation.

        3.3.1   Criteria. Describe the rules to be used to evaluate test results, such as range of data values used, combinations of input types used, maximum number of allowable interrupts or halts.

        3.3.2   Data Reduction. Describe the techniques to be used for manipulating the test data into a form suitable for evaluation, such as manual or automated methods, to allow comparison of the results that should be produced to those that are produced.

4. TEST DESCRIPTIONS

    4.1   Test (Identify). Describe the test to be performed (format will vary for on-line test script).

        4.1.1   Control. Describe the test control, such as manual, semiautomatic or automatic insertion of inputs, sequencing of operations, and recording of results.

        4.1.2   Inputs. Describe the input data and input commands used during the test.

        4.1.3   Outputs. Describe the output data expected as a result of the test and any intermediate messages that may be produced.

        4.1.4   Procedures. Specify the step-by-step procedures to accomplish the test. Include test setup, initialization, steps and termination.

    4.2   Test (Identify). Describe the second and subsequent tests in a manner similar to that used in paragraph 4.1.

Figure 3.6   *(Continued)*

8. Build the Unit Test Plan

During internal design, the system is divided into the components or units that perform the detailed processing. Each of these units should have its own test plan. The plans can be as simple or as complex as the organization requires based on its quality expectations.

The importance of a unit test plan is to determine when unit testing is complete. It is a bad idea economically to submit units that contain defects to higher levels of testing. Thus, extra effort spent in developing unit test plans, testing units, and assuring that units are defect free prior to integration testing can have a significant payback in reducing overall test costs.

A suggested unit test plan is presented in Figure 3.7. This unit test plan is consistent with the most widely accepted unit test plan standards. Note that the test reporting in Chapter 14 for units assumes that a standardized unit test plan is utilized.

1. **PLAN**

   1.1   Unit Description. Provide a brief description and flowchart of the unit which describes the input, outputs, and functions of the unit being tested as a frame of reference for the specific tests.

   1.2   Milestones. List the milestone events and dates for testing.

   1.3   Budget. List the funds allocated to test this unit.

   1.4   Test Approach. The general method or strategy used to test this unit.

   1.5   Functions not Tested. List those functions which will not be validated as a result of this test.

   1.6   Test Constraints. Indicate anticipated limitations on the test due to test conditions, such as interfaces, equipment, personnel, and data bases.

2. **BUSINESS AND STRUCTURAL FUNCTION TESTING**

   2.1   Business Functions. List the business functional requirements included in this unit.

   2.2   Structural Functions. List the structural functions included in the unit.

   2.3   Test Descriptions. Describe the tests to be performed in evaluating business and structural functions.

   2.4   Expected Test Results. List the desired result from each test. That which will validate the correctness of the unit functions.

   2.5   Conditions to Stop Test. The criteria which if occurs will result in the tests being stopped.

   2.6   Test Number Cross-Reference. A cross-reference between the system test identifiers and the unit test identifiers.

3. **INTERFACE TEST DESCRIPTIONS**

   3.1   Interface. List the interfaces that are included in this unit.

   3.2   Test Description. Describe the tests to be performed to evaluate the interfaces.

   3.3   Expected Test Results. List the desired result from each test. That which will validate the correctness of the unit functions.

   3.4   Test Number Cross-Reference. A cross-reference between the system test identifiers and the unit test identifiers.

4   **TEST PROGRESSION**

   List the progression in which the tests must be performed. Note that this is obtained from the system test plan. This section may be unnecessary if the system test plan progression worksheet can be carried forward.

Figure 3.7   Unit test plan standard.

Testing Tactics Checklist

This chapter focused on the tactics needed to test any kind of software. Once you're familiar with these tactics, you need to incorporate them into a test plan.

Work Paper 3.5 is a self-assessment checklist for test tactics that you can use in the test planning process. Use this checklist as you develop your test plan, for it will ensure that the test team considers and decides which test tactics you'll use. A Yes response to any checklist items means that you've chosen an effective test tactic for your project. If you don't want to use a particular item as you test, insert No for that item. Use the comments column to clarify your response and to provide guidance to the test plan committee. A blank worksheet has been provided for your use at the end of this chapter.

Chapter 6 will help you put all the pieces together to design your testing team, and apply the concepts of verification and validation and structural and functional testing directly to the software testing process.

Summary

The time spent in test planning is normally recouped in more efficient and effective testing. As a guideline, about one-third of the total test time should be spent in strategic and tactical planning. This chapter describes testing methodology concepts and considerations. Chapters 4 and 5 will address the testing techniques and tools that are an integral part of a testing methodology. These two chapters will complete the establishment of the environment in which the proposed 11-step software testing process will be discussed in Chapters 7 through 17.

WORK PAPER 3.1   Structural Risk Assessment

TEST DOCUMENT
Structural Risk Assessment

		RATING × WEIGHT=
Ratings: L - Low M - Medium H - High NA - Not Applicable		
RISK	RATINGS	SCORE

RISK	RATINGS	SCORE
1. Amount of time since last major change to existing area of business		3
• More than 2 years	L=1	
• 1 to 2 years; unknown	M=2	
• Less than 1 year	H=3	
• No automated system	H=3	
2. Estimated frequency of change to proposed/existing systems		3
• No existing automated system; or development effort insufficient for estimate	NA=0	
• Fewer than 2 per year	L=1	
• 2 to 10 per year	M=2	
• More than 20 per year	H=3	
3. Estimated extent of total changes in business area methods in last year in percentage of methods affected		3
• No changes	NA=0	
• Less than 10%	L=1	
• 10 to 25%	M=2	
• More than 25%	H=3	
4. Magnitude of changes in business area associated with this project		3
• Minor change(s)	L=1	
• Significant but manageable change	M=2	
• Major changes to system functionality and/or resource needs	H=4	
5. Project performance site		2
• Company facility	L=1	
• Local noncompany facility	M=2	
• Not in local area	H=5	
6. Critical staffing of project		2
• In-house	L=1	
• Contractor, sole-source	M=2	
• Contractor, competitive-bid	H=6	
7. Type of project organization		2
• Line and staff: project has total management control of personnel	L=1	
• Mixture of line and staff with matrix-managed elements	M=2	
• Matrix: no management control transferred to project	H=3	

(Continues)

WORK PAPER 3.1 *(Continued)*

TEST DOCUMENT
Structural Risk Assessment

Ratings: L - Low M - Medium H - High NA - Not Applicable		RATING × WEIGHT=
RISK	**RATINGS**	**SCORE**
8. Potential problems with subcontractor relationship		5
• Not applicable to this project	NA=0	
• Subcontractor not assigned to isolated or critical task: prime contractor has previously managed subcontractor successfully	L=1	
• Subcontractor assigned to all development tasks in subordinate role to prime contractor: company has favorable experience with subcontractor on other effort(s)	M=2	
• Subcontractor has sole responsibility for critical task; subcontractor new to company	H=3	
9. Status of the ongoing project training		2
• No training plan required	NA=0	
• Complete training plan in place	L=1	
• Some training in place	M=2	
• No training available	H=3	
10. Level of skilled personnel available to train project team		3
• No training required	NA=0	
• Knowledgeable on all systems	L=1	
• Knowledgeable on major components	M=2	
• Few components understood	H=3	
11. Accessibility of supporting reference and or compliance documents and other information on proposed/existing system		3
• Readily available	L=1	
• Details available with some difficulty and delay	M=2	
• Great difficulty in obtaining details, much delay	H=3	
12. Status of documentation in the user areas		3
• Complete and current	L=1	
• More than 75% complete and current	M=2	
• Nonexistent or outdated	H=6	
13. Nature of relationship with users in respect to updating project documentation to reflect changes that may occur during project development		3
• Close coordination	L=1	
• Manageable coordination	M=2	
• Poor coordination	H=5	
14. Estimated degree to which project documentation reflects actual business need		3
• Excellent documentation	L=1	
• Good documentation but some problems with reliability	M=2	
• Poor or inadequate documentation	H=3	

WORK PAPER 3.1   *(Continued)*

TEST DOCUMENT
Structural Risk Assessment

Ratings: L - Low M - Medium H - High NA - Not Applicable		RATING × WEIGHT=
RISK	RATINGS	SCORE
15. Quality of documentation for the proposed system		3
• Excellent standards: adherence and execution are integral part of system and program development	L=1	
• Adequate standards: adherence is not consistent	M=2	
• Poor or no standards: adherence is minimal	H=3	
16. Quality of development and production library control		3
• Excellent standards: superior adherence and execution	L=1	
• Adequate standards: adherence is not consistent	M=2	
• Poor or no standards: adherence is minimal	H=3	
17. Availability of special test facilities for subsystem testing		2
• Complete or not required	L=1	
• Limited	M=2	
• None available	H=3	
18. Status of project maintenance planning		2
• Current and complete	L=1	
• Under development	M=2	
• Nonexistent		H=3
19. Contingency plans in place to support operational mission should application fail		2
• None required	NA=0	
• Complete plan	L=1	
• Major subsystems addressed	M=2	
• Nonexistent		H=3
20. User approval of project specifications		4
• Formal, written approval based on structured, detailed review processes	L=1	
• Formal, written approval based on informal unstructured, detailed review processes	M=2	
• No formal approval; cursory review	H=3	
21. Effect of external systems on the system		5
• No external systems involved	NA=0	
• Critical intersystem communications controlled through interface control documents; standard protocols utilized: stable interfaces	L=1	
• Critical intersystem communications controlled through interface control documents: some nonstandard protocols: interfaces change infrequently	M=2	
• Not all critical intersystem communications controlled through interface control documents: some nonstandard protocols: some interfaces change frequently	H=3	

(Continues)

WORK PAPER 3.1 *(Continued)*

TEST DOCUMENT
Structural Risk Assessment

Ratings: L - Low M - Medium H - High NA - Not Applicable		RATING × WEIGHT=
RISK	RATINGS	SCORE
22. Type and adequacy of configuration management planning		2
• Complete and functioning	L=1	
• Undergoing revisions for inadequacies	M=2	
• None available	H=3	
23. Type of standards and guidelines to be followed by project		4
• Standards use structured programming concepts, reflect current methodology, and permit tailoring to nature and scope of development project	L=1	
• Standards require a top-down approach and offer some flexibility in application	M=2	
• Standards are out of date and inflexible	H=3	
24. Degree to which system is based on well-specified requirements		5
• Detailed transaction and parametric data in requirements documentation	L=1	
• Detailed transaction data in requirements documentation	M=2	
• Vague requirements documentation	H=5	
25. Relationships with those who are involved with system (e.g., users, customers, sponsors, interfaces) or who must be dealt with during project effort		3
• No significant conflicting needs: system primarily serves one organizational unit	L=1	
• System meets limited conflicting needs of cooperative organization units	M=2	
• System must meet important conflicting needs of several cooperative organization units	H=3	
• System must meet important conflicting needs of several uncooperative organizational units	H=4	
26. Changes in user area necessary to meet system operating requirements		3
• Not applicable	NA=0	
• Minimal	L=1	
• Somewhat	M=2	
• Major	H=3	
27. General user attitude		5
• Good: values data processing solution	L=1	
• Fair: some reluctance	M=2	
• Poor: does not appreciate data processing solution	H=3	

WORK PAPER 3.1 *(Continued)*

TEST DOCUMENT
Structural Risk Assessment

RISK		RATINGS	RATING × WEIGHT= SCORE
Ratings: L - Low M - Medium H - High NA - Not Applicable			
28. Status of people, procedures, knowledge, discipline, and division of details of offices that will be using system			4
	• Situation good to excellent	L=1	
	• Situation satisfactory but could be improved	M=2	
	• Situation less than satisfactory	H=3	
29. Commitment of senior user management to system			3
	• Extremely enthusiastic	L=1	
	• Adequate	M=3	
	• Some reluctance; or level of commitment unknown	H=3	
30. Dependence of project on contributions of technical effort from other areas (e.g., database administration)			2
	• None	L=1	
	• From within IT	M=2	
	• From outside IT	H=3	
31. User's IT knowledge and experience			2
	• Highly capable	L=1	
	• Previous exposure but limited knowledge	M=2	
	• First exposure	H=3	
32. Knowledge and experience of user in application area			2
	• Previous experience	L=1	
	• Conceptual understanding	M=2	
	• Limited knowledge	H=4	
33. Knowledge and experience of project team in application area			3
	• Previous experience	L=1	
	• Conceptual understanding	M=2	
	• Limited knowledge	H=4	
34. Degree of control by project management			2
	• Formal authority commensurate with assigned responsibility	L=1	
	• Informal authority commensurate with assigned responsibility	M=2	
	• Responsibility but no authority	H=3	
35. Effectiveness of project communications			2
	• Easy access to project manager(s): change information promptly transmitted upward and downward	L=1	
	• Limited access to project manager(s); downward communication limited	M=2	
	• Aloof project management, planning information closely held	H=3	

(Continues)

WORK PAPER 3.1   *(Continued)*

TEST DOCUMENT
Structural Risk Assessment

Ratings: L - Low M - Medium H - High NA - Not Applicable		RATING × WEIGHT=
RISK	RATINGS	SCORE
36. Test team's opinion about conformance of system specifications to business needs based on early tests and/or reviews		3
• Operational tests indicate that procedures and operations produce desired results	L=1	
• Limited tests indicate that procedures and operations differ from specifications in minor aspects only	M=2	
• Procedures and operations differ from specifications in important aspects: specifications insufficient to use for testing	H=3	
37. Sensitivity of information		1
• None L=0		
• High H=3		

PREPARED BY:	DATE:	Total	107.00
		Total Score / Total Weight = Risk Average	

WORK PAPER 3.2   Technical Risk Assessment

TEST DOCUMENT
Technical Risk Assessment

Ratings: L - Low M - Medium H - High NA - Not Applicable		RATING × WEIGHT=
RISK	RATINGS	SCORE
1. Ability to fulfill mission during hardware or software failure		2
• Can be accomplished without system	L=1	
• Can be accomplished without fully operational system, but some minimum capability required	M=2	
• Cannot be accomplished without fully automated system	H=6	
2. Required system availability		2
• Periodic use (weekly or less frequently)	L=1	
• Daily use (but not 24 hours per day)	M=2	
• Constant use (24 hours per day)	H=5	
3. Degree to which system's ability to function relies on exchange of data with external systems		2
• Functions independently: sends no data required for the operation of other systems	L=0	
• Must send and/or receive data to or from another system	M=2	
• Must send and/or receive data to or from multiple systems	H=3	
4. Nature of system-to-system communications		1
• System has no external interfaces	L=0	
• Automated communications link using standard protocols	M=2	
• Automated communications link using nonstandard protocals	H=3	
5. Estimated system's program size limitations		2
• Substantial unused capacity	L=1	
• Within capacity	M=2	
• Near limits of capacity	H=3	
6. Degree of specified input data control procedures		3
• Detailed error checking	L=1	
• General error checking	M=2	
• No error checking	H=3	
7. Type of system hardware to be installed		3
• No hardware needed	NA=0	
• Standard batch or on-line systems	L=1	
• Nonstandard peripherals	M=2	
• Nonstandard peripherals and mainframes	H=3	
8. Basis for selection of programming and system software		3
• Architectural analysis of functional and performance requirements	L=1	
• Similar system development experience	M=2	
• Current inventory of system software and existing programming language skills	H=3	

(Continues)

WORK PAPER 3.2   *(Continued)*

TEST DOCUMENT
Technical Risk Assessment

	Ratings: L - Low M - Medium H - High NA - Not Applicable	RATINGS	RATING × WEIGHT= SCORE
RISK			
9.	Complexity of projected system		2
	• Single function (e.g., word processing only)	L=1	
	• Multiple but related function (e.g., message generation, editing, and dissemination)	M=2	
	• Multiple but not closely related functions (e.g., database query, statistical manipulation, graphics plotting, text editing)	H=3	
10.	Projected level of programming language		2
	• High level, widely used	L=1	
	• Low-level or machine language, widely used	M=2	
	• Special-purpose language, extremely limited use	H=3	
11.	Suitability of programming language to application(s)		2
	• All modules can be coded in straightforward manner in chosen language	L=1	
	• All modules can be coded in a straightforward manner with few exit routines, sophisticated techniques, and so forth	H=3	
	• Significant number of exit routines, sophisticated techniques, and so forth are required to compensate for deficiencies in language selected	H=3	
12.	Familiarity of hardware architecture		2
	• Mainframe and peripherals widely used	L=1	
	• Peripherals unfamiliar	M=2	
	• Mainframe unfamiliar	H=4	
13.	Degree of pioneering (extent to which new, difficult, and unproven techniques are applied)		5
	• Conservative: no untried system components; no pioneering system objectives or techniques	L=1	
	• Moderate: few important system components and functions are untried; few pioneering system objectives and techniques	H=3	
	• Aggressively pioneering: more than a few unproven hardware or software components or system objectives	H=3	
14.	Suitability of hardware to application environment		2
	• Standard hardware	NA=0	
	• Architecture highly comparable with required functions	L=1	
	• Architecture sufficiently powerful but not particularly efficient	M=2	
	• Architecture dictates complex software routines	H=3	

WORK PAPER 3.2   *(Continued)*

TEST DOCUMENT
Technical Risk Assessment

RISK	RATINGS	RATING × WEIGHT= SCORE
Ratings: L - Low M - Medium H - High NA - Not Applicable		
15. Margin of error (need for perfect functioning, split-second timing, and significant cooperation and coordination)		5
• Comfortable margin	L=1	
• Realistically demanding	M=2	
• Very demanding; unrealistic	H=3	
16. Familiarity of project team with operating software		2
• Considerable experience	L=1	
• Some experience or experience unknown	M=2	
• Little or no experience	H=3	
17. Familiarity of project team with system environment supporting the application		2
• Considerable experience	L=1	
• Some experience or experience unknown	M=2	
• Little or no experience with:		
Operating System	H=3	
DBMS	H=3	
Data Communications	H=3	
18. Knowledgeability of project team in the application area		2
• Previous experience	L=1	
• Conceptual understanding	M=2	
• Limited knowledge	H=3	
19. Type of test tools used		5
• Comprehensive test/debut software, including path analyzers	L=1	
• Formal, documented procedural tools only	M=2	
• None	H=3	
20. Realism of test environment		4
• Tests performed on operational system: total database and communications environment	L=1	
• Tests performed on separate development system: total database, limited communications	M=2	
• Tests performed on dissimilar development system: limited database and limited communications	H=3	
21. Communications interface change testing		4
• No interfaces required	NA=0	
• Live testing on actual line at operational transaction rates	L=1	
• Loop testing on actual line, simulated transactions	M=2	
• Line simulations within development system	H=3	

(Continues)

WORK PAPER 3.2   *(Continued)*

TEST DOCUMENT
Technical Risk Assessment

Ratings: L - Low M - Medium H - High NA - Not Applicable		RATING × WEIGHT=
RISK	**RATINGS**	**SCORE**
22. Importance of user training to the success of the system		1
• Little training needed to use or operate system: documentation is sufficient for training	L=1	
• Users and or operators need no formal training, but experience is required in addition to documentation	M=2	
• Users essentially unable to operate system without formal, hands-on training in addition to documentation	H=3	
23. Estimated degree of system adaptability to change		3
• High: structured programming techniques used: relatively unpatched, well documented	L=1	
• Moderate M=2		
• Low: monolithic program design, high degree of inner/ intrasystem dependency, unstructured development, minimal documentation	H=4	
		Total 61.00
PREPARED BY:	DATE:	Total Score / Total Weight = Risk Average

WORK PAPER 3.3   Size Risk Assessment

TEST DOCUMENT
Size Risk Assessment

RISK	Ratings: L - Low M - Medium H - High NA - Not Applicable	RATINGS	RATING × WEIGHT= SCORE
1.	Ranking of this project's total worker-hours within the limits established by the organization's smallest andlargest system development projects (in number of worker-hours)		3
	• Lower third of systems development projects	L=1	
	• Middle third of systems development projects	M=2	
	• Upper third of systems development projects	H=3	
2.	Project implementation time		3
	• 12 months or less	L=1	
	• 13 months to 24 months	M=2	
	• More than 24 months, with phased implementation	H=3	
	• More than 24 months; no phasing	H=4	
3.	Estimated project adherence to schedule		1
	• Ahead of schedule	L=1	
	• On schedule	M=2	
	• Behind schedule (by three months or less)	H=3	
	• Behind schedule (by more than three months)	H=4	
4.	Number of systems interconnecting with the application		3
	• 1 to 2	L=1	
	• 3 to 5	M=2	
	• More than 5	H=3	
5.	Percentage of project resources allocated to system testing		2
	• More than 40%	L=1	
	• 20 to 40%	M=2	
	• Less than 20%	H=3	
6.	Number of interrelated logical data groupings (estimate if unknown)		1
	• Fewer than 4	L=1	
	• 4 to 6	M=2	
	• More than 6	H=3	
7.	Number of transaction types		1
	• Fewer than 6	L=1	
	• 6 to 25	M=2	
	• More than 25	H=3	
8.	Number of output reports		1
	• Fewer than 10	L=1	
	• 10 to 20	M=2	
	• More than 20	H=3	

(Continues)

WORK PAPER 3.3 *(Continued)*

TEST DOCUMENT
Size Risk Assessment

Ratings: L - Low M - Medium H - High NA - Not Applicable	RATING × WEIGHT=	
RISK	RATINGS	SCORE
9. Ranking of this project's number of lines of program code to be maintained within the limits established by the organization's smallest and largest systems development projects (in number of lines of code)		3
• Lower third of systems development projects	L=1	
• Middle third of systems development projects	M=2	
• Upper third of systems development projects	H=3	

			Total	18.00
PREPARED BY:	DATE:		Total Score / Total Weight = Risk Average	

WORK PAPER 3.4   Risk Score Analysis

<table>
<tr><td colspan="7" align="center">**TEST DOCUMENT**
Risk Score Analysis</td></tr>
<tr><td colspan="7">APPLICATION SYSTEM _____</td></tr>
</table>

RISK AREA	SCORE		COMPARATIVE RATING WITH COMPANY APPLICATIONS			COMMENTS
	TOTAL	AVERAGE	HIGH	MEDIUM	LOW	
STRUCTURE						
TECHNOLOGY						
SIZE						
TOTAL RISK SCORE						

HIGH RISK ATTRIBUTES		
RISK AREA	RISK ATTRIBUTES	TEST CONCERN

PREPARED BY:	DATE:

WORK PAPER 3.5   Testing Tactics Checklist

Number	Test Tactic	Include in Test Plan		Comments
		Yes	No	
1	Did you use your test strategy as a guide for developing the test tactics?			
2	Did you decompose your strategy into test tactics? (May not fully occur until the test planning step.)			
3	Did you consider trade-offs between test factors when developing test tactics (e.g., choosing between continuity of processing and accuracy)?			
4	Did you compare your test tactics to the test strategy to ensure they support the strategy?			
5	Have you identified the individuals who can perform the tests?			
6	Did you compose a strategy for recruiting those individuals?			
7	Did management agree to let the team members accept the proposed responsibilities on your project team?			
8	Has a test plan for testing been established? If so does the test team have the following responsibilities:			
	Set test objectives.			
	Develop a test strategy.			
	Develop the test tactics.			
	Define the test resources.			
	Execute tests needed to achieve the test plan.			
9	Modify the test plan and test execution as changes occur.			
	Manage use of test resources.			
	Issue test reports.			
	Ensure the quality of the test process.			
	Maintain test statistics.			
10	Does the test team adequately represent the following:			
	User personnel			
	Operation's staff			
	Data administration			
	Internal auditors			
	Quality assurance staff			
	Information technology			
	Management			
	Security administrator			
	Professional testers			

(Continues)

WORK PAPER 3.5   *(Continued)*

		Include in Test Plan		
Number	Test Tactic	Yes	No	Comments
11	Did you develop test team assignments for each test member?			
	Does the test team accept responsibility for finding users/customer type defects?			
12	Does the test team accept responsibility for finding defects?			
13	Does the team recognize the benefit of removing defects earlier in the correction life cycle process?			
14	Will testing begin when the development process begins?			
15	Does one person have primary responsibility for testing?			
16	Will the test team perform validation tests?			
17	Will the test team perform verification tests?			
18	Will verification tests include requirement reviews?			
19	Will verification tests include design reviews?			
20	Will verification tests include code walkthroughs?			
21	Will verification tests include code inspections?			
22	Will validation tests include unit testing?			
23	Will validation tests include integration testing?			
24	Will validation tests include system testing?			
25	Will validation tests include user acceptance testing?			
26	Will testers develop a testers' workbench?			
27	Will the workbench identify the deliverables/products to be tested?			
28	Will the workbench include test procedures?			
29	Will the workbench check accuracy of test implementation?			
30	Will you identify test deliverables?			
31	Does your workbench identify the tools you'll use?			
32	Have the testers identified a source of these generic test tools?			

Determining Your Software Testing Techniques

Testing is performed to determine the existence, quality, or genuineness of the attributes of the application system. The practice of testing utilizes tools and techniques. The less structured the process, the more an art, while the more structured the process becomes, the more the organization can rely upon the results of testing.

This chapter describes the more common testing techniques used in evaluating computerized applications. The techniques are divided into three categories: (1) system structural testing techniques, (2) system functional techniques, and (3) unit testing techniques. The chapter explains the need for techniques to help ensure that the application fits the organizational requirements. The chapter also shows the interrelationship between the test factors and the techniques in order to illustrate the purpose for which each of the described techniques is most valuable.

Concept of Application Fit

The effectiveness of a computer application in a business environment is determined by how well that application fits into the environment in which it operates. Fit is a concept that implies how usable, helpful, and meaningful the application is in the performance of the day-to-day function of the user. The more valuable the application in performing the user's function, the better the fit, while the less valuable the application, the poorer the fit.

The concept of fit is important in both design and testing. Design must attempt to build the application that fits into the user's business process, and the test process must ensure the degree of fit. Testing that concentrates on structure and requirements may fail to assess fit, and thus fail to test the value of the automated application to the business. The four components of fit are:

1. **Data.** The reliability, timeliness, consistency, and usefulness of the data included in the automated application to the user

2. **People.** The skills, training, aptitude, and desire to properly use and interact with the automated application

3. **Structure.** The proper development of application systems to optimize technology and satisfy requirements

4. **Rules.** The procedures that are to be followed in processing the data

The application system must fit into these four components of the business environment (see Figure 4.1). If any of the components fail to fit properly, the success of the application system will be diminished. Therefore, testing must ensure that all the components are adequately prepared and/or developed, and that the four components fit together to provide the best possible solution to the business problem.

Testing Techniques/Tool Selection Process

The third dimension of the testing cube is tactics. This dimension outlines in detail the criteria that should be tested for each of the identified risks. To evaluate these risks,

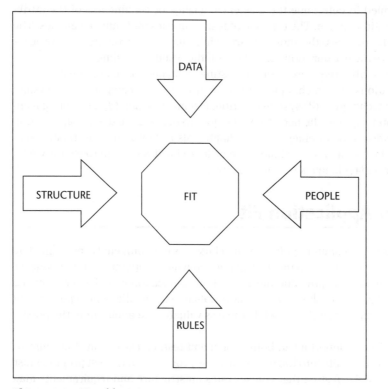

Figure 4.1 Testable components.

testing techniques and tools are needed. Chapters 9, 10, and 11 outline the testing for each phase in the systems development life cycle and identify the test criteria for those phases, together with the tools and techniques recommended for evaluating the identified criteria. These chapters provide a predetermined structured test methodology.

Individuals responsible for testing may prefer to select their own technique and tool based on the test situation. For this purpose, a Testing Techniques/Tool Selection Process flowchart is provided in Figure 4.2. However, prior to reviewing the flowchart it is necessary to review three testing concepts:

1. Structural versus functional testing

2. Dynamic versus static testing

3. Manual versus automatic testing

Structural versus Functional Testing

The properties that the test set is to reflect are classified according to whether they are derived from a description of the program's function or from the program's internal structure. Both structural and functional analysis should be performed to ensure adequate testing. Structural analysis-based test sets tend to uncover errors that occur during "coding" of the program, while functional analysis-based test sets tend to uncover errors that occur in implementing requirements or design specifications.

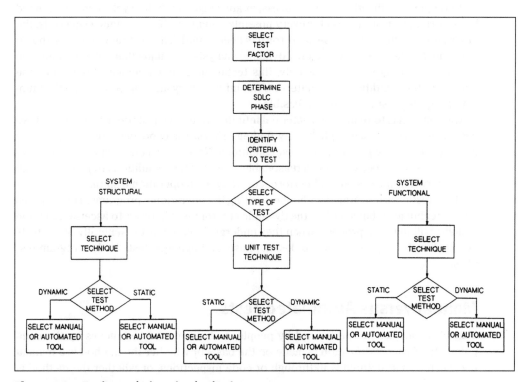

Figure 4.2   Testing technique/tool selection process.

Functional testing ensures that the requirements are properly satisfied by the application system. The functions are those tasks that the system is designed to accomplish. Functional testing is not concerned with how processing occurs, but rather, with the results of processing.

Structural testing ensures sufficient testing of the implementation of a function. Although used primarily during the coding phase, structural analysis should be used in all phases of the life cycle where the software is represented formally in some algorithmic, design, or requirements language. The intent of structural testing is to assess the implementation by finding test data that will force sufficient coverage of the structures present in the implemented application. Structural testing evaluates both that all aspects of the structure have been tested and that the structure is sound. Determining that all tasks through a structure are tested is a difficult process and one requiring extensive test data. However, determining if the structure functions properly is a test task that is more easily accomplished.

Dynamic versus Static Testing

Test methods can be classified into dynamic and static techniques. Dynamic analysis requires that the program be executed and hence involves the traditional notion of programming testing. That is, the program is run on some test cases and the results of the program's performance are examined to check whether the program operated as expected. Static analysis does not usually involve actual program execution. Common static analysis techniques include such tasks as syntax checking.

A complete verification of the process, at any stage in the life cycle, can be obtained by performing a test process for every possible condition. If the instance succeeds, the program is verified, otherwise, an error has been found. This testing method is known as exhaustive testing and is the only dynamic analysis technique that will guarantee the validity of a program. Unfortunately, this technique is not practical. Frequently, the number of test conditions is infinite, or if not infinite, very large, so as to make the number of required test conditions infeasible.

The solution is to reduce this potential infinite exhaustive test process to a finite testing process. This is accomplished by finding criteria for choosing representative test cases from the total population of test conditions. Normally a combination of static and dynamic tests is used, selecting a reasonable subset of test conditions to provide a high probability that the system will perform correctly in an operational status.

Static testing is performed without executing the operational programs. This requires testing techniques that simulate the dynamic environment in order to ascertain that the systems will function properly when they undergo dynamic tests. Generally, static tests are used in the requirements and design phase, and dynamic tests in the program test phase.

Manual versus Automated Tests

Manual techniques are performed by people, and automated techniques by the computer. This final classification is made on the basis of whether the method is a manual one, such as a structured walkthrough or code inspections, or whether the method is automated. The more automated the developmental process, the easier it becomes to automate the test process. On the other hand, the greater reliance on people to analyze, document, and develop computer systems manually, the more it becomes necessary to test manually.

Selecting Techniques/Tools

Testing tools should be selected based upon their ability to accomplish test objectives. The flowchart illustrated in Figure 4.2 outlines the steps required to select the most appropriate techniques and tools for accomplishing the test objectives. This flowchart is applicable to all phases in a systems development life cycle.

The technique/tool selection process begins with selecting the test factor. In developing a test plan, the factors need to be evaluated to determine which are the appropriate factors for the application system being tested. Once the factor has been selected, the test concerns/risks can be determined by identifying the systems development life cycle phase in which the tool will be utilized.

The third dimension of the test cube is the tactics to be used during testing. These tactics are described in Chapters 4 and 5; plus Chapters 9 to 11 are devoted to each phase of the systems development life cycle. Each concern has criteria to be tested to determine whether the concern has been adequately addressed by the developmental process.

Once an individual concern has been identified, it must be determined whether to perform a structural or functional test. The structural test evaluates how the system performs its requirements, while the functional testing is more concerned with what the system does. Both types of testing are important, but different tools are used depending on the type of testing selected.

Both structural and functional testing can be accomplished using a predetermined set of techniques. Once the technique has been selected, the test method for implementing that technique needs to be determined. The test method can be dynamic or static. Dynamic techniques attempt to determine whether the application system functions properly while the programs are being operated, and static testing looks at the system in a nonoperating environment.

The last step is to select for either the dynamic or static test method a manual or automated tool. The tools will be selected from among the available testing tools. Chapter 5 describes the more common testing tools.

Difference between Testing Techniques and Tools

A tool is a vehicle for performing a test process. The tool is a resource to the tester, but by itself is insufficient to conduct testing. For example, a hammer is a tool, but until the technique for using that hammer is determined the tool will lie dormant.

A testing technique is a process for ensuring that some aspect of an application system or unit functions properly. There are few techniques, but many tools. For example, a technique would be the leverage provided by swinging an instrument to apply force to accomplish an objective—the swinging of a hammer to drive in a nail. The hammer is the tool used by the swinging technique to drive in a nail. On the other hand, a swinging technique can also be used to split a log using an axe or to drive a stake in the ground with a sledge hammer.

The concept of tools and techniques is important in the testing process. It is a combination of the two that enables the test process to be performed. The tester should first understand the testing techniques and then understand the tools that can be used with each of the techniques.

Structural System Testing Techniques

Structural system testing is designed to verify that the developed system and programs work. The objective is to ensure that the product designed is structurally sound and will function correctly. It attempts to determine that the technology has been used properly and that when all the component parts are assembled they function as a cohesive unit. The structural system testing techniques provide the facility for determining that the implemented configuration and its interrelationship of parts functions so that they can perform the intended tasks. The techniques are not designed to ensure that the application system is functionally correct, but rather, that it is structurally sound. The structural system testing techniques are listed below, briefly described in Figure 4.3, and then individually explained:

- Stress testing
- Execution testing
- Recovery testing
- Operations testing
- Compliance testing (to process)
- Security testing

Stress Testing Technique

Stress testing is designed to determine if the system can function when subject to large volumes—larger than would be normally expected. The areas that are stressed include input transactions, internal tables, disk space, output, communications, computer capacity, and interaction with people. If the application functions adequately under test, it can be assumed that it will function properly with normal volumes of work.

Objectives

The objective of stress testing is to simulate a production environment. Specific objectives of stress testing include:

- Normal or above-normal volumes of transactions can be processed through the transaction within the expected time frame.
- The application system is structurally able to process large volumes of data.

TECHNIQUE	DESCRIPTION	EXAMPLE
STRESS	Determine system performs with expected volumes	• Sufficient disk space allocated • Communication lines adequate
EXECUTION	System achieves desired level of proficiency	• Transaction turnaround time adequate • Software/hardware use optimized
RECOVERY	System can be returned to an operational status after a failure	• Induce failure • Evaluate adequacy of backup data
OPERATIONS	System can be executed in a normal operational status	• Determine systems can run using document • JCL adequate
COMPLIANCE (TO PROCESS)	System is developed in accordance with standards and procedures	• Standards followed • Documentation complete
SECURITY	System is protected in accordance with importance to organization	• Access denied • Procedures in place

Figure 4.3   Structural testing techniques.

- System capacity, including communication lines, has sufficient resources available to meet expected turnaround times.
- People can perform their assigned tasks and maintain the desired turnaround time.

How to Use Stress Testing

Stress testing should simulate as closely as possible the production environment. On-line systems should be stress tested by having people enter transactions at a normal or above-normal pace. Batch systems can be stress tested with large input batches. Error conditions should be included in tested transactions. Transactions for use in stress testing can be obtained from one of the following three sources:

1. Test data generators
2. Test transactions created by the test group
3. Transactions previously processed in the production environment

In stress testing, the system should be run as it would in the production environment. Operators should use standard documentation, and the people entering transactions or working with the system should be the clerical personnel that will work with the system after it goes into production. On-line systems should be tested for an extended period of time, and batch systems tested using more than one batch of transactions.

Stress Testing Examples

Stress tests can be designed to test all or parts of an application system. Some specific examples of stress testing include:

- Enter transactions to determine that sufficient disk space has been allocated to the application.
- Ensure that the communication capacity is sufficient to handle the volume of work by attempting to overload the network with transactions.
- Test system overflow conditions by entering more transactions than can be accommodated by tables, queues, internal storage facilities, and so on.

When to Use Stress Testing

Stress testing should be used when there is uncertainty regarding the volume of work the application system can handle without failing. Stress testing attempts to break the system by overloading it with a large volume of transactions. Stress testing is most common with on-line applications because it is difficult to simulate heavy-volume transactions using the other testing techniques. The disadvantage of stress testing is the amount of time it takes to prepare for the test plus the amount of resources consumed during the actual execution of the test. These costs need to be weighed against the risk of not identifying volume-related failures until the application is placed into an operational mode.

Execution Testing Technique

Execution testing is designed to determine whether the system achieves the desired level of proficiency in a production status. Execution testing can verify response times, turnaround times, as well as design performance. The execution of a system can be tested in whole or in part, using the actual system or a simulated model of a system.

Objectives

Execution testing is used to determine whether the system can meet the specific performance criteria. Specific objectives of execution testing include:

- Determining the performance of the system structure
- Verifying the optimum use of hardware and software
- Determining response time to on-line use requests
- Determining transaction processing turnaround time

How to Use Execution Testing

Execution testing can be conducted in any phase of the system development life cycle. The testing can evaluate a single aspect of the system, for example, a critical routine in the system, or the ability of the proposed structure to satisfy performance criteria. Execution testing can be performed in any of the following manners:

- Using hardware and software monitors
- Simulating the functioning of all or part of the system using a simulation model
- Creating a quick and dirty program(s) to evaluate the approximate performance of a completed system

Execution testing may be executed in one's own installation, or may use nonowned facilities for the performance of the test. For example, execution testing can be performed on hardware and software before being acquired, or may be done after the application system has been completed. The earlier the technique is used, the higher the assurance that the completed application will meet the performance criteria.

Execution Testing Examples

Some specific examples of execution testing include:

- Calculating turnaround time on transactions processed through the application
- Determining that the hardware and software selected provide the optimum processing capability
- Using software monitors to determine that the program code is effectively used

When to Use Execution Testing

Execution testing should be used early in the developmental process. While there is value in knowing that the completed application does not meet performance criteria, if that assessment is not known until the system is operational, it may be too late or too costly to make the necessary modifications. Therefore, execution testing should be used at that point in time when the results can be used to affect or change the system structure.

Recovery Testing Technique

Recovery is the ability to restart operations after the integrity of the application has been lost. The process normally involves reverting to a point where the integrity of the system is known, and then reprocessing transactions up until the point of failure. The time required to recover operations is affected by the number of restart points, the volume of applications run on the computer center, the training and skill of the people conducting the recovery operation, and the tools available for recovery. The importance of recovery will vary from application to application.

Objectives

Recovery testing is used to ensure that operations can be continued after a disaster. Recovery testing not only verifies the recovery process, but also the effectiveness of the component parts of that process.

Specific objectives of recovery testing include the following:

- Adequate backup data is preserved.
- Backup data is stored in a secure location.
- Recovery procedures are documented.
- Recovery personnel have been assigned and trained.
- Recovery tools have been developed and are available.

How to Use Recovery Testing

Recovery testing can be conducted in two modes. First, the procedures, methods, tools, and techniques can be assessed to evaluate whether they appear adequate; and second, after the system has been developed, a failure can be introduced into the system and the ability to recover tested. Both types of recovery testing are important. The implementation of the technique is different depending upon which type of recovery testing is being performed.

Evaluating the procedures and documentation is a process using primarily judgment and checklists. On the other hand, the actual recovery test may involve off-site facilities and alternate processing locations. Testing the procedures is normally done by skilled systems analysts, professional testers, or management personnel. On the other hand, testing the actual recovery procedures should be performed by computer operators and other clerical personnel who would, in fact, be involved had it been an actual disaster instead of a test disaster.

A simulated disaster is usually performed on one aspect of the application system. For example, the test may be designed to determine whether people using the system can continue processing and recover computer operations after computer operations cease. While several aspects of recovery need to be tested, it is better to test one segment at a time rather than induce multiple failures at a single time. When multiple failures are induced, and problems are encountered, it may be more difficult to pinpoint the cause of the problem than when only a single failure is induced.

It is preferable not to advise system participants when a disaster test will be conducted. For example, a failure might be intentionally introduced during a normal system test to observe reaction and evaluate the recovery test procedures. When people are prepared, they may perform the recovery test in a manner different from the performance when it occurs at an unexpected time. Even if the participants know that recovery may be part of the test, it is not recommended to let them know specifically when it will occur, or what type of recovery will be necessary.

Recovery Testing Examples

Recovery testing can involve the manual functions of an application, loss of input capability, loss of communication lines, hardware or operating system failure, loss of database integrity, operator error, or application system failure. It is desirable to test all aspects of recovery processing. Some specific examples of recovery testing include:

- Inducing a failure in one of the application system programs during processing. This could be accomplished by inserting a special instruction to look for a transaction code that upon identification would cause an abnormal program termination.

- The recovery could be conducted from a known point of integrity to ensure that the available backup data was adequate for the recovery process. When the recovery had been completed, the files at the point where the exercise was requested could be compared to the files recreated during the recovery process.

When to Use Recovery Testing

Recovery testing should be performed whenever the user of the application states that the continuity of operation of the application is essential to the proper functioning of the user area. The user should estimate the potential loss associated with inability to recover operations over various time spans; for example, the inability to recover within five minutes, one hour, eight hours, and a week. The amount of the potential loss should determine both the amount of resources to be put into disaster planning as well as recovery testing.

Operations Testing Technique

After testing, the application will be integrated into the operating environment. At this point in time, the application will be executed using the normal operations staff, operations procedures, and documentation. Operations testing is designed to verify prior to production that the operating procedures and staff can properly execute the application.

Objectives

Operations testing is primarily designed to determine whether the system is executable during normal systems operations. Specific objectives of operations testing include:

- Determining the completeness of computer operator documentation
- Ensuring that the necessary support mechanisms, such as job control language, have been prepared and function properly
- Evaluating the completeness of operator training
- Testing to ensure that operators using prepared documentation can, in fact, operate the system

How to Use Operations Testing

Operations testing evaluates both the process and the execution of the process. During the requirements phase, operational requirements can be evaluated to determine the reasonableness and completeness of those requirements. During the design phase, the operating procedures should be designed and thus can be evaluated. This continual definition of the operating procedures should be subjected to continual testing.

The execution of operations testing can normally be performed in conjunction with other tests. However, if operations testing is included, the operators should not be prompted or helped by outside parties during the test process. The test needs to be executed as if it was part of normal computer operations in order to adequately evaluate the effectiveness of computer operators in running the application in a true-to-life operations environment.

Operations Testing Examples

Operations testing is a specialized technical test of executing the application system. Some specific examples of operations testing include:

- Determining that the operator instructions have been prepared and documented in accordance with other operations instructions, and that computer operators have been trained in any unusual procedures
- Testing that the job control language statements and other operating systems support features perform the predetermined tasks
- Verifying that the file labeling and protection procedures function properly

When to Use Operations Testing

Operations testing should occur prior to placing any application into a production status. If the application is to be tested in a production-type setting, operations testing can piggyback that process at a very minimal cost. It is as important to identify an operations flaw as it is to identify an application flaw prior to placing the application into production.

Compliance Testing Technique

Compliance testing verifies that the application was developed in accordance with information technology standards, procedures, and guidelines. The methodologies are used to increase the probability of success, to enable the transfer of people in and out of the project with minimal cost, and to increase the maintainability of the application system. The type of testing conducted varies on the phase of the systems development life cycle. However, it may be more important to compliance test adherence to the process during requirements than at later stages in the life cycle because it is difficult to correct applications when requirements are not adequately documented.

Objectives

Compliance testing is performed to both ensure compliance to the methodology and to encourage and help the information technology professional to comply with the methodology. Specific objectives of compliance testing include:

- Determining that systems development and maintenance methodologies are followed

- Ensuring compliance to departmental standards, procedures, and guidelines
- Evaluating the completeness and reasonableness of application system documentation

How to Use Compliance Testing

Compliance testing requires that the prepared document/program is compared to the standards for that particular program/document. A colleague would be the most appropriate person to do this comparison. The most effective method for compliance testing is the inspection process.

Compliance Testing Examples

A peer group of programmers would be assembled to test line-by-line that a computer program is compliant with programming standards. At the end of the peer review, the programmer would be given a list of noncompliant information that would need to be corrected.

When to Use Compliance Testing

Compliance to information technology application system development standards and procedures is dependent upon management's desire to have the procedures followed and the standards enforced. Therefore, if management really wants compliance they should perform sufficient tests to both determine the degree of compliance with the methodology and identify violators for management action. However, lack of compliance should also be used from the perspective that the standards may be misunderstood, or not adequately instructed or publicized, or may, in fact, be poor standards inhibiting the development of application systems. In these instances, it may be desirable to change the methodology.

Security Testing Technique

Security is a protection system that is needed for both secure confidential information and for competitive purposes to assure third parties that their data will be protected. The amount of security provided will be dependent upon the risks associated with compromise or loss of information. Protecting the confidentiality of the information is designed to protect the resources of the organization. However, information such as customer lists or improper disclosure of customer information may result in a loss of customer business to competitors. Security testing is designed to evaluate the adequacy of the protective procedures and countermeasures.

Objectives

Security defects do not become as obvious as other types of defects. Therefore, the objectives of security testing are to identify defects that are very difficult to identify. Even failures in the security system operation may not be detected, resulting in a loss or compromise of information without the knowledge of that loss.

Specific objectives of security testing include:

- Determining that adequate attention has been devoted to identifying security risks

- Determining that a realistic definition and enforcement of access to the system has been implemented

- Determining that sufficient expertise exists to perform adequate security testing

- Conducting reasonable tests to ensure that the implemented security measures function properly

How to Use Security Testing

Security testing is a highly specialized part of the test process. Most organizations can evaluate the reasonableness of security procedures to prevent the average perpetrator from penetrating the application. However, the highly skilled perpetrator using sophisticated techniques may use methods undetectable by novices designing security measures and/or testing those measures.

The first step in testing is the identification of the security risks and the potential loss associated with those risks. If either the loss is low or the penetration method mere routine, the information technology personnel can conduct the necessary tests. On the other hand, if either the risks are very high or the technology that might be used is sophisticated, specialized help should be acquired in conducting the security tests.

Security Testing Examples

Security testing involves a wide spectrum of conditions. Testing can first be divided into physical and logical security. Physical security deals with the penetration by people in order to physically gather information, while logical security deals with the use of computer processing and/or communication capabilities to improperly access information. Second, access control can be divided by type of perpetrator, such as employee, consultant, cleaning or service personnel, as well as categories of employees. The type of test to be conducted will vary upon the condition being tested.

Some specific examples of security testing include:

- Determination that the resources being protected are identified, and access is defined for each resource. Access can be defined by program or individual.

- Evaluation as to whether the designed security procedures have been properly implemented and function in accordance with the specifications.

- Unauthorized access can be attempted in on-line systems to ensure that the system can identify and prevent access by unauthorized sources.

When to Use Security Testing

Security testing should be used when the information and/or assets protected by the application system are of significant value to the organization. The testing should be performed both prior to the system going into an operational status and after the system is placed into an operational status. The extent of testing should depend on the security risks, and the individual assigned to conduct the test should be selected based on the estimated sophistication that might be used to penetrate security.

Functional System Testing Techniques

Functional system testing is designed to ensure that the system requirements and specifications are achieved. The process normally involves creating test conditions for use in evaluating the correctness of the application. The types of techniques useful in performing functional testing include:

- Requirements testing
- Regression testing
- Error-handling testing
- Manual-support testing
- Intersystems testing
- Control testing
- Parallel testing

These techniques are briefly described with examples in Figure 4.4 and in addition, each of these is individually explained below.

Requirements Testing Technique

Requirements testing must verify that the system can perform its function correctly and that the correctness can be sustained over a continuous period of time. Unless the system can function correctly over an extended period of time, management will not be able to rely upon the system. The system can be tested for correctness throughout the life cycle, but it is difficult to test the reliability until the program becomes operational.

Objectives

Successfully implementing user requirements is only one aspect of requirements testing. The responsible user is normally only one of many groups having an interest in the application system.

Specific objectives of requirements testing include the following:

- User requirements are implemented.
- Correctness is maintained over extended processing periods.
- Application processing complies with the organization's policies and procedures.
- Secondary user needs have been included, such as:
    - Security officer

TECHNIQUE	DESCRIPTION	EXAMPLE
REQUIREMENTS	System performs as specified	• Prove system requirements • Compliance to policies, regulations
REGRESSION	Verifies that anything unchanged still performs correctly	• Unchanged system segments function • Unchanged manual procedures correct
ERROR HANDLING	Errors can be prevented or detected, and then corrected	• Error introduced into test • Errors reentered
MANUAL SUPPORT	The people-computer interaction works	• Manual procedures developed • People trained
INTERSYSTEMS	Data is correctly passed from system to system	• Intersystem parameters changed • Intersystem documentation updated
CONTROL	Controls reduce system risk to an acceptable level	• File reconciliation procedures work • Manual controls in place
PARALLEL	Old system and new system are run and the results compared to detect unplanned differences	• Old and new system can reconcile • Operational status of old system maintained

Figure 4.4   Functional testing techniques.

■ Database administrator
■ Internal auditors
■ Records retention
■ Comptroller

■ System processes accounting information in accordance with generally accepted accounting procedures.

■ Application systems process information in accordance with governmental regulations.

How to Use Requirements Testing

Requirements testing is primarily performed through the creation of test conditions and functional checklists. Test conditions are generalized during requirements, and become more specific as the SDLC progresses, leading to the creation of test data for use in evaluating the implemented application system.

As proposed in this book, functional testing is more effective when the test conditions are created directly from user requirements. When test conditions are created from the system documentation, defects in that documentation will not be detected through testing. When the test conditions are created from other than the system documentation, defects introduced into the documentation will be detected. Much of the emphasis in this book will be directed toward requirements testing.

Requirements Testing Examples

Some specific requirements testing examples include:

- Creating a test matrix to prove that the system requirements as documented are the requirements desired by the user

- Using a checklist prepared specifically for the application to verify the application's compliance to organizational policies and governmental regulations

- Determining that the system meets the auditability requirements established by the organization's department of internal auditors

When to Use Requirements Testing

Every application should be requirements tested. The process should begin in the requirements phase, and continue through every phase of the life cycle into operations and maintenance. It is not a question as to whether requirements must be tested but, rather, the extent and methods used in requirements testing.

Regression Testing Technique

One of the attributes that has plagued information technology professionals for years is the snowballing or cascading effect of making changes to an application system. One segment of the system is developed and thoroughly tested. Then a change is made to another part of the system, which has a disastrous effect on the thoroughly tested portion. Either the incorrectly implemented change causes a problem, or the change introduces new data or parameters that cause problems in a previously tested segment. Regression testing retests previously tested segments to ensure that they still function properly after a change has been made to another part of the application.

Objectives

Regression testing involves assurance that all aspects of an application system remain functional after testing. The introduction of change is the cause of problems in previously tested segments.

Specific objectives of regression testing include:

- Determining whether systems documentation remains current
- Determining that system test data and test conditions remain current
- Determining that previously tested system functions perform properly after changes are introduced into the application system

How to Use Regression Testing

Regression testing is retesting unchanged segments of the application system. It normally involves rerunning tests that have been previously executed to ensure that the same results can be achieved currently as were achieved when the segment was last tested. While the process is simple in that the test transactions have been prepared and the results known, unless the process is automated it can be a very time-consuming and tedious operation. It is also one in which the cost/benefit needs to be carefully evaluated or large amounts of effort can be expended with minimal payback.

Regression Testing Examples

Some specific examples of regression testing include:

- Rerunning of previously conducted tests to ensure that the unchanged system segments function properly
- Reviewing previously prepared manual procedures to ensure that they remain correct after changes have been made to the application system
- Obtaining a printout from the data dictionary to ensure that the documentation for data elements that have been changed is correct

When to Use Regression Testing

Regression testing should be used when there is a high risk that new changes may affect unchanged areas of the application system. In the developmental process, regression testing should occur after a predetermined number of changes are incorporated into the application system. In maintenance, regression testing should be conducted if the potential loss that could occur due to affecting an unchanged portion is very high. The determination as to whether to conduct regression testing should be based upon the significance of the loss that could occur due to improperly tested applications.

Error-Handling Testing Technique

One of the characteristics that differentiates automated from manual systems is the predetermined error-handling features. Manual systems can deal with problems as they occur, but automated systems must preprogram error handling. In many instances the completeness of error handling affects the usability of the application. Error-handling testing determines the ability of the application system to properly process incorrect transactions.

Objectives

Errors encompass all unexpected conditions. In some systems, approximately 50 percent of the programming effort will be devoted to handling error conditions.

Specific objectives of error-handling testing include:

- Determining that all reasonably expected error conditions are recognizable by the application system

- Determining that the accountability for processing errors has been assigned and that the procedures provide a high probability that the error will be properly corrected

- Determining that reasonable control is maintained over errors during the correction process

How to Use Error-Handling Testing

Error-handling testing requires a group of knowledgeable people to anticipate what can go wrong with the application system. Most other forms of testing involve verifying that the application system conforms to requirements. Error-handling testing uses exactly the opposite concept.

A successful method for developing test error conditions is to assemble, for a half-day or a day, people knowledgeable in information technology, the user area, and auditing or error tracking. These individuals are asked to brainstorm what might go wrong with the application. The totality of their thinking must then be organized by application function so that a logical set of test transactions can be created. Without this type of synergistic interaction on errors, it is difficult to develop a realistic body of problems prior to production.

Error-handling testing should test the introduction of the error, the processing of the error, the control condition, and the reentry of the condition properly corrected. This requires error-handling testing to be an iterative process in which errors are first introduced into the system, then corrected, then reentered into another iteration of the system to satisfy the complete error-handling cycle.

Error-Handling Testing Examples

Error handling requires the tester to think negatively. The testers must try to determine how the system might fail due to errors, so they can test to determine if the software can properly process the erroneous data.

Some specific examples of error-handling include the following:

- Produce a representative set of transactions containing errors and enter them into the system to determine whether the application can identify the problems.

- Through iterative testing, enter errors that will result in corrections, and then reenter those transactions with errors that were not included in the original set of test transactions.

- Enter improper master data, such as prices or employee pay rates, to determine that errors that will occur repetitively are subjected to greater scrutiny than those causing single-error results.

When to Use Error-Handling Testing

Error testing should occur throughout the system development life cycle. At all points in the developmental process the impact from errors should be identified and appropriate action taken to reduce those errors to an acceptable level. Error-handling testing assists in the error management process of systems development and maintenance. Some organizations use auditors, quality assurance, or professional testing personnel to evaluate error processing.

Manual-Support Testing Technique

Systems commence when transactions originate and conclude with the use of the results of processing. The manual part of the system requires the same attention to testing as does the automated segment. Although the timing and testing methods may be different, the objectives of manual testing remain the same as testing the automated segment of the application system.

Objectives

Manual-support testing involves all the functions performed by people in preparing data for and using data from automated applications. Specific objectives of manual-support testing include:

- Verifying that the manual-support procedures are documented and complete
- Determining that manual-support responsibility has been assigned
- Determining that the manual-support people are adequately trained
- Determining that the manual support and the automated segment are properly interfaced

How to Use Manual-Support Testing

Manual testing involves first the evaluation of the adequacy of the process, and second, the execution of the process. The process itself can be evaluated in all segments of the systems development life cycle. The execution of the process can be done in conjunction with normal systems testing. Rather than prepare and enter test transactions, the system can be tested having the actual clerical and supervisory people prepare, enter, and use the results of processing from the application system.

Manual testing normally involves several iterations of the process. To test people processing requires testing the interface between people and the application system. This means entering transactions, getting the results back from that processing, and taking additional action based on the information received, until all aspects of the manual computer interface have been adequately tested.

The manual-support testing should occur without the assistance of the systems personnel. The manual-support group should operate using the training and procedures provided them by the systems personnel. However, the results should be evaluated by the systems personnel to determine if they have been adequately performed.

Manual-Support Testing Examples

Some specific examples of manual-support testing include the following:

- Provide input personnel with the type of information they would normally receive from their customers and then have them transcribe that information and enter it into the computer.
- Output reports are prepared from the computer based on typical conditions, and the users are then asked to take the necessary action based on the information contained in computer reports.
- Users can be provided a series of test conditions and then asked to respond to those conditions. Conducted in this manner, manual support testing is like an examination in which the users are asked to obtain the answer from the procedures and manuals available to them.

When to Use Manual-Support Testing

Verification that the manual systems function properly should be conducted throughout the systems development life cycle. This aspect of system testing should not be left to the latter stages of the life cycle. However, extensive manual-support testing is best done during the installation phase so that the clerical people do not become involved with the new system until immediately prior to its entry into operation. This avoids the confusion of knowing two systems and not being certain which rules to follow. During the maintenance and operation phases, manual-support testing may only involve providing people with instructions on the changes and then verifying with them through questioning that they properly understand the new procedures.

Intersystem Testing Technique

Application systems are frequently interconnected to other application systems. The interconnection may be data coming into the system from another application, leaving for another application, or both. Frequently multiple applications—sometimes called cycles or functions—are involved. For example, there is a revenue function or cycle that interconnects all of the income-producing applications such as order entry, billing, receivables, shipping, and returned goods. Intersystem testing is designed to ensure that the interconnection between applications functions correctly.

Objectives

Many problems exist in intersystem testing. One is that it is difficult to find a single individual having jurisdiction over all of the systems below the level of senior management. Also, the process is time-consuming and costly.

Specific objectives of intersystem testing include:

- Determining that the proper parameters and data are correctly passed between applications

- Ensuring that proper coordination and timing of functions exists between the application systems

- Determining that the documentation for the involved systems is accurate and complete

How to Use Intersystem Testing

Intersystem testing involves the operation of multiple systems in the test. Thus, the cost may be expensive, especially if the systems have to be run through several iterations. The process is not difficult, in that files or data used by multiple systems are passed from one another to verify that they are acceptable and can be processed properly. However, the problem can be magnified during maintenance when two or more of the systems are undergoing internal changes concurrently.

One of the best testing tools for intersystem testing is the integrated test facility. This permits testing to occur during a production environment and thus the coupling of systems can be tested at minimal cost. The integrated test facility is described in the next chapter.

Intersystem Testing Examples

Some specific examples of intersystem testing include:

- Developing a representative set of test transactions in one application for passage to another application for processing verification

- Entering test transactions in a live production environment using the integrated test facility so that the test conditions can be passed from application to application, to verify that the processing is correct

- Manually verifying that the documentation in the affected systems is updated based upon the new or changed parameters in the system being tested

When to Use Intersystem Testing

Intersystem testing should be conducted whenever there is a change in parameters between application systems. The extent and type of testing will depend on the risk associated with those parameters being erroneous. If the integrated test facility concept is used, the intersystem parameters can be verified after the changed or new application is placed into production.

Control Testing Technique

Approximately one-half of the total system development effort is directly attributable to controls. Controls include data validation, file integrity, audit trail, backup and recovery, documentation, and the other aspects of systems related to integrity. Although control testing will be included in the other testing techniques, that control testing technique is designed to ensure that the mechanisms that oversee the proper functioning of an application system work.

Objectives

Control is a management tool to ensure that processing is performed in accordance with the intents of management.

Specific objectives of control testing include:

- Accurate and complete data
- Authorized transactions
- Maintenance of an adequate audit trail of information
- Efficient, effective, and economical process
- Process meeting the needs of the user

How to Use Control Testing

Control can be considered a system within a system. The term "system of internal controls" is frequently used in accounting literature to describe the totality of the mechanisms that ensure the integrity of processing. Controls are designed to reduce risks; therefore, in order to test controls the risks must be identified. The individual designing the test then creates the risk situations in order to determine whether the controls are effective in reducing them to a predetermined acceptable level of risk.

One method that can be used in testing controls is to develop a risk matrix. The matrix identifies the risks, the controls, and the segment within the application system in which the controls reside. The risk matrix is described in Chapter 5.

Control Testing Examples

Control testing is frequently done by control-oriented people. Like error handling, it requires a negative look at the application system to ensure that those "what-can-go-wrong" conditions are adequately protected. Error handling is a subset of controls oriented toward the detection and correction of erroneous information. Control in the broader sense looks at the totality of the system.

Specific examples of control testing include:

- Determining that there is adequate assurance that the detailed records in a file equal the control total. This is normally done by running a special program that accumulates the detail and reconciles it to the total.
- Determining that the manual controls used to ensure that computer processing is correct are in place and working.
- Selecting transactions and verifying that the processing for those transactions can be reconstructed on a test basis.

When to Use Control Testing

Control testing should be an integral part of system testing. Controls must be viewed as a system within a system, and tested in parallel with other systems tests. Knowing that approximately 50 percent of the total development effort goes into controls, a proportionate part of testing should be allocated to evaluating the adequacy of controls.

Parallel Testing Technique

In the early days of computer systems, parallel testing was one of the more popular testing techniques. However, as systems become more integrated and complex, the difficulty in conducting parallel tests increases and thus the popularity of the technique diminishes. Parallel testing is used to determine that the results of the new application are consistent with the processing of the previous application or version of the application.

Objectives

Specific objectives of parallel testing include:

- Conducting redundant processing to ensure that the new version or application performs correctly
- Demonstrating consistency and inconsistency between two versions of the same application system

How to Use Parallel Testing

Parallel testing requires that the same input data be run through two versions of the same application. Parallel testing can be done with the entire application or with a segment of the application. Sometimes a particular segment, such as the day-to-day interest calculation on a savings account, is so complex and important that an effective method of testing is to run the new logic in parallel with the old logic.

If the new application changes data formats, then the input data will have to be modified before it can be run through the new application. This also makes it difficult to automatically check the results of processing through a tape or disk file compare. The more difficulty encountered in verifying results or preparing common input, the less attractive the parallel testing technique becomes.

Parallel Testing Examples

Specific examples of parallel testing include:

- Operating a new and old version of a payroll system to determine that the paychecks from both systems are reconcilable.
- Running the old version of the application system to ensure that the operational status of the old system has been maintained in the event that problems are encountered in the new application.

When to Use Parallel Testing

Parallel testing should be used when there is uncertainty regarding the correctness of processing of the new application, and the old and new versions of the application are similar. In applications like payroll, banking, and other heavily financial applications where the results of processing are similar, even though the methods may change significantly—for example, going from batch to on-line banking—parallel testing is one of the more effective methods of ensuring the integrity of the new application.

Unit Testing Technique

This section examines the techniques, assessment, and management of unit testing and analysis. Testing and analysis strategies are categorized according to whether their coverage goal is functional, structural, error-oriented, or a combination of these. Mastery of the material in this section assists the software engineer to define, conduct, and evaluate unit tests and analyses and to assess new unit testing techniques.

Program testing and analysis are the most practiced means of verifying that a program possesses the features required by its specification. *Testing* is a dynamic approach to verification in which code is executed with test data to assess the presence (or absence) of required features. *Analysis* is a static approach to verification in which required features are detected by analyzing, but not executing, the code. Many analysis techniques, such as proof of correctness, safety analysis, and the more open-ended analysis procedures represented by code inspections and reviews, have become established technologies with their own substantial literature. These techniques are not discussed in this section.

This section focuses on unit-level verification. What constitutes a "unit" has been left imprecise—it may be as little as a single statement or as much as a set of coupled subroutines. The essential characteristic of a unit is that it can meaningfully be treated as a whole. Some of the techniques presented here require associated documentation that states the desired features of the unit. This documentation may be a comment in the source program, a specification written in a formal language, or a general statement of requirements. Unless otherwise indicated, this documentation should not be assumed to be the particular document in the software life cycle called a "software specification," "software requirements definition," or the like. Any document containing information about the unit may provide useful information for testing or analysis.

Functional Testing and Analysis

Three major classes of testing and analysis are discussed—functional, structural, and error oriented—as well as some hybrid approaches. Functional testing and analysis ensure that major characteristics of the code are covered. Error-oriented testing and analysis ensure that the range of typical errors is covered. The potential benefits of each major class are complementary, and no single technique is comprehensive. By specifying the criteria that must be satisfied by a test, each technique acts both as specifier and evaluator—as specifier by indicating features that must be satisfied by the test data, and as evaluator by indicating deficiencies in the test data. Exploring this dual role of test criteria is an important facet of this section. Assessment of unit testing and analysis techniques can be theoretical or empirical. This section presents both of these forms of assessment, and discusses criteria for selecting methods and controlling the verification process. Management of unit testing and analysis should be systematic. It proceeds in two stages. First, techniques appropriate to the project must be selected. Then these techniques must be systematically applied.

Functional Analysis

Functional analysis seeks to verify, without execution, that the code faithfully implements the specification. Various approaches are possible. In proof of correctness, a formal proof is constructed to verify that a program correctly implements its intended function. In safety analysis, potentially dangerous behavior is identified and steps are taken to ensure such behavior is never manifested. Functional analysis is mentioned here for completeness, but a discussion of it is outside the scope of this section.

Functional Testing

Program testing is functional when test data is developed from documents that specify a module's intended behavior. These documents include, but are not limited to, the actual specification and the high- and low-level design of the code to be tested. The goal is to test for each software feature of the specified behavior, including the input domains, the output domains, categories of inputs that should receive equivalent processing, and the processing functions themselves.

Testing Independent of the Specification Technique

Specifications detail the assumptions that may be made about a given software unit. They must describe the interface through which access to the unit is given, as well as the behavior once such access is given. The interface of a unit includes the features of its inputs, its outputs, and their related value spaces (called domains). The behavior of a module always includes the function(s) to be computed (its semantics), and sometimes the runtime characteristics, such as its space and time complexity. Functional testing derives test data from the features of the specification.

Testing Based on the Interface

Testing based on the interface of a module selects test data based on the features of the input and output domains of the module and their interrelationships.

Input domain testing. In external testing, test data is chosen to cover the extremes of the input domain. Similarly, midrange testing selects data from the interiors of domains. The motivation is inductive—it is hoped that conclusions about the entire input domain can be drawn from the behavior elicited by some of its representative members. For structured input domains, combinations of extreme points for each component are chosen. This procedure can generate a large quantity of data, though considerations of the inherent relationships among components can ameliorate this problem somewhat.

Equivalence partitioning. Specifications frequently partition the set of all possible inputs into classes that receive equivalent treatment. Such partitioning is called equivalence partitioning. A result of equivalence partitioning is the identification of a finite set of functions and their associated input and output domains. For example, the specification

```
{(x,y)|x=0⊃y=x&x<0⊃y=-x}
```

partitions the input into two sets, associated, respectively, with the identity and negation functions. Input constraints and error conditions can also result from this partitioning. Once these partitions have been developed, both extremal and midrange testing are applicable to the resulting input domains.

Syntax checking. Every robust program must parse its input and handle incorrectly formatted data. Verifying this feature is called syntax checking. One means of accomplishing this is to execute the program using a broad spectrum of test data. By describing the data with documentation language, instances of the input language can be generated using algorithms from automata theory.

Testing Based on the Function to Be Computed

Equivalence partitioning results in the identification of a finite set of functions and their associated input and output domains. Test data can be developed based on the known characteristics of these functions. Consider, for example, a function to be computed that has fixed points, that is, certain of its input values are mapped into themselves by the function. Testing the computation at these fixed points is possible, even in the absence of a complete specification. Knowledge of the function is essential in order to ensure adequate coverage of the output domains.

Special-value testing. Selecting test data on the basis of features of the function to be computed is called special-value testing. This procedure is particularly applicable to mathematical computations. Properties of the function to be computed can aid in selecting points that will indicate the accuracy of the computed solution.

Output domain coverage. For each function determined by equivalence partitioning there is an associated output domain. Output domain coverage is performed by selecting points that will cause the extremes of each of the output domains to be achieved. This ensures that modules have been checked for maximum and minimum output conditions and that all categories of error messages have, if possible, been produced. In general, constructing such test data requires knowledge of the function to be computed and, hence, expertise in the application area.

Testing Dependent on the Specification Technique

The specification technique employed can aid in testing. An executable specification can be used as an oracle and, in some cases, as a test generator. Structural properties of a specification can guide the testing process. If the specification falls within certain limited classes, properties of those classes can guide the selection of test data. Much work remains to be done in this area of testing.

Algebraic

In algebraic specification, properties of a data abstraction are expressed by means of axioms or rewrite rules. In one testing system, the consistency of an algebraic specification with an implementation is checked by testing. Each axiom is compiled into a procedure, which is then associated with a set of test points. A driver program supplies each of these points to the procedure of its respected axiom. The procedure, in turn, indicates whether the axiom is satisfied. Structural coverage of both the implementation and the specification is computed.

Axiomatic

Despite the potential for widespread use of predicate calculus as a specification language, little has been published about deriving test data from such specifications. A relationship between predicate calculus specifications and path testing has been explored.

State Machines

Many programs can be specified as state machines, thus providing an additional means of selecting test data. Since the equivalence problem of two finite automata is decidable, testing can be used to decide whether a program that simulates a finite automation with a bounded number of nodes is equivalent to the one specified. This result can be used to test those features of programs that can be specified by finite automata, for example, the control flow of a transaction-processing system.

Decision Tables

Decision tables are a concise method of representing an equivalence partitioning. The rows of a decision table specify all the conditions that the input may satisfy. The columns specify different sets of actions that may occur. Entries in the table indicate whether the actions should be performed if a condition is satisfied. Typical entries are "Yes," "No," or "Don't care." Each row of the table suggests significant test data. Cause-effect graphs provide a systematic means of translating English specifications into decision tables, from which test data can be generated.

Structural Testing and Analysis

In structural program testing and analysis, test data is developed or evaluated from the source code. The goal is to ensure that various characteristics of the program are adequately covered.

Structural Analysis

In structural analysis, programs are analyzed without being executed. The techniques resemble those used in compiler construction. The goal here is to identify fault-prone code, to discover anomalous circumstances, and to generate test data to cover specific characteristics of the program's structure.

Complexity measures. As resources available for testing are always limited, it is necessary to allocate these resources efficiently. It is intuitively appealing to suggest that the more complex the code, the more thoroughly it should be tested. Evidence from large projects seems to indicate that a small percentage of the code typically contains the largest number of errors. Various complexity measures have been proposed, investigated, and analyzed in the literature.

Data flow analysis. A program can be represented as a flowgraph annotated with information about variable definitions, references, and indefiniteness. From this representation, information about data flow can be deduced for use in code optimization, anomaly detection, and test data generation. Data flow anomalies are flow conditions that deserve further investigation, as they may indicate problems. Examples include: defining a variable twice with no intervening reference, referencing a variable that is undefined, and undefining a variable that has not been referenced since its last definition. Data flow analysis can also be used in test data generation, exploiting the relationship between points where variables are defined and points where they are used.

Symbolic execution. A symbolic execution system accepts three inputs: a program to be interpreted, symbolic input for the program, and the path to follow. It produces two outputs: the symbolic output that describes the computation of the selected path, and the path condition for that path. The specification of the path can be either interactive or preselected. The symbolic output can be used to prove the program correct with respect to its specification, and the path condition can be used for generating test data to exercise the desired path. Structured data types cause difficulties, however, since it is sometimes impossible to deduce what component is being modified in the presence of symbolic values.

Structural Testing

Structural testing is a dynamic technique in which test data selection and evaluation are driven by the goal of covering various characteristics of the code during testing. Assessing such coverage involves the instrumentation of the code to keep track of which characteristics of the program text are actually exercised during testing. The inexpensive cost of such instrumentation has been a prime motivation for adopting this technique. More importantly, structural testing addresses the fact that only the program text reveals the detailed decisions of the programmer. For example, for the sake of efficiency, a programmer might choose to implement a special case that appears nowhere in the specification. The corresponding code will be tested only by chance using functional testing, whereas use of a structural coverage measure such as statement coverage should indicate the need for test data for this case. Structural coverage measures form a rough hierarchy, with higher levels being more costly to perform and analyze, but being more beneficial, as described below.

Statement testing. Statement testing requires that every statement in the program be executed. While it is obvious that achieving 100 percent statement coverage does not ensure a correct program, it is equally obvious that anything less means that there is code in the program that has never been executed!

Branch testing. Achieving 100 percent statement coverage does not ensure that each branch in the program flowgraph has been executed. For example, executing an **if . . . then** statement (no **else**) when the tested condition is true, tests only one of two branches in the flowgraph. Branch testing seeks to ensure that every branch has been executed. Branch coverage can be checked by probes inserted at points in the program that represent arcs from branch points in the flowgraph. This instrumentation suffices for statement coverage as well.

Conditional testing. In conditional testing, each clause in every condition is forced to take on each of its possible values in combination with those of other clauses. Conditional testing thus subsumes branch testing and, therefore, inherits the same problems as branch testing. Instrumentation for conditional testing can be accomplished by breaking compound conditional statements into simple conditions and nesting the resulting **if** statements.

Expression testing. Expression testing requires that every expression assume a variety of values during a test in such a way that no expression can be replaced by a simpler expression and still pass the test. If one assumes that every statement contains an expression and that conditional expressions form a proper subset of all the program expressions, then this form of testing properly subsumes all the previously mentioned techniques. Expression testing does require significant run-time support for the instrumentation.

Path testing. In path testing, data is selected to ensure that all paths of the program have been executed. In practice, of course, such coverage is impossible to achieve, for a variety of reasons. First, any program with an indefinite loop contains an infinite number of paths, one for each iteration of the loop. Thus, no finite set of data will execute all paths. The second difficulty is the infeasible path problem: It is undecided whether an arbitrary path in an arbitrary program is executable. Attempting to generate data for such infeasible paths is futile, but it cannot be avoided. Third, it is undecided whether an arbitrary program will halt for an arbitrary input. It is therefore impossible to decide whether a path is finite for a given input.

In response to these difficulties, several simplifying approaches have been proposed. Infinitely many paths can be partitioned into a finite set of equivalence classes based on characteristics of the loops. Boundary and interior testing require executing loops zero times, one time, and, if possible, the maximum number of times. Linear sequence code and jump criteria specify a hierarchy of successively more complex path coverage.

Path coverage does not imply condition coverage or expression coverage since an expression may appear on multiple paths but some subexpressions may never assume more than one value. For example, in

if a / b **then** S_1 **else** S_2

b may be false and yet each path may still be executed.

Error-Oriented Testing and Analysis

Testing is necessitated by the potential presence of errors in the programming process. Techniques that focus on assessing the presence or absence of errors in the programming process are called error oriented. There are three broad categories of such techniques: statistical assessment, error-based testing, and fault-based testing. These are stated in order of increasing specificity of what is wrong with the program. Statistical methods attempt to estimate the failure rate of the program without reference to the number of remaining faults.

Error-based testing attempts to show the absence of certain errors in the programming process. Fault-based testing attempts to show the absence of certain faults in the code. Since errors in the programming process are reflected as faults in the code, both techniques demonstrate the absence of faults. They differ, however, in their starting point: Error-based testing begins with the programming process, identifies potential errors in that process, and then asks how those errors are reflected as faults. It then seeks to demonstrate the absence of those reflected faults. Fault-based testing begins with the code and asks what are the potential faults in it, regardless of what error in the programming process caused them.

Statistical Methods

Statistical testing employs statistical techniques to determine the operational reliability of the program. Its primary concern is how faults in the program affect its failure rate in its actual operating environment. A program is subjected to test data that statistically models the operating environment, and failure data is collected. From the data, a reliability estimate of the program's failure rate is computed. This method can be used in an incremental development environment. A statistical method for testing paths that compute algebraic functions has also been developed. There has been a prevailing sentiment that statistical testing is a futile activity, since it is not directed toward finding errors. However, studies suggest it is a viable alternative to structural testing. Combining statistical testing with an oracle appears to represent an effective tradeoff of computer resources for human time.

Error-based Testing

Error-based testing seeks to demonstrate that certain errors have not been committed in the programming process. Error-based testing can be driven by histories of programmer errors, measures of software complexity, knowledge of error-prone syntactic constructs, or even error guessing. Some of the more methodical techniques are described below.

Fault estimation. Fault seeding is a statistical method used to assess the number and characteristics of the faults remaining in a program. Harlan Mills originally proposed this technique, and called it error seeding. First, faults are seeded into a program. Then the program is tested and the number of faults discovered is used to estimate the number of faults yet undiscovered. A difficulty with this technique is that the faults seeded must be representative of the yet-undiscovered faults in the program. Techniques for predicting the quantity of remaining faults can also be based on a reliability model.

Domain testing. The input domain of a program can be partitioned according to which inputs cause each path to be executed. These partitions are called path domains. Faults that cause an input to be associated with the wrong path domain are called domain faults. Other faults are called computation faults. (The terms used before attempts were made to rationalize nomenclature were "domain errors" and "computation errors.") The goal of domain testing is to discover domain faults by ensuring that the test data limits the range of undetected faults.

Perturbation testing. Perturbation testing attempts to decide what constitutes a sufficient set of paths to test. Faults are modeled as a vector space, and characterization theorems describe when sufficient paths have been tested to discover both computation and domain errors. Additional paths need not be tested if they cannot reduce the dimensionality of the error space.

Fault-based Testing

Fault-based testing aims at demonstrating that certain prescribed faults are not in the code. It functions well in the role of test data evaluation: Test data that does not succeed in discovering the prescribed faults is not considered adequate. Fault-based testing methods differ in both extent and breadth. One with local extent demonstrates that a fault has a local effect on computation; it is possible that this local effect will not produce a program failure. A method with global extent demonstrates that a fault will cause a program failure. Breadth is determined by whether the technique handles a finite or an infinite class of faults. Extent and breadth are orthogonal, as evidenced by the techniques described below.

Local extent, finite breadth. Input-output pairs of data are encoded as a comment in a procedure, as a partial specification of the function to be computed by that procedure. The procedure is then executed for each of the input values and checked for the output values. The test is considered adequate only if each computational or logical expression in the procedure is determined by the test; that is, no expression can be replaced by a simpler expression and still pass the test. Simpler is defined in a way that allows only a finite number of substitutions. Thus, as the procedure is executed, each possible substitution is evaluated on the data state presented to the expression. Those that do not evaluate the same as the original expression are rejected. The system allows methods of specifying the extent to be analyzed.

Global extent, finite breadth. In mutation testing, test data adequacy is judged by demonstrating that interjected faults are caught. A program with interjected faults is called a mutant, and is produced by applying a mutation operator. Such an operator changes a single expression in the program to another expression, selected from a finite class of expressions. For example, a constant might be incremented by one, decremented by one, or replaced by zero, yielding one of three mutants. Applying the mutation operators at each point in a program where they are applicable forms a finite, albeit large, set of mutants. The test data is judged adequate only if each mutant in this set is either functionally equivalent to the original program or computes different output than the original program. Inadequacy of the test data implies that certain faults can be introduced into the code and go undetected by the test data.

Mutation testing is based on two hypotheses. The competent-programmer hypothesis says that a competent programmer will write code that is close to being correct; the correct program, if not the current one, can be produced by some straightforward syntactic changes to the code. The coupling-effect hypothesis says that test data that reveals simple faults will uncover complex faults as well. Thus, only single mutants need be eliminated, and combinatoric effects of multiple mutants need not be considered. Studies formally characterize the competent-programmer hypothesis as a function of the probability of the test set's being reliable, and show that under this characterization, the hypothesis does not hold. Empirical justification of the coupling effect has been attempted, but theoretical analysis has shown that it does not hold, even for simple programs.

Local extent, infinite breadth. Rules for recognizing error-sensitive data are described for each primitive language construct. Satisfaction of a rule for a given construct during testing means that all alternate forms of that construct have been distinguished. This has an obvious advantage over mutation testing—elimination of all mutants without generating a single one! Some rules even allow for infinitely many mutants. Of course, since this method is of local extent, some of the mutants eliminated may indeed be the correct program.

Global extent, infinite breadth. We can define a fault-based method based on symbolic execution that permits elimination of infinitely many faults through evidence of global failures. Symbolic faults are inserted into the code, which is then executed on real or symbolic data. Program output is then an expression in terms of the symbolic faults. It thus reflects how a fault at a given location will impact the program's output. This expression can be used to determine actual faults that could not have been substituted for the symbolic fault and remain undetected by the test.

Managerial Aspects of Unit Testing and Analysis

Administration of unit testing and analysis proceeds in two stages. First, techniques appropriate to the project must be selected. Then these techniques must be systematically applied.

Selecting Techniques

Selecting the appropriate techniques from the array of possibilities is a complex task that requires assessment of many issues, including the goal of testing, the nature of the software product, and the nature of the test environment. It is important to remember the complementary benefits of the various techniques and to select as broad a range of techniques as possible, within imposed limits. No single testing or analysis technique is sufficient. Functional testing suffers from inadequate code coverage, structural testing suffers from inadequate specification coverage, and neither technique achieves the benefits of error coverage.

Goals. Different design goals impose different demands on the selection of testing techniques. Achieving correctness requires use of a great variety of techniques. A goal of reliability implies the need for statistical testing using test data representative of that of the anticipated user environment. It should be noted, however, that proponents of this technique still recommend judicious use of "selective" tests to avoid embarrassing or disastrous situations. Testing may also be directed toward assessing the utility of proposed software. This kind of testing requires a solid foundation in human factors. Performance of the software may also be of special concern. In this case, extremal testing is essential. Timing instrumentation can prove useful.

Often, several of these goals must be achieved simultaneously. One approach to testing under these circumstances is to order testing by decreasing benefit. For example, if reliability, correctness, and performance are all desired features, it is reasonable to tackle performance first, reliability second, and correctness third, since these goals require increasingly difficult-to-design tests. This approach can have the beneficial effect of identifying faulty code with less effort expended.

Nature of the product. The nature of the software product plays an important role in the selection of appropriate techniques.

Nature of the testing environment. Available resources, personnel, and project constraints must be considered in selecting testing and analysis strategies.

Control

To ensure quality in unit testing and analysis, it is necessary to control both documentation and the conduct of the test.

Configuration control. Several items from unit testing and analysis should be placed under configuration management, including the test plan, test procedures, test data, and test results. The test plan specifies the goals, environment, and constraints imposed on testing. The test procedures detail the step-by-step activities to be performed during the test. Regression testing occurs when previously saved test data is used to test modified code. Its principal advantage is that it ensures previously attained functionality has not been lost during a modification. Test results are recorded and analyzed for evidence of program failures. Failure rates underlie many reliability models; high failure rates may indicate the need for redesign.

Conducting tests. A test bed is an integrated system for testing software. Minimally, such systems provide the ability to define a test case, construct a test driver, execute the test case, and capture the output. Additional facilities provided by such systems typically include data flow analysis, structural coverage assessment, regression testing, test specification, and report generation.

Test Factor/Test Technique Matrix

The objective of testing applications is to verify that the test factors have been adequately addressed. In accomplishing the test process, it is necessary to conduct tests. The testing technique options available for testing have been described in this chapter as both structural and functional testing techniques.

The recommended test process is first to determine the test factors to be evaluated in the test process; and second, to select the techniques that will be used in performing the test. Figure 4.5 is a test factor/test technique matrix that shows which techniques are most valuable in evaluating the various test factors.

The test factor/test technique matrix is designed to show the better techniques for use in evaluating each of the identified test factors. For example, if one wanted to evaluate the system structure for reliability, then the execution and recovery testing techniques are recommended. On the other hand, if one wanted to evaluate the functional aspects of reliability, then the requirements, error handling, manual support, and control testing techniques are recommended. (Note: Use Figure 4.5 to select and identify the recommended test techniques.)

The matrix is provided as a guide to help the tester in selecting the appropriate technique for each test factor. Once the testing technique has been selected, then a test tool will need to be selected. The following chapter identifies and describes the more popular testing tools and provides a matrix that shows which tools are most effective in accomplishing the objectives of the identified testing techniques.

Summary

Techniques are the means by which testers perform their job tasks. This chapter describes the more common testing techniques used for structural, functional, and unit testing. The chapter then shows which techniques are most effective in testing the implementation of the 15 test factors. This technique selection needs to be considered in the 11-step testing process when deciding how to test a specific test factor.

TEST FACTOR	STRUCTURAL TESTING						FUNCTIONAL TESTING							UNIT TESTING
	Stress	Execution	Recovery	Operations	Compliance	Security	Requirements	Regression	Error Handling	Manual Support	Inter-systems	Control	Parallel	
Reliability	x	x	x				x		x					x
Authorization						x	x							x
File Integrity			x				x		x					x
Audit Trail			x				x							x
Continuity of Processing	x		x	x										x
Service Level	x	x		x										
Access Control						x								
Methodology					x									
Correctness							x	x	x	x	x	x	x	x
Ease of Use					x		x			x				x
Maintainable					x									x
Portable				x	x									
Coupling				x							x	x		
Performance	x	x			x									x
Ease of Operation				x	x									

Figure 4.5 Test factor/test technique matrix.

# CHAPTER 5

Selecting and Installing Software Testing Tools

Much effort in the last twenty years has been expended on the developmental process. This has left testing primarily a manual operation and often an inefficient function in many organizations. However, new test methods are being developed to improve testing effectiveness and productivity.

Testing, like program development, generates large amounts of information, necessitates numerous computer executions, and requires coordination and communication between workers. Testing tools can ease the burden of test production, test execution, general information handling, and communication. This section discusses the more common testing tools.

This chapter proposes the job of a tool manager for each tool. The role of the tool manager, and how to establish a tool manager is explained. A more detailed explanation of the most often used tools will be covered in the specific test step for which that tool is most applicable.

Testing Tools—The Hammers of Testing

The selection of the appropriate tool in testing is an important aspect of the test process. Techniques are few in number and broad in scope, while tools are large in number and narrow in scope. Each provides different capabilities; each tool is designed to accomplish a specific testing objective.

Selection of the tool affects the effectiveness and efficiency of testing. The technique for hammering a nail into a piece of wood is well understood. However, if the wrong hammer is selected the entire process can be inefficient. For example, visualize a large piece of wood with a five-inch nail to be driven in. The tool selected is a tack hammer, and the hammering process becomes tedious and extensive. Visualize the same situation, but this time with a two-pound heavy-duty hammer. The nail flows smoothly into the wood with less effort than was used with the tack hammer. The difference is the tool, and the efficiency achieved depends on selecting the proper tool.

Most information technology professionals can only name a handful of testing techniques. The objective of this chapter is to broaden the perspective on available testing tools. A knowledge of the available testing tools should be part of the knowledge base of information technology professionals having testing responsibility.

Overview

Testing tools are the aids used by individuals with testing responsibility to fulfill that responsibility. The tools cover a wide range of activities and are applicable for use in all phases of the systems development life cycle. Some of the techniques are manual, some automated; some perform static tests, others dynamic; some evaluate the system structure, and others, the system function.

The skill required to use the tools and the cost of executing the tools vary significantly. Some of the skills are highly technical and involve an in-depth knowledge of computer programming and the system being tested. Other tools are general in nature and are useful to almost anyone with testing responsibilities. The cost of some techniques only involves a short expenditure of people time, while others must be conducted by a team and make heavy use of computer resources in the test process.

Listed below, and summarized in Figure 5.1, are the more common testing tools. The objective of the explanation is to familiarize the tester with the repertoire of available testing tools. Other parts of the book explain how, where, and when these tools should be used.

1. **Acceptance Test Criteria.** The development of system standards that must be achieved before the user will accept the system for production purposes.

2. **Boundary Value Analysis.** A method of dividing application systems into segments so that testing can occur within the boundaries of those segments. The concept complements top-down system design.

3. **Cause-Effect Graphing.** Attempts to show the effect of each event processed in order to categorize events by the effect that will occur as a result of processing. The objective is to reduce the number of test conditions by eliminating the need for multiple test events that all produce the same effects.

4. **Checklist.** A series of probing questions designed for use in reviewing a predetermined area or function.

5. **Code Comparison.** Identifies differences between two versions of the same program. It can be used with either object or source code.

6. **Compiler-based Analysis.** Utilizes the diagnostics produced by a compiler or diagnostic routines added to a compiler to identify program defects during the compilation of the program.

7. **Complexity-based Metric Testing.** Uses statistics and mathematics to develop highly predictive relationships that can be used to identify the complexity of computer programs and the completeness of testing in evaluating the complex logic.

8. **Confirmation/Examination.** Verifies the correctness of many aspects of the system by contacting third parties, such as users, or examining a document to verify that it exists.

9. **Control Flow Analysis.** Requires the development of a graphic representation of a program to analyze the branch logic within the program to identify logic problems.

10. **Correctness Proof.** Involves developing a set of statements or hypotheses that define the correctness of processing. These hypotheses are then tested to determine whether the application system performs processing in accordance with these correctness statements.

11. **Coverage-based Metrics Testing.** Uses mathematical relationships to show what percent of the application system has been covered by the test process. The resulting metric should be usable for predicting the effectiveness of the test process.

12. **Data Dictionary.** The documentation tool for recording data elements and the attributes of the data elements that, under some implementations, can produce test data to validate the system's data edits.

13. **Data Flow Analysis.** A method of ensuring that the data used by the program has been properly defined, and the defined data is properly used.

14. **Design-based Functional Testing.** Recognizes that functions within an application system are necessary to support the requirements. This process identifies those design-based functions for test purposes.

15. **Design Reviews.** Reviews conducted during the systems development process, normally in accordance with systems development methodology. The primary objective of design reviews is to ensure compliance to the design methodology.

16. **Desk Checking.** Reviews by the originator of the requirements, design, or program as a check on the work performed by that individual.

17. **Disaster Test.** A procedure that predetermines a disaster as a basis for testing the recovery process. The test group then causes or simulates the disaster as a basis for testing the procedures and training for the recovery process.

18. **Error Guessing.** Uses the experience or judgment of people to predetermine through guessing what the most probable errors will be and then test to ensure whether the system can handle those test conditions.

19. **Executable Specs.** Requires a special language for writing system specifications so that those specifications can be compiled into a testable program. The compiled specs have less detail and precision than will the final implemented programs, but are sufficient to evaluate the completeness and proper functioning of the specifications.

20. **Exhaustive Testing.** Performs sufficient testing to evaluate every possible path and condition in the application system. This is the only test method that guarantees the proper functioning of the application system.

21. **Fact-Finding.** Information needed to conduct a test or provide assurance of the correctness of information on a document, achieved through an investigative process requiring obtaining information, look-up, or search for the facts regarding a predetermined condition.

22. **Flowchart.** Graphically represents the system and/or program flow in order to evaluate the completeness of the requirements, design, or program specifications.

23. **Inspections.** A highly structured step-by-step review of the deliverables produced by each phase of the systems development life cycle in order to identify potential defects.

24. **Instrumentation.** The use of monitors and/or counters to determine the frequency with which predetermined events occur.

25. **Integrated Test Facility.** A concept that permits the introduction of test data into a production environment so that applications can be tested at the same time they are running in production. The concept permits testing the accumulation of data over many iterations of the process, and facilitates intersystem testing.

26. **Mapping.** Process that analyzes which parts of a computer program are exercised during the test and the frequency of execution of each statement or routine in a program. Can be used to detect system flaws, determine how much of a program is executed during testing, and to identify areas where more efficient code may reduce execution time.

27. **Modeling.** Method of simulating the functioning of the application system and/or its environment to determine if the design specifications will achieve the system objectives.

28. **Parallel Operation.** Runs both the old and new version within the same time frame in order to identify differences between the two processes. The tool is most effective when there is a minimal number of changes between the old and new processing versions of the system.

29. **Parallel Simulation.** Develops a less precise version of a segment of a computer system in order to determine whether the results produced by the test are reasonable. Effective when used with large volumes of data to automatically determine the correctness of the results of processing. Normally only approximates actual processing.

30. **Peer Review.** A review process that uses peers to review that aspect of the systems development life cycle with which they are most familiar. Normally the peers review compliance to standards, procedures, guidelines, and the use of good practices as opposed to efficiency, effectiveness, and economy of the design and implementation.

31. **Risk Matrix.** Tests the adequacy of controls through the identification of risks and the controls implemented in each part of the application system to reduce those risks to a level acceptable to the user.

32. **SCARF (System Control Audit Review File).** Evaluates the operational system over a period of time, or compares the operation of like entities at a specific

point in time. The tool uses information collected during operations to perform the analysis. For example, all data entry errors would be collected over a period of time to show whether the quality of input is improving or degrading over time.

33. **Scoring.** Method used to determine what aspects of the application system should be tested by determining the applicability of problem criteria to the application being tested. The process can be used to determine the degree of testing (for example, high-risk systems would be subject to more tests than low-risk systems) or to identify areas within the application system to determine the amount of testing needed.

34. **Snapshot.** A method of printing the status of computer memory at predetermined points during processing. Computer memory can be printed when specific instructions are executed, or when data with specific attributes are processed.

35. **Symbolic Execution.** Permits the testing of programs without test data. The symbolic execution of a program results in an expression that can be used to evaluate the completeness of the programming logic.

36. **System Logs.** Uses information collected during the operation of a computer system for analysis purposes to determine how well the system performed. The logs used are those produced by operating software such as database management systems, operating systems, and job accounting systems.

37. **Test Data.** System transactions that are created for the purpose of testing the application system.

38. **Test Data Generator.** Software systems that can be used to automatically generate test data for test purposes. Frequently, these generators only require parameters of the data element values in order to generate large amounts of test transactions.

39. **Tracing.** A representation of the paths followed by computer programs as they process data or the paths followed in a database to locate one or more pieces of data used to produce a logical record for processing.

40. **Utility Programs.** A general-purpose software package that can be used in the testing of an application system. The most valuable utilities are those that analyze or list data files.

41. **Volume Testing.** The creation of specific types of test data in order to test predetermined system limits to verify how the system functions when those limits are reached or exceeded.

42. **Walkthroughs.** A process that asks the programmer or analyst to explain the application system to a test team normally using a simulation of the execution of the application system. The objective of the walkthrough is to provide a basis for questioning by the test team as a basis of identifying defects.

A further explanation of many of the tools in Figure 5.1 is provided on the companion Web site, as well as a specific example of how some of these tools function. In addition, the more effective tools are described in detail in several chapters where the use of that tool is most appropriate; some examples follow:

#	TOOL NAME	TESTING USE
1.	Acceptance Test Criteria	Provides the standards that must be achieved for the system to be acceptable to the user.
2.	Boundary Value Analysis	Divides system top down into logical segments and then limits testing within the boundaries of each segment.
3.	Cause-Effect Graphing	Limits the number of test transactions by determining which of the number of variable conditions pose minimal risk based on system actions.
4.	Checklist	Provides a series of questions designed to probe potential system problem areas.
5.	Code Comparison	Compares two versions of the same program in order to identify differences between the two versions.
6.	Compiler-based Analysis	Detects errors during the program compilation process.
7.	Complexity-based Metric Testing	Uses relationships to demonstrate the degree of system processing complexity provided by the test process.
8.	Confirmation/Examination	Verifies that a condition has or has not occurred.
9.	Control Flow Analysis	Identifies processing inconsistencies such as routines with no entry point, potentially unending loops, branches into the middle of a routine, etc.
10.	Correctness Proof	Requires a proof hypothesis to be defined and then used to evaluate the correctness of the system.
11.	Coverage-based Metric Testing	Uses relationships to demonstrate the degree of system processing complexity provided by the test process.
12.	Data Dictionary	Generates test data to verify data validation programs based on the data contained in the dictionary.
13.	Data Flow Analysis	Identifies defined data not used and used data that is not defined.
14.	Design-based Functional Testing	Evaluates functions attributable to the design process as opposed to design requirements; for example, capability may be a design process.
15.	Design Reviews	Requires reviews at predetermined points throughout systems development in order to examine progress and ensure the development process is followed.
16.	Desk Checking	Provides an evaluation by programmer or analyst of the propriety of program logic after the program is coded or the system is designed.

Figure 5.1   Testing tools.

#	TOOL NAME	TESTING USE
17.	Disaster Test	Simulates an operational or systems failure to determine if the system can be correctly recovered after the failure.
18.	Error Guessing	Relies on the experience of testers and the organization's history of problems to create test transactions that have a high probability of detecting an error.
19.	Executable Specs	Provides a high-level interpretation of the system specs in order to create the response to test data. Interpretation of expected software packages requires system specs to be written in a high-level language.
20.	Exhaustive Testing	Attempts to create a test transaction for every possible condition and every path in the program.
21.	Fact Finding	Performs those steps necessary to obtain facts to support the test process.
22.	Flowchart	Pictorially represents computer systems logic and data flow.
23.	Inspections	Requires a step-by-step explanation of the product with each step checked against a predetermined list of criteria.
24.	Instrumentation	Measures the functioning of a system structure by using counters and other monitoring instruments.
25.	Integrated Test Facility	Permits the integration of test data in a production environment to enable testing to run during production processing.
26.	Mapping	Identifies which part of a program is exercised during a test and at what frequency.
27.	Modeling	Simulates the functioning of the environment or system structure in order to determine how efficiently the proposed system solution will function.
28.	Parallel Operation	Verifies that the old and new version of the application system produce equal or reconcilable results.
29.	Parallel Simulation	Approximates the expected results of processing by simulating the process to determine if test results are reasonable.
30.	Peer Review	Provides an assessment by peers of the efficiency, style, adherence to standards, etc. of the product which is designed to improve the quality of the product.

Figure 5.1   *(Continued)*   *(Continues)*

#	TOOL NAME	TESTING USE
31.	Risk Matrix	Produces a matrix showing the relationship between system risk, the segment of the system where the risk occurs, and the presence or absence of controls to reduce that risk.
32.	SCARF (System Control Audit Review File)	Builds a history of potential problems in order to compare problems in a single unit over a period of time and/or compares like units.
33.	Scoring	Identifies areas in the application that require testing, through the rating of criteria that have been shown to correlate to problems.
34.	Snapshot	Shows the content of computer storage at predetermined points during processing.
35.	Symbolic Execution	Identifies processing paths by testing the programs with symbolic rather than actual test data.
36.	System Logs	Provides an audit trail of monitored events occurring in the environment area controlled by system software.
37.	Test Data	Creates transactions for use in determining the functioning of a computer system.
38.	Test Data Generator	Provides test transactions based on the parameters that need to be tested.
39.	Tracing	Follows and lists the flow of processing and data-base searches.
40.	Utility Program	Analyzes and prints the result of a test through the use of a general-purpose program (i.e., utility program).
41.	Volume Testing	Identifies system restriction (e.g., internal table size) and then creates a large volume of transactions designed that exceed those limits.
42.	Walkthroughs	Leads a test team through a manual simulation of the product using test transactions.

Figure 5.1 (Continued)

Chapter 9—Requirements Phase Testing: Risk matrix; walk-through

Chapter 10—Design Phase Testing: Scoring; design reviews

Chapter 11—Program Phase Testing: Desk checking; peer reviews

Chapter 12—Test Phase Testing: Test data; volume testing

Selecting and Using the Test Tools

This chapter presents an extensive array of tools for systems testing. Many of these tools have not seen wide use. The principal reasons for this include their specialization (simulation), the high cost of their use (symbolic execution), and their unproven applicability (formal proof of correctness). Many of these tools represent the state of the art and are in areas where research is continuing. However, this should not prevent organizations from experimenting with some of the newer test concepts. The tools attracting the most interest and activity at present include automated test support systems (test data generator) and automated analysis (compiler-based analysis).

As more formal techniques are used during requirements and design, an increase in automatic analysis is possible. In addition, more sophisticated analysis tools are being applied to the code during construction. More complete control and automation of the actual execution of tests, both in assistance in generating the test cases and in the management of the testing process and result, are also taking place.

It is important that validation occur throughout the life cycle. One of the reasons for the great success of disciplined manual techniques is the uniform applicability at requirements, design, and coding phases. These tools can be used without massive capital expenditure. However, to be most effective they require a serious commitment and a disciplined application. Careful planning, clearly stated testing objectives, precisely defined tools, good management, organized record keeping, and a strong commitment are critical to successful testing. A disciplined approach must be followed during both planning and execution of the testing activities.

An integral part of this process is the selection of the appropriate testing tool. The four steps involved in selecting the appropriate testing tool are:

1. Matching the tool to its intended use.
2. Selecting a tool appropriate to the life cycle phase in which it will be used.
3. Matching the tool to the skill level of the tester.
4. Selecting an affordable tool.

Step 1: Matching the Tool to Its Use

A tool is an aid to accomplish a task. The better that tool is suited to accomplish the task, the more efficient the test process. The wrong tool not only decreases the efficiency of testing; it may not permit the test objectives to be achieved.

The testing use for each of the identified tools is described in Figure 5.2. The tester needs to be familiar with both the tool and its use in order to make a proper selection. This figure can be used to help select the proper tool for the intended purpose. The testing technique should be selected prior to the tool. Chapter 4 shows the relationship between the testing factor and the testing technique. The objective of the matrices in this book is to lead the tester to the appropriate tool.

Figure 5.3 is a matrix showing tools that are appropriate for the identified testing techniques. This matrix can be used to select the tools that have proven most beneficial for each of the identified testing techniques. From this list of tools, a knowledge of the

TEST TECHNIQUE

TEST TOOL	Stress	Execution	Recovery	Operations	Compliance	Security	Requirements	Regression	Error Handling	Manual Support	Inter-systems	Control	Parallel
1. Acceptance Test Criteria		x			x		x		x				
2. Boundary Value Analysis							x		x				
3. Cause Effect Graphing			x			x	x		x	x		x	
4. Checklist	x	x	x	x	x	x	x	x	x	x	x	x	
5. Code Comparison								x				x	x
6. Compiler-based Analysis					x		x						
7. Complexity-based Metric Testing							x						
8. Confirmation/Examination		x	x	x	x	x	x			x	x	x	
9. Control Flow Analysis							x						
10. Correctness Proof							x		x	x	x	x	
11. Coverage-based Metric Testing							x						
12. Data Dictionary							x		x				

Figure 5.2 Testing technique/tool matrix.

(Continues)

TEST TOOL	Stress	Execution	Recovery	Operations	Compliance	Security	Requirements	Regression	Error Handling	Manual Support	Inter-systems	Control	Parallel
13. Data Flow Analysis							x						
14. Design-based Functional Testing							x						
15. Design Reviews					x								
16. Desk Checking							x	x	x		x	x	
17. Disaster Test			x	x						x			
18. Error Guessing	x	x	x	x	x	x	x	x	x	x	x	x	
19. Executable Specs							x						
20. Exhaustive Testing						x	x	x	x	x	x	x	
21. Fact Finding			x	x	x	x	x			x	x	x	
22. Flowchart						x	x		x	x	x	x	
23. Inspections	x	x	x	x	x	x	x	x	x	x	x	x	x
24. Instrumentation	x	x		x		x	x		x	x	x	x	
25. Integrated Test Facility				x		x	x	x	x	x	x	x	
26. Mapping							x						
27. Modeling							x						

Figure 5.2 *(Continued)*

(Continues)

TEST TECHNIQUE

TEST TOOL	Stress	Execution	Recovery	Operations	Compliance	Security	Requirements	Regression	Error Handling	Manual Support	Inter-systems	Control	Parallel
28. Parallel Operation													x
29. Parallel Simulation													x
30. Peer Review			x	x	x	x							
31. Risk Matrix						x						x	
32. SCARF		x					x			x			
33. Scoring							x						
34. Snapshot							x						
35. Symbolic Execution							x						
36. System Logs		x		x	x	x	x		x		x		
37. Test Data							x	x	x	x	x	x	
38. Test Data Generator							x	x	x	x	x	x	
39. Tracing							x						
40. Utility Programs		x		x			x						
41. Volume Testing	x												
42. Walkthroughs							x		x	x	x	x	

Figure 5.2 *(Continued)*

specific use outlined in Figure 5.2 can be used to narrow the choice to the more appropriate tools. This does not mean that the tester should be restricted to the tools identified in Figure 5.3, but rather, that they form a good basis for narrowing the selection process.

Step 2: Selecting a Tool Appropriate to the Life Cycle Phase

The type of testing varies by the life cycle in which that test occurs. Just as the methods change, so do the tools. Thus, it becomes necessary to select the tool appropriate for the life cycle in which that tool will be used.

As the life cycle progresses, the tools tend to shift from manual to automatic. However, this should not imply that the manual tools are less effective than the automatic, because some of the most productive testing can occur during the early phases of the life cycle using manual tools.

The life cycle phases in which the identified test tools are most effective are listed in Figure 5.3. This matrix shows the 42 test tools and for which of the six systems development life cycle phases each tool is most appropriate. This matrix can be used for the second step of the selection process, in which the population of tools identified in step 1 can be reduced to those tools that are effective in the life cycle phase where the test will be occurring.

Step 3: Matching the Tool to the Skill Level of the Tester

The individual performing the test must select a tool that conforms to his or her skill level. For example, it would be inappropriate for a user to select a tool that requires programming skills when the user does not possess those skills. This does not mean that an individual will not have to be trained before the tool can be used, but rather, that he or she possesses the basic skills necessary to undertake the training to use the tool. The tools divided according to the skill required are presented in Figure 5.4. This figure divides skills into user skill, programming skill, system skill, and technical skill.

User skill. Requires the individual to have an in-depth knowledge of the application and the business purpose for which that application is used. Skills needed include general business specializing in the area computerized, general management skills used to achieve the mission of the user area, and a knowledge of identifying and dealing with user problems.

Programming skill. Requires understanding of computer concepts, flowcharting, programming in the languages used by the organization, debugging, and documenting computer programs.

System skill. Requires the ability to translate user requirements into computer system design specifications. Specific skills include flowcharting, problem analysis, design methodologies, computer operations, some general business skills, error identification and analysis in automated applications, and project management. The individual normally possesses a programming skill.

TESTING TOOL	SDLC PHASE					
	Re-quire-ments	Design	Pro-gram	Test	Instal-lation	Main-tain
1. Acceptance Test Criteria				X	X	
2. Boundary Value Analysis			X	X		
3. Cause-Effect Graphing		X	X			
4. Checklist	X	X	X	X	X	X
5. Code Comparison						X
6. Compiler-based Analysis			X			
7. Complexity-based Metric Testing			X	X		
8. Control Flow Analysis			X			
9. Confirmation/Examination	X	X	X	X	X	X
10. Correctness Proof		X		X		
11. Coverage-based Metric Testing			X	X		
12. Data Dictionary				X		
13. Data Flow Analysis			X			
14. Design-based Functional Testing		X		X		
15. Design Reviews		X				
16. Desk Checking	X	X	X			X
17. Disaster Test				X		X
18. Error Guessing	X	X	X	X	X	X
19. Executable Specs		X				
20. Exhaustive Testing				X		
21. Fact Finding	X	X	X	X	X	X
22. Flowchart	X	X	X			
23. Inspections	X	X	X	X	X	X
24. Instrumentation				X	X	X
25. Integrated Test Facility						X
26. Mapping			X			

Figure 5.3   SDLC phase/test tool matrix.

TESTING TOOL	SDLC PHASE					
	Re-quire-ments	Design	Pro-gram	Test	Instal-lation	Main-tain
27. Modeling	x	x				
28. Parallel Operation					x	
29. Parallel Simulation				x		
30. Peer Review	x	x	x	x	x	x
31. Risk Matrix	x	x				
32. SCARF						x
33. Scoring	x	x				
34. Snapshot				x		
35. Symbolic Execution			x			
36. System Logs				x	x	x
37. Test Data		x	x	x		x
38. Test Data Generator				x		x
39. Tracing			x			x
40. Utility Programs				x	x	x
41. Volume Testing				x		
42. Walkthroughs	x	x	x			

Figure 5.3   *(Continued)*

Technical skill. Understands a highly technical specialty and can exhibit reasonable performance at that specialty. Examples of technical skills needed for testing (note that the individual may only need to possess a single skill) include systems programming, database administration, statistics, accounting, and operating software packages.

The skills indicated in Figure 5.4 are those needed to execute the tool. In some instances, different skills are needed to develop the tool, and if this is the case, that has been indicated in the comments column. The comments also indicate any skill qualification or specific technical skill needed.

Step 4: Selecting an Affordable Tool

Testing normally must be accomplished within a budget or time span. An extremely time-consuming and hence costly tool, while desirable, may not be affordable under the test budget and schedule. Therefore, the last selection criterion is to pick those tools that are affordable from the population of tools remaining after step 3.

SKILL REQUIRED	TESTING TOOL	COMMENTS
User Skill	Acceptance Test Criteria	
	Checklist	
	Integrated Test Facility	
	Peer Review	
	Risk Matrix	
	SCARF	
	Scoring	
	Walkthroughs	
Programmer Skill	Boundary Value Analysis	
	Checklist	
	Code Comparison	
	Compiler-based Analysis	
	Complexity-based Metric Testing	Requires statistical skills to develop
	Control Flow Analysis	
	Correctness Proof	
	Coverage-based Metric Testing	
	Data Dictionary	
	Data Flow Analysis	
	Design-based Functional Testing	
	Desk Checking	
	Error Guessing	
	Exhaustive Testing	Hard to hold programmer interest
	Flowchart	
	Instrumentation	
	Mapping	
	Modeling	
	Parallel Simulation	
	Peer Review	
	SCARF	
	Snapshot	
	Symbolic Execution	
	System Logs	
	Test Data	
	Test Data Generator	
	Tracing	
	Utility Programs	
	Volume Testing	
	Walkthroughs	

Figure 5.4   Skill levels for use of testing tools.   *(Continues)*

SKILL REQUIRED	TESTING TOOL	COMMENTS
Systems Skill	Boundary Value Analysis	Skill needed for design of system, not testing
	Cause-Effect Graphing	
	Checklist	
	Confirmation/Examination	
	Correctness Proof	
	Design-based Functional Testing	
	Design Reviews	
	Desk Checking	
	Disaster Test	
	Error Guessing	
	Executable Specs	Few such languages in existence
	Fact Finding	
	Flowchart	
	Inspections	Helpful to have application knowledge
	Integrated Test Facility	Skills needed to develop by not using ITF
	Mapping	
	Modeling	
	Parallel Simulation	
	Peer Review	
	SCARF	
	System Logs	
	Test Data	
	Tracing	
	Volume Testing	
	Walkthroughs	
Technical Skill (e.g., system programmer)	Checklist	Needs to understand how to use checklist
	Complexity-based Metric Testing	Requires statistical skill to develop
	Coverage-based Metric Testing	Requires statistical skill to develop
	Instrumentation	System programmer skill
	Parallel Operation	Requires operations skill
	Peer Review	Must be taught how to conduct review

Figure 5.4   *(Continued)*

Some of the test tools are extremely costly to execute, while others only involve nominal costs. It is difficult to put a specific price tag on many of the tools because they require the acquisition of hardware or software, and the cost of what is acquired may vary significantly from vendor to vendor. Therefore, only a category of cost has been given (see Figure 5.5).

Three categories of cost are used—high, medium, and low. The cost categories are relational, meaning that tools categorized as high cost will cost more than those categorized as medium, and the medium more than the low-cost categories. Where costs are extremely high or low, the comments column is used to further clarify the cost category. At this point, select the most appropriate tool from the selectable list.

What if You Finish Step 4 and All Tools Are Excluded?

It is possible that you will have gone through the selection process and ended up with no tools to select from. In this instance, you have two options. First, you can repeat the process and be more generous in your selection criteria. In other words, be more inclined to include tools as you move from step to step. Second, you can ignore the formal selection process and from the available 42 tools use judgment and experience to select the tool that appears most appropriate to accomplish the test objective.

Appointing Managers for Testing Tools

It is recommended that an individual be appointed manager of each acquired significant software tool. The objective of appointing a tool manager is threefold, as follows:

Objective 1. Create a source of competency about how to use the tool.

Objective 2. Assign someone accountable to oversee tool usage. Without someone accountable to ensure tools are properly used, tools may fall into disuse.

Objective 3. Provide a training ground for future managers.

Managing a tool should involve budgeting, planning, training, and related managerial responsibilities.

The workbench for managing testing tools using a tool manager is illustrated in Figure 5.6. The three steps involve appointing a tool manager; assigning the duties the tool manager will perform; and limiting the tool manager tenure. This concept not only facilitates the use of tools, but builds future managers at the same time.

Once management has determined that a specific tool is needed, and that tool has been selected, a tool manager can be appointed. There are two inputs needed for this workbench. First is a clear definition of the objective for acquiring and using the tool; second is a list of potential tool manager candidates.

Tool usage should be mandatory. In other words, work processes should indicate when to use a specific tool. If a tool user can select among two or more recommended tools, that should be indicated in the work process. The tool manager should not be in the mode of marketing a tool, but rather assisting and making tool usage more effective.

COST	TESTING TOOL	COMMENTS
High	Complexity-Based Metric Testing	Cost to develop metrics is high—not usage
	Correctness Proof	
	Coverage-based Metric Testing	Cost to develop metrics is high—not usage
	Executable Specs	
	Exhaustive Testing	
	Inspections	
	Modeling	
	Parallel Operation	
	Parallel Simulation	
	SCARF	Requires building an analysis computer system
	Symbolic Execution	
	Test Data	Cost varies by volume of test transactions
Medium	Cause-Effect Graphing	
	Code Comparison	Major cost is acquisition of utility program
	Control Flow Analysis	
	Design-based Functional Testing	
	Design Reviews	Cost varies with size of review team
	Disaster Test Instrumentation	Cost varies with size of test
	Integrated Test Facility	Major cost is building ITF
	Mapping	Software is major cost
	Peer Review	
	Risk Matrix	
	Snapshot	Major cost is building snap-shot routines into programs
	Systems Logs	Assumes logs already in operation
	Test Data Generator	Major cost is acquiring software
	Utility Programs	Assumes utility already available
	Volume Testing	
	Walkthroughs	Cost varies with size of walkthrough team

Figure 5.5   Cost to use testing tools.   *(Continues)*

COST	TESTING TOOL	COMMENTS
Low	Acceptance Test Criteria	Byproduct of requirements
	Boundary Value Analysis	Requires establishing boundaries during development
	Checklist	
	Compiler-based Analysis	
	Confirmation/examination	
	Data Dictionary	Assumes cost of DD is not a test cost
	Desk Checking	
	Error Guessing	
	Fact Finding	
	Flowchart	Assumes software available
	Scoring	

Figure 5.5 *(Continued)*

A three-step process for using a manager to manage the use of IT tools follows (use Work Paper 5.1 to record selection criteria).

Step 1: Tool Manager Selection

Ideally, the tool manager would be selected during the process of selecting the tool, and have ownership in the selection decision. The tool manager should possess the following skills:

- Organization
- Training abilities
- Tool proficiency
- Managerial qualities
  - Planning
  - Organizing
  - Directing
  - Controlling

If the tool manager candidate lacks the above skills, they can be developed during the tool manager tenure. If the tool manager position is used to train future managers then technical proficiency and competency in tool usage is the only real skill requirement. The other skills can be developed during the tenure as tool manager. A mentor must be assigned to a tool manager to develop the missing skills.

In addition to the tool manager, an assistant tool manager should also be named for each tool. This individual will not have any direct managerial responsibilities, but will serve as backup for the tool manager. The primary responsibility of the assistant tool manager will be to gain competency in the use of the tool. Normally, the assistant tool

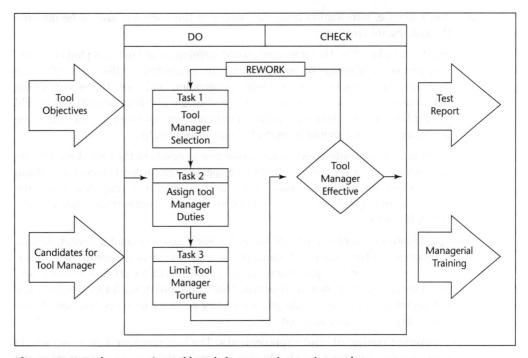

Figure 5.6 Tool manager's workbench for managing testing tools.

manager is a more junior person than the tool manager. The assistant is the most logical person to become the next manager for the tool.

Step 2: Assign the Tool Manager Duties

A tool manager can be assigned any or all of the following duties:

Assisting colleagues in the use of the tool. The tool manager should be available to assist other staff members in the use of the tool. This is normally done using the concept of a "hotline." Individuals having problems in using the tool or experiencing operational problems with the tool can call the tool manager for assistance. *Note:* The hours of "hot-line" activities may be restricted; for example, 8 to 9 A.M. and 2 to 5 P.M. This restriction will be dependent upon the other responsibilities of the tool manager and the expected frequency of the calls.

Tool training. The initial tool training normally comes from the vendor. However, additional tool training is the responsibility of the tool manager. Note that the tool manager may subcontract this training to the training department, the tool vendor, or other competent people. The tool manager has the responsibility to ensure the training occurs and may or may not do it personally.

Tool vendor contact. The tool manager would be the official contact for the tool vendor. Questions from staff regarding the use of the tool that can only be answered by the vendor should be funneled through the tool manager to the vendor. Likewise, information from the vendor to the company should be directed through the tool manager.

Annual tool plan. The tool manager should develop an annual tool plan complete with planned tool usage, schedule, and resources needed to effectively utilize the tool. Tool managers may want to define penetration goals (i.e., the percent of the department who will use the tool by the end of the planning period) and should budget for upgrades, training, and other expenditures involved in tool usage. The tool manager's time should be budgeted and accounted for.

Installing tool upgrades. As vendors issue new versions of the tool, the tool manager is responsible for ensuring that those upgrades are properly incorporated and that the involved parties are made aware and trained, if necessary. Note again, the tool manager may not have to do a lot of this personally, but is responsible to make sure it happens.

Preparing annual tool reports. At the end of each year, or planning period, the tool manager should prepare for IT management an overview of the use of the tool during the year. This will require the tool manager to maintain statistics on tool usage, problems, costs, upgrades, and so forth. (Note that tool usage for mainframe tools can normally be obtained from job accounting software systems. Non-mainframe usage may have to be estimated.)

Determining timing of tool replacements. The tool manager, being responsible for a specific software tool, should also be responsible for determining when the tool is no longer effective or when better tools can be acquired to replace it. When these situations occur, the tool manager should prepare proposals to senior IT management regarding tool replacement.

Step 3: Limiting the Tool Manager's Tenure

It is recommended that an individual serve two years as a manager for a specific tool. The rationale for the two years is that individuals tend to lose interest over a period of time. Also, after a period of time the manager tends to lose perspective of new uses for the tool or deficiencies in the tool. Bringing in a new tool manager every two years tends to revitalize the use of that tool in the organization. Note that the tool managers can be transferred to manage another tool.

In instances where tools are highly specialized, very complex, or have minimal usage, it may be desirable to keep an individual manager for longer than a two-year period.

To verify that the practice was performed as specified, the following questions should be answered positively:

1. Has IT management established objectives for the tool to be managed?

2. Has the use of the tool been specified in IT work procedures?

3. Has a training program been established for using the tool?

4. Have the potential candidates for tool manager been trained in the use of the tool that they would manage?

5. Have potential candidates for tool manager effectively used the tool in a production environment?

6. Do the candidates for tool manager have managerial potential?

7. Does the individual selected for tool manager want to be manager of the tool?

8. Does the candidate selected for tool manager believe that this tool is effective in accomplishing the IT mission?

9. Will the candidate for manager have sufficient time to perform the tool manager duties?

10. Have reasonable duties been assigned to the tool manager?

11. Does the tool manager understand and agree that these are reasonable duties to perform?

12. Has a tenure been established on the length of service for tool managers?

The deliverables from this work practice are important but subjective in nature. Thus, evaluating the benefits from a tool manager will require the time to perform a subjective analysis. The two subjective deliverables are:

1. **More effective tool usage.** Having a tool manager is in fact establishing a help desk for tools. Since the tool manager is knowledgeable in what the tool does and how it works, that individual can speed the learning of other users and minimize problems associated with the tool usage. Also, if an individual gets into trouble using the tool, the tool manager is available for assistance.

2. **Impart managerial training.** The individual appointed tool manager should have total responsibility for that tool. This includes contact with the vendor, budgeting for maintenance and support, overseeing training, and providing supervisory support. It is an effective way to provide managerial training for individuals; it is also effective in evaluating future managerial candidates.

The role of a tool manager can be enhanced in the following ways:

Allow individuals adequate time to perform the tool manager's role. The assignment of a tool manager should be scheduled and budgeted, so that the individual knows the amount of time and resources that can be allocated to it.

Incorporate tool manager performance into individual performance appraisals. The performance of the tool manager's duties should be considered an important part of an individual's work.

Summary

Efficient testing necessitates the use of testing tools. Each testing organization should have a portfolio of tools used in testing. This chapter describes the more common testing tools—both static and dynamic tools. It also proposes the establishment of a test manager function for each tool. Chapters 6 through 17 describe in more detail the tools most applicable for the recommended 11-step testing process.

WORK PAPER 5.1 Tool Manager Selection Worksheet

Name of Tool:

Tool Objectives:

Vendor Name:

Vendor Contact:

Potential Tool Managers										
Name	**Skills Possessed**								**Selected**	
	Organizational		Training		Tool Proficiency		Managerial			
	Yes	No	Yes	No	Yes	No	Yes	No	Yes	No

Tool Manager Duties:

Duty	Assigned	
	Yes	No
• Assisting colleagues in the use of the tool		
• Tool training		
• Tool vendor contact		
• Annual tool plan		
• Installing tool upgrades		
• Preparing annual tool reports		
• Determining timing of tool replacements		

Comments:

PART

Three

The Eleven-Step Testing Process

# CHAPTER 6

Eleven-Step Software Testing Process Overview

In Chapters 2 through 5 we explained how to establish a test environment. Now we're ready to:

- Form the test team that will tackle a software testing assignment for your company.
- Introduce the 11-step process that will take you through identifying, testing, and solving your testing assignment.

The process for software testing described in this chapter is based on experience with more than 1,000 corporate members of the Quality Assurance Institute.

The Cost of Computer Testing

There are two general categories of testing—pre-implementation and post-implementation testing. The first encompasses those activities that occur prior to placing the application system in an operational status. The objective of pre-implementation testing is to determine that the system functions as specified and that defects in the system are removed prior to placing the system into production. The second type of testing occurs after the system goes into operation and is normally considered part of systems maintenance.

The cost of removing system defects prior to the system going into production includes:

- Building the defect into the system
- Identifying existence of the defect
- Correcting the defect
- Testing to determine that the defect is removed

Defects uncovered after the system goes into operation generate the following costs:

- Specifying and coding the defect into the system
- Detecting the problem within the application system
- Reporting the problem to information services and/or the user
- Correcting the problems caused by the defect
- Operating the system until the defect is corrected
- Correcting the defect
- Testing to determine that the defect no longer exists
- Integrating the corrected program(s) into production

Testing should include the cost to test *plus* the cost of undetected defects. Few organizations consolidate all of the named costs as testing costs. Therefore, the true cost of testing is rarely known to an organization. Testing is normally considered to be that process used to find defects and assure that the system functions properly. However, as illustrated, the cost of building and correcting defects may far exceed the cost of detecting those defects.

The National Bureau of Standards has estimated that testing, including the correction of defects not uncovered until the application goes into production, accounts for at least one-half of the total system development effort.

The high cost of system defects poses the following two challenges to organizations: how to quantify the true cost of removing defects, and how to reduce the cost of testing.

Quantifying the Cost of Removing Defects

Quality Assurance Institute surveys indicate that there are approximately 60 defects in an application system per 1,000 source statements or equivalent. These surveys indicate that approximately two-thirds, or 40 out of the 60 defects per 1,000 lines of source code, occur in the requirements and design phase of application systems. Thus, while the defects are normally caught in the test phase of the systems development life cycle, they occur early in the development process.

The defects built into application systems include:

Improperly interpreted requirements. The information technology (IT) people misinterpret what the user wants, but correctly implement what the IT people believe is wanted.

Users specify wrong requirements. The specifications given to IT are erroneous.

Requirements are incorrectly recorded. Information services people fail to record the specifications properly.

Design specifications incorrect. The application system design does not achieve the system requirements, but the design as specified may be correctly implemented.

Program specifications incorrect. The design specifications are incorrectly interpreted, making the program specifications inaccurate, but the program can be properly coded to achieve the correct program specifications.

Program coding error. The program is not coded according to the program specifications.

Program structural or instruction error. The programming capabilities are improperly utilized, resulting in defects attributable to misuse of a program instruction or the method in which the instruction is used.

Data entry error. The system and/or program information is incorrectly entered into the computer.

Testing error. The test either detects an error where there is no error or fails to detect an existing error in the application system.

Error correction mistake. In the process of correcting an error, the corrected condition contains a defect.

Corrected condition causes another defect. In the process of correcting a defect, the correction process itself causes additional defects to be entered into the application system.

The areas associated with the test process can usually be readily identified. It is the estimation of the costs associated with these areas that is difficult to obtain. However, until the total cost of testing is known, the cost of uncovering and correcting defects will be unknown.

There are two methods for developing a more realistic estimate of testing. The first is to ask information services personnel to identify all of the above conditions and allocate their time and effort accordingly. While this concept works in theory, in practice it is difficult to record the time and effort associated with incurring defects until that defect is actually known. Since the point of uncovering may be many weeks or months after the actual defect was built into the system, it may be difficult to go back and recover these costs.

The second, and more practical, approach is to record the number of defects encountered as a result of testing. As each defect is uncovered, it would be noted, as well as the point in the system life cycle process where it was uncovered.

The actual cost to redesign and correct the system is then recorded. These are the costs required for correcting the programs by some recompilation and change of documentation. The costs are then multiplied by a factor that represents the totality of the error and problems associated with the defect as follows:

Defects encountered during design requirements phase. The cost to correct will be the totality of the cost associated with the correction of the defect.

Defects corrected during the system test phase. The cost to correct should be multiplied by a factor of 10.

Defects corrected after the system goes into production. The cost to correct should be multiplied by a factor of 100.

The cost of error correction increases as the system life cycle progresses (see Figure 6.1). While this is an old study it is still accepted as valid in the industry.

Reducing the Cost of Testing

The economics of computer testing clearly demonstrate that the method to reduce the cost of defects is to locate those defects as early in the system development life cycle as possible. This involves beginning testing during the requirements phase of the life cycle and continuing testing throughout the life cycle. The objective of testing would then become to detect the error as early in the life cycle as possible.

Life Cycle Testing Concept

Life cycle testing involves continuous testing of the system during the developmental process. At predetermined points, the results of the development process are inspected to determine the correctness of the implementation. These inspections identify defects at the earliest possible point.

Life cycle testing cannot occur until a formalized system development process has been incorporated. Life cycle testing is dependent upon the completion of predetermined deliverables at specified points in the developmental life cycle. If information services personnel have the discretion to determine the order in which deliverables are developed, the life cycle test process becomes ineffective. This is due to variability in the process, which normally increases cost.

The life cycle testing concept can best be accomplished by the formation of a test team. The team is comprised of members of the project who may be both implementing and testing the system. However, when members of the team are testing the system, they must use a formal testing methodology to clearly distinguish the implementation mode from the test mode, and they also must follow a structured methodology when approaching testing the same as when approaching system development. Without a specific structured test methodology, the test team concept would be ineffective because team members would follow the same methodology for testing as they used for developing the system. Experience shows people are blind to their own mistakes, so the effectiveness of the test team is dependent upon developing the system under one methodology and testing it under another.

The life cycle testing concept is illustrated in Figure 6.2. This illustration shows that when the project starts both the system development process and system test process begins. The team that is developing the system begins the systems development process and the team that is conducting the system test begins planning the system test process. Both teams start at the same point using the same information. The systems development team has the responsibility to define and document the requirements for developmental purposes. The test team will likewise use those same requirements, but for the purpose of testing the system. At appropriate points during the developmental process, the test team will test the developmental process in an attempt to uncover defects. The test team should use the structured testing techniques outlined in this book as a basis of evaluating the system development process deliverables.

During the system test process an appropriate set of test transactions should be developed to be completed at the same time as the completion of the application system. When the application meets the acceptance criteria it can be integrated into the operating environment. During this process, the systems development team and the systems test team work closely together to ensure that the application is properly integrated into the production environment. At that point, the teams again split to ensure the correctness of changes made during the maintenance phase. The maintenance team will make whatever changes and enhancements are necessary to the application system, and the test team will continue the test process to ensure that those enhancements are properly implemented and integrated into the production environment.

Define a Process

The workbench described in Chapter 3 is a graphic representation of a process that defines the input and the procedures to produce output and check that it was properly developed. You must define all four components (i.e., input, do procedures, check procedures, and output) to have a complete process.

The do and check procedures are the core of the testers' workbench, and are proportional to each other; the more do procedures a phase has, the more check procedures you'll have to perform. Figure 6.1 illustrates this relationship, which also applies to product development. When you create a new product, you base much of your work on theory. For example, when the first jet aircraft was built, many developers weren't certain how it would perform. To make sure their concept would function correctly, they developed a prototype (thereby developing a prototype process as a byproduct) and devoted much of those expenses to testing the aircraft, modifying it, and testing it again.

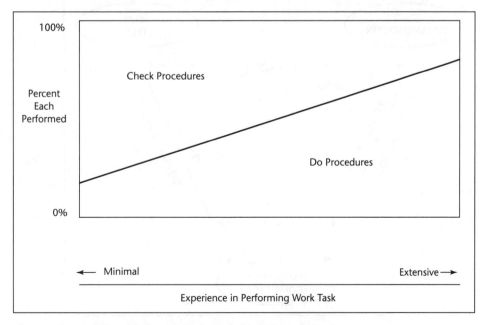

Figure 6.1   Relationship between do and check procedures.

Use the V-Testing Concept

In the V-testing concept, your project's do and check procedures slowly converge from start to finish (see Figure 6.2), which indicates that as the do team attempts to implement a solution, the check team concurrently develops a process to minimize or eliminate the risk. If the two groups work closely together, the high level of risk at a project's inception will decrease to an acceptable level by the project's conclusion.

We'll expand on V-testing later in the chapter, but first let's set up your test team.

Form the Software Development Project Team

Effectively solving user needs begins with assembling a project team to oversee the implementation process. The project team is responsible for all aspects of the implementation effort including requirements gathering, design, and implementation. The team should include representatives of the staff or departments for whom the project is being developed, but designated members of the IT department will comprise the core of the team. Note that it's not necessary to assign representatives from every department: You could, for example, have one or two end users represent all end-user departments, as long as they understand the needs of all affected groups.

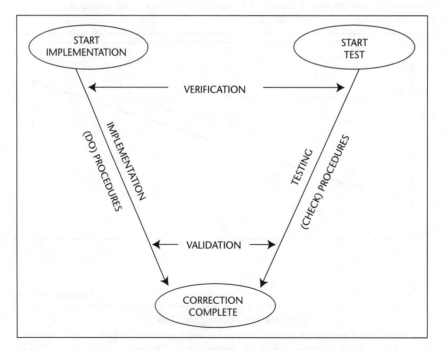

Figure 6.2   Using verification and validation in software testing.

Organize the Software Development Test Team

Normally, a member of the project team with testing experience organizes the test team (we refer to this team as the test team throughout the book). In many IT organizations, testing will be performed by an independent test organization. The test team is separate from the project team, but may report to and obtains its resources from the project team. The test team should do the following:

- Ensure that the project plan includes testing capabilities.
- Confirm that management allocates adequate resources for testing.
- Review the implementation schedule to determine that testing can be done effectively within the timeframe.
- Develop and present the test plan to the project team.
- Evaluate the implementation plan to confirm that the implementation is testable.
- Report testing status to the project team.
- Ensure that testing occurs throughout the development process.

The scope of the project effort should define the size of the test team and the other resources needed for the project. The number of team members varies, depending on the number of systems to test and the project's timeframe. Even if your software is well documented, the test effort will still consume about 50 percent of your project resources; and if your documentation is subpar, it could easily consume two-thirds.

Select Test Team Members

The test team members obviously need the skills to fulfill the responsibilities just listed; ideally they will thoroughly know the applications the project team plans to change. For example, if your payroll system will undergo extensive changes, you'd want the payroll system designer or manager on your test team. Other personnel you should include on the test team are:

- User personnel
- Computer operation staff
- Data administrators
- Internal auditors
- Quality assurance staff
- Information services management
- Security administrators
- Professional testers

Gathering a good test team is essential to the successful testing of your project solution. Any number of problems—lack of interest by prospective members, lack of awareness from management, or lack of resources to invest in testing the solution—could significantly hinder your test team. Here are three steps to forming the best test team for your purposes:

1. **Identify potential test team members.** Brainstorm a list of potential team members who would make the ideal test team. Don't consider restrictions or constraints. Work Paper 6.1 helps you make this list, providing space to indicate highly desirable test team members, their department and phone number, skills they must possess, time commitment, and role each member will play.

2. **Recruit test team members and develop tentative test assignments.** Work Paper 6.1 allows you to plot out the role each member will play to ensure effective testing. This will also help you build the case to persuade management to assign the people you want to the team.

3. **Define individual work assignments.** Once management assigns your candidate to the test team, complete a test assignment Work Paper for him or her (Work Paper 6.2). Include his or her department and telephone number, as well as the specific test assignment from Work Paper 6.1.

Figure 6.3 shows an entry on Work Paper 6.1, based on your payroll example from Chapter 2. The test team needs an individual who can, in the shortest time period and with the greatest accuracy, identify where the project team must change the payroll system. The figure identifies Bill Smith as a test team candidate and builds the case for placing him on the team by indicating his years of experience as it relates to the role he'll play. The test team coordinator successfully placed Bill on the test team.

After you've identified a candidate, the person assembling the test team should approach him or her and explain why his or her participation is important. You must get a candidate's consent before seeking management approval because management will take the person's preference into account before making a decision. Therefore, each time you request a team member, make sure management is aware of the following information:

Date:			Needed			Assigned	
Project: Payroll System Changes							
Name	**Dept.**	**Phone**	**Skills**	**Time Commitment**	**How person will be utilized**	**Yes**	**No**
Bill Smith	Payroll	425-1000	23 years working with corp. benefit programs & payroll systems	40 hours	Bill's experience is needed to ensure all date concerns are addressed in the test plan for payroll and benefit systems.	X	

Figure 6.3   Identifying a sample test team member.

- The candidate's specific importance to the effort
- The tasks he or she will perform (from Work Paper 6.1)
- The correlation between the candidate's skills and the testing skills needed
- The candidate's willingness to participate on the test team
- The amount of time the candidate will have to devote to the effort (from the Time Commitment column in Work Paper 6.1)

Obviously Work Papers 6.1 and 6.2 overlap; this is intentional. You'll use Work Paper 6.1 to identify candidates and Work Paper 6.2 to assign an official task to a test team member. As you do this, record only official team members on Work Paper 6.2 and use the forms when you compose your test plan. Remember the test strategy we created in Chapter 2? If you use your test strategy to assign responsibilities to team members, their roles won't change significantly when you create the official test plan, thereby lowering costs and saving time.

Establish a Test Objective

Once your test team is in place and they're ready to create their test plan, it's a good idea to state a test objective to drive the plan's development and isolate what the testers must accomplish. This objective follows the establishment of the test strategy. For direction in establishing this objective, or policy, review Chapter 2.

We create a formal test plan in Chapter 7, at which time you should create your objective, but it is important at this point to have the general idea of the test strategy, team, tactics, and policy firmly in mind as you learn to use verification and validation in tests, and while overviewing the 11-step testing process for performing the check procedures.

Verification and Validation in the Software Development Process

Generally, in testing, you'll use verification to examine interim deliverables and validation to assess the performance of executable code. Table 6.1 gives examples as to how you might use verification and validation in different software development phases.

Introducing the 11-Step Software Testing Process

The software testing process (see Figure 6.4) follows the aforementioned V-concept of testing. The V represents both the software development process and the 11-step software testing process. The first five steps use verification as the primary means to evaluate the correctness of the interim development deliverables. Validation is used to test the software in an executable mode. Results of both verification and validation should be documented in a test report. Both verification and validation will be used to test the

Table 6.1   Using Verification and Validation

SOFTWARE DEVELOPMENT PHASES	HOW TO USE VERIFICATION	HOW TO USE VALIDATION
Requirements gathering	• Verify completeness of requirements	• Not usable
Project Planning	• Verify vendor capability, if applicable • Verify completeness of project test plan	• Not usable
Project Implementation	• Verify correctness and completeness of Interim Deliverables • Verify contingency plan	• Validate correctness of changes • Validate regression • Validate meets user acceptance criteria • Validate supplier's software processes correctly • Validate software interfaces

installation of the software as well as changes to the software. The final step of the V process represents both the development and test team evaluating the effectiveness of testing.

The 11 steps are described below:

1. **Assess development plan and status.** This is a prerequisite to building the test plan that will be used to evaluate the implemented software solution. During this step, testers will challenge the completeness and correctness of the development plan. Based on the extensiveness and completeness of the project plan, the testers will be in a position to estimate the amount of resources they will need to test the implemented software solution.

2. **Develop the test plan.** Forming the plan for testing will follow the same pattern as any software planning process. The structure of all plans should be the same, but the content will vary based on the degree of risk the testers perceive as associated with the software being developed.

3. **Test software requirements.** Incomplete, inaccurate, or inconsistent requirements lead to most software failures. The inability to get prerequisites right during the requirements-gathering phase can also increase the cost of implementation significantly. Testers, through verification, must determine that the requirements are accurate and complete, and that they do not conflict with one another.

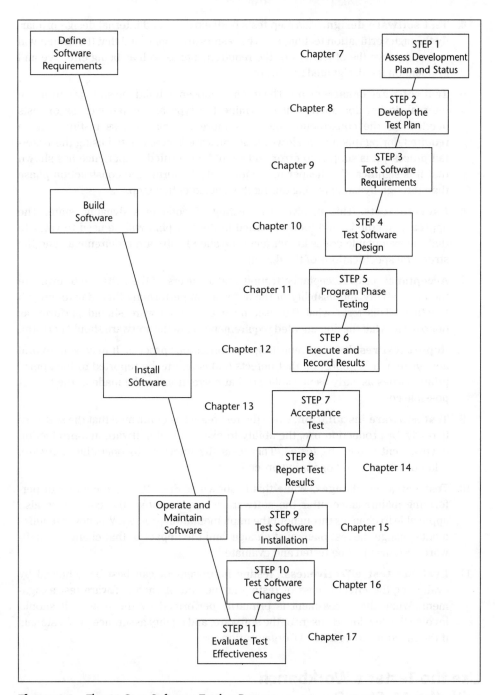

Figure 6.4 The 11-Step Software Testing Process.

4. **Test software design.** This step tests both external and internal design primarily through verification techniques. The testers are concerned that the design will in fact achieve the objectives of the requirements as well as being effective and efficient on the designated hardware.

5. **Test software construction.** The method chosen to build the software from the internal design document will determine the type and extensiveness of tests needed. As the construction becomes more automated, less testing will be required during this phase. However, if software is constructed using the waterfall process, it is subject to error and should be verified. Experience has shown that it is significantly cheaper to identify defects during the construction phase than through dynamic testing during the test execution step.

6. **Execute tests.** This involves the testing of code in a dynamic state. The approach, methods, and tools specified in the test plan will be used to validate that the executable codes in fact meet the stated software requirements and the structural specifications of the design.

7. **Acceptance test.** Acceptance testing enables users of the software to evaluate the applicability and usability of the software in performing their day-to-day job functions. This tests what the user believes the software should perform, as opposed to what the documented requirements state the software should perform.

8. **Report test results.** Test reporting is a continuous process. It may be both oral and written. It is important that defects and concerns be reported to the appropriate parties as early as possible, so that correction can be made at the lowest possible cost.

9. **Test software installation.** Once the test team has confirmed that the software is ready for production use, the ability to execute that software in a production environment should be tested. This tests the interface to operating software, related software, and operating procedures.

10. **Test software changes.** While this is shown as Step 10 in the context of performing maintenance after the software is implemented, the concept is also applicable to changes throughout the implementation process. Whenever requirements change the test plan must change, and the impact of that change on software systems must be tested and evaluated.

11. **Evaluate test effectiveness.** Testing improvement can best be achieved by evaluating the effectiveness of testing at the end of each software test assignment. While this assessment is primarily performed by the testers, it should involve the developers, users of the software, and quality assurance professionals if the function exists in the IT organization.

Use the Tester's Workbench with the 11-Step Process

Chapter 3 introduced the testers' workbench, which forms the template describing the procedures your test team will perform within the 11 test steps. Chapters 7 through 17 are set up as follows:

- **Overview.** A brief description of the step. This will repeat the overview just given for each step.

- **Objective.** A detailed description of the purpose of the step, to use as a ruler against which to measure your progress at each step.

- **Concerns.** Specific challenges that testers will have to overcome to complete the step effectively.

- **Workbench.** A description of the process that the testers should follow to complete the step.

- **Input.** The documents, information, and skills needed to complete the step.

- **Do procedures.** Detailed, task-by-task procedures that testers must follow to perform this step. (If you'll need to use a vendor tool, it will be described in this subsection.)

- **Check procedures.** A checklist that testers use to verify that they have performed a step correctly. These procedures will be related to the test step objective.

- **Output.** The deliverables that the testers must produce at the conclusion of each step.

- **Guidelines.** Suggestions for performing each step more effectively and for avoiding problems.

Workbench Requirement Skills

Manufacturing positions are frequently designed so that workers require minimal skills to perform their tasks effectively. Often, descriptions for these positions are accompanied by extensive documentation so that any worker could perform a function at any time. Professional positions, however, require much more advanced skills, and are usually accompanied by far inferior documentation (it's assumed that the person coming into the position will bring in a certain level of knowledge.)

A surgeon, for example, has to undergo 12 years of training before becoming licensed. Though there are detailed do and check procedures for performing a given operation, much of the execution depends on the person. The same is true when the systems analyst defines end-user requirements. The systems analyst is guided by work papers, but much of the innovative work needed to properly define requirements depends on his or her years of experience and skill level.

Figure 6.5 illustrates the relationship between tester skill competency and the testers' workbench. The workbench assumes an average skill level on the part of the reader, incorporating these assumptions into its descriptions of procedures and tools. The skills that a professional tester should possess are defined in the "common body of knowledge" for an information system software testing professional. Developed by the Quality Assurance Institute Certification Board, the common body of knowledge is the basis used for evaluating the competency of your testers.

If the people involved in the test workbench do not possess the basic testing skills in the common body of knowledge, one or more of the following recommendations should be pursued to improve testing skills:

Figure 6.5   Relationship between testing skills and the workbench.

- Attend a basic course on software testing.
- Take the necessary courses from the Quality Assurance Institute to prepare for the Certified Software Test Engineering examination (contact the Quality Assurance Institute at its web site, www.qaiusa.com, or by telephone, at 407-363-1111).

Summary

Software testing is a process. This chapter defines an 11-step testing process that demonstrates how software testing occurs throughout the software development process. A software test team that possesses all the needed skills will be in a good position to execute the proposed 11-step testing process described in Chapters 7 through 17.

WORK PAPER 6.1   Test Team Selection

Field Requirements

FIELD	INSTRUCTIONS FOR ENTERING DATA
Date	The date that the worksheet is developed.
Project	The software system(s) and the specific activity within that system that needs to be performed during testing. (Note: This is normally cryptic and should relate to the test plan.)
Name	The name of the candidate for the test team.
Department	The name of the candidate's department.
Phone	The candidate's phone number.
Skills Needed	The skills that make the candidate uniquely qualified to be a member of the testing team.
Time Commitment	The approximate number of hours that the candidate will need to spend on test team activities.
How person will be utilized	The specific test need that the candidate can meet in accomplishing the testing objectives. (Note: This should be written in a manner that justifies having that person join the test team.)
Assigned	After the candidate is agreed to be a desired member of the test team, management must approve or disapprove (yes or no) that person for assignment to the test team.

Date: **Project: System Changes**

Name	Dept.	Phone	Needed Skills	Needed Time Commitment	How person will be utilized	Assigned Yes	No

WORK PAPER 6.2   Test Team Selection

Field Requirements

FIELD	INSTRUCTIONS FOR ENTERING DATA
Date	The date that the worksheet is developed.
Project	The software system(s) and the specific activity within that system that needs to be performed during testing. (Note: This is normally cryptic and should relate to the test plan.)
Name	The name of the candidate for the test team.
Department	The name of the candidate's department.
Phone	The candidate's phone number.
Test Assignment	The specific task(s) that will be assigned to the candidate related to testing. Normally, a preliminary test plan will have been prepared before staff are assigned to perform testing. Thus, the test assignment on worksheet 2 should relate to a test task incorporated into the test plan.

Date: **Project:**

Name	Dept.	Phone	Test Assignments

Step 1: Assess Project Management Development Estimate and Status

Project management is a process involving a series of tasks that navigate a project throughout the development activities. Problems in performing the project management tasks can have a direct effect on the quality of the software. Using testers to identify these problems early enables project management to make the adjustments necessary to keep the project on schedule. This step (see Figure 7.1) enables the testers to identify estimating and status problems early in the project.

Overview

This chapter identifies two areas in which testers can help manage the project. Test programs are provided to aid in testing two critical project management areas:

1. **Testing the validity of a software cost estimate.** An inaccurate estimate, particularly in estimating effort, can force developers to compromise software quality.

2. **Testing the status of the software system.** If the project manager cannot accurately determine the status of the project, decisions based on incorrect status may not allow needed adjustments.

Objective

The objective of testing software cost estimating is to determine what resources will be available to produce and to maintain the software associated with a project. Resources

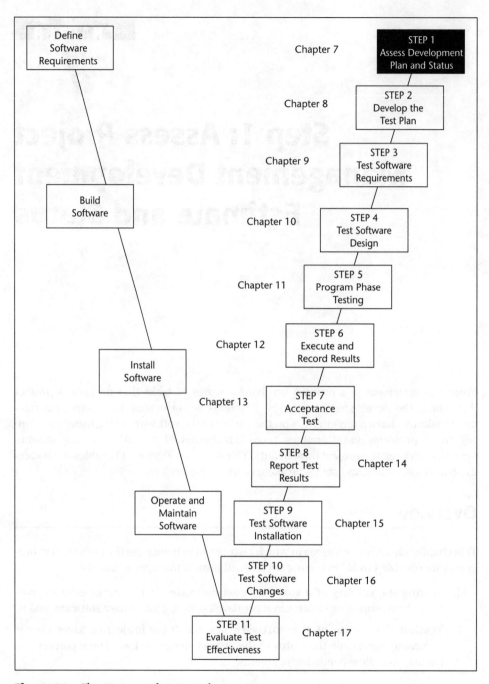

Figure 7.1   The 11-step software testing process.

of particular relevance in software cost estimating are staff, computer time, and elapsed time. A good estimate will also show when and how costs will be incurred, so that the estimate can be used not only to provide justification for software development, but also as a management control tool. This test step will also explain why cost estimating is error prone.

The tester needs to know the progress of the system under development. It is the purpose of project management systems and accounting systems to monitor this progress. However, many of these systems are more budget and schedule oriented than they are project completion oriented. The purpose of this test is to provide the test group with a simple tool for measuring the status of software development.

Concerns

The tester's main concern during the development is that inadequate resources and time will be allocated to testing. Since much of the testing will be performed after development is complete, the time period between completing development and the due date for production may be inadequate for testing. There are three general concerns regarding available time and resources for testing:

1. **Inaccurate estimate.** The estimate for resources in time will not be sufficient to complete the project as specified.

2. **Inadequate development process.** The tools and procedures given developers will not enable them to complete the project with the available resources and time constraints.

3. **Incorrect status reporting.** The project leaders will not know the correct status of the project during early developmental stages and thus cannot take the necessary corrective action in time to meet the scheduled completion dates.

Workbench

Figure 7.2 provides a workbench for assessing the project estimate and status. The workbench requires the testers to be knowledgeable about the project planning process, the project estimating process, and the project development process. This knowledge enables them to test the correctness of the estimate and the accuracy of the project's status reports. Deficiencies identified by the testers can be reported to the project personnel so that corrective action can be taken early in the development process.

Input

Three inputs are needed to perform this workbench. The first is the project plan as completed by the project personnel. The task on testing the project estimate will use the key planning components from the project plan. The second input is the project estimate

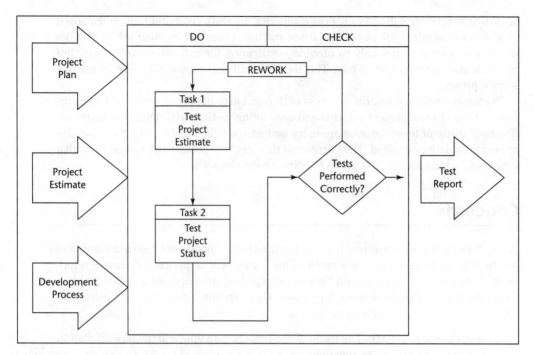

Figure 7.2   Workbench for assessing development estimate and status.

and the method used for developing that estimate. The last input is a knowledge of development processes that will be used by the project personnel in building the software to meet user requirements.

Do Procedures

This test process involves the following two tasks:

1. Testing the validity of the software estimate
2. Testing the status of the software system

Let's take a closer look at each task.

Task 1: Testing the Validity of the Software Estimate

Many software projects are essentially innovative, and both history and logic suggest that cost overruns may be due to an ineffective estimating system. Software cost estimating is a complicated process because project development is influenced by a large number of variables, many of which are subjective, nonquantifiable, and interrelated in complex ways.

Some reasons for not obtaining a good estimate are:

- A lack of understanding of the process of software development and maintenance.
- A lack of understanding of the effects of various technical and management constraints.
- A view that each project is unique, which inhibits project-to-project comparisons.
- Lack of historic data against which the model can be checked.
- Lack of historic data for calibration. The process by which a model is fitted to a given cost-estimating situation is called calibration. The calibration of a model may be performed using formal curve-fitting methods on a representative historical data set, by selecting values from experience, or, with some models, by running the model in calibration mode to assign values to selected parameters using appropriate historical data.

In addition to these reasons, current estimating techniques suffer from:

- Inadequate definition of the objective of the estimate (whether it is intended as a project management tool or needed purely to aid in making a go-ahead decision) and at what stage the estimate is required, needed so that inputs and outputs can be chosen appropriately
- Inadequate specifications of the scope of the estimate (what is included and what is excluded)
- Inadequate definition of and understanding of the premises on which the estimate is based

Strategies for Software Cost Estimating

There are five commonly used methods for estimating the cost of developing and maintaining a software system:

1. Seat-of-the-pants and personal experience, using analogy with similar historic projects and extrapolation, based mainly on size and difficulty
2. Constraint method
3. Percentage of hardware method
4. Simulation
5. Parametric modeling

The first method (sometimes referred to as a WAG, or "wildly aspiring guess") has been and still is very popular because no better method has been proven. One of its problems is that each estimate is based on different experience, and therefore different estimates of the cost of a single project may vary widely. A second problem is that the estimator must have experience of a similar project, of a similar size. Experience does not work on systems larger than those in the base used for comparison, nor on systems with a totally different content.

The constraint method is equivalent to taking an educated guess. Based on schedule, cost, or staffing constraints, a manager agrees to develop the software within the constraints. The constraints are not related to the complexity of the project. In general, this method will result in delivery of the software within the specified constraints, but with the specification adjusted to fit the constraints.

The percentage of hardware method is based on two assumptions:

1. Software costs are a fixed percentage of hardware costs.

2. Hardware cost estimates are usually reasonably accurate.

A study on estimating has indicated that the first of these assumptions is not justified. Simulating is widely used in estimating life cycle support costs for hardware systems, but it is not appropriate for software cost estimating because it is based on a statistical analysis of hardware failure rates and ignores logistics for which there is no software equivalent.

The most commonly used models are all parametric models (sometimes called SWAG, or "scientific WAG"). SWAG is the method used by most software estimating packages such as ESTIMACS.

It has been suggested that there is some universal model or formula that represents all types of software and all organizations. However, each estimator must tailor the universal model to take account of the idiosyncrasies of his or her own organization and the characteristics of his or her own application. This can be a difficult task since organizations are not static, but change with time.

Types of Parametric Models

Parametric models (SWAG) may be divided into three classes: regression models, heuristic models, and phenomenological models. The models considered do not necessarily fit tidily into one or another of the three classes, but if a model fits more into one class than into either of the others it will be regarded as a member of that class.

    Regression Models. The quantity to be estimated is mathematically related to a set of input parameters. The parameters of the hypothesized relationship are arrived at by statistical analysis and curve fitting on an appropriate historical database. There may be more than one relationship to deal with different databases, different types of applications, and different developer characteristics.

    Heuristic Models. In a heuristic model observation and interpretation of historical data are combined with supposition and experience. Relationships between variables are stated without justification. The advantage of heuristic models is that they need not wait for formal relationships to be established describing how the cost-driving variables are related. Over a period, a given model can become very effective in a stable predicting environment. If the model fails, it is adjusted to deal with the situation. It therefore becomes a repository for the collected experiences and insights of the designers.

    Phenomenological Models. The phenomenological model is based on a hypothesis that the software development process can be explained in terms of some more widely applicable process or idea. For example, the Putnam model is based on the belief that the distribution of effort during the software life cycle has the same characteristics as the distribution of effort required to solve a given number of problems given a constant learning rate.

General Pattern Followed by the Models

Most of the estimating models follow a similar pattern, based on the following six steps:

1. Estimate software size.
2. Convert size estimate to labor estimate (and possibly also a money estimate).
3. Adjust estimate for special project characteristics.
4. Divide the total estimate into the different project phases.
5. Estimate nontechnical labor costs and costs of computer time.
6. Sum the costs.

Not all steps occur in all models. For example, some models do not initially perform a total project labor or cost estimate, but start by estimating the different phases separately, so step 4 aggregates the separate estimates instead of dividing up the total estimate. Similarly the adjustments for special project characteristics may occur between steps 1 and 2 as well as or instead of between steps 2 and 3.

Estimate Software Size

Most models start from an estimate of project size, although some models include algorithms for computing size from various other system characteristics, such as units of work.

Convert Size Estimate to Labor Estimate

Some models convert from size to labor; others go directly from size to money estimates. In regression models, these conversions are either derived from productivity measures using the *cost per instruction* type of equation or they are derived using the *general summing equation*. The cost per instruction equation has the form:

```
e=a#s#b+c
```

where # is multiply; * is raise to the power; e = effort needed, for example, staff-months of effort or cost in money terms, to develop the program; s = size of project, for example, number of machine-level instructions; and values are chosen for a, b, and c by curve fitting on as large a historical database as possible. Different values of a, b, and c are appropriate to different development organizations, different project types, different sets of units for measuring e and s, and different items included in the estimates.

The general summing equation has the form:

```
e=a1#21+a2*f2+a3#f3+....+ai*fi+.....+am*fm
```

where ai are input parameters derived from the description of the software characteristics (including size) and the characteristics of the development environment, and the values of fi are chosen by curve fitting on a suitable historical database.

In heuristic models the relationship of size estimate to labor estimate is not necessarily based on a statistically derived expression. In a phenomenological model the relationship would derive from the underlying theory.

Adjust Estimate for Special Project Characteristics

In some models an effective size is calculated from the basic size estimate obtained in step 1; in others an effective labor or cost estimate is calculated from the estimates obtained in step 2. The effective estimate is an adjustment of the basic estimate intended to take account of any special project characteristics that make it dissimilar to the pattern absorbed in the underlying historical database. Such variations, which include the effect of volatility of the requirements, different software tools, difficulty above the level of projects in the database, or a different method of dealing with support costs, are frequently based on intuitively derived relationships, unsupported by statistical verification.

The adjustment may precede amalgamation of the costs of the different phases, or a single adjustment may be applied to the total.

Divide the Total Estimate into the Different Project Phases

Each model dealing with a project's schedule makes assumptions about the allocation of effort in the different project phases. The simplest assumption defines a percentage of the effort for each phase, for example, the much-quoted 40 percent design, 20 percent code, and 40 percent test rule. It should be noted that this is not a universally agreed-on rule. Some estimating research shows that other percentages may be more appropriate, and the percentage in each phase may depend on other software characteristics. Some models assume that staffing allocation with respect to time follows a rectangular distribution, others assume that it follows a beta distribution, or a Rayleigh distribution. In general, the assumptions on staffing allocation with respect to time are based on historical data. The effect of deviating from historical patterns has not been considered.

Estimate Nontechnical Labor Costs and Costs of Computer Time

Where these costs are explicitly included, they are often calculated as a percentage of the technical labor costs. Sometimes such costs are included implicitly because they were included in the database from which the model was derived.

Sum the Costs

The nontechnical labor costs and the cost of computer time, where these are included in the estimates, are added to the technical costs of the different phases of the software life cycle to obtain an aggregated cost estimate.

Testing the Validity of the Software Cost Estimate

An improper cost estimate can do more damage to the quality of a software project than almost any other single factor. People tend to do that which they are measured on. If they are measured on meeting a software cost estimate, they will normally meet that estimate. If the estimate is incorrect, the project team will make whatever compromises are necessary to meet that estimate. This process of compromise can significantly undermine the quality of the delivered project. The net result is increased maintenance costs, dissatisfied customers, increased effort in the customer area to compensate for software system weaknesses, and discouraged, demoralized project personnel.

Estimating software costs is just that—estimating. No one can guarantee that the software estimate will be correct for the work to be performed. However, testing can increase the validity of the estimate, and thus is a worthwhile testing task. Testing of a software estimate is a three-part process, as follows:

1. Validate the reasonableness of the estimating model.

2. Validate that the model includes all the needed factors.

3. Verify the correctness of the cost-estimating model estimate.

Validate the Reasonableness of the Estimating Model

Organizations need to use a model for estimating. In some organizations, this is an internally developed procedure, in others the estimating system has been purchased. Purchased estimating methods can be included in system development methodologies, maintenance methodologies, or special software packages such as ESTIMACS can be acquired for the purpose of estimating software costs.

The objective of this first part of estimate testing is to validate the reasonableness of the estimating model. This test will challenge the model using 14 desirable characteristics of a cost-estimating model. The more of these characteristics included in the cost-estimating model in your organization, the more reliance you can place on that model. The fewer of these 14 characteristics included, the less reliance you can place on that model. The amount of testing included in part 3 of the test process will be dependent upon the reliance you can place on the cost-estimating model. The less reliance you can place on the model (i.e., the fewer of the 14 characteristics included in your model), the more testing you should perform.

Work Paper 7.1 (at the end of the chapter) lists the 14 characteristics. The worksheet provides a place to indicate whether the characteristics are present or absent, and any comments you care to make about the inclusion or exclusion of those characteristics. The closer the number comes to 14, the more reliance you can place on your software-estimating model.

Validate that the Model Includes All the Needed Factors

The factors that influence the cost of a software project may be divided into those contributed by the development and maintenance organization, many of which are subjective, and those inherent in the software project itself. Current models differ in respect to the factors that are required as specific inputs. Many different factors may be subsumed in a single parameter in some models, particularly the more subjective parameters.

Software cost-estimating models can be properly used, or intentionally or unintentionally abused. Depending on the information fed to the model, the estimate produced can vary significantly. It is important that models are used correctly, and that all of the factors that influence software costs are properly inputted into the model. Models can produce incorrect results based on these influencing factors in two ways. First, the factor can be excluded from the model, resulting in an incorrect estimate. Second, the factor can be incomplete or incorrectly entered into the model, again causing incorrect software cost estimates to be produced.

Work Paper 7.2 lists the factors that can influence software costs. The work paper provides a space to indicate whether the factor has been adequately or inadequately addressed in the software model. A comments column is provided to explain the potential impact of incomplete or inadequate use of these factors in the software model.

No generalization can be made about the impact of inadequately or improperly considering one of these influencing factors. The impact of each factor not adequately addressed by the model needs to be considered individually. If a factor has not been included, the tester must make a determination as to whether that factor will significantly affect the actual costs of building the software.

Factors that influence the software system include:

1. **Size of the software.** A favorite measure for software system size is lines of operational code, or deliverable code (operational code plus supporting code, for example, for hardware diagnostics) measured either in object code statements or in source code statements. It is rarely specified whether source code statements include nonexecutable code, such as comments and data declarations. Other measures are lines of code, including nondeliverable code (i.e., all code written during project development, whether deliverable or not, including support software and test software), number of functions to be performed or number of modules (where function and module are intuitive measures), or number of inputs and outputs.

   Parametric cost-estimating models relate cost in some way to the size estimate, and are therefore heavily dependent on the accuracy of the size estimate. In some models a reasonable check of the size estimate is included. The size is indicated in more than one way, and the different estimates are checked for consistency. One way to do this is by indicating the class of function to be performed by the software system and the languages to be employed. A database of past projects is then searched to see what range of sizes has previously been achieved for that type of software. Most databases so far available do not include the size or cost of nondeliverable software.

   Another size indicator that is sometimes used is related to the size and structure of the database to be handled by the operational software.

   Some models include algorithms for computing project size, either by splitting the project into smaller parts, or by analogy with other similar software. Other models use size estimates as the starting point.

   One study on estimating showed that size estimated can vary by as much as ten times if the units are not well defined. Since some support software, test software, and diagnostic software may be nondeliverable although developed on the project, size estimates for the same project will be very different if such software is included in one size estimate and not in another. Similarly, if a model makes an assumption about the proportion of the total software that is included because it assumes a certain percentage of software for simulation of the environment, or other nonoperational software, this should be clearly stated. This study found that deliverable code averaged 70 percent of total code developed, but with a standard deviation of about 30 percent.

2. **Percentage of the design and/or code that is new.** This is relevant when moving existing software systems to new computer hardware, when planning an extension to or modification of an existing software system, or when using software prototypes.

3. **Complexity of the software system.** It is recognized in the software industry that different software projects have different degrees of complexity, usually measured by the amount of interaction between the different parts of the software system, and between the software and the external world. The complexity affects programmer productivity, and is an input parameter for several models.

4. **Difficulty of design and coding.** Different application areas are considered to have different levels of difficulty in design and coding, affecting programmer productivity. For example, operating system software is usually regarded as more difficult than standalone commercial applications. Software projects might be given a difficulty or an application mix rating, according to the degree to which they fall into one (or more) of the following application areas:

- Real-time systems
- Operating systems
- Self-contained real-time projects
- Standalone non-real-time applications
- Modifications to an existing software system
- Rewrite of an existing system for new target machine

There are, of course, other categories. Each different model deals with the difficulty in its own way, some requiring estimates of the percentage of each type of software system, others asking for a number on a predefined scale. Others merge the factor with the complexity rating.

5. **Quality.** Quality, documentation, maintainability, and reliability standards required are all included in a single factor. This factor is sometimes called the platform type, reflecting the fact that the documentation and reliability requirements for software in a manned spacecraft are higher than in a standalone statistical package. The documentation and reliability requirements may be given a defined numeric scale from 1 to 10 (for example). In some estimating models there is also a parameter for the number of different locations at which the software will be run.

One estimating study found that as the number of pages of external documentation required per thousand lines of source code increased by 10 percent, programmer productivity decreased by 63 percent. If independent validation and verification were required, then the cost of the software increased by about 20 percent.

6. **Languages to be used.** The class of programming language used affects the cost, size, time scale, and documentation effort. Some models require that the

language input to be used in the majority of the software be known. Some models only apply to projects using assembler code. The study estimates that the ratio of the total life cycle cost of a project programmed entirely in assembler to the total life cycle cost of the same project programmed entirely in a high-level language could be as high as 5:1.

7. **Security classification level of the project.** The higher the security classification of the project, the more it will cost because of the additional precautions required. The security classification is not an input factor in most models.

8. **Target machine.** A few models require information about the target machine, in particular the word length and whether the machine has an established architecture.

9. **Utilization of the target hardware.** Several models include a parameter for target hardware utilization. As the percentage utilization, either in terms of processor time or in terms of storage space on the target machine, increases above about 50 percent, the estimated software development cost increases. The study shows programmer productivity decreasing exponentially as the percentage of target hardware utilization increases.

10. **Volatility of the requirement.** The firmness of the requirement specification and the interface between developer and customer affect the amount of rework that will be needed before the software is delivered. This highly subjective but nonetheless important factor is an input factor to several models. The following are included in this factor:

   ■ Amount of change expected in the requirement
   ■ Amount of detail omitted from the requirement specification
   ■ Concurrent development of associated hardware, causing changes in the software specification
   ■ Unspecified target hardware (One study indicated that productivity can decrease by up to 50 percent if requirements are vague rather than detailed.)

Organization-dependent factors include:

1. **Project schedule.** Software projects cannot be speeded up to occupy less than some minimum time. Attempts to compress time scales below the minimum by applying more people to the project prove counterproductive, since more time and effort are expended in communication between members of the project team than can be gained by adding extra people. There must therefore be either a minimum time below which the project cannot be completed, or at least a time below which the costs of saving a small amount of time become prohibitive. Conversely, if more time is allocated to a project than is required, it has been argued that the cost decreases. However, other models show costs increasing if more than some optimum time is allocated, because more personnel are consumed. One effect of the compression of time scales is that work that should be done in series is undertaken in parallel, with the increased risk that some of the work will have to be scrapped (e.g., if coding is started before design is complete).

   Not all models deal with project schedules. Of those which do, some assume the 40-20-40 rule (40 percent design, 20 percent coding, and 40 percent testing), and others use more elaborate scheduling assumptions. Some research throws doubt on the validity of the 40-20-40 rule, and indicates that phases are strongly interrelated, so that effort skimped in one phase will probably result in a considerable increase in the effort needed in a later phase.

Few models require input of a proposed development schedule. In the PRICE-S model the proposed development schedule is an optional input. Some models actually deliver a recommended or assumed development schedule.

2. **Personnel.** The personnel assigned to a project contribute to the cost, depending on staffing levels. Most projects are resource limited, in that the number of people with a given skill who are available to the project is limited. The level of personnel available at any stage in a project will affect the time scales, and hence the cost, but it is not a required input for most models.

   - *Technical competence*—Several statistical analyses have shown that for large projects the experience of the technical personnel makes very little difference to their productivity. However, several models use the technical expertise of the personnel and the experience of the developer on similar applications as an input, although this is a highly subjective judgment. The study indicates that an extra six months should be added to the development time for personnel to gain experience of new hardware or an unfamiliar application area.

   - *Nontechnical staff*—Estimates of the nontechnical personnel levels required by a project are frequently made as a percentage of the technical personnel levels. Although some models compute nontechnical staffing requirements as a function of project size, some use the documentation and maintenance requirements to derive a relationship between technical staffing requirements and the requirements for support personnel, and some ignore the question.

3. **Development environment.** The adequacy of the development environment, both in hardware and software, depends largely on the management of the development organization. This factor is not usually requested as an explicit input to a model, but may be implicit in the calibration of the model, or in some general management parameter. Three aspects of the development environment that are sometimes required as inputs to models are described as follows:

   - *Development machine*—The adequacy of the development machine as a host for developing software for the selected target, and the availability of the development machine to the software development personnel, will affect both the schedule and the cost of a software development. The study showed that time sharing, where the development machine is constantly available, is 20 percent more productive than batch systems for software development.

   - *Availability of associated software and hardware*—Projected late delivery of some item of associated hardware or software can affect schedules and costs. Models that use development schedules cater to this by rerunning with different input parameters.

   - *Software tools and techniques to be used during system design and development*—It has been demonstrated that newer tools and techniques, properly applied, can reduce development effort. One IBMer estimates that savings of up to 40 percent can be achieved by the application of modern techniques. Among techniques to be considered are:

   a. Host/target development systems. A study on estimating indicates that development on a different machine from the target has an adverse effect on cost unless the target has inadequate facilities for software development.

   b. High-level languages.

   c. Design and test methodology.

   d. Prototyping.

   e. Development libraries.

   f. Development databases.

   g. Work processors for documentation.

   h. Adequate programming support environment.

(This list is not meant to be complete.)

4. **Resources not directly attributable to technical aspects of the project.** The management style of the development organization affects the amount of effort expended in communication between team members (meetings) and the level of nontechnical effort involved as well as the cost of bought software/hardware tools, costs of subcontracting, and profit. These factors are usually ignored, are implicit in the database from which the model is derived, or are taken care of by a general management factor. The geographical distribution of the development organization may affect costs because of travel and the cost of transmitting data between sites, and is therefore input to some models.

5. **Computing resources.** Many models ignore the cost of computing (hardware and computer time). Others assume a fixed percentage of the total cost will be consumed by this item, while yet others take an average cost per staff-month with different average costs for each phase in the development.

6. **Labor rates.** If the model estimate costs in terms of money, rather than staff-hours, the relationship of labor costs to staff-hours within the development organization may be required by the model. The model may be capable of reflecting increased rates for staff required to work irregular hours because of decreases in the development time scale or lack of availability of development tools.

7. **Inflation.** Costs estimated in terms of money rather than staff-hours may take inflation rates into account, as well as the costs in a base year. If inflation is not built into the model, the rate of inflation may be required as an input.

Verify the Correctness of the Cost-Estimating Model Estimate

The amount of testing of the produced estimate will depend on: the reasonableness of the estimating model, and the completeness of the influencing factors included in the model. The less the tester can rely on the model, the more testing that needs to be performed on the validity of the estimate produced by the model.

The following four tests are suggested for use in testing the validity of the estimate produced by the software cost-estimating model:

1. **Recalculate the estimate.** The tester can validate the processing of the estimate by rerunning the estimating model. The purpose of this is to:

   - Validate the input was entered correctly.
   - Validate the input was reasonable.
   - Validate the mathematical computation was performed correctly.

   This test can be done in totality, or in part. For example, the tester can completely recalculate the estimate, check that the input going into the estimating model was correct, test the reasonableness of some of the input test by recalculating all or parts of the estimate, and so forth.

2. **Compare produced estimate to like projects.** The tester can determine how long it took to develop projects of similar size and complexity. These actual project costs should be available from the organization's accounting system. The estimate produced by the estimating system is then compared to the actual costs for like projects completed in the past. If there is any significant difference the tester can challenge the validity of the estimate. This challenge may result in a recalculation, or change of the estimate based on previous organization experience.

3. **The prudent person test.** This test is similar to test 2, in that past experience is utilized. The tester documents the factors influencing the cost estimate, documents the estimate produced by the estimating system, and then validates the reasonableness of that estimate by asking experienced project leaders for their opinions regarding the validity of the estimate. It is recommended that three experienced project leaders be asked to validate the estimate. If one or more does not feel that the estimate is reasonable, then the validity of the estimate should be challenged. The challenge in this case might be a challenge of the validity of the estimation model based on the characteristics of the system being estimated.

4. **Redundancy in software cost estimating.** This test has the tester recalculate the estimate using another cost-estimating model. For example, let's assume that your organization has developed a cost-estimating model. The project people have used that model to develop the cost estimate. The tester uses another method, for example, the software package ESTIMACS. If the two estimating systems produce approximately the same estimate, the reliance on that estimate is increased. On the other hand, if there is a significant variance between the estimates using the two methods, then additional investigation needs to be undertaken.

   Sources of software estimating models include:

   - Organization-developed estimating models
   - Estimating models included in system development methodologies
   - Software packages for developing software estimates
   - Use of function points in estimating software costs

Task 2: Testing the Status of the Software System

The suggested test for project status is a simple point accumulation system for measuring progress. This system of accumulating points can then be compared to the project management or accounting system progress reporting. If there is a significant difference between the two progress measurement systems, the tester can challenge the validity of the results produced by the project management and/or accounting system.

The point system for performance measurement during software development provides an objective, accurate, efficient means of collecting and reporting performance data in an engineering field that often lacks visibility. The method uses data based on deliverable software items and collected as a normal part of the development process. The results are easily interpreted and can be presented in a number of formats and subdivisions. The scheme is flexible and can be modified to meet the needs of projects, both large and small.

Overview of the Point Accumulation Tracking System

The increasing complexity of software systems, combined with the requirements for structured and modular designs, has increased manyfold the number of software elements developed and delivered on recent simulator programs. The increased number of elements, plus the traditionally "soft" milestones used to measure progress, have made monitoring software development and predicting future progress time-consuming, subjective, and often unreliable.

A software progress tracking system that uses an earned point scheme has been successfully used to monitor software development on several large tests. Points are assigned for each step in the software development cycle on a per-element basis. The steps are "hard" milestones in which a generated product is accepted by program management. As the products are accepted, the associated points are earned. The ratio of earned points to total possible points is compiled on an element, functional area, or total software system basis to determine progress achieved. A report generator program, usually resident on the simulator computational system, tabulates the data in a variety of management reports.

The system as implemented is flexible and highly automated, and is closely coupled to configuration management systems and software quality assurance procedures to ensure validity of data. The accumulated point values are quickly ascertained, objective, and based on the current state of program development. Simple calculations or comparisons of the accumulated point values provide an accurate measure of progress, deviation from schedule, and prediction of future progress.

Typical Methods of Measuring Performance

Performance in software development is measured typically either by estimating percent of a task completed or by counting the number of predetermined milestones that have been reached. In either method a schedule of tasks and/or milestones is used as a baseline with which measured performance is compared.

In the estimate of percent completed method the person actually doing the work estimates the percent of the work that has been accomplished in reaching a milestone or completing a task. The percent completed method has several faults. The major fault is that the measurement is subjective. The manager is asking a person with a vested interest in completing the task as early as possible to make an educated guess as to how nearly complete it is. Most people tend to be optimistic in their ability to complete a task—particularly if their manager subtly encourages optimism. The old bromide of a task being 95 percent complete for months is all too true.

While not necessarily a characteristic of the percent completed method, a potential shortcoming of this method when used with tasks rather than milestones is that the definition of completion is not always stated. Therefore, the person making the estimate may have one perception of what the task includes, while his or her manager may have another. Hence, when the programmer states the task is 100 percent complete—written, tested, and documented—the manager may have an unpleasant surprise when he or she asks to see the installation guide. Therefore, since the end of the task may not be clearly defined, the estimates of completion may be quite inaccurate.

Since the estimates are subjective, the interpretation of the results may also be subjective. In trying to ascertain the degree of completeness of a job, a manager may ask who made the estimate and then apply a "correction factor" to the estimate for that person to get a number he feels comfortable with.

The second method, or milestone method, attempts to alleviate these problems by defining specific milestones that must be met and measuring performance by summing the number of milestones that have been met. This method is much more objective, tends to describe the overall task more fully, and as a result is easier to interpret. The shortcomings of this method are more in the area of resolution of the measurement versus the efficiency of collecting, collating, and presenting the results in a meaningful way.

In order to get the resolution of measurement fine enough to show incremental progress on a periodic basis, a large number of milestones need to be defined. However, the large number of milestones makes it more difficult to collect and present the data in a timely and meaningful way. A common method is to present the data on bar graphs, but on a large project with thousands of milestones, the upkeep of bar graphs can be a slow, expensive effort.

Another potential problem is that the milestone may not accurately reflect the real task. If care is not taken to define the milestone, the milestone may not be based on deliverable items, but based on something that appears to show progress, such as lines of code generated. Also, if the milestones are not carefully chosen, it may be difficult to determine if the milestone has been reached.

These performance measurement tools and techniques emphasize functions performed early in the life of a project. Less information is available on the ongoing management function of control. Control can be thought of as a three-step process: An attribute or characteristic of interest is measured, the measured value is compared with an expected or baseline value, and an appropriate action is taken if an unacceptable deviation exists. Any number of items of interest during software development may be controlled in this manner. Development time, development costs, computer memory usage, and computer time are some of the more common items.

The purpose of this section is to describe a method of measuring the performance of the software development team and comparing the measured performance to a baseline schedule. Performance here refers to the effectiveness of software development personnel in meeting established schedule and cost targets. By providing an objective, timely measure of actual performance with a comparison to expected performance, project management will have the means to pinpoint schedule and cost deviations, thus enabling them to take action to assure schedule and cost targets are met.

A performance measurement scheme should meet several criteria. First and most important, the scheme should be objective. The person claiming performance should not be required to estimate degree of completion. Likewise, the person monitoring performance should know exactly what a performance measurement represents. Ideally, the state of development should be sufficiently visible and the measurement means sufficiently clear to enable any project member to make the actual measurement.

Second, the scheme should measure performance in accomplishing the real task (i.e., the development of deliverable software). Further, the resolution of the measuring scheme should be sufficiently fine to measure incremental progress on a weekly or monthly basis, and the measurement should be timely in that it measures the current state of development. Providing accurate, current performance information on a periodic basis can be a positive motivating factor for a programming staff.

Finally, the scheme needs to be efficient. It should require minimal resources to collect, collate, and report performance data and should require minimum time to interpret the results. Systems that require constant inputs from the programming staff, updates by clerical personnel, or integration of large amounts of data by management are not used.

How to Use the Point System

A method of overcoming these problems is a point system, which has been successfully used on several large simulator programs. The point system is really an extension to the milestone system that lends itself to automation. In its simplest form it is assumed that each software module goes through a similar development process and there are a number of clearly identifiable milestones within that process. For the purpose of illustration, assume ten modules will be developed and four milestones will define the development process. The milestones may represent design reviewed and accepted, code walkthrough complete, test results verified, and module released.

In the simple case each milestone for each software item is worth a point. In the case of the system with ten modules, 40 points can be earned. As part of each design review, code walkthrough, test verification, or release audit, the milestone is achieved and the corresponding point earned. By listing all of the modules and milestones achieved (points earned) in a computer file, and creating a few simple report generators, an objective, accurate, and timely measure of performance can be acquired. Figure 7.3 shows what a simple status report might look like.

This simplified scheme works well for a homogeneous set of modules where all modules are of the same complexity and each of the milestones represents an approximately equal amount of work. Through an introduction of weighting factors, modules of varying complexity or milestones representing unequal effort to complete can be easily handled.

SOFTWARE STATUS REPORT				
	DESIGN	CODE	TEST	RELEASE	POINTS EARNED
Module A	1	1			2
Module B	1				1
Module C	1				1
Module D	1	1	1		3
Module E	1	1			2
Module F	1				1
Module G	1	1			2
Module H	1	1	1	1	4
Module I	1				1
Module J	1	1			2
TOTALS	10	6	2	1	19
PERCENT COMPLETE = 19/40 = 48%					

Figure 7.3   Simple status report.

Before this and other extensions are discussed, however, a brief description of implementation is in order. The heart of the system is a computer data file and a few simple report generators. The data file is simply a collection of records, one for each item that is to be tracked, that contains fields to indicate whether a particular milestone has been met. Usually, it is advantageous to include fields that allow for description of the item, responsible analyst, work package identification, and various file identification fields. Figure 7.4 shows a sample record layout. Often such a file will serve multiple uses, particularly if a few additional fields are added. Typical uses are family tree definition, specification cross-references, configuration control list, documentation cross-reference, and any one of a number of uses where a comprehensive list of deliverable software items is needed.

Maintenance or updating of the file can be as straightforward as modifying records with a line editor or as complex as building a special-purpose interactive update program. Some means of limited access should be used to restrict unauthorized modification of the file, particularly if some of the other uses of the file are sensitive to change.

Once the file is updated to include an entry of the module under development, the milestone status fields are updated as the milestones are met. In some cases this may be a manual process; once an event has occurred and the milestone achieved, a program librarian or other authorized person updates the status file. In other instances, in a more sophisticated system, a computer program could determine that a milestone event has occurred (error-free compilation or successful test run) and automatically update the milestone status.

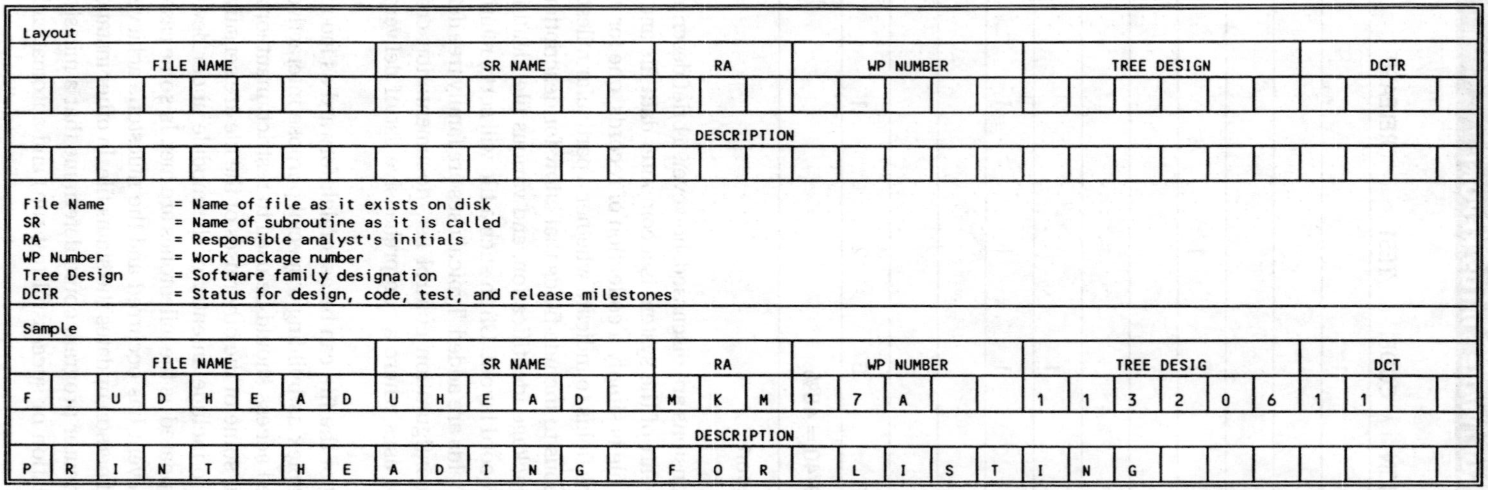

Figure 7.4 File layout.

After the file has been built, report generator programs are written to print the status. For smaller projects, a program that simply prints each record, sums the earned and defined points, and calculates the percent points earned, may be sufficient. Larger projects may need several reports for different subsystems or summary reports that emphasize change.

Extensions

A number of extensions can be added to the scheme as described so far. The first is to add a method of weighting modules and/or milestones. While weighting all modules equally on a large program where many (over 1,000) modules exist appears to give good results, smaller programs with few modules may need to weight the modules to give a sufficiently accurate measurement of performance. Also, depending on the level of visibility of the measuring system and the attitude of the personnel involved, there may be a tendency to do all the "easy" modules first to show early performance.

A similar argument can be made for weighting milestones. Depending on the acceptance criteria, some milestones may involve more work than others. Therefore, achieving those milestones represents accomplishing a greater amount of work than in meeting other milestones. Further, there may be instances where a combination of module weight and milestone weight may interact. An example is a module that was previously written on another project in a different language. The amount of design work for that module may be considerably less than a module designed from scratch, but the amount of effort to code the routine might be more since an unfamiliar language may be involved.

The weighting scheme is easily implemented by assigning points to each milestone for all modules. Then as a milestone is earned, the assigned points are added to the total earned and divided by the total defined points to compute percent completion. The number of points assigned to each milestone is in proportion to the difficulty in achieving the milestone, and, in fact, relates directly to the estimated number of hours needed to complete the milestone. In assigning points it is recommended that points first be assigned to each of the modules and then reapportioned to the milestones.

A second extension is to add selecting and sorting options to the report generator programs. Selecting options allows the user to select all entries in the file by some field such as work package number, file name, software family tree component, or responsible analyst. Once the entries of interest are selected, the sort option allows the user to order the entries by some key. The points earned and points defined are summed from the selected entries and the percent complete calculated. Therefore, reports can be printed listing all modules and percent complete for a certain analyst, work package, or other selected criteria. It has been found valuable to allow Boolean operations on selection fields (analyst A and subsystem B) and to provide for major and minor sort fields. (List modules in alphabetical order by analyst.)

A third extension that has been useful is to add target dates and actual completion dates to each module record. In this extension the individual milestone status fields are replaced by two dates. The first date field is a target date indicating when the milestone should be met. The target dates do not have to be used for all modules or milestones, but are useful where an interdependency exists between a particular module milestone and some other element in the system. These interdependencies may exist in the design stage to some extent, but they become very important during the integration phase of a project.

The actual completion date field becomes a flag identifying when the milestone is achieved. By adding up the points assigned to a milestone that have an actual date entered in the file, the percent complete can be computed.

Using the two date fields has two advantages: Schedule interdependence can be monitored and a historical record exists for future analysis. By making the date fields selectable and sortable, additional interesting reports can be generated. Assuming that an integration milestone has been identified, a list of all modules of interest can be selected by WBS work package number, family tree identification, or individual module name. Target dates for the milestone of interest can then be entered. As the date of the integration milestone comes closer, lists of all modules of interest that have a particular due date and have not been completed can be provided to the responsible analyst or work package manager. Judicious use of these lists on a periodic basis can be used to monitor and motivate the programming staff to assure the milestone is met. Usually, several of these lists in various stages are active at once as key milestones are coming up. It has been found that choosing approximately one major milestone a month and starting the list several months in advance of the target date is very effective. More milestones than this tend to set up multiple or conflicting goals for the individual analysts. Also, the lists need to be started well enough in advance to allow suitable time for the work to be completed and institute workarounds if problems arise.

It should be noted that the meeting of these interdependency dates is really separate from performance measurement. It is possible that in a given subsystem the performance may be fully adequate, say 75 percent complete, but a key integration event may have been missed. The manager must be aware of both elements. If performance is where it should be, but an integration event has been missed, it may mean the manager's people are not concentrating on the right item and need to be redirected.

Rolling Baseline

A potential problem with the point system described thus far has to do with an effect known as a rolling baseline. The rolling baseline occurs over the life of a program as new items are continually defined and added to the status file. This has the effect of changing the baseline, which causes percent complete to vary independently of milestones earned. During periods when few new items are added to the file, the percent complete accurately reflects real performance. At other times, as new items are added as quickly as previously defined milestones are met, reported progress tends to flatten out. In some instances where more new items were added than old items completed, negative progress is reported.

This problem is overcome by freeing the baseline for a unit of work or work package basis and reporting progress on the unit. That is, once a package of work is defined, no new points are allocated to the package. If, for some reason, it is decided certain modules have to be split up for sake of modularity or computing efficiency, the points are likewise split up in a replanning effort. In the instance where the scope of work changes due to an oversight or contract change, the effort is reprogrammed and either new work packages are created or existing work packages are expanded with a corresponding increase of points.

This has the effect of measuring performance on active or open work packages only, and not on the system as a whole. However, since performance is being compared to an established schedule, which is also made up of units of work, the comparison is valid and useful.

Reports

Several informative detail and summary reports can be generated from the data file. The most encompassing detail report, of course, is a listing of all elements. Such a list may be useful in creating inventory lists of software items to be delivered and might be used during physical configuration audits. Other lists may be sorted and/or selected by work package or family tree identification number. Such lists show status of specific modules within subsets of the work breakdown structure or functional items of the system. Other sorts or selections by a responsible analyst show status of a particular individual's effort. Figures 7.5 through 7.8 show sample summary reports. Collecting data from several summary runs allows rates of completion to be calculated, upon which trends or predictions of future performance can be made.

Using the Point System As a Test Method

The point method for tracking software progress can be used by the tester in the following three ways:

1. **Validating the project leader's software progress tracking results.** Use of the point system by the test group develops a progress evaluation that can be compared against the project leader's progress reports. If progress tracking using the two results is approximately the same, the tester can validate the reasonableness of the project reports produced by the project team. This is an extension of what testing normally does, but can be a very valuable extension from the perspective of information services management. Note that if there is a significant difference in the project progress estimate, the difference can be either the point system or the project leader's system. The purpose of doing the two estimates is to provide the project leader and information services management with greater assurance of the validity of the progress report results.

2. **Test planning.** The point method of progress tracking indicates when testing will be occurring. Having a system that enables the test manager to track progress can assist in planning the use of test resources. The point system does not require many resources to calculate; yet it is designed to assist the test manager in indicating when programs/subsystems will be available for testing.

3. **Test status reporting.** The point system also indicates when testing is done and modules are released for production purposes. The information contained in the point system is the same information the test manager will need for reporting test results.

FILENAME	ID	RA	CLASS	DESCRIPTION	DESIGN	CODE	TEST	RELEASE
F.UDHEAD	DF-U150	MKM	U	PRINT HEADING FOR DELTA LISTING (CONFIG)	--/--/--	--/--/--	--/--/--	04/15/00
					01/27/00	02/08/00	03/15/00	04/21/00
F.UDLIST	DF-U151	MKM	U	PRINT DELTA LISTING (CONFIG)	--/--/--	--/--/--	--/--/--	04/15/00
					01/31/00	02/10/00	03/15/00	04/21/00
F.UDLTST	DF-U152	MKM	U	START UDELTA SUBTASKING (CONFIG)	--/--/--	--/--/--	--/--/--	04/15/00
					01/31/00	02/15/00		
F.UDMAT	DF-U153	MKM	U	CHECK BUFFERS FOR MATCH (CONFIG)	--/--/--	--/--/--	--/--/--	04/15/00
					01/14/00			
F.UDMOVE	DF-U154	MKM	U	MOVE DATA INTO MEMORY (CONFIG)	--/--/--	--/--/--	--/--/--	04/15/00
					02/02/00	03/01/00	04/04/00	04/11/00
F.UDOPT	DF-U155	MKM	U	SET OPTIONS IN DELTA (CONFIG)	--/--/--	--/--/--	--/--/--	04/15/00
					02/01/00	02/28/00	04/14/00	04/11/00

Detail Interdependency Listing

Figure 7.5 Detail interdependency listing.

WORK PACKAGE	FILENAME	WEIGHT	MILESTONES				MODULE STATUS		
			DESIGN	CODE	TEST	RELE-ASE	STATUS CODE	SCORE	% COMPLETE
173F	F.LEDCPY	8	2	2	2	2	3	4	50
173F	F.LEDEL	8	2	2	2	2	3	4	50
173F	F.LEDFIL	44	11	11	11	11	1	11	25
173F	F.LEDINF	20	5	5	5	5	1	5	25
173F	F.LEDPRT	12	3	3	3	3	15	12	100
173F	F.LIBEDT	16	4	4	4	4	3	8	50
173F	F.LIBGEN	28	7	7	7	7	15	28	100
173F	F.LTACGN	16	4	4	4	4	3	8	50
173F	F.LTACID	8	2	2	2	2	15	8	100
173F	F.LTASTA	32	8	8	8	8	3	16	50
173F	F.LTCMPR	16	4	4	4	4	15	16	100
173F	F.LTCMST	56	14	14	14	14	0	0	0
173F	F.LTCVRT	12	3	3	3	3	0	0	0
173F	F.LTGNUM	12	3	3	3	3	0	0	0
173F	F.LTINIT	12	3	3	3	3	0	0	0
173F	F.LTMDID	16	4	4	4	4	0	0	0
173F	F.LTREC	32	8	8	8	8	0	0	0
173F	F.LTSSTM	48	12	12	12	12	3	24	50
173F	F.LTUCHK	8	2	2	2	2	7	5	63
173F	F.LTUCVT	12	3	3	3	3	7	11	92
173F	F.LTVALU	8	2	2	2	2	15	8	100
TOTALS:	21	424	106	106	106	106	15	168	40

Figure 7.6   Detail status listing.

WORK PACKAGE: 1234

	DESIGN		CODE		TEST		RELEASE		TOTAL	
TOTAL ITEMS	24		24		24		24		96	
TARGET COMPLETE	10	42%	7	29%	3	13%	0	0%	20	21%
ACTUAL COMPLETE	9	38%	5	21%	1	4%	0	0%	15	16%
LATE	1	4%	2	8%	2	8%	0	0%	5	5%
LESS THAN 1 WEEK LATE	0		1		0		0		0	
1-2 WEEKS LATE	1		0		2		0		0	
2-4 WEEKS LATE	0		1		0		0		0	
4-8 WEEKS LATE	0		0		0		0		0	
MORE THAN 8 WEEKS LATE	0		0		0		0		0	

Figure 7.7 Summary report.

| WORK PACKAGE | DESCRIPTION | MGR | WEIGHT | ------MILESTONES------ | | | | ------WP STATUS------ | |
				DESIGN	CODE	TEST	RELEASE	SCORE	% COMPLETE
173G	SCAN LIBRARY SOFTWARE	NFB	480	120	120	120	120	150	31
173H	PPG LIBRARY SOFTWARE	NFB	296	74	74	74	74	74	25
173K	EMITTER SCRIPTING: EMTR 1-50	NFB	2500	2250	250	0	0	1055	42
17A1	TD REPORTING CPPS	TJR	310	155	155	0	310	310	100
17A3	TD REPORTING SW DEVELOP- MENT	TJR	1230	375	375	240	240	575	47
17A4	SCAN PROCESSOR DOCUMENTA- TION	TJR	1078	863	215	0	0	0	0
17A5	TIMS, DEBUG, SVL DOCUMEN- TATION	TJR	7420	6550	870	0	0	3465	47
17A7	SOFTWARE DEV TOOLS DOCU- MENT	TJR	4818	3563	1255	0	0	3563	73
TOTALS:			18132	13950	3314	434	434	9192	51

Figure 7.8 Summary status report.

Check Procedures

Work Paper 7.3 is a quality control checklist for this step. It is designed so that Yes responses indicate good test practices; No responses warrant additional investigation. A Comments column is provided to explain No responses and to record results of investigation. The N/A column is used when the checklist item is not applicable to the test situation.

Output

The only output from this step is a report to the project personnel on the adequacy of the test estimate and the reasonableness of the project status. Note that this step may need to be repeated periodically as the project plan changes. The testers may also want to evaluate the reasonableness of the status report multiple times during the development process.

Guidelines

This test step is generally not performed by testers. However, the lack of a correct estimate or providing project managers with realistic status reports are essential for successful project completion. It is also essential to assure that adequate test resources and schedule will be available for testing. Testers should include this step in their test plan and obtain management's support for performing this step.

Summary

Step 1 in the 11-step process provides for testing the reasonableness of the project estimate, and testing the reasonableness of the status of the project as reported by the project status system. Testers need some degree of confidence that the project estimate is correct, and that project status will be reported correctly prior to developing a test plan. Creating a test for which adequate resources will not be available because the overall estimate is incorrect, or developing a test plan that is dependent upon the project meeting predefined milestones are prerequisites to the test planning process.

WORK PAPER 7.1   Characteristics Included/Excluded from Your Organization's Software Estimating Model

Field Requirements

FIELD	INSTRUCTIONS FOR ENTERING DATA
Name of Model	Indicate the estimating model that was used to calculate the estimate for the project being tested.
#	The sequential number of the model characteristics.
Characteristics	These are the characteristics of an estimating model that are desirable to be included in that model.
Characteristic Included/ Excluded	The test should indicate whether this desirable characteristic is included within the model that was used for estimating or whether it was excluded.
Comments	The testers should provide more specific information about characteristics excluded from the model used to develop the project estimate. The information should be a clarification of the specific characteristic as it relates to the project being tested.
Total Characteristics Included	This should be a total of the number of characteristics included and excluded. The combined total of the two columns should equal 14.

WORK PAPER 7.1 *(Continued)*

Name of Model: _____

#	CHARACTERISTIC	CHARACTERISTIC INCLUDED	EXCLUDED	COMMENTS
1.	The model should have well-defined scope. (It should be clear which activities associated with the software life cycle are taken into account in the model and which are excluded. It should also be clear which resources—manpower, computer time, and elapsed time—are being estimated, and whether costs of support software are included.)			
2.	The model should be widely applicable. (It should be possible to tailor a model to fit individual organizations, and types of software development.)			
3.	The model should be easy to use. (Input requirements should be kept to a minimum, and output should be provided in an immediately useful format.)			
4.	The model should be able to use actual project data as it becomes available. (Initial project cost estimates are likely to be based on inadequate information. As a project proceeds, more accurate data becomes available for cost estimating. It is essential that any estimating model be capable of using actual data gathered at any stage in the project life to update the model and provide refined estimates, probably with a lower likely range of values than achieved initially.			
5.	Estimating is based on a probabilistic model. This means that an estimate is a number in the likely range of the quantity being estimated, and confidence in the estimate depends on the likely range of the quantity being estimated. The better the information we have on which to base an estimate, the smaller the likely range and the greater the confidence.)			
6.	The model should allow for the use of historic data in the calibration for a particular organization and type of software.			
	The model should have been checked against a reasonable number of historic projects.			

Name of Model: _____

#	CHARACTERISTIC	CHARACTERISTIC INCLUDED	EXCLUDED	COMMENTS
7.	The model should only require inputs based on properties of the project which are well defined and can be established with a reasonable degree of certainty at the time the estimate is required.			
8.	The model should favor inputs based on objective rather than subjective criteria.			
9.	The model should not be oversensitive to subjective input criteria.			
10.	The model should be sensitive to all the parameters of a project which have been established as having a market effect on the cost, and should not require input of parameters which do not have a marked effect on cost.			
11.	The model should include estimates of how and when the resource will be needed.			
	(This is particularly important if the estimates are to be used for resource allocation, but also important if the results are given in financial terms since inflation needs to be taken into account.)			
12.	The model should produce a range of likely values for the quantity being estimated.			
	(It is important to realize that an estimate cannot provide a precise prediction of the future. It must, of course, predict sufficiently closely to be useful, and to do this it should ideally be able to place bounds on either side of the estimate within a stated probability that the actual figures will lie within the stated bounds.)			
13.	The model should include possibilities for sensitivity analysis, so that the response of the estimates to variation of selected input parameters can be seen.			
14.	The model should include some estimate of the risk of failure to complete within the estimated time or cost.			
	TOTAL CHARACTERISTICS INCLUDED			

WORK PAPER 7.2   Factors that Influence Software Cost Estimate

Field Requirements

FIELD	INSTRUCTIONS FOR ENTERING DATA
#	The sequential number of the software cost estimate factor-by-factor category.
Factor Included/Excluded	Testers should indicate whether these specific factors have been included in the software cost estimate or whether they are excluded from the estimating process.
Comments Regarding Impact of Excluded Factors	The tester should indicate whether or not they believe excluded factors will have a negative impact on the accuracy and completeness of the cost estimate. That rationale should be described in this column.

#	FACTOR	FACTOR INCLUDED EXCLUDED	COMMENTS REGARDING IMPACT OF EXCLUDED FACTORS
Project-Specific Factors			
1.	Size of the software		
2.	Percentage of the design and/or code which is new		
3.	Complexity of the software system		
4.	Difficulty of design and coding		
5.	Quality		
6.	Languages to be used		
7.	Security classification level of the project		
8.	Target machine		
9.	Utilization of the target hardware		
10.	Volatility of the requirement		
Organization-Dependent Factors			
1.	Project schedule		
2.	Personnel		
	• Technical competence		
	• Nontechnical manpower		
3.	Development environment		
	• Development machine		
	• Availability of associated software and hardware		
	• Software tools and techniques to be used during design and development		
4.	Resources not directly attributable to technical aspects of the project		
5.	Computing resources		
6.	Labor rates		
7.	Inflation		

WORK PAPER 7.3   Assessing a Development Estimate and Status Quality Control Checklist

Field Requirements

FIELD	INSTRUCTIONS FOR ENTERING DATA
Number	A number that sequentially identifies the quality control items, which if positively addressed would indicate that this step has been performed correctly.
Item	The specific quality control item that is used to measure the effectiveness of performing this step.
Response	The testers should indicate in this column whether or not they have performed the referenced item. The response can be "yes," "no," or "n/a" if it is not appropriate for your organization's testing process.
Comments	This column is used to clarify the "yes, no, or n/a" response for the item indicated. Generally the comments column need only be completed for "no" responses. "No" responses should be investigated and a determination made as to whether or not this item needs to be performed before this step considered complete.

#	ITEM	YES	NO	N/A	COMMENTS
1.	Does project management support the concept of having the test team assess the development estimate and status?				
2.	If so, is the test team knowledgeable in the estimation process?				
3.	If so, is the test team knowledgeable in the method that will be used to report project status?				
4.	Does the test team understand how the software estimate was calculated?				
5.	Has the test team performed a reasonable test to determine the validity of the estimate?				
6.	If the test team disagrees with the validity of the estimate, will a reasonable process be followed to resolve that difference?				
7.	Does the project team have a reasonable status reporting system?				
8.	Have the testers determined that the project status system will be utilized on a regular basis?				
9.	Is there a process to follow if the status reporting system indicates that the project is ahead or behind estimates?				
10.	Have the test team taken into account the influencing factors in evaluating the estimate (e.g., size of the software and so forth)?				

(Continues)

WORK PAPER 7.3   *(Continued)*

#	ITEM	RESPONSE			COMMENTS
		YES	NO	N/A	
11.	Will the team receive copies of the status reports?				
12.	Is there a process in the test plan to act upon the status reports when received?				
13.	Does the test team have a knowledge of how projects are planned and how the content of a project is planned?				
14.	Does the test team have an understanding of the project estimating process used to estimate this project?				
15.	Does the project team have an understanding of the developmental process that will be used to build the software specified in this project?				
16.	Is the project plan complete?				
17.	Is the project estimate fully documented?				
18.	Is the developmental process documented?				
19.	Is the estimating method used for this project reasonable for the project characteristics?				
20.	Is the estimate reasonable to complete the project as specified in the plan?				
21.	Has the project been completed using the development process?				
22.	Does the project team have a method for determining and reporting project status?				
23.	Is that project status method used?				
24.	Do the testers agree that the project status as reported is representative of the actual status?				

Step 2: Develop Test Plan

The scope of the test effort to determine if the software is ready to be placed into production should be defined in a test plan. To expend the resources needed for testing without a plan will almost certainly lead to waste and the inability to make an evaluation of the status of the correction effort prior to installation. An old proverb states, "If you fail to plan—plan to fail." The test planning effort should follow the normal test planning process; however, while the structure of the plan will be the same, the content will vary, because it will involve not only in-house developed software, but also vendor-developed software and software embedded into computer chips. See Figure 8.1.

Overview

The test plan describes how testing will be accomplished. Its creation is essential to effective testing, and should take about one-third of the total test effort. If the plan is developed carefully, test execution, analysis, and reporting will flow smoothly. Furthermore, the time you spend developing the test plan will be worthwhile because the results will be effective test execution, analysis, and report preparation.

Consider the test plan an evolving document. As the developmental effort changes in scope, the test plan must change accordingly. It is important to keep the test plan current and to follow it, for it is the execution of the test plan that management must rely on to assure that testing is effective; and it is from this plan that the testers will ascertain the status of the test effort and base opinions on the results of the test effort.

This chapter contains a test plan standard that defines what to include in the test plan. The procedures described here are amplified with work papers and checklists detailing how to develop the planning material. The assessment described in Step 1 will assist in developing the test plan. Steps 3 through 11 of the test approach involve executing the test plan and summarizing and reporting the results of that test execution.

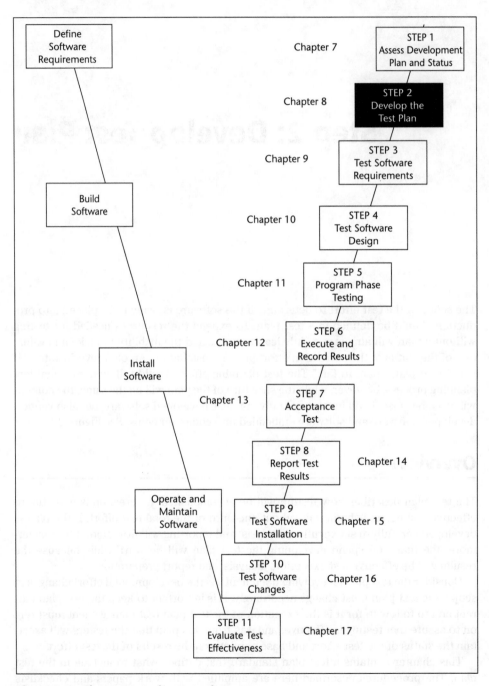

Figure 8.1 The 11-step software testing process.

Objective

The objective of a test plan is to describe all testing that is to be accomplished, together with the resources and schedule necessary for completion. The test plan should provide background information on the software being tested, a test objective and risks, and specific tests to be performed. Properly constructed, the test plan is a contract between the testers and the project team/users describing the role of testing in the project. Thus, status reports and final reports will be based on that contract, which is the status of the planned test activities.

Concerns

The concerns testers face in assuring that the test plan will be complete include the following:

Not enough training. The majority of IT personnel have not been formally trained in testing, and only about half of full-time independent testing personnel have been trained in testing techniques. This causes a great deal of misunderstanding and misapplication of testing techniques.

Us-versus-them mentality. This common problem arises when developers and testers are on opposite sides of the testing issue. Each feels that it is "out to get" the other. Often, the political infighting takes up energy, sidetracks the project, and accomplishes little except to negatively impact relationships.

Lack of test tools. IT management may have the attitude that test tools are a luxury. Manual testing can be an overwhelming task. Although more than just tools are needed, trying to test effectively without tools is like trying to dig a trench with a spoon.

Lack of management understanding/support of testing. Support for testing must come from the top, otherwise staff will not take the job seriously and testers' morale will suffer. Management support goes beyond financial provisions; management must also make the tough calls to deliver the software on time with defects or take a little longer and do the job right.

Lack of customer and user involvement. Users and customers may be shut out of the testing process, or perhaps they don't want to be involved. Users and customers play one of the most critical roles in testing: making sure the software works from a business perspective.

Not enough time for testing. This is common complaint. The challenge is to prioritize the plan to test the right things in the given time.

Overreliance on independent testers. Sometimes called the "throw it over the wall" syndrome, developers know that independent testers will check their work, so they focus on coding and let the testers do the testing. Unfortunately, this results in higher defect levels and longer testing times.

Rapid change. In some technologies, especially Rapid Application Development (RAD), the software is created and/or modified faster than the testers can test it.

This highlights the need for automation, but also for version and release management.

Testers are in a lose–lose situation. On the one hand, if the testers report too many defects, they are blamed for delaying the project. Conversely, if the testers do not find the critical defects, they are blamed for poor quality.

Having to say no. This is the single toughest dilemma for testers, having to say, "No, the software is not ready for production." Nobody on the project likes to hear that, and frequently, testers succumb to the pressures of schedule and cost.

Workbench

Test planning is an activity that should begin when a project commences. The plan needs to be developed and updated throughout the project as the project changes. The workbench in Figure 8.2 shows the development of the initial test plan. As the project changes throughout the development cycle, the plan itself should be updated using the process outlined in this step. However, the updating process should be much simpler than the development of the initial plan.

The workbench shows the project plan and the tester's assessment of that plan as input. Four steps are required to complete the test plan. Note that if the test team has been formed during the assessment step it will not be necessary to repeat that task during this test planning step.

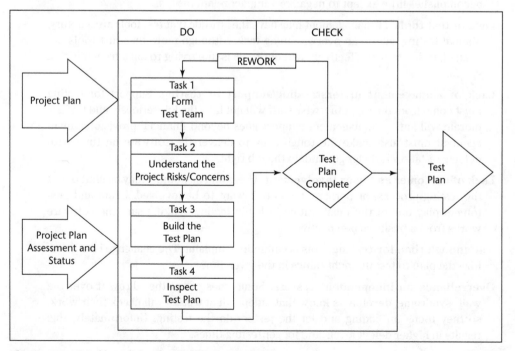

Figure 8.2 Workbench for developing a test plan.

Input

Accurate and complete inputs are critical to developing an effective test plan, as the planning process assumes they are and builds the plan based on those inputs. The two inputs used in developing the test plan are:

1. **Project plan**. This plan should address the totality of activities needed to implement the project and control that implementation. The plan should also include testing.

2. **Project plan assessment and status**. This report (developed from Step 1 of the 11 step process) evaluates the completeness and reasonableness of the project plan. It also indicates the status of the plan as well as the method for reporting status throughout the development effort.

Do Procedures

The following four tasks should be completed during the execution of this step (note: If the test team has been formed prior to this step, the workbench begins with task 2).

Task 1: Form the Test Team

The process for forming a test team is described in Chapter 6. The purpose of this task is to emphasize that the test team leadership must be selected and in place prior to developing the test plan. This task supplements the material in Chapter 6 with a discussion of the composition of the test team.

The test team is an integral part of the test process. Without the formalization of the test team, it is difficult to introduce a formalized testing concept into the development process. Extensive "desk checking" by the individual who developed the work being checked has not proven to be a cost-effective method of testing. The disadvantages of a person checking his or her own work using his or her own documentation are as follows:

- Misunderstandings will not be detected, because the checker will assume that what the other individual heard from him or her was correct.

- Improper use of the development process may not be detected because the individual may not understand the process.

- The individual may be "blinded" into accepting erroneous system specifications and coding because he or she falls into the same trap during testing that led to the introduction of the defect in the first place.

- Information services people are optimistic in their ability to do defect-free work and thus sometimes underestimate the need for extensive testing.

- Without a formal division between development and test, an individual may be tempted to improve the system structure and documentation, rather than allocate that time and effort to the test.

The test team can be organized using one of four different approaches (see Figure 8.3), which are described in the following sections.

1. *Internal IT Test Team Approach*

The members of the project team become the members of the test team. In most instances, the systems development project leader is the test team project leader. However, it is not necessary to have all of the development team members participate on the test team, although there is no reason why they would not participate. What is important is that one member of the test team will be primarily responsible for testing other members' work. The objective of the team is to establish a test process that is independent of the people who developed the particular part of the project being tested.

The advantage of the internal IT test team approach is that it minimizes the cost of the test team. The project is already responsible for testing, so using project members on the test team is merely an alternate method for conducting the tests. Testing using the test team approach not only trains the project people in good test methods, but

TEST TEAM APPROACH	COMPOSITION OF TEST TEAM MEMBERS	ADVANTAGES	DISADVANTAGES
Internal IT	Project team	• Minimize cost • Training • Knowledge of project	• Time allocation • Lack of independence • Lack of objectivity
External IT	Quality assurance Professional testers	• Independent view • IT professionals • Multiple project testing experience	• Cost • Overreliance • Competition
Non-IT	Users Auditors Consultants	• Independent view • Independence in assessment • Ability to act	• Cost • Lack of IT knowledge • Lack of project knowledge
Combination	Any or all of the above	• Multiple skills • Education • Clout	• Cost • Scheduling reviews • Diverse backgrounds

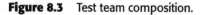

Figure 8.3   Test team composition.

cross-trains them in other parts of the project. The internal IT test team approach uses those people in testing who are most knowledgeable about the project. The disadvantage of the internal IT test team approach is the need for ensuring that the project team allocates appropriate time for testing. In addition, the project team members may lack independence and objectivity in conducting the test. There is a tendency for the project team members to believe that the project solution is correct and thus find it difficult to challenge the project assumptions.

2. External IT Test Team Approach

Testing performed by information services personnel independently of the project does not relieve the project personnel of responsibility for the correctness of the application system. The external testing is designed to provide independent testing in order to provide extra assurance of the correctness of processing. The external testing normally occurs after the project team has performed the testing they deem necessary. Frequently the system development team verifies that the system structure is correct, and the independent test team verifies that the system satisfies user requirements.

External IT testing is normally performed by either information services quality assurance or a professional testing group in the IT department. While the project team is involved in all aspects of the development, the quality assurance professional test teams specialize in the testing process. However, most individuals in these testing groups have had systems design and programming experience.

The advantage of external information services testing is the independent perspective they bring to the test process. The group is comprised of information services professionals who have specialized in the area of testing. In addition, these groups have testing experience in multiple projects, and thus are better able to construct and execute tests than those individuals who only test periodically.

The disadvantage of external IT testing is the additional cost that may be required to establish and administer a testing function. Also, the development team may place too much reliance on the test team and thus fail to perform adequate testing themselves, resulting in overburdening the professional testers. In addition, the competition between the test team and the project team may result in a breakdown of cooperation, making it difficult for the test team to function properly.

3. Non-IT Test Team Approach

Testing can be performed by groups external to the information services department. The three most common groups that test application systems are users, auditors, and consultants. These groups represent the organizational needs and test on behalf of the organization. They are concerned with protecting the interest of the entire organization. The advantage of a non-IT test team is that they provide an independent view and at the same time can offer independence in assessment. The non-IT group is not restricted by loyalty or charter to report unfavorable results to only the information services department. The non-IT group has greater ability to act and to cause action to occur once problems are detected than does a group within an information services department.

The disadvantage of non-IT testing is the cost of the test. Generally, these groups are not familiar with the application and must first learn the application, and then learn how to test within the organization. The non-IT group may encounter difficulties in testing due to lack of information services knowledge and lack of project knowledge.

4. Combination Test Team Approach

Any or all of the above groups can participate on a test team. The combination team can be drawn together to meet specific testing needs. For example, if the project had significant financial implications, an auditor could be added to the test team; if it had communication concerns a communication consultant could be added.

The advantage of drawing on multiple skills for the test team is to enable a multidisciplined approach to testing. In other words, the skills and backgrounds of individuals from different disciplines can be drawn into the test process. For some of the test participants, particularly users, it can be an educational experience to make them aware of both the system and the potential pitfalls in an automated system. In addition, a combination test team has greater clout in either approving, disapproving, or modifying the application system based upon the test.

The disadvantage of the combination test team is the cost associated with assembling and administering the test team. It also may pose some scheduling problems determining when the tests will occur. Finally, the diverse backgrounds of the test team may make the determination of a mutually acceptable test approach difficult.

Task 2: Understand the Project Risks

The test factors describe the broad objectives of testing. These are the risks/concerns that the testers need to be evaluating to assure the objectives identified by that factor have been achieved. For example, if reliability is a factor for a specific project and up-time was a reliability measure then the testers would need to evaluate the system's capability to meet that up-time objective. The risk/concern expressed by that factor might become a reality, causing the system to go down when needed.

The following discussion of the 15 test factors delineates the type of system characteristics the tester would need to evaluate to determine whether that test factor/objective has been met. (Note: These factors need to be customized in the detailed test plan for the specific system being developed.) See the matrix in Figure 8.4.

1. **Reliability test factor**
   - The level of accuracy and completeness expected in the operational environment is established.
   - The data integrity controls to achieve the established processing tolerances are designed.
   - Data integrity controls are implemented in accordance with the design.
   - Manual, regression, and functional tests are performed to ensure the data integrity controls work.
   - The accuracy and completeness of the system installation are verified.
   - The accuracy requirements are maintained as the applications are updated.

TEST FACTOR	REQUIREMENTS	DESIGN	PROGRAM	TEST	INSTALLATION	MAINTAIN
RELIABILITY	Tolerances established	Data integrity controls designed	Data integrity controls implemented	Manual regression and functional testing	Accuracy and completeness of installation verified	Update accuracy requirements
AUTHORIZATION	Authorization rules defined	Authorization rules designed	Authorization rules implemented	Compliance testing	Prohibit data changes during installation	Preserve authorization rules
FILE INTEGRITY	File integrity requirements defined	File integrity controls designed	File integrity controls implemented	Functional testing	Verify integrity of production files	Preserve file integrity
AUDIT TRAIL	Reconstruction requirements defined	Audit trail designed	Implement audit trail	Functional testing	Record installation audit trail	Update audit trail
CONTINUITY OF PROCESSING	Impact of failure defined	Contingency plan designed	Write contingency plan and procedures	Recovery testing	Assure integrity of previous testing	Update contingency plan
SERVICE LEVEL	Desired service level defined	Method to achieve service level designed	Design system to achieve service level	Stress testing	Implement fail-safe installation plan	Preserve service level
ACCESS CONTROL	Access defined	Access procedure designed	Implement security procedures	Compliance testing	Control access during integration	Preserve security
METHODOLOGY	Requirements comply with methodology	Design complies with methodology	Programs comply with methodology	Testing complies with methodology	Integration complies with methodology	Maintenance complies with methodology

Figure 8.4 Testing concerns matrix.

(Continues)

TEST FACTOR	REQUIREMENTS	DESIGN	PROGRAM	TEST	INSTALLATION	MAINTAIN
CORRECTNESS	Functional specifications designed	Design conforms to requirements	Programs conform to design	Functional testing	Proper programs and data are placed into production	Update requirements
EASE OF USE	Usability specifications determined	Design facilitates use	Programs conform to design	Manual support testing	Usability instructions disseminated	Preserve ease of use
MAINTAINABLE	Maintenance specifications determined	Design is maintainable	Programs are maintainable	Inspection	Documentation complete	Preserve maintainability
PORTABLE	Portability needs determined	Design is portable	Programs conform to design	Disaster testing	Documentation complete	Preserve portability
COUPLING	Systems interface defined	Interface design complete	Programs conform to design	Functional and regression testing	Interface coordinated	Assure proper interface
PERFORMANCE	Performance criteria established	Design achieves criteria	Programs achieve criteria	Compliance test	Integration performance monitored	Preserve level of performance
EASE OF OPERATION	Operational needs defined	Communicate needs to operations	Develop operating procedures	Operations test	Implement operating procedures	Update operating procedures

Figure 8.4 (Continued)

2. **Authorization test factor**
   - The rules governing the authorization of transactions that enable the transaction to be processed are defined.
   - The application is designed to identify and enforce the authorization rules.
   - The application programs implement the authorization rules design.
   - The system is compliance tested to ensure that the authorization rules are properly executed.
   - Unauthorized data changes are prohibited during the installation process.
   - The method and rules for authorization are preserved during maintenance.

3. **File integrity test factor**
   - Requirements for file integrity are defined.
   - The design provides for the controls to ensure the integrity of the file.
   - The specified file integrity controls are implemented.
   - The file integrity functions are tested to ensure they perform properly.
   - The integrity of production files is verified prior to placing those files into a production status.
   - The integrity of the files is preserved during the maintenance phase.

4. **Audit trail test factor**
   - The requirements to reconstruct processing are defined.
   - The audit trail and information in the audit trail needed to reconstruct processing are designed.
   - The audit trail requirements are incorporated into the system.
   - The audit trail functions are tested to ensure the appropriate data is saved.
   - The audit trail of events during installation is recorded.
   - The audit trail requirements are updated during systems maintenance.

5. **Continuity-of-processing test factor**
   - The impact of each system failure has been defined.
   - A contingency plan has been designed to address the identified failures.
   - The contingency plan and procedures have been written.
   - Recovery testing verifies that the contingency plan functions properly.
   - The integrity of the previous systems is assured until the integrity of the new system has been verified.
   - The contingency plan is updated and tested as systems requirements change.

6. **Service level test factor**
   - The desired service level for all aspects of the system is defined.
   - The method to achieve the predefined service levels is incorporated into the systems design.
   - The programs and manual systems are designed to achieve the specified service level.
   - Stress testing is conducted to ensure that the system can achieve the desired service level when both normal and above normal volumes of data are processed.

- A fail-safe plan is used during installation to ensure service will not be disrupted.
- The predefined service level is preserved as the system is maintained.

7. **Access control test factor**

- The access to the system has been defined including those individuals/programs authorized access and the resources they are authorized.
- The procedures to enforce the access rules are designed.
- The defined security procedures are implemented.
- Compliance tests are utilized to ensure that the security procedures function in production.
- Access to the computer resources is controlled during installation.
- The procedures controlling access are preserved as the system is updated.

8. **Methodology test factor**

- The system requirements are defined and documented in compliance with the system development methodology.
- The system design is performed in accordance with the system design methodology.
- The programs are constructed and documented in compliance with the programming methodology.
- The testing is performed in compliance with the test methodology.
- The integration of the application system in a production environment is performed in accordance with the installation methodology.
- Maintenance is performed in compliance with the system maintenance methodology.

9. **Correctness test factor**

- The user has fully defined the functional specifications.
- The developed design conforms to the user requirements.
- The developed program conforms to the system design specifications.
- Functional testing ensures that the requirements are properly implemented.
- The proper programs and data are placed into production.
- The user-defined requirement changes are properly implemented in the operational system.

10. **Ease-of-use test factor**

- The usability specifications for the application system are defined.
- The system design attempts to optimize the usability of the implemented requirements.
- The programs conform to the design in order to optimize ease of use.
- The interrelationship between the manual and automated system is tested to ensure the application is easy to use.
- The usability instructions are properly prepared and disseminated to the appropriate individuals.
- As the system is maintained, ease of use is preserved.

11. **Maintainable test factor**
    - The desired level of maintainability of the system is specified.
    - The design is developed to achieve the desired level of maintainability.
    - The programs are coded and designed to achieve the desired level of maintainability.
    - The system is inspected to ensure that it is prepared to be maintainable.
    - The application system documentation is complete.
    - Maintainability is preserved as the system is updated.

12. **Portable test factor**
    - The portability in moving the application system from one piece of hardware or software to another is determined.
    - The design is prepared to achieve the desired level of portability.
    - The programs are designed and implemented to conform with the portability design.
    - The implemented system is subjected to a disaster test to ensure that it is portable.
    - The documentation is complete to facilitate portability.
    - Portability is preserved as the system is maintained.

13. **Coupling test factor**
    - The interface between the system being developed and other related systems is defined.
    - The design takes into account the interface requirements.
    - The designed programs conform to the interface design specifications.
    - Functional and regression testing are performed to ensure that the interface between systems functions properly.
    - The interface between systems is coordinated prior to the new system being placed into production.
    - The interface between systems is preserved during the systems maintenance process.

14. **Performance test factor**
    - The performance criteria are established.
    - The design specifications are prepared to ensure that the desired level of performance is achieved.
    - The programs are designed and implemented to achieve the performance criteria.
    - The system is compliance tested to ensure that the desired performance levels are achieved.
    - The performance is monitored during the installation phase.
    - The desired level of performance is preserved during systems maintenance.

15. **Ease-of-operation test factor**
    - The operational needs are incorporated into the system design.
    - The operational needs are communicated to operations.

- The needed operating procedures are developed.
- The operational procedures are tested to ensure they achieve the desired level of operational usability.
- The operating procedures are implemented during the installation phase.
- The changes to the operational system are reflected in changes to operating procedures.

The test team should undertake an investigation of the system characteristics in order to evaluate the potential magnitude of the risk. The types of things that the testers should do during that investigation are as follows:

1. **Define what meeting project objectives means.** These are the objectives to be accomplished by the project team.

2. **Understand the core business areas and processes.** All information systems are not created equal. Systems that support mission-critical business processes are clearly more important than systems that support mission support functions (usually administrative), although these, too, are necessary functions. A focus on core business areas and processes is essential to the task of assessing the impact of the problem on the enterprise and for establishing the priorities for the program.

3. **Assess the severity of potential failures.** This must be done for each core business area and its associated processes.

4. **Identify the components for this system:**
   - Links to core business areas or processes
   - Platforms, languages, and database management systems
   - Operating system software and utilities
   - Telecommunications
   - Internal and external interfaces
   - Owners
   - Availability and adequacy of source code and associated documentation

5. **Identify, prioritize, and estimate needed test resources.** Achieving test objectives will require significant investment in two vital resources: money and people. Accordingly, the organization will have to make informed choices about information technology priorities by assessing the costs, benefits, and risks of competing projects. In some instances, it may be necessary to defer or cancel new system development efforts and reprogram the freed resources to achieve and test this project.

6. **Develop validation strategies and testing plans for all converted or replaced systems and their components; identify and acquire automated test tools and write test scripts.** The testing and validation of the converted or replaced systems require a phased approach. As you recall, virtually all testing tactics include four phases. Consider the specific objectives for:
   - *Phase 1, unit testing.* Focuses on functional and compliance testing of a single application or software module.

- *Phase 2, integration testing.* Test the integration of related software modules and applications.
- *Phase 3, system testing.* Test all integrated components of an information system.
- *Phase 4, acceptance testing.* Test the information system with live operational data.

Regardless of the selected validation and testing strategy, the scope of the testing and validation effort will require careful planning and use of automated tools, including test case analyzers and test data libraries.

7. **Define requirements for the test facility.** Organizations may have to acquire an adequate testing environment to avoid potential contamination or interference with the operation of production systems.

8. **Identify and acquire tools.** Organizations should identify and acquire tools to facilitate the conversion and testing processes.

9. **Address implementation schedule issues.** Include:
   - Identification and selection of conversion facilities
   - Time needed to put converted systems into production
   - The conversion of backup and archival data

10. **Address interface and data exchange issues.** Include:
    - Development of a model showing the internal and external dependency links among enterprise core business areas, processes, and information systems
    - Notification of all outside data exchange entities
    - Data bridges and filters
    - Contingency plans if no data is received from an external source
    - Validation process for incoming external data
    - Contingency plans for invalid data

11. **Evaluate contingency plans for this system and activities.** These should be realistic contingency plans, including the development and activation of manual or contract procedures, to ensure the continuity of core business processes.

12. **Identify vulnerable parts of the system and processes operating outside the information resource management area.** Include telephone and network switching equipment and building infrastructure systems. Develop a separate plan for their testing.

Task 3: Build the Test Plan

The development of an effective test plan involves the four subtasks described in the following subsections.

Subtask 1: Set Test Objectives

To establish test objectives, the objectives of conducting testing will have been agreed on, and so can be viewed as strategic in nature. These objectives must be measurable, and the means for measuring defined; in addition, the objectives must be prioritized.

Testing objectives should restate the project objectives from the project plan. In fact, the test plan objectives should determine whether those project plan objectives have been achieved. If the project plan does not have clearly stated objectives, then the testers must develop their own. In that case, testers must have them confirmed as the project objectives by the project team. The testers can:

- Set objectives to minimize the project risks.
- Brainstorm to identify project objectives.
- Relate objectives to the testing policy, if established.

Normally, 10 or fewer test objectives is a good number; too many scatters the testers' focus.

Test Objectives Using Work Paper 8.1

Work Paper 8.1 is designed for documenting test objectives. To complete the Work Paper:

- Itemize the objectives so that they can be referred to by a number.
- Write the test objectives in a measurable statement, to focus testers on accomplishing the objective.
- Assign a priority to the objectives as follows:
  - **High:** The most important objectives to be accomplished during testing
  - **Average:** Objectives to be accomplished only after the high-priority test objectives have been accomplished
  - **Low:** The least important of the test objectives

NOTE Establish priorities so that approximately one-third are high, one-third are average, and one-third are low.

- Define the completion criteria for each objective. This should state quantitatively how the testers will determine whether the objective has been accomplished. The more specific the criteria, the easier it will be for the testers to follow through.

Work Paper 8.1 also provides a general objective for a project, stating that all dates are compliant with the completion criteria and that all software will function correctly when dates are entered. This example shows how the form is to be used. In practice, there would probably be several objectives of this type: One might be in-house developed software, another purchased software or contracted software, and so on.

During test plan development and reporting, there will be constant decomposition from test objectives down to test transaction; then, test transaction results will be consolidated back up through the test objectives.

When the test objectives are completed, the testers should review the materials in Chapters 1 to 5 to gain insight from reviewing awareness criteria, risks, areas to address, and so forth. This will help in determining whether the test objectives are complete and to assign a priority to specific test objectives.

Subtask 2: Develop Test Matrix

The test matrix is the key component of the test plan. On one side it lists what is to be tested; on the other, it indicates which test is to be performed, or "how" software will be tested. Between the two dimensions of the matrix are the tests applicable to the software; for example, one test may test more than one software module. The test matrix is also a test "proof." It proves that each testable function has at least one test, and that each test is designed to test a specific function.

An example of a test matrix is illustrated in Table 8.1. This shows four functions in a payroll system, with three tests to validate the functions. Since payroll is a batch system, batched test data is used with various dates, the parallel test is run when posting to the general ledger, and all changes are verified through a code inspection. The check marks in the matrix indicate which test is applicable to which software module.

The test matrix can be prepared using the following work papers. (Note: The modules that contain the function(s) to be tested will be identified.)

Individual Software Module(s) Using Work Paper 8.2

Work Paper 8.2 lists the software modules that will be tested. The work paper contains the name of the module, a brief description of the module, and the criteria that will be used to evaluate the module's correct processing. The Number column can be used to sequentially identify the modules; or, if your organization has a numbering system, it would be the number that your software library uses to identify the module.

> **NOTE** For the purpose of documenting software modules, include three categories of software modules, as follows:
>
> 1. Modules written by the central information technology (IT) development group.
>
> 2. Modules written by noninformation services department personnel.
>
> 3. Software capabilities embedded in hardware chips.

Table 8.1 Test Matrix Example

SOFTWARE FUNCTION	TEST DECK TRANSACTION	TEST PARALLEL TEST	CODE INSPECTION
FICA Calculation	√		√
Gross Pay	√		√
Tax Deduction	√		√
General Ledger Charges		√	√

Structural Attributes Using Work Paper 8.3

Work Paper 8.3 will identify the structural attributes of software that may be impacted and thus require testing. The structural attributes can be those described earlier, such as maintainability, reliability, efficiency, usability, and so on, or specific processing concerns regarding how changes can affect operating performance of the software.

Structural attributes also include the impact the processing of one software system has on another software system, for example, input from another organization to software processing in your organization, or information transmitted by your organization to another. This is classified as a structural attribute because the structure of one system may be incompatible with the structure of another.

Work Paper 8.3 relates to response time. The structural concern would be that the software processing would negatively impact performance. The concern is defined in the Description column and the criteria to evaluate the structural concern are indicated in the Evaluation Criteria column.

Batch Tests Using Work Paper 8.4

Batch tests are high-level tests. They must be composed during the execution phase in specific test transactions. For example, a test identified at the test plan level might "validate that all dating in a software module is correct." During execution, each date-related instruction in a software module would require a test transaction. (It is not necessary for test descriptions at the test planning level to be that detailed.)

Work Paper 8.4 describes each batch test to perform during testing. Using our previous example of the testing-related processing date, that task can be described in the test plan and related to all of the software modules in which that test will occur. However, during execution, the test data for each module that executes that test will be a different transaction. In order to complete Work Paper 8.4, the software project must be identified, unless it is applicable to *all* software projects, in which case the word "all" should be used to describe the software project.

Each test should be named and numbered. In our example, it might be called Date Compliance test and given a unique number. Numbering is important both to control tests and to roll test results back to the high-level test described in the test plan.

Figure 8.5 shows a completed test document for a hypothetical test of data validation routines. Although all the detail is not yet known because the data validation routines have not been specified at this point, there is enough information to enable a group to prepare the data validation routines.

Conceptual Test Script for On-Line System Test Using Work Paper 8.5

Work Paper 8.5 serves approximately the same purpose for on-line systems as Work Paper 8.4 does for batch systems. Work Paper 8.4 is a high-level description of the test script, not the specific transaction that will be entered during on-line testing. For the test planning perspective, it is unimportant whether the individual items will be manually prepared, or generated and controlled using a software tool.

Software Project: <u>Payroll Application</u>

Name of Test: Validate Input   **Test No. 1**

Test Objective

Exercise data validation routines.

Test Input

Prepare the following types of input data for each input field:

- valid data
- invalid data
- range of codes
- validation of legitimate values and tables

Test Procedures

Create input transactions that contain the conditions described in test input.
Run the entire test deck until all conditions are correctly processed.

Test Output

Reject all invalid conditions and accept all valid conditions.

Test Controls

Run the entire test run each time the test is conducted. Rerun the test until all
specified output criteria have been achieved.

Software or Structure Attribute Tested

The data validation function.

Figure 8.5   Conducting batch tests.

The example given for entering a batch test to validate date-related processing is also
appropriate for test scripts. The primary differences are the sequence in which the
events must occur and the source or location of the origin of the on-line event.

Figure 8.6 shows an example of developing test scripts for the data validation function of an audit-entry software project. It lists two scripting events, the evaluation criteria, and comments that would be helpful in developing these tests.

Verification Tests Using Work Paper 8.6

Verification is a static test performed on a document developed by the team responsible
for creating software. Generally, for large complex documents, the verification process

is a review; for smaller documents, the verification process comprises inspections. Other verification methods include:

- Static analyzers incorporated into the compilers
- Independent static analyzers
- Walkthroughs
- Confirmation in which a third party attests to the accuracy of the document

Verification tests normally relate to a specific software project, but because of the extensiveness of testing, a single verification test may be applicable to many software projects. For example, it may be determined that each source code listing that is changed will be inspected prior to unit test. In this case, the software project will be indicated as "all."

Software/Test Matrix Using Work Paper 8.7

The objective of this matrix is to illustrate that the tests validate and verify all of the software modules, including the structural attributes to those models (Work Paper 8.7). The matrix also illustrates which tests exercise which software modules. The

---

Software Project: _Order Entry_

Software Module: Test No.: 2

SEQUENCE	SOURCE	SCRIPT EVENT	EVALUATION CRITERIA	COMMENTS
1	Data Entry Clerk	The data entry clerk enters an invalid customer order.	The customer number should be rejected as invalid.	A help routine would help to locate the proper customer number.
2	Data Entry Clerk	The data entry clerk enters a correct order into the system for one or more invalid company products.	The system should, first, confirm that the information entered is valid and for legitimate values, and, second, ask the data entry clerk to verify that all the information has been entered correctly.	This tests the entry of a valid order through the data validation routines.

Figure 8.6   Example of a test script for a data validation function.

information to complete this matrix has already been recorded in Work Papers 8.2 through 8.6.

The vertical axis of the matrix lists the software modules and structural attributes from Work Papers 8.2 and 8.3. The horizontal axis lists the tests indicated on Work Papers 8.4, 8.5, and 8.6. The intersection of the vertical and horizontal axes indicates whether the test exercises the software module/structural attributes listed. This can be indicated by a check mark or via a reference to a more detailed description that relates to the specific test and software module.

Subtask 3: Define Test Administration

The administrative component of the test plan identifies the schedule, milestones, and resources needed to execute the test plan as illustrated in the test matrix. This cannot be undertaken until the technical part (i.e., the test matrix) has been completed.

Prior to developing the test plan, the test team has to be organized. This initial test team is responsible for developing the test plan and then defining the administrative resources needed to complete the plan. Thus, part of the plan will be executed as the plan is being developed; that part is the creation of the test plan, which itself consumes resources.

The test plan, like the implementation plan, is a dynamic document, meaning it changes as the implementation plan changes and the test plan is being executed. The test plan must be viewed as a "contract" in which any modifications must be incorporated.

Work Papers 8.8 through 8.10 are provided to develop and document the administrative component of the test plan. The instructions to complete these workpapers follow.

Test Plan General Information
Using Work Paper 8.8

Work Paper 8.8 is designed to provide background and reference data on testing. Because of the scope of this testing, in many organizations this background information will be necessary to acquaint testers with the project. It is recommended that, along with this background data, testers be required to read all or parts of Chapters 1 through 4.

1: Define Test Milestones
Using Work Paper 8.9

Work Paper 8.8 is designed to indicate the start and completion date of each test. These tests are derived from the matrix in Work Papers 8.4, 8.5, and 8.6. The start/completion milestones in Work Paper 8.9 are listed as numbers. If you prefer, these may be days or dates. For example, milestone 1 could just be week 1 or day 1, or November 18. The tests from the test matrix are then listed in this work paper in the Test column; a start and completion milestone are checked for each test.

NOTE Organizations that have scheduling software should use that in lieu of this work paper. Both the work paper and the scheduling software should include the person responsible for performing that test as the assignment becomes known.

2: Define Checkpoint Administration Using Work Paper 8.10

Work Paper 8.10 should be defined for each test milestone. This workpaper, which is completed for each milestone, can be used to schedule work as well as to monitor its status. Work Paper 8.10 also covers the administrative aspects associated with each testing milestone. If the test plan calls for a different test at six milestones, six different workpapers must be prepared. Because budgeting information should be summarized, a total budget figure for testing is not identified in the administrative part of the plan.

Test administration contains all of the attributes associated with any other project. Test administration is, in fact, project management; the project is testing. Administration involves identifying what is to be tested, who will test it, when it will be tested, when it is to be completed, the budget and resources needed for testing, any training the testers need, and the materials and other support for conducting testing.

Subtask 4: Write the Test Plan

The test plan may be as formal or informal a document as the organization's culture dictates. When a test team has completed Work Papers 8.1 through 8.10, they have completed the test plan. The test plan can either be the 10 work papers or the information on those work papers transcribed to a more formal test plan. Generally, if the test team is small, the work papers are more than adequate. As the test team grows in size, it is generally better to formalize the test plan.

A four-part test plan standard is provided as Table 8.2. It is a restatement and slight clarification of the information contained on the 11 test planning work papers provided in this chapter. Note this standard is also included in test documentation in Chapter 26.

Table 8.2   System Test Plan Standard

1. General Information

    1.1   Summary. Summarize the functions of the software and the tests to be performed.

    1.2   Environment and pretest background. Summarize the history of the project. Identify the user organization and computer center where the testing will be performed. Describe any prior testing and note results that may affect this testing.

    1.3   Test objectives. State the objectives to accomplish by testing.

Table 8.2   *(Continued)*

1.4   Expected defect rates. State the estimated number of defects for software of this type.

1.5   References. List applicable references, such as:
   a.   Project request authorization.
   b.   Previously published documents on the project.
   c.   Documentation concerning related projects.

2.   Plan

2.1   Software description. Chart and briefly describe the inputs, outputs, and functions of the software being tested as a frame of reference for the test descriptions.

2.2   Test team. State who is on the test team and their test assignment(s).

2.3   Milestones. List the locations, milestone events, and dates for the testing.

2.4   Budgets. List the funds allocated to test by task and checkpoint.

2.5   Testing (systems checkpoint). Identify the participating organizations and the system checkpoint where the software will be tested.

   2.5.1   Schedule (and budget). Detail schedule of dates and events for the testing at this location. Events may include familiarization, training, and data, as well as the volume and frequency of the input. Show resources allocated.

   2.5.2   Requirements. State the resource requirements, including:
      a.   Equipment. Show the expected period of use, types, and quantities of the equipment needed.
      b.   Software. List other software that will be needed to support the testing, which is not part of the software to be tested.
      c.   Personnel. List the number and skills of staff expected to be available during the test from both the user and development groups. Include any special requirements such as multishift operation or key personnel.

   2.5.3   Testing materials. List the materials needed for the test, such as:
      a.   System documentation.
      b.   Software to be tested and its medium.
      c.   Test inputs.
      d.   Test documentation.
      e.   Test tools.

   2.5.4   Test training. Describe or reference the plan for providing training to use the software being tested. Specify the types of training, personnel to be trained, and the training staff.

   2.5.5   Tests to be conducted. Reference specific tests to be conducted at this checkpoint.

(Continues)

Table 8.2   *(Continued)*

2.6   Testing (system checkpoint). Describe the plan for the second and subsequent system checkpoint where the software will be tested in a manner similar to item 2.5.

3.   Specifications and Evaluation

   3.1   Specifications

      3.1.1   Business functions. List the business functional requirement established as part of software requirements.

      3.1.2   Structural functions. List the detailed structural functions to be exercised during the overall test.

      3.1.3   Test/function relationships. List the tests to be performed on the software and relate them to the functions in item 3.1.1 and 3.1.2.

      3.1.4   Test progression. Describe the manner in which progress is made from one test to another so that the entire test cycle is completed.

   3.2   Methods and Constraints

      3.2.1   Methodology. Describe the general method or strategy of the testing.

      3.2.2   Test tools. Specify the type of test tools to be used.

      3.2.3   Extent. Indicate the extent of the testing, such as total or partial. Include any rationale for partial testing.

      3.2.4   Data recording. Discuss the method used to record the test results and other information about the testing.

      3.2.5   Constraints. Indicate anticipated limitations on the test caused by conditions such as interfaces, equipment, personnel, databases.

   3.3   Evaluation

      3.3.1   Criteria. Describe the rules to be used to evaluate test results, such as range of data values, combinations of input types, and maximum number of allowable interrupts or halts.

      3.3.2   Data reduction. Describe the techniques to be used for manipulating the test data into a form suitable for evaluation, such as manual or automated methods, to enable comparison of the results that should be produced to those that are produced.

4.   Test Descriptions

   4.1   Test (identify). Describe the test to be performed (format will vary for on-line test script).

      4.1.1   Control. Describe the test control, such as manual, semiautomatic, or automatic insertion of inputs, sequencing of operations, and recording of results.

Table 8.2   *(Continued)*

        4.1.2   Inputs. Describe the input data and input commands used during the test.

        4.1.3   Outputs. Describe the output data expected as a result of the test and any intermediate messages that may be produced.

        4.1.4   Procedures. Specify the step-by-step procedures to accomplish the test. Include test setup, initialization, steps, and termination.

    4.2   Test (identify). Describe the second and subsequent tests in a manner similar to that used in item 4.1.

Task 4: Inspect the Test Plan

This task describes how to inspect the corrected software prior to its execution. This process is used, first, because it is more effective in identifying defects than validation methods; and second, it is much more economical to remove the defects at the inspection stage than to wait until unit or system testing. This task describes the inspection process, including the role and training of the inspectors, and the step-by-step procedures to complete the process.

The implementation/rework step of the project team involves modifying software and supporting documentation to make it compliant. Thereafter, the software needs to be tested. However, as already noted, identifying defects in dynamic testing is more costly and time-consuming than to do so by performing a static inspection of the changed products or deliverables.

Inspection then is a process by which completed but untested products are evaluated as to whether the specified changes were installed correctly. To accomplish this, inspectors examine the unchanged product, the change specifications, and the changed product to determine the outcome. They look for three types of defects: errors, meaning the change has not been made correctly; missing, meaning something should have been changed but was not changed; and extra, meaning something not intended was changed or added.

The inspection team reviews the product after each inspector has reviewed it individually. The team then reaches a consensus on the errors, missing, and extra defects. The author (the person implementing the project change) is given those defect descriptions so that the product can be changed prior to dynamic testing. After the changes are made, they are reinspected to verify correctness; then dynamic testing can commence. The purpose of inspections is twofold: to conduct an examination by peers, which normally improves the quality of work because the synergy of a team is applied to the solution; and to remove defects during inspection.

Inspection Concerns

The concerns regarding the project inspection process are basically the same associated with any inspection process. They are as follows:

Inspections may be perceived to delay the start of testing. Because inspection is a process that occurs after a product is complete, but before testing, it does in fact impose a delay to dynamic testing. Therefore, many people have trouble acknowledging that the inspection process will ultimately reduce implementation time. But in practice, the time required for dynamic testing is reduced when the inspection process is used. Thus, the total time is reduced.

There is resistance to accepting the inspection role. There are two drawbacks to becoming an inspector. The first is time. An inspector loses time on his or her own work assignments. The second is that inspectors are often perceived as criticizing their peers. Management must provide inspectors with the time they need to perform inspections; and they must encourage a synergistic team environment in which inspectors are members offering suggestions, as opposed to being critics.

Space may be difficult to obtain for conducting inspections. Each deliverable is inspected individually by a team; therefore meeting space is needed in which to conduct inspections. Most organizations have limited meeting space, so this need may be difficult to fulfill. Some organizations use cafeteria space during off hours; or if the group is small enough, they can meet in someone's work area. However, it is important to hold meetings in an environment that does not impact others' work.

Change implementors may resent having their work inspected prior to test. Traditional software implementation methods have encouraged sloppy developments, which rely on testing to identify and correct problems. Thus, people instituting changes may resist having their products inspected prior to having the opportunity to identify and correct the problems themselves. The solution is to encourage team synergism with the goal of developing optimal solutions, not criticizing the work of individuals.

Inspection results may impact individual performance appraisal. The results of an inspection in a sense are also a documented list of a person's defects, which can result in a negative performance appraisal. Management must emphasize that performance appraisals will be based on the final product, not an interim defect list.

Product/Deliverables to Inspect

Each software project team determines the products to be inspected, unless specific inspections are mandated by the project plan. Consider inspecting the following products:

- Project requirements specifications
- Software rework/maintenance documents
- Updated technical documentation
- Changed source code
- Test plans
- User documentation (including on-line help)

Formal Inspection Roles

The selection of the inspectors is critical to the effectiveness of the process. It is important to include appropriate personnel from all impacted functional areas and to carefully assign the predominant roles and responsibilities (project, operations, external testing, etc.). There should never be fewer than three, not more than five, inspection participants.

Each role must be filled on the inspection team, although one person may take on more than one role. The following subsections outline the participants and identify their roles and responsibilities in the inspection process:

Moderator

The moderator is trained to coordinate, lead, and control the inspection process, and oversee any necessary follow-up. It is recommended that the moderator *not* be a member of the project team. Specifically, the moderator:

1. Organizes the inspection by selecting the participants; verifying the distribution of the inspection materials; and scheduling the overview, inspection, and required follow-up sessions.

2. Leads the inspection process; ensures that all participants are prepared; encourages participation; maintains focus on finding defects; controls flow and direction; and maintains objectivity.

3. Controls the inspection by enforcing adherence to the entry and exit criteria; seeks consensus on defects; makes the final decision on disagreements; directs the recording and categorizing of defects; summarizes inspection results; and limits inspections to one to two hours.

4. Ensures the author completes the follow-up tasks.

5. Completes activities listed in moderator checklist (reference Work Paper 8.11).

   - Determine if the product is ready for inspection, based on entry criteria for the type of inspections to be conducted.
   - Select inspectors and assign the roles of reader and recorder.
   - Estimate inspection preparation time (e.g., 20 pages of written documentation per two hours of inspections).
   - Schedule the inspection meeting and send inspection meeting notices (reference Work Paper 8.14) to participants.
   - Determine if overview is required (e.g., if the product is lengthy or complex) with author and project leader.
   - Oversee the distribution of the inspection material, including the meeting notice.

Reader

The reader is responsible for setting the pace of the inspection. He or she does this by paraphrasing or reading the product being inspected. Specifically, the reader:

- Is not also the moderator or author
- Has a thorough familiarity with the material to be inspected
- Objectively presents the product
- Paraphrases or reads the product material line by line or paragraph by paragraph, pacing for clarity and comprehension

Recorder

The recorder is responsible for listing defects and summarizing the inspection results. He or she must have ample time to note each defect, since this is the only information that the author will have to find and correct the defect. The recorder should avoid using abbreviations or shorthand that may not be understood by other team members. Specifically, the recorder:

- May also be the moderator, but cannot be the reader or the author
- Records every defect found
- Presents the defect list for consensus by all participants in the inspection
- Classifies the defects as directed by the inspectors by type, class, and severity based on predetermined criteria

Author

The author is the originator of the product being inspected. Specifically, the author:

- May also act as an inspector during the inspection meeting
- Determines when the product is ready for inspection
- Assists the moderator in selecting the participants for the inspection team
- Meets all entry criteria outlined in the appropriate inspection package cover sheet
- Provides an overview of the material prior to the inspection for clarification if requested
- Clarifies inspection material during the process, if requested
- Corrects the defects and presents finished rework to the moderator for sign-off
- Initiates the inspection process by informing the moderator, who has been appointed by project management, that the product is ready for inspection
- Forwards all materials required for the inspection as indicated in the entry criteria to the moderator

Inspectors

The inspectors should be trained staff who can effectively contribute to meeting objectives of the inspection. The moderator, reader, and recorder may also be inspectors. Specifically, inspectors do the following:

- Must prepare for the inspection by carefully reviewing and understanding the material.
- Maintain objectivity toward the product.

- Review the product.
- Record all preparation time.
- Present potential defects and problems encountered before and during the inspection meeting.

Formal Inspection Defect Classification

The classification of defects provides meaningful data for their analysis and gives the opportunity for identifying and removing their cause. This results in overall cost savings and improved product quality.

Each defect should be classified by origin, type, class, and severity, as defined here.

- **Origin.** Indicates where the defect was generated (e.g., requirements, design, code, etc.).
- **Type.** Indicates the cause of the defect. For example, code defects could be errors in procedural logic, or code that does not satisfy requirements or deviates from standards.
- **Class.** Indicates whether the defect was missing, wrong, or extra. Missing means an absence of a requirement; wrong means the requirement was not met; extra means the requirement was not requested but was present in the product.
- **Severity.** There are two severity levels: major, those that either interrupt system operation or cause an incorrect result; and minor, all those that are not major.

Inspection Procedures

The formal inspection process is segmented into the following five subtasks, each of which is distinctive and essential to the successful outcome of the overall process:

1. Planning and organizing
2. Overview session (optional)
3. Individual preparation
4. Inspection meeting
5. Rework and follow-up

1. Planning and Organizing

The planning step defines the participants' roles and defines how defects will be classified. It also initiates, organizes, and schedules the inspection.

2. Overview Session

This task is optional, but recommended. Its purpose is to acquaint all inspectors with the product to be inspected and to minimize individual preparation time. This task is especially important if the product is lengthy, complex, or new; if the inspection process is new; or if the participants are new to the inspection process. Here is the breakdown of the participant's responsibilities:

Moderator. Requests the authority to present an overview of the product.

Author. Organizes, schedules, and presents the overview.

Inspector. Attends the overview session to gain an understanding of the product, not to find defects.

This task also is to allow the author to give a minipresentation regarding his or her product. Recommended guidelines for the author are to:

- Be brief.
- Give a broad overview of specifications and product.
- Highlight anything unique to the product or task.
- Give the software developer/maintainer's concerns about quality.
- Ask inspector to concentrate on areas of concern.
- Solicit inspector's help.

3. Individual Preparation

The purpose of this task is to allot time for each inspection participant to acquire a thorough understanding of the product to be inspected and identify any defects found (per exit criteria).

The inspectors' responsibilities are to:

- Familiarize themselves with the inspection material.
- Record all defects found and time spent on the inspection preparation report (reference Work Paper 8.12) and inspection defect list (reference Work Paper 8.13).

Each inspector performs a "desk review" of the material. Recommended guidelines in conducting this individual review are that:

- It should be performed in one continuous time span.
- The inspector must disregard style of the work product; for example, the way a programmer chooses to build a report.
- The emphasis should be on meeting information systems standards and assuring that output meets the product specification.
- Every defect must be identified.

The activities involved in performing an individual inspection are to:

- Review input product (product specification).
- Review output product (author's work).
- Identify each input specification by a unique identifier on the input product document.
- Trace specifications one by one to output product, essentially repeating the author's process.
- Cross-reference output to input specification (block out output that relates to the input specification).

- Continue this process until all specifications have been traced and all output has been referenced; make comments on input and output documents.

During the individual inspection, each inspector records defects, questions, and concerns to be addressed during the inspection meeting. Recommended guidelines for recording these items are that:

- Every defect should be recorded, no matter how small.

- Areas of concern regarding correctness of input specifications should be noted as issues to discuss.

- Significant inefficiencies in output product should be noted as issues to discuss.

- Any output that does not have an input specification should be marked as a defect (i.e., extra).

4. Inspection Meeting

The purpose of the inspection meeting is to find defects in the product, not to correct those defects or suggest alternatives for correction. A notice is sent to all participants notifying them of the meeting (see Work Paper 8.14). Listed below are the responsibilities of the meeting participants, in the sequence they occur, followed by the actions that must be taken during each inspection meeting.

The moderator's responsibilities at the beginning of the inspection include the following:

- Introduce participants and identifies roles.

- Restate objective of the inspection.

- Verify inspectors' readiness by checking time spent in preparation and whether all material was reviewed prior to the meeting (as indicated on each inspector's inspection preparation report). If any of the participants are not prepared, the moderator must decide whether to continue with the inspection or reschedule it to allow for further preparation.

The reader's responsibilities include:

- Paraphrase or read the material.

The inspector's responsibilities include:

- State potential defects found, discuss the defect, and reach a consensus as to whether the defect actually exists.

The recorder's responsibilities include:

- Record defects found, by origin, type, class, and severity, on the inspection defect list (reference Work Paper 8.9).

- Classify each defect found, with concurrence from all inspectors.

- Prepare the inspection defect summary (reference Work Paper 8.15).

The author's responsibilities include:

- Clarify the product, when requested.

The moderator's responsibilities at the end of the inspection include:

- Call the inspection to an end if a number of defects are found early, indicating that the product is not ready for inspection. The author then is responsible for reinitiating an inspection, through the moderator, once the product is ready.

- Determine the disposition of the inspection and any follow-up required.

- Approve the inspection defect list and the inspection summary, then forward a copy to the author and project quality assurance.

- Sign off on the inspection certification report (reference Work Paper 8.16) if no defects were found.

The moderator determines that all of the necessary prerequisites to the meeting have been met:

- Determine whether all inspectors are present.

- Ensure that meeting starts on time.

- Determine that all inspectors have fully performed their preparatory work, by asking each inspector how much time he or she spent preparing for the inspection. The inspector should have previously recorded this information on the inspection preparation log.

The reader either reads through or paraphrases the (output) product description for the other inspectors:

- All commentary should be paraphrased.

- Any product segment containing a defect (noted by the reader) should be read word for word.

- All complex, difficult, or important parts of the product documentation should be read word for word.

Rules-of-thumb for reading:

- Reading or paraphrasing should not exceed one minute.

- Better to paraphrase too much than read word for word.

- Have other inspectors give insight into effectiveness of reader (e.g., reading word for word too much, paraphrasing too much, covering too much at one time, and so forth).

- Be prepared to stop reading if interrupted (encourage inspectors to interrupt to discuss defects).

NOTE Readers will spend much more time in preparation than the other inspectors because they must be much more familiar with the output product than the other inspectors.

The recorder lists and classifies defects:

- Whenever the reader stops reading or paraphrasing, the moderator interjects and asks if any defects have been noted.
- Any inspector can cite a potential defect.
- All inspectors are encouraged by the moderator to discuss the defect.
- The moderator cuts off discussion once he or she has determined that what is being discussed is or is not a defect. If the moderator determines it to be a defect, he or she instructs the recorder to add the defect to the inspection defect list.
- The recorder lists the defect by location, narrative description, and classification. Table 8.3 details the classification of defects.

During this action it is determined whether the product passes inspection, needs minor rework, or will have to be reinspected. The dispositions are as follows:

- Moderator certification.
- Meets specifications/standards.
- No rework required.
- Moderator reexamination.
- Does not meet specs/standards.
- Limited rework required.
- Reinspection.
- Does not meet specs/standards.
- Rework required.
- The product must be defect-free to be certified at this point.
- The frequency and type of defects will determine whether the product needs to be reexamined or reinspected.
- Normally reexamination occurs when there are limited minor defects or, possibly one or two major defects, depending on their importance.

Table 8.3 Classification of Defects

CATEGORY	SEVERITY
(M) Missing—The defect is the result of material that should be in the component but isn't.	(MAJ) Major—A defect that will cause an observable product failure or departure from requirements.
(W) Wrong—The material that is and should be present contains an error.	(MIN) Minor—A defect that will not cause a failure in execution of the product.
(E) Extra—The defect is material that should not be included in the component and exceeds the specifications.	

- A significant number of major errors or combination of major and minor errors calls for reinspection.
- Moderator completes inspection report, indicating the inspection result.
- The inspection report is given to the author with a copy of the inspection defect list.
- The product cannot go to the next developmental task until the moderator has certified the product as meeting specifications and requiring no more rework.

5. Rework and Follow-up

The purpose of this task is to complete required rework, obtain a sign-off, or initiate a reinspection and capture inspection results. Listed next are the participants' responsibilities in order of occurrence.

The author's responsibilities include the following:

- Complete all rework to correct defects found during the inspection.
- Reinitiate the inspection process if the inspection ended with a disposition of major rework required.
- Contact the moderator to approve the rework if the inspection ended with a disposition of minor rework required.

The moderator's responsibilities include:

- Review all rework completed and sign off on the inspection report when all defects have been corrected.

The recorder's responsibilities include:

- Summarize defect data and ensure its entry into an inspection defect database.

Inspection Guidelines

These guidelines are given to help make inspections effective:

- Trace each defect to its correction in the product.
- If any defects have not been corrected, request additional rework.
- If defects have been corrected, certify the product.

Check Procedures

Work Paper 8.17 contains the items to evaluate to determine the accuracy and completeness of performing this step. The questions are designed so that a Yes response is desirable; and a No response requires evaluation as to whether that item should be addressed. If the item is not applicable, a check mark should be placed in the N/A column. For No responses, a comment should be prepared; and if action is required, the results of the action should also be recorded in the Comments column.

There are two parts to performing any task. The first is to do it, called "do procedures" in this book; the second is to check it, which are the "check procedures." The do procedures approach a task positively; in other words, defining what a person must do in order to complete a job. The check procedures approach the same task negatively; in other words, they ask, "Did you do those things that you should have to perform the tasks you were assigned?" Thus, the check procedures become a series of questions that challenge whether the job has been performed correctly.

There are two types of check procedure questions. The first is a literal query. It asks whether some definitive task has been completed, such as "Was Work Paper 8.7 completed?" The second type of check procedure question is subjective; for example, whether the information contained on Work Paper 8.7 is reasonable based on the task assignment. In answering the questions for the check procedures, you should first determine whether it is a literal or subjective question. In this book, Yes responses are considered desirable and No responses undesirable; therefore, if you answer No to an item on the check procedure, you should ask yourself, "Should additional work be done on this task?"

Output

The single deliverable from this step is the test plan. It should be reviewed with appropriate members of management to determine its adequacy. Once approved, the testers' primary responsibility is to execute the test in accordance with that plan, and then report the results of the execution. Once the test plan is approved, the testers should not be held responsible for potential omissions.

Guidelines

Test planning can be one of the most challenging aspects of testing. These guidelines can help make the job a little easier.

Start early. Even though you might not have all of the details at hand, you can complete a great deal of the planning effort by starting on the general and working toward the specific. By starting early, you can also identify resource needs and plan for them before they are subsumed by other areas of the project.

Keep the test plan flexible. Make it easy to add test cases, test data, and so on. The test plan itself should be changeable, but subject to change control.

Frequently review the test plan. Other people's observations and input greatly facilitate achieving a comprehensive test plan. The test plan should be subject to quality control just like any other project deliverable.

Keep the test plan concise and readable. The test plan does not need to be large and complicated. In fact, the more concise and readable it is, the more useful it will be. Remember, the test plan is intended to be a communication document. The details should be kept in a separate reference document.

Calculate the planning effort. You can count on roughly one-third of the testing effort being spent on each of the following test activities: planning, execution, and evaluation.

Spend the time to do a complete test plan. The better the test plan, the easier it will be to execute the tests.

Summary

The test plan drives the remainder of the testing effort. Well-planned test projects tend to cost less, and get completed earlier than projects with incomplete test plans. It is not unusual to spend approximately one-third of the total test effort on planning, but that time reaps rewards during test execution and reporting which will be discussed in Steps 3 to 11 of the 11-step process.

This chapter approaches test planning from a risk oriented approach. Test objectives are designed to address the significant risks. The objectives are decomposed into test transactions. The test plan is completed when the administrative data, such as schedule and budget, are added to the written test plan.

WORK PAPER 8.1   Test Objective

Field Requirements

FIELD	INSTRUCTIONS FOR ENTERING DATA
Number	A number that uniquely identifies each test objective.
Test Objective	A specific test objective that the testers are responsible for accomplishing during their testing effort.
Test Priority	Indicate whether this objective is of high, medium, or low priority. One-third of the test objectives should fall within each of the three categories.
Completion Criteria	Define how the testers will know whether a specific test objective has been correctly completed.

Number	Test Objective	Test Priority	Completion Criteria

WORK PAPER 8.2   Software Module

Field Requirements

FIELD	INSTRUCTIONS FOR ENTERING DATA
Software Project	The name or number that uniquely identifies the project or system that will be tested for compliance.
Number	A sequential number used to uniquely identify a software module.
Software Module Name	A name or number to uniquely identify the software module that will be tested.
Description	A brief statement of the processing performed by this software module.
Evaluation Criteria	Factors that will enable the tester to know whether the results of testing are correct and complete.

Software Project: _____

Number	Software Module Name	Description	Evaluation Criteria

WORK PAPER 8.3   Structural Attribute

Field Requirements

FIELD	INSTRUCTIONS FOR ENTERING DATA
Software Project	The name or number that uniquely identifies the project or system that will be tested for compliance.
Software Module Number	The number of the software module, taken from the Number column in Work Paper 8.2.
Structural Attribute	The attribute of the structural architecture that needs to be evaluated during testing. Note that for a single software module, there may be multiple structural attributes requiring testing.
Description	A more detailed explanation of the structural attribute being tested.
Evaluation Criteria	Factors to enable the tester to know that the structural attribute does or does not work as specified.

Software Project: _____

Software Model Number	Structural Attribute	Description	Evaluation Criteria

WORK PAPER 8.4   Batch Tests

Field Requirements

FIELD	INSTRUCTIONS FOR ENTERING DATA
Software Project	The name or number that uniquely identifies the project or system that will be tested for compliance.
Name of Test	A brief description of the test (e.g., to validate input).
Test Number	A unique identifying number, usually assigned sequentially.
Test Objective	A brief statement of the test's purpose (e.g., to perform data validation routines).
Test Input	A detailed description of the input data and conditions that drive the test.
Test Procedures	The methods used to conduct the test.
Test Output	The expected results of the test.
Test Controls	How the test group ensures the test is run correctly.
Software module tested	The software module or structural attribute to be validated through the test.

Software Project: _____

Name of Test: _____   **Test No.** _____

Test Objective

Test Input

Test Procedures

Test Output

Test Controls

Software or Structure Attribute Tested

WORK PAPER 8.5   Conceptual Test Script for Online System Test

Field Requirements

FIELD	INSTRUCTIONS FOR ENTERING DATA
Software Project	The name or number that uniquely identifies the project or system that will be tested for compliance.
Software Module	The name of the software module.
Test Number	A unique identifying number, usually assigned sequentially.
Sequence	The sequence of test events.
Source	The staff responsible for entering the transaction.
Script Event	The online actions.
Evaluation Criteria	Factors used to determine that a scripted event was performed successfully.
Comments	Any additional information that would help in preparing or evaluating the online test script.

Software Project: _____

Software Module:_____ Test No. _____

Sequence	Source	Script Event	Evaluation Criteria	Comments

WORK PAPER 8.6. Verification Tests

Field Requirements

FIELD	INSTRUCTIONS FOR ENTERING DATA
Software Project	The name of the software project.
Test Number	A unique number for each verification test, usually assigned sequentially.
Verification Test	The test to be performed. (Often, this is tied to a system checkpoint development document.)
System Product	The specific document or product to be verified.
Purpose	A brief description of the purpose of the verification test.
Responsibility	The group responsible for conducting this test.
Test Point and Schedule	The time when the test will take place.

Software Project: _____

Test No.	Verification Test	System Product	Purpose	Responsibility	Test Point/ Schedule

WORK PAPER 8.7   Software/Test Matrix

Field Requirements

FIELD	INSTRUCTIONS FOR ENTERING DATA
Software Project	The name or number that uniquely identifies the project or system that will be tested for compliance.
Software Module	The name or number of the module to be tested, from Work Paper 8.2.
Test	The tests that will be conducted on the software module, from Work Paper 8.4, 8.5, and/or 8.6. The horizontal column can name the test or give the test number.
Interface Block between Software Module and Test	A simple checkmark as indicated in Table 8.1 (test matrix example) or reference information indicating the completion criteria for the test.

Software Project: _____

Tests

Software Module	1	2	3	4	5	6	7	8	9	10

WORK PAPER 8.8   Test Plan General Information

Field Requirements

FIELD	INSTRUCTIONS FOR ENTERING DATA
Software Project	The name or number that uniquely identifies the project or system that will be tested for compliance.
Summary	A one- or two-paragraph overview of what is to be tested and how the testing will be performed.
Pretest Background	Summary of any previous test experiences that might prove helpful with testing.The assumption is, if there were problems in the past, they will probably continue; however, if there were few problems with test tools, the test team can expect to use those tools effectively.
Test Environment	The computer center or facilities used to test the application. In a single computer center installation, this subsection is minimal. If the software is used in multiple installations, the test environments may need to be described extensively.
Test Constraints	Certain types of testing may not be practical or possible during testing. For example, in banking systems in which the software ties into the Fed Wire system, it is not possible to test software with that facility. In other cases, the software cannot yet interface directly with production databases, and therefore the test cannot provide assurance that some of those interfaces work. List all known constraints.
References	Any documents, policies, procedures, or regulations applicable to the software being tested or the test procedures. It is also advisable to provide a brief description of why the reference is being given and how it might be used during the testing process.
When to stop testing	What type of test results or events should cause testing to be stopped and the software returned to the implementation team for more work.

Software Project:_____

Summary

Pretest Background

Test Environment

Test Constraints

References

When to stop testing

WORK PAPER 8.9   Test Milestones

Field Requirements

FIELD	INSTRUCTIONS FOR ENTERING DATA
Tests	Tests to be conducted during execution (the tests described on Work Papers 8.4, 8.5, and 8.6 and shown in matrix format in Work Paper 8.7). The vertical column can contain either or both the test number and/or name.
Start/Completion Milestone	The names to identify when tests start and stop. The milestones shown in Work Paper 8.9 are numbers 1–30, but these could be week numbers, day numbers, or specific dates such as November 18, 1999, included in the heading of the vertical columns.
Intersection between Tests and Start/ Completion Milestones	Insert a check mark in the milestone where the test starts, and a check mark in the column where the tests are to be completed.

Tests   **Start/Completion Milestones**

	1	2	3	4	5	6	7	8	9	10	11	12	13	14	15	16	17	18	19	20	21	22	23	24	25	26	27	28	29	30

WORK PAPER 8.10   Administrative Checkpoint

Field Requirements

FIELD	INSTRUCTIONS FOR ENTERING DATA
Software Project	The name or number that uniquely identifies the project or system that will be tested for compliance.
Project	The name of the project being tested.
Checkpoint for Test	The name of the systems development checkpoint at which testing occurs. Unless the test team knows which development documents have been completed, testing is extremely difficult to perform.
Schedule	The dates on which the following items need to be started and completed: • plan • train test group • obtain data • test execution • test report(s)
Budget	The test resources allocated at this milestone, including both test execution and test analysis and reporting.
Resources	The resources needed for this checkpoint, including: • equipment (computers and other hardware needed for testing) • software and test personnel (staff to be involved in this milestone test, designated by name or job function)
Testing Materials	Materials needed by the test team to perform the test at this checkpoint, including: • system documentation (specific products and documents needed to perform the test at this point) • software to be tested (names of the programs and subsystems to be tested at this point) • test input (files or data used for test purposes) • test documentation (any test documents needed to conduct a test at this point) • test tools (software or other test tools needed to conduct the test at this point) *Note:* Not all these materials are needed for every test.
Test Training	It is essential that the test team be taught how to perform testing. They may need specific training in the use of test tools and test materials, the performance of specific tests, and the analysis of test results.

(Continues)

WORK PAPER 8.10 *(Continued)*

Software Project: _____

Test Milestone Number: _____

	Start	Finish
Schedule: Test Plan: _____		
Tester Training: _____		
Obtaining Data: _____		
Execution: _____		
Report: _____		

Budget:
_____

Resources

Equipment:

Support Personnel:

Test Personnel:
_____

Testing Materials

Project Documentation:

Software to be tested:

Test Input:

Test Documentation:

Test Tools:
_____

Test Training

_____

WORK PAPER 8.11   Moderator Checklist

Field Requirements

FIELD	INSTRUCTIONS FOR ENTERING DATA
Items to Be Completed by Moderator During the Inspection	Eleven items that the moderator should complete during execution of the inspection process, listed in the sequence in which they should be performed. The chapter text explains these tasks.

_____ Check that entry criteria (inspection package cover sheet) have been met.

_____ Meet with author and team leader to select qualified inspection participants and assign roles.

_____ Determine need for an overview session.

_____ Schedule inspection meeting; complete inspection meeting notice.

_____ Gather materials from author, and distribute to inspection participants.

_____ Talk with inspectors to assure preparation time.

_____ Complete self-preparation of material for inspection.

_____ Conduct inspection meeting.

_____ Ensure completion and distribution of inspection defect list and inspection summary.

_____ Verify conditional completion (moderator review or reinspection).

_____ Complete inspector certification report.

WORK PAPER 8.12   Inspection Preparation Report

Field Requirements

FIELD	INSTRUCTIONS FOR ENTERING DATA
Project Name	The name of the project in which an interim deliverable is being inspected.
Date	The date on which this workpaper is completed.
Name of Item Being Inspected	The number or name by which the item being inspected is known.
Item Version Identification	The version number, if more than one version of the item is being inspected.
Material Size	The size of the item being inspected. Code is frequently described as number of lines of executable code. Written documentation is frequently described as number of pages.
Expected Preparation Time	The number of hours that an inspector should spend preparing for the inspection.
Preparation Log	Dates on which the inspector did preparation work, and the amount of time spent.
Total Preparation Time	Number of hours expended by the inspector in preparing for the inspection.
Defect List	Defects that the inspector uncovered during preparation. The list should contain the location of the defect; a description of the defect; and the exit criteria violated, meaning the condition that should have existed, but did not.

Project name: _____   Date: _____

Name of item being inspected: _____

Item version identification: _____

Material size (lines/pages): _____   Expected preparation time: _____

Preparation Log:

Date   Time Spent

_____   _____

_____   _____

Total preparation time: _____

Defect List:

Location	Defect Description	Exit Criteria Violated
_____	_____	_____
_____	_____	_____
_____	_____	_____
_____	_____	_____
_____	_____	_____
_____	_____	_____
_____	_____	_____

Note: For additional defects, use reverse side of form.

WORK PAPER 8.13   Inspection Defect List

Field Requirements

FIELD	INSTRUCTIONS FOR ENTERING DATA
Project Name	The name of the project in which an interim deliverable is being inspected.
Date	The date on which this workpaper is completed.
Name of Item Being Inspected	The number or name by which the item being Inspected is known.
Item Version Identification	The version number if more than one version of the item is being inspected.
Material Size	The size of the item being inspected. Code is frequently described as number of lines of executable code. Written documentation is frequently described as number of pages.
Expected Preparation Time	Total expected preparation time of all the inspectors.
Moderator	The name of the person leading the inspection.
Phone	The phone number of the moderator.
Inspection Type	Indicates whether an initial inspection or a reinspection of the item to verify defect correction.
Release #	A further division of version number indicating the sequence in which variations of a version are released into test.
Product Type	The type of product being inspected, such as source code.
Location	The location of a defect determined to be a defect by the formal inspection meeting.
Origin/Defect Description	The name by which the defect is known in the organization; inspectors' opinion as to where that defect originated.
Defect Phase	The phase in the development process at which the defects were uncovered.
Defect Type	A formal name assigned to the defect. This Work Paper suggests 17 different defect types. Your organization may wish to modify or expand this list.
Severity Class	Indicate whether the defect is an extra, missing, or wrong class. (See Chapter 8 for explanation of defect class.)
Severity MAJ/MIN	Indicate whether the defect is of major or minor severity. (See Chapter 8 for a discussion of the meaning of major and minor.
	Note: This form is completed by the inspector filling the reporter role during the formal inspection process.

(Continues)

WORK PAPER 8.13 *(Continued)*

Project name _____ Date: _____

Name of item being inspected: _____

Item version identification: _____

Material size (lines/pages): _____ Expected preparation time: _____

Moderator: _____ Phone: _____

Inspection type: _____ Inspection   Release #: _____

                 _____ Reinspection   Product Type: _____

Location	Origin Defect Description	Defect Phase	Defect Type	Severity	
				Class	Maj/Min
_____	_____	_____	_____	_____	_____
_____	_____	_____	_____	_____	_____
_____	_____	_____	_____	_____	_____
_____	_____	_____	_____	_____	_____
_____	_____	_____	_____	_____	_____
_____	_____	_____	_____	_____	_____
_____	_____	_____	_____	_____	_____
_____	_____	_____	_____	_____	_____
_____	_____	_____	_____	_____	_____
_____	_____	_____	_____	_____	_____
_____	_____	_____	_____	_____	_____
_____	_____	_____	_____	_____	_____

Defect Types:

CM	Comments	LO	Logic	PF	Performance
DA	Data	LR	Linkage Requirements	RQ	Requirements
DC	Documentation	MN	Maintainability	SC	Spec Clarification
EN	English Readability	MS	Messages/Return Codes	ST	Standards
IF	Interface	OT	Other	TP	Test Plan
LD	Logical Design	PD	Physical Design		

Defect Class: E   Extra   M   Missing   W   Wrong

WORK PAPER 8.14   Inspection Meeting Notice

Field Requirements

FIELD	INSTRUCTIONS FOR ENTERING DATA
Project Name	The name of the project in which an interim deliverable is being inspected.
Name of Item Inspected	The number or name by which the item being inspected is known.
Item Version Identification	Version number, if there is more than one version of the item being inspected.
Material Size	The size of the item being inspected. For example, code is frequently described by number of lines. Written documentation is frequently described in number of pages.
Anticipated Preparation Time	The number of hours that an inspector should spend preparing for the inspection.
Moderator	The name of the individual leading the inspection.
Phone	The phone number of the moderator.
Inspection Type	Indicates whether it is an initial inspection or a reinspection to verify defect correction.
This Inspection Has Been Scheduled For	The date, time, location, and expected duration of the formal inspection meeting.
The Following Individuals Are Scheduled to Participate	The names, phone numbers, and roles of the inspectors involved in the inspection.
Comments	Any guidance from moderator to the inspectors to help them to prepare for or perform the inspection. For example, the moderator may tell inspectors that a specific part of a program being inspected has a very complex logic component.

Project name: _____   Date: _____

Name of item being inspected: _____

Item version identification: _____

Material size (lines/pages): _____   Expected preparation time: _____

Moderator: _____   Phone: _____

Inspection type: _____ Inspection

            _____ Reinspection

This inspection has been scheduled for:

Date: _____

Time: _____

Location: _____

Duration: _____

(Continues)

WORK PAPER 8.14 *(Continued)*

The following Individuals are scheduled to participate:

Name	Phone	Role
_____	_____	_____
_____	_____	_____
_____	_____	_____
_____	_____	_____
_____	_____	_____

Comments

_____

_____

_____

_____

_____

_____

_____

WORK PAPER 8.15   Inspection Defect Summary

Field Requirements

FIELD	INSTRUCTIONS FOR ENTERING DATA
Project Name	The name of the project in which an interim deliverable is being inspected.
Date	The date on which this work paper is completed.
Name of Item Being Inspected	The number or name by which the item being inspected is known.
Item version identification	The version number, if more than one version of the item is being inspected.
Moderator	The name of the person leading the inspection.
Phone	The phone number of the moderator.
Inspection Type	Indicates whether it is an initial inspection or a reinspection of the item to verify defect correction.
Defect Types	The formal names and mnemonics assigned to defect type.
Minor Defect Class	A summation of minor defects by class from Work Paper 8.13.
Major Defect Class	A summation of the major defects by class for the defects recorded in Work Paper 8.13.
	Note: This work paper is prepared by the inspector filling the recorder role at the end of the formal inspection process, using Work Paper 8.13 as input.

Project name: _____ Date: _____

Name of item being inspected: _____

Item version identification: _____

Material size (lines/pages): _____

Moderator: _____ Phone: _____

Inspection type: _____ Inspection

_____ Reinspection

(Continues)

WORK PAPER 8.15   *(Continued)*

Defect Types	Minor Defect Class				Major Defect Class			
	E	M	W	Total	E	M	W	Total
CM Comments								
DA Data								
DC Documentation								
EN English Readability								
IF Interfaces								
LD Logical Design								
LO Logic								
LR Linkage Requirements								
MN Maintainability								
MS Messages/Return Codes								
OT Other								
PD Physical Design								
PF Performance								
RQ Requirements								
SC Spec Clarification								
ST Standards								
TP Test Plan								
Totals:								

WORK PAPER 8.16   Inspection Certification Report

Field Requirements

FIELD	INSTRUCTIONS FOR ENTERING DATA
Project Name	The name of the project in which an interim deliverable is being inspected.
Date	The date on which this work paper is completed.
Name of Item Being Inspected	The number or name by which the item being inspected is known.
Item Version Identification	The version number, if more than one version of the item is being inspected.
Moderator	The name of the person leading the inspection.
Inspector	The name of the inspector and the role that inspector played during the inspection process. For example, the inspector serving as moderator would go on the moderator's line.
Moderator's Signature/Date	The name of the moderator and the date on which he or she certified the item being inspected that passed the inspection process.
	Note: This inspection certification report is prepared by the inspection moderator.

Project name: _____   Date: _____

Name of item being inspected: _____

Item version identification: _____

The following people have inspected the named item and have agreed that all technical, contractual, quality, and other requirements and inspection criteria have been satisfied:

Moderator: _____

Recorder: _____

Reader: _____

Author: _____

Software Quality Representative: _____

Inspectors: _____

_____

_____

_____

_____

_____

_____

_____
Moderator Signature/Date

WORK PAPER 8.17   Quality Control Checklist

Field Requirements

FIELD	INSTRUCTIONS FOR ENTERING DATA
Number	A number that sequentially identifies the quality control items, which if positively addressed would indicate that this step had been performed correctly.
Item	The specific quality control item used to measure the effectiveness of performing this step.
Response	Indicate whether testers have performed the referenced item. The response can be yes, no, or N/A, if not appropriate for the organization's testing process.
Comments	Clarify the yes, no, or N/A response for the item indicated. Generally, comments need only be completed for no responses. They also should be investigated to determine whether this item needs to be performed before this step is considered complete.

Item	Response Yes	No	N/A	Comments
Software Function/Software Attribute Work Papers				
1. Have all the business software functions been identified?				
2. Does the sponsor/user agree that these are the appropriate software functions?				
3. Is the software function identified by a commonly used name?				
4. Are all the software functions described?				
5. Have the criteria for evaluating the software functions been identified?				
6. Are the evaluation criteria measurable (i.e., a decision can be made as to whether the criteria have been met)?				
7. Has the structure addressed: Reliability? Efficiency? Integrity? Usability?				

(Continues)

WORK PAPER 8.17   *(Continued)*

	Response			
Item	**Yes**	**No**	**N/A**	**Comments**
Maintainability? Testability? Flexibility? Portability? Reusability? Interoperability?				
8. Have the criteria for each structural attribute been stated?				
9. Are the evaluation criteria measurable?				
10. Has the description for each structural attribute been given?				
Work Papers on Tests to Be Conducted				
1. Has the test been named?				
2. Has the test been given a unique identifying number?				
3. Has the test objective been stated clearly and distinctly?				
4. Are the tests appropriate to evaluate the functions defined?				
5. Is the level of detail on the document adequate for creating actual test conditions once the system is implemented?				
6. Are the verification tests directed at project products?				
7. Is the verification test named?				

(Continues)

WORK PAPER 8.17   *(Continued)*

Item	Yes	No	N/A	Comments
8. Is the name of the verification test adequate for test personnel to understand the intent of the test?				
9. Have the products to be tested been identified?				
10. Has the purpose of the verification test been stated?				
11. Has the sequence in which each online test will be performed been identified?				
12. Has the name for each test been included (optional)?				
13. Have the criteria that would cause testing to be stopped been indicated?				
14. Are the stop criteria measurable (i.e., there is no question that the criteria have been met)?				
15. Are the stop criteria reasonable?				
Software Function/Test Matrix				
1. Does the matrix contain all the software functions defined on Work Paper 8.2?				
2. Does the matrix contain all the structural attributes defined on Work Paper 8.3?				
3. Does the matrix contain all the tests described in test Work Papers 8.4, 8.5, and 8.6?				

(Continues)

WORK PAPER 8.17 *(Continued)*

Item	Response			Comments
	Yes	**No**	**N/A**	
4. Are the tests related to the functions?				
5. Are there tests for evaluating each software function?				
6. Are there tests for evaluating each structural attribute?				
Administrative Work Papers				
1. Has a work paper been prepared for each test milestone (time sequence for which test will be scheduled)?				
2. Has the date for starting the testing been identified?				
3. Has the date for starting test team training been identified?				
4. Has the date for collecting the testing material been identified?				
5. Has the concluding date of the test been identified?				
6. Has the test budget been calculated?				
7. Is the budget consistent with the test workload?				
8. Is the schedule reasonably based on the test workload?				
9. Have the equipment requirements for the test been identified?				

WORK PAPER 8.17   *(Continued)*

Item	Yes	No	N/A	Comments
	Response			
10. Have the software and documents needed for conducting the test been identified?				
11. Have the personnel for the test been identified? (Personnel can be assigned by job title and/or group.)				
12. Have the system documentation materials for testing been identified?				
13. Has the software to be tested been identified?				
14. Has the test input been defined?				
15. Have the needed test tools been identified?				
16. Has the type of training that needs to be conducted been defined?				
17. Have the personnel who require training been identified?				
18. Will the test team be notified of the expected defect rate at each checkpoint?				
19. Has a test summary been described?				
20. Does this summary indicate which software is to be included in the test?				
21. Does the summary indicate the general approach to testing?				

(Continues)

WORK PAPER 8.17 *(Continued)*

Item	Yes	No	N/A	Comments
	Response			
	Yes	No	N/A	
22. Has the pretest background been defined?				
23. Does the pretest background describe previous experience in testing?				
24. Does the pretest background describe the sponsor's/user's attitude to testing?				
25. Has the test environment been defined?				
26. Does the test environment indicate which computer center will be used for testing?				
27. Does the test environment indicate permissions needed before beginning testing (if appropriate)?				
28. Does the test environment state all the operational requirements that will be placed on testing?				
29. Have all appropriate references been stated?				
30. Has the purpose for listing references been stated?				
31. Has the use, that the group should make of those references, been stated?				
32. Are the number of references complete?				
33. Are the test tools consistent with the departmental standards?				

WORK PAPER 8.17 *(Continued)*

Item	Response Yes	No	N/A	Comments
34. Are the test tools complete?				
35. Has the extent of testing been defined?				
36. Have the constraints of testing been defined?				
37. Are the constraints consistent with the resources available for testing.				
38. Are the constraints reasonable based on the test objectives?				
39. Has the general method for recording test results been defined?				
40. Is the data reduction method consistent with the test plan?				
41. Is the information needed for data reduction easily identifiable in the test documentation?				
Test Milestones Work Paper				
1. Has the start date of testing been defined?				
2. Are all the test tasks defined?				
3. Are the start and stop dates for each test indicated?				
4. Is the amount of time allotted for each task sufficient to perform the task?				
5. Will all prerequisite tasks be completed before the task depending on them is started?				

Step 3: Requirements Phase Testing

Testing during systems development should begin during the requirements phase. It is during this phase that most of the critical system decisions are made. The requirements are the basis for the systems design, which is then used for programming to produce the final implemented application. If the requirements contain errors the entire application will be erroneous.

Testing the system requirements increases the probability that the requirements will be good ones. Testing at this point is designed to ensure the requirements are properly recorded, have been correctly interpreted by the information services project team and are reasonable when measured against good practices, and are recorded in accordance with the department's guidelines, standards, and procedures. This step (see Figure 9.1) provides a test process for assessing the accuracy and completeness of requirements.

Overview

The requirements phase should be a user-dominated phase. In other words, the user should be specifying the needs and the information services personnel should be recording the needs and counseling about the alternative solutions, just as the builder and architect would counsel the homeowner on building options. This means that the user, being the dominant party, should take responsibility for requirements phase testing.

During the life cycle, the participants play different roles. In some phases, the user is dominant, while in other phases information services is dominant. The determination of who is the dominant party in each phase is an important consideration regarding who

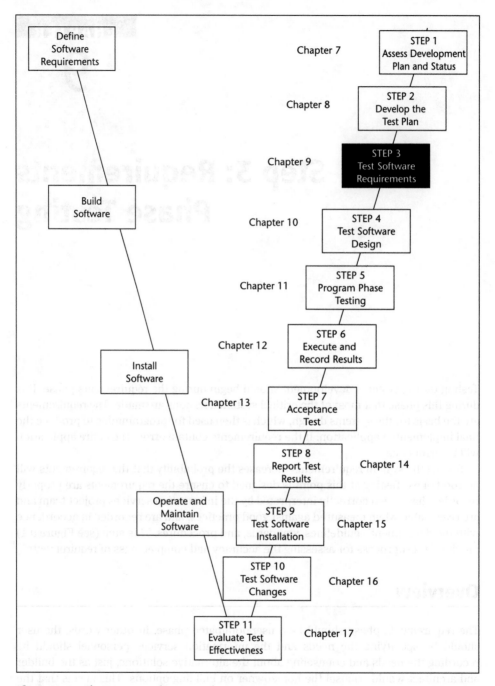

Figure 9.1 The 11-step software testing process.

should have test responsibility. To assign responsibility for verifying the correctness of a process for which the person or group is not the dominant party is a misplacement of responsibility. For example, to ask the user to verify that the programs are properly constructed would be impractical.

Having responsibility for testing does not necessarily mean responsibility for performing the test. Performance of the test is differentiated from the party having responsibility for the test—responsibility meaning the acceptance or rejection of the product based upon the test results.

Life cycle testing is a new concept in information services. Therefore, testing responsibility in all phases of the life cycle has not been established by standards or practice. Organizations must assign responsibility for testing in each phase of the development life cycle within the test plan.

It is recommended that the user be assigned requirements phase test responsibility. If there are multiple users, responsibility may be assigned to a committee, which may be the same committee that develops the requirements. One of the primary objectives of testing during requirements is to ensure that the requirements have been properly stated and recorded. Normally only the user can look at recorded requirements and make that determination. Thus, it becomes important for the user to accept testing responsibility during requirements, and also to be an active participant in the test process.

Objective

Testing during the requirements phase is a new concept to many developmental teams. However, experience has shown that the requirements phase is the most cost-effective phase in which to detect a system flaw. Located at this point, the defect will not be incorporated into the design and coded into a program, but rather, caught at the earliest possible point.

The primary objectives of testing during the requirements phase are to:

- Determine that the requirements fairly represent what the user needs.
- Determine that the needs have been defined and documented.
- Verify that a cost/benefit study has been performed and that it is reasonable.
- Determine that the business problem has been solved.
- Verify that the control requirements have been specified.
- Verify that a reasonable process was followed in developing the business solution.
- Verify that a reasonable alternative was selected among the most probable alternative solutions.

The task being required during requirements testing is a higher-level task than frequently occurs during program testing. For this reason it may take a higher-caliber person to perform the test. The test process also requires new testing methods. Although a wide range of tools does not currently exist, the testers should be continually alert to new test methods.

Concerns

People undertaking the test process must understand the requirements phase objectives and then evaluate those objectives through testing. Should the requirements phase be found inadequate as a result of testing, the phase should be continued until requirements are complete. Without testing, inadequacies in the requirements phase may not be detected.

Customarily, a management review occurs after the requirements phase is complete. Frequently this is done by senior management, who are not as concerned with the details as with the economics and the general business solution. Unfortunately, inadequate details can significantly affect the cost and timing of implementing the proposed solution.

The recommended test process outlined in this book is based on the 15 requirements phase test factors and the test concerns for each factor (see Task 2 of the do procedures). The test team determines which of those factors apply to the application being tested, and then conducts those tests necessary to determine whether the test factor has been adequately addressed during the requirements phase. This chapter defines the test factors and recommends tests that can be used to address the requirements phase testing concerns.

Workbench

The workbench for testing requirements is illustrated in Figure 9.2. This workbench shows that the testers need the project requirements and the methods for gathering requirements as input. The major requirements test task is a walkthrough, which is preceded by preparing a risk matrix and performing an analysis of the test factors. The risk matrix and the test factor analysis will be used in conducting the requirements walkthrough. The results of the workbench will be a report indicating deficiencies in the accuracy and completeness of requirements.

Input

The requirements phase is undertaken to solve a business problem. The problem and its solution drives the systems development process. Therefore, it is essential that the business problem is well defined. For example, the business problem might be to improve accounts receivable collections, reduce the amount of on-hand inventory through better inventory management, or improve customer service.

The analogy of building a home illustrates the phases in the systems development life cycle. The homeowner's needs may be increased living space, and the results of the requirements phase offer a solution for that need. The requirements phase in building a home would specify the number of rooms, the location of the lot on which the house will be built, the approximate cost to construct the house, the type of architecture, and so on. At the completion of the requirements phase, the potential homeowner's needs

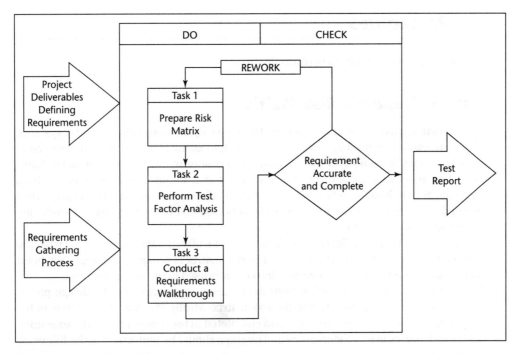

Figure 9.2   Workbench for testing requirements.

would be specified. The deliverables produced from the homeowner's requirements phase would be a functional description of the home and a plot map of the lot on which the home is to be constructed. These are the inputs that go to the architect to design the home.

The requirements phase should be initiated by management request, and should conclude with a proposal to management on the recommended solution for the business need. The requirements team should study the business problem, the previous methods of handling the problem, and the consequences of that method, together with any other input pertinent to the problem. Based on this study, the team develops a series of solutions. The requirements team should then select a preferred solution from among these alternatives and propose that solution to management.

The most common deliverables from the requirements phase needed by the testers for this step include:

- Proposal to management describing the problem, the alternatives, and proposing a solution

- Cost/benefit study describing the economics of the proposed solution

- Detailed description of the recommended solution, highlighting the recommended method for satisfying those needs (Note: This becomes the input to the systems design phase)

- List of system assumptions, such as the life of the project, the value of money, the average skill of the user, and so on

Do Procedures

Three tasks are necessary to perform this step:

Task 1: Prepare a Risk Matrix

A risk matrix is a tool designed to assess the adequacy of controls in computer systems. The term *controls* is used in its broadest context, meaning all of the mechanisms, methods, and procedures used in the application to ensure that it functions in accordance with the intent of management. It is estimated that in automated systems controls account for at least one-half of the total developmental effort. Therefore, effort expended to ensure the adequacy of controls is essential to the success and credibility of the application system.

One of the major benefits of the risk matrix is the identification of risks and what the system must do for each of those risks. The risk matrix is primarily a design tool, but it can be used as a test tool because it is infrequently used in the design process.

The risk matrix can be used in both the requirements phase and the design phase. The following explains how to use the risk matrix. Ideally, the risk matrix starts in the requirements phase and is expanded and completed in the design phase. The execution of the risk matrix is a five-step process. The steps should be performed in the following sequence.

1. Identify Risk Team

The key to a successful risk matrix is the establishment of the correct risk team, whose responsibility will be to complete the matrix. The objective of completing the matrix is to determine the adequacy of the control requirements and design to reduce the risks to an acceptable level.

The risk team may be part of the requirements team, or part of the test team, or it may be a team specifically selected for the purpose of completing the risk matrix. The team should be comprised of three to six members, and at a minimum possess the following skills:

- Knowledge of the user application
- Understanding of risk concepts
- Ability to identify controls
- Familiarity with both application and information services risks
- Understanding of information services concepts and systems design
- Understanding of computer operations procedures

The candidates included on the risk team should at a minimum include someone from the user area and any or all of the following:

- Internal auditor
- Risk consultant

- Data processor
- Security officer
- Computer operations manager

2. Identify Risks

The objective of the risk team is first to identify the application-oriented, not environmental, risks associated with the application system. For example, the risks that relate to all applications equally (i.e., environmental risks) need not be identified unless they have some special relevance to the applicants. The risk team can use one of the following two methods for risk identification:

1. **Risk analysis scenario.** In this method, the risk team "brainstorms" the potential application risks using their experience, judgment, and knowledge of the application area. It is important to have the synergistic effect of a group so that group members can challenge one another to develop a complete list of risks that are realistic for the application.

2. **Risk checklist.** The risk team is provided with a list of the more common risks that occur in automated applications. From this list, the team selects those risks that are applicable to the application. In this method, the team needs fewer skills because the risk list provides the stimuli for the process, and the objective of the team is to determine which of the risks on the list are applicable to the application. Figure 9.3 provides a list of risks for the purpose of identification.

CATEGORY: Uncontrolled System Access

1. Date or programs may be stolen from the computer room or other storage areas.

2. Information services facilities may be destroyed or damaged by either intruders or employees.

3. Individuals may not be adequately identified before they are allowed to enter the information services area.

4. Remote terminals may not be adequately protected from use by unauthorized persons.

5. An unauthorized user may gain access to the system via a dial-in line and an authorized user's password.

6. Passwords may be inadvertently revealed to unauthorized individuals. A user may write his or her password in some convenient place, or the password may be obtained from card decks, discarded printouts, or by observing the user as he or she types it.

7. A user may leave a logged-in terminal unattended, allowing an unauthorized person to use it.

Figure 9.3 List of generalized application risks. *(Continues)*

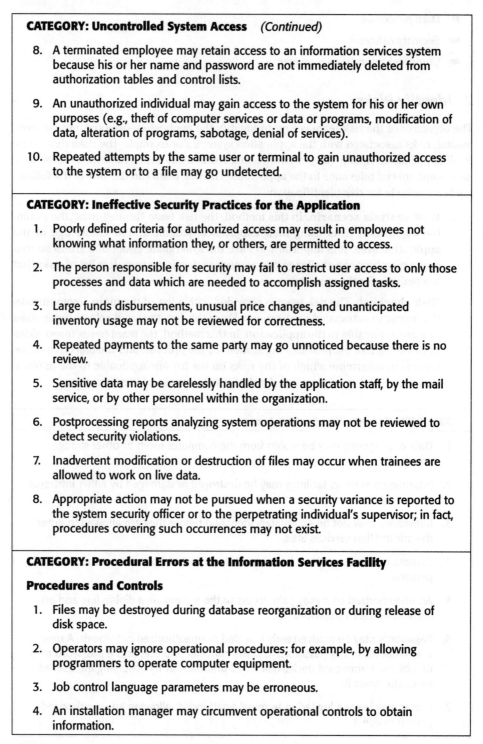

CATEGORY: Uncontrolled System Access   *(Continued)*

8. A terminated employee may retain access to an information services system because his or her name and password are not immediately deleted from authorization tables and control lists.

9. An unauthorized individual may gain access to the system for his or her own purposes (e.g., theft of computer services or data or programs, modification of data, alteration of programs, sabotage, denial of services).

10. Repeated attempts by the same user or terminal to gain unauthorized access to the system or to a file may go undetected.

CATEGORY: Ineffective Security Practices for the Application

1. Poorly defined criteria for authorized access may result in employees not knowing what information they, or others, are permitted to access.

2. The person responsible for security may fail to restrict user access to only those processes and data which are needed to accomplish assigned tasks.

3. Large funds disbursements, unusual price changes, and unanticipated inventory usage may not be reviewed for correctness.

4. Repeated payments to the same party may go unnoticed because there is no review.

5. Sensitive data may be carelessly handled by the application staff, by the mail service, or by other personnel within the organization.

6. Postprocessing reports analyzing system operations may not be reviewed to detect security violations.

7. Inadvertent modification or destruction of files may occur when trainees are allowed to work on live data.

8. Appropriate action may not be pursued when a security variance is reported to the system security officer or to the perpetrating individual's supervisor; in fact, procedures covering such occurrences may not exist.

CATEGORY: Procedural Errors at the Information Services Facility

Procedures and Controls

1. Files may be destroyed during database reorganization or during release of disk space.

2. Operators may ignore operational procedures; for example, by allowing programmers to operate computer equipment.

3. Job control language parameters may be erroneous.

4. An installation manager may circumvent operational controls to obtain information.

Figure 9.3   List of generalized application risks.   *(Continues)*

CATEGORY: Procedural Errors at the Information Services Facility
(Continued)

5. Careless or incorrect restarting after shutdown may cause the state of a transaction update to be unknown.

6. An operator may enter erroneous information at CPU console (e.g., control switch in wrong position, terminal user allowed full system access, operator cancels wrong job from queue).

7. Hardware maintenance may be performed while production data is on-line and the equipment undergoing maintenance is not isolated.

8. An operator may perform unauthorized acts for personal gain (e.g., make extra copies of competitive bidding reports, print copies of unemployment checks, delete a record from a journal file).

9. Operations staff may sabotage the computer (e.g., drop pieces of metal into a terminal).

10. The wrong version of a program may be executed.

11. A program may be executed twice using the same transactions.

12. An operator may bypass required safety controls (e.g., write rings for tape reels).

13. Supervision of operations personnel may not be adequate during nonworking hour shifts.

14. Due to incorrectly learned procedures, an operator may alter or erase the master files.

15. A console operator may override a label check without recording the action in the security log.

Storage Media Handling

1. Critical tape files may be mounted without being write protected.

2. Inadvertently or intentionally mislabeled storage media are erased. In a case where they contain backup files, the erasure may not be noticed until the backup is needed.

3. Internal labels on storage media may not be checked for correctness.

4. Files with missing or mislabeled expiration dates may be erased.

5. Incorrect processing of data or erroneous updating of files may occur when card decks have been dropped, partial input decks are used, write rings are mistakenly placed in tapes, paper tape is incorrectly mounted, or wrong tape is mounted.

6. Scratch tapes used for jobs processing sensitive data may not be adequately erased after use.

Figure 9.3   List of generalized application risks.   *(Continues)*

CATEGORY: Procedural Errors at the Information Services Facility *(Continued)*

7. Temporary files written during a job step for use in subsequent steps may be erroneously released or modified through inadequate protection of the files or because of an abnormal termination.

8. Storage media containing sensitive information may not get adequate protection because operations staff is not advised of the nature of the information content.

9. Tape management procedures may not adequately account for the current status of all tapes.

10. Magnetic storage media that have contained very sensitive information may not be degaussed before being released.

11. Output may be sent to the wrong individual or terminal.

12. Improperly operating output or postprocessing units (e.g., bursters, decollators, or multipar forms) may result in loss of output.

13. Surplus output material (e.g., duplicates of output data, used carbon paper) may not be disposed of properly.

14. Tapes and programs that label output for distribution may be erroneous or not protected from tampering.

CATEGORY: Program Errors

1. Records may be deleted from sensitive files without a guarantee that the deleted records can be reconstructed.

2. Programmers may insert special provisions in programs that manipulate data concerning themselves (e.g., payroll programmer may alter his or her own payroll records).

3. Data may not be stored separately from code with the result that program modifications are more difficult and must be made more frequently.

4. Program changes may not be tested adequately before being used in a production run.

5. Changes to a program may result in new errors because of unanticipated interactions between program modules.

6. Program acceptance tests may fail to detect errors that only occur for unusual combinations of input (e.g., a program that is supposed to reject all except a specified range of values actually accepts an additional value).

7. Programs, the contents of which should be safeguarded, may not be identified and protected.

8. Code, test data with its associated output, and documentation for certified programs may not be filed and retained for reference.

9. Documentation for vital programs may not be safeguarded.

Figure 9.3 List of generalized application risks.   *(Continues)*

CATEGORY: Program Errors *(Continued)*

10. Programmers may fail to keep a change log, to maintain back copies, or to formalize recordkeeping activities.

11. An employee may steal programs he or she is maintaining and use them for personal gain (e.g., sale to a commercial organization, hold another organization for extortion).

12. Poor program design may result in a critical data value being initialized twice. An error may occur when the program is modified to change the data value—but only changes it in one place.

13. Production data may be disclosed or destroyed when it is used during testing.

14. Errors may result when the programmer misunderstands requests for changes to the program.

15. Errors may be introduced by a programmer who makes changes directly to machine code.

16. Programs may contain routines not compatible with their intended purpose, which can disable or bypass security protection mechanisms. For example, a programmer who anticipates being fired inserts code into a program which will cause vital system files to be deleted as soon as his/her name no longer appears in the payroll file.

17. Inadequate documentation or labeling may result in wrong version of program being modified.

CATEGORY: Operating System Flaws

1. User jobs may be permitted to read or write outside assigned storage area.

2. Inconsistencies may be introduced into data because of simultaneous processing of the same file by two jobs.

3. An operating system design or implementation error may allow a user to disable audit controls or to access all system information.

4. An operating system may not protect a copy of information as thoroughly as it protects the original.

5. Unauthorized modification to the operating system may allow a data entry clerk to enter programs and thus subvert the system.

6. An operating system crash may expose valuable information such as password lists or authorization tables.

7. Maintenance personnel may bypass security controls while performing maintenance work. At such times the system is vulnerable to errors or intentional acts of the maintenance personnel, or anyone else who might also be on the system and discover the opening (e.g., microcoded sections of the operating system may be tampered with or sensitive information from on-line files may be disclosed).

Figure 9.3   List of generalized application risks.   *(Continues)*

CATEGORY: Operating System Flaws   *(Continued)*

8. An operating system may fail to record that multiple copies of output have been made from spooled storage devices.

9. An operating system may fail to maintain an unbroken audit trail.

10. When restarting after a system crash, the operating system may fail to ascertain that all terminal locations which were previously occupied are still occupied by the same individuals.

11. A user may be able to get into monitor or supervisory mode.

12. The operating system may fail to erase all scratch space assigned to a job after the normal or abnormal termination of the job.

13. Files may be allowed to be read or written without having been opened.

CATEGORY: Communication System Failure

Accidental Failures

1. Undetected communications errors may result in incorrect or modified data.

2. Information may be accidentally misdirected to the wrong terminal.

3. Communication nodes may leave unprotected fragments of messages in memory during unanticipated interruptions in processing.

4. Communication protocol may fail to positively identify the transmitter or receiver of a message.

Intentional Acts

1. Communication lines may be monitored by unauthorized individuals.

2. Data or programs may be stolen via telephone circuits from a remote job entry terminal.

3. Programs in the network switching computers may be modified to compromise security.

4. Data may be deliberately changed by individuals tapping the line (requires some sophistication, but is applicable to financial data).

5. An unauthorized user may "take over" a computer communication port as an authorized user disconnects from it. Many systems cannot detect the change. This is particularly true in much of the currently available communication protocols.

6. If encryption is used, keys may be stolen.

7. A terminal user may be "spoofed" into providing sensitive data.

8. False messages may be inserted into the system.

9. True messages may be deleted from the system.

10. Messages may be recorded and replayed into the system.

Figure 9.3   List of generalized application risks.

3. Establish Control Objectives (Requirements Phase Only)

During the requirements phase, the control objectives for each risk should be established. These objectives define the acceptable level of loss for each of the identified risks. Another way of stating the acceptable level of loss is the measurable objective for control. When control can be stated in terms that are measurable, the controls to achieve that objective have a requirement to use for control-decision purposes.

The adequacy of control cannot be tested until the acceptable level of loss from each risk has been defined. Thus, while the definition of the control objectives is a user and project responsibility, it may take the formation of a risk team to get them defined. Once the control objectives have been defined, the requirements can be tested to determine whether those objectives are achievable.

An example of a risk matrix at the end of the requirements phase for a typical billing and distribution system is illustrated in Figure 9.4. This matrix lists four risks for the billing and distribution system, and control objectives for each of those risks. For example, one of the risks is that product will be shipped but not billed. In this instance, the control objective is to ensure that all shipments are billed. In other words, the acceptable level of loss for this risk is zero, and the project team must install a system that will ensure that for each shipment leaving the distribution area an invoice will be prepared. However, note that the next risk is that the product will be billed at the wrong price or quantity and that the controls have a greater than zero level of loss established, as do the other two risks.

4. Identify Controls in Each System Segment (Design Phase Only)

During the design phase, the risk team will identify the controls in each phase of the application system for each identified risk. The common system segments are:

Origination. The creation of the source document plus the authorization associated with that transaction origination.

Data entry. The transfer of information to machine-readable media.

Communication. The movement of data from one point in the system to another. Movement may be manual or electronic.

RISK	CONTROL OBJECTIVES
Shipped but not billed	Ensure *all* shipments are billed
Billed for wrong quantity or price	Bill at current price on 99% of line items and have error pricing less than plus or minus 10%
Billed to wrong customer	Reduce misbillings to less than .1% of invoices
Shipped wrong product or quantity	Ship correct product and quantity on 99% of line items

Figure 9.4   Risk matrix example (requirements)—billing and distribution system.

Processing. Application of the system logic to the data.

Storage. The retention of data, for both temporary and extended periods of time.

Output. The translation of data from computer media to media understandable and usable by people.

Use. Satisfaction of the business need through the results of system processing.

The risk team will determine which controls are applicable to which risk and record them in the correct segment of the system. At the conclusion of the development of the risk matrix, the risk team will make an assessment as to whether the controls are adequate to reduce the risk to the acceptable level identified in the control objective. This will test the adequacy of the controls at the conclusion of the design process. An example of a risk matrix for billing and distribution systems at the end of the design phase is illustrated in Figure 9.5.

The same four risks that were identified during the requirements phase (Figure 9.4) are listed on this matrix also, as are the controls associated with each risk. In this example, the shipped but not billed risk shows that three controls, 1, 2, and 3, will help reduce that risk. (Note that for an actual matrix these controls must be described.) The matrix shows in which segment of the application system those controls reside. After the controls have been identified and recorded, the risk team must determine whether those three controls and the segments in which they exist are adequate to reduce the shipped but not billed risk to the point where all shipments will be billed.

5. Determine Adequacy of Controls

The test concludes when the risk team assesses whether controls are adequate to reduce each of the identified risks to the acceptable level.

SYSTEM SEGMENT RISK	ORIGINATION	DATA ENTRY	COMMUNICATION	PROCESSING	STORAGE	OUTPUT	USE
Shipped but not billed	#1			#2			#6
Billed for wrong quantity or price		#6		#7 #8	#10	#11	
				#9			
Billed to wrong customer				#12 #3	#14	#15	#16
Shipped wrong product or quantity	#17	#18		#19 #20		#21	#22

Figure 9.5   Risk matrix example (design)—billing and distribution system.

Task 2: Perform a Test Factor Analysis for the Requirements Phase

A process for assessing the concerns associated with the requirements phase of the systems development life cycle is included as Work Paper 9.1. A test program is included for each concern. There are 15 concerns, covering each phase of the developmental process. For each concern there is a test program comprising eight criteria. The test program lists those criteria that, if proved to be adequately addressed through testing, should assure the test team that the magnitude of the concern is minimal. The criteria are questions that the test team must answer. The test team must perform sufficient testing in order to evaluate the adequacy with which the project team has handled each of the test criteria. For example, in the requirements phase one test criterion is "Have the significant financial fields been identified?" To determine that the project team has adequately addressed this criterion, the test team would conduct such tests as necessary to assure themselves that the significant financial fields have been identified. The testing may require fact-finding in the accounting department to verify that the fields indicated as financial fields are complete.

Fifteen Requirements Phase Test Factors

A brief description of the 15 requirement phase test factors (concerns) follows.

1. Requirements Comply with Methodology (Methodology Test Factor)

The process used by the information services function to define and document requirements should be adhered to during the requirements phase. The more formal these procedures, the easier the test process. The requirements process is one of fact gathering, analysis, decision making, and recording the requirements in a predefined manner for use in design.

2. Functional Specifications Defined (Correctness Test Factor)

User satisfaction can only be assured when system objectives are achieved. The achievement of these objectives can only be measured when the objectives are measurable. Qualitative objectives—such as improving service to users—are unmeasurable objectives, while processing a user order in four hours is measurable.

3. Usability Specifications Determined (Ease-of-Use Test Factor)

The amount of effort required to use the system and the skill level necessary should be defined during requirements. Experience shows that difficult-to-use applications or features are not often used, while easy-to-use functional systems are highly used. Unless included in the specifications, the ease-of-use specifications will be created by default by the systems analyst or programmer.

4. Maintenance Specifications Determined (Maintainable Test Factor)

The degree of expected maintenance should be defined, as well as the areas where change is most probable. Specifications should then determine the methods of maintenance—such as user-introduced change of parameters—and the time span in which certain types of maintenance changes need to be installed; for example, a price change must be operational within 24 hours after notification to information services.

5. Portability Needs Determined (Portable Test Factor)

The ability to operate the system on different types of hardware, move it at a later time to another type of hardware, or to move from version to version of software should be stated as part of the requirements. The need to have the application developed as a portable one can significantly affect the implementation of the requirements.

6. System Interface Defined (Coupling Test Factor)

The information expected as input from other computer systems, and the output to be delivered to other computer systems, should be defined. This definition not only includes the types of information passed, but the timing of the interface and the expected processing to occur as a result of that interface. Other interface factors that may need to be addressed include privacy, security, and retention of information.

7. Performance Criteria Established (Performance Test Factor)

The expected efficiency, economy, and effectiveness of the application system should be established. These system goals are an integral part of the design process and, unless established, default to the systems analyst/programmer. When this happens, user dissatisfaction is almost guaranteed to occur with the operational system. An end product of the requirements phase should be a calculation of the cost/benefit to be derived from the application. The financial data should be developed based on procedures designed to provide consistent cost and benefit information for all applications.

8. Operational Needs Defined (Ease-of-Operations Test Factor)

The operational considerations must be defined during the requirements phase. This becomes especially important in user-driven application systems. The processes that must be followed at terminals to operate the system—in other words, the procedures needed to get the terminal into a state ready to process transactions—should be as simple as possible. Central site operating procedures also need to be considered.

9. Tolerances Established (Reliability Test Factor)

The expected reliability from the system controls should be defined. For example, the requirements phase should determine the control requirements for the accuracy of invoicing, the percent of orders that need to be processed within 24 hours, and other such concerns. An invoicing tolerance might state that invoices are to be processed with a tolerance of plus or minus 1 percent from the stated current product prices. Without establishing these tolerances, there is no basis to design and measure the reliability of processing over an extended period of time. Without defining an expected level of defects, zero defects are normally expected. Controls to achieve zero defects are normally not economical. It is usually more economical and to the advantage of the user to have some defects occur in processing, but to control and measure the number of defects.

10. Authorization Rules Defined (Authorization Test Factor)

Authorization requirements specify the authorization methods to ensure that transactions are, in fact, processed in accordance with the intent of management.

11. File Integrity Requirements Defined (File Integrity Test Factor)

The methods of ensuring the integrity of computer files need to be specified. This normally includes the control totals that are to be maintained both within the file and independently of the automated application. The controls must ensure that the detail records are in balance with the control totals for each file.

12. Reconstruction Requirements Defined (Audit Trail Test Factor)

Reconstruction involves both substantiating the accuracy of processing and recovery after an identified problem. Both of these needs involve the retention of information to backup processing. The need to substantiate processing evolves both from the organization and regulatory agencies, such as tax authorities requiring that sufficient evidential matter be retained to support tax returns.

Application management needs to state if and when the system recovery process should be executed. If recovery is deemed necessary, management needs to state the time span in which the recovery process must be executed. This time span may change based upon the time of the day and the day of the week. These recovery requirements affect the type and availability of data retained.

13. Impact of Failure Defined (Continuity-of-Processing Test Factor)

The necessity to ensure continuity of processing is dependent upon the impact of failure. If system failure causes only minimal problems, ensuring continuous processing may be unnecessary. On the other hand, where continuity of operations is essential, it may be necessary to obtain duplicate data centers so that one can continue processing should the other experience a failure.

14. Desired Service Level Defined (Service Level Test Factor)

Service level implies response time based on the requirements. The service level required will vary based on the requirements. Each level of desired service needs to be stated; for example, there is a service level to process a specific transaction, a service level to correct a programming error, a service level to install a change, and a service level to respond to a request.

15. Access Defined (Security Test Factor)

Security requirements should be developed showing the relationship between system resources and people. Requirements should state all of the available system resources subject to control, and then indicate who can have access to those resources and for what purposes. For example, access may be authorized to read, but not change, data.

At the conclusion of the testing, the test team can make a judgment about the adequacy of each of the criteria, and thus of all of the test concerns included in the test process for the requirements phase. The test team should make one of the following four judgments about each criterion:

1. **Very adequate**. The project team has done more than normally would be expected for the criterion.

2. **Adequate evaluation**. The project team has done sufficient work to ensure the reasonableness of control over the criterion.

3. **Inadequate assessment**. The project team has not done sufficient work, and should do more work in this criterion area.

4. **Not applicable (N/A)**. Due to the type of application or the system design philosophy by the organization, the implementation of this criterion is not applicable to the application being reviewed.

Each test process contains a test that can be performed for each evaluation criterion. The objective of the test is to assist the team in evaluating each criterion. The test should be conducted prior to assessing the adequacy of the project being tested. It should be noted that because of time limitations, review experience, and tests previously performed, the test team may choose not to assess each criterion.

The 15 test processes are recommended in Work Paper 9.1 as a basis for testing the requirements phase. One test program is constructed to evaluate each of the requirements phase concerns.

Task 3: Conduct a Requirements Walkthrough

The requirements phase involves creativity, experience, and judgment, as well as a methodology to follow. During this phase, the methodology helps, but it is really creativity and problem solving that is needed. Of the review processes, the walkthrough is the least structured and the most prone to creativity. Therefore, the walkthrough becomes a review process that complements the objectives of the requirements phase. The objective of the walkthrough is to create a situation in which a team of skilled individuals can help the project team in the development of the project solutions. The walkthrough attempts to use the experience and judgment of the review team as an adjunct or aid in the developmental process. The walkthrough in the requirements phase is oriented toward assistance in problem solving as opposed to compliance to methodology.

The walkthrough is a five-step process which is to be completed in the sequence listed below. The amount of time allocated to each step will be dependent upon the size of the application being reviewed and the degree of assistance desired from the walkthrough team.

Step 1. Establish Ground Rules

The walkthrough concept requires the project people to make a presentation explaining the functioning of the system as developed at the time of the presentation. The presentation, or reading of the requirements, is the vehicle for initiating discussion between the project team and the walkthrough team. The prime objective is to initiate questions, comments, and recommendations by the walkthrough team.

The walkthrough is most productive when ground rules are established before the actual walkthrough. The ground rules should be understood by both the project team and the walkthrough team, and normally include:

- Size and makeup of the walkthrough team (three to six skilled participants is a good size)

- Responsibility of the walkthrough team, which is usually limited to recommendations, comments, and questions

- Obligation of the project team to answer all questions and respond to recommendations

- Approximate length, time, and location of the walkthrough

- Confidentiality of information discussed at the walkthrough

- Aspects of the system that are not challengeable or discussible

- Who will receive the results of the walkthrough and how are those results to be used? For example, if the report is to be prepared, who will receive it, what is the purpose of the report, and what is the most likely action based on that report?

Step 2. Select Team/Notify Participants

The ground rules establish the size and makeup of the team. The ground rules are normally generic in nature, and must be converted into action. For example, if the ground rules say that the team should be comprised of two members of user management and two project leaders, the most appropriate individuals must then be selected.

The walkthrough team should be selected based upon the objectives to be accomplished. Any of the involved parties (i.e., users, information services, and senior management) may wish to recommend walkthrough team participants. These tend to be selected based upon the concerns about the projects. For example, if operations is a major concern, then operations people should be selected for the walkthrough team.

The most common participants on a walkthrough team include:

- Information services project manager/systems analyst.

- Senior management with responsibility over the computerized area.

- Operations management.

- User management.

- Consultants possessing needed expertise. (The consultants may be from inside or outside the corporation. For example, the consultants may be internal auditors, database administrators, or independent computer consultants.)

The size of the walkthrough team should be between three and six members. Three members are needed to get sufficient perspective and discussion, but more than six members makes the process too large and unwieldy. A good review team has at least one member of user management, one senior member of information services, and one member of senior management. Additional participants can be added as necessary.

The team participants should be notified as soon as possible that they have been selected for the walkthrough, and advised of the responsibility and time commitments and the date for the walkthrough. Generally, if people do not want to participate in the walkthrough, they should be relieved of that responsibility and another individual selected. If there is a major conflict between selected individuals and the review time, it may be more advisable to move the time of the review than to change the participants.

Step 3. Project Presentation

The project personnel should present the project requirements to the walkthrough team. A good walkthrough includes presentation of the following:

- Statement of the goals and objectives of the project.

- Background information including appropriate statistics on the current and proposed application area. Note that these statistics should be business statistics and not computer system statistics.

- List of any exceptions made by the project team.

- Discussion of the alternatives considered and the alternative selected.

- A walkthrough of the requirements using representative transactions as a basis. Rather than describing the system, it is better to select the more common transaction types and explain how those transactions will be processed based upon the defined requirements.

Step 4. Questions/Recommendations

The project presentation should be interrupted with questions, comments, and recommendations as they occur to the walkthrough team. The objective of the walkthrough is to evoke discussion and not to instruct the walkthrough team on the application requirements. The project team should be prepared to deviate from any presentation plan to handle questions and recommendations as they occur.

It is generally good to appoint one individual as recorder for the walkthrough. This is normally a member of the project team. The recorder's duty is to capture questions for which appropriate answers are not supplied during the walkthrough, and to indicate recommendations for which acceptance and implementation are possible.

Step 5. Final Report (Optional)

The ground rules determine whether a report will be issued, and if so, to whom. However, if it is determined that a walkthrough report should be issued, responsibility should be given to a single individual to write the report. It should be stated in advance to whom the report is to be issued. The entire walkthrough team should agree on the contents of the report; if they do not, the report should state minority opinions. The information captured by the recorder may prove valuable in developing the report. To be most valuable to the project team, the report should be issued within five days of the conclusion of the walkthrough.

Check Procedures

Work Paper 9.2 is a quality control checklist for this step. It is designed so that Yes responses indicate good test practices; No responses warrant additional investigation. A Comments column is provided to explain No responses and to record results of investigation. The N/A column is used when the checklist item is not applicable to the test situation.

Output

The only output from this step is a report indicating requirements deficiencies. These will indicate where requirements are not accurate and/or complete. It is important that this report be prepared prior to completing the requirements checkpoint.

Guidelines

The walkthrough test tool and risk matrix are recommended as two of the more effective test tools for the requirements phase. The use of these tools will help determine whether the requirements phase test factors have been adequately addressed during the requirements phase. These recommendations are not meant to exclude from use the other test tools applicable to the requirements phase, but rather to suggest and explain in detail two of the more effective tools for this phase.

Summary

This chapter provides a process for assessing the accuracy and completeness of requirements. The cost of uncovering and correcting requirement deficiencies at this phase of development is significantly less than during acceptance testing. Estimates indicate that it would cost at least 10 times as much to correct a requirement deficiency in acceptance testing than during this phase. If testers can increase the accuracy and completeness of requirements at this point of development the test effort during the design phase can emphasize structural concerns and implementation concerns as opposed to identifying improper requirements at later test phases.

WORK PAPER 9.1 Requirements Test Phase Process

Field Requirements

FIELD	INSTRUCTIONS FOR ENTERING DATA
Test Criteria	The questions to be answered by the test team.
Assessment	The test team's evaluation of the test criteria.
Recommended Test	The recommended test to be conducted to assess the test criteria.
Test Technique	The recommended technique to be used in evaluating the test criteria. Other techniques may be helpful and should be used based on the attributes of the application being tested.
Test Tool	The tool(s) to be used to accomplish the test technique (options may be indicated).

(Continues)

WORK PAPER 9.1 (Continued)

TEST FACTOR: REQUIREMENTS COMPLY WITH METHODOLOGY

#	TEST CRITERIA	ASSESSMENT				RECOMMENDED TEST	TEST TECHNIQUE	TEST TOOL
		Very Adequate	Adequate	Inadequate	N/A			
1.	Have the applicable organization's policies and procedures been identified?					Confirm with those individuals responsible for developing the policies and procedures that all the applicable policies have been identified.	Compliance	Confirmation/ examination
2.	Do the requirements comply with these policies and procedures?					Review requirement to ensure compliance	Compliance	Fact finding
3.	Have the requirements been documented in accordance with the requirements methodology?					Examine requirement to ensure all needed documentation is complete.	Compliance	Checklist
4.	Is the cost/benefit analysis prepared in accordance with the appropriate procedures?					Examine cost/benefit analysis to ensure it was prepared in accordance with procedures.	Compliance	Checklist
5.	Has the requirements phase met the intent of the requirements methodology?					Review the deliverables from requirements and assess if it meets the intent of the methodology.	Compliance	Checklist
6.	Is the requirements phase staffed according to procedures?					Verify that the project is appropriately staffed.	Compliance	Peer review
7.	Will all of the applicable policies, procedures, and requirements be in effect at the time the system goes in operation?					Confirm with the appropriate parties the effective dates of existing policies, procedures, and regulations.	Compliance	Fact finding
8.	Will there be new standards, policies, and procedures in effect at the time the system goes operational?					Confirm with the appropriate parties the effective dates of new standards, policies, and procedures.	Compliance	Fact finding

(Continues)

WORK PAPER 9.1 (Continued)

TEST FACTOR: Functional Specifications Defined

#	TEST CRITERIA	ASSESSMENT				RECOMMENDED TEST	TEST TECHNIQUE	TEST TOOL
		Very Adequate	Adequate	Inadequate	N/A			
1.	Can the data required by the application be collected with the desired degree of reliability?					Confirm with the people who would generate the data that it can be generated with the desired degree of reliability.	Requirements	Fact finding
2.	Can the data be collected within the time period specified?					Confirm with the people generating the data that it can be collected within the required time frame.	Requirements	Fact finding
3.	Have the user requirements been defined in writing?					Confirm with the user that the requirements in writing are complete.	Requirements	Checklist
4.	Are the requirements stated in measurable terms?					Examine the reasonableness of the criteria for measuring successful completion of the requirements.	Requirements	Walkthroughs
5.	Has the project solution addressed the user requirements?					Examine the system specifications to confirm they satisfy the user's stated objectives.	Requirements	Walkthroughs
6.	Could test data be developed to test the achievement of the objectives?					Verify that the requirements are stated in enough detail that they could generate test data to verify compliance.	Requirements	Test data
7.	Have procedures been specified to evaluate the implemented system to ensure the requirements are achieved?					Examine the specifications that indicate a postinstallation review will occur.	Requirements	Confirmation/ examination
8.	Do the measurable objectives apply to both the manual and automated segments of the application system?					Examine to verify that the system objectives cover both the manual and automated segments of the application.	Requirements	Confirmation/ examination

WORK PAPER 9.1 (Continued)

TEST FACTOR: Usability Specifications Defined

#	TEST CRITERIA	ASSESSMENT				RECOMMENDED TEST	TEST TECHNIQUE	TEST TOOL
		Very Adequate	Adequate	Inadequate	N/A			
1.	Have the user functions been identified?					Confirm with the user that all user functions are defined in requirements.	Manual support	Confirmation/ examination
2.	Have the skill levels of the users been identified?					Examine requirements documentation describing user skill level.	Manual support	Confirmation/ examination
3.	Have the expected levels of supervision been identified?					Examine requirements documentation describing expected level of supervision.	Manual support	Confirmation/ examination
4.	Has the time span for user function been defined?					Confirm with the user that the stated time span for processing is reasonable.	Manual support	Confirmation/ examination
5.	Will the counsel of an industrial psychologist be used in designing user functions?					Confirm that the industrial psychologist's services will be used.	Manual support	Confirmation/ examination
6.	Have user clerical people been interviewed during the requirements phase to identify their concerns?					Confirm with clerical personnel that their input has been obtained.	Manual support	Confirmation/ examination
7.	Have tradeoffs between computer and people processing been identified?					Examine reasonableness of identified tradeoffs.	Manual support	Design reviews
8.	Have the defined user responsibilities been presented to the user personnel for comment?					Confirm with the user that they have examined defined user responsibilities	Manual support	Confirmation/ examination

(Continues)

WORK PAPER 9.1 (Continued)

TEST FACTOR: Maintenance Specifications Defined

#	TEST CRITERIA	ASSESSMENT				RECOMMENDED TEST	TEST TECHNIQUE	TEST TOOL
		Very Ade-quate	Ade-quate	Inade-quate	N/A			
1.	Has the expected life of the project been defined?					Confirm with the user that the stated project life is reasonable.	Compliance	Confirmation/examination
2.	Has the expected frequency of change been defined?					Confirm with the user that the expected frequency of change is reasonable.	Compliance	Confirmation/examination
3.	Has the importance of keeping the system up to date functionally been defined?					Confirm with the user that the stated importance of functional update is correct.	Compliance	Confirmation/examination
4.	Has the importance of keeping the system up to date technologically been defined?					Confirm with IS management that the importance of technological update is correct.	Compliance	Confirmation/examination
5.	Has it been decided who will perform maintenance on the project?					Confirm with IS management who will perform maintenance.	Compliance	Confirmation/examination
6.	Are the areas of greatest expected change identified?					Examine documentations for areas of expected change.	Compliance	Peer review
7.	Has the method of introducing change during development been identified?					Examine project change procedures.	Compliance	Checklist
8.	Have provisions been included to properly document the application for maintenance purposes?					Examine completeness of project maintenance documentation.	Compliance	Peer review

WORK PAPER 9.1 *(Continued)*

TEST FACTOR: Portability Needs Determined

#	TEST CRITERIA	ASSESSMENT				RECOMMENDED TEST	TEST TECHNIQUE	TEST TOOL
		Very Adequate	Adequate	Inadequate	N/A			
1.	Are significant hardware changes expected during the life of the project?					Confirm with computer operations expected hardware changes.	Operations	Confirmation/ examination
2.	Are significant software changes expected during the life of the project?					Confirm with computer operations expected software changes.	Operations	Confirmation/ examination
3.	Will the application system be run in multiple locations?					Confirm with the user the locations where the application will be operated.	Compliance	Confirmation/ examination
4.	If an on-line application, will different types of terminals be used?					Examine terminal hardware requirements.	Compliance	Confirmation/ examination
5.	Is the proposed solution dependent on specific hardware?					Review requirements to identify hardware restrictions.	Compliance	Inspections
6.	Is the proposed solution dependent on specific software?					Review requirements to identify software restrictions.	Compliance	Inspections
7.	Will the application be run in other countries?					Confirm with the user the countries in which the application will be run.	Compliance	Confirmation/ examination
8.	Have the portability requirements been documented?					Examine requirements documentation for portability requirements.	Compliance	Inspections

(Continues)

301

WORK PAPER 9.1 *(Continued)*

TEST FACTOR: Systems Interface Defined

#	TEST CRITERIA	ASSESSMENT				RECOMMENDED TEST	TEST TECHNIQUE	TEST TOOL
		Very Adequate	Adequate	Inadequate	N/A			
1.	Have data to be received from other applications been identified?					Confirm with project team interfaced applications have been identified.	Intersystems	Confirmation/ examination
2.	Have data going to other applications been identified?					Confirm with project team interfaced applications have been identified.	Intersystems	Confirmation/ examination
3.	Has the reliability of interfaced data been defined?					Confirm with other applications reasonableness of reliability requirements.	Control	Fact finding
4.	Has the timing of transmitting data been defined?					Confirm with other applications reasonableness of timing requirements.	Control	Fact finding
5.	Has the timing of data being received been defined?					Confirm with other applications reasonableness of timing requirements.	Control	Fact finding
6.	Has the method of interfacing been defined?					Examine documentation to ensure completeness of interface methods.	Intersystems	Walkthroughs
7.	Have the interface requirements been documented?					Verify completeness of interface requirements documentation.	Intersystems	Walkthroughs
8.	Have future needs of interfaced systems been taken into consideration?					Confirm with interfaced projects need to consider future requirements.	Intersystems	Fact finding

WORK PAPER 9.1 *(Continued)*

TEST FACTOR: Performance Criteria Established

#	TEST CRITERIA	ASSESSMENT				RECOMMENDED TEST	TEST TECHNIQUE	TEST TOOL
		Very Adequate	Adequate	Inadequate	N/A			
1.	Will hardware and software be obtained through competitive bidding?					Examine the reasonableness of the competitive bidding procedures.	Compliance	Acceptance test criteria
2.	Have cost-effectiveness criteria been defined?					Examine the cost-effectiveness criteria.	Compliance	Confirmation/ examination
3.	Has the cost-effectiveness for this application system been calculated in accordance with the procedures?					Examine the calculation and confirm that it has been prepared in accordance with the procedures.	Compliance	Checklist
4.	Are the cost-effectiveness procedures applicable to this application?					Confirm with the user that the procedures are applicable to this application.	Compliance	Confirmation/ examination
5.	Could application characteristics cause the actual cost to vary significantly from the projections?					Confirm with the user that there are no unusual characteristics that could cause the cost to vary significantly.	Compliance	Confirmation/ examination
6.	Are there application characteristics that could cause the benefits to vary significantly from the projected benefits?					Confirm with the user that there are no characteristics that would cause the actual benefits to vary significantly from the projected benefits.	Compliance	Confirmation/ examination
7.	Is the expected life of the project reasonable?					Confirm with the user the reasonable life for the project.	Compliance	Confirmation/ examination
8.	Does a design phase schedule exist which identifies tasks, people, budgets, and costs?					Examine the completeness of the design phase work program.	Compliance	Design review

(Continues)

303

WORK PAPER 9.1 (Continued)

TEST FACTOR: Operational Needs Defined

#	TEST CRITERIA	ASSESSMENT				RECOMMENDED TEST	TEST TECHNIQUE	TEST TOOL
		Very Adequate	Adequate	Inadequate	N/A			
1.	Have the volume of transactions been identified?					Confirm with user volume of transactions is correct.	Compliance	Confirmation/ examination
2.	Has the timing of processing been determined?					Confirm with user the timing is reasonable.	Compliance	Confirmation/ examination
3.	Has the frequency of processing been determined?					Confirm with user the frequency is reasonable.	Compliance	Confirmation/ examination
4.	Has the number of documents that need to be stored on-line been determined?					Confirm with user the storage requirements are correct.	Compliance	Confirmation/ examination
5.	Will communication capabilities be required for processing?					Confirm with user the communication needs are correct.	Compliance	Confirmation/ examination
6.	Will special processing capabilities such as optical scanners be required?					Review documentation to identify special processing needs.	Operations	Peer review
7.	Will computer operations be expected to perform special tasks, such as data entry?					Review documentation to identify special operating requirements.	Operations	Peer review
8.	Has it been confirmed with computer operations that they have been advised of project requirements?					Confirm with computer operations that they have been advised of project requirements.	Operations	Confirmation/ examination

WORK PAPER 9.1 (Continued)

TEST FACTOR: Tolerances Established

#	TEST CRITERIA	ASSESSMENT				RECOMMENDED TEST	TEST TECHNIQUE	TEST TOOL
		Very Adequate	Adequate	Inadequate	N/A			
1.	Have the significant financial fields been identified?					Confirm with the accounting department that the indicated financial fields are the key financial fields for the application system.	Control	Confirmation/examination
2.	Has responsibility for the accuracy and completeness of each financial field been assigned?					Examine system documentation indicating individual responsible for each key financial field.	Control	Inspections
3.	Have the accuracy and completeness risks been identified?					Assess the completeness of the identified risks.	Requirements	Walkthroughs
4.	Has the individual responsible for each field stated the required precision for financial accuracy?					Review the system documentation to determine that the stated accuracy precision is recorded.	Control	Confirmation/examination
5.	Has the accounting cutoff method been determined?					Confirm with the user that the projected cutoff procedure is realistic.	Control	Confirmation/examination
6.	Have procedures been established to ensure that all of the transactions will be entered on a timely basis?					Examine the reasonableness of the procedures to ensure the timely recording of transactions.	Control	Walkthroughs
7.	Has a procedure been specified to monitor the accuracy of financial information?					Review the reasonableness of the procedures to monitor financial accuracy.	Control	Walkthroughs
8.	Are rules established on handling inaccurate and incomplete data?					Review the reasonableness of the procedures to handle inaccurate and incomplete data.	Error handling	Inspections

(Continues)

WORK PAPER 9.1 (Continued)

TEST FACTOR: Authorization Rules Defined

#	TEST CRITERIA	ASSESSMENT				RECOMMENDED TEST	TEST TECHNIQUE	TEST TOOL
		Very Adequate	Adequate	Inadequate	N/A			
1.	Have all of the key transactions been identified?					Confirm with the user that all of the key transactions are identified.	Security	Confirmation/ examination
2.	Have the rules for authorizing each of the key transactions been determined?					Verify that the authorization rules comply with organizational policies and procedures.	Control	Confirmation/ examination & Peer review
3.	Are the authorization rules consistent with the value of the resources controlled by the transaction?					Review the reasonableness of the authorization rules in relationship to the resources controlled.	Requirements	Walkthroughs and Peer review
4.	Have the individuals been identified who can authorize each transaction?					Verify that the individuals have been granted that specific authorization by management.	Control	Confirmation/ examination & Peer review
5.	Have specifications been determined requiring the name of the individual authorizing the transaction to be carried with the transaction?					Review the documentation to verify the specifications require the system to maintain records on who authorized each transaction.	Requirements	Inspection
6.	Have the transactions that will be automatically generated by the system been identified?					Confirm with the user that all of the transactions that will be computer generated have been identified.	Security	Confirmation/ examination
7.	Have the rules for authorizing computer-generated transactions been identified?					Verify that these authorization rules are consistent with the organization's policies and procedures.	Control	Confirmation/ examination
8.	Have procedures been specified to monitor the reasonableness of computer-generated transactions?					Review the reasonableness of the procedures that will monitor computer-generated transactions.	Requirements	Walkthroughs

WORK PAPER 9.1 (Continued)

TEST FACTOR: File Integrity Requirements

#	TEST CRITERIA	ASSESSMENT				RECOMMENDED TEST	TEST TECHNIQUE	TEST TOOL
		Very Ade-quate	Ade-quate	Inade-quate	N/A			
1.	Have key computer files been identified?					Confirm with the user that the identified files are the key files.	Requirements	Confirmation/examination
2.	Has the composition of the data on each of the key files been identified?					Confirm with the user that the major data fields have been identified.	Requirements	Confirmation/examination
3.	Have the key control fields been identified?					Confirm with the user that the identified key fields are the key control fields.	Requirements	Confirmation/examination
4.	Has the method of internal file integrity for each of the key fields been determined?					Verify the reasonableness of the method to ensure the integrity of the key fields within the automated system.	Control	Walkthroughs
5.	In a multiuser system, has one user been assigned data integrity responsibility?					Determine the reasonableness of assigning responsibility to the named individual.	Control	Fact finding
6.	Has a decision been made as to whether the integrity of the field warrants an external independently maintained control total?					Confirm with the organization's comptroller the importance of the key fields with which independent external control totals are not maintained.	Control	Confirmation/examination
7.	Has the method of maintaining independent control totals on the key fields been determined?					Examine the reasonableness of the method for maintaining independent control totals on key fields.	Control	Fact finding
8.	Have tolerances been established on the degree of reliability expected from file integrity controls?					Confirm the reasonableness of the integrity tolerances with the organization's comptroller.	Control	Confirmation/examination

(Continues)

307

WORK PAPER 9.1   (Continued)

TEST FACTOR: Reconstruction Requirements Defined

#	TEST CRITERIA	ASSESSMENT				RECOMMENDED TEST	TEST TECHNIQUE	TEST TOOL
		Very Adequate	Adequate	Inadequate	N/A			
1.	Does the organization's record retention policy include automated applications?					Review the applicability of the record retention policy to automated applications.	Control	Walkthroughs
2.	Have the criteria for reconstructing transaction processing been determined?					Review the reasonableness of the reconstruction criteria with the application user.	Requirements	Fact finding
3.	Have the criteria for reconstructing computer files been determined?					Verify the reasonableness of reconstruction procedures with the manager of computer operations.	Requirements	Fact finding
4.	Is requirements documentation adequate and in compliance with standards?					Verify the completeness and adequacy of requirements documentation.	Requirements	Inspections
5.	Have the criteria for reconstructing processing from a point of known integrity been determined?					Confirm the reasonableness of the processing reconstruction requirements with the manager of computer operations.	Requirements	Confirmation/ examination
6.	Has the project stated a requirement to trace transactions to application control totals?					Verify that the system specifications include this requirement.	Control	Confirmation/ examination
7.	Has the project stated a requirement specifying that control totals must be supportable by identifying all the transactions comprising that control total?					Verify that the system specifications include this requirement.	Control	Confirmation/ examination
8.	Has the retention period for all of the reconstruction information been specified?					Confirm that the retention periods are in accordance with the organization's record retention policy.	Requirements	Inspections

WORK PAPER 9.1 (Continued)

TEST FACTOR: Impact of Failure Defined

#	TEST CRITERIA	ASSESSMENT				RECOMMENDED TEST	TEST TECHNIQUE	TEST TOOL
		Very Adequate	Adequate	Inadequate	N/A			
1.	Has the dollar loss of an application system failure been defined?					Examine the reasonableness of the dollar loss.	Recovery	Fact finding
2.	Has the dollar loss calculation for a failure been extended to show the loss at different time intervals, such as one hour, eight hours, one day, one week, etc.?					Examine the reasonableness of the loss amounts at various time intervals.	Recovery	Fact finding
3.	Is the proposed system technology reliable and proven in practice?					Confirm with independent sources the reliability and track record of the recommended hardware and software.	Recovery	Confirmation/ examination
4.	Has a decision been made as to whether it is necessary to recover this application in the event of a system failure?					Confirm the correctness of the decision with the system user.	Recovery	Confirmation/ examination
5.	Are alternate processing procedures needed in the event that the system becomes unoperational?					Confirm the need for alternate processing procedures with the user.	Recovery	Confirmation/ examination
6.	If alternate processing procedures are needed, have they been specified?					Confirm with the user the reasonableness of those alternate processing procedures.	Recovery	Confirmation/ examination
7.	Has a procedure been identified for notifying users in the event of a system failure?					Confirm with the user the reasonableness of the notification procedure.	Recovery	Confirmation/ examination
8.	Has the desired percent of up-time for the system been specified?					Confirm the reasonableness of the up-time with the user.	Recovery	Confirmation/ examination

WORK PAPER 9.1 *(Continued)*

TEST FACTOR: Desired Service Level Defined

#	TEST CRITERIA	ASSESSMENT				RECOMMENDED TEST	TEST TECHNIQUE	TEST TOOL
		Very Adequate	Adequate	Inadequate	N/A			
1.	Has the response time for each transaction been identified?					Confirm with the user that the response times are reasonable.	Operations	Confirmation/ examination
2.	Has a schedule been established indicating which part of the system is run on which day?					Confirm with computer operations that there is sufficient capacity to meet these service levels.	Operations	Confirmation/ examination
3.	Do all vendor contracts indicate maintenance support for key hardware and software?					Review contractual specifications to ensure they include maintenance.	Operations	Confirmation/ examination
4.	Have processing tolerances been established for each part of the system, such as a particular report is to be delivered within plus/minus two hours of the scheduled time?					Confirm with the user that these service level tolerances are correct.	Operations	Confirmation/ examination
5.	Can computer operations process the requirements within the expected tolerances?					Confirm with the manager of computer operations the reasonableness of the tolerances.	Operations	Confirmation/ examination
6.	Has the priority of each part of system processing been decided to determine which segment runs first in the event computer time is limited?					Confirm with the user the reasonableness of the priorities.	Operations	Confirmation/ examination
7.	Has the priority of each application been established in relationship to other applications to determine priority of processing after a failure and in the event of limited computer time?					Confirm with a member of executive management the reasonableness of the application system priority.	Operations	Confirmation/ examination
8.	Has the volume of processing requirements been projected for a reasonable period of time in the future?					Confirm with the manager of operations there will be sufficient capacity to meet these increased volumes.	Operations	Confirmation/ examination

WORK PAPER 9.1 *(Continued)*

TEST FACTOR: Access Defined

#	TEST CRITERIA	ASSESSMENT				RECOMMENDED TEST	TEST TECHNIQUE	TEST TOOL
		Very Ade-quate	Ade-quate	Inade-quate	N/A			
1.	Have the application resources been identified?					Confirm with the user that the identified resources are complete.	Security	Risk matrix & Confirmation/ examination
2.	Have the users of those resources been identified?					Confirm with the individual responsible for those resources that the users are authorized users.	Security	Risk matrix & Confirmation/ examination
3.	Have the individuals responsible for those resources been identified?					Confirm with user management that these are the individuals responsible for those resources.	Security	Risk matrix & Confirmation/ examination
4.	Has a profile been established matching resources with the users authorized to access those resources?					Examine the completeness of the user profile.	Security	Risk matrix & Peer review
5.	Have procedures been identified to enforce the user profile?					Confirm with the manager of computer operations that the procedures are workable.	Security	Confirmation/ examination
6.	Has the importance of each resource been identified (e.g., a resource security classification procedure)?					Confirm with the individual responsible that the security classifications are correct.	Security	Confirmation/ examination
7.	Has a procedure been established for monitoring access violations?					Evaluate the reasonableness of the monitoring procedures.	Control	Fact finding
8.	Has a process been established to punish access violators?					Confirm with management that they intend to enforce those violation procedures.	Control	Confirmation/ examination

WORK PAPER 9.2   Quality Control Checklist

Field Requirements

FIELD	INSTRUCTIONS FOR ENTERING DATA
Number	A number that sequentially identifies the quality control items, which if positively addressed would indicate that this step has been performed correctly.
Item	The specific quality control item that is used to measure the effectiveness of performing this step.
Response	The testers should indicate in this column whether they have performed the referenced item. The response can be Yes, No, or N/A if it is not appropriate for your organization's testing process.
Comments	This column is used to clarify the Yes, No, or N/A response for the item indicated. Generally the comments column need only be completed for No responses; No responses should be investigated and a determination made as to whether this item needs to be performed before this step can be considered complete.

NUMBER	ITEM	RESPONSE			COMMENTS
		YES	NO	N/A	
1	Are the defined requirements testable?				
2	Does the user agree the defined requirements are correct?				
3	Do the developers understand the requirements?				
4	Do the stated requirements meet the stated business objectives for the project?				
5	Have the project risks been identified?				
6	Was a reasonable process followed in defining the requirements?				
7	Are project control requirements adequate to minimize project risks?				
8	Was a project requirements walkthrough conducted?				

# CHAPTER 10

Step 4: Design Phase Testing

The design phase provides the opportunity to test the structure (both internal and external) of the computerized application. At this point, requirements are converted into a system structure that will be implemented on the computer. The greater the assurance of the project team that the structure is sound and efficient, the higher the probability that the project will be successful.

Current test tools permit the structure to be tested in both a static and a dynamic mode. It is possible through modeling and simulation to execute the structure on the computer in order to analyze the performance characteristics of the structure. However, the testing concepts must be developed hand-in-hand with the design process in order to gain maximum test advantages.

Overview

The design phase involves a close working relationship between the user and the system designer. Neither party should be dominant during this phase, which is responsible for converting the defined user requirements into a process that can be accomplished by a computer. It is important that both the user and systems designer work as partners to develop not only an efficient application system, but also one that is acceptable to the user.

Testing during the design phase should be jointly shared by the user and the information services project team. If the team is comprised of both users and IT personnel, then the project team can accept test responsibility.

The system design is an IT responsibility. It is therefore logical to assume that IT should accept responsibility for the adequacy of that design, and thus have test responsibility. Unfortunately, this logic shifts responsibility from the user to information services. The danger is that the system may become information services' system, as opposed to the user's system. When the user is involved in establishing test criteria, the ultimate responsibility for the application is more clearly established. (See Figure 10.1.)

Objective

This chapter describes testing during the system design phase. Design phase concerns are described and a testing process is proposed to assess whether those concerns have been adequately addressed by the project team. A detailed test process is provided for each of the concerns. The test process recommends scoring the design success factor, conducting a design review, and inspecting design deliverables.

Concerns

The design phase can be viewed as a funnel that takes the broad system requirements at the wide end of the funnel and narrows them down through a design process to very detailed specifications. This is a creative phase of the life cycle. Along with this creativity is a concern that some important design aspects will be overlooked.

Understanding design phase concerns produces more effective testing. Testing can then be directed at specific concerns rather than attempting broad-based testing. This enables the test process to be more productive, create a more professional image, and develop more meaningful findings and recommendations.

Workbench

The workbench for conducting a test of the design phase is illustrated in Figure 10.2. This workbench is a static test of the deliverables produced during the design phase. The workbench proposes scoring the success and failure factors in order to estimate the probability of success during this phase. That's followed by analyzing the test factors. The results of these two tasks are incorporated into the design review and an inspection of design deliverables. The report produced would indicate whether the design is accurate and complete.

Input

There are two inputs to the design phase test process. The first is an understanding on the part of the test team as to how design, both internal and external, is constructed. Since there is great variance in the methods and tools used for creating designs, it is

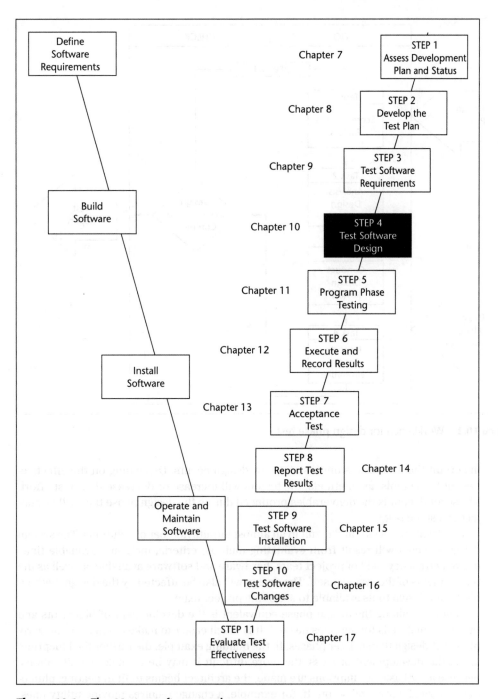

Figure 10.1 The 11-step software testing process.

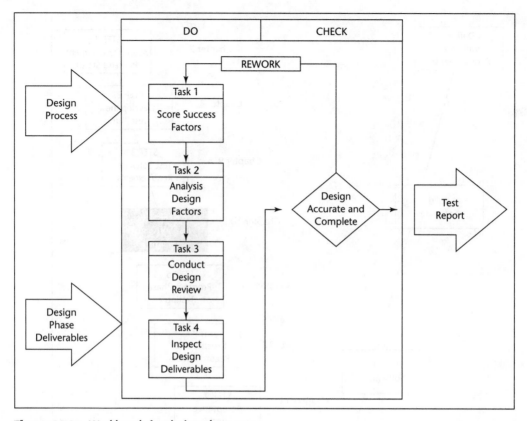

Figure 10.2 Workbench for design phase test.

important that the testers understand how design occurs. Depending on the effectiveness of those tools and methods, the testers will increase or decrease their test effort. The second input is the deliverables produced during the design phase that will be subject to a static test.

The design process could result in an almost infinite number of solutions. The system design selected will result from evaluating multiple criteria, including available time, desired efficiency, skill of project team, hardware and software available, as well as the requirements of the system itself. The design will also be affected by the design methodology and design tools available to assist the project team.

In home building the design phase equivalent is the development of blueprints and the bill of materials for supplies needed. It is much easier to make changes in the early phases of design than in later phases. In the building example, the further the blueprints are in the development process, the more difficult it may be to make modifications, because after basic assumptions are made, the architect begins to fit in heating, plumbing, electrical work, and so on. If, for example, a change requires moving utility lines, the architectural process becomes more difficult. However, it is still significantly cheaper than attempting to make a change after construction commences. Testers must understand the design process.

From a project perspective the most successful testing is that conducted early in the design phase. The sooner the project team becomes aware of potential defects, the cheaper it is to correct those defects. If the project waited until the end of the design phase to begin testing, it would fall into the same trap as many projects that wait until the end of programming to conduct their first tests: When defects are found, the corrective process can be so time-consuming and painful that it may appear cheaper to live with the defects than to correct them.

Testing normally occurs using the deliverables produced by the design phase. The more common design phase deliverables include:

- Input specifications
- Processing specifications
- File specifications
- Output specifications
- Control specifications
- System flowcharts
- Hardware and software requirements
- Manual operating procedure specifications
- Data retention policies

Do Procedures

There are four tasks that need to be completed during the design phase testing:

1. Score success factors.
2. Analyze test factors.
3. Conduct design review.
4. Inspect design deliverables.

Task 1: Score Success Factors

Scoring is a predictive tool that utilizes previous systems experience. Existing systems are analyzed to determine the attributes of those systems and their correlation to the success or failure of that particular application. Once the attributes correlating to success or failure can be identified, they can be used to predict the behavior of systems under development.

The concept is the same as that used for predicting the outcome of elections. The people making the predictions attempt to identify election districts that show a high historical correlation to the outcomes of previous elections. Knowing the voting record of a specific district and the outcomes of previous elections provides the basis for making future predictions. Those districts with a record of picking winners can be sampled, and then, based on that sample, the outcome of an election can be predicted long before all the votes have been counted.

These types of predictors in computer systems are well known, but they had not been properly utilized until the scoring concept was developed. For example, we know there is a positive correlation between user involvement and the success of the computer system: The more heavily the user is involved, the higher the probability that the system will be successful. We also know that there will be problems with computer systems that push the current bounds of technology. For example, the first system to use a new technology could be identified as a high-risk system because of the high probability that problems will be encountered during the implementation.

The scoring concept uses the following criteria for making a prediction:

Sampling. The criteria that will be used will be a sample of all of the criteria encompassed in the implementation of an automated application system. The criteria are not meant to be complete.

High positive correlation. The criteria picked will have shown a high positive correlation in the past with either success or failure of an automated application. These criteria should not be judgmental or intuitive, but rather, those criteria for which it can be demonstrated that the absence or presence of that attribute has shown a high correlation to the outcome of the project.

Ease of use. To be effective the process of scoring must be simple. People will use an easy predictive concept, but will be hesitant to invest large amounts of time and effort.

Develop risk score. The score for each attribute should be determined in a measurable format so that a total risk score can be developed for each application. This will indicate the degree of risk, the area of risk, as well as a comparison of risk among application systems.

The scoring test tool is prepared for use in evaluating all applications. The tool should be general in nature so that it will apply to diverse applications, because the degree of risk must be compared against a departmental norm.

The scoring test tool can be used in one of the following two ways under the direction of the test team:

1. **Project leader assessment.** The application project leader can be given the scoring mechanism and asked to rate the degree of risk for each of the attributes for his or her project. The project leader need not know the importance of any of the attributes in a risk score, but only needs to measure the degree of project risk based on his or her in-depth knowledge of the project.

2. **Test team assessment.** A member of the test team can be assigned the responsibility to develop the risk score. If the test team has worked on the project from the beginning, that individual member may be knowledgeable enough to complete the scoring instrument personally. However, if the test team member lacks knowledge, investigation may be needed to gather sufficient evidence to score the project.

At the conclusion of the scoring process, the result can be used in any of the following ways:

Estimate extent of testing. The higher the risk, the more testing that management may desire. Knowing that an application is high risk alerts management to the need to take those steps necessary to reduce that risk to an acceptable level.

Identify areas of test. Depending upon the sophistication of the scoring instrument, specific areas may be identified for testing. For example, if computer logic is shown to be high risk, testing should thoroughly evaluate the correctness of that processing.

Identify composition of test team. The types of risks associated with the application system help determine the composition of the test team. For example, if the risks deal more with technology than with logic, the test team should include individuals thoroughly knowledgeable in that technology.

A scoring instrument for application systems is presented in Work Paper 10.1 at the end of the chapter. This scoring instrument develops a computer application system profile on many different system characteristics or attributes. The user is then asked to determine whether the system being reviewed is high, medium, or low risk for the identified characteristic. For example, the first characteristic deals with the importance of the function being computerized. If that function is important to several organizational units, it is a high-risk application. If the requirements are only of limited significance to cooperating units, the risk drops to medium; if there are no significant conflicting needs and the application is primarily for one organizational unit, the risk is low. The individual doing the assessment circles the appropriate indicator. At the conclusion, a score can be developed indicating the number of high-risk, medium-risk, and low-risk indicators.

A risk score is achieved by mathematically developing a score by using the following table:

RISK OF CHARACTERISTIC	# OF CHARACTERISTICS RATED	FACTOR FOR MULTIPLICATION	FACTOR FOR RISK SCORE
High		3	
Medium		2	
Low		1	
TOTAL SCORE			

To use this table, the number of characteristics rated high, medium, and low should be totaled, and the totals entered in the "number of characteristics rated" column. Each number is then multiplied by the factor to arrive at a risk score. For example, the total number of characteristics defined by high risk should be multiplied by 3. The three numbers are then added together to arrive at a total risk score, which can be used for comparison between application systems or against a norm. Another way to use the information is to divide the total score by the total number of risk characteristics to obtain a score between 1 and 3. The higher the score is to 3, the higher the risk, and conversely, the lower the score, the lower the risk.

Task 2: Analyze Test Factors

A test process for each of the design phase test factors (concerns) is contained in Work Paper 10.2 at the end of the chapter. The individual conducting the test can select the concerns of interest and use the appropriate test programs, keeping in mind the following general objectives for the design phase:

- Develop a solution to the business problem.
- Determine the role of the computer in solving the business problem.
- Develop specifications for the manual and automated segments of the system.
- Comply with policies, procedures, standards, and regulations.
- Define controls that will reduce application risks to an acceptable level.
- Complete the project within budgetary, staffing, and scheduling constraints.

The concerns to be analyzed during the design phase are described in the following subsections.

Data Integrity Controls Designed

Data integrity commences with risk identification, followed by management decisions on the acceptability of that risk, stated in terms of the amount of loss that is acceptable. The data integrity controls are then designed to these risk tolerance specifications.

Authorization Rules Designed

Authorization in automated systems may be manual and/or automated. The procedures for manual authorization should be specified during the design phase. Automated authorization methods must be specified in more detail than manual procedures because they cannot rely on people to react to unexpected situations.

File Integrity Controls Designed

File integrity is ensured by file identification methods, automated file controls, and independently maintained file integrity controls. The specifications for this three-part integrity process must be determined during the design phase.

Audit Trail Designed

The audit trail provides the capability to trace transactions from their origination to control totals, and to identify all of the transactions substantiating a control total. In addition, the audit trail is used to substantiate individual transaction processing, and to recover the integrity of computer operations after it has been lost. Frequently, governmental agencies will specify the types of information that need to be retained for audit trail purposes—this information must be defined during the design phase. The audit trail should be designed to achieve those purposes.

Contingency Plan Designed

The contingency plan outlines the actions to be performed in the event of problems. This plan includes the manual methods to be followed while the automated applications are not in operation, the backup and recovery procedures, as well as physical site considerations. Contingency plan specifications should be outlined during the design phase.

Method to Achieve Service Level Designed

The requirements phase defined the service levels to be achieved during the operation of the application. The method of achieving those service levels is developed during the design phase. This concern deals primarily with the performance of the system and its ability to satisfy user needs on a timely basis.

Access Procedures Defined

Security in an automated system is achieved by predefining who can have access and for what purpose and then enforcing those access rules. A security profile indicates who can have access to what resources. During the design phase, the procedures, tools, and techniques necessary to develop and implement a security profile must be developed.

Design Complies with Methodology

The system design process should be performed and documented in accordance with information services (IS) methodology. Standardized design procedures ensure ease of understanding by all parties trained in that methodology, and at the same time help ensure the completeness of the design process. The purpose of the methodology is to develop better systems at a lower cost.

Design Conforms to Requirements

The system design is a translation of the user requirements into detailed system specifications. During any translation, misunderstandings or misinterpretations can occur. Steps need to be taken to ensure that the completed design achieves the objectives and intent of the defined requirements.

Design Facilitates Use

The final product must be used by people. The easier the system is to use, the more likely that the features will be utilized and the transactions processed correctly. The design must take into consideration the skill levels and job motivation of the people using the application system.

Design Is Maintainable

The cost of maintaining a computer application normally far exceeds the cost to develop. Identifying those system aspects that are most likely to be changed and building those parts of the system for ease of maintenance is an important aspect of the design process. The system design needed for maintainability may change significantly depending upon the expected frequency of change.

Design Is Portable

If the requirements indicate that the application system should be transferable from one piece of hardware to another, or one version of software to another, the design should incorporate those portability features. When future hardware and software is uncertain, the design should be generalized, and not attempt to take advantage of features or facilities of existing hardware and software.

Interface Design Is Complete

The interface to other applications needs to be identified and the specifications for that interface designed. Interface specifications should also consider secondary uses of application information. Understanding these secondary uses may result in additional capabilities included within the design process.

Design Achieves Criteria

The cost/benefit study performed during the requirements phase may not supply a high-precision evaluation. One organization stated to their management that the requirements phase estimate could be off by plus or minus 50 percent. During the design phase, the performance estimates can be more accurately stated so that a better prediction can be made as to whether the performance criteria can be achieved. A guideline used by one corporation is that the accuracy of estimating the achievement of the performance criteria at the end of the design phase should be within plus or minus 10 percent.

Needs Communicated to Operations

Operations needs to identify future processing requirements in order to prepare to handle those requirements when the system becomes operational. The larger the processing requirements, the greater the need to involve operations in the design alternative considerations.

A detailed work program is provided for each of the 15 design phase test concerns. These work programs follow and outline the criteria to be assessed for each concern, together with the recommended test, test technique, and test tool to be used in evaluating each criterion. Note that the person conducting the test should use judgment regarding the extent of testing relative to the importance of the criteria to the application. (Note: To do this task follow the instructions for Task 2 in Chapter 9.)

Task 3: Conduct Design Review

The design review is structured using the same basic information that formed the basis for scoring. However, in the case of the design review the criteria will be more specific. The objective is to preidentify those attributes of design that correlate to system problems. The design review then investigates those attributes to determine that they have been appropriately addressed by the project team.

The design review is conducted by a team of individuals knowledgeable in the design process. They are charged with the responsibility of reviewing the application system for completeness and reasonableness. It is not necessary that the team is knowledgeable about the specific application, but they must be knowledgeable about the design methodology.

In conducting a design review, the team follows a predetermined review process. The design review is normally formal and highly structured in nature, in that the review team has predetermined investigations to make and has known start and stop points. The design review normally follows the design methodology. Team members attempt to determine that all the tasks have been properly performed. At the conclusion of the design review, the team normally issues a formal report indicating their findings and recommendations about the project. The design review team may be comprised of the following members:

Project personnel. The project personnel can conduct their own design review. Normally the individual on the project assigned review responsibility is not the same person that actually designed the system; however, the reviewer may have had partial design responsibility. This requires individuals to accept different roles and responsibilities during the review process than they have held during the design process. Because of the possible ties to the actual design of the system, having the design review checklist as a self-assessment tool normally fulfills a valuable function for the reviewer(s).

Independent review team. The members of this review team are not members of the project being reviewed. They can be from other projects or quality assurance groups, or they can be professional testers. This mode of operation provides a greater degree of independence in conducting the review in that there is no conflict of interest between the design and review roles. On the other hand, it is frequently difficult for peers to be critical of each other, especially in situations where a reviewer might eventually work for the person being reviewed.

These general guidelines should be followed in conducting a review:

1. **Select the review team.** The members of the review team should be selected in advance of the review process.

2. **Train the review team members.** The individuals who will be conducting the review should be trained in how to conduct the review. At a minimum this means reviewing the checklist and explaining the objective and intent of each question. It is also advisable to train the people in the interpersonal relationships involved in conducting a review so that the review can be held in a nonthreatening environment.

3. **Notify the project team.** The project team should be notified several days in advance of the review as to when the review will occur and the responsibility of the project team during the review. Obviously, if the project team conducts the review this task is less important, but it is still necessary to formally schedule the review so that all members will be present.

4. **Allot adequate time.** The review should be conducted in a formal, businesslike manner, as efficiently as possible, but should not be rushed. Sufficient time should be allocated to probe and investigate areas of concern. Even when the same people conduct the review that designed the system, the interpersonal relationships and synergistic effect of a review can produce many positive effects if sufficient time is allocated to enable appropriate interaction.

5. **Document the review facts.** All of the factual findings of the review should be recorded. Normally this can be done on the review checklist unless the comments are lengthy or supporting evidence is required. In any case, facts should be referenced to the specific checklist questions that uncovered them.

6. **Review the facts with the project team.** The correctness of the facts should be substantiated with all individuals involved, and the review should not proceed until this is done. It is better to do this at the end of the review for important findings than intermittently during the review process.

7. **Develop review recommendations.** Based upon the facts, the review team should offer their recommendations to correct any problem situation. These recommendations are an important part of the review process.

8. **Review recommendations with the project team.** The project team should be the first to receive the recommendations and have an opportunity to accept, modify, or reject the recommendations.

9. **Prepare a formal report.** A report documenting the findings, the recommendations, and the action taken or to be taken on the recommendations should be prepared. This report may or may not be sent to higher levels of management, depending upon the review ground rules established by the organization. However, it is important to have a formal record of the review process, what it found, and the actions taken on recommendations.

One or more reviews may occur during the design phase. The number of reviews will depend on the importance of the project and the time span of the design phase. A program for a two-point design phase review is shown in Work Papers 10.3 and 10.4. This provides for the first review at the end of the business system design (Work Paper 10.3) that part of the design where it is determined how the business problem will be solved. The second review point would occur after the computer system design (Work Paper 10.4) is complete. Note that the questions in the two review checklists are taken from an actual organization's review process, and thus may not be applicable to all organizations. Normally, the review process needs to be customized based upon the design methodology, information services policies and procedures, and the criteria found to be causing problems in the organization.

Task 4: Inspect Design Deliverables

Inspection is a process by which completed but untested design products are evaluated as to whether the specified changes were installed correctly. To accomplish this, inspectors examine the unchanged product, the change specifications, and the changed product to determine the outcome. They look for three types of defects: errors, meaning the change has not been made correctly; missing, meaning something that should have been changed, but was not changed; and extra, meaning something not intended was changed or added.

The inspection team reviews the product in a team after each inspector has reviewed it individually. The team then reaches a consensus on the errors, missing, and extra defects. The author (the person implementing the project change) is given those defect descriptions so that the product can be changed prior to dynamic testing. After the changes are made, they were reinspected to verify correctness; then dynamic testing can commence. The purpose of inspections is twofold: to conduct an examination by peers, which normally improves the quality of work because the synergy of a team is applied to the solution; and to remove defects during inspection. Chapter 8 contains the detailed procedures for conducting a design inspection.

Check Procedures

Workpaper 10.5 is a quality control checklist for this step. It is designed so that Yes responses indicate good test practices; No responses warrant additional investigation. A Comments column is provided to explain No responses and to record results of investigation. The N/A column is used when the checklist item is not applicable to the test situation.

Output

There are two categories produced from this step. The first is the deficiencies uncovered in the design review, and the second is the defects and assessment produced by the inspection process.

Both the design review and the design deliverables inspection process will produce a defects list. Since the review is more general in nature it may include some recommendations and areas of concern. Since inspections are more specific and tied to standards, these defects are usually variances from standards and are nonargumentive.

One of three categories of results can be produced from each design deliverables inspection. This is one of the following three assessments of the product being inspected:

1. **No defects found.** Product has passed the inspection.

2. **Minor work required.** Only minor defects were found and a reinspection is not required. The author will correct all defects, and then the moderator will verify the results.

3. **Major rework required.** Major defects were found, and a reinspection is required.

After all the tasks in this step have been performed, there should be only one deliverable: the moderator's certification of the product, releasing the product to the next phase of the process to make the organization software compliant.

Guidelines

Many of the available test tools for systems design are relatively new and unproven. Some of the more promising techniques require design specifications to be recorded in predetermined formats. While the long-run potential for design phase testing is very promising, there are few proven design phase test tools.

Two design phase test tools that are receiving widespread acceptance are scoring and design reviews. Scoring is a tool designed to identify the risk associated with an automated application. The design review concept involves a formal assessment of the completeness of the process followed during the design phase.

These two recommended test tools complement each other. Scoring is a process of identifying the system attributes that correlate to risk and then determining the extent to which those attributes are present or absent in the system being scored. The result of scoring is a determination of the degree of risk in the application system, and thus establishes the extent to which testing is needed. The design review then becomes the vehicle for testing the design specifications. The higher the risk, the more detailed the design review should be; for minimal-risk systems the design review could be limited or even nonexistent.

The following items can enhance the benefits of formal inspections:

- **Training.** Use inspections to train new staff members in the department's standards and procedures.

- **Product quality.** Do not inspect obviously poor products; that is, the inspectors should not do the developers' work. Developers should not submit a product for inspection if they are not satisfied with the quality of the product.

Summary

The requirements phase outputs define the customer's needs in a format that can be used to create design specifications. External design is a concept, and internal design is the system architecture. Depending on the methods and tools used, all or parts of the internal design may be generated from the external design. Thus, the two designs are combined in this same chapter. This chapter describes a process for testers to evaluate the accuracy and completeness of the design process. Once verified as accurate and complete, the design can be moved to the build phase to create the code that will produce the needed results from the user-provided input.

WORK PAPER 10.1   Computer Applications Risk Scoring Form[1]

SIGNIFICANT CHARACTERISTICS	INDICATIVE OF HIGH RISK	INDICATIVE OF MEDIUM RISK	INDICATIVE OF LOW RISK	COMMENTS
System Scope and Complexity				
Organizational breadth				
a) Important functions	Must meet important conflicting needs of several organizational units.	Meets limited conflicting requirements of cooperative organizational units.	No significant conflicting needs, serves primarily one organizational unit.	
b) Unrelated organizational units deeply involved	Dependent upon data flowing from many organizational units not under unified direction.	Dependent upon data from a few organizational units with a common interest; if not unified control.	Virtually all input data comes from a small group of sections under unified control.	
Information services breadth				
a) Number of transaction types	More than 25	6 to 25	Less than 6	
b) Number of related record segments	More than 6	4 to 6	Less than 4	
c) Output reports	More than 20	10 to 20	Less than 10	
Margin of error				
a) Necessity for everything to work perfectly, for "split-second timing" for great cooperation (perhaps including external parties), etc.	Very demanding	Realistically demanding	Comfortable margin	
Technical complexity	**High, aggressive**	**Moderate**	**Conservative**	
a) Number of programs including sort/merge	More than 35	20 to 35	Less than 20	

[1]Risk scoring method developed by the General Accounting Office.

(Continues)

WORK PAPER 10.1 *(Continued)*

SIGNIFICANT CHARACTERISTICS	INDICATIVE OF HIGH RISK	INDICATIVE OF MEDIUM RISK	INDICATIVE OF LOW RISK	COMMENTS
b) Programming approach (number of module/functions interacting within an update/file maintenance program)	More than 20	10 to 20	Less than 10	
c) Size of largest program	More than 60K	25K to 60K	Less than 25K	
d) Adaptability of program to change	Low, due to monolithic program design.	Can support problems with adequate talent and effort.	Relatively high; program straightforward, modular, roomy, relatively unpatched, well-documented, etc.	
e) Relationship to equipment in use	Pushes equipment capacity near limits.	Within capacities.	Substantial unused capacity.	
f) Reliance on on-line data-entry automatic document reading or other advanced techniques	Heavy, including direct entry of transactions and other changes into the master files.	Remote-batch processing under remote operations control.	None or limited to file inquiry.	
Pioneering aspects Extent to which the system applies new, difficult, and unproven techniques on a broad scale or in a new situation, thus placing great demands on the non-IS departments, systems and programming groups, IS operations personnel, customers, or vendors, etc.	**Aggressively pioneering** More than a few relatively untried equipment or system software components or system techniques or objectives, at least one of which is crucial.	**Moderate** Few untried systems components and their functions are moderately important; few, if any, pioneering system objectives and techniques.	**Conservative** No untried system components, no pioneering system objectives or techniques.	

WORK PAPER 10.1   *(Continued)*

SIGNIFICANT CHARACTERISTICS	INDICATIVE OF HIGH RISK	INDICATIVE OF MEDIUM RISK	INDICATIVE OF LOW RISK	COMMENTS
System stability	**Unstable, much is new**	**Moderate change, most is not new**	**Stable, little is new**	
a) Age of system (since inception or last big change)	Less than 1 year	1 to 2 years	Over 2 years	
b) Frequency of significant change	More than 4 per year	2 to 4 per year	Less than 2 per year	
c) Extent of total change in last year	Affecting more than 25% of programs.	Affecting 10 to 25% of programs.	Affecting less than 10% of programs.	
d) User approval of specifications	Cursory, essentially uninformed.	Reasonably informed as to general but not detailed specifications; approval apt to be informal.	Formal, written approval, based on informed judgment and written, reasonably precise specifications.	
Satisfaction of user requirements	**Low satisfaction, many problems**	**Reasonable satisfaction, some problems**	**High satisfaction**	
a) Completeness	Incomplete, significant number of items not processed in proper period.	Occasional problems but normally no great difficulties.	No significant data omitted or processed in wrong period.	
b) Accuracy	Considerable error problem, with items in suspense or improperly handled.	Occasional problems but normally not great difficulties.	Errors not numerous or of consequence.	
c) Promptness in terms of needs	Reports and documents delayed so as to be almost useless; forced to rely on informal records.	Reports and documents not always available when desired; present timetable inconvenient but tolerable.	Reports and documents produced soon enough to meet operational needs.	

(Continues)

329

SIGNIFICANT CHARACTERISTICS	INDICATIVE OF HIGH RISK	INDICATIVE OF MEDIUM RISK	INDICATIVE OF LOW RISK	COMMENTS
d) Accessibility of details (to answer inquiries, review for reasonableness, make corrections, etc.)	Great difficulty in obtaining details of transactions or balances except with much delay.	Complete details available monthly; in interim, details available with some difficulty and delay.	Details readily available.	
e) Reference to source documents (audit trail)	Great difficulty in locating documents promptly.	Audit trail excellent; some problems with filing and storage.	Audit trail excellent; filing and storage good.	
f) Conformity with established system specifications	Actual procedures and operations differ in important respects.	Limited tests indicate that actual procedures and operations differ in only minor respects and operations produce desired results.	Limited tests indicate actual procedures and operations produce desired results.	
Source data origin and approval	**Leaves much to be desired**	**Reasonable**	**Sound procedures, well carried out**	
a) People, procedures, knowledge, discipline, division of duties, etc. in departments that originate and/or approve data	Situation leaves much to be desired.	Situation satisfactory, but could stand some improvement.	Situation satisfactory.	
b) Data control procedures outside the information services organization	None or relatively ineffective; e.g., use of noncritical fields, loose liaison with IS department, little concern with rejected items.	Control procedures based on noncritical fields; reasonably effective liaison with IS department.	Control procedures include critical fields; good tie-in with IS department; especially good on rejected items.	
c) Error rate	Over 7% of transactions rejected after leaving source data department.	4–7% of transactions rejected after leaving source data department.	Less than 4% of transactions rejected after leaving source data department.	

SIGNIFICANT CHARACTERISTICS	INDICATIVE OF HIGH RISK	INDICATIVE OF MEDIUM RISK	INDICATIVE OF LOW RISK	COMMENTS
d) Error backing	Many 30-day-old items.	Mostly 10–15-day-old items.	Items primarily less than 7 days old.	
Input data control (within information services department)	**Leaves much to be desired**	**Reasonable**	**Sound, well executed**	
a) Relationship with external controls	Loose liaison with external control units; little concern with rejected items; batch totals not part of input procedures; only use controls like item counts; no control totals of any kind.	Reasonably effective liaison with external data control units; good control over new items, but less satisfactory control over rejected items; batch totals received, but generated by computer.	Good tie-in with external control units for both valid and rejected items; batch totals received as part of input process.	
b) Selection of critical control fields.	Control based on noncritical fields.	Control based on a mixture of critical and noncritical fields, with effective supplementary checks.	Control established on critical fields.	
c) Controls over key transcription	Control based on batch totals	Control based on transmittal sheets; batch totals and key verification of critical fields not batch controlled.	Control based on transmittal sheets, batch totals maintained on data logs, key verification of all critical fields, and written "sign-off" procedures.	
Data validation (computer editing)	**Few, relatively simple tests**	**Reasonably effective tests**	**Extensive, well-designed tests**	
a) Edit tests	Alphanumeric tests.	Range and alphanumeric tests.	Range, alphanumeric, and check-digit tests.	
b) Sophistication	Simple, based on edit of one field at a time.	Simple editing, plus some editing based on the interrelationship of two.	Simple editing, plus extensive edit tests based on the interrelationship of two or more fields.	

(Continues)

SIGNIFICANT CHARACTERISTICS	INDICATIVE OF HIGH RISK	INDICATIVE OF MEDIUM RISK	INDICATIVE OF LOW RISK	COMMENTS
c) Application to critical data	A considerable amount of critical data is not edited.	A few critical fields are edited only indirectly.	Editing performed on critical fields.	
d) Error balancing, retrieval, and correction procedures	Error rejected by system and eliminated from controls; treated as new items when reintroduced.	Number and value of rejected items carried in suspense account without electronically maintained details.	Error carried in suspense account in total and in detail until removed by correction.	
Computer processing control procedure	**Limited—excessive reliance on manual**	**Reasonable**	**Comprehensive and automatic**	
a) Controls within machine room	Informal operating instructions.	Written operating procedures.	Operations are based on a schedule, use up-to-date instructions.	
b) Manual and electronic safeguards against incorrect processing of files	Tape library controls by serial number; no programmed checks.	Tape library controls by serial number; programmed checks applied to file identification.	Programmed label check applied to serial number, expiration date, and the identification.	
c) Recording of run-to-run debit, credit, and balance totals for both transaction processing and master field records	Run-to-run totals not used.	Run-to-run totals printed and compared manually.	Run-to-run totals printed and compared by program.	
d) Documentation status	Poor or no standards; uneven adherence; not part of system and program development.	Adequate practices not uniformly adhered to; documentation done "after the fact."	Excellent standards closely adhered to and carried out as part of system and program development.	
e) System test practices	Some transaction paths not tested.	Each transaction path tested individually.	Each transaction path tested in combination with all other transactions.	

WORK PAPER 10.1 *(Continued)*

SIGNIFICANT CHARACTERISTICS	INDICATIVE OF HIGH RISK	INDICATIVE OF MEDIUM RISK	INDICATIVE OF LOW RISK	COMMENTS
Output control	**Essentially lacking**	**Reasonable**	**Good in information services and user department**	
a) Quantitative controls				
• In IS department	Virtually nonexistent.	Hard to tie back meaningfully to input controls.	Tied back to input controls.	
• In user department	Virtually nonexistent.	Hard to tie back meaningfully to input controls.	Tied back to input controls.	
b) Qualitative controls	Documents and reports accepted virtually without review.	Sample documents and reports receive limited review.	Documents and reports tested in detail, in addition to receiving a "common sense" review of reasonable data limits.	
c) Distribution controls	No routine report distribution procedures.	Routine procedures for distribution limited to list of users and frequency of report delivery.	Written procedures requiring that control log indicate receipt by user, time of accounting for each copy, etc.	
On-line processing controls				
a) Data transmission controls, including error detection, error recovery, and data security	The front-end control program does not validate operator identification codes or message sequence number, and does not send acknowledgment to origin.	The front-end control program checks terminal and operator identification codes and message sequence number, sends acknowledgment to origin, and provides a transaction log.	The front-end control program validates terminal/operator identification codes plus transaction authorization codes and message sequence number and count, corrects errors, sends acknowledgment to origin, and provides log of transactions plus copies of updated master file records.	

(Continues)

WORK PAPER 10.1 (Continued)

SIGNIFICANT CHARACTERISTICS	INDICATIVE OF HIGH RISK	INDICATIVE OF MEDIUM RISK	INDICATIVE OF LOW RISK	COMMENTS
b) Data validation controls, including error detection and correction	Neither the front-end control nor the application processing program checks for authorization approval codes; no check digits are used with identification keys; there is little use of extensive data relationship tests; erroneous transactions are rejected without analysis or suspense entry.	The application program checks approval codes for key transaction types only, but check digits are not used with identification keys; extensive data relationship tests are used; erroneous transactions are sent back to terminal with a note, but no suspense entry is made.	The application program validates approval codes for all transactions, and check digits are used with identification keys; data relationship tests are used extensively; erroneous transactions are noted in error suspense file when sent back to terminal with note.	
c) Information services controls, including error detection, transaction processing controls, master file processing controls, and file recovery provisions	Application program produces a total number of transactions processed; no master file processing controls; file recovery provisions limited to periodic copy of master file.	Application program produces a summary record of all debit and credit transactions processed; no master file processing controls; file recovery provisions limited to transaction log and periodic copy of master file.	Stored validation range values are used to validate transaction fields; application program summarizes all transactions processed by type, with credit and debit values for each terminal, and uses a master file control trailer record that is balanced by program routine; end-of-processing file recovery provisions include transaction log of active master file records.	

WORK PAPER 10.2   Design Phase Test Process

TEST FACTOR: Data Integrity Controls Designed

#	TEST CRITERIA	ASSESSMENT				RECOMMENDED TEST	TEST TECHNIQUE	TEST TOOL
		Very Adequate	Adequate	Inadequate	N/A			
1.	Are controls established over accuracy and completeness during the transaction origination process?					Review the adequacy of the transaction origination accuracy and completeness control.	Control	Risk matrix & Checklist
2.	Are input transactions controlled, such as through a sequential input number, to ensure that all transactions are entered?					Review the adequacy of the input controls to ensure that all input is entered.	Control	Risk matrix & Checklist
3.	Are communication controls established to ensure the accurate and complete transmission of data?					Review the adequacy of transmission accuracy and completeness controls.	Control	Risk matrix & Checklist
4.	For key entry transactions, such as cash receipts, are batch control totals prepared?					Verify the adequacy of the batch control total procedures.	Requirements	Control flow analysis
5.	For key entry input transactions, such as purchases orders, are batch numbers prepared to ensure that batches of input are not lost?					Verify the adequacy of the batch numbering procedures.	Requirements	Control flow analysis
6.	Are check digits or equivalent controls used on key control field, such as product number, to ensure the accurate entry of product number?					Verify that key fields use procedures that ensure the accurate entry of that information.	Requirements	Error guessing & Design-based functional testing

(Continues)

335

WORK PAPER 10.2 *(Continued)*

TEST FACTOR: Data Integrity Controls Designed *(continued)*

#	TEST CRITERIA	ASSESSMENT				RECOMMENDED TEST	TEST TECHNIQUE	TEST TOOL
		Very Ade-quate	Ade-quate	Inade-quate	N/A			
7.	Is each field subject to extensive data validation checks?					Examine the type and scope of data validation checks for each key field to determine that they are adequate.	Error handling	Acceptance test criteria, Error guessing. Checklist, & Data dictionary
8.	Are input numbers, batch numbers, and batch totals verified by the data validation programs to ensure the accurate and complete input of transactions?					Verify that the controls established at the time of manual input preparation are verified by the computer program.	Control	Inspections

WORK PAPER 10.2 *(Continued)*

TEST FACTOR: Authorization Rules Designed

#	TEST CRITERIA	ASSESSMENT				RECOMMENDED TEST	TEST TECHNIQUE	TEST TOOL
		Very Ade-quate	Ade-quate	Inade-quate	N/A			
1.	Has the method for authorizing each transaction been documented?					Review the documentation to ensure authorization rules are complete.	Security	Checklist & Inspections
2.	For those documents whose authorization is dependent upon the source of origination as opposed to a signature, can that source of origination be verified by the application system?					Determine that for transactions whose entry itself indicates authorization, that those transactions can only originate from the properly authorized source.	Security	Checklist, Error guessing, & Inspections
3.	In a multiple user system, has responsibility for authorization been assigned to single individuals?					Determine the adequacy of the assigned authorization responsibilities in a multiuser system.	Control	Inspections & Fact finding
4.	Is the authorization method consistent with the value of the resources being authorized?					Review the reasonableness of the authorization method in relationship to the resources being controlled.	Requirements	Cause effect graphing, Walkthroughs, & Scoring
5.	If passwords are used for authorization, are procedures adequate to protect passwords?					Review the adequacy of the password protection procedures.	Control	Error guessing
6.	If passwords are used will they be changed at reasonable frequencies?					Determine the reasonableness of the frequency for changing passwords.	Control	Error guessing

(Continues)

WORK PAPER 10.2 *(Continued)*

TEST FACTOR: Authorization Rules Designed *(Continued)*

#	TEST CRITERIA	ASSESSMENT				RECOMMENDED TEST	TEST TECHNIQUE	TEST TOOL
		Very Ade-quate	Ade-quate	Inade-quate	N/A			
7.	Are the authorization rules verified by the automated segment of the application?					Examine the documentation indicating the methods for verifying authorization rules.	Security	Checklist, Risk matrix, & Inspections
8.	Are procedures established to report authorization violations to management?					Examine the reasonableness of the procedure to report authorization violations to management.	Control	Error guessing & Inspections

338

WORK PAPER 10.2 *(Continued)*

TEST FACTOR: File Integrity Controls Designed

| # | TEST CRITERIA | ASSESSMENT | | | | RECOMMENDED TEST | TEST TECHNIQUE | TEST TOOL |
		Very Adequate	Adequate	Inadequate	N/A			
1.	Have the fields been identified that will be used to verify file integrity?					Confirm with users that there are sufficient file integrity checks based upon the importance of data.	Control	Error guessing Confirmation/ examination
2.	Are procedures established to verify the integrity of key files?					Examine the documentation indicating the file integrity verification procedures to determine they are adequate.	Requirements	Inspections
3.	Are procedures established to verify the integrity of files on a regular basis?					Confirm with the user that the file integrity verification frequency is adequate to protect the integrity of the file.	Requirements	Confirmation/ examination
4.	Are procedures established to report file integrity variances to management?					Examine the specifications and procedures for reporting file integrity variances to management.	Control	Inspections
5.	For key files, such as cash receipts, have procedures been established to maintain independent control totals?					Verify for key files that independent control total procedures are adequate.	Control	Checkpoint & Inspections
6.	Have procedures been established to reconcile independent control totals to the totals produced by the automated segment?					Verify the adequacy of the reconciliation procedures.	Control	Cause-effect graphing, Checklist, & Desk checking
7.	Will the independent control totals be reconciled regularly to the automated control totals?					Confirm with the user that the frequency of independent reconciliation is adequate.	Requirements	Confirmation/ examination

(Continues)

339

WORK PAPER 10.2 *(Continued)*

TEST FACTOR: File Integrity Controls Designed *(Continued)*

#	TEST CRITERIA	ASSESSMENT				RECOMMENDED TEST	TEST TECHNIQUE	TEST TOOL
		Very Adequate	Adequate	Inadequate	N/A			
8.	Are simple accounting proofs (i.e., old total, plus additions, minus deletions, equals new total) performed regularly to ensure that the updating procedures are properly performed?					Review the adequacy of the methods to ensure that updating is performed correctly.	Error handling	Boundary value analysis & Desk checking

WORK PAPER 10.2 *(Continued)*

TEST FACTOR: Audit Trail Designed

#	TEST CRITERIA	ASSESSMENT				RECOMMENDED TEST	TEST TECHNIQUE	TEST TOOL
		Very Adequate	Adequate	Inadequate	N/A			
1.	Have the detailed specifications been documented for each review trail objective (e.g., individual transaction reconstruction)?					Review the completeness of the documentation in relationship to the review trail objectives.	Requirements	Walkthroughs
2.	Have the data fields and records for each review trail been defined?					Review the reasonableness of the included data fields to satisfy the review trail objective.	Requirements	Walkthroughs
3.	Has the length of time to save each review trail been defined?					Verify that the length of time is consistent with the organization's record retention policy.	Control	Confirmation/ examination & Fact finding
4.	Have the instructions been defined for utilizing the review trail?					Review the completeness of the specifications to instruct people in using the review trail.	Requirements	Checklist & Data flow analysis
5.	Does the review trail include both the manual and automated segments of the system?					Review the review trail specifications to verify that both the manual and automated segments are included.	Requirements	Flowchart & Tracing
6.	Is the review trail stored in a sequence and format making the retrieval and use easy?					Confirm with review trail users that the form and sequence is consistent with the use they would make of the review trail.	Requirements	Confirmation/ examination & Fact finding
7.	Will sufficient generations of the review trail be stored away from the primary site so that if the primary site is destroyed processing can be reconstructed?					Examine the adequacy of the off-site facility.	Requirements	Inspections
8.	Have procedures been established to delete review trails in the prescribed manner at the completion of their usefulness?					Assess the adequacy of the review trail destruction procedures.	Requirements	Checklist & Error guessing

341

WORK PAPER 10.2 *(Continued)*

TEST FACTOR: Contingency Plan Designed

#	TEST CRITERIA	ASSESSMENT				RECOMMENDED TEST	TEST TECHNIQUE	TEST TOOL
		Very Ade-quate	Ade-quate	Inade-quate	N/A			
1.	Has responsibility for the preparation of a contingency plan been assigned?					Verify that the assigned individual has the sufficient skills and time to prepare a contingency plan.	Operations	Fact finding
2.	Does the contingency plan define all of the causes of failure?					Confirm with the computer operations manager that the list of potential failures is complete.	Operations	Error guessing & Confirmation/ examination
3.	Does the contingency plan define responsibilities during the contingency period?					Review the completeness of the assigned responsibilities.	Operations	Checklist
4.	Does the contingency plan identify contingency resources?					Confirm with the computer operations manager that the assigned resources will be available in the event of a contingency.	Operations	Confirmation/ examination
5.	Does the contingency plan predetermine the operating priorities after a problem?					Confirm with a member of executive management that the recovery priorities are reasonable.	Recovery	Confirmation/ examination
6.	Are all the parties involved in a failure included in the development of the contingency plan?					Review the list of contingency plan participants for completeness.	Recovery	Checklist
7.	Are procedures established to test the contingency plan?					Review the adequacy of the contingency plan test procedures.	Recovery	Checklist & Disaster test
8.	Will the contingency plan be developed at the time the application goes operational?					Review the schedule for developing the contingency plan to ensure it will be complete when the system goes operational.	Recovery	Inspections

WORK PAPER 10.2 (Continued)

TEST FACTOR: Method to Achieve Service Level Designed

#	TEST CRITERIA	ASSESSMENT				RECOMMENDED TEST	TEST TECHNIQUE	TEST TOOL
		Very Adequate	Adequate	Inadequate	N/A			
1.	Can the system design achieve the desired service level?					Either confirm the reasonableness with computer operations personnel or run a simulation of the system to verify service levels.	Execution	Confirmation/ examination & Modeling
2.	Do peak period volumes impact upon the desired service level?					Develop a simulation to test service levels based upon maximum processed volumes.	Execution	Modeling
3.	Can user personnel manually handle their part of peak volume periods?					Develop a model to demonstrate the amount of time required to perform the manual part of processing.	Execution	Modeling
4.	Will expected errors impact upon service levels?					Determine the expected number of errors and include that in the system simulation.	Execution	Checklist, Error guessing, Inspections, & Modeling
5.	Has the cost of failing to achieve service levels been determined?					Confirm with user the cost of failure to meet service levels has been calculated.	Execution	Confirmation/ examination
6.	Are desired and projected service levels recalculated as the system is changed?					Examine the requests for system changes and determine their impact on the service level.	Execution	Inspections & Modeling
7.	Are procedures established to monitor the desired service level?					Review the adequacy of the monitoring procedure.	Execution	Checklist & Inspections
8.	Will sufficient computer resources be installed to meet the service levels as the volumes increase?					Confirm with the computer operations manager that computer resources will be increased in proportion to increased volumes of data.	Operations	Confirmation/ examination & Fact finding

(Continues)

WORK PAPER 10.2 *(Continued)*

TEST FACTOR: Access Procedures Designed

#	TEST CRITERIA	ASSESSMENT				RECOMMENDED TEST	TEST TECHNIQUE	TEST TOOL
		Very Adequate	Adequate	Inadequate	N/A			
1.	Have advanced security techniques such as cryptography been considered?					Confirm with the individual responsible for data security that advanced security measures have been considered and implemented where necessary.	Security	Confirmation/ examination
2.	Have operating software features (such as operating system features) been evaluated for security purposes and implemented where necessary?					Confirm with system programmers that a systematic process was used to evaluate systems software features needed for security.	Security	Risk matrix & Confirmation/ examination
3.	Have procedures been designed to protect the issuance and maintenance of passwords?					Confirm with the data security officer the adequacy of password protection procedures.	Security	Risk matrix & Confirmation/ examination
4.	Are procedures defined to monitor security violations?					Review the adequacy of the procedures to monitor security violations.	Control	Checklist & Fact finding
5.	Does senior management intend to prosecute security violators?					Confirm with senior management their intent to monitor security and prosecute violators.	Control	Confirmation/ examination
6.	Have the security needs of each application resource been defined?					Review the completeness and adequacy of the security for each application resource.	Control	Risk matrix & Scoring
7.	Has one individual been assigned the responsibility for security of the application?					Confirm that the individual appointed has sufficient skill and time to monitor security.	Security	Checklist & Confirmation/ examination
8.	Is the system designed to protect sensitive data?					Confirm with the user the completeness of the design to protect sensitive data.	Security	Cause-effect graphing, Correctness proof, Inspections, & Scoring

WORK PAPER 10.2 (Continued)

TEST FACTOR: Design Complies with Methodology

#	TEST CRITERIA	ASSESSMENT				RECOMMENDED TEST	TEST TECHNIQUE	TEST TOOL
		Very Adequate	Adequate	Inadequate	N/A			
1.	Have the appropriate methodology specifications been determined?					Confirm with the responsible party that the specifications are correct.	Compliance	Correctness proof, Error guessing, & Confirmation/ examination
2.	Has the required level of compliance to the methodology been achieved?					Verify that the project complies with the methodology.	Compliance	Design reviews
3.	Will the standards, policies, etc. be monitored during implementation?					Confirm with the involved parties that they will monitor compliance to the methodology.	Compliance	Confirmation/ examination & Fact finding
4.	Has the cost of compliance been determined so that it can be measured against the benefit, sanction, etc.?					Review with the involved parties the cost/benefit of compliance.	Compliance	Fact finding
5.	Are procedures established to substantiate compliance to the methodology?					Review the adequacy of the specified method of substantiating compliance.	Compliance	Fact finding
6.	Will the methodology be in use when the system becomes operational?					Confirm with information services management the applicability of using all or part of the methodology based on the application's expected implementation data.	Compliance	Confirmation/ examination
7.	Have deviations from the methodology been documented and approved?					Verify variances from the methodology are approved.	Compliance	Design reviews & Confirmation/ examination
8.	Is design documentation adequate and in compliance with standards?					Verify the completeness and adequacy of design documentation.	Compliance	Design reviews

WORK PAPER 10.2 (Continued)

TEST FACTOR: Design Conforms to Requirements

#	TEST CRITERIA	ASSESSMENT				RECOMMENDED TEST	TEST TECHNIQUE	TEST TOOL
		Very Adequate	Adequate	Inadequate	N/A			
1.	Has the systems design group made changes to the application system without gaining user approval?					Examine all of the program change requests to verify they have been approved by the user.	Requirements	Confirmation/ examination
2.	Is there a formal change request procedure that must be followed to make all system changes?					Examine the adequacy and compliance to the program change procedure.	Control	Checklist & Inspections
3.	Are the objectives of the system reevaluated and changed where necessary based on each approved change request?					Determine the effect of the approved system changes on the objectives, and determine if the objectives have been changed accordingly.	Requirements	Inspections & Walkthroughs
4.	Does the user continually reevaluate the application system objectives in regard to changing business conditions?					Confirm with the user that the objectives are changed based on changing business conditions.	Requirements	Acceptance test criteria, Confirmation/ examination, & Fact finding
5.	Are user personnel heavily involved in the design of the application system?					Confirm with the information services project personnel that the user is heavily involved in the system design.	Requirements	Confirmation/ examination & Fact finding
6.	If user management changes, does the new management reconfirm the system objectives?					Verify that the design specifications achieve the intent of the application requirements.	Requirements	Acceptance test criteria, Confirmation/ examination

WORK PAPER 10.2 *(Continued)*

TEST FACTOR: Design Conforms to Requirements *(Continued)*

#	TEST CRITERIA	ASSESSMENT				RECOMMENDED TEST	TEST TECHNIQUE	TEST TOOL
		Very Adequate	Adequate	Inadequate	N/A			
7.	If the objectives are changed, is the means of measuring those objectives changed accordingly?					Examine the new objectives to determine that the criteria to measure the objectives are reasonable.	Requirements	Acceptance test criteria, Cause-effect graphing, Design-based functional testing, Executable specs, & Symbolic execution
8.	Do the design specifications achieve the intent of the requirements?					Verify that the design specifications achieve the intent of the application requirements.	Requirements	Correctness proof, Data flow analysis, Design-based functional testing, Desk checking, Executable specs, & Symbolic execution

(Continues)

WORK PAPER 10.2 *(Continued)*

TEST FACTOR: Design Facilitates Use

#	TEST CRITERIA	ASSESSMENT				RECOMMENDED TEST	TEST TECHNIQUE	TEST TOOL
		Very Ade-quate	Ade-quate	Inade-quate	N/A			
1.	Have the people tasks been defined?					Examine manual processing documentation.	Manual support	Inspections
2.	Are the tasks realistic based on the skill level of the people?					Review the application system processing.	Manual support	Peer review
3.	Is the timing of the tasks realistic?					Calculate adequacy of manual turnaround time.	Requirements	Modeling
4.	Will the information needed to do the people tasks be available?					Confirm with user expected availability of needed information.	Requirements	Confirmation/examination
5.	Is the workload reasonable based on the expected staffing?					Estimate time required to complete assigned tasks.	Requirements	Modeling
6.	Have the people involved been presented their tasks for comment?					Confirm with user their independence in systems design.	Manual support	Confirmation/examination
7.	Could some of the people tasks be better performed on the computer?					Review the application system processing.	Requirements	Cause-effect graphing & Error guessing
8.	Will adequate instruction manuals be prepared for these tasks?					Review design specifications for preparation of instructions for people-tasks manual.	Manual support	Checklist

WORK PAPER 10.2 (Continued)

TEST FACTOR: Design Is Maintainable

#	TEST CRITERIA	ASSESSMENT				RECOMMENDED TEST	TEST TECHNIQUE	TEST TOOL
		Very Adequate	Adequate	Inadequate	N/A			
1.	Is system design logically constructed?					Review application design structure.	Compliance	Peer review
2.	Are data attributes fully defined?					Examine data documentation for completeness.	Compliance	Inspections
3.	Is computer logic presented in an easy-to-follow manner?					Review the application system logic.	Compliance	Peer review
4.	Are changes to the system incorporated into the design documentation?					Trace changes to the system specifications.	Compliance	Inspections
5.	Have areas of expected high frequency of change been designed to facilitate maintenance?					Review maintainability of logic in areas of expected high change.	Compliance	Fact finding
6.	Are business functions designed using a standalone concept?					Review application design structure.	Compliance	Inspections
7.	Is design documentation complete and usable?					Examine design documentation for usability.	Compliance	Inspections
8.	Are maintenance specialists involved in the design process?					Confirm with maintenance specialists that they are involved in the design process.	Compliance	Confirmation/ examination

(Continues)

349

WORK PAPER 10.2   *(Continued)*

TEST FACTOR: Design Is Portable

| # | TEST CRITERIA | ASSESSMENT | | | | RECOMMENDED TEST | TEST TECHNIQUE | TEST TOOL |
		Very Ade-quate	Ade-quate	Inade-quate	N/A			
1.	Does the design avoid specialized hardware features?					Review hardware specifications for special features.	Operations	Inspections
2.	Does the design avoid specialized software features?					Review software specifications for special features.	Operations	Inspections
3.	Will the system be coded in a common computer language?					Examine coding rules for the project.	Operations	Fact finding
4.	Will the system be restricted to common features of the language?					Examine coding rules for the project.	Operations	Fact finding
5.	Does the system avoid the use of specialized software packages?					Review software specifications for specialized software.	Operations	Inspections
6.	Are data values restricted to normal data structures?					Review data documentation for type of data structure used.	Operations	Inspections
7.	Does documentation avoid specialized jargon?					Review documentation for use of specialized jargon.	Operations	Inspections
8.	Have the portability implementation considerations been documented?					Review the adequacy of the portability documentation.	Operations	Inspections

WORK PAPER 10.2 (Continued)

TEST FACTOR: Interface Design Complete

#	TEST CRITERIA	ASSESSMENT				RECOMMENDED TEST	TEST TECHNIQUE	TEST TOOL
		Very Ade-quate	Ade-quate	Inade-quate	N/A			
1.	Have the transactions to be received from other applications been defined?					Examine interfaced input data documentation.	Intersystems	Checklist
2.	Have the transactions going to other applications been defined?					Examine interfaced output data documentation.	Intersystems	Checklist
3.	Has the timing of interfaced transactions been defined?					Review system specifications for definition of timing.	Intersystems	Flowchart
4.	Is the timing of interfaced transactions realistic?					Confirm with interfaced application personnel that timing is reasonable.	Operations	Confirmation/ examination
5.	Has the media for transferring data to interfaced applications been defined?					Review system specifications for documentation of media.	Operations	Inspections
6.	Are common data definitions used on interfaced data?					Compare common data definitions of interfaced applications.	Control	Fact finding
7.	Are common value attributes used on interfaced data?					Compare common value attributes description of interfaced applications.	Control	Fact finding
8.	Has interface documentation been exchanged with interfaced applications?					Confirm with interfaced projects that documentation has been exchanged.	Intersystems	Confirmation/ examination

(Continues)

351

WORK PAPER 10.2 *(Continued)*

TEST FACTOR: Design Achieves Criteria

#	TEST CRITERIA	ASSESSMENT				RECOMMENDED TEST	TEST TECHNIQUE	TEST TOOL
		Very Adequate	Adequate	Inadequate	N/A			
1.	Have the systems development and acceptance criteria costs been recalculated based on the systems design?					Confirm with the user that the new system costs and acceptance criteria are reasonable.	Execution	Acceptance test criteria & Confirmation/examination
2.	Have the criteria for developing the manual processing segments been confirmed?					Confirm with the user that the manual effort has been defined and the cost confirmed.	Execution	Acceptance test criteria & Confirmation/examination
3.	Has the cost of operating the computer programs been confirmed based on the systems design?					Confirm with computer operations that the operational costs are reasonable.	Execution	Acceptance test criteria & Confirmation/examination
4.	Have the costs to operate the manual segments of the system been confirmed?					Confirm with the user that the cost to operate the manual segments of the application are reasonable.	Execution	Acceptance test criteria & Confirmation/examination
5.	Have the benefits of the system been confirmed based upon the systems design?					Confirm with the user the reasonableness of the benefits.	Execution	Acceptance test criteria & Confirmation/examination
6.	Has the useful life of the system been confirmed based upon the systems design?					Confirm with the user the reasonableness of the expected life of the application	Execution	Acceptance test criteria & Confirmation/examination

WORK PAPER 10.2 (Continued)

TEST FACTOR: Design Achieves Criteria (Continued)

#	TEST CRITERIA	ASSESSMENT				RECOMMENDED TEST	TEST TECHNIQUE	TEST TOOL
		Very Adequate	Adequate	Inadequate	N/A			
7.	Has the cost-effectiveness of the new system been recalculated if changes in the factors have occurred?					Confirm with the organization's accountants that the cost is correct.	Execution	Confirmation/examination
8.	Does the cost-effectiveness after design warrant the continuance of the system?					Confirm with senior management that the system design is still cost-effective	Execution	Confirmation/examination

(Continues)

WORK PAPER 10.2 *(Continued)*

TEST FACTOR: Needs Communicated to Operations

#	TEST CRITERIA	ASSESSMENT				RECOMMENDED TEST	TEST TECHNIQUE	TEST TOOL
		Very Adequate	Adequate	Inadequate	N/A			
1.	Have special hardware needs been defined?					Review specifications for special hardware needs.	Operations	Inspections
2.	Have special software needs been defined?					Review specifications for special software needs.	Operations	Inspections
3.	Have operations timing specifications been defined?					Review specifications for operations timing specifications.	Operations	Inspections
4.	Have system volumes been projected over an extended time period?					Confirm with user reasonableness of projections.	Compliance	Confirmation/ examination
5.	Have operations capacity requirements been specified?					Review specifications to determine capacity requirements are reasonable.	Operations	Checklist
6.	Have computer test requirements been specified?					Examine test specifications for reasonableness.	Operations	Fact finding
7.	Have supplies/forms been specified?					Review specifications to determine all supplies/ forms have been identified.	Operations	Fact finding
8.	Has computer operations been notified of anticipated operations workload and other requirements?					Confirm with computer operations their awareness of operation requirements.	Operations	Confirmation/ examination

WORK PAPER 10.3   Business System Design Review Checklist[2]

ITEM	YES	NO	N/A	COMMENTS
		RESPONSE		

Systems Overview

1. Is there a brief description of interfaces with other systems?
2. Is there an outline of the major functional requirements of the system?
3. Are the major functions defined into discrete steps with no boundary overlapping?
4. Have manual and automatic steps been defined?
5. Has the definition of what data is required to perform each step been indicated along with a description of how the data is obtained?

System Description

6. Has a system structure chart been developed, showing the logical breakdown into subsystems and interfaces with other systems?
7. Have the major inputs and outputs been defined as well as the functional processing required to produce the output?
8. Is there a narrative description of the major functions of the system?
9. Have subsystem functional flow diagrams been developed showing the inputs, processing, and outputs relevant to the subsystem?
10. Has subsystem narrative description been developed?
11. Do the functional outlines follow the logical structure of the system?
12. Are they hierarchical in nature, that is, by function and by steps within function?

Design Input and Output Data—Data Structure:

13. Has the data been grouped into logical categories (i.e., customer product, accounting, marketing sales, etc.)?
14. Has the data been categorized as follows:
    a) Static
    b) Historical data likely to be changed
    c) Transaction related
15. Have standard data names (if possible) been used?
16. Has the hierarchical relationship among data elements been defined and described?

[2]Based on case study included in *Effective Methods of EDP Quality Assurance*.

(Continues)

WORK PAPER 10.3 *(Continued)*

ITEM	RESPONSE			COMMENTS
	YES	NO	N/A	
Design Output Documents:				
17. Are there headings?				
18. Do the headings include report titles, department, date, page number, etc.?				
19. Are the output documents adaptable to current filing equipment?				
20. Are processing dates, system identification, titles, and page numbers shown?				
21. Has consideration been given to COM or other output devices?				
22. Is each data column identified?				
23. Where subtotals are produced (e.g., product within customer) are they labeled by control break?				
Design Input Elements:				
24. Are the data elements clearly indicated?				
25. Has the source of the data been defined (department and individual)?				
26. Have input requirements been documented?				
27. Is the purpose of the input document clear (e.g., enter orders, process salary action)?				
28. Is the sequence (if applicable) indicated?				
Design Computer Processing:				
29. Has each function been described using functional terminology (e.g., if salary exceeds maximum, print message)?				
30. Has validity checking been defined with reference to the data element dictionary?				
31. In cases where the same data may be coming from several sources, have the sources been identified as to priorities for selection by the system?				
32. Has processing been classified according to type of function (e.g., transaction, calculation, editing, etc.)?				
Design Noncomputer Processing:				
33. Has the preparation of input been described?				
34. Has the distribution of output been described?				
35. Has an error correction procedure been described?				
Organizational Controls:				
36. Have organizational controls been established?				

WORK PAPER 10.3   *(Continued)*

ITEM		RESPONSE			COMMENTS
		YES	NO	N/A	
37.	Have controls been established across department lines?				
38.	Have the control fields been designed?				
39.	Are there control validation procedures prior to proceeding to the next step?				
Overall System Controls:					
40.	Have controls been designed to reconcile data received by the computer center?				
41.	Have controls for error correction and reentry been designed?				
42.	Have controls been designed that can be reconciled to those of another system (e.g., accounting transactions whose various categories should equal general ledger totals)?				
Input Controls:					
43.	Have some or all of the following criteria been used for establishing input controls?				
	a) Sequence numbering				
	b) Prepunched cards				
	c) Turnaround documents				
	d) Batch numbering				
	e) By type of input				
	f) Predetermined totals				
	g) Self-checking numbers				
	h) Field length checks				
	i) Limit checks				
	j) Reasonability checks				
	k) Existence/nonexistence checks				
44.	Do controls and totals exist for:				
	a) Each value column				
	b) Where appropriate, cross-foot totals				
	c) Counts of input transactions, errors, accepted transactions				
	d) Input transactions, old master, new master				
45.	Are the results of all updates listed for each transaction showing the before and after condition?				
46.	As the result of an update, are the number of adds, deletes, and changes processed shown?				
47.	If relationship tests have been used, are they grouped and defined?				
48.	If used, have control total records been utilized to verify that all records have been processed between runs?				

(Continues)

WORK PAPER 10.3 *(Continued)*

ITEM	RESPONSE			COMMENTS
	YES	NO	N/A	
Output Controls:				
49. Have output controls been established for all control fields?				
50. Is there a separate output control on errors rejected by the system?				
System Test Plan:				
51. Have acceptance criteria (user-defined conditions) been identified?				
52. Has a tentative user acceptance strategy been developed?				
53. Have test data requirements been defined?				
54. Have data element dictionary forms been completed?				
55. Have organizational changes been defined (if required)?				
56. Have new organization charts or new positions been required?				
57. If required, have areas for special user procedures been identified?				
58. Has a timetable for operating the system been developed?				
59. Were separate timetables developed for different cycles (weekly, monthly)?				
60. Has the documentation been gathered and organized?				
61. Has a financial analysis been performed?				
Plan User Procedures—Conversion Design:				
62. Have the scope, objectives, and constraints been developed?				
63. Has a plan for user procedures and conversion phases been completed?				
64. Has the plan been broken down into approximate work units (days) to serve as a basis for a schedule for the other phases?				
65. Have the resources and responsibilities been arranged (who is doing what)?				
66. Have schedules been prepared for the next phases?				
67. Have appropriate budgets for the next phases been prepared?				
68. Has a project authorization been properly prepared for remaining phases?				

WORK PAPER 10.4   Computer Systems Design Review Checklist[3]

ITEM	RESPONSE			COMMENTS
	YES	NO	N/A	

Develop Outline Design:

1. Has a detailed review of the business system design resulted in requiring additional information or changes?

2. Have these revisions been reviewed by the user?

3. Have existing sources of data been identified?

4. Has a data management alternative been considered because of the nature of the system?

5. Have the data elements been grouped by category of data?

6. Have the record layout forms been used for listing the data elements?

7. Has the file description form been used to show the characteristics of each file?

8. Have the access methods been determined?

9. Has use been made of blocking factors to reduce accesses for a sequential file?

10. If a data base has been used, has the relationship between segments (views of the data base) been included?

11. If new data elements have been required, have they been included as part of the data dictionary?

12. Has the description of processing been translated into system flowcharts showing programs and their relationships, as well as reports?

13. Has the processing been isolated by frequency as well as function?

14. Does each file requiring updating have an associated unique transaction file?

15. Does each main file have a separate validation and update function?

16. Have the following been addressed in order to reduce excessive passing of files:
    a) Sort verbs (statements)
    b) Input procedure
    c) Output procedure
    d) Random updating

17. Has a matrix been prepared showing which programs create, access, and update each file?

[3]ibid.

(Continues)

WORK PAPER 10.4   *(Continued)*

ITEM				RESPONSE			COMMENTS
				YES	NO	N/A	
18.	Has a separate program section been set up for each program in the system showing:						
	a)	Cover page showing the program name, systems and/or subsystem name, run number, and a brief description of the program					
	b)	Input/output diagram					
	c)	Processing description					
19.	Does the processing description contain a brief outline of the processing that the program is going to perform?						
20.	Has the content and format of each output been defined?						
21.	Conversely, has the same been completed for each input?						
22.	Have data items been checked out to the rules specified in the data dictionary?						
23.	Have transactions that update master files been assigned record types?						
24.	For multirecord transactions have the following been done:						
	a)	Identifying record types that define the records comprising one transaction					
	b)	Development of a sequence number if required					
	c)	Defining mandatory and optional records					
Hardware/Software Configuration:							
25.	Has the hardware configuration been defined showing:						
	a)	CPU					
	b)	Minimum core storage					
	c)	Number and type of peripherals					
	d)	Special hardware					
	e)	Numbers of tapes and/or disk packs					
	f)	Terminals, minicomputers, microfilm, microfiche, optical scanning, etc.					
26.	Has the software been defined specifically:						
	a)	Operating system					
	b)	Telecommunications (CICS, TSO, etc.)					
	c)	Data base management (IMS)					
27.	If telecommunications equipment is involved, has a communications analyst been consulted regarding type, number, speed, etc.?						

WORK PAPER 10.4   *(Continued)*

	RESPONSE			
ITEM	YES	NO	N/A	COMMENTS

File Conversion Computer System:

28. If applicable, have the file conversion requirements been specified?

29. If required, have program specifications for the file conversion programs been completed?

30. If applicable, can the main program(s) be utilized to perform the file conversion?

31. Has a schedule been established?

Design System Tests:

32. Has the user's role for testing been defined, namely:
    a) Has the user described what he/she expects from the system output?
    b) Has the user agreed to provide system test data and to check system output?

33. Have responsibilities and schedules for preparing test data been agreed to by the user?

34. Has the input medium been agreed to (cards, on-line entry, other)?

35. Is special hardware/software required, and if so, will programmers and/or users require additional training?

36. Have turnaround requirements been defined?

37. Have testing priorities been established?

38. If an on-line system, has an investigation of required space as opposed to available space been made?

39. Has an analysis of the impact upon interfacing systems been made and have arrangements been made for acquiring required information and data?

40. Have testing control procedures been established (logs, tapes, disks, etc.)?

41. Has the possibility of utilizing existing code (prewritten subroutines) been investigated?

42. Has a system test plan been prepared consisting of a description of each run (program or a number of programs) to be made and specifically does each show:
    a) Test run identification
    b) Test run description (program/job title)
    c) Programs and utilities required for the test

(Continues)

WORK PAPER 10.4   *(Continued)*

ITEM	RESPONSE			COMMENTS
	YES	NO	N/A	
d) Dependencies (runs which must be completed prior to testing) e) Inputs and their sources f) Outputs; content and destination g) List of conditions to be tested (e.g., validation rules)				
43. Has the user prepared the system test data as defined by the conditions to be tested in the system test plan?				
44. Has computer operations been consulted regarding keypunching and/or verification?				
Revise and Complete Design:				
45. Have all required forms from previous phases as well as previous task activities in this phase been completed?				
46. Has the processing description for program specifications been categorized by function (e.g., validation, error handling, reports, updating end of file)?				
47. For validation routines have the editing rules been specified for:				
a) Field format and content (data element description) b) Interfield relationships c) Intrafield relationships d) Interrecord relationships e) Sequence f) Duplicates g) Control reconciliation				
48. Have the rejection criteria been indicated for each type of error situation, as follows:				
a) Warning message but transaction is accepted b) Use of the default value c) Outright rejection of record within a transaction set d) Rejection of an entire transaction e) Rejection of a batch of transactions f) Program abort				
Revise and Complete Design:				
49. Have the following validation techniques been included in the specifications:				
a) Validation of entire transaction before any processing b) Validation to continue regardless of the number of errors on the transaction unless a run abort occurs				

WORK PAPER 10.4   *(Continued)*

ITEM			RESPONSE			COMMENTS
			YES	NO	N/A	
	c)	Provide information regarding an error so the user can identify the source and determine the cause				
50.		If applicable, has a procedure been developed for correction of rejected input either by deletion, reversal, or reentry?				
51.		Do the specifications for each report (output) define:				
	a)	The origin of each item including the rules for the selection of optional items				
	b)	The rules governing calculations				
	c)	The rules for printing and/or print suppression				
52.		Have the following been defined for each intermediate (work) file:				
	a)	Origins or alternative origins for each element				
	b)	Calculations				
	c)	Rules governing record types, sequence, optional records, as well as inter- and intrarecord relationships				
53.		Have the following audit controls been built in where applicable:				
	a)	Record counts (in and out)				
	b)	Editing of all source input				
	c)	Hash totals on selected fields				
	d)	Sequence checking of input files				
	e)	Data checking				
	f)	Listing of errors and review				
	g)	Control records				
Determine Tentative Operational Requirements:						
54.		Has the impact of the system upon existing computer resources been evaluated?				
55.		Have the computer processing requirements been discussed with computer operations (e.g., volumes, timeframes, turnaround, etc.)?				
56.		Have backup procedures been developed?				
On-line Systems:						
57.		Have testing plans been discussed with computer operations to ensure that required resources (core, disk space) for "sessions" will be available?				
58.		Have terminal types been discussed with appropriate technical support personnel?				
59.		Have IMS considerations (if applicable) been coordinated with computer operations, technical support, and DBA representatives?				

(Continues)

WORK PAPER 10.4   *(Continued)*

ITEM	RESPONSE			COMMENTS
	YES	NO	N/A	
60. Has a user training program been developed?				
61. Have run schedules been prepared to provide computer operations with the basic information necessary to schedule computer usage?				
62. Have run flowcharts including narrative (where required) been prepared?				
63. Have "first cut" estimates of region sizes, run times, etc. been provided on the flowcharts or some other documentations?				
64. Has the following information been shown for either input or output tapes and disks: a) DDNAME, DSNAME, LABEL, UNIT, DCB, RECFM, BLKSIZE, DISP, RETPD, estimated volumes of records, concatenation, source, destination b) In addition to the above, for disk files: 1) Input, output, or input/output 2) Space (number of blocks)				
65. Where appropriate, have restart procedures been described for each step of the job?				
66. If appropriate, have restart procedures been appended to the security and backup section of the documentation?				
Plan Program Design:				
67. Has all relevant documentation for each program been gathered?				
68. Has the sequence in which programs are to be developed been defined in accordance to the system test plan?				
69. Has the number of user and project personnel (including outside vendors) required been ascertained?				
70. Has computer time required for program testing (compiles, test runs) been estimated?				
71. Have data preparation requirements been discussed with computer operations regarding data entry?				
72. Has a development cost worksheet been prepared for the next phase or phases?				
73. Have personnel been assigned and project work schedules been prepared?				
74. Has the project schedule and budget been reviewed and updated if required?				
Prepare Project Authorization:				
75. If required, has a project authorization form been completed?				

WORK PAPER 10.5   Quality Control Checklist

Field Requirements

FIELD	INSTRUCTIONS FOR ENTERING DATA
Number	A number that sequentially identifies the quality control items, which if positively addressed would indicate that this step has been performed correctly.
Item	The specific quality control item that is used to measure the effectiveness of performing this step.
Response	The testers should indicate in this column whether they have performed the referenced item. The response can be Yes, No, or N/A if it is not appropriate for your organization's testing process.
Comments	This column is used to clarify the Yes, No, or N/A response for the item indicated. Generally the comments column need only be completed for No responses; No responses should be investigated and a determination made as to whether this item needs to be performed before this step can be considered complete.

#	ITEM	YES	NO	N/A	COMMENTS
		RESPONSE			
1.	Is the test team knowledgeable in the design process?				
2.	If tools are used in creating the design, are the testers knowledgeable about those tools?				
3.	Have the testers received all of the design phase deliverables needed to perform this test?				
4.	Do the users agree that the design is realistic?				
5.	Does the project team believe that the design is realistic?				
6.	Have the testers identified the success factors, both positive and negative, that can affect the success of the design?				
7.	Have the testers used those factors in scoring the probability of success?				
8.	Do the testers understand the 15 test factors related to design?				
9.	Have the testers analyzed those design test factors to evaluate their potential impact on the success of the design?				
10.	Do the testers understand the design review process?				
11.	Has a review team been established that represents all vested interest in the success of the design?				

(Continues)

WORK PAPER 10.5 *(Continued)*

#	ITEM	YES	NO	N/A	COMMENTS
		RESPONSE			
12.	Does management support using the design review process?				
13.	Is the design review process conducted at an appropriate time?				
14.	Were the items identified in the design review process reasonable?				
15.	Does the project team agree that the identified items need to be addressed?				
16.	Does management support performing inspections on project rework?				
17.	Has appropriate time been allotted in the project scheduling for performing inspections?				
18.	Have the individuals responsible for project rework been educated in the importance of participating in the inspection process?				
19.	Does management view inspections as an integral part of the process rather than as an audit to identify participants' performance?				
20.	Has the inspection process been planned?				
21.	Have the inspectors been identified and assigned their specific roles?				
22.	Have the inspectors been trained to perform their role?				
23.	Have the inspectors been given the necessary materials to perform the review?				
24.	Have the inspectors been given adequate time from their normal activities to complete both the preparation and the review meeting inspection process?				
25.	Did the individual inspectors adequately prepare for the inspection?				
26.	Did the individual inspectors prepare a defect list?				
27.	Was the inspection scheduled at a time convenient for all inspectors?				
28.	Did all inspectors come to the inspection meeting?				
29.	Did all inspectors agree on the final list of defects?				

WORK PAPER 10.5   *(Continued)*

#	ITEM	YES	NO	N/A	COMMENTS
		RESPONSE			
30.	Have the inspectors agreed upon one of the three acceptable inspection dispositions (i.e., moderator's certification, moderator reexamination, or reinspection)?				
31.	Were the defects identified during the review meeting recorded and given to the author?				
32.	Has the author agreed to make the necessary corrections?				
33.	Has a reasonable process been developed to determine that those defects have been corrected satisfactorily?				
34.	Has a final moderator certification been issued for the product/deliverable inspected?				

Step 5: Program Phase Testing

Programming is purely an information technology function. There is little need for user involvement during this phase, except where questions exist regarding the design specifications and/or requirements. In those instances, it may be necessary to involve the user.

A continual concern, although a fact of life, is user-requested changes during the programming phase. Wherever possible, these should be discouraged through more complete design reviews, or postponed until the system is placed into operation. Where changes cannot be postponed, they should be implemented through the regular development process, and possibly tested prior to changing the original program specifications.

The complexity of performing the programming phase depends on the thoroughness of the design phase and the tool used to generate code. Well-defined and measurable design specifications greatly simplify the programming task. On the other hand, the failure to make decisions during the early phases necessitates those decisions being made during the programming phase. Unfortunately, if not made earlier, these decisions may be made by the wrong individual—the programmer.

Testing during the programming phase may be static or dynamic. During most of the phase, programs are being specified, designed, and coded. In this programming phase, the resultant code may not be executable, and thus require different test tools. The efficiency gained from early testing is just as appropriate to the programming phase as it is to other phases. For example, problems detected during program design can be corrected more economically than when the same problem is detected during the test of the executable program.

NOTE The importance of this step will vary based on the means of code generation. The more automated code generation becomes, the less emphasis needs to be placed on program phase testing. Since many organizations use a variety of methods for code generation, this chapter is designed to incorporate all of the program phase components needed. The user of this test process must adjust this step according to the method used to generate code.

Overview

The programming phase encompasses three segments. First, the program specifications are written from the design specifications. Second, a programmer converts the program specifications into machine-executable instructions. Third, the programmer verifies that these instructions perform in accordance with the program specifications.

The programming phase may involve the writing of several thousand computer instructions. Because many of the programming tasks are repetitious, they are subject to error; therefore, software systems are being developed that automatically generate program code from specifications. Unfortunately, it may be a number of years before these systems are in general use. During that time, extensive program testing will be necessary.

The programming equivalent in home construction is the building of the house by masons, carpenters, plumbers, and electricians. These are the craftsmen who take the design specifications and materials and convert them into the desired product. However, just as aids are available to the programmer, aids are also available to the construction worker. For example, preconstructed roof trusses and other parts of the house can be purchased. The more pieces that can be produced automatically, the greater the probability of a successfully built home, and the fewer tests that need to be conducted on the home.

The programming phase in the construction of a system produces a large volume of deliverables. It is during this phase that the number of items to be tested increases significantly. Therefore, it becomes important to understand the deliverables, their risk, and which segments of the deliverables need to be tested.

Objective

The information technology project leader should be responsible for testing during the programming phase. The primary objective for this testing is to ensure that the design specifications have been correctly implemented. Program testing is not concerned with achieving the user's needs, but rather that the developed structure satisfies the design specifications and works. Much of the testing will be conducted by the programmer. Testing at this point is highly technical, and it normally requires someone with programming experience. These tests should be complete prior to interconnecting the entire application and testing the application system.

This chapter describes a test process to use during programming. Desk debugging and peer reviews are recommended as effective test methods during the programming phase. This relatively low-cost test approach has proven to be very effective in detecting problems and can be used at any point during the programming activity. The chapter includes a complete test program addressing all of the programming phase concerns. Figure 11.1 shows this step in relationship to the other steps in the proposed 11-step testing process.

Concerns

There are three concerns that testers need to consider during this step:

1. **Program testing will be comprised exclusively of dynamic testing as opposed to including static testing.** Static testing using techniques such as desk debugging and peer reviews is much more effective in uncovering defects than is dynamic testing. The concern is that the proper testing technique will not be used for the needed test objective.

2. **Program testing will be too costly.** Programmers have a tendency to identify defects, assume there are no more, and then correct those defects and retest. This has proven to be a time-consuming and costly approach to testing. Using static methods to remove defects and dynamic testing to verify functionality is a much more efficient method of program testing. (Note: This chapter will concentrate on static testing, and Chapter 12 will concentrate on dynamic testing.)

3. **Programs will be released for string, system, and acceptance testing before they are fully debugged.** The shortest and most economical testing is to remove all the defects at one level of testing before moving to the next level. For example, it is much more economical to continue program testing to remove program defects than to identify those defects in string testing.

Workbench

Figure 11.2 is a workbench used for testing during the programming phase. The tests shown are static in nature. To perform effective static testing of programs, the testers need to understand how the program was constructed, and receive current program phase deliverables. Note that these deliverables should be free of compiler errors.

The three tasks in this step are the more commonly used static tests for program testing. However, inspections are highly recommended as a more effective technique. Testers wishing to use the inspection process should refer to Chapter 8 where that technique is described in detail.

Input

The more common programming phase deliverables that are input for testing are:

- Program specifications
- Program documentation

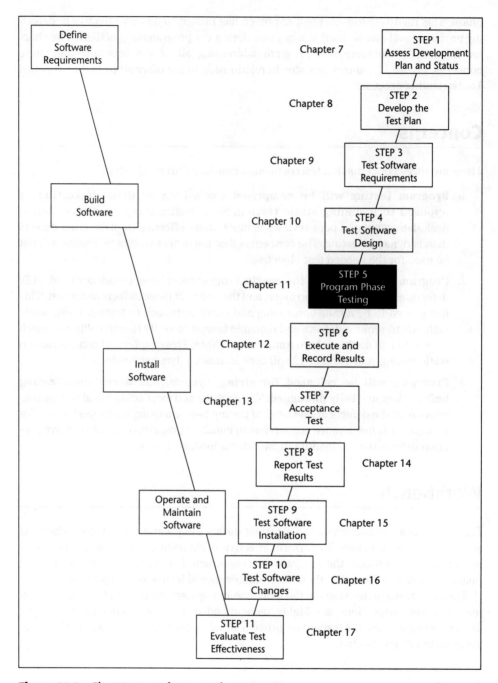

Figure 11.1 The 11-step software testing process.

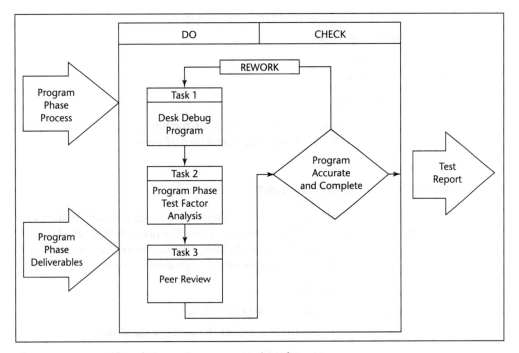

Figure 11.2   Workbench for testing programming phase.

- Computer program listings
- Executable programs
- Program flowcharts
- Operator instructions

In addition the testers need to understand the process used to build the program under test.

Do Procedures

Completion of programming phase testing involves the following three tasks.

Task 1: Desk Debug the Program

Desk debugging enables the programmer to evaluate the completeness and correctness of the program prior to conducting more expensive program testing. In addition, desk debugging can occur at any point in the programming process, including both program design and coding. Desk debugging can be as extensive or as minimal as desired. The amount of desk debugging performed will depend on:

- Wait time until the next program deliverable is received
- Implementation schedule
- Testing resources
- Efficiency of test tools
- Departmental policy

Desk debugging can be syntactical, structural, or functional. Let us examine how each of these three types of desk debugging should be performed.

1. Syntactical Desk Debugging

Program specifications and program statements must be developed in accordance with departmental methodology and compiler requirements. The programmer can check the appropriate syntax of the documentation and statements to ensure they are written in compliance with the rules. Syntactical checking asks questions such as:

- Is the job identification correct?
- Are program statements appropriately identified?
- Are program statements constructed using the appropriate structure?
- Are data elements properly identified?
- Do the program statements use the proper data structure; for example, do mathematical instructions work on mathematical fields?
- Are the data structures adequate to accommodate the data values that will be used in those structures?

2. Structural Desk Debugging

Structural problems account for a significant number of defects in most application systems. These defects also mask functional defects so that their detection becomes more difficult. The types of questions to be asked during structural desk debugging include:

- Are all instructions entered?
- Are all data definitions used in the instructions defined?
- Are all defined data elements used?
- Do all branches go to the correct routine entrance point?
- Are all internal tables and other limits structured so that when the limit is exceeded processing can continue?

3. Functional Desk Debugging

The functions are the requirements that the program is to perform. The questions to be asked about the function when desk debugging include:

- Will the program perform the specified function in the manner indicated?
- Are any of the functions mutually exclusive?
- Will the system detect inaccurate or unreasonable data?
- Will functional data be accumulated properly from run to run?

Task 2: Perform Program Phase Test Factor Analysis

The depth of testing in the program phase depends on the adequacy of the system at the end of the design phase. The more confidence the test team has in the adequacy of the application at the end of the design phase, the less concern they will have during the program phase. This can minimize testing. During requirements and design testing, the concerns over the test factors may change based upon test results. In the program phase, the test team should identify the concerns of most interest, and then develop the test process to address those concerns. In identifying these concerns, the test team must take into account changes that have occurred in the system specifications since the last test was conducted. The objectives that the test team members should continually consider when testing during the programming phase include:

- Are the systems maintainable?
- Have the system specifications been implemented properly?
- Do the programs comply with information services standards and procedures as well as good practice?
- Is there a sufficient test plan to evaluate the executable programs?
- Are the programs adequately documented?

The test concerns to be considered during this task are described in the following subsections.

Data Integrity Controls Implemented

Specific controls need to be implemented in a manner that will achieve the desired processing precision. Improperly implemented controls may not achieve the established level of control tolerance, and because of the widespread misunderstanding of the purpose of controls (i.e., reduced risk), simplistic solutions might be implemented where complex controls are needed to achieve the control objectives.

Authorization Rules Implemented

Authorization rules need to be implemented in a manner that makes it difficult to circumvent them. For example, when authorization limits are set, people should not be able to circumvent these limits by entering numerous items under the prescribed limit. Therefore, authorization rules must not only consider the enforcement of the rules, but also take into account the more common methods to circumvent those rules.

File Integrity Controls Implemented

File integrity controls should be implemented in a manner that minimizes the probability of loss of file integrity, and they should both prevent the loss of integrity and detect that loss, should it occur, on a timely basis.

Audit Trail Implemented

The audit trail needs to be implemented in a manner that facilitates retrieval of audit trail information. If the audit trail contains needed information, but it is too costly or time-consuming to use, its value diminishes significantly. The implementation considerations include the amount of information retained, sequencing for ease of retrieval of that information, cross-referencing of information for retrieval purposes, as well as the length of time that the audit trail information needs to be retained.

Contingency Plan Written

The contingency plan is a set of detailed procedures in step-by-step format outlining those tasks to be executed in the event of problems. The plan should describe the preparatory tasks so that the necessary data and other resources are available when the contingency plan needs to be activated. The design contingency approach is of little value until it is documented and in the hands of the people who need to use it.

System to Achieve Service Level Designed

The desired service level can only become a reality when the procedures and methods are established. One procedure that should be set up is the monitoring of the level of service to ensure that it meets specifications. The inclusion of monitoring routines provides assurance over an extended period of time that service levels will be achieved, or if not, that fact will be detected early so corrective action can be taken.

Security Procedures Implemented

Security is the combination of employee awareness and training, plus the necessary security tools and techniques. The procedures ensuring that these two parts are available and working together must be developed during the program phase.

Program Complies with Methodology

Procedures should be implemented that ensure compliance to developmental standards, policies, procedures, and methods. If noncompliance is detected, appropriate measures must be taken to either obtain a variance from the methodology or modify the system or design so that compliance is achieved. While methodology does not necessarily satisfy user objectives, it is necessary to satisfy information services design objectives.

Program Conforms to Design (Correctness)

Changing conditions cause many information services project personnel to ignore project objectives during the program phase. The argument is that there are sufficient changes so that monitoring compliance to system objectives is meaningless. The test team should discourage this thinking and continually monitor the implementation of objectives. If objectives have not been met, either they should be changed or the system changed to bring it into compliance with the functional specifications of the application.

Program Conforms to Design (Ease of Use)

The implementation of system specs may negate some of the ease-of-use design aspects unless those aspects are specifically defined. Programming is a translation of design specifications and it may fail to achieve the ease-of-use intent. Programming must achieve this ease-of-use design spec as it does other functional specifications.

Program Is Maintainable

The method of program design and coding may have a greater significance for maintainability than the design specifications themselves. The rules of maintainable code should be partially defined by departmental standards, and partially defined by system specifications. In addition, the programmer should use judgment and experience in developing highly maintainable code.

Program Conforms to Design (Portability)

The portability of programs depends on the language selected and how that language is used. The specifications should indicate the do's and don'ts of programming for portability, and the coding should conform to those design specifications. If portability is a major concern and the program specifications fail to define portability coding adequately, the programmer should make every effort to write in as straightforward a method as possible.

Program Conforms to Design (Coupling)

The design specifications should indicate parameters passing to and from other application systems. It is normally good practice for the programmer to verify that the system's specifications are up-to-date prior to coding intersystem functions. This assures not only that the programs conform to the design, but that the specifications of interconnected applications have not changed since the design was documented.

Operating Procedures Developed

Procedures should be developed during programming to operate the application system. During the next phase, the executable programs will be operated, and the necessary instructions should be developed prior to that phase of the SDLC. The operating procedures should be consistent with the application system operational requirements.

Program Achieves Criteria (Performance)

The creation of the program provides the first operational opportunity for users to assess whether the system can achieve the desired performance level. At this point, the instructions to perform the requirements have been defined and can be evaluated. An early assessment of potential performance provides an opportunity to make performance adjustments if necessary.

A detailed test process is illustrated in Work Paper 11.1 for each of the 15 identified program phase test concerns. The test process includes test criteria, recommended test processes, techniques, and tools. The team conducting the test is urged to use judgment in determining the extent of tests and the applicability of the recommended techniques and tools to the application being tested. The testers should use the same process for this task as described in Task 2, in Chapter 9.

Task 3: Conduct a Program Peer Review

The peer review provides a vehicle for knowledgeable people (peers) to contribute to the construction of the computer program by informally but effectively reviewing the functioning of the program in a nonthreatening environment. The peer review provides a static analysis that evaluates both the structure and the functioning of the program. The peer review can detect syntactical errors, but more through personal observation than as a direct result of the walkthrough.

Peer reviews can also be formal. Whether the formal or informal version is used, management should approve the peer review concept. Formal peer reviews are an integral task in the programming process, while informal peer reviews are called for at the discretion of the lead programmer.

The peer review team should be comprised of between three and six members. It is important to have at least three members on the peer review team in order to obtain sufficiently varied opinion and to keep discussion going. Individuals who should be considered for the peer review team include:

- Computer programmers (at least two)
- Job control specialists
- Computer operator
- Control clerk
- Programming supervisor

Program peer reviews are performed by executing the following tasks.

Establish Peer Review Ground Rules

This need not be done for every peer review, but it is important to have good ground rules. Among the ground rules that need to be decided are:

- Areas included and excluded from the peer review, for example, whether efficiency of programs will be included
- Whether reports will be issued
- Method for selecting peer review team leader
- Location of conducting the peer review
- Method for selecting a peer review

Select Peer Review Team

The members of the peer review team should be selected sufficiently in advance so that they can arrange their schedules to allocate sufficient time and acquire training for the peer review exercise.

Train Team Members

If an individual on the team has not participated in the program peer review previously, that individual should be trained in the process. Training includes an understanding of the peer review ground rules, preferably some training in interpersonal relationships such as how to interview and work with people in a peer review process, and training in the intent of the standards and program methodologies.

Select Review Method

The team leader should select the review method. The review itself consists of two parts. The first part is a general explanation of the objectives and functioning of the program. The second part is the review of the program(s) using the selected method. Four methods can be used to conduct the peer review:

1. **Flowchart.** The program is explained from a flowchart of the program logic. This is most effective when the flowchart is produced directly from the source code.
2. **Source code.** The review examines each line of source code in order to understand the program.
3. **Sample transactions.** The lead programmer explains the programs by explaining the processing that occurs on a representative sample of transactions.
4. **Program specifications.** The program specifications are reviewed as a means of understanding the program.

Conduct Peer Review

The project lead programmer normally oversees the peer review. The peer review commences by having the lead programmer briefly review the ground rules, explain the program's objectives, and then lead the team through the program processing. The review team is free to question and comment on any aspect of the project programmer's explanations and to make recommendations and suggestions about the program. Generally, the peer review is conducted in a democratic manner. The role of the team leader is to ensure that the team's questions and comments are in order, ensure the team members' rights to ask questions, to make recommendations, or to stop interrogation on a specific point if, in the opinion of the inspection team leader, there is no benefit from continuing discussion.

Draw Conclusions

At the end of the formal peer review, the lead programmer will indicate that he or she has no more comments to make and turn the meeting over to the peer review team leader. The peer review team leader now takes control of the meeting and summarizes the factual information drawn from the review and presents the review team's recommendations. Ideally, this is done as a group activity, but some peer review teams, especially when the process is formalized, may want some time alone to discuss among themselves what they have heard and what they are going to recommend. The findings and recommendations are then presented to the project team for their consideration.

Prepare Report

In the formal peer review process, reports may be prepared documenting the results. However, this is optional and not an essential part of the peer review process.

Check Procedures

Work Paper 11.2 is a quality control checklist for this step. It is designed so that Yes responses indicate good test practices; No responses warrant additional investigation. A Comments column is provided to explain No responses and to record results of investigation. The N/A column is used when the checklist item is not applicable to the test situation.

Output

Two outputs should occur from this step. The first is a fully debugged program using static testing to uncover and remove defects. The second is a list of the defects uncovered during testing. Note that if the organization has a quality assurance activity, that list of defects should be forwarded to them, so that they may address weaknesses in processes to eliminate reoccurrence of the same defects in other programs.

Guidelines

Two test tools have proven themselves over the years in programming phase testing: desk debugging and peer review. These two tools are closely related and complement each other. Desk debugging is performed by the individual programmer prior to peer reviews, which are normally performed by other members of the information services department. A combination of the two tools is effective in detecting both structural and functional defects.

Summary

The method of generating computer code varies significantly from organization to organization, and from project to project. In some organizations statement level languages, such as COBOL, are still used. In other organizations or projects, code is generated from design languages.

The program phase testing approach outline in this chapter is designed to cover all methods of code generation. However, all of the techniques should be used when code is generated through statement languages. When code generators are used from design specifications the program testing will be minimal. Some of these programming testing techniques maybe incorporated in design phase testing. When this is done the testing emphasis shifts to dynamic testing, which is covered in Chapter 12.

WORK PAPER 11.1   Initial Supplier Capability Assessment

Field Requirements

FIELD	INSTRUCTIONS FOR ENTERING DATA
Test criteria	The questions to be answered by the test team.
Assessment	The test team's evaluation of the test criteria.
Recommended test	The recommended test to be conducted to assess the test criteria.
Test technique	The recommended technique to be used in evaluating the test criteria. Other techniques may be helpful and should be used based on the attributes of the application being tested.
Test tool	The tool(s) to be used to accomplish the test technique (options may be indicated).

(Continues)

WORK PAPER 11.1 (Continued)

TEST FACTOR: Data Integrity Controls Implemented

#	TEST CRITERIA	ASSESSMENT				RECOMMENDED TEST	TEST TECHNIQUE	TEST TOOL
		Very Adequate	Adequate	Inadequate	N/A			
1.	Have procedures been written indicating how to record transactions for entry into the automated system?					Examine the usefulness of data error messages and listing.	Manual support	Correctness proof, Exhaustive testing, & Flowchart
2.	Have data validation checks been implemented to ensure that input complies with system specifications?					Review the completeness of the data validation checks.	Requirements	Compiler-based analysis, Data dictionary, & Inspections
3.	Have anticipation controls been installed where appropriate, to ensure that valid, but unreasonable, data is noted for manual investigation?					Examine the extensiveness of anticipation controls to identify potential problems.	Error handling	Correctness proof, Error guessing, & Inspections
4.	Are errors properly identified and explained so that follow-up action can be readily conducted?					Examine the completeness of the data entry procedures.	Error handling	Exhaustive testing
5.	Have procedures been established to take corrective action on data errors?					Examine the reasonableness of the procedures to take corrective action on identified errors.	Error handling	Cause-effect graphing
6.	Are procedures established to ensure that errors are corrected on a timely basis?					Verify that the procedures will ensure that errors are corrected on a timely basis.	Error handling	Correctness proof & Flowchart

(Continues)

WORK PAPER 11.1 *(Continued)*

TEST FACTOR: Data Integrity Controls Implemented

#	TEST CRITERIA	ASSESSMENT				RECOMMENDED TEST	TEST TECHNIQUE	TEST TOOL
		Very Ade-quate	Ade-quate	Inade-quate	N/A			
7.	Are run-to-run controls installed to ensure the completeness and accuracy of transactions as they move from point to point in the system?					Examine the reasonableness of the procedures that ensure accuracy and completeness of transactions as they flow through the system.	Requirements	Control flow analysis & Data flow analysis
8.	Have procedures been implemented that will verify the installed input controls, such as sequence numbers, batch numbers, etc., to ensure that complete and accurate input is recorded?					Verify the adequacy of the procedures to ensure that controls established during data origination are verified during processing.	Control	Correctness proof & Exhaustive testing

WORK PAPER 11.1 (Continued)

TEST FACTOR: Authorization Rules Implemented

#	TEST CRITERIA	ASSESSMENT				RECOMMENDED TEST	TEST TECHNIQUE	TEST TOOL
		Very Ade-quate	Ade-quate	Inade-quate	N/A			
1.	Have the authorization methods been divided between manual and automated?					Evaluate the reasonableness of the authorization method selected.	Security	Fact finding
2.	Have procedures been prepared to specify the manual authoriza-tion process for each trans-action?					Review the adequacy of the manual authorization procedures.	Security	Inspections
3.	Are the methods implemented in programs for authorizing trans-actions in the automated seg-ment of the system?					Examine the program specifications, or actual pro-grams, to determine that authorization method has been properly implemented.	Requirements	Inspections
4.	Have manual procedures been established to indicate violations of manual authorization pro-cedures?					Examine the reasonableness of the violation pro-cedures for manual authorization.	Control	Checklist & Fact finding
5.	Have procedures been estab-lished to identify and act upon violations of automated authori-zation procedures?					Examine the adequacy of the automated authoriza-tion violation procedures.	Requirements	Walkthroughs

(Continues)

WORK PAPER 11.1 (Continued)

TEST FACTOR: Authorization Rules Implemented

#	TEST CRITERIA	ASSESSMENT				RECOMMENDED TEST	TEST TECHNIQUE	TEST TOOL
		Very Ade-quate	Ade-quate	Inade-quate	N/A			
6.	Do the implemented authorization methods conform to the authorization rules defined in the requirements phase?					Verify compliance of implemented authorization methods to the defined authorization rules.	Requirements	Inspections
7.	Have procedures been implemented to verify the source of transactions where the source becomes the basis for authorizing the transaction?					Verify that the system authenticates the source of transaction where that source itself authorizes the transaction.	Security	Inspections
8.	Does the system maintain a record of who authorized each transaction?					Verify that procedures are implemented to identify the authorizer of each transaction.	Requirements	Inspections

WORK PAPER 11.1 *(Continued)*

TEST FACTOR: File Integrity Controls Implemented

#	TEST CRITERIA	ASSESSMENT				RECOMMENDED TEST	TEST TECHNIQUE	TEST TOOL
		Very Adequate	Adequate	Inadequate	N/A			
1.	Has someone been appointed accountable for the integrity of each file?					Verify that the assigned individual has the necessary skills and time available.	Control	Fact finding
2.	Have the file integrity controls been implemented in accordance with the file integrity requirements?					Compare the implemented controls to the integrity requirements established during the requirements phase.	Requirements	Inspections
3.	Have procedures been established to notify the appropriate individual of file integrity problems?					Examine the adequacy of the procedures to report file integrity problems.	Error handling	Walkthroughs
4.	Are procedures established to verify the integrity of files on a regular basis?					Review the reasonableness of the file integrity verification frequency.	Requirements	Walkthroughs
5.	Are there subsets of the file that should have integrity controls?					Confirm with the user that all file subsets are appropriately safeguarded through integrity controls.	Control	Error guessing & Confirmation/ examination
6.	Are procedures written for the regular reconciliation between automated file controls and independently maintained control totals?					Verify the reasonableness and timeliness of procedures to reconcile automated to manually maintained controls.	Control	Walkthroughs
7.	Are interfile integrity controls maintained where applicable (e.g., cash receipts and accounts receivable applied cash)?					Confirm with the user that all applicable file relationships are reconciled as a means of verifying file integrity.	Control	Confirmation/ examination
8.	Are sensitive transactions subject to special authorization controls?					Verify with legal counsel that sensitive transaction authorization controls are adequate.	Control	Confirmation/ examination

WORK PAPER 11.1 (Continued)

TEST FACTOR: Implement Audit Trail

#	TEST CRITERIA	ASSESSMENT				RECOMMENDED TEST	TEST TECHNIQUE	TEST TOOL
		Very Ade-quate	Ade-quate	Inade-quate	N/A			
1.	Has the audit trail relationship from source record to control total been documented?					Examine the completeness of the audit trail from source document to control total.	Requirements	Walkthroughs
2.	Has the audit trail from the control total to the supporting source transaction been documented?					Examine the completeness of the audit trail from the control total to the source document.	Requirements	Walkthroughs
3.	Have all the defined fields for inclusion on the audit trail been included in the audit trail?					Verify that the audit trail records include all of the defined audit trail fields.	Requirements	Walkthroughs
4.	Does the implemented audit trail satisfy the defined reconstruction requirements?					Verify that the implemented audit trail is in compliance with the reconstruction requirements phase.	Requirements	Inspections
5.	Have procedures been defined to test the audit trail?					Verify that an audit trail test plan has been devised.	Requirements	Fact finding
6.	Are procedures defined to store part of the audit trail off-site?					Examine the reasonableness of the procedures that require application audit trail records to be stored off-site.	Recovery	Cause-effect graphing & Peer review
7.	Does the implemented audit trail permit reconstruction of transaction processing?					Review the completeness of the transaction reconstruction process.	Requirements	Exhaustive testing & Inspections
8.	Does the audit trail contain the needed information to restore a failure?					Confirm with the computer operations manager that the audit trail information is complete.	Requirements	Confirmation/ examination

WORK PAPER 11.1 *(Continued)*

TEST FACTOR: Write Contingency Plan

#	TEST CRITERIA	ASSESSMENT				RECOMMENDED TEST	TEST TECHNIQUE	TEST TOOL
		Very Adequate	Adequate	Inadequate	N/A			
1.	Does the contingency plan identify the people involved in recovering processing after a failure?					Confirm with the operations manager that all the appropriate people are identified in the contingency plan.	Recovery	Confirmation/ examination
2.	Has the contingency plan been approved by the operations manager?					Examine the evidence indicating the operations manager approves of the plan.	Recovery	Confirmation/ examination
3.	Does the plan identify all the resources needed for recovery?					Confirm with the operations manager that all the needed resources are identified.	Recovery	Confirmation/ examination
4.	Does the contingency plan include the priority for restarting operations after a failure?					Review the reasonableness of the priority with senior management.	Recovery	Error guessing & Fact finding
5.	Does the recovery plan specify an alternate processing site?					Confirm with alternate site that it is available for backup processing.	Recovery	Confirmation/ examination
6.	Does the contingency plan provide for security during a recovery period?					Review the reasonableness of the security plan with the security officer.	Recovery	Inspections
7.	Has a plan been developed to test the contingency plan?					Examine the completeness of the test plan.	Operations	Inspections
8.	Has the role of outside parties, such as the hardware vendor, been included in the test plan, and confirmed with those outside parties?					Confirm with outside parties they can supply the support indicated in the contingency plan.	Operations	Confirmation/ examination

WORK PAPER 11.1 (Continued)

TEST FACTOR: Design System to Achieve Service Level

#	TEST CRITERIA	ASSESSMENT				RECOMMENDED TEST	TEST TECHNIQUE	TEST TOOL
		Very Ade-quate	Ade-quate	Inade-quate	N/A			
1.	Do the implemented programs perform in accordance with the desired service level?					Verify the performance criteria of the programs during testing.	Stress	Instrumentation
2.	Does the system performance achieve the desired level of service?					Verify the performance of the system during testing.	Stress	Instrumentation
3.	Have the training programs been prepared for the people who will use the application system?					Examine the completeness of the training programs.	Execution	Checklist & Inspections
4.	Is the support software available and does it meet service-level requirements?					Confirm with computer operations personnel that the support software is available and does meet performance criteria.	Operations	Confirmation/examination
5.	Is the support hardware available and does it provide sufficient capacity?					Confirm with computer operations personnel that the support hardware is available and does meet the capacity requirements.	Operations	Confirmation/examination
6.	Is sufficient hardware and software on order to meet anticipated future volumes?					Confirm with computer operations that sufficient hardware and software is on order to meet anticipated future volumes.	Operations	Confirmation/examination
7.	Has a test plan been defined to verify that service-level performance criteria can be met?					Examine the completeness of the test plan.	Execution	Checklist & Inspections
8.	Can the required input be delivered to processing in time to meet production schedules?					Confirm with the individuals preparing input that they can prepare input in time to meet production schedules.	Execution	Confirmation/examination

WORK PAPER 11.1 (Continued)

TEST FACTOR: Implement Security Procedures

#	TEST CRITERIA	ASSESSMENT				RECOMMENDED TEST	TEST TECHNIQUE	TEST TOOL
		Very Adequate	Adequate	Inadequate	N/A			
1.	Is the required security hardware available?					Confirm with the security officer that the needed security hardware is available.	Security	Confirmation/examination
2.	Is the required security software available?					Confirm with the security officer that the needed security software is available.	Security	Confirmation/examination
3.	Has a procedure been established to disseminate and maintain passwords?					Examine the completeness and adequacy of the password dissemination and maintenance plan.	Security	Exhaustive testing
4.	Have the involved personnel been trained in security procedures?					Examine the adequacy and completeness of the security training procedures.	Security	Exhaustive testing
5.	Has a security violation procedure been established to monitor violations?					Examine the completeness and adequacy of the test violation procedure.	Control	Exhaustive testing
6.	Has management been instructed on the procedure for punishing security violators?					Confirm with management that they have been adequately instructed on how to implement security prosecution procedures.	Control	Confirmation/examination
7.	Have procedures been established to protect the programs, program listings, data documentation, and other systems documentation defining how the system works?					Verify with the security officer the adequacy of the procedures to protect the system documentation and program.	Security	Risk matrix & Confirmation/examination
8.	Has one individual been appointed accountable for security of the application when it becomes operational?					Verify that the accountable individual has the necessary skills and the time available.	Security	Fact finding

WORK PAPER 11.1   (Continued)

TEST FACTOR: Programs Comply with Methodology

#	TEST CRITERIA	ASSESSMENT				RECOMMENDED TEST	TEST TECHNIQUE	TEST TOOL
		Very Ade-quate	Ade-quate	Inade-quate	N/A			
1.	Have the organization's policies and procedures been incorporated into the application programs?					Examine the programs to ensure that they comply with the necessary organization policies and procedures.	Compliance	Inspections
2.	Have the organization's information services methods, policies, and procedures been incorporated into the application programs?					Examine the programs to ensure that they comply with the necessary information services methods, policies, and procedures.	Compliance	Inspections
3.	Have the organization's accounting policies and procedures been incorporated into the application programs?					Examine the programs to ensure that they comply with the necessary accounting policies and procedures.	Compliance	Inspections
4.	Have the governmental regulations been incorporated into the application program?					Examine the programs to ensure that they comply with the necessary government regulations.	Compliance	Inspections
5.	Have the industry standards been incorporated into the application programs?					Examine the programs to ensure that they comply with the necessary industry standards.	Compliance	Inspections
6.	Have the organization's user department policies and procedures been incorporated into the application programs?					Examine the programs to ensure that they comply with the user department's policies and procedures.	Compliance	Inspections

TEST FACTOR: Programs Comply with Methodology

#	TEST CRITERIA	ASSESSMENT				RECOMMENDED TEST	TEST TECHNIQUE	TEST TOOL
		Very Ade-quate	Ade-quate	Inade-quate	N/A			
7.	Are the policies, procedures, and regulations used as a basis for system specifications the most up-to-date version?					Confirm with the appropriate party that the regulations used for specifications are the most current requirements.	Compliance	Confirmation/ examination
8.	Are there anticipated changes to the policies, standards, or regulations between this phase and the time the system will become operational?					Confirm with the involved parties the probability of, or known changes to the policies, standards, or regulations that will occur prior to the system's becoming operational.	Compliance	Confirmation/ examination

(Continues)

393

WORK PAPER 11.1 *(Continued)*

TEST FACTOR: Programs Conform to Design (Correctness)

#	TEST CRITERIA	ASSESSMENT				RECOMMENDED TEST	TEST TECHNIQUE	TEST TOOL
		Very Adequate	Adequate	Inadequate	N/A			
1.	Have changes in user management affected their support of system objectives?					Confirm with user management that the stated objectives are still desired.	Requirements	Confirmation/examination
2.	Does the program implementation comply with stated objectives?					Compare program results to stated objectives.	Requirements	Design reviews
3.	Will the implemented systems produce correct results?					Verify that the implemented systems will produce correct results	Requirements	Correctness proof
4.	Have the desired reports been produced?					Confirm that the reports produced by the application program comply with user-defined specifications.	Requirements	Design reviews
5.	Does the system input achieve the desired data consistency and reliability objectives?					Confirm with the user that the input to the system achieves the desired consistency and reliability objectives.	Requirements	Design reviews
6.	Are the manuals explaining how to use the computer outputs adequate?					Confirm with the user the adequacy of the output use manuals.	Requirements	Checklist & Confirmation/examination
7.	Are the input manuals and procedures adequate to ensure the preparation of valid input?					Confirm with the input preparers that the manuals appear adequate to produce valid input.	Requirements	Checklist & Confirmation/examination
8.	Has the user involvement in the developmental process continued through the programming phase?					Confirm with the project personnel that the user participation has been adequate to ensure user satisfaction.	Requirements	Checklist & Confirmation/examination

WORK PAPER 11.1   (Continued)

TEST FACTOR: Programs Conform to Design (Ease of Use)

#	TEST CRITERIA	Very Adequate	Adequate	Inadequate	N/A	RECOMMENDED TEST	TEST TECHNIQUE	TEST TOOL
		ASSESSMENT						
1.	Do the application documents conform to design specifications?					Verify that the implemented ease of use segment of the application conforms to design.	Compliance	Design reviews
2.	Have easy-to-use instructions been prepared for interfacing with the automated application?					Examine the usability of the people interface instructions.	Manual support	Checklist
3.	Have provisions been made to provide assistance to input clerks if needed?					Verify provisions are implemented to assist input clerks in the proper entry of data.	Manual support	Checklist & Walkthroughs
4.	Are the training sessions planned to train personnel on how to interact with the computer system?					Examine the course content to verify the appropriateness of the material for the user.	Manual	Walkthroughs
5.	Are the output documents implemented for ease of use?					Verify the ease of use of the output documents.	Requirements	Checklist & Walkthroughs
6.	Do the output documents indicate the importance of information contained on the document?					Verify the importance of message will be indicated on system documents.	Requirements	Inspections
7.	Are the input documents implemented for ease of use?					Verify the ease of use of the input documents.	Requirements	Checklist & Walkthroughs
8.	Do user clerical personnel accept the application system as usable?					Confirm with user clerical personnel their acceptance of the usability of the application.	Manual support	Confirmation/examination

395

WORK PAPER 11.1 *(Continued)*

TEST FACTOR: Programs Are Maintainable

#	TEST CRITERIA	ASSESSMENT				RECOMMENDED TEST	TEST TECHNIQUE	TEST TOOL
		Very Adequate	Adequate	Inadequate	N/A			
1.	Do the programs conform to the maintenance specifications for the application?					Verify that the programs conform to the maintenance specifications.	Compliance	Inspections
2.	Is the program documentation complete and usable?					Review the documentation for completeness and usability.	Compliance	Compiler-based analysis & Inspections
3.	Do the programs contain a reasonable number of explanatory statements?					Review the programs to determine they contain a reasonable number of explanatory statements.	Compliance	Inspections
4.	Is each processing segment of the program clearly identified?					Verify that each processing segment of the program is adequately identified.	Compliance	Inspections
5.	Do the programs avoid complex program logic wherever possible?					Review programs for complex programming logic.	Compliance	Checklist & Inspections
6.	Are the expected high-frequency change areas coded to facilitate maintenance?					Determine ease of maintenance of high-change areas.	Compliance	Peer review
7.	Have the programs been reviewed from an ease of maintenance perspective?					Review programs to determine the maintainability	Compliance	Peer review
8.	Are changes introduced during programming incorporated into the design documentation?					Review changes and determine they have been incorporated into the design documentation.	Compliance	Design reviews & Confirmation/examination

WORK PAPER 11.1 (Continued)

TEST FACTOR: Programs Conform to Design (Portable)

#	TEST CRITERIA	ASSESSMENT				RECOMMENDED TEST	TEST TECHNIQUE	TEST TOOL
		Very Adequate	Adequate	Inadequate	N/A			
1.	Does the system avoid the use of any manufacturer-special hardware features?					Review application for special hardware restrictions.	Operations	Inspections
2.	Does the system avoid the use of any vendor-special software features?					Review application for special software restrictions.	Operations	Inspections
3.	Are the programs written using the common program language statements?					Review programs for use of uncommon programming statements.	Compliance	Inspections
4.	Are all portability restrictions documented?					Determine completeness of the portability documentation.	Compliance	Inspections
5.	Are all operating characteristics documented (e.g., program size)?					Determine completeness of operating characteristics documentation.	Compliance	Inspections
6.	Does program documentation avoid technical jargon?					Review documentation for use of technical jargon.	Compliance	Inspections
7.	Are the data values used in the program machine independent?					Review data values to determine they are machine independent.	Compliance	Checklist, Confirmation/ examination & Fact finding
8.	Are the data files machine independent					Review data files to determine they are machine independent.	Compliance	Checklist, Confirmation/ examination & Fact finding

WORK PAPER 11.1 *(Continued)*

TEST FACTOR: Programs Conform to Design (Coupling)

#	TEST CRITERIA	ASSESSMENT				RECOMMENDED TEST	TEST TECHNIQUE	TEST TOOL
		Very Adequate	Adequate	Inadequate	N/A			
1.	Are common record layouts used for interfaced programs?					Verify that common record layouts are used by interfaced applications.	Intersystems	Inspections
2.	Are the values in the data fields common to interfaced programs?					Verify that common data values are used by interfaced applications.	Intersystems	Inspections
3.	Do the interfaced systems use the same file structure?					Verify that common file structures are used by interfaced applications.	Intersystems	Inspections
4.	Have the interfaced segments been implemented as designed?					Verify that the interface segments of the application are implemented as designed.	Intersystems	Correctness proof, Desk checking, & Inspections
5.	Have changes to the interfaced system been coordinated with any affected application?					Confirm that changes affecting interfaced applications are coordinated with those applications	Intersystems	Exhaustive testing & Confirmation/examination
6.	Is the program/interface properly documented?					Verify that the interface document is complete.	Intersystems	Error guessing & Inspections
7.	Is the data transfer media common to interfaced applications?					Verify that common media is used for interfaced application files.	Operations	Confirmation/examination & Fact finding
8.	Can the required timing for the transfer of data be achieved?					Verify that the data transfer timing between interfaced applications is reasonable.	Intersystems	Error guessing & Fact finding

WORK PAPER 11.1 *(Continued)*

TEST FACTOR: Develop Operating Procedures

#	TEST CRITERIA	ASSESSMENT				RECOMMENDED TEST	TEST TECHNIQUE	TEST TOOL
		Very Adequate	Adequate	Inadequate	N/A			
1.	Has the size of the largest program been identified?					Review programs to determine maximum program size.	Operations	Inspections
2.	Have changes made during programming affected operations?					Review changes to ascertain if they affect operations.	Operations	Inspections
3.	Have any deviations from designed operations been communicated to computer operations?					Review application for operation design variations and confirm operations has been notified of these changes.	Operations	Error guessing
4.	Have operations documentation been prepared?					Review completeness of operations documentation.	Compliance	Design reviews
5.	Have special forms and other needed media been ordered?					Determine if needed media has been ordered.	Operations	Confirmation/ examination & Fact finding
6.	Have data media retention procedures been prepared?					Review adequacy of data retention procedures.	Compliance	Inspections
7.	Has needed computer time for tests been scheduled?					Examine computer schedule to ascertain if needed test time has been scheduled.	Operations	Fact finding
8.	Have off-site storage needs been defined?					Determine reasonableness of off-site storage requirements.	Operations	Fact finding

(Continues)

399

WORK PAPER 11.1 (Continued)

TEST FACTOR: Programs Achieve Criteria (Performance)

#	TEST CRITERIA	ASSESSMENT				RECOMMENDED TEST	TEST TECHNIQUE	TEST TOOL
		Very Adequate	Adequate	Inadequate	N/A			
1.	Has the cost to design and test the system approximated the cost estimate?					Examine the projected budget to verify that actual costs approximate budget costs.	Execution	Fact finding
2.	Does the operational cost as represented by information services tests approximate the projected operational costs?					Use the data from the job accounting system to substantiate that the actual test operational costs approximate the projected operational costs.	Execution	Fact finding
3.	Are the costs monitored during the developmental process?					Confirm with the information services manager that project costs are monitored.	Compliance	Confirmation/ examination
4.	Will changes made during the programming phase affect anticipated system costs?					Confirm with the project manager that changes during the program phase will not affect operational costs.	Execution	Confirmation/ examination & Fact finding
5.	Are the projected benefits still reasonable?					Confirm with user management that projected benefits are still reasonable.	Execution	Confirmation/ examination & Fact finding
6.	Is the projected life of the project still reasonable?					Confirm with user management that the expected life of the project is still reasonable.	Execution	Confirmation/ examination
7.	Is the project on schedule?					Compare the current status versus projected status in the schedule.	Execution	Fact finding
8.	Are there any expected changes in the test or conversion phases that would impact the projected return on investment?					Confirm with the project leader whether there would be any changes during the test or conversion phase that could affect project return on investment.	Execution	Error guessing & Confirmation/ examination

WORK PAPER 11.2   Quality Control Checklist

Field Requirements

FIELD	INSTRUCTIONS FOR ENTERING DATA
Number	A number that sequentially identifies the quality control items, which if positively addressed would indicate that this step has been performed correctly.
Item	The specific quality control item that is used to measure the effectiveness of performing this step.
Response	The testers should indicate in this column whether they have performed the referenced item. The response can be Yes, No, or N/A if it is not appropriate for your organization's testing process.
Comments	This column is used to clarify the Yes, No, or N/A response for the item indicated. Generally the comments column need only be completed for No responses; No responses should be investigated and a determination made as to whether this item needs to be performed before this step can be considered complete.

#	ITEM	RESPONSE			COMMENTS
		YES	NO	N/A	
1.	Is verifying and validating programs considered to be a responsibility of the programmer?				
2.	Does the programmer understand the difference between static and dynamic testing?				
3.	Will the program be subject to static testing as the primary means to remove defects?				
4.	Does the programmer understand the process that will generate the program code (e.g., does the programmer understand the strength and weakness of the compiler/program generating tool)?				
5.	Does the programmer understand and use desk debugging?				
6.	Does the programmer understand the 15 programming concerns, and will they be incorporated into programming testing?				
7.	Is the program tested using either the peer review technique or code inspections?				
8.	Will the program be subject to full testing prior to moving to a higher-level testing (e.g., string testing)?				
9.	Are all of the uncovered defects recorded in detail?				
10.	Are all of the uncovered defects corrected prior to moving to the next level of testing?				

Step 6: Execute Test and Record Results

This step provides the opportunity to evaluate executable programs as a system. Effective testing in the previous steps provides a high degree of assurance that the executable programs will function as specified. However, it is not until they are executed as a system that there is complete assurance they will function properly. For this reason, it is important to test the completed system. (See Figure 12.1.)

Testing tradeoffs can be made between the various phases of the life cycle. The more testing that is performed during the requirements, design, and program phases, the less testing that needs to be performed during the test phase. On the other hand, when only minimal testing is performed during the early phases, extensive testing may be needed during the test phase.

Overview

During the programming test step, information services personnel test the programs in accordance with the specifications as they understand them. Even if the program testing was performed perfectly, there could still be defects in the system because there can be misunderstandings in the translations between the user, design, and programming, as well as time and budget constraints that can result in defects existing in the system at the beginning of the test phase. Thus, the test phase can be a time-consuming and costly process.

Continuing the analogy from previous chapters between building a home and a computer system, the test execution step would be equivalent to the final walkthrough of

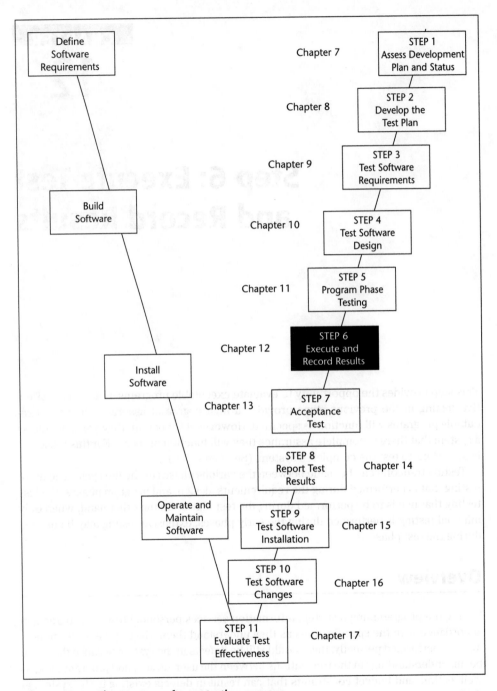

Figure 12.1   The 11-step software testing process.

the home by the purchaser, verifying that the home conforms to specifications. The homeowner has the opportunity to try all of the utilities, to verify that all the expected components have been delivered, and that the quality of the construction conforms to specifications. Unfortunately, if the user has not performed some aspects of previous testing, they cannot occur during the final phase. For example, many of the electrical lines and much of the plumbing will be hidden behind wallboards and cannot be evaluated during the final testing.

Objective

The objective of this step is to determine whether the software system will perform correctly in an executable mode. The software is executed in a test environment in approximately the same operational mode as it would be in an operational environment. The test should be executed in as many different ways as necessary to address the 15 concerns described in this test process. Any deviation from the expected results should be recorded during this step. Depending on the nature and severity of those problems, uncovered changes may need to be made to the software before it is placed in a production status. If the findings/problems are extensive it may be necessary to stop testing completely and return the software to the developers to make the needed changes prior to restoring testing.

Concerns

There are three major concerns testers have on entering the test execution step:

1. **Software not in a testable mode.** The previous testing steps will not have been performed adequately to remove most of the defects and/or the necessary functions will not have been installed, or correctly installed in the software. Thus, testing will become bogged down in identifying problems that should have been identified earlier.

2. **Inadequate time/resources.** Because of delays in development or failure to adequately budget sufficient time and resources for testing, the testers will not have the time or resources necessary to effectively test the software. In many IT organizations management relies on testing to assure that the software is ready for production prior to being placed in production. When adequate time or resources are unavailable, management may still rely on the testers when they are unable to perform their test as expected.

3. **Significant problems will not be uncovered during testing.** Unless testing is adequately planned and executed according to that plan, the problems that can cause serious operational difficulties may not be uncovered. This can happen because testers at this step spend too much time uncovering defects rather than evaluating the operational performance of the application software.

Workbench

The workbench for executing tests and recording results is illustrated in Figure 12.2. This shows that the testers use a test environment at this point in the testing life cycle. The more closely this environment resembles the actual operational environment the more effective the testing becomes. If test data has not been created earlier in the testing process it needs to be created as part of this step. Tests are then executed and the results recorded. The test report should indicate what works and what does not work. The test report should also give the tester's opinion regarding whether he or she believes the software is ready for operation at the conclusion of this test step.

Input

The testing of an application system during the test execution steps has few new inputs. Like the home, many aspects of the developmental process are unavailable for evaluation during the test phase. Therefore, the testing during this phase must rely upon the adequacy of the work performed during the earlier phases. The deliverables that are available during the test phase include:

- Test execution step test plan
- Test data (if available)

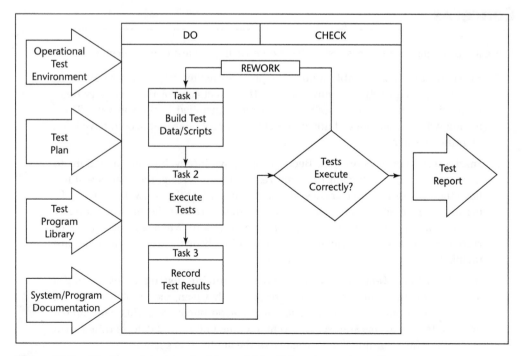

Figure 12.2 Workbench to execute (dynamic) test(s) and record results.

- Results of previous test (primarily verification tests)
- Third-party inputs, such as computer operator

Do Procedures

The execution of this step involves performing the following three tasks:

Task 1: Build Test Data

Information services personnel and users have been using test data since the inception of computer programming. The concept of test data is a simple one—creating representative processing conditions using test transactions. The complex part of creating test data is determining which transactions to make test transactions. Experience shows that it is uneconomical to test all conditions in an application system. Experience further shows that most testing exercises fewer than one-half of the computer instructions. Therefore, optimizing testing through selecting the most important test transactions is the key aspect of the test data test tool.

Several of the test tools are structured methods for designing test data. For example, correctness proof, data flow analysis, and control flow analysis are all designed to develop extensive sets of test data, as is exhaustive testing. Unfortunately, all of these tools, while extremely effective, require large amounts of time and effort to implement. Few organizations allocate sufficient budgets for this type of testing. In addition, information services personnel are not trained in the use of these test tools.

Test File Design

To design an adequate test file, the tester must be familiar with information services test standards and other relevant policies, include their provisions in the simulated transactions and information services procedures, and supply input and output formats for all types of transactions to be processed. Also helpful is a preliminary knowledge of system objectives and operating procedures obtained by reviewing and analyzing system flowcharts, operating instructions, and other documentation. This knowledge can alert the test team to possible system weaknesses for which unique test transactions should be designed.

To be effective, a test file should use transactions having a wide range of valid and invalid input data—valid data for testing normal processing operations and invalid data for testing programmed controls.

Only one test transaction should be processed against each master record. This permits an isolated evaluation of specific program controls by ensuring that test results will not be influenced by other test transactions processed against the same master record. General types of conditions that should be tested follow.

> **Tests of normally occurring transactions.** To test a computer system's ability to accurately process valid data, a test file should include transactions that normally occur. For example, in a payroll system, normally occurring transactions include

the calculation of regular pay, overtime pay, and some other type of premium pay (such as shift pay), as well as setting up master records for newly hired employees and updating existing master records for other employees.

Tests using invalid data. Testing for the existence or effectiveness of programmed controls requires using invalid data. Examples of tests for causing invalid data to be rejected or "flagged" are:

- Entering alphabetic characters when numeric characters are expected and vice versa.
- Using invalid account or identification numbers.
- Using incomplete or extraneous data in a specific data field or omitting it entirely.
- Entering negative amounts when only positive amounts are valid and vice versa.
- Entering illogical conditions in data fields that should be related logically.
- Entering a transaction code or amount that does not match the code or amount established by operating procedures or controlling tables. For example, if the valid codes for employee status in a payroll system are A, B, and C, the code to be entered would be something other than A, B, or C. Another example is entering a salary amount which is incompatible with a controlling salary table.
- Entering transactions or conditions that will violate limits established by law or by standard operating procedures. An example in a payroll system would be the entry of X + 2 dollars as an employee's gross pay when X dollars is the maximum gross pay allowed by law for the highest grade.

Tests to violate established edit checks. From system documentation, the auditor should be able to determine what edit routines are included in the computer programs to be tested. He or she should then create test transactions to violate these edits to see whether they, in fact, exist.

Entering Test Data

After the types of test transactions have been determined, the test data should be put into correct entry form. If the test team wishes to test controls over both input and computer processing, they should feed the data into the system on basic-source documents for the organization to convert into machine-readable form (on disk, magnetic tape, etc.). When testing only computer processing controls, data should both violate and conform to the processing rules.

Analyzing Processing Results

Before processing test data through the computer, the test team must predetermine the correct result for each test transaction for comparison with actual results. Any difference between actual and predetermined results indicates a weakness in the system. The test team should determine the effect of the weakness on the accuracy of master file data and on the reliability of reports and other computer products.

Applying Test Files against Programs that Update Master Records

There are two basic approaches to test programs for updating master records. In one approach, copies of actual master records and/or simulated master records are used to set up a separate master file for the test. In the second approach, special audit records, kept in the organization's current master file, are used.

To use the first approach, the test team must have a part of the organization's master file copied to create a test master file. From a printout of this file, the team selects records suitable for the test. The tester then updates the test file with both valid and invalid data by using the organization's programs to process the transactions making up the test file. Master records can be simulated most easily by preparing source documents and processing them with the program the organization uses to add new records to its master file. Procedures for using simulated records as test data are the same as those for copied records. An advantage of using simulated records is that they can be tailored for particular conditions and they eliminate the need to locate and copy suitable organization records. This advantage is usually offset when many records are needed because their creation can be complex and time-consuming when compared to the relatively simple procedure of copying a part of the organization's master file.

Often, the most practical approach is to use a test master file that is a combination of copied and simulated master records. In this approach, copied records are used whenever possible and simulated records are used only when necessary to test conditions not found in the copied records.

By using copied and simulated master records in a separate test file, the tester avoids the complications and dangers of running test data in a regular processing run against the current master file. A disadvantage of copied and simulated records is that computer programs must be loaded and equipment set up and operated for audit purposes only, thus involving additional cost.

Test File Process

The recommended nine-step process for the creation and use of test data is as follows:

1. **Identify test resources.** Testing using test data can be as extensive or limited a process as desired. Unfortunately, many programmers approach the creation of test data from a "we'll do the best job possible" perspective and then begin developing test transactions. When time expires, testing is complete. The recommended approach suggests that the amount of resources allocated for the test data test tool be determined and then a process developed that optimizes that time.

2. **Identify test conditions.** A testing matrix is recommended as the basis for identifying conditions to test. As these matrices cascade through the developmental process, they identify all possible test conditions. If the matrix concept is not used, then the possible test conditions should be identified during the use of this test tool. These should be general test conditions, such as in a payroll application to test the FICA deductions.

3. **Rank test conditions.** If resources are limited, the maximum use of those resources will be obtained by testing the most important test conditions. The objective of ranking is to identify high-priority test conditions that should be tested first.

   Ranking does not mean that low-ranked test conditions will not be tested. Ranking can be used for two purposes: first, to determine which conditions should be tested first; and second, and equally important, to determine the amount of resources allocated to each of the test conditions. For example, if testing the FICA deduction was a relatively low-ranked condition, only one test transaction might be created to test that condition, while for the higher-ranked test conditions several test transactions may be created.

4. **Select conditions for testing.** Based on the ranking, the conditions to be tested should be selected. At this point, the conditions should be very specific. For example, "testing FICA" is a reasonable condition to identify and rank, but for creating specific test conditions it is too general. Three test situations might be identified—such as employees whose year-to-date earnings exceed the maximum FICA deduction; an employee whose current-period earnings will exceed the difference between the year-to-date earnings and the maximum deduction; and an employee whose year-to-date earnings are more than one pay period amount below the maximum FICA deductions. Each test situation should be documented in a testing matrix. This is a detailed version of the testing matrix that was started during the requirements phase.

5. **Determine correct results of processing.** The correct processing results for each test situation should be determined. Each test situation should be identified by a unique number, and then a log made of the correct results for each test condition. If a system is available to automatically check each test situation, special forms may be needed as this information may need to be converted to machine-readable media.

   The correct time to determine the correct processing results is before the test transactions have been created. This step helps determine the reasonableness and usefulness of test transactions. The process can also show if there are ways to extend the effectiveness of test transactions, and whether the same condition has been tested by another transaction.

6. **Create test transactions.** Each test situation needs to be converted into a format suitable for testing. In some instances, this requires the creation of a test transaction and master information to be stored by the program for the purpose of processing the transaction. The method of creating the machine-readable transaction will vary based on the application and the test rules available in the information systems department.

   The most common methods of creating test transactions include:
   - Key entry via card, tape, disk, or terminal
   - Test data generator
   - Preparation of an input form which will be given to user personnel to enter

7. **Document test conditions.** Both the test situations and the results of testing should be documented. (See Chapter 26 for recommended test documentation.)

8. **Conduct test.** The executable system should be run, using the test conditions. Depending on the extent of the test, it can be run under a test condition or in a simulated production environment.

9. **Verify and correct.** The results of testing should be verified and any necessary corrections to the programs performed. Problems detected as a result of testing can be attributable not only to system defects, but to test data defects. The individual conducting the test should be aware of both situations.

Creating a Test File Example–Payroll Application

In making two reviews of automated civilian payroll systems, the U.S. General Accounting Office used test files to test the agencies' computer programs for processing pay and leave data. This case shows their test file development approach.

First, all available documentation was reviewed for the manual and automated parts of each system. To understand the manual operations, they interviewed payroll supervisors and clerks, reviewed laws and regulations relating to pay and leave, and familiarized themselves with standard payroll operating procedures. For the automated part of each system they interviewed system designers and programmers and reviewed system and program documentation and operating procedures.

After acquiring a working knowledge of each system, they decided to test computer programs used to update payroll master records and those used to calculate biweekly pay and leave entitlements. Although they were concerned primarily with these particular programs, they decided that other programs used in the normal biweekly payroll processing cycle (such as programs for producing pay and leave history reports, leave records, and savings bond reports) should also be tested to see how they would handle test data.

They then designed a test file of simulated pay and leave transactions to test the effectiveness of internal controls, compliance with applicable laws and regulations, and the adequacy of standard payroll operating procedures. The test file included transactions made up of both valid and invalid data. These transactions were based on specified procedures and regulations and were designed to check the effectiveness of internal controls in each installation's payroll processing. They used one transaction for each master record chosen.

The best method of obtaining suitable payroll master records for the test, they decided, would be to use copies of actual master records, supplemented with simulated records tailored for test conditions not found in the copied records.

Accordingly, they obtained a duplicate of each agency's payroll master file and had a section of it printed in readable copy. From this printout, they selected a specific master record to go with each test transaction. When none of the copied records appearing on the printout fitted the specifics of a particular transaction, they made up a simulated master record by preparing source documents and processing them with the program used by each installation to add records for new employees to its master file. They then added the simulated records to the copied records to create the test master file.

They next prepared working papers on which were entered, for each test transaction, the control number assigned to the transaction, the type of input document to be used, and the nature and purpose of the test. They predetermined the correct end results for all test transactions and recorded these results in the working papers for comparison with actual results.

With some help from payroll office personnel, they next coded the test transactions onto source documents. The data was then key entered and key verified. They then processed the test data against actual agency payroll programs and compared the test results with the predetermined results to see whether there were any differences.

They found both systems accepted and processed several invalid test transactions that should have been rejected or flagged by programmed computer controls. Alternative manual controls were either nonexistent or less than fully effective because they could be bypassed or compromised through fraud, neglect, or inadvertent error. They recommended that the systems' automated controls be strengthened to ensure accurate payrolls and protect the government from improper payments.

A copy of their work papers outlining the test conditions is illustrated in Figure 12.3.

Volume Test Tool

Volume testing is a tool that supplements test data. The objective is to verify that the system can perform properly when internal program or system limitations have been exceeded. This may require that large volumes of transactions be entered during testing.

The types of internal limitations that can be evaluated with volume testing include:

- Internal accumulation of information, such as tables
- Number of line items in an event, such as the number of items that can be included within an order
- Size of accumulation fields
- Data-related limitations, such as leap year, decade change, switching calendar years, and so on
- Field size limitations, such as number of characters allocated for people's names
- Number of accounting entities, such as number of business locations, state/country in which business is performed, and so on

The concept of volume testing is as old as the processing of data in information services. What is necessary to make the concept work is a systematic method of identifying limitations. The recommended steps for determining program/system limitations follows.

1. **Identify input data used by the program.** A preferred method to identify limitations is to evaluate the data. Each data element is reviewed to determine if it poses a system limitation. This is an easier method than attempting to evaluate the programs. The method is also helpful in differentiating between system and program limitations. It also has the advantage that data may only need to be evaluated once, rather than evaluating numerous individual programs.

   All of the data entering an application system should be identified. Those data elements not used by the applications, but merely accessible to it, should be deleted, resulting in a list of input data used by the application system.

		NATURE OF TEST TRANSACTION	PURPOSE OR EXPLANATION OF TEST TRANSACTION	Reject	Print error message	Reject in certain circumstances	Cut back to allow-able maximum	Process without cutback	Automatically compute correct amount	Automatically adjust leave records
	1.	Leave a mandatory field blank on a new employee's master record.	To determine whether the system will accept a master record with essential data missing. If missing data will cause an incorrect payment, the master record should be rejected with appropriate warning; if missing data is for administrative purposes only, the condition should be flagged by an error message.		X	X				
	2.	Enter erroneous codes, such as charity, life insurance, union dues, marital status, etc. (Note: One erroneous code per master record.)	To determine whether the system will accept invalid data into employees' master records. The program should print error messages to identify invalid data and reject further processing of such transactions.		X	X				
	3.	Enter an invalid annual leave category	To determine whether the system will accept an invalid annual leave category. Federal regulations have established annual leave categories as 4, 6, or 8, depending on the amount of creditable service.	X	X					

(Continues)

Figure 12.3 Typical payroll transactions to be included in a test deck.

	NATURE OF TEST TRANSACTION	PURPOSE OR EXPLANATION OF TEST TRANSACTION	**HOW A SYSTEM WITH EFFECTIVE CONTROLS WILL HANDLE THE TRANSACTION**						
			Reject	Print error message	Reject in certain circumstances	Cut back to allowable maximum	Process without cutback	Automatically compute correct amount	Automatically adjust leave records
4.	Change a field in an inactive master record.	To determine whether it is possible to change fields in inactive master records and whether adequate controls exist over such changes. Processing of inactive records should be separated from the normal processing of active records to eliminate the possibility of unearned salary payments or the manipulation of records for persons who are not in a pay status.	x	x					
5.	Change an employee's annual leave category before it is due to be changed.	To determine whether the system will reject invalid updates. The annual leave category is based on the amount of creditable service an employee has, computed from the employee's service computation date. Employees with less than 3 years of service are in category 4; employees with 3 to 15 years of service are in category 6; employees with more than 15 years of service are in category 8. The program should reject any attempt to change a leave category before it is due to be changed.							

Figure 12.3 (Continued)

(Continues)

	NATURE OF TEST TRANSACTION	PURPOSE OR EXPLANATION OF TEST TRANSACTION	HOW A SYSTEM WITH EFFECTIVE CONTROLS WILL HANDLE THE TRANSACTION						
			Reject	Print error message	Reject in certain circumstances	Cut back to allowable maximum	Process without cutback	Automatically compute correct amount	Automatically adjust leave records
6.	Promote a general schedule (GS) employee above grade 5 before one year in grade has passed.	To determine whether the system rejects an invalid transaction. Federal regulations state that GS employees above grade 5 must be in grade at least one year before they can be promoted.	x	x					
7.	Give a GS employee a within-grade salary increase before one year in grade has passed.	To determine how the system handles this transaction. Federal regulations state that a GS employee must be in grade at least one year before being eligible for a within-in-grade salary increase. The system should "flag" the transaction as being a quality step increase (which has the same effect as within-grade increase but can occur without the employee's having been in grade for one year).		x					
8.	Change an employee's grade or annual salary so that the grade/step and annual salary rate are incompatible.	To determine whether the system accepts incompatible data. The program should have salary and grade controls which will reject transactions of this type from further processing (except for payments under the Civil Service "retained rate" provision, which allows certain down-graded employees to retain their old salaries for a time).		x	x				

Figure 12.3 (Continued)

(Continues)

	NATURE OF TEST TRANSACTION	PURPOSE OR EXPLANATION OF TEST TRANSACTION	HOW A SYSTEM WITH EFFECTIVE CONTROLS WILL HANDLE THE TRANSACTION						
			Reject	Print error message	Reject in certain circumstances	Cut back to allowable maximum	Process without cutback	Automatically compute correct amount	Automatically adjust leave records
9.	Change an employee's service computation date to indicate that that leave category is due to change.	To determine whether the annual leave category is correctly changed, with a message printed to indicate the change. If the leave category is not automatically changed, a message should be printed.		x					
10.	Pay an inactive employee.	To determine whether the system will compute pay for an inactive employee (an employee who has been separated but whose record is maintained in the same master file used for active employees).	x	x					
11.	Pay a nonexistent employee.	To determine whether the system will compute pay for an employee with no record in the master file.	x	x					
12.	Input two time and attendance cards for the same employee.	To determine whether the system will compute pay twice for the same employee.	x	x					
13.	Pay a GS employee for 80 hours of work on a second-shift entitlement for a wage board (WB) employee.	To determine whether the system rejects WB entitlements for GS employees.	x	x					

(Continues)

Figure 12.3 *(Continued)*

	NATURE OF TEST TRANSACTION	PURPOSE OR EXPLANATION OF TEST TRANSACTION	Reject	Print error message	Reject in certain circumstances	Cut back to allowable maximum	Process without cutback	Automatically compute correct amount	Automatically adjust leave records
14.	Pay a GS employee for 80 hours work on a third-shift entitlement for a WB employee.	Same as above.	X	X					
15.	Pay a WB employee for 80 hours work on a night-shift differential entitlement for a GS employee.	To determine whether the system rejects GS entitlements for WB employees.	X	X					
16.	Pay a WB employee for 20 hours of overtime.	To verify the accuracy of premium (overtime) pay computation. Overtime pay is 1 and 1/2 times regular pay.						X	
17.	Pay a GS employee for 20 hours of night-differential pay.	Same as above. Premium = 10 percent.						X	
18.	Pay a WB employee for 80 hours on second shift.	Same as above. Premium = 7 1/2 percent.						X	
19.	Pay a WB employee for 80 hours on third shift.	Same as above. Premium = 10 percent.						X	

HOW A SYSTEM WITH EFFECTIVE CONTROLS WILL HANDLE THE TRANSACTION

(Continues)

Figure 12.3   (Continued)

Nature of Test Transaction	Purpose or Explanation of Test Transaction	Reject	Print error message	Reject in certain circumstances	Cut back to allowable maximum	Process without cutback	Automatically compute correct amount	Automatically adjust leave records
20. Pay a GS employee for 8 hours of holiday pay	Same as above. Holiday pay is double regular pay.						x	
21. Pay a WB employee for 8 hours of holiday pay.	Same as above.						x	
22. Pay a GS employee for 8 hours of Sunday pay (for Sunday work that is not overtime work).	Same as above. Sunday premium is 25 percent of regular pay if Sunday is a regularly scheduled workday.						x	
23. Pay a WB employee for 8 hours of Sunday pay.	Same as above.						x	
24. Pay GS employees for 10 hours of environmental pay at the following premiums: a) 4 percent b) 8 percent c) 25 percent d) 50 percent	Same as above.						x	

HOW A SYSTEM WITH EFFECTIVE CONTROLS WILL HANDLE THE TRANSACTION

(Continues)

Figure 12.3 (Continued)

418

#	NATURE OF TEST TRANSACTION	PURPOSE OR EXPLANATION OF TEST TRANSACTION	HOW A SYSTEM WITH EFFECTIVE CONTROLS WILL HANDLE THE TRANSACTION						
			Reject	Print error message	Reject in certain circumstances	Cut back to allow-able maximum	Process without cutback	Automatically compute correct amount	Automatically adjust leave records
25.	Pay WB employees for 10 hours of environmental pay at the following premiums: a) 4 percent b) 8 percent c) 25 percent d) 50 percent	Same as above.						x	
26.	Pay a GS-1, 2, 3, 4, 5, 6, or 7 employee for 10 hours of overtime.	To verify accuracy of premium pay computation. For GS employees whose basic pay rate does not exceed the salary of a GS-10/1, the overtime rate is 1 and 1/2 times the basic pay rate. (FPM 550-5)						x	
27.	Pay a GS-10, 11, 12, or 13 employee for 10 hours of overtime.	Same as above. For a GS employee whose basic pay rate is equal to or exceeds the rate of a GS-10/1, the overtime rate is one and 1/2 times the hourly rate for a GS-10/1. (FPM 550-5)						x	

Figure 12.3 (Continued)

(Continues)

		HOW A SYSTEM WITH EFFECTIVE CONTROLS WILL HANDLE THE TRANSACTION						
	NATURE OF TEST TRANSACTION	PURPOSE OR EXPLANATION OF TEST TRANSACTION	Reject	Print error message	Reject in certain circumstances	Cut back to allow-able maximum	Process without cutback	Automatically compute correct amount	Automatically adjust leave records
28.	Pay a GS-14 employee enough overtime pay to exceed the maximum salary limitation.	To test maximum salary limitation. Additional pay, such as overtime, night differential, holiday and Sunday pay, may be paid to the extent that it does not cause the aggregate pay for a biweekly period to exceed the rate of a GS-15/10. (FPM 550.105). The program should cut back pay to this maximum.		x		x			
29.	Pay a GS-14 employee enough environmental pay to exceed the maximum salary limitation.	Same as above. Program should not cut back environmental pay because it is not subject to the maximum salary limitation.					x		
30.	Pay a WB employee enough premium pay to exceed the maximum salary limitation.	Same as above. Program should not cut pay because WB employees have no maximum salary limitation.					x		
31.	Pay a GS employee for one hour of holiday pay.	To determine whether the system will pay less than the two-hour minimum of holiday pay. (FPM 990-1)		x				x	

(Continues)

Figure 12.3 *(Continued)*

420

	NATURE OF TEST TRANSACTION	PURPOSE OR EXPLANATION OF TEST TRANSACTION	Reject	Print error message	Reject in certain circumstances	Cut back to allowable maximum	Process without cutback	Automatically compute correct amount	Automatically adjust leave records
								HOW A SYSTEM WITH EFFECTIVE CONTROLS WILL HANDLE THE TRANSACTION	
32.	Pay a WB employee for one hour of holiday pay	Same as above.		x				x	
33.	Pay a GS employee for 40 hours of Sunday pay.	To determine whether the system limits Sunday pay to 32 hours maximum allowed. (FPM 990-2)		x		x			
34.	Pay a WB employee for 80 hours on second shift and 10 hours for overtime into the third shift.	To verify the accuracy of premium pay. Federal regulations state that overtime pay for an employee regularly working the second or third shift will be computed at 1 and 1/2 times the second or third shift rate, respectively. (FPM 532-1)						x	
35.	Pay a WB employee for 80 hours on third shift and 10 hours for overtime into the first shift.	Same as above.						x	
36.	Charge a full-time employee for 80 hours of leave without pay. (LWOP)	To determine whether sick and annual leave will accrue when a full-time employee charges 80 LWOP. The sick leave credit should be reduced by 4 hours, and the annual leave credit should be reduced by 4, 6, or 8 hours, depending on the annual leave category.							x

(Continues)

Figure 12.3 *(Continued)*

NATURE OF TEST TRANSACTION	PURPOSE OR EXPLANATION OF TEST TRANSACTION	Reject	Print error message	Reject in certain circumstances	Cut back to allowable maximum	Process without cutback	Automatically compute correct amount	Automatically adjust leave records
37. Charge a full-time employee for more than annual leave than the employee has.	To determine whether excess annual leave is charged to LWOP. (The system should automatically reduce employee's pay for LWOP.)		X				X	X
38. Charge a full-time employee for more sick leave than the employee has.	To determine whether excess sick leave is charged to annual leave or LWOP. (The system should automatically adjust leave records and reduce pay for LWOP, if required.)		X				X	X
39. Charge a full-time employee for 99 hours of annual leave (19 hours more than a regular biweekly period).	To determine whether the system will cut back to the maximum of 80 hours for regular pay in a pay period.		X		X			
40. Charge a full-time employee for 99 hours of sick leave.	Same as above.		X		X			

Figure 12.3 *(Continued)*

(Continues)

NATURE OF TEST TRANSACTION	PURPOSE OR EXPLANATION OF TEST TRANSACTION	HOW A SYSTEM WITH EFFECTIVE CONTROLS WILL HANDLE THE TRANSACTION						
		Reject	Print error message	Reject in certain circumstances	Cut back to allowable maximum	Process without cutback	Automatically compute correct amount	Automatically adjust leave records
41. Charge a full-time employee for 80 hours of regular pay and 80 hours of annual leave in the same pay period.	Same as above. Total hours of work and leave cannot exceed 80 in a pay period.	X	X					
42. Charge a full-time employee for enough hours of military leave to exceed 120 hours total.	To determine whether the system flags military leave in excess of 120 hours. Federal regulations state that an employee cannot charge more than 120 hours to military leave in a pay year. Because there are certain exceptions (such as duty in the District of Columbia National Guard) which permit military leave to exceed 120 hours, the system should alert payroll clerks to the excess and should not reject or cut back the transaction.		X					
43. Make a lump-sum annual leave payment to a separated employee in excess of annual leave balance.	To determine whether the system appropriately excludes excess annual leave in a lump-sum leave payment.		X		X			

Figure 12.3 (Continued)

(Continues)

NATURE OF TEST TRANSACTION	PURPOSE OR EXPLANATION OF TEST TRANSACTION	Reject	Print error message	Reject in certain circumstances	Cut back to allowable maximum	Process without cutback	Automatically compute correct amount	Automatically adjust leave records
44. Pay a GS part-time employee for 32 hours of regular pay.	To determine whether the system correctly accrues annual and sick leave for part-time employees. For each 20 hours worked, a part-time employee receives one hour of sick leave. If in leave category 4, an employee needs 20 hours of work to earn one hour of annual leave; if in leave category 6, the employee needs 15 hours worked to earn one hour of annual leave; and if in leave category 8, the employee needs 10 hours worked to earn one hour of annual leave.							x
45. Make a lump-sum annual leave payment to an active employee.	To determine whether the system will make a lump-sum annual leave payment to an active employee. These payments should be made only to separated employees.	x	x					

Figure 12.3 *(Continued)*

2. **Identify data created by the program.** Data generated by application systems should be identified. These would be data elements that are not input into the system but are included in internal or output data records. Knowing the input data and the output data, it is a relatively simple process to identify newly created data elements.

3. **Challenge each data element for potential limitations.** A key step in determining program/system limitations is in the challenge process. The individual using volume test tools should ask the following questions about each data element:

   - Can the data value in a field entering the system exceed the size of this data element? (If so, a limitation is identified.)
   - Is the value in a data field accumulated? (If so, a limitation is identified.)
   - Is data temporarily stored in the computer? (If so, a limitation is identified.)
   - Is the information in a data element(s) stored in the program until a following transaction is entered? (If so, a limitation is identified.)
   - If a data element represents an accounting entity, for example, the number of sales financial accounts, etc., does the number used to identify the accounting entity in itself provide a future limitation, such as using a one-character field to identify sales districts? (If so, a limitation is identified.)

4. **Document limitations.** All of the limitations identified in step 3 should be documented. This forms the basis for volume testing. Each of these limitations must now be evaluated to determine the extent of testing on those limitations.

5. **Perform volume testing.** The testing to be performed follows the same nine steps outlined in the test file method. The limitations documented in step 4 above become the test conditions that need to be identified in step 2 of the test file methodology. The test process then follows steps 3–9.

Creating Test Scripts

The following five tasks are needed to develop, use, and maintain test scripts.

1. Determine Testing Levels

There are five levels of testing for scripts, as follows:

1. **Unit scripting.** Develop a script to test a specific unit/module.

2. **Pseudoconcurrency scripting.** Develop scripts to test when there are two or more users accessing the same file at the same time.

3. **Integration scripting.** Determine that various modules can be properly linked.

4. **Regression scripting.** Determine that the unchanged portions of systems remain unchanged when the system is changed. (Note: This is usually performed with the information captured on capture/playback software systems.)

5. **Stress/performance scripting.** Determine whether the system will perform correctly when it is stressed to its capacity. This validates the performance of the software when stressed by large numbers of transactions.

The testers need to determine which (or all) of these five levels of scripting to include in the script.

2. Develop Script

This task, too, is normally done using the capture/playback tool. The script is a complete series of related terminal actions. The development of a script involves a number of considerations, as follows:

- Script components
- Terminal input
- Programs to be tested
- Files involved
- On-line operating environment
- Terminal output
- Manual entry of script transactions
- Date setup
- Secured initialization
- File restores
- Password entry
- Update
- Automated entry of script transactions
- Edits of transactions
- Navigation of transactions through the system
- Inquiry during processing
- External considerations
- Program libraries
- File states/contents
- Screen initialization
- Operating environment
- Security considerations
- Complete scripts
- Start and stop considerations
- Start; usually begins with a clear screen
- Start; begins with a transaction code
- Scripts; end with a clear screen
- Script contents
- Sign-on

- Setup
- Menu navigation
- Function
- Exit
- Sign-off
- Clear screen
- Security considerations
- Changing passwords
- User identification/security rules
- Reprompting
- Single-terminal user identifications
- Sources of scripting transactions
- Terminal entry of scripts
- Operations initialization of files
- Application program interface (api) communications
- Special considerations
- Single versus multiple terminals
- Date and time dependencies
- Timing dependencies
- Inquiry versus update
- Unit versus regression test
- Organization of scripts (recommended by purpose; see Figure 10.3)
- Unit test organization
  - Single functions (transactions)
  - Single terminal
  - Separate inquiry from update
  - Self-maintaining
- Pseudoconcurrent test
  - Single functions (transactions)
  - Multiple terminals
  - Three steps: setup (manual/script), test (script), and reset (manual/script)
- Integration test (string testing)
  - Multiple functions (transactions)
  - Single terminal
  - Self-maintaining
- Regression test
  - Multiple functions (transactions)

Table 12.1   Script Development Strategies

TEST LEVEL	SINGLE TRANSACTION	MULTIPLE TRANSACTION	SINGLE TERMINAL	MULTIPLE TERMINALS
Unit	X		X	
Concurrent	X			X
Integration		X	X	
Regression		X		X
Stress		X		X

- Multiple terminals
- Three steps: setup (external), test (script), and reset (external)
- Stress/performance test
  - Multiple functions (transactions)
  - Multiple terminals (2x rate)
  - Iterative/vary arrival rate; three steps: setup (external), test (script), and collect performance data

Work Paper 12.1 can also be used for script development. Table 12.1 summarizes the script development strategies. The table shows for the five levels of testing using scripts described in Task 1 which level is best suited for single transaction tests and which is best suited for testing multiple transactions. The table also shows for each level whether testing occurs from a single terminal or from multiple terminals.

3. Execute Script

The script can be executed manually or by using the capture/playback tools. Caution: Be reluctant to use scripting extensively unless a software tool drives the script. Some of the considerations to incorporate into script execution are:

- Environmental setup
- Program libraries
- File states/contents
- Date and time
- Security
- Multiple terminal arrival modes
- Serial (cross-terminal) dependencies
- Pseudoconcurrent
- Processing options
- Stall detection
- Synchronization

- Rate
- Arrival rate
- Think time

4. Analyze Results

After executing the test script, the results must be analyzed. However, much of this should have been done during the execution of the script, using the operator instructions provided. Please note that if a capture/playback software tool is used, analysis will be more extensive after execution. The result analysis should include the following:

- System components
- Terminal outputs (screens)
- File content at conclusion of testing
- Environment activities, such as:
    - Status of logs
    - Performance data (stress results)
- On-screen outputs
- Individual terminal screen outputs
- Multiple screen outputs
- Order of outputs processing
- Compliance of screens to specifications
- Ability to process actions
- Ability to browse through data

The main results checking will be the actual results against the expected results. The preceding lists highlight some of the specific considerations included in this.

5. Maintain Scripts

Once developed, scripts need to be maintained so that they can be used throughout development and maintenance. The areas to incorporate into the script maintenance procedure are:

- Programs
- Files
- Screens
    - Insert (transactions)
    - Delete
    - Arrange
- Field
    - Changed (length, content)
    - New
    - Moved
- Expand test cases

The following questions can be used to determine the completeness of the scripts. If items in the checklist are not addressed by the script, you should consider extending the script. A No response indicates that you have not included a test condition of that type, and you may want to indicate the reason for not including this test condition. Thus, ask yourself the following questions:

1. Does the script include unit testing?
2. Does the script include pseudoconcurrency testing?
3. Does the script include integration testing?
4. Does the script include regression testing?
5. Does the script include stress testing?
6. Does manual entry of transactions include:
   - Date setup?
   - Secured initialization?
   - File restores?
   - Password entry?
   - Updates?
7. Does automated entry of scripts include the appropriate navigation through the system?
8. Do the scripts include references to the program libraries?
9. Do the scripts address the various file states?
10. Do the scripts address initialization of screens?
11. Do the scripts address the operating environment?
12. Do the scripts address security considerations?
13. Do the scripts contain the appropriate sign-on and setup procedures?
14. Do the scripts include the appropriate sign-off and clear screen procedures?
15. Do the scripts address all items on the menu?
16. Do the scripts address changing user identification?
17. Do the scripts address changing passwords?
18. Do the scripts include the use of the prompting routines?
19. Do the scripts include multiple terminal processing?
20. Do the scripts include time and date dependencies?
21. Do the scripts include single-function transactions?
22. Do the scripts include multiple-function transactions?
23. Do the scripts include inquiry?
24. Do the scripts include update?
25. Do the scripts include deletion?
26. Do the scripts include multiple-terminal testing?

27. Do the scripts include single-terminal testing?

28. Do the scripts include single-transaction testing?

29. Do the scripts include multiple-transaction testing?

The output from this workbench will be a description of the results of the scripting test, which might include:

- Performance and/or problems in manual entry

- Performance and/or problems in the data entry process

- Performance and/or problems associated with the hardware, menu navigation, sign-on and sign-off procedures

- Problems with quality characteristics such as ease of use and security

- Capability of the on-line system to perform in accordance with specifications

Several characteristics of scripting are different from batch test data development. These differences are:

- **Data entry procedures required.** The test procedures take on greater significance in scripting. The person using the script needs to know in detail how to enter the transaction via the terminal. This may be more complex than simply creating a test condition.

- **Use of software packages.** Scripting is a very difficult and complex task to do manually, particularly when the script has to be repeated multiple times. Therefore, most testers use a capture/playback type of software package, which enables the capture of transactions as they are entered via terminal, and then repeats them as the scripts are reused. There are many of these on the market, although they are aimed primarily at the IBM mainframe.

- **Sequencing of events.** Scripts require the sequencing of transactions. In batch systems, sequencing is frequently handled by sorting during systems execution; however, with scripts, the sequence must be predefined.

- **Stop procedures.** Batch testing continues until the batch is complete or processing abnormally terminates. Scripting may be able to continue, but the results would be meaningless; therefore, the script has to indicate when to stop, or if specific conditions occur, where to go in the script to resume testing.

Task 2: Execute Tests

The recommended test process to follow for the test step to execute the code is shown in Work Paper 12.2. It contains a completed test program for each test concern, listing the test criteria, together with the recommended tests, plus the test techniques and tools to use. The test team should use judgment in selecting the appropriate test technique and tool based upon application system test needs.

Effective testing during the test phase should use a test plan created much earlier in the life cycle. The test phase testing is a culmination of the previous work preparing for this phase. Without this preparation, tests may be uneconomical and ineffective. To utilize Work Paper 12.2 follow the process described in Task 2 of Chapter 9.

There are many methods of testing an application system. The test team is concerned that all of these forms of testing occur so that the organization has the highest probability of success when installing a new application system. The following types of tests should be addressed by the test team during the test phase.

Manual, Regression, and Functional Testing (Reliability)

Manual testing ensures that the people interacting with the automated system can perform their functions correctly. Regression testing is the verification that what is being installed does not affect any portion of the application already installed or other applications interfaced by the new application. Functional testing verifies that the system requirements can be performed correctly when subjected to a variety of circumstances and repetition of the transactions.

Compliance Testing (Authorization)

Testing should verify that the authorization rules have been properly implemented and evaluate compliance with them. Test conditions should include unauthorized transactions or processes to ensure that they are rejected, as well as ensuring authorized transactions are accepted.

Functional Testing (File Integrity)

The controls over the integrity of computer files should be verified during testing. For example, if integrity is dependent upon the proper functioning of an independent control total, that function should be tested along with the automated segment of the application system. In addition, sufficient updates of the file should be performed so that the integrity controls can be tested during several iterations of executing the application system.

Functional Testing (Audit Trail)

The audit trail function should be tested to ensure that a source transaction can be traced to a control total, that the transaction supporting a control total can be identified, and that the processing of a single transaction or the entire system can be reconstructed using audit trail information. It is normally advisable to list part of the audit trail file to ensure that it is complete based upon the test transactions entered.

Recovery Testing (Continuity of Testing)

If processing must continue during periods when the automated system is not operational, then alternate processing procedures should be tested during the test phase. In addition, the users of application systems should be involved in a complete recovery test so that not only the automated system is tested, but the procedures for performing the manual aspects of recovery are tested. This may involve intentionally causing the system to fail so that the recovery procedures can be tested.

Stress Testing (Service Level)

Acceptance testing should put the application under stress to verify that the system can handle high-volume processing. Stress testing should attempt to find those levels of processing at which the system can no longer function effectively. In on-line systems, this may be determined by the volume of transactions, while in batch systems the size of the batch or large volumes of certain types of transactions can test internal tables or sort capabilities.

Compliance Testing (Security)

The adequacy of the security procedures should be tested by attempting to violate those procedures. For example, testing should attempt to access or modify data by an unauthorized individual. If more sophisticated penetration attempts are of concern, it may be necessary to use the services of security specialists in order to ensure that security is adequate.

Testing Complies with Methodology

Testing should be performed in accordance with the organization's testing policies, procedures, standards, and guidelines. The methodology should specify the type of test plan required, the recommended test techniques and tools, as well as the type of documentation required during the test phase. The methodology should also specify the method of determining whether the test is successful.

Functional Testing (Correctness)

Functional correctness testing verifies that the application functions in accordance with user-specified requirements. Because information services personnel normally concentrate their testing on verifying that the mainline requirements function properly, test phase testing may wish to emphasize the other test concerns, or emphasize improperly entered transactions to test the data validation and error detection functions.

Manual Support Testing (Ease of Use)

The ultimate success of the system will depend heavily on the ability of people to use it. Testing the ease of use of the system is an important aspect of the test phase. Because this is difficult to evaluate prior to the test phase, it is important that the people aspect of the system is evaluated in as realistic a test environment as possible.

Inspections (Maintainability)

Modifications made during the systems development life cycle provide one method of testing the maintainability of the application system. Fortunately, these changes are made by the developers who are intimately familiar with the application system. The completed system should be inspected by an independent group, preferably systems maintenance specialists, in order to evaluate the maintainability of the application system. The system development standards should be devised with maintainability in mind.

Disaster Testing (Portability)

The only method that ensures the application will function in a second operating environment is to run the application in that different environment. Disaster testing is a mechanism that simulates problems in the original environment so that an alternative processing environment can be tested. While it is not possible to simulate all environments into which an application system may be moved, knowing that it can transfer between two different environments provides a high probability that other moves will not cause major complications.

Functional and Regression Testing (Coupling)

The test phase should verify that the application being tested can correctly communicate with interrelated application systems. Both functional and regression testing are recommended. Functional testing verifies that any new function properly interconnects, while regression testing verifies that unchanged segments of the application system that interconnect with other applications still function properly.

Compliance Testing (Performance)

Performance criteria are established during the requirements phase. These criteria should be updated if the requirements change during later phases of the life cycle. Many of the criteria can be evaluated during the test phase, and those that can be tested should be tested. However, it may be necessary to wait until the system is placed into production to verify that all of the criteria have been achieved.

Operations Testing (Ease of Operations)

Testing in this phase should be conducted by the normal operations staff. Project development personnel should not be permitted to coach or assist during the test process. It is only through having normal operation personnel conduct the test that the completeness of operator instructions and the ease with which the system can be operated can be properly evaluated.

Task 3: Record Test Result

A test problem is a condition that exists within the software system that needs to be addressed. Carefully and completely documenting a test problem is the first step in correcting the problem.

The following four attributes should be developed for all test problems:

1. **Statement of condition.** Tells what is.
2. **Criteria.** Tells what should be.

These two attributes are the basis for a finding. If a comparison between the two gives little or no practical consequence, no finding exists.

3. **Effect.** Tells why the difference between what is and what should be is significant.
4. **Cause.** Tells the reasons for the deviation. Identification of the cause is necessary as a basis for corrective action.

A well-developed problem statement will include each of these attributes. When one or more of these attributes is missing, questions almost always arise, such as:

Condition. What is the problem?

Criteria. Why is the current state inadequate?

Effect. How significant is it?

Cause. What could have caused the problem?

Documenting a statement of a user problem involves three subtasks, which are explained in the following paragraphs.

1. Document Deviation

Problem statements begin to emerge by a process of comparison. Essentially, the user compares "what is" with "what should be." When a deviation is identified between what is found to actually exist and what the user thinks is correct or proper, the first essential step toward development of a problem statement has occurred. It is difficult to visualize any type of problem that is not in some way characterized by this deviation. The "what is" can be called the statement of condition. The "what should be" shall be called the criteria. These concepts are the first two, and most basic, attributes of a problem statement.

The documenting of deviation is describing the conditions as they currently exist, and the criteria, which represents what the user desires. The actual deviation will be the difference or gap between "what is" and "what is desired."

The statement of condition is uncovering and documenting the facts as they exist. What is a fact? If somebody tells you something happened, is that "something" a fact? Or is it only a fact if someone told you it's a fact? The description of the statement of condition will of course depend largely on the nature and extent of the evidence or support that is examined and noted. For those facts making up the statement of condition, the IT professional will obviously take pains to be sure that the information is accurate, well-supported, and worded as clearly and precisely as possible.

The statement of condition should document as many of the following attributes as appropriate for the problem:

Activities involved. The specific business or administrated activities that are being performed

Procedures used to perform work. The specific step-by-step activities that are utilized in producing output from the identified activities

Outputs/deliverables. The products that are produced from the activity

Inputs. The triggers, events, or documents that cause this activity to be executed

Users/customers served. The organization, individuals, or class of users/customers serviced by this activity

Deficiencies noted. The status of the results of executing this activity and any appropriate interpretation of those facts

The criterion is the user's statement of what is desired. It can be stated in either negative or positive terms. For example, it could indicate the need to reduce the complaints or delays as well as desired processing turnaround time.

There are often situations where what "should be" can relate primarily to common sense or general reasonableness, and the statement of condition virtually speaks for itself. These situations must be carefully distinguished from personal whims or subjective, fanciful notions. There is no room for such subjectivity in defining what is desired.

As much as possible the criteria should be directly related to the statement of condition. For example, if volumes are expected to increase, the number of users served has changed, or the user processes have changed, they should be expressed in the same terms as used in documenting the statement of condition.

Work Paper 12.3 provides space to describe the problem and document the statement of condition and the statement of criteria. Note that an additional section could be added to Work Paper 12.3 to describe the deviation. However, if the statement of condition and statement criteria are properly worded, the deviation should be readily determinable.

2. Document Effect

Whereas the legitimacy of a problem statement may stand or fall on criteria, the attention that the problem statement gets after it is reported depends largely on its significance. Significance is judged by effect.

Efficiency, economy, and effectiveness are useful measures of effect and frequently can be stated in quantitative terms such as dollars, time, units of production, number of procedures and processes, or transactions. Where past effects cannot be ascertained, potential future effects may be presented. Sometimes effects are intangible but nevertheless of major significance.

In thought processes, effect is frequently considered almost simultaneously with the first two attributes of the problem. Reviewers may suspect a bad effect even before they have clearly formulated these other attributes in their minds. After the statement of condition is identified, reviewers may search for a firm criterion against which to measure the suspected effect. They may hypothesize several alternative criteria, which are believed to be suitable based on experiences in similar situations elsewhere. They may conclude that the effects under each hypothesis are so divergent or unreasonable that what is really needed is a firmer criterion—say, a formal policy in an area where no policy presently exists. The presentation of the problem statement may revolve around this missing criterion, although suspicions as to effect may have been the initial path.

The reviewer should attempt to quantify the effect of a problem wherever practical. While the effect can be stated in narrative or qualitative terms, that frequently does not convey the appropriate message to management; for example, statements like "Service will be delayed," or "Extra computer time will be required" do not really tell what is happening to the organization.

3. Document Cause

The cause is the underlying reason for the condition. In some cases the cause may be obvious from the facts presented. In other instances investigation will need to be undertaken to identify the origin of the problem.

Most findings involve one or more of the following causes:

- Nonconformity with standards, procedures, or guidelines
- Nonconformity with published instructions, directives, policies, or procedures from a higher authority
- Nonconformity with business practices generally accepted as sound
- Employment of inefficient or uneconomical practices

The determination of the cause of a condition usually requires the scientific approach, which encompasses the following steps:

- Define the problem (the condition that results in the finding).
- Identify the flow of work and/or information leading to the condition.
- Identify the procedures used in producing the condition.
- Identify the people involved.
- Recreate the circumstances to identify the cause of a condition.

Document the cause for the problem on Work Paper 12.3.

Check Procedures

Work Paper 12.4 is a quality control checklist for this step. It is designed so that Yes responses indicate good test practices; No responses warrant additional investigation. A Comments column is provided to explain No responses and to record results of investigation. The N/A column is used when the checklist item is not applicable to the test situation.

Output

There are three outputs from this step:

1. The test transactions needed to validate the software system
2. The results from executing those transactions
3. Variances from expected results

Guidelines

The test phase is the last line of defense against defects entering the operational environment. If no testing has occurred prior to the test phase, it is unreasonable to expect testing at this point to remove all of the defects. Experience has shown that it is difficult for the test phase to be more than 80 percent effective in reducing defects. Obviously, the fewer the number of defects entering the test phase, the fewer the number of defects getting into the production environment.

At the end of the test phase, the application system will be placed into production for the purpose of satisfying user needs. The test phase provides the last opportunity for the user to ensure that the system functions properly. For this reason, the user should be heavily involved in testing the application system.

The information services department has an opportunity to evaluate the application system during the program phase. During this phase, they determine whether the system functions properly in accordance with information services' interpretation of the requirements. The test step is best performed by a group other than the project team. This is not to indicate that the project team should not be involved or help, but rather, that the team should not be the dominant party in the test phase. If the same individual was responsible for both the program phase testing and the test phase testing, there would be no need to have two different phases. If information services assume test responsibility during the program phase, and the user accepts it during the test phase, the two phases become complementary to one another.

An independent test group should be given the responsibility to test the system to determine if the system performs according to its needs. Due to communication problems, there may be differences between the specifications to which the system was built and the requirements that the user expected. Ideally, the test team will have been developing test conditions from the requirements phase, and during the test phase should uncover any remaining defects in the application system.

Summary

This chapter describes a process for dynamically testing the application software. The process should focus on determining that the software executes as specified when placed in a operational type mode. This test step should not focus on defect removal, but rather whether the system can, in operational status, perform as specified. Because full testing is impractical the step must concentrate on those operational aspects that are most important to the application system user. This step concentrates on testing against requirements/specifications as understood by the development team and test team. The next step, called acceptance testing (Chapter 13), is designed to determine whether the software meets the real needs of the user regardless of system requirements and specifications.

WORK PAPER 12.1   Test Script

Field Requirements

FIELD	INSTRUCTIONS FOR ENTERING DATA
Test Item	A unique identifier of the test condition.
Entered by	Who will enter the script item via the terminal.
Sequence	The sequence in which the actions are to be entered.
Action	The action or scripted item to be entered on the terminal.
Expected Result	The result expected from entering the action.
Operator Instructions	What the operator is to do if the proper result is received, or if an improper result is returned.

Test Item	Entered By	Sequence	Action	Expected Result	Operator Instructions

WORK PAPER 12.2 Test Phase Test Process

TEST FACTOR: Manual, Regressional, and Functional Testing (Reliability)

#	TEST CRITERIA	ASSESSMENT				RECOMMENDED TEST	TEST TECHNIQUE	TEST TOOL
		Very Adequate	Adequate	Inadequate	N/A			
1.	Has data been tested which does not conform to individual data element specifications?					Verify that data validation programs reject data not conforming to data element specifications.	Error handling	Test data & Test data generator
2.	Have tests been performed testing data relationships to reject those not conforming to system specifications?					Verify that the system rejects data relationships which do not conform to system specifications.	Error handling	Test data & Test data generator
3.	Have invalid identifiers been tested?					Verify that program rejects invalid identifiers.	Error handling	Test data & Test data generator
4.	Have tests been made to verify that missing sequence numbers will be detected?					Confirm that the system detects missing sequence numbers.	Requirements	Test data
5.	Have tests been conducted to verify that inaccurate batch totals will be detected?					Verify that the system will detect inaccurate batch totals.	Error handling	Test data
6.	Have tests been conducted to determine that data missing from a batch or missing scheduled data will be detected?					Verify that the programs will defect data missing from batches and scheduled data which does not arrive on time.	Manual support	Test data & Test data generator
7.	Have tests been made to verify that the unchanged parts of the system are not affected by invalid data?					Conduct regression test to ensure that unchanged portions of the program are not affected by invalid data.	Execution	Inspections, Test data, & Test data generator
8.	Are the results obtained from the recovery process correct?					Verify the correctness of the results obtained from the recovery process.	Recovery	Disaster test & Inspections

WORK PAPER 12.2 *(Continued)*

TEST FACTOR: Compliance Testing (Authorization)

#	TEST CRITERIA	ASSESSMENT				RECOMMENDED TEST	TEST TECHNIQUE	TEST TOOL
		Very Adequate	Adequate	Inadequate	N/A			
1.	Do manual procedures ensure that the proper authorization is received?					Test manual procedures to verify that authorization procedures are followed.	Security	Cause-effect graphing
2.	Have automated authorization rules been tested?					Verify that programs enforce automated authorization rules.	Control	Test data & Test data generator
3.	Have the current authorization names and identifiers been included as part of the test?					Confirm that the actual identifiers for authorization are included in the programs.	Control	Inspections & Confirmation/ examination
4.	Have unauthorized transactions been entered into the system to determine if they will be rejected?					Verify that the authorization programs reject unauthorized transactions.	Security	Symbolic execution
5.	If multiple authorization is required, do the procedures function properly?					Verify that multiple authorization procedures perform properly.	Control	Exhaustive testing
6.	If authorizers are limited in the size of transactions they can authorize, have multiple transactions below that limit been entered to determine if the system checks against limit violations?					Verify that the system can identify potential violations of authorization limits caused by entering multiple transactions below the limit.	Security	Exhaustive testing

(Continues)

441

WORK PAPER 12.2 *(Continued)*

TEST FACTOR: Compliance Testing (Authorization)

#	TEST CRITERIA	ASSESSMENT				RECOMMENDED TEST	TEST TECHNIQUE	TEST TOOL
		Very Adequate	Adequate	Inadequate	N/A			
7.	Have the procedures been tested to change the name or identifier of individuals authorized to change a transaction?					Verify that the procedure to change the authorization rules of a program performs properly.	Control	Test data
8.	Have the procedures to report authorization violations to management been tested?					Verify that the authorization reports are properly prepared and delivered.	Control	Test data & Confirmation/ examination

WORK PAPER 12.2 *(Continued)*

TEST FACTOR: Functional Testing (File Integrity)

#	TEST CRITERIA	ASSESSMENT				RECOMMENDED TEST	TEST TECHNIQUE	TEST TOOL
		Very Adequate	Adequate	Inadequate	N/A			
1.	Have the file balancing controls been tested?					Verify that the procedures to balance the files function properly.	Requirements	Test data & Test data generator
2.	Have the independently maintained control totals been tested?					Verify that the independently maintained control totals can confirm the automated file control totals.	Requirements	Inspections
3.	Have integrity procedures been tested to ensure that updates are properly recorded?					Verify that the new control totals properly reflect the updated transactions.	Requirements	Test data & Test data generator
4.	Have tests been performed to ensure that integrity can be retained after a program failure?					Cause a program to fail to determine if it affects the file integrity.	Recovery	Disaster test
5.	Has erroneous data been entered to determine if it can destroy the file integrity?					Enter erroneous data to determine that it cannot affect the integrity of the file totals.	Error handling	Test data & Test data generator
6.	Have the manual procedures developing independent control totals been tested?					Verify that the manual procedures can be properly performed to produce correct independent control totals.	Control	Test data & Test data generator
7.	If multiple files contain the same data, will all like elements of data be changed concurrently to ensure the integrity of all computer files?					Change a data element in one file that is redundant in several files to verify that the other files will be changed accordingly.	Requirements	Test data
8.	Have nil and one record file conditions been tested?					Run system with one and no records on each file.	Requirements	Test data

WORK PAPER 12.2 (Continued)

TEST FACTOR: Functional Testing (Audit Trail)

#	TEST CRITERIA	ASSESSMENT				RECOMMENDED TEST	TEST TECHNIQUE	TEST TOOL
		Very Adequate	Adequate	Inadequate	N/A			
1.	Has a test been conducted to verify that source documents can be traced to control totals?					Verify that a given source transaction can be traced to the appropriate control total.	Requirements	Tracing
2.	Has a test been conducted to verify that all of the supporting data for a control total can be identified?					Determine for a control total that all the supporting transactions can be identified.	Requirements	Inspections
3.	Can the processing of a single transaction be reconstructed?					Verify that the processing of a single transaction can be reconstructed.	Recovery	Disaster test
4.	Has a test been conducted to verify that the review trail contains the appropriate information?					Examine the review trail to verify that it contains the appropriate information.	Requirements	Inspections
5.	Will the review trail be saved for the appropriate time period?					Verify that a review trail is marked to be saved for the appropriate time frame.	Control	Checklist & Fact finding
6.	Have review trail procedures been tested to determine that people can reconstruct processing from the review trail procedures?					Verify that by using the review trail procedures people can reconstruct processing.	Recovery	Disaster test
7.	Have tests been conducted to verify that the review trail is economical to use?					Determine the cost of using the review trail to determine it is economical to use.	Requirements	Fact finding
8.	Does the review trail satisfy review requirements?					Verify with the auditors that the review trail is satisfactory for their purpose.	Control	Confirmation examination

TEST FACTOR: Recovery Testing (Continuity of Processing)

#	TEST CRITERIA	ASSESSMENT				RECOMMENDED TEST	TEST TECHNIQUE	TEST TOOL
		Very Ade-quate	Ade-quate	Inade-quate	N/A			
1.	Has a simulated disaster been created to test recovery procedures?					Simulate a disaster to verify that recovery can occur after a disaster.	Recovery	Disaster test
2.	Can people perform the recovery operation from the recovery procedures?					Verify that a recovery can be performed directly from the recovery procedures.	Operations	Disaster test
3.	Has a test been designed to determine recovery can occur within the desired time frame?					Conduct a recovery test to determine that it can be performed within the required time frame.	Recovery	Disaster test
4.	Have operation personnel been trained in recovery procedures?					Confirm with operation personnel that they have received appropriate recovery training.	Operations	Confirmation/ examination
5.	Has each type of system failure been tested?					Verify that the system can recover from each of the various types of system failures.	Recovery	Disaster test
6.	Have the manual backup procedures been tested using full volume for system failures?					Simulate a system disaster to verify that the manual procedures are adequate.	Stress	Volume testing
7.	Have the manual procedures been tested for entering data received during downtime into the system after the integrity of the system has been restored?					Verify that the system users can properly enter data that has been accumulated during system failures.	Recovery	Disaster test
8.	Can alternate processing procedures be performed using the manual procedures?					Require the manual alternate processing procedures to be performed exclusively from the manual procedures.	Recovery	Disaster test

WORK PAPER 12.2 (Continued)

TEST FACTOR: Stress Testing (Service Level)

#	TEST CRITERIA	ASSESSMENT				RECOMMENDED TEST	TEST TECHNIQUE	TEST TOOL
		Very Adequate	Adequate	Inadequate	N/A			
1.	Have the limits of all internal tables and other restrictions on volume been documented?					Confirm with the project leader that all the project limits are documented.	Operations	Confirmation/ examination
2.	Have tests been conducted to test each of the documented units?					Verify that the application limits have been tested.	Stress	Volume testing
3.	Have programmed procedures been included so that transactions which cannot be processed within current capacity are retained for later processing?					Confirm that when more transactions are entered than the system can handle they are stored for later processing.	Stress	Volume testing
4.	Has the input portion of the system been subject to stress testing?					Verify that excessive input will not result in system problems.	Stress	Volume testing
5.	Has the manual segment of the system been subject to stress testing?					Verify that when people get more transactions than they can process, no transactions will be lost.	Stress	Volume testing
6.	Have communication systems been stress tested?					Verify that when communication systems are required to process more transactions than their capability, transactions are not lost.	Stress	Volume testing
7.	Have procedures been written outlining the process to be followed when system volume exceeds capacity?					Evaluate the reasonableness of the excess capacity procedures.	Operations	Fact finding
8.	Have tests using backup personnel been performed to verify that the system can process normal volumes without the regular staff present?					Test the functioning of the system when operated by backup personnel.	Execution	Disaster test

WORK PAPER 12.2 (Continued)

TEST FACTOR: Compliance Test (Performance)

#	TEST CRITERIA	ASSESSMENT				RECOMMENDED TEST	TEST TECHNIQUE	TEST TOOL
		Very Ade-quate	Ade-quate	Inade-quate	N/A			
1.	Can systems be operated at expected volumes with the anticipated manual support?					Verify that the systems can be operated within anticipated manual effort.	Stress	Test data & Test data generator
2.	Can transactions be processed at expected volumes for the expected cost?					Verify that the transaction processing costs are within expected tolerances.	Stress	Test data & Test data generator
3.	Has the test phase been conducted within the test budget?					Verify from the accounting reports that the test phase has been performed within budget.	Execution	Test data & Test data generator
4.	Have problems been encountered in testing that will affect the cost-effectiveness of the system?					Confirm with the project leader that uncovered problems will not significantly affect the cost-effectiveness of the system.	Execution	Confirmation/ examination & Fact finding
5.	Does the test phase indicate that the expected benefits will be received?					Confirm with user management that the expected benefit should be received.	Execution	Confirmation/ examination
6.	Will projected changes to hardware and software significantly reduce operational or maintenance costs?					Confirm with computer operations whether projected changes to hardware and software will significantly reduce operations and maintenance costs.	Execution	Confirmation/ examination & Fact finding
7.	Does a test phase schedule exist which identifies tasks, people, budgets, and costs?					Examine the completeness of the test phase work program.	Compliance	Inspections
8.	Is the technology used for implementation sound?					Confirm with an independent source the soundness of the implementation technology.	Execution	Confirmation/ examination & Fact finding

WORK PAPER 12.2   *(Continued)*

TEST FACTOR: Compliance Testing (Security)

#	TEST CRITERIA	ASSESSMENT				RECOMMENDED TEST	TEST TECHNIQUE	TEST TOOL
		Very Adequate	Adequate	Inadequate	N/A			
1.	Do the identified security risks have adequate security protection?					Examine the completeness of the protection against the identified security risks.	Security	Cause-effect graphing & Risk matrix
2.	Have tests been made to violate physical security?					Attempt to violate physical security to determine adequacy of security.	Security	Error guessing & Inspections
3.	Have tests been conducted to violate access security?					Conduct procedures that violate access security to test whether security procedures are adequate	Security	Error guessing & Inspections
4.	Have tests been conducted to determine if computer resources can be used without authorization?					Attempt to utilize computer resources without proper authorization	Security	Error guessing & Inspections
5.	Have tests been conducted to determine if security procedures are adequate during off hours?					Conduct security violations during nonworking hours to determine adequacy of security procedures.	Security	Error guessing & Inspections
6.	Are repetitive tests conducted to attempt to violate security by continual attempts?					Conduct repetitive security violations to determine if you can break security through repetitive attempts.	Security	Error guessing & Inspections
7.	Are tests conducted to obtain access to programs and systems documentation?					Attempt to gain access to computer programs and systems documentation.	Security	Error guessing & Inspections
8.	Are employees adequately trained in security procedures?					Verify that employees know and follow security procedures.	Control	Confirmation/ examination

WORK PAPER 12.2 *(Continued)*

TEST FACTOR: Test Complies with Methodology

#	TEST CRITERIA	ASSESSMENT				RECOMMENDED TEST	TEST TECHNIQUE	TEST TOOL
		Very Adequate	Adequate	Inadequate	N/A			
1.	Does testing verify that the system processing is in compliance with the organization's policies and procedures?					Verify that the operational system results are in compliance with the organization's policies and procedures.	Compliance	Checklist & Inspections
2.	Does testing verify that the system processing is in compliance with the information services processing policies and procedures?					Verify that the operational system results are in compliance with the information services policies and procedures.	Compliance	Checklist & Inspections
3.	Does testing verify that the system processing is in compliance with the accounting policies and procedures?					Verify that the operational system results are in compliance with the accounting policies and procedures.	Compliance	Checklist & Inspections
4.	Does testing verify that the system processing is in compliance with governmental regulations?					Verify that the operational system results are in compliance with governmental regulations.	Compliance	Checklist & Inspections
5.	Does testing verify that the system processing is in compliance with industry standards?					Verify that the operational system results are in compliance with industry standards.	Compliance	Checklist & Inspections
6.	Does testing verify that the system processing is in compliance with the user department policies and procedures?					Verify that the operational system results are in compliance with the user department policies and procedures.	Compliance	Checklist & Inspections

(Continues)

WORK PAPER 12.2   *(Continued)*

TEST FACTOR: Test Complies with Methodology

| # | TEST CRITERIA | ASSESSMENT | | | | RECOMMENDED TEST | TEST TECHNIQUE | TEST TOOL |
		Very Ade-quate	Ade-quate	Inade-quate	N/A			
7.	Did testing procedures conform to the test plan?					Verify that the test plan was fully implemented.	Compliance	Confirmation/ examination & Fact finding
8.	Has the testing verified that sensitive data is adequately protected?					Confirm with the user the completeness of the test to verify sensitive data is protected.	Compliance	Confirmation/ examination

WORK PAPER 12.2 *(Continued)*

TEST FACTOR: Functional Testing (Correctness)

#	TEST CRITERIA	ASSESSMENT				RECOMMENDED TEST	TEST TECHNIQUE	TEST TOOL
		Very Adequate	Adequate	Inadequate	N/A			
1.	Do the normal transaction origination procedures function in accordance with specifications?					Verify that the transaction origination procedures perform in accordance with systems requirements.	Requirements	Test data & Test data generator
2.	Do the input procedures function in accordance with specifications?					Verify that the input procedures perform in accordance with systems requirements.	Requirements	Test data & Test data generator
3.	Do the processing procedures function in accordance with specifications?					Verify that the processing procedures perform in accordance with systems requirements.	Requirements	Test data & Test data generator
4.	Do the storage retention procedures function in accordance with specifications?					Verify that the storage retention procedures perform in accordance with systems requirements.	Requirements	Test data & Test data generator
5.	Do the output procedures function in accordance with specifications?					Verify that the output procedures perform in accordance with systems requirements.	Requirements	Test data & Test data generator
6.	Do the error-handling procedures function in accordance with specifications?					Verify that the error-handling procedures perform in accordance with systems requirements.	Error handling	Test data & Test data generator
7.	Do the manual procedures function in accordance with specifications?					Verify that the manual procedures perform in accordance with systems requirements.	Manual support	Test data & Test data generator
8.	Do the data retention procedures function in accordance with specifications?					Verify that the data retention procedures perform in accordance with systems requirements.	Requirements	Test data & Test data generator

451

WORK PAPER 12.2 *(Continued)*

TEST FACTOR: Manual Support Testing (Ease of Use)

#	TEST CRITERIA	ASSESSMENT Very Ade-quate	ASSESSMENT Ade-quate	ASSESSMENT Inade-quate	N/A	RECOMMENDED TEST	TEST TECHNIQUE	TEST TOOL
1.	Do the clerical personnel understand the procedures?					Confirm with clerical personnel that they understand the procedures.	Manual support	Confirmation/ examination
2.	Are the reference documents easy to use (e.g., error message explanations)?					Examine results of using reference documents.	Manual support	Inspections
3.	Can input document be completed correctly?					Examine processing for correctness.	Requirements	Inspections
4.	Are output documents used properly?					Examine correctness of use of output documents.	Requirements	Checklist
5.	Is manual processing completed within the expected time frame?					Identify time span for manual processing.	Requirements	Fact finding
6.	Do the outputs indicate which actions should be taken first?					Examine outputs for priority of use indications.	Requirements	Fact finding
7.	Are documents clearly identified regarding recipients and use?					Examine documents for clarity of identification.	Requirements	Fact finding
8.	Are the clerical personnel satisfied with the ease of use of the system?					Confirm with clerical personnel the ease of use of the system.	Manual support	Confirmation/ examination

WORK PAPER 12.2 (*Continued*)

TEST FACTOR: Inspections (Maintainability)

#	TEST CRITERIA	ASSESSMENT Very Adequate	Adequate	Inadequate	N/A	RECOMMENDED TEST	TEST TECHNIQUE	TEST TOOL
1.	Do the programs contain nonentrant code?					Determine all program statements are entrant.	Compliance	Compiler-based analysis & mapping
2.	Are the programs executable?					Examine reasonableness of program processing results.	Compliance	Test data
3.	Can program errors be quickly located?					Introduce an error into the program.	Compliance	Test data
4.	Does the program conform to the program documentation?					Verify the executable version of the program conforms to the program documentation.	Compliance	Inspections
5.	Is a history of program changes available?					Examine completeness of history of program changes.	Compliance	Inspections
6.	Are test criteria prepared so that they can be used for maintenance?					Examine usability of test data for maintenance.	Compliance	Peer review
7.	Are self-checking test results prepared for use during maintenance?					Examine usability of expected test results for maintenance.	Compliance	Peer review
8.	Are all errors detected during testing corrected?					Verify errors detected during testing have been corrected.	Compliance	Inspections

WORK PAPER 12.2 (Continued)

TEST FACTOR: Disaster Testing (Portability)

# TEST CRITERIA	ASSESSMENT				RECOMMENDED TEST	TEST TECHNIQUE	TEST TOOL
	Very Adequate	Adequate	Inadequate	N/A			
1. Have alternate processing sites and/or requirements been identified?					Confirm that alternate site requirements have been identified.	Operations	Confirmation/ examination
2. Are data files readable on the new facilities?					Execute data files on new facilities.	Operations	Parallel operation
3. Are programs executable on the new facilities?					Execute programs on new facilities.	Operations	Parallel operation
4. Are operating instructions usable at the new facilities?					Request normal operators execute system on new facilities.	Operations	Parallel operation
5. Are outputs usable after printing/display on the new facilities?					Examine usability of outputs produced using the new facilities.	Operations	Inspections
6. Is execution time acceptable at the new facilities?					Monitor execution time of new facility.	Operations	Fact finding
7. Are programs recompilable on the new facilities?					Recompile programs using new facility.	Operations	Parallel operation
8. Are the user procedures usable with the new facilities?					Request users to operate system using new facilities.	Operations	Parallel operation

WORK PAPER 12.2   *(Continued)*

TEST FACTOR: Functional and Regression Testing (Coupling)

#	TEST CRITERIA	ASSESSMENT				RECOMMENDED TEST	TEST TECHNIQUE	TEST TOOL
		Very Adequate	Adequate	Inadequate	N/A			
1.	Are inputs from other appliance systems correct?					Verify correctness of computerized data.	Intersystems	Test data & Test data generator
2.	Are outputs going to other applications correct?					Verify correctness of computerized data.	Intersystems	Test data & Test data generator
3.	Does input from other applications conform to specifications documents?					Verify actual input conforms to specifications.	Intersystems	Inspections
4.	Does output going to other applications conform to specifications documents?					Verify actual output conforms to specifications.	Intersystems	Inspections
5.	Does input from other applications impact nonrelated functions?					Perform appropriate regression testing.	Operations	Test data
6.	Can the intersystem requirements be processed within time frame specifications?					Monitor time span of processing for adherence to specifications.	Intersystems	Fact finding
7.	Are intersystem operation instructions correct?					Verify intersystem operation instructions are correct.	Intersystems	Confirmation/ examination & Fact finding
8.	Are the retention dates on intersystem files correct?					Confirm that intersystem file retention dates are correct.	Control	Confirmation/ examination & Fact finding

WORK PAPER 12.2 *(Continued)*

TEST FACTOR: Operations Test (Ease of Operations)

#	TEST CRITERIA	ASSESSMENT				RECOMMENDED TEST	TEST TECHNIQUE	TEST TOOL
		Very Adequate	Adequate	Inadequate	N/A			
1.	Are operation instructions in the proper format?					Verify documented instructions conform to standards.	Compliance	Inspections
2.	Have operators been instructed in how to operate the new applications?					Confirm with operators completeness of instructions.	Operations	Confirmation/ examination & Fact finding
3.	Has a trouble call-in list been prepared?					Examine call-in list.	Operations	Confirmation/ examination
4.	Are operations instructions complete?					Determine operator instructions are complete.	Operations	Inspections
5.	Has appropriate operations and test time been scheduled?					Examine schedule for reasonable allocation of time.	Operations	Fact finding
6.	Are data retention procedures prepared?					Verify completeness of retention procedures.	Operations	Inspections
7.	Have normal operators successfully executed the application?					Verify that operators can operate the system by only using operator instructions.	Operations	Test data
8.	Have operator recommendations for improvements been reviewed?					Verify that operator recommendations have been adequately reviewed.	Operations	Confirmation/ examination & Fact finding

WORK PAPER 12.3　Test Problem Documentation

Field Requirements

FIELD	INSTRUCTIONS FOR ENTERING DATA
Name of Software Tested	Put the name of the software system or subsystem tested here.
Problem Description	Write a brief narrative description of the variance uncovered from expectations.
Statement of Conditions	Put the results of actual processing that occurred here.
Statement of Criteria	Put what the testers believe was the expected result from processing.
Effect of Deviation	If this can be estimated, testers should indicate what they believe the impact or effect of the problem will be on computer processing.
Cause of Problem	The testers should indicate what they believe is the cause of the problem, if known. If the testers are unable to do this the work paper will be given to the development team and they should indicate the cause of the problem.
Location of Problem	The testers should document where the problem occurred as closely as possible. It can be related to a specific instruction or processing section that is desirable. If not, the testers should try and find the location as accurately as possible.
Recommended Action	The testers should indicate any recommended action they believe would be helpful to the project team. If the testers feel unable to indicate the action needed, the project team would record the recommended action here. Once approved, then the action would be implemented. If not approved, an alternate action should be listed or the reason for not following the recommended action should be documented.

Name of Software Tested: _____

**Problem
Description**

_____

**Statement of Condition (i.e.,
what is)**

_____

**Statement of Criteria (i.e., what
is wanted)**

_____

**Effect of
Deviation**

_____

Cause of Problem

_____

**Location of
Problem**

_____

**Recommended
Action**

_____

WORK PAPER 12.4   Quality Control Checklist

Field Requirements

FIELD	INSTRUCTIONS FOR ENTERING DATA
Number	A number that sequentially identifies the quality control items, which if positively addressed would indicate that this step has been performed correctly.
Item	The specific quality control item that is used to measure the effectiveness of performing this step.
Response	The testers should indicate in this column whether they have performed the referenced item. The response can be Yes, No, or N/A if it is not appropriate for your organization's testing process.
Comments	This column is used to clarify the Yes, No, or N/A response for the item indicated. Generally the comments column need only be completed for No responses; No responses should be investigated and a determination made as to whether this item needs to be performed before this step can be considered complete.

#	ITEM	RESPONSE			COMMENTS
		YES	NO	N/A	
1.	Have all of the previous steps been performed as specified?				
2.	If the previous steps have not been performed as specified, have extra resources been allocated for uncovering defects during the execution step?				
3.	Has an appropriate test environment been established to perform the dynamic test of the application software?				
4.	Are the testers trained in the test tools that will be used during this step?				
5.	Has adequate time been allocated for this step?				
6.	Have adequate resources been assigned to this step?				
7.	Have the methods for creating test data been appropriate for this system?				
8.	Has sufficient test data been developed to adequately test the application software?				
9.	Have all of the testing techniques (e.g., regression testing) that were indicated in the test plan been scheduled for execution during this step?				
10.	Have the expected results from testing been determined?				
11.	Has a process been established to determine variance/deviation between expected results and actual results?				

WORK PAPER 12.4   *(Continued)*

#	ITEM	YES	NO	N/A	COMMENTS
			RESPONSE		
12.	Have both the expected and actual results been documented when there's a deviation between the two?				
13.	Has the potential impact of any deviation (i.e., test problem) been determined?				
14.	Has a process been established to ensure that appropriate action/resolution will be taken on all identified test problems?				

Step 7: Acceptance Test

Acceptance testing is formal testing conducted to determine whether a software system satisfies its acceptance criteria and to enable the buyer to determine whether to accept the system. Software acceptance testing at delivery is usually the final opportunity for the buyer to examine the software and to seek redress from the developer for insufficient or incorrect software. Frequently the software acceptance test period is the only time the buyer is involved in acceptance and the only opportunity the buyer has to identify deficiencies in a critical software system. (The term *critical* implies economic or social catastrophe, such as loss of life; as used in this chapter it implies the strategic importance to an organization's long-term economic welfare.) The buyer is thus exposed to the considerable risk that a needed system will never operate reliably (because of inadequate quality control during development). To reduce the risk of problems arising at delivery or during operation, the buyer must become involved with software acceptance early in the acquisition process. Figure 13.1 shows this step in relationship to the other 10 testing steps.

Overview

Software acceptance is an incremental process of approving or rejecting software systems during development or maintenance, according to how well the software satisfies predefined criteria. In this chapter, for the purpose of software acceptance, the activities of software maintenance are assumed to share the properties of software development. "Development" and "developer" include "maintenance" and "maintainer."

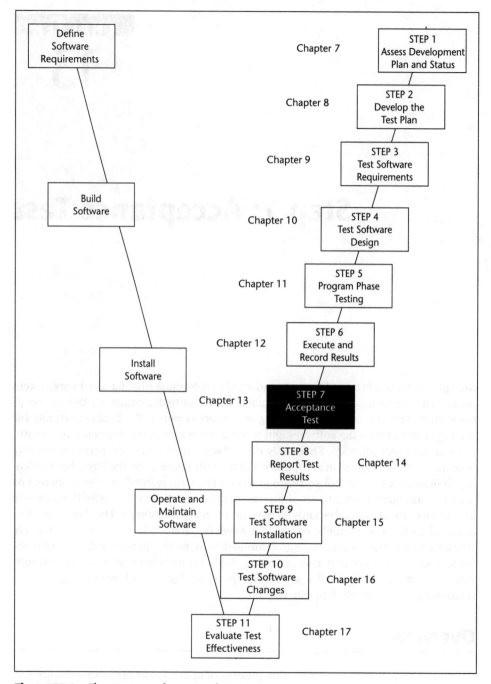

Figure 13.1   The 11-step software testing process.

Acceptance decisions occur at prespecified times when processes, support tools, interim documentation, segments of the software, and finally the total software system must meet predefined criteria for acceptance. Subsequent changes to the software may affect previously accepted elements. The final acceptance decision occurs with verification that the delivered documentation is adequate and consistent with the executable system and that the complete software system meets all buyer requirements. This decision is usually based on software acceptance testing. Formal final software acceptance testing must occur at the end of the development process. It consists of tests to determine whether the developed system meets predetermined functionality, performance, quality, and interface criteria. Criteria for security or safety may be mandated legally or by the nature of the system.

Objective

This step describes procedures for identifying acceptance criteria for interim life cycle products and for accepting them. Final acceptance not only acknowledges that the entire software product adequately meets the buyer's requirements but also acknowledges that the process of development was adequate. As a life cycle process, software acceptance enables:

- Early detection of software problems (and time for the buyer to plan for possible late delivery)
- Preparation of appropriate test facilities
- Early consideration of the user's needs during software development

Accountability for software acceptance belongs to the customer/user of the software, whose responsibilities are as follows:

- Ensure user involvement in developing system requirements and acceptance criteria.
- Identify interim and final products for acceptance, their acceptance criteria, and schedule.
- Plan how and by whom each acceptance activity will be performed.
- Plan resources for providing information on which to base acceptance decisions.
- Schedule adequate time for buyer staff to receive and examine products and evaluations prior to acceptance review.
- Prepare the acceptance plan.
- Respond to the analyses of project entities before accepting or rejecting.
- Approve the various interim software products against quantified criteria at interim points.
- Perform the final acceptance activities, including formal acceptance testing, at delivery.
- Make an acceptance decision for each product.

The customer/user must be actively involved in defining the type of information required, evaluating that information, and deciding at various points in the development activities if the products are ready for progression to the next activity.

Acceptance testing is designed to determine whether the software is "fit" for the user to use. The concept of fit is important in both design and testing. Design must attempt to build the application to fit into the user's business process; the test process must ensure a prescribed degree of fit. Testing that concentrates on structure and requirements may fail to assess fit, and thus fail to test the value of the automated application to the business. The four components of fit are:

1. **Data.** The reliability, timeliness, consistency, and usefulness of the data included in the automated application

2. **People.** The skills, training, aptitude, and desire to properly use and interact with the automated application

3. **Structure.** The proper development of application systems to optimize technology and satisfy requirements

4. **Rules.** The procedures to follow in processing the data

The system must fit into these four components of the business environment (see Figure 13.2). If any of the components fails to fit properly, the success of the application system will be diminished. Therefore, testing must ensure that all the components are adequately prepared and/or developed, and that the four components fit together to provide the best possible solution to the business problem.

The objective of acceptance testing is to determine throughout the development cycle that all aspects of the development process meet the user's needs. There are many ways to accomplish this. The user may require that the implementation plan be subject to an independent review of which the user may choose to be a part, or simply prefer to input acceptance criteria into the review process.

Acceptance testing occurs not only at the end point of the development process; it should be an ongoing activity that tests both interim and final products, so that unnecessary time is not expended making corrections that will prove unacceptable to the system user.

Concerns

The concerns that the software user faces in making the acceptance decision include the following:

Acceptance testing must be integrated into the overall development process. Software acceptance is an incremental process of approving or rejecting software systems, according to how well the software satisfies predefined criteria. If the acceptance test criteria are not incorporated into the project plan, the probability that the final software will be unacceptable to the software user is increased.

Cost and time for acceptance testing will not be available. Each testing activity appears to extend the time it will take to complete the project. Thus, it becomes

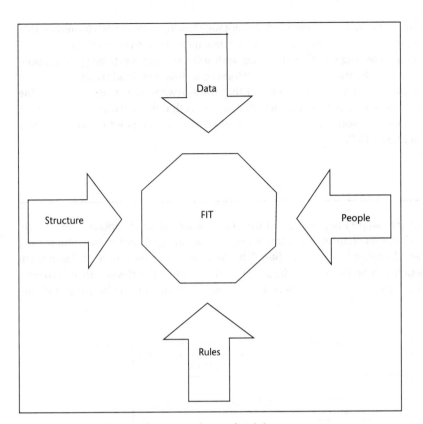

Figure 13.2   Software change testing and training.

very important that the acceptance testing phase be planned for and incorporated into all aspects of the project plan.

The implementors of the project plan will be unaware of the acceptance criteria. Either because the acceptance criteria has been developed late in the development cycle or has not been effectively communicated to the implementors, software may be made that is unacceptable to the software user.

The users will not have the skill sets needed to perform acceptance testing. Performing effective acceptance testing requires knowledge of the business application, how software is constructed, and how to perform testing. It also requires software users to develop acceptance criteria. Lack of experience in any of these areas may result in ineffective acceptance testing.

Workbench

For the purposes of this chapter, acceptance testing is used in the broadest sense. The workbench in Step 6 of the 11-step process was designed to validate that the installed changes did in fact perform as specified. Acceptance testing is designed to validate that the software, when placed in an operational environment, meets the user's needs.

The acceptance testing workbench begins with software that has been system tested for the system specifications. The tasks performed in this step lead to an acceptance decision, which does not necessarily mean that the software works as desired by the user, or that all problems have been corrected; it means that the software user is willing to accept and use the software in its current state. The acceptance test workbench is illustrated in Figure 13.3.

Input

The input to this step is dependent on the scope assigned to acceptance testing. As already noted, in this chapter, acceptance testing is an integral part of the total testing effort, and so, though it is aligned as Step 7 in the 11-step process, some of the tasks in this workbench can be performed during an earlier part of the development process. For example, if the user wanted to perform acceptance testing during the project imple-

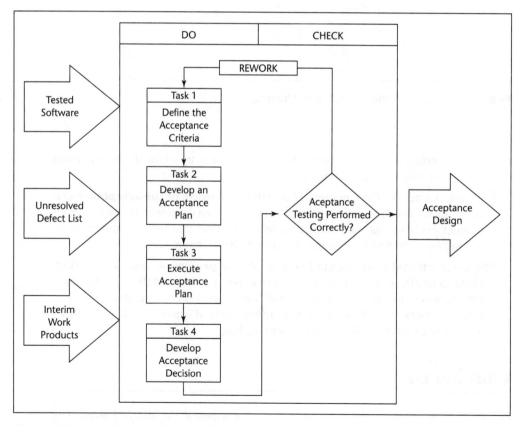

Figure 13.3   Acceptance testing workbench.

mentation plan, that planning activity would be input. However, final acceptance testing occurs only after the validation testing has been done (Step 6).

The three inputs to this step are:

1. **Interim work products.** All of the work products produced during the development process can be acceptance tested. Early acceptance testing done by the software user will help ensure that the entire effort is moving toward user acceptance.

2. **Tested software.** The output of Step 6 becomes input to Step 7. At that point, any corrections should have been made and validated. When Step 6 testing has been satisfactorily completed, acceptance testing begins.

3. **Unresolved defect list.** It may not be prudent to wait until all corrections work properly before beginning acceptance testing. In this case, acceptance testers receive an unresolved defects list, which will enable them to anticipate incorrect processing and focus on the main acceptance criteria before acceptance testing.

Do Procedures

This step involves four tasks. Normally, Task 1 would occur early in the project effort, and be performed by the software user. Basically, it is a contract that says, "If the software, when completed, meets this criteria, I will accept it." Tasks 2 and 3 involve developing an acceptance plan and executing that plan, which may be performed repetitively throughout the development cycle. The final task, reaching an acceptance decision, is performed only at the conclusion of acceptance testing. However, if the software user performs acceptance testing early in the development cycle, he or she can issue opinions regarding specific interim implementation products. The four tasks are individually described next.

Task 1: Define the Acceptance Criteria

The user must assign the criteria the software must meet to be deemed acceptable. (Note: Ideally, this is included in the software requirements specifications.) In preparation for developing the acceptance criteria, the user should:

- Acquire full knowledge of the application for which the system is intended.

- Become fully acquainted with the application as it is currently implemented by the user's organization.

- Understand the risks and benefits of the development methodology that is to be used in correcting the software system.

- Fully understand the consequences of adding new functions to enhance the system.

Acceptance requirements that a system must meet can be divided into these four categories:

1. Functionality requirements, which relate to the business rules that the system must execute.

2. Performance requirements, which relate to operational requirements such as time or resource constraints.

3. Interface quality requirements, which relate to a connection to another component of processing (e.g., human/machine, machine/module).

4. Overall software quality requirements are those that specify limits for factors or attributes such as reliability, testability, correctness, and usability.

The criterion that a requirements document may have no more than five statements with missing information is an example of quantifying the quality factor of completeness.

Assessing the criticality of a system is important in determining quantitative acceptance criteria. The user should determine the degree of criticality of the requirements in the six generic categories of acceptance criteria (see Table 13.1). By definition, all safety criteria are critical; and by law, certain security requirements are critical. Some typical factors affecting criticality include:

- Importance of the system to organization or industry
- Consequence of failure
- Complexity of the project
- Technology risk
- Complexity of the user environment

Products or pieces of products with critical requirements do not qualify for acceptance if they do not satisfy their acceptance criteria. A product with failed noncritical requirements may qualify for acceptance, depending upon quantitative acceptance criteria for quality factors. Clearly, if a product fails a substantial number of noncritical requirements, the quality of the product is questionable.

The user has the responsibility of ensuring that acceptance criteria contain pass or fail criteria. The acceptance tester should approach testing assuming that the least acceptable corrections have been made; while the developer believes the corrected system is fully acceptable. Similarly, a contract with what could be interpreted as a range of acceptable values could result in a corrected system that might never satisfy the user's interpretation of the acceptance criteria. Table 13.1 identifies some acceptance issues for each of the four generic categories with respect to the basic model stages.

For specific software systems, users must examine their projects' characteristics and criticality in order to develop expanded lists of acceptance criteria for those software systems. Some of the criteria may change according to the phase of correction for which criteria are being defined. For example, for requirements, the "testability" quality may mean that test cases can be developed automatically.

The user must also establish acceptance criteria for individual elements of a product. These criteria should be the acceptable numeric values or ranges of values. The buyer should compare the established acceptable values against the number of problems presented at acceptance time. For example, if the number of inconsistent requirements exceeds the acceptance criteria, then the requirements document should be rejected. At that time, the established procedures for iteration and change control go into effect.

Work Paper 13.1 is designed to document the acceptance criteria. It should be prepared for each hardware or software project within the overall project, where the

Table 13.1 Examples of Acceptance Issues by Category

Functionality:	Internal consistency of documents and code and between stages; traceability of functionality; adequate verification of logic; functional evaluation and testing; preservation of functionality in the operating environment.
Performance:	Feasibility analysis of performance requirements; correct simulation and instrumentation tools; performance analysis in the operating environment.
Interface Quality:	Interface documentation; interface complexity; interface and integration test plans; interface ergonomics; operational environment interface testing.
Overall Software Quality:	Quantification of quality measures; criteria for acceptance of all software products; adequacy of documentation and software system development standards; quality criteria for operational testing.

acceptance criteria requirements should be listed and uniquely numbered for control purposes. After defining the acceptance criteria, a determination should be made as to whether meeting the criteria is critical to the success of the system. This is indicated by placing a check mark in the Yes or No columns under Critical. Note that if an acceptance criterion is critical, then the system would not be accepted if that requirement has not been met.

The following example is for a payroll project. It lists two acceptance criteria and shows that they are both critical for the project. The Test Result column is blank, indicating the test has not yet been performed; the Comments column reports that the table will not be run unless these two critical requirements are met.

No.	Acceptance Requirement	Critical Yes No	Test Result Accept Reject	Comments
1	The system must execute to end of job during a payroll production run after January 1, 2000.	X		Payroll will not be run in a production status until this requirement has been met.
2	The results of payroll must be correct even if there are date problems in the report or other processing components.	X		Payroll will not be run in a production status until this requirement is met.

Task 2: Develop an Acceptance Plan

The first step to achieve software acceptance is the simultaneous development of a software acceptance plan, general project plans, and software requirements to ensure that user needs are represented correctly and completely. This simultaneous development will provide an overview of the acceptance activities, to ensure that resources for them are included in the project plans. Note that the initial plan may not be complete and may contain estimates that will need to be changed, as more complete project information becomes available.

Acceptance managers define the objectives of the acceptance activities and a plan for meeting them. Knowing how the software system is intended to be used in the operational environment and the risks associated with the project's life cycle provide a basis for determining these acceptance objectives. Because most of this information may be provided by users, initial planning sessions may be interactive between acceptance managers and users to assure that all parties fully understand what the acceptance criteria should be.

After the initial software acceptance plan has been prepared, reviewed, and approved, the acceptance manager is responsible for implementing the plan and for assuring that the plan's objectives are met. It may have to be revised before this assurance is warranted.

Table 13.2 lists examples of information that should be included in a software acceptance plan. The first section of the plan is an overview of the software development or maintenance project, followed by major sections for management responsibilities and administrative matters. The plan's overview section describes the technical program for software acceptance. Details for each software acceptance activity or review appear in separate sections as supplements to the overview.

Table 13.2   Acceptance Plan Contents

Project Description:	Type of system; life cycle methodology; user community of delivered system; major tasks system must satisfy; major external interfaces of the system; expected normal usage; potential misuse; risks; constraints; standards and practices.
User Responsibilities:	Organization and responsibilities for acceptance activities; resource and schedule requirements; facility requirements; requirements for automated support, special data, training; standards, practices, and conventions; updates and reviews of acceptance plans and related products.
Administrative Procedures:	Anomaly reports; change control; recordkeeping; communication between developer and manager organizations.
Acceptance Description:	Objectives for entire project; summary of acceptance criteria; major acceptance activities and reviews; information requirements; types of acceptance decisions; responsibility for acceptance decisions.

The plan must include the techniques and tools that will be utilized in acceptance testing. Normally, testers will use the organization's current testing tools, which should be oriented toward specific testing techniques.

Two categories of testing techniques can be used in acceptance testing: structural and functional. (Again, acceptance testing must be viewed in its broadest context; it should not be the minimal testing that some users perform after the information system professionals have concluded their testing.)

The functional testing techniques help ensure that the requirements/specifications are properly satisfied by the software system. Functional testing is not concerned with how processing occurs, but with the results of processes.

Structural testing ensures sufficient checking of the implementation of the function by finding test data that will force sufficient coverage of the structured presence in the implemented software. It evaluates all aspects of this structure to verify that the structure is sound.

Task 3: Execute the Acceptance Plan (Conduct Acceptance Tests and Reviews)

The objective of this step is to determine whether the acceptance criteria have been met in a delivered product. This can be accomplished through reviews, which involve looking at interim products and partially developed deliverables at various points throughout the developmental process. It can also involve testing the executable software system. The determination of which (or both) of these techniques to use will depend on the criticality of the software, the size of the software program, the resources involved, and the time period over which the software is being developed.

Software acceptance criteria should be specified in the formal project plan. The plan identifies products to be tested, the specific pass/fail criteria, the reviews, and the types of testing that will occur throughout the entire life cycle.

Acceptance decisions need a framework in which to operate; items such as contracts, acceptance criteria, and formal mechanisms are part of this framework. Software acceptance must state or refer to specific criteria that products must meet in order to be accepted. A principal means of reaching acceptance in the development of critical software systems is to hold a periodic review of interim software documentation and other software products.

A disciplined acceptance program for software of any type may include reviews as a formal mechanism. When the acceptance decision requires change, another review becomes necessary to ensure that the required changes have been properly configured and implemented, and that any affected segments are acceptable. For large or complicated projects, several reviews may be necessary during the development of a single product.

Some software acceptance activities may include testing pieces of the software; formal software acceptance testing occurs at the point in the development life cycle when the user accepts or rejects the software. This means a contractual requirement between the user and the project team has been met. Rejection normally means additional work must be done on the system in order to render it acceptable to the user. Final software acceptance testing is the last opportunity for the user to examine the software for functional, interface, performance, and quality features prior to the final acceptance review. The system at this time must include the delivered software, all user documentation, and final versions of other software deliverables.

Developing Test Cases (Use Cases) Based on How Software Will Be Used*

Incomplete, incorrect, and missing test cases can cause incomplete and erroneous test results. Flawed test results causes rework, at minimum, and at worst, a flawed system to be developed. There is a need to ensure that all required test cases are identified so that all system functionality requirements are tested.

A *use case* is a description of how a user (or another system) uses the system being designed to perform a given task. A system is described by the sum of its use cases. Each instance or scenario of a use case will correspond to one test case. Incorporating the use case technique into the development life cycle will address the effects of incomplete, incorrect, and missing test cases. Use cases are an easy-to-use approach that is applicable to both conventional and object-oriented system developments.

Use cases provide a powerful means of communication between customer, developers, testers, and other project personnel. Test cases can be developed with system users and designers as the use cases are being developed. Having the test cases this early in the project provides a baseline for the early planning of acceptance testing. Another advantage to having test cases early on is that, if a packaged software solution is indicated, then the customer can use them to evaluate purchased software earlier in the development cycle. Using the use case approach will ensure not only meeting requirements, but also expectations.

Subtask 1: Build System Boundary Diagram

A system boundary diagram depicts the interfaces between the software being tested and the individuals, systems, and other interfaces. These interfaces or external agents in this work practice will be referred to as "actors." The purpose of the system boundary diagram is to establish the scope of the system and to identify the actors (i.e., the interfaces) that need to be developed.

An example of a system boundary diagram for an automatic automated teller machine for an organization called "Best Bank" is illustrated in Figure 13.4.

Work Paper 13.2 is designed to document a system boundary diagram for the software under test. For that software each system boundary needs to be defined. System boundaries can include:

- Individuals/groups that manually interface with the software
- Other systems that interface with the software
- Libraries
- Objects within object-oriented systems

*The material in this chapter on developing "use case" test data was developed by Larry Creel, Sprint Corp. The test practice was awarded the Quality Assurance Institute's Best of the Best test practice award in 1998.

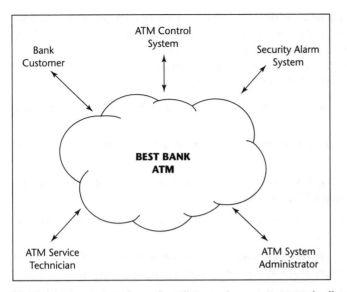

Figure 13.4 System boundary diagram for an automated teller machine (ATM) example.

Each system boundary should be described. For each boundary an actor must be identified.

Two aspects of actor definition are required. The first is the actor description, and the second is the name of an individual or group who can play the role of the actor (i.e., represent that boundary interface). For example, in Figure 13.4 the security alarm system is identified as an interface. The actor is the security alarm company. The name of a person in the security alarm company or the name of someone who can represent the security alarm company must be identified. Note that in some instances the actor and the individual may be the same, such as the ATM system administrator listed in Figure 13.4.

Subtask 2: Define Use Cases

An individual use case consists of:

- Preconditions that set the stage for the series of events that should occur for the use case
- Postconditions that state the expected outcomes of the above process
- Sequential narrative of the execution of the use case

Use cases are used to:

- Manage (and trace) requirements
- Identify classes and objects (OO)
- Design and code (Non-OO)
- Develop application documentation
- Develop training
- Develop test cases

The use case definition is done by the actor. The actor represents the system boundary interface and prepares all of the use cases for that system boundary interface. Note that this can be done by a single individual or a team of individuals.

Work Paper 13.3 is used for defining a use case. The information about each use case that needs to be determined for defining the case follows:

- **Last Updated By**. The name of the individual who updated the initial use case definition.

- **Last Update On**. The date on which the original use case definition was most recently changed.

- **Use Case ID (UC ID)**. A unique identifier for this use case. (Note: Many organizations just use a sequential number.)

- **Name**. A short phrase in business terms that identifies and describes the use case.

- **Actor**. Anything that needs to exchange information with the system. Often it is a role played by the user of the system or it could be another system.

- **Objective**. A description of what a use case accomplishes given a defined set of conditions.

- **Preconditions**. The entrance criteria or state that the system must be in for the use case to execute.

- **Results (Postconditions)**. The expected completion criteria of the use case.

- **Detailed Description**
  - The sequence of steps (performed by the actor) necessary to execute the use case.
  - The model (system) response for each step.
  - This is the basic course of events that support the pre- and postconditions.
  - The description is from a user's ("black-box") point of view and does not include details about the events of the internal system.

- **Exceptions**. Errors or deviations that may occur that cause the actor to deviate from the basic course.

- **Alternative Courses**
  - A deviation from the step-by-step events of the Detailed Description that generally inserts extra steps or omits steps.
  - These are valid events, but are not the basic course of events.

- **Original Author**. The name of the individual who originally completed this form.

- **Original Date**. The date on which the individual originally completed this work paper.

An example of a completed Work Paper 13.3 for an ATM system is illustrated in Figure 13.5. This example is for an ATM system. The case is a bank customer making a withdrawal from the checking account on an ATM.

Use Case Definition		
Last Updated By:	Last Updated On:	
Use Case Name: Withdraw From Checking		UC ID: ATM-01
Actor: Bank Customer		
Objective: To allow a bank customer to obtain cash and have the withdrawal taken from their checking account.		
Preconditions: Bank customer must have an ATM cash card, valid account, valid PIN and their available checking account balance must be greater than, or equal to, withdrawal amount. ATM in idle mode with greeting displayed (main menu).		
Results (Postconditions): The cash amount dispensed must be equal to the withdrawal amount. The ATM must print a receipt and eject the cash card. The checking account is debited by amount dispensed.		

Detailed Description	
Action	Model (System) Response
1. Customer inserts ATM cash Card.	1. ATM reads cash card and prompts customer to enter PIN.
2. Customer enters PIN.	2. ATM validates PIN and displays menu with a list of transactions that can be selected.
3. Customer selects <u>Withdraw From Checking</u> transacton.	
4. Customer enters withdrawal amount.	3. ATM validates account and prompts customer for withdrawal amount.
5. Customer takes cash.	4. ATM validates account balance is greater than, or equal to, withdrawal amount. ATM dispenses cash equal to withdrawal amount and prompts customer to take cash.
6. Customer indicates not to continue.	
7. Customer takes card and receipt.	
	5. ATM asks customer whether they want to continue.
	6. ATM prints receipt, ejects cash, prompts customer to take card, sends debit message to ATM Control System, returns to idle mode and displays main menu.

| Exceptions:
If ATM cannot read cash card, then ATM ejects cash card.
  If incorrect PIN is entered, then customer is given two additional chances to enter correct PIN. If correct PIN not entered on third try, then ATM keeps cash card and informs customer that they must retrieve card from bank personnel during business hours.
  If account is not valid, ATM ejects card and informs customer that they must contact bank personnel during business hours regarding their invalid account.
If account balance is less than withdrawal amount, ATM informs customer that the withdrawal amount exceeds their account balance and to reenter a withdrawal amount that does not exceed account balance. If amount reentered still exceeds account balance, ATM ejects card, informs customer that amount requested still exceeds account balance and bank policy does not permit exceptions. | |

| Alternative Courses:
At any time after reaching the main menu and before finishing a transaction, including before selecting a transaction, the customer may press the cancel key. If the cancel key is pressed, the specified transaction (if there is one) is canceled, the customer's cash card is returned, the ATM returns to idle mode and the main menu is displayed. | |

| Original Author: Larry Creel | Original Date: 9-25-X |

Figure 13.5   Example of completed Work Paper 13.3 (use case definition) for an ATM system.

Subtask 3: Develop Test Cases

A test case is a set of test inputs, execution conditions, and expected results developed for a particular test objective. There should be a one-to-one relationship between use case definitions and test cases. There needs to be at least two test cases for each use case: one for successful execution of the use case and one for an unsuccessful execution of a test case. However, there may be numerous test cases for each use case.

Additional test cases are derived from the exceptions and alternative courses of the use case. Note that additional detail may need to be added to support the actual testing of all the possible scenarios of the use case.

The use case description is the input to the test case work paper. The actor who prepared the use case description also prepares the test case work paper. There will be at least two test conditions for each use case description and normally many more. The actor tries to determine all of the possible scenarios that occur for each use case. To complete Work Paper 13.4, the following needs to be determined:

- Test Case ID—A unique identifier for this particular test case. Note, many organizations use sequential numbers, which become appended to the parent Use Case ID.

- Original Author, Original Date, Last Updated By, and Last Updated On portions of Work Paper 13.4 are posted from Work Paper 13.3.

- Parent Use Case ID—The Use Case ID number from the use case description.

- Test Objective—The specific objectives of the test case. The test objective is related to the use case definition that details the description action.

- Item Number—A subdivision of the Test Case ID number.

- Test Condition—One of the possible scenarios as a result of the action being tested from the use case description worksheet.

- Operator Action—The detailed steps that the operator performing the test condition performs to execute the test condition.

- Input Specifications—The input that is necessary in order for the test case to be executed.

- Output Specifications—The results expected from performing the operator actions on the input specified.

- Pass or Fail—The results of executing the test.

- Comments—Guidance from the actor to the individual who will actually perform the test.

Figure 13.6 is an example of a test case work paper designed to test the function "withdrawal from checking from a ATM." Note that this is Action 3 from Figure 13.5.

At the conclusion of acceptance testing, a decision must be made on each acceptance criterion as to whether it has been achieved. In Work Paper 13.1, if the acceptance criterion has been met, a check mark is placed in the Test Results Accept column; if the criterion has not been met, a check mark is placed in the Test Result Reject column. This work paper becomes the input to Task 4 during which the acceptance decision is made. An example of Work Paper 13.4 is in Figure 13.7.

Test Case Worksheet

Test Case ID: T-ATM-01		Original Author: Larry Creel	Last Updated By:
Parent Use Case ID: ATM-01		Original Date: 9-26-XX	Last Updated On:

Test Objective: To test the function *Withdraw From Checking*, the associated exceptions and alternative courses.

ITEM NO.	TEST CONDI-TION	OPERATOR ACTION	INPUT SPECIFI-CATIONS	OUTPUT SPECIFICATIONS (EXPECTED RESULTS)	PASS OR FAIL	COMMENTS
1	Successful withdrawal.	1-Insert card. 2-Enter PIN. 3-Select Withdraw From Checking transaction. 4-Enter withdrawal amount. 5-Take cash. 6-Indicate not to continue. 7-Take card and receipt.	1-ATM can read card. 2-Valid account. 3-Valid PIN. 4-Account balance greater than, or equal to, withdrawal amount.	1-ATM reads card and prompts customer to enter PIN. 2-ATM validates PIN and displays menu with a list of transactions that can be selected. 3-ATM validates account and prompts customer to enter withdrawal amount. 4-ATM validates account balance greater than, or equal to, withdrawal amount. ATM dispenses cash equal to withdrawal amount and prompts customer to take cash. 5-ATM asks customer whether they want to continue. 6-ATM prints receipt, ejects cash card, prompts customer to take card, sends debit message to ATM Control System. ATM returns to idle mode and displays Main Menu.		Re-execute test and use the Continue option Verify correct debit message received by ATM Control System.
2	Unsuccess-ful with-drawal due to unread-able card.	1-Insert card. 2-Take card.	1-ATM cannot read card. 2-Valid account. 3-Valid PIN. 4-Account bal-ance greater than or equal to, with-drawal amount.	1-ATM ejects card, prompts customer to take card and displays message "Cash Card unreadable. Please contact bank personnel during business hours." ATM returns to idle mode and displays Main Menu.		

Figure 13.6 Example of completed Work Paper 13.4 (test case work paper) for an ATM withdrawal.

(Continues)

ITEM NO.	TEST CONDITION	OPERATOR ACTION	INPUT SPECIFICATIONS	OUTPUT SPECIFICATIONS (EXPECTED RESULTS)	PASS OR FAIL	COMMENTS
3	Unsuccessful withdrawal due to incorrect PIN entered three times.	1-Insert Card. 2-Enter PIN. 3-Reenter PIN. 4-Reenter PIN.	1-ATM can read card. 2-Valid account. 3-Invalid PIN. 4-Account balance greater than, or equal to, withdrawal amount.	1-ATM reads card and prompts customer to enter PIN. 2-ATM does not validate PIN and prompts customer to reenter PIN. 3-ATM does not validate PIN and prompts customer to reenter PIN. 4-ATM does not validate PIN, keeps card, displays message "For return of your card, please contact bank personnel during business hours." ATM returns to idle mode and displays Main Menu.		
4	Unsuccessful withdrawal due to invalid account.	1-Insert card. 2-Enter PIN. 3-Select Withdrawal transaction. 4-Enter withdrawal amount. 5-Take card.	1-ATM can read card. 2-Invalid account. 3-Valid PIN. 4-Account balance greater than, or equal to, withdrawal amount.	1-ATM reads card and prompts customer to enter PIN. 2-ATM validates PIN and displays menu with a list of transactions that can be selected. 3-ATM prompts customer for withdrawal. 4-ATM does not validate account, ejects card, prompts customer to take card and displays message "Your account is not valid. Please contact bank personnel during business hours." ATM returns to idle mode and displays Main Menu.		
5	Unsuccessful withdrawal due to account balance less than	1-Insert card. 2-Enter PIN. 3-Select Withdraw From Checking transaction. 4-Enter withdrawal amount that is greater	1-ATM can read card. 2-Valid account. 3-Valid PIN. 4-Account balance less	1-ATM reads card and prompts customer to enter PIN. 2-ATM validates PIN and displays menu with a list of transactions that can be selected. 3-ATM prompts customer for withdrawal amount.		

Figure 13.6 (Continued)

(Continues)

ITEM NO.	TEST CONDITION	OPERATOR ACTION	INPUT SPECIFICATIONS	OUTPUT SPECIFICATIONS (EXPECTED RESULTS)	PASS OR FAIL	COMMENTS
	withdrawal amount.	than account balance. 5-Reenter withdrawal amount that is greater than account balance. 6-Take card.	than withdrawal amount.	4-ATM ejects card and displays message informing customer that the withdrawal amount exceeds their account balance and to reenter a withdrawal amount that does not exceed account balance. 5-ATM ejects card, prompts customer to take card and displays message "Amount requested still exceeds account balance and bank policy does not permit exceptions." ATM returns to idle mode and displays Main Menu.		
6	Unsuccessful withdrawal due to customer pressing Cancel key before entering PIN.	1-Insert card. 2-Press Cancel key. 3-Take card.	1-ATM can read card. 2-Valid account. 3-Valid PIN 4-Account balance greater than, or equal to, withdrawal amount.	1-ATM reads card and prompts customer to enter PIN. 2-ATM ejects card and prompts customer to take card. ATM returns to idle mode and displays Main Menu.		
7	Unsuccessful withdrawal due to customer pressing Cancel key after entering PIN.	1-Insert card. 2-Enter PIN. 3-Press Cancel key. 4-Take card.	1-ATM can read card. 2-Valid account. 3-Valid PIN. 4-Account balance greater than, or equal to, withdrawal amount.	1-ATM reads card and prompts customer to enter PIN. 2-ATM validates PIN and displays menu with a list of transactions that can be selected. 3-ATM ejects card and prompts customer to take card. ATM returns to idle mode and displays Main Menu.		

(Continues)

Figure 13.6 *(Continued)*

ITEM NO.	TEST CONDI- TION	OPERATOR ACTION	INPUT SPECIFI- CATIONS	OUTPUT SPECIFICATIONS (EXPECTED RESULTS)	PASS OR FAIL	COMMENTS
8	Unsuccess- ful with- drawal; due to customer pressing Cancel key after enter- ing PIN and selecting Withdrawal transaction.	1-Insert card. 2-Enter PIN. 3-Select Withdraw From Checking transaction. 4-Press Cancel key. 5-Take card.	1-ATM can read card. 2-Valid account. 3-Valid PIN. 4-Account balance greater than, or equal to, withdrawal amount.	1-ATM reads card and prompts customer to enter PIN. 2-ATM validates PIN and displays menu with a list of transactions that can be selected. 3-ATM validates account and prompts customer to enter withdrawal amount. 4-ATM ejects card and prompts customer to take card. ATM returns to idle mode and displays Main Menu.		

Figure 13.6 *(Continued)*

No.	Acceptance Requirement	Critical Yes No	Test Result Accept Reject	Comments
1	The system must execute to end of job during a payroll production run after January 1, 2000.	X		Payroll will not be run in a production status until this requirement has been met.
2	The results of payroll must be correct even if there are date problems in the report or other processing components.	X		Payroll will not be run in a production status until this requirement is met.

Figure 13.7   Acceptance criteria.

Task 4: Reach an Acceptance Decision

Final acceptance of software based on software acceptance testing usually means that the software project has been completed, with the exception of any caveats or contingencies. Final acceptance for the software occurs, and the developer has no further development obligations (except, of course, for maintenance, which is a separate issue).

Typical acceptance decisions include:

- Required changes are accepted before progressing to the next activity.

- Some changes must be made and accepted before further development of that section of the product; other changes may be made and accepted at the next major review.

- Progress may continue and changes may be accepted at the next review.

- No changes are required and progress may continue.

The goal is to achieve and accept "perfect" software, but usually some criteria will not be completely satisfied for each product, in which case the user may choose to accept less-than-perfect software. The user must have established in advance individual and collections of requirements.

Software acceptance is a contractual process during which users and developers identify criteria for the acceptance of software systems. Developers must agree to the users' acceptance criteria. The users must define the acceptance criteria based on the system requirements for functionality, performance, interface quality, and overall software quality, as well as other project characteristics such as the correction methodology (or variant). The buyer bases acceptance decisions on analyses and reviews of the products and on results from software product assurance activities.

The users must plan and manage the software acceptance program carefully to assure that adequate resources are available throughout the acceptance activities. Early in the process, they must include detailed plans for software acceptance testing. Such early planning enables all those involved in the software project to focus on the requirements and how well the evolving system is satisfying those requirements. Software acceptance requires adequate resources and commitment from the beginning. Its completion will result in software that delivers to its users the services they require.

Check Procedures

An acceptance testing quality control checklist is provided as Work Paper 13.5. It is designed so that Yes responses indicate satisfactory acceptance testing practices; No responses indicate additional investigation is necessary. The N/A column is provided for quality control items that are not applicable to this acceptance test step in your organization. The Comments column is for explaining No responses and the action taken on those responses.

Output

Two outputs are produced from this step at various times, as follows:

1. **Interim product acceptance opinion.** An opinion as to whether an interim product is designed to meet the acceptance criteria.

2. **Final acceptance decision.** Relates to a specific hardware or software component regarding whether it is acceptable for use in production.

Guidelines

Acceptance testing is a critical part of testing. Guidelines to make it effective include:

Incorporate acceptance criteria into the test plan. Although this chapter suggests a separate test plan and acceptance test plan, they can in fact be incorporated, in which case the test plan will use the acceptance criteria as the test plan objectives.

Include information systems professionals on the acceptance test team. The acceptance test team needs information system skills as well as business skills for the areas affected by the hardware/software being acceptance tested. Acceptance testers must be able to understand information systems and to effectively communicate with information systems professionals.

Summary

Once the user unconditionally accepts the software system the project is complete. The test report as described in Chapter 14 may be prepared prior to acceptance testing, then updated at the conclusion of acceptance testing. However, problems may still occur when the software is placed into a production status—which is addressed in Chapter 15.

WORK PAPER 13.1　Acceptance Criteria

Field Requirements

FIELD	INSTRUCTIONS FOR ENTERING DATA
Hardware/Software Project	The name of the project being acceptance-tested. This is the name the user/customer calls the project.
Number	A sequential number identifying acceptance criteria.
Acceptance Requirement	A user requirement that will be used to determine whether the corrected hardware/software is acceptable.
Critical	Indicate whether the acceptance requirement is critical, meaning that it must be met, or noncritical, meaning that it is desirable but not essential.
Test Result	Indicates after acceptance testing whether the requirement is acceptable or not acceptable, meaning that the project is rejected because it does not meet the requirement.
Comments	Clarify the criticality of the requirement; or indicate the meaning of test result rejection. For example, the software cannot be run; or management will make a judgment after acceptance testing as to whether the project can be run.

Hardware/Software Project: _____

Number	Acceptance Requirement	Critical Yes	No	Test Result Accept	Reject	Comments

WORK PAPER 13.2 System Boundary Diagram

Software under test: _____

SYSTEM BOUNDARY	BOUNDARY DESCRIPTION	ACTOR DESCRIPTION	NAME OF INDIVIDUAL/GROUP REPRESENTING ACTOR

WORK PAPER 13.3   Use Case Definition

Last Updated by:	Last Updated On:	

Use Case Name:		UC ID:

Actor:

Objective:

Preconditions:

Results (Postconditions):

Detailed Description

Action	Model (System) Response
1.	1.
2.	2.
3.	3.
4.	4.
5.	5.

Exceptions:

Alternative Courses:

Original Author:	Original Date:

WORK PAPER 13.4   Test Case Work Paper

Test Case ID: _____   Original Author: _____   Last Updated By: _____

Parent Use Case ID: _____   Original Date: _____   Last Updated On: _____

Test Objective: _____

Item No.	Test Condition	Operator Action	Input Specifications	Output Specifications (Expected Results)	Pass or Fail	Comments

WORK PAPER 13.5   Quality Control Checklist

Field Requirements

FIELD	INSTRUCTIONS FOR ENTERING DATA
Number	A number that sequentially identifies the quality control items, which if positively addressed would indicate that this step has been performed correctly.
Item	The quality control item used to measure the effectiveness of performing this step.
Response	Testers indicate whether they have performed the referenced item. The response can be Yes, No, or N/A, if it is not applicable to the organization's testing process.
Comments	Clarify the Yes, No, or N/A response for the item. Generally, the Comments column need only be completed for No responses, which should be investigated to determine whether the item needs to be performed before this step can be considered complete.

#	ITEM	YES	NO	N/A	COMMENTS
1.	Has acceptance testing been incorporated into the test plan?				
2.	Is acceptance testing viewed as a project process, rather than as a single step at the end of testing?				
3.	Have the appropriate users of the software or hardware components been selected to develop the acceptance criteria for those components?				
4.	Does the group that defines the acceptance criteria represent all uses of the component to be tested?				
5.	Do those individuals accept the responsibility of identifying acceptance criteria?				
6.	Have the acceptance criteria been identified early enough in the project so that they can influence planning and implementation?				
7.	Has an acceptance test plan been developed?				
8.	Does that plan include the components of acceptance test plan as outlined in this chapter?				
9.	Is the acceptance test plan consistent with the acceptance criteria?				
10.	Have appropriate interim products been reviewed by the acceptance testers before being used for the next implementation task?				
11.	Have the appropriate testing techniques been selected for acceptance testing?				

(Continues)

WORK PAPER 13.5   *(Continued)*

#	ITEM	RESPONSE			COMMENTS
		YES	NO	N/A	
12.	Do the acceptance testers have the skill sets necessary to perform acceptance testing?				
13.	Have adequate resources for performing acceptance testing been allocated?				
14.	Has adequate time to perform acceptance testing been allocated?				
15.	Have interim acceptance opinions been issued?				
16.	Has the project team reacted positively to the acceptance testers' concerns?				
17.	Has a final acceptance decision been made?				
18.	Is that decision consistent with the acceptance criteria that have been met and not met?				
19.	Have the critical acceptance criteria been identified?				
20.	Are the requirements (in user documentation supporting the software to be tested) documented in enough detail that the software interfaces can be determined?				
21.	Does both user management and customer management support use case testing?				
22.	Has a system boundary diagram been prepared for the software being tested?				
23.	Does the system boundary diagram identify all of the interfaces?				
24.	Have the individuals responsible for each interface on the new system boundary diagram been identified?				
25.	Do the actors agree to participate in developing use cases?				
26.	Has a use case been defined for each system boundary?				
27.	Do the users of the software agree that the use case definitions are complete?				
28.	Have at least two test cases been prepared for each use case?				
29.	Have both a successful and unsuccessful test condition been identified for each use case?				
30.	Do the users of the software agree that the test case work paper identifies all of the probable scenarios?				

# CHAPTER 14

Step 8: Report Test Results

Both interim and final test reports should be written. Interim test reports are necessary for both testers and management; testers need to know testing defect identification and correction status; management needs to know the status of the overall project effort. Management also needs to know, just prior to placing the software into production development, the status of the software system change efforts and what risks the organization is facing as a consequence of that status.

Overview

This chapter builds upon the material presented so far in this book. (See Figure 14.1.) In earlier steps, the test objectives are decomposed into a test plan, which eventually is decomposed into specific tests; tests are executed, then the results are rolled up into test reports. The test results are compared against the expected results and experience with similar software systems. Reports are then prepared to provide the information that the user of the software system needs to make effective business decisions.

The user of the software system has the responsibility to make decisions regarding whether the software system should be used as presented; and if so, which precautions must be taken to ensure high-quality results. It is the testers who provide the information on which those decisions will be based. Thus, the testers have a responsibility not only to perform testing, but to also consolidate and present data in a format that is conducive to good business decision making.

The project team is responsible for reporting the status of the project. However, experience has shown that project teams tend to be overly optimistic about their ability

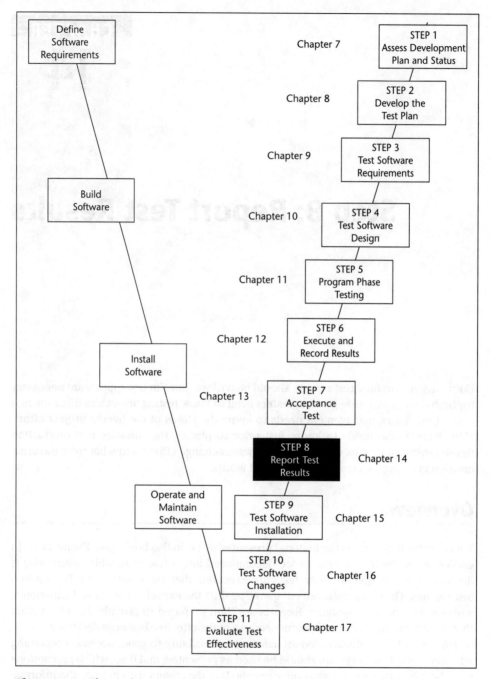

Figure 14.1 The testing process.

to complete projects on time and within budget. Testers can provide management with independent assessment regarding the status of the project.

If testers maintain a status report of their test activities, they can report regularly to management what works and what does not work. Not working may mean a variety of statuses, including not tested, partially working, and not working at all.

Reporting on how the system will perform in operation uses the results of acceptance testing. Management may be interested in knowing only that the software system is acceptable to the system users. Math-oriented management may want statistical reliability measures, in addition to user acceptance. Reliability assessment would include such statistical measures as expected mean time between failure, meaning how much time will elapse between failures.

Whether to place a software system in production is a user management decision, although testers can offer factual data about the status of the system together with their opinion regarding that decision.

Objective

By now you know that testing is a continuous activity that commences with project launch and concludes when the project ends. The verb "to test" means to measure. Throughout the project, testing is continually measuring various aspects of the project.

Management wants four questions answered:

1. What is the status of the project?
2. What has testing determined to work and not to work?
3. How will the system perform in operation (i.e., how reliable will it be)?
4. When should the software systems be placed into production?

Testing can be designed to answer any or all of these questions. To do this, a test plan must be constructed to discover the data that answers them. From that data, reports are prepared during and at the conclusion of testing to provide management with the answers to these questions.

Concerns

The individuals responsible for assuring that software projects are accurate, complete, and meet users' true needs have these concerns regarding the status of project:

Test results will not be available when needed. The individuals that need to make decisions will not have the appropriate information to make those decisions at the time they should be made.

Test information is inadequate. Information needed by decision makers will not be included in the test report.

Test status is not delivered to the right people. The individuals making decisions regarding project implementation and/or developmental actions will not get the information to make those decisions.

Workbench

The workbench for reporting the results of testing is illustrated in Figure 14.2. It shows that to report the results of testing, testers not only need the data collected during testing, but the plans and the expected processing results. Tasks 1 and 2, which report project status and interim test results, are reports that should be prepared on a regular basis. In the early stages of testing, reports may be prepared only monthly, but during the later stages of testing the reports may become more frequent.

The type and number of final reports prepared will vary based on the scope of the project and the number of software systems involved. There may be a final report for each software system, or a single report if all of the software systems are placed into production concurrently.

Input

There are three types of input needed to answer management's questions about the status of the software system. They are described in the following subsections.

1. Test Plan(s) and Project Plan(s)

Testers need both the test plan and the project plan, both of which should be viewed as contracts. The project plan is the project's contract with management for work to be

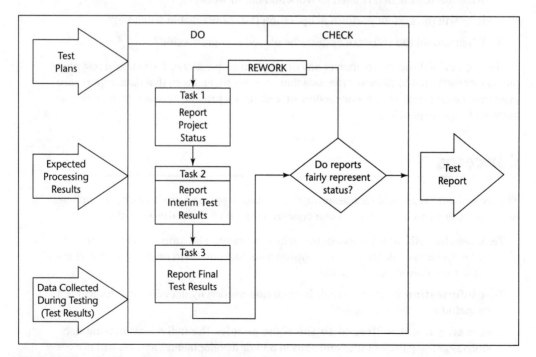

Figure 14.2 Workbench for reporting test results.

performed; and the test plan is a contract indicating what the testers will do to determine whether the software is complete and correct. It is against these two plans that testers will report status.

2. Expected Processing Results

Testers report status of actual results against expected results. To make these reports, the testers need to know what results are expected. For software systems the expected results are the business results.

3. Data Collected During Testing

Four categories of data will be collected during testing. These are explained in the following sections:

1. Test Results Data

This data will include, but not be limited to:

Test factors. The factors incorporated in the plan, the validation of which becomes the test objective.

Business objectives. The validation that specific business objectives have been met.

Interface objectives. Validation that data/objects can be correctly passed among software components.

Functions/subfunctions. Identifiable software components normally associated with the requirements for the software.

Units. The smallest identifiable software components.

Platform. The hardware and software environment in which the software system will operate.

2. Test Transactions, Test Suites, and Test Events

These are the test products produced by the test team to perform testing. They include, but are not limited to:

Test transactions/events. The type of tests that will be conducted during the execution of tests, which will be based on software requirements.

Inspections. A verification of process deliverables against deliverables specifications.

Reviews. A verification that the process deliverables/phases are meeting the user's true needs.

3. Defects

This category includes a description of the individual defects uncovered during testing. (Work Paper 14.1 represents a computer screen that can be used to record defects as uncovered, and then for monitoring purposes.) This description includes, but is not limited to:

- Data the defect uncovered
- Name of the defect
- Location of the defect
- Severity of the defect
- Type of defect
- How the defect was uncovered (i.e., test data/test script)

The results of later investigations should add to this information in the form of where the defect originated, when it was corrected, and when it was entered for retest.

4. Efficiency

Two types of efficiency can be evaluated during testing: software system and test. As the system is being developed, a process decomposes requirements into lower and lower levels. These levels normally include high- and low-level requirements, external and internal design, and the construction or build phase. While these phases are in progress, the testers are decomposing the requirements through a series of test phases, which have been described as Steps 3 through 7 of the 11-step process.

Conducting testing is normally the reverse of the test development process. In other words, testing begins at the lowest level and the results are rolled up to the highest level. The final test report determines whether the requirements were met. Documenting, analyzing, and rolling up test results depends partially on the process of decomposing testing through a detailed level. The roll-up is the exact reverse of the test strategy and tactics.

Storing Data Collected During Testing

It is recommended that a database be established in which to store the results collected during testing. It is also suggested that the database be put on-line through client/server systems so that those individuals with a vested interest in the status of the project can readily access that database for status update.

As described, the most common test report is a simple spreadsheet which indicates the project component for which status is requested, the test that will be performed to determine the status of that component, and the results of testing at any point in time. Interim report examples in this chapter will show how to use such a spreadsheet.

Do Procedures

Three tasks are involved in reporting test results. They are described here as individual steps because each is a standalone effort. For example, reporting the status of the project is an activity independent of other test reports. Testers could issue interim and final test reports without reporting or knowing the status of the project. However, Tasks 2 and 3 are more closely linked. Interim test results will normally be used in developing the final test report. On the other hand, some testers prepare only interim reports and others only final reports.

The three tasks and their associated reports detailed in this chapter are representative of what testers *could* report. Testers should not limit themselves to these reports, but rather use their creativity to develop others appropriate to the project and the organization.

What is important about test reports is that they supply management with the information they need for decision-making purposes. To report extraneous information is a waste of testers' time, and not reporting information needed by management is an ineffective use of testing. Testers are encouraged early in the project to consult with management to learn the types of reports they should prepare during and at the conclusion of testing. Descriptions of the three tasks included in this workbench follow.

Task 1: Report Software Status

This task offers an approach for reporting project status information. These reports enable senior IT management to easily determine the status of the project, and can be issued as needed.

There are two levels of project status reports:

1. **Summary Status report.** Provides a general view of all project components. It is used to determine which projects need immediate attention and which are on schedule with no apparent problems.

2. **Project Status report.** Shows detailed information about a specific project component, allowing the reader to see up-to-date information about schedules, budgets, and project resources. Each report is limited to one page so that only vital statistics are included.

Both reports are designed to present information clearly and quickly. Colorful graphics can be used to highlight status information. Senior management does not have time to read and interpret lengthy status reports from all project teams in the organization. Therefore, this step describes a process that enables management to quickly and easily assess the status of all projects.

> **NOTE** An individual software system needing rework is referred to as a "project."

The best way to produce such "user-friendly" reports is to incorporate simple graphics and color-coding similar to a traffic stoplight. Projects represented in green graphics would be those with no apparent problems; projects in yellow would indicate those potentially problematic situations; projects in red graphics would indicate those needing immediate management attention.

This step describes reporting on three status conditions for each project: technical, schedule, and budgets. These conditions are defined later in this step. The number of status conditions should be kept as low as possible; four is still manageable. Some organizations list quality as the fourth, beginning with system testing in later development phases.

In addition to being the input to project status reports, the data collected can be used for internal benchmarking, in which case the collective data from all projects is used to determine the mean level of performance for all enterprise projects. This benchmark is used for comparison purposes, to make judgments on the performance of individual projects.

Prior to effectively implementing a project reporting process, two inputs must be in place.

1. **Measurement units.** Information services must have established reliable units of measure that can be validated. Management must be willing to use this quantitative data as an integral part of the management decision-making process. All those involved in IT projects must be trained in collecting and using this data.

2. **Process requirements.** Process requirements for a project reporting system must include functional, quality, and constraint attributes. Functional attributes describe the results the process is to produce; quality attributes define particular attributes that must be contained in the requirement product to make it unambiguous, complete, consistent, modifiable, and traceable.

The six subtasks for this task are described in the following subsections.

1. Establish a Measurement Team

The measurement team should include individuals who:

- Have a working knowledge of quality and productivity measures
- Are knowledgeable in the implementation of statistical process control tools
- Have a working understanding of benchmarking techniques
- Know of the organization's goals and objectives
- Are respected by their peers and management

The measurement team may consist of two or more individuals, relative to the size of the organization. Representatives should come from management and development and maintenance projects. For an average-size organization, the measurement team should be between three and five members.

2. Inventory Existing Project Measures

The inventory of existing measures should be performed in accordance with a plan. Should problems arise during the inventory, the plan and the inventory process should be modified accordingly. The formal inventory is a systematic and independent review of all existing measures and metrics captured and maintained. All identified data must be validated to determine if they are valid and reliable.

The inventory process should start with an introductory meeting of the participants. The objective of this meeting is to review the inventory plan with management and representatives of the projects that are to be inventoried. A sample agenda for the introductory meeting is:

1. Introduce all members.
2. Review scope and objectives of the inventory process.
3. Summarize the inventory processes to be used, including work papers and data repositories.
4. Establish communication channels to use.
5. Confirm the inventory schedule with major target dates.

The inventory involves these activities:

1. **Review all measures being captured and recorded.** Measures should include, but not be limited to, functionality, schedule, budgets, and quality.
2. **Document all findings.** Measures should be defined, samples captured, and related software and methods of capture documented. Data file names and media location should be recorded. It is critical that work papers be as complete as possible in order to determine the consistency of activities among different projects.
3. **Conduct interviews to determine what and how measurement data is captured and processed.** Through observation, the validity of the data can be determined.

3. Develop a Consistent Set of Project Metrics

To implement a common management system that enables senior management to quickly access the status of each project, it is critical to develop a list of consistent measures spanning all project lines. Initially, this can be challenging, but with cooperation and some negotiating, a reasonable list of measures can be drawn up. Organizations with development and maintenance standards will have an easier time completing this step, as well as those with commonly used tools.

4. Define Process Requirements

The objective of this step is to use the management criteria and measurement data developed in steps 2 and 3 to define the process requirements for the management project reporting system. Major criteria of this specification will include:

- Description of desired output reports
- Description of common measures
- Source of common measures and associated software tools for capture
- Definition of data repositories (centralized and/or segregated)

5. Develop and Implement the Process

The objective of this step is to document the work process used to output the reports of the project data. The implementation will involve these activities:

1. Document the workflow of the data capture and reporting process.

2. Procure software tool(s) to capture, analyze, and report the data, if such tools are not currently available.

3. Develop and test system and user documentation.

4. Beta-test the process using a small to medium-size project.

5. Resolve all management and project problems.

6. Conduct training sessions for management and project personnel on how to use the process and interrelate the reports.

7. Roll out the process across all project lines.

6. Monitor the Process

Monitoring the reporting process is very important because software tools are being upgraded, and manual supporting activities sometimes break down. It is essential to monitor the outputs of the system to ensure reasonableness. The more successful the system, the better the chance that management will want to use it and perhaps expand the reporting criteria (e.g., quality).

The two primary reports from this step are Summary Status and Project Status.

Summary Status Report

The Summary Status report (see Figure 14.3) provides general information about all projects. Figure 14.4 uses graphics to summarize the status of each project component, and is divided into four sections:

1. **Report date information.** Report information is located at the top of the report. The information that is contained in the report is listed as current as of the date in the top left corner. The date the report was produced appears in the top right corner.

2. **Project information.** Project information appears in a column on the left side of the report. Each project has its own "cell" where information about the project appears. Each cell contains the official project name, the name of the project manager, the phase of the project (e.g., planning, requirements, development, and implementation), and the name of the executive sponsor.

3. **Time line information.** Time line information appears in a chart that displays project status over a 16-month period. It shows project status by measuring technical, budgeting, and scheduling considerations. The year and month (abbreviated with initials) appear along the top of the chart to indicate the month-by-month status of each project.

   Technical (T), scheduling (S), and budget (B) information also appears in the chart, and is specific to each project. These three considerations measure the status of each project:

   ■ Technical status (T) shows the degree to which the project is expected to function within the defined technical and/or business requirements.

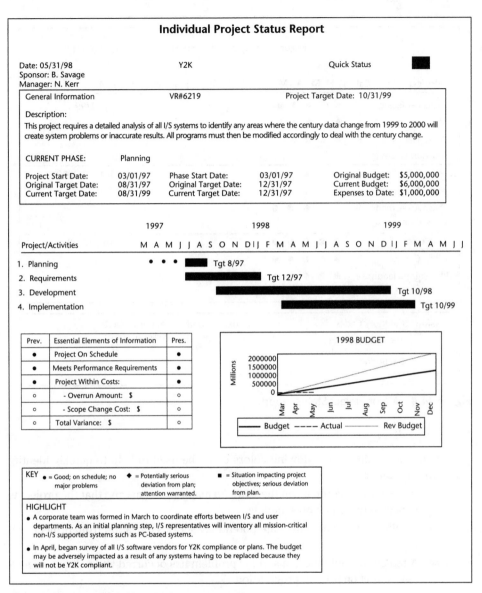

Individual Project Status Report

Date: 05/31/98   Y2K   Quick Status   ▮

Sponsor: B. Savage
Manager: N. Kerr

| General Information | VR#6219 | Project Target Date: 10/31/99 |

Description:
This project requires a detailed analysis of all I/S systems to identify any areas where the century data change from 1999 to 2000 will create system problems or inaccurate results. All programs must then be modified accordingly to deal with the century change.

CURRENT PHASE: Planning

Project Start Date:	03/01/97	Phase Start Date:	03/01/97	Original Budget:	$5,000,000
Original Target Date:	08/31/97	Original Target Date:	12/31/97	Current Budget:	$6,000,000
Current Target Date:	08/31/99	Current Target Date:	12/31/97	Expenses to Date:	$1,000,000

1997   1998   1999

Project/Activities   M A M J J A S O N D|J F M A M J J A S O N D|J F M A M J J

1. Planning   • • • ▬ Tgt 8/97
2. Requirements   ▬▬▬ Tgt 12/97
3. Development   ▬▬▬▬▬▬▬▬▬ Tgt 10/98
4. Implementation   ▬▬▬▬▬▬▬ Tgt 10/99

Prev.	Essential Elements of Information	Pres.
•	Project On Schedule	•
•	Meets Performance Requirements	•
•	Project Within Costs:	•
○	- Overrun Amount: $	○
○	- Scope Change Cost: $	○
○	Total Variance: $	○

1998 BUDGET

Millions
2000000
1500000
1000000
500000
0

Mar Apr May Jun Jul Aug Sep Oct Nov Dec

——— Budget   – – – Actual   ·········· Rev Budget

KEY   • = Good; on schedule; no   ◆ = Potentially serious   ■ = Situation impacting project
        major problems   deviation from plan;   objectives; serious deviation
                                                    attention warranted.   from plan.

HIGHLIGHT
• A corporate team was formed in March to coordinate efforts between I/S and user departments. As an initial planning step, I/S representatives will inventory all mission-critical non-I/S supported systems such as PC-based systems.

• In April, began survey of all I/S software vendors for Y2K compliance or plans. The budget may be adversely impacted as a result of any systems having to be replaced because they will not be Y2K compliant.

Figure 14.3   Individual Project Status report.

- ■ Scheduling status (S) shows the degree to which the project is adhering to the current approved schedule.

- ■ Budgeting status (B) shows the degree to which the project is adhering to the current approved budget. Expenditures for the budget include funds, human resources, and other resources.

4. **Legend information.** The report legend, which is located along the bottom of the page, defines the colors and symbols used in the report, including category

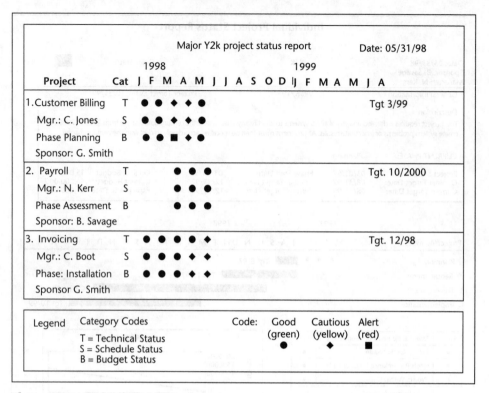

Figure 14.4   Major Project Status report.

and color codes. The following colors could be used to help to quickly identify project status:

- A green circle could mean there are no major problems and that the project is expected to remain on schedule.
- A yellow circle could indicate potentially serious deviation from project progression.
- A red circle could mean a serious problem has occurred and will have a negative effect on project progression.

Project Status Report

The Project Status report provides information related to a specific project component. The design of the report and use of color enables the reader to quickly and easily access project information. It is divided into the following six sections:

1. **Vital project information.** Vital project information appears along the top of the report. This information includes:
   - Date the report is issued
   - Name of the executive sponsoring the project

- Name of project manager
- Official name of project
- Quick-status box containing a color-coded circle indicating the overall status of the project

2. **General project information.** This section of the report appears inside a rectangular box that contains general information about the project. The work request number and a brief description of the project appear in the top half of the box. The lower half of the box shows the phase of the project (e.g., planning, requirements, development, and implementation), as well as important project dates and figures, which include:

- Project start date, determined by official approval, sponsorship, and project management
- Original target date for project completion
- Current target date for project completion
- Phase start date of the current phase
- Original target date for completion of the current phase
- Current target date for completion of the current phase
- Original budget allotted for the project
- Current budget allotted for the project
- Expenses to date for the project

3. **Project Activities information.** The Project Activities section of the report appears in the center of the page and gives a history of the project over a 16-month period. The Project Activities chart measures the status according to the phase of the project. The following four project phases appear along the left side of the chart:

- Planning
- Requirements
- Development
- Implementation

Comments may be added below each phase to track specific project developments or occurrences. A 16-month time line appears along the top of the chart, to measure each phase of the project. Color-coded circles could indicate the status of each phase.

Future activities for the project are indicated by a bar, which extends to the expected date of project completion, or the current target date, identified by the abbreviation TGT inside a shield symbol.

4. **Essential Elements information.** The Essential Elements section of the report also contains a chart. It measures the current status of the project by comparing it to the previous status of the project. The chart could use the color-coded circles and list considerations that allow the reader to quickly gather project statistics. These considerations ask:

- Is the project on schedule?
- Do the current project results meet the performance requirements?
- Are the project costs within the projected budget?
- Are the project costs over budget?
- What is the dollar amount of the project budget overrun?

These questions can be answered by comparing the previous report results (on the left side of the chart) to the current report results (on the right side of the chart).

This section of the report also includes a graph that compares projected costs to actual costs. The projected cost line appears in one color; the actual cost line appears in another. The dollar amounts appear on the left side of the graph; and the time line, which spans a 14-month period, appears along the bottom of the graph. This graph shows you whether the project is adhering to the current approved budget.

5. **Legend information.** The report legend, which is located along the bottom of the page, defines the colors and symbols used in the report, including category and color codes. The following symbols are used to quickly identify project status:

- The ● indicates there are no major problems and that the project is expected to remain on schedule.
- The ♦ means there is a potentially serious deviation from project progression.
- The ■ indicates a serious problem has occurred and will have a negative effect on project progression.

6. **Project highlights information.** The project highlights appear in a rectangular box located at the bottom of the report. This section may also contain comments explaining specific project developments of occurrences that affect progression.

Task 2: Report Interim Test Results

The test process should produce a continuous series of reports that describe the status of testing. The test reports are for use by the testers, the test manager, and the software development team. The frequency of the test reports should be at the discretion of the team, and based on the extensiveness of the test process. Generally, large projects will require much more interim reporting than will small test projects with a very limited test staff.

Nine interim reports are proposed here. Testers can use all nine or select specific ones to meet individual test needs. However, it is recommended, if available test data permits at the end of the testing phase, that all nine test reports be prepared and incorporated into the final test report. Each of the nine reports is described in the following pages, with examples.

1. Function/Test Matrix

The function/test matrix was described earlier in this book as part of test planning and execution. This function/test matrix shows which tests must be performed in order to validate the functions. Its matrix will be used to determine which tests are needed, as well as their sequencing. It will also be used to determine the status of testing.

Many organizations use a spreadsheet package to maintain test results. The intersection can be color coded or coded with a number or symbol to indicate the following:

- 1 = Test is needed, but not performed.
- 2 = Test is currently being performed.
- 3 = Minor defect noted.
- 4 = Major defect noted.
- 5 = Test complete and function is defect-free for the criteria included in this test.

Example of Report

The defect report work paper or on-screen form should be completed each time the testers uncover a defect. A sample work paper/screen is presented as Work Paper 14.1. It is recommended that this information be maintained electronically so that it can be reviewed by test managers and/or users of the software system. The information collected about each defect can be as simple or as complex as desired. For simplification purposes, it is suggested that the following guidelines be used:

- **Defect naming.** Name defects according to the phase in which the defect most likely occurred, such as a requirements defect, design defect, documentation defect, and so forth.
- **Defect severity.** Use three categories of severity as follows:

  1. *Critical.* Would stop the software system from operating.

  2. *Major.* Would cause incorrect output to be produced.

  3. *Minor.* Would be a problem, but would not cause improper output to be produced, such as a system documentation error.
- **Defect type.** Use the following three categories:

  1. *Missing.* A specification not included in the software.

  2. *Wrong.* A specification improperly implemented in the software.

  3. *Extra.* Element in the software not requested by a specification.

The information from Work Paper 14.1 is used to produce the function/test matrix (see Table 14.1 for an example of a function/matrix). In this example, the intersection between the function and test is check marked. It could also be color-coded or numbered 1 to 5, as described in the objective for this report.

Table 14.1   Function Test Matrix

TEST FUNCTION	1	2	3	4	5	6	7	8	9	10
A	√			√				√		√
B		√		√				√		
C		√				√	√			
D		√							√	
E	√		√					√		√

How to Interpret the Report

The report is designed to show the results of performing a specific test on a function. A low-level report indicates the results of each test. It is considered the lowest-level matrix of the three matrices described in Chapter 10. The report is designed to show the status of each test; therefore no interpretation can be made about the results of the entire software system, only about the results of individual tests. However, if all of the tests for a specific function are successful, one could assume that function works. Nevertheless, "working" means that it has met the criteria in the test plan.

2. Functional Testing Status Report

The purpose of this report is to list the functions that have been fully tested; the functions that have been tested, but contain errors; and the functions that have not been tested. The report should include 100 percent of the functions to be tested in accordance with the test plan.

Example of Report

A sample of this test report is illustrated in Figure 14.5. It shows that 50 percent of the functions tested have errors, 40 percent were fully tested, and 10 percent were not tested.

How to Interpret the Report

The report is designed to show status to the test manager and/or customer of the software system. How status is interpreted will depend heavily on the point in the test process at which the report was prepared. As the implementation date approaches, a high number of functions tested with uncorrected errors and functions not tested should raise concerns about meeting the implementation date.

3. Functions Working Time Line

The purpose of this report is to show the status of testing and the probability that the development and test groups will have the system ready on the projected implementation date.

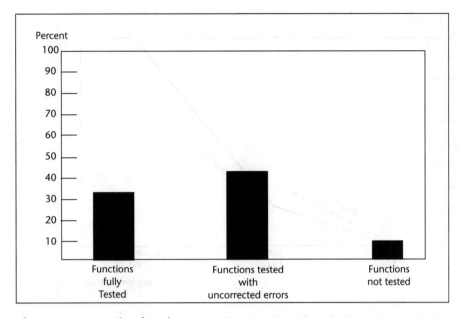

Figure 14.5   Functional Testing Status report.

Example of Report

The example of the Functions Working Time Line (Figure 14.6) shows the normal projection for having functions working. This report assumes a September implementation date and shows from January through September the percent of functions that should be working correctly at any point in time. The actual line shows that the project is doing better than anticipated.

How to Interpret the Report

If the actual performance is better than that planned, the probability of meeting the implementation date is high. On the other hand, if the actual percent of functions working is less than planned, both the test manager and development team should be concerned, and may want to extend the implementation date or add resources to testing and/or development.

4. Expected versus Actual Defects Uncovered Time Line

The purpose of this report is to show whether the number of defects uncovered is above or below the expected number. This assumes that the organization has sufficient historical data to project defect rates. It also assumes that the development process is sufficiently stable so that the defect rates from that process are relatively consistent.

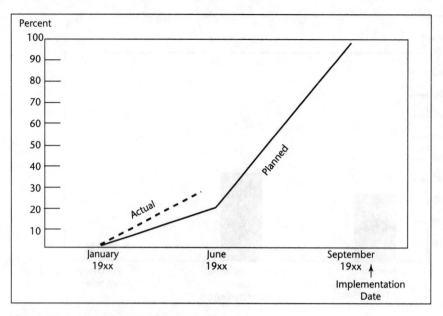

Figure 14.6   Functions Working Time Line report.

Example of Report

The example chart for the Expected versus Actual Defects Uncovered Time Line in Figure 14.7 shows a project beginning in January with a September implementation date. For this project, 500 defects are expected; the expected line shows the cumulative anticipated rate for uncovering those defects. The actual line shows that a higher number of defects than expected have been uncovered early in the project.

How to Interpret the Report

If the actual defect rate varies from the expected rate, generally there is a special cause, and investigation is warranted. In Figure 14.7, the cause may be due to the fact that a very inexperienced project team is developing the software. Even when the actual defects are significantly less than expected, testers should be concerned, because it may mean that the tests have not been effective and therefore a large number of undetected defects remain in the software.

5. Defects Uncovered versus Corrected Gap Time Line

The purpose of this report is to list the backlog of detected but uncorrected defects. It requires recording defects as they are detected, and then again when they have been successfully corrected.

Example of Report

The example in Figure 14.8 shows a project beginning in January with a projected September implementation date. One line on the chart shows the cumulative number of

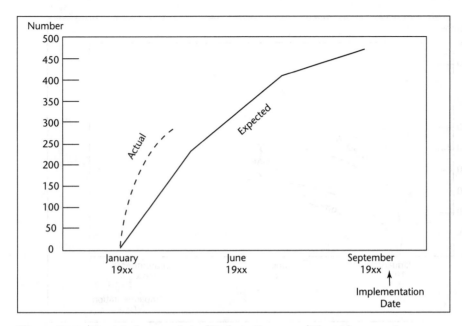

Figure 14.7 Expected versus Actual Defects Uncovered Time Line report.

defects uncovered during testing, and the second line shows the cumulative number of defects corrected by the development team, which have been retested to demonstrate that correctness. The gap represents the number of uncovered but uncorrected defects at any point in time.

How to Interpret the Report

The ideal project would have a very small gap between these two time lines. If the gap becomes wide, it indicates that the backlog of uncorrected defects is growing, and that the probability the development team will be able to correct them prior to implementation date is decreasing. The development team must manage this gap to ensure that it remains narrow.

6. Average Age of Uncorrected Defects by Type

The purpose of this report (Figure 14.9) is to show the breakdown of the gap presented in Figure 14.8 by defect type, that is, the actual number of defects by the three severity categories.

Example of Report

The Average Age of Uncorrected Defects by Type report example shows the three severity categories aged according to the average number of days since the defect was detected. For example, it shows that the average critical defect is about 3 days old, the average major defect is about 10 days old, and the average minor defect is about 20 days

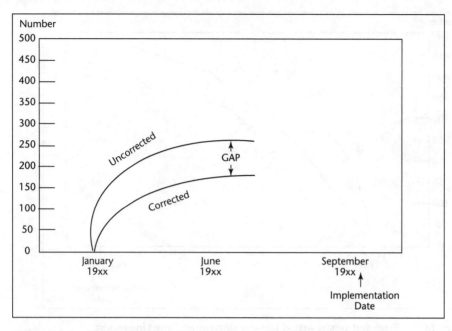

Figure 14.8   Defects Uncovered versus Corrected Gap Time Line report.

old. The calculation is to accumulate the total number of days each defect has been waiting to be corrected, divided by the number of defects. Average days should be working days.

How to Interpret the Report

Figure 14.9 shows a desirable result, demonstrating that critical defects are being corrected faster than major defects, which are being corrected faster than minor defects.

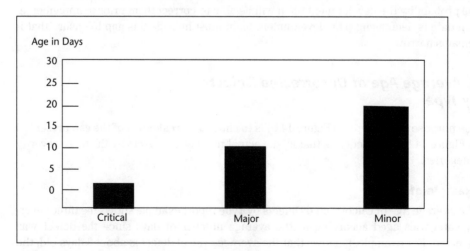

Figure 14.9   Average Age of Uncorrected Defects by Type report.

Organizations should have guidelines for how long defects at each level should be maintained before being corrected. Action should be taken accordingly based on actual age.

7. Defect Distribution Report

The purpose of this report is to explain how defects are distributed among the modules/units being tested. It lists the total cumulative defects uncovered for each module being tested at any point in time.

Example of Report

The Defect Distribution report example (Figure 14.10) shows eight units under test along with the number of defects uncovered in each of those units to date. The report could be enhanced to show the extent of testing that has occurred on the modules, for example, by color-coding the number of tests; or by incorporating the number of tests into the bar as a number, such as 6 for a unit that has undergone six tests when the report was prepared.

How to Interpret the Report

This report can help identify modules that have an excessive defect rate. A variation of the report could list the cumulative defects by test: for example, defects uncovered in test 1, the cumulative defects uncovered by the end of test 2, the cumulative defects uncovered by test 3, and so forth. Frequently, modules that have abnormally high defect rates are those that have ineffective architecture, and thus are candidates for rewrite rather than additional testing.

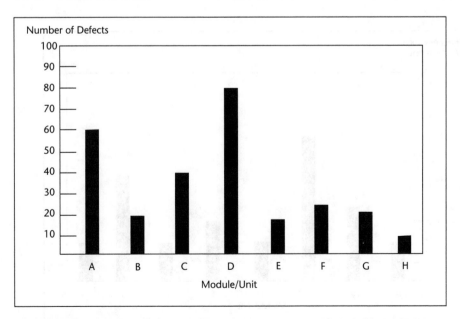

Figure 14.10 Defect Distribution report.

8. Relative Defect Distribution Report

The purpose of this report is to normalize the defect distribution presented in Figure 14.10. The normalization can be by function points or lines of code. This will permit comparison of defect density among the modules/units.

Example of Report

The normalized Defect Distribution report example (Figure 14.11) shows the same eight modules presented in Figure 14.10. However, in this example, the defect rates have been normalized to defects per 100 function points or defects per 1,000 lines of code, to enable the reader of the report to compare defect rates among the modules. This was not possible in Figure 14.10 because there was no size consideration. Again, a variation that shows the number of tests can be helpful in drawing conclusions.

How to Interpret the Report

This report can help identify modules that have excessive defect rates. A variation of the report could show the cumulative defects by test: for example, the defects uncovered in test 1, the cumulative defects uncovered by the end of test 2, the cumulative defects uncovered by test 3, and so forth. Frequently, modules that have abnormally high defect rates are those that have ineffective architecture, and thus are candidates for rewrite rather than additional testing.

9. Testing Action Report

This is a summary action report prepared by the test team. It is designed for the test manager and the software development manager. The information contained in the

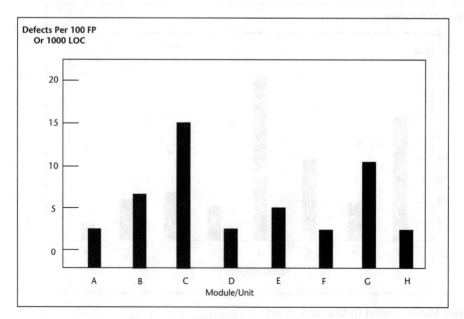

Figure 14.11 Normalized Defect Distribution report.

report should be listed as necessary to the test manager and/or the development manager to properly direct the team toward a successful implementation date.

Example of Report

The Testing Action report example (Figure 14.12) lists four pieces of information helpful to most test managers: total number of tests behind schedule (meaning either they have not been performed or contain an excessive number of defects that prevent their completion on the scheduled date); uncorrected critical defects (the total number of critical defects not yet corrected); major uncorrected defects more than five days old (the absolute number of major defects waiting more than five days to be corrected); number of uncovered defects not corrected (the total number of defects awaiting correction).

These items are examples of what could be included in the Testing Action report. Most are included in the other reports, but this report is a summation, or a substitute, for the other reports.

How to Interpret the Report

The test manager should carefully monitor the status of testing and take action when testing falls behind schedule.

Individual Project Component Test Results

As testing is completed on each project, component test reports could be issued for the individual projects. Figure 14.13 describes a standard for such a report, indicating it

Tests Behind Schedule:
Uncorrected Critical Defects:
Major Uncorrected Defects over 5 Days Old:
Number of Uncovered Defects Not Corrected:

Figure 14.12 Testing Action report.

should discuss the scope of the test, the test results, what works and does not work, and recommendations.

In any report on testing it is important to show the scope; otherwise, the reader will assume that exhaustive testing has occurred, which is never the case. Testing is a risk-oriented activity in which resources should be expended to minimize the major risks. Exhaustive testing is neither possible, practical, nor economical. Thus testing is never designed to assure that there are no defects remaining in the software and the scope will explain what the testers accomplished.

The remainder of the report is straightforward, describing the result of the testing—specifically, what works and what does not work in recommendations. Where detailed interim test reports are available, the "what works" and "what does not work" sections may merely reference those reports or attach those reports.

The recommendations section is a critical part of the report, because the reader is usually removed from the project being tested and the technical recommendations provided by the testers can help with the reader's business decision. For example, testers may indicate that there is a 50/50 probability that the system will terminate abnormally in production due to dating problems. A business decision might then be made to put

1. Scope of Test This section indicates which functions were and were not tested.
2. Test Results This section indicates the results of testing, including any variance between what is and what should be.
3. What Works/What Does Not Work This section defines the functions that work and do not work and the interfaces that work and do not work.
4. Recommendations This section recommends actions that should be taken to: a. Fix functions/interfaces that do not work. b. Make additional improvements.

Figure 14.13   Individual Project and Interface report.

the software into operation, but develop effective backup recovery procedures in case the termination occurs.

Task 3: Report Final Test Results

A final test report should be prepared at the conclusion of each test activity. This might include:

- Individual Project test report (e.g., a single software system)
- Integration Test report
- System Test report
- Acceptance Test report

The test reports are designed to document the results of testing as defined in the test plan. Without a well-developed test plan, which has been executed in accordance with its criteria, it is difficult to develop a meaningful test report. It is designed to accomplish three objectives: define the scope of testing, normally a brief recap of the test plan; present the results of testing; and draw conclusions and make recommendations based on those results. The test report may be a combination of electronic data and hard copy. For example, if the function test matrix is maintained electronically, there is no reason to print it because the paper report will summarize that data, draw the appropriate conclusions, and present recommendations.

The test report has one immediate and two long-term purposes. The immediate purpose is to provide information to the customers of the software system so that they can determine whether the system is ready for production; and if so, to assess the potential consequences and initiate appropriate actions to minimize those consequences. The first of the two long-term uses is for the project, to trace problems in the event the application malfunctions in production. Knowing which functions have been correctly tested and which ones still contain defects can assist in taking corrective action. The second long-term purpose is to use the data to analyze the rework process for making changes to prevent defects from occurring in the future. This is done by accumulating the results of many test reports to identify which components of the rework process are defect prone. These defect-prone components identify tasks/steps that, if improved, could eliminate or minimize the occurrence of high-frequency defects.

Individual Project Test Report

This report focuses on individual projects (e.g., software system). When different testers test individual projects, they should prepare a report on their results. The Integration Test report can document interface testing. See Figure 14.13 for a sample report format.

Integration Test Report

Integration testing tests the interfaces between individual projects. A good test plan will identify the interfaces and institute test conditions that will validate interfaces. Given this, the interface report follows the same format as the individual Project Test report, except that the conditions tested are the interfaces.

System Test Report

Chapter 8 presented a system test plan standard that identified the objectives of testing, what was to be tested, how it was to be tested, and when tests should occur (see Figure 14.14). The System Test report should present the results of executing that test plan. Sections 2 and 3 of the test plan standard identified the functions and tests to be performed; thus, those sections report the results of that testing. If this is maintained electronically, it need only be *referenced*, not included in the report.

Acceptance Test Report

There are two primary objectives for testing. The first is to ensure that the system as implemented meets the real operating needs of the user/customer. If the defined requirements are those true needs, the testing should have accomplished this objective. The second objective is to ensure that the software system can operate in the real-world user environment, which includes people skills and attitudes, time pressures, changing business conditions, and so forth. This final report should answer these questions.

Check Procedures

A quality control questionnaire that will assist testers in verifying that the test reporting processes have been performed correctly is provided as Work Paper 14.2. The report is designed so that Yes responses are indicative of following the process; No responses indicate that additional work may be needed, and should include appropriate comments to clarify them and the action taken. An N/A is for questions that are not applicable to a specific report or organization.

The checklist is divided into three parts. Part 1 is Quality Control over Writing the Status Report; Part 2 is Quality Control for Developing Interim Test Result Reports; Part 3 is Control over Writing Final Test Reports; and Work Paper 14.3 is a general checklist on Good Report Writing Practices.

Output

Three categories of reports are to be produced from this step.

1. **Project status reports.** These reports are designed both for the project team and senior management. Senior management includes information services management, user/customer management, and organizational executive management. These reports provide a check and balance against the status reports submitted by the project team. Discrepancies between the two reports should be reconciled.

1. General Information
    1.1 *Summary*. Summarize both the general functions of the software tested and the test analysis performed.

    1.2 *Environment*. Identify the software sponsor, developer, user organization, and the computer center where the software is to be installed. Assess the manner in which the test environment may be different from the operation environment, and the effects of this difference on the tests.

    1.3 *References*. List applicable references, such as:
        a. Project request (authorization).
        b. Previously published documents on the project.
        c. Documentation concerning related projects.
        d. FIPS publications and other reference documents.

2. Test Results and Findings

Identify and present the results and findings of each test separately in paragraphs 2.1 through 2.*n*.

    2.1 Test (identify)

        2.1.1 *Validation tests*. Compare the data input and output results, including the output of internally generated data, of this test with the data input and output requirements. State the findings.

        2.1.2 *Verification tests*. Compare what is shown on the document to what should be shown.

    2.n *Test (identify)*. Present the results and findings of the second and succeeding tests in a manner similar to that of paragraph 2.1.

3. Software Function Findings

Identify and describe the findings on each function separately in paragraphs 3.1 through 3.*n*.

    3.1 Function (identify).

        3.1.1 *Performance.* Describe briefly the function. Describe the software capabilities designed to satisfy this function. State the findings as to the demonstrated capabilities from one or more tests.

        3.1.2 *Limits*. Describe the range of data values tested. Identify the deficiencies, limitations, and constraints detected in the software during the testing with respect to this function.

    3.n Function (identify). Present the findings on the second and succeeding functions in a manner similar to that of paragraph 3.1.

Figure 14.14 System Test report standard.   *(Continues)*

4. Analysis Summary

    4.1 *Capabilities*. Describe the capabilities of the software as demonstrated by the tests. Where tests were to demonstrate fulfillment of one or more specific performance requirements, compare the results with these requirements. Compare the effects any differences in the test environment versus the operational environment may have had on this test demonstration of capabilities.

    4.2 *Deficiencies*. Describe the deficiencies of the software as demonstrated by the tests. Describe the impact of each deficiency on the performance of the software. Describe the cumulative or overall impact on performance of all detected deficiencies.

    4.3 *Risks*. Describe the business risks if the software is placed in production.

    4.4 *Recommendations and estimates*. For each deficiency, provide any estimates of time and effort required for its correction, and any recommendations as to:
    a. The urgency of each correction.
    b. Parties responsible for corrections.
    c. How the corrections should be made.

    4.5 *Option*. State the readiness for implementation of the software.

Figure 14.14   *(Continued)*

2. **Interim test reports.** These reports describe the status of testing. They are designed so that the test team can track their progress in completing the test plan. They are also important for the project implementors, as the test reports will identify defects requiring corrective action. Other staff may wish to access the reports to evaluate the project's status.

3. **Final test reports.** These reports are designed for staff who need to make decisions regarding the implementation of developed software. The report should indicate whether the software is complete and correct; and if not, which functions are not working.

Guidelines

Two guidelines are provided for writing and using the report information:

1. **Develop a baseline.** The data extracted from individual project reports can be used to develop a baseline for the enterprise based on mean scores of the reporting criteria. Rather than comparing quality, productivity, budget, defects, or other categories of metrics to external organizations, valuable management information can be made available. From this baseline, individual projects can be compared. Information from projects consistently scoring above the enterprise baseline can be used to improve those projects that are marginal or fall below the enterprise baseline.

2. **Prepare the test report and follow these guidelines:**

- Use the report writing and good practices checklist to ensure effective report writing.
- Allow project team members to review the draft and make comments before the report is finalized.
- Don't include names or assign blame.
- Stress quality.
- Limit the report to two or three pages stressing important items; include other information in appendices and schedules.
- Eliminate small problems from the report and give these directly to the project people.
- Hand-carry the report to the project leader.
- Offer to have the testers work with the project team to explain their findings and recommendations.

Summary

The emphasis of this chapter has been on summation, analysis, and reporting the results of testing used for informational and decision-making purposes. Once the decision is made to implement software, the next step (in Chapter 15) is designed to monitor installation to ensure the correctness and completeness of the installation process.

WORK PAPER 14.1   Defect Reporting

Field Requirements

FIELD	INSTRUCTIONS FOR ENTERING DATA
Software/System Tested	Name of software being tested.
Date	Date on which the test occurred.
Defect Found (Name/Type)	The name and type of a single defect found in the software being tested.
Location Found (Unit/Module)	The individual unit or system module in which the defect was found.
Severity of Defect	Critical, major, or minor. Critical means the system cannot run without correction; major means the defect will impact the accuracy of operation; minor means it will not impact the operation.
Type of Defect	Whether the defect represents something missing, something wrong, or something extra.
Test Data/Script Locating Defect	Which test was used to uncover the defect.
Origin of Defect/Phase of Development	The phase in which the defect occurred.
Date Corrected	The date on which the defect was corrected.
Retest Date	The date on which the testers were scheduled to validate whether the defect had been corrected.
Result of Retest	Whether the software system functions correctly and the defect no longer exists; or if additional correction and testing will be required. If so, the "To be added later" section will need to be reentered.

(Continues)

WORK PAPER 14.1 *(Continued)*

Software system being tested: _____

_____

Date: _____

_____

Defect Found (Name/Type): _____

_____

Location Found (Unit/Module): _____

_____

Severity of Defect: ❑ Critical
                        ❑ Major
                        ❑ Minor

Type of Defect: ❑ Missing
                        ❑ Wrong
                        ❑ Extra

Test Data/Script Locating Defect:

_____

_____

Origin of Defect/Phase of Development: _____

_____

Date Corrected: _____

_____

Date for Retest: _____

_____

Result of Retest: _____

_____

WORK PAPER 14.2   Report Writing Quality Control Checklist

Field Requirements

FIELD	INSTRUCTIONS FOR ENTERING DATA
Number	A number that sequentially identifies the quality control items, which if positively addressed would indicate that this step had been performed correctly.
Item	The questions in this field represent what is needed to write effective status reports, effective interim test result reports, and effective final test reports.
Response	Testers indicate whether they have performed the referenced item. The response can be Yes, No, or N/A, if not applicable to your organization's testing process.
Comments	Clarify the Yes, No, or N/A response for the item indicated. Generally, the Comments column need only be completed for No responses, which should be investigated to determine whether the item needs to be performed before this step can be considered complete.

# ITEM	YES	NO	N/A	COMMENTS
Part 1: Quality Control over Writing Status Reports				
1. Has management been involved in defining the information to be used in the management decision-making process?				
2. Have the existing units of measure been validated?				
3. Are software tools in place for collecting and maintaining a database to support the project reporting process?				
4. Has the completed requirements document been signed off by management and project personnel?				
5. Have management and project personnel been trained in collecting quantitative data and using the reports?				
Part 2: Quality Control for Developing Interim Test Result Reports				
1. Do the report writers have the expected results from testing?				
2. Is there a method of reporting uncovered defects?				
3. Is there a method of reporting the status of defects?				
4. Is there a method to relate the defects to the function that is defective?				
5. Have the testers consulted with management to determine what type of reports are wanted?				

WORK PAPER 14.2   *(Continued)*

#	ITEM	YES	NO	N/A	COMMENTS
6.	If the following reports are wanted, have they been prepared: • Function Test Matrix report • Function Testing Status report • Function Working Time Line • Expected vs. Actual Defects Uncovered Time Line • Defects Uncovered vs. Corrected Gap Time Line • Average Age of Uncorrected Defects by Type • Defect Distribution Report • Relative Defect Distribution Report • Testing Action Report				
7.	Do the reports appear reasonable to those involved in testing?				
8.	Have the reports been delivered to the person desiring the report?				
9.	Have the reports been delivered on a timely basis?				
Part 3: Control over Writing Final Test Reports					
1.	Have reports been issued for the final results of individual project testing?				
2.	Have reports been issued for the final results of integration testing?				
3.	Has a summary report been issued on the overall results of testing?				
4.	Did these reports identify the scope of testing?				
5.	Did these reports indicate what works and what doesn't?				
6.	Do these reports provide recommendations on actions to take if appropriate?				
7.	Do these reports provide an opinion to management on whether the software system should be placed into the production?				

WORK PAPER 14.3   Quality Control Checklist for Writing Test Reports

Field Requirements

FIELD	INSTRUCTIONS FOR ENTERING DATA
Number	A number that sequentially identifies the quality control items, which if positively addressed would indicate that this step had been performed correctly.
Item	These questions represent good writing practices that when followed increase the probability of readability and acceptance of test reports.
Response	Testers indicate in this column they have performed the referenced item. The response can be Yes, No, or N/A, not applicable to your organization testing process.
Comments	Clarify the Yes, No, or N/A response for the item indicated. Generally the Comments column need only be completed for No responses, which should be investigated to determine whether the item needs to be performed before this step can be considered complete.

#	ITEM	RESPONSE			COMMENTS
		YES	NO	N/A	
Reporting Complete					
1.	Does it give all necessary information?				
2.	Is it written with the reader in mind, and does it answer all his or her questions?				
3.	Is there a plan for a beginning, middle, and end?				
4.	Are specific illustrations, cases, or examples used to best advantage?				
5.	Are irrelevant ideas and duplications excluded?				
6.	Are the beginning and the ending of the report effective?				
Clarity					
7.	Are the ideas presented in the best order?				
8.	Does each paragraph contain only one main idea?				
9.	Is a new sentence started for each main idea?				
10.	Are the thoughts tied together so the reader can follow from one to another without getting lost?				
11.	Are most sentences active? Are the verbs mostly action verbs?				
12.	Is the language adapted to the readers; are the words the simplest to carry the thought?				
13.	Is underlining used for emphasis, or parentheses for casual mention?				
14.	Will your words impart exact meaning to the reader?				

WORK PAPER 14.3   *(Continued)*

#	ITEM	YES	NO	N/A	COMMENTS
		RESPONSE			
Concise					
15.	Does report contain only essential facts?				
16.	Are most of the sentences kept short?				
17.	Are most paragraphs kept short?				
18.	Are unneeded words eliminated?				
19.	Are short words used for long ones?				
20.	Are roundabout and unnecessary phrases eliminated?				
21.	Is the practice followed of using pronouns instead of repeating nouns?				
22.	Is everything said in the fewest possible words?				
Correct					
23.	Is the information accurate?				
24.	Do the statements conform to policy?				
25.	Is the writing free from errors in grammar, spelling, and punctuation?				
Tone					
26.	Is the tone natural? Is conversational language used?				
27.	Is it personal? Are the "we" and "you" appropriately emphasized?				
28.	Is it friendly, courteous, and helpful?				
29.	Is it free from words that arouse antagonism?				
30.	Is it free from stilted, hackneyed, or technical words and phrases?				
Effectiveness					
31.	Is there variety in the arrangement of words, sentences, and pages so that it is interesting to read?				
32.	Was it given the ear test?				
Conclusion					
33.	Is the report satisfactory and ready for publication?				

Step 9: Testing Software Installation

The installation phase is the primary responsibility of the information services department. Specifically, computer operations has the responsibility for getting the system into operation. However, the project team and the users may share responsibility for developing the appropriate data files and user and operator instructions for the application system.

As with other aspects of the life cycle, there are many parties involved in the installation. Assigning one of those parties to be responsible for the installation pinpoints both accountability and action. The recommended party for that responsibility would be a key individual in computer operations.

However, in some on-line systems the user operations personnel may have primary operating responsibilities due to initiating work at terminals, and in that instance, it may be more appropriate to assign user operations personnel installation responsibility than to assign responsibility to a centralized operations group.

The installation team performs a standalone, onetime process. This enables them to be independent of the development team so that they can perform their installation tasks concurrently with the development process. This does not prohibit both teams from being comprised of the same individuals.

Most phases in the systems development life cycle are sequential in nature, and the execution of the installation phase is part of this sequential life cycle process. However, preparing for the installation can overlap with any or all of the previous phases. This installation process may encompass requirements, design, programming, and testing, all of which become the responsibility of the individual in charge of the installation process. See Figure 15.1 for positioning of this step within the 11-step testing process.

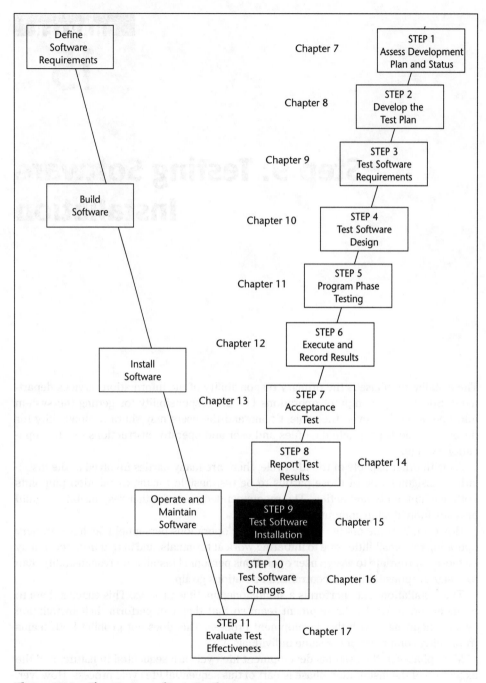

Figure 15.1 The 11-step software testing process.

Overview

Placing a system under development into an operational status may require a minisystem to handle the process. The installation phase specifications need to be determined and the mechanism developed to install the new system. Programming may be required to convert files from an old format to a new format. Those programs should be tested prior to executing the actual system conversion. However, because this is a onetime process the attention to detail and control exhibited in the system being developed may not exist in the development of the installation system.

Many organizations have experienced loss and inconvenience due to an improperly planned and executed installation process. While the installation process is normally short in duration, it may be a complex process to complete. The installation process should be tested to ensure the completeness of the installation procedures and the accuracy of changes to data and files made during the installation phase.

Objective

This chapter provides a complete test program for the installation phase of both the original and changed versions of a software system. The test program for each of the identified installation test criteria includes a recommended test together with the suggested techniques and tools. This process needs to be well planned because of the short time span for execution of the installation process.

Concerns

The installation phase testing does not verify the functioning of the application system, but rather, the process that places that application system into a production status. The process is attempting to validate that:

- Proper programs are placed into the production status.
- Needed data is properly prepared and available.
- Operating and user instructions are prepared and used.

An effective test of the installation phase cannot be performed until the results expected from the phase have been identified. The results should be predetermined and then tests performed to validate that what is expected has happened. For example, a control total of records updated for installation might be determined, and then an installation phase test would be performed to validate that the detailed records in the file support the control total.

Workbench

Both new systems and changed systems need to be placed into production. Both types of systems follow approximately the same process. However, new systems have all new

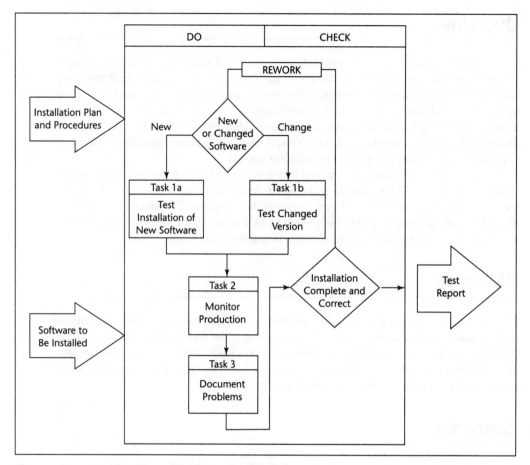

Figure 15.2 Workbench to test software installation.

documentation, while changed systems necessitate that existing operational and user documentation be updated to represent the change.

The input to the workbench (see Figure 15.2) is either the new or changed software and associated documentation, plus the plan and procedures to install the software. The first task will vary depending on whether it is new or changed software. The workbench shows that once the software is placed into production, a monitoring process (the second task) occurs to determine whether the software is operating correctly. The final task is documenting problems arising in Tasks 1a, 1b, or 2. The end result of this step is the test report indicating any problems uncovered.

Input

The installation phase is the process of getting a new system operational. The process may involve any or all of the following areas:

Changing old data to a new format. This may involve developing a special program(s) to read in the old records and create the new records.

Creating new data. Data needed by the new system not currently on computer media must be keyed and entered into the computer. This may require special programs to place the information into existing records and to validate and format new data.

Installing new and/or change programs. The new or changed programs must be placed into a production status, while the old programs should be deleted from the production status.

Updating computer instructions. The new computer operator instructions must be installed and the old instructions should be deleted.

Installing new user instructions. New instructions for users of application data must be installed and the old instructions should be deleted.

The installation process may be difficult to execute within the time constraints. For example, many system installations are performed over a weekend. If the installation cannot be successfully completed within this two-day weekend period, the organization may face serious operational problems Monday morning. For this reason, many organizations have adopted a fail-safe method. They pick a point in time at which the new system must be successfully installed; if it is not, they revert back and use the old system. This process has saved many organizations from serious operational problems in attempting to execute programs with known problems.

Much of the test process will be evaluating and working with installation phase deliverables. The more common deliverables produced during the installation phase include:

- Installation plan

- Installation flowchart

- Installation program listings and documentations (assuming special installation programs are required)

- Test results from testing special installation programs

- Documents requesting movement of programs into the production library and removal of current programs from that library

- New operator instructions

- New user instructions and procedures

- Results of installation process

Do Procedures

Three tasks are needed to complete this step. The first task will vary depending on whether it is a new or changed system. The procedures to be conducted for the three tasks follow.

Task 1a: Test Installation of New Software

The installation phase poses two difficulties to the test team. First, installation is a process separate from the rest of the application development. Its function relates not to satisfying user needs, but to placing a completed and tested application into production. In many instances, this test will be performed by a group different from that which has tested the other portions of the application system. Second, installation normally occurs in a very short time span. It is not uncommon for an installation to occur within an hour or several hours. Therefore, tests must be well planned and executed if they are to be meaningful and helpful to the installation process.

Test results that are not available until hours or days after the installation are worthless. It is important that the test results be available prior to the completion of the installation. The objective of testing is to determine whether the installation is successful; therefore the results must be available as quickly as possible. In many instances, this means that the test results must be predetermined before the test starts.

The 15 installation concerns needing testing are as follows:

1. **Accuracy and completeness of installation verified (reliability).** The integrity of the data before, during, and after installation, should be ensured through the implementation of accuracy and completeness controls. For example, if a data file is reformatted, the installation process needs to ensure that the integrity has not been lost during that reformatting process. This may involve the use of utility programs to verify the accuracy and completeness of the file.

2. **Data changes during installation prohibited (authorization).** The normal audit trail produced as data is added, deleted, or modified is normally nonexistent during the installation process. Therefore, installation is not the appropriate time to add, delete, or modify data other than reformatting data or entering new data fields currently nonexistent. The processes of deleting, adding, or modifying the types of data currently existing within the system—such as deleting an accounts payable record, changing the amount owed, or adding a cash payment—should be prohibited.

3. **Integrity of production files verified.** The integrity of production files should be verified before the new system becomes operational. This provides a base point for controlling the application system. In addition to determining that the detailed records equal the control totals, the control totals should be verified against independently maintained control totals to ensure that the computer application is in balance with the official records of the organization.

4. **Installation audit trail recorded.** Those processes and changes that occur during the installation process should be recorded on a special installation audit trail so that if it becomes necessary to revert back to a previous point in time for assurance of data integrity that known point is attainable. The installation audit trail will contain records of all the installation processing. The installation audit trail may be manual, automated, or a combination of both.

5. **Integrity of previous system assured (continuity of processing).** The installation process may not be successful, which could necessitate reverting

back to the previous system. In addition, the integrity of the installed system may be lost during the first few days of processing, again necessitating reverting to the older system. The integrity of the old system must be maintained until it can be ascertained that the integrity of the new system has been achieved. Normally, this only involves the retention of programs, data, and instructions; however, in rare cases it may involve running the two systems in parallel.

6. **Fail-safe installation plan implemented (service level).** The installation process should be handled in such a manner that it is possible to stop it if it becomes apparent that it will not be successful. It is far better to revert to the previous system than to continue installing the system that is known not to operate correctly, or which cannot be installed in the allotted time. The fail-safe concept connotes that if the installation is not successful at a point where processing can still be performed on the old system, the installation stops, and the necessary procedures are taken to revert back to the previous system.

7. **Access controlled during installation (security).** The installation process is a vulnerable time because neither the old nor the new security procedures may be operational. In addition, the installation procedures that govern the security of all applications may not be operational. The security installation risk should be assessed and appropriate procedures implemented to ensure integrity during that time span.

8. **Installation complies with methodology.** Tests should be performed to ensure that the installation process is performed in accordance with the departmental standards, policies, procedures, and guidelines. Those procedures are normally selected to ensure success in placing a new system in production. If the procedures are not followed, the probability of an unsuccessful installation is increased.

9. **Proper programs and dates placed into production.** An important aspect of the installation process is the movement of the programs from a test library to a production library. The effective operational dates of each program should be indicated so that the old programs will cease operation on the date the new programs are placed into operation. Testing normally involves evaluating the library documentation to ensure that the appropriate movement of programs has occurred.

10. **Usability instructions disseminated.** Normally, the clerical people are not instructed in the new procedures until immediately prior to the new system going into production. This avoids confusion regarding what the people are supposed to do. However, it requires that all the instructions and training material be ready so that they can be disseminated to all involved parties at the appropriate time. Testing should verify that the dissemination of the manual instructions has occurred.

11. **Documentation complete (maintainability).** Maintainable programs are well documented. One of the easy-to-delay developmental tasks is documentation, yet the cost of incomplete documentation may be high after the system becomes operational. Testing should ensure that the documentation is complete and that it reasonably satisfies the intent of the documentation guidelines. It is advisable to

assess the completeness of maintenance documentation from the perspective of having to maintain that program/system.

12. **Documentation complete (portability).** A system that is to be moved from one operating environment to another must be adequately documented to identify both areas of potential change and the operating characteristics. If portability is an important factor, special documentation is normally required for this purpose. The documentation should identify any environment-dependent characteristics of the application system, and the operational characteristics of that system, such as the current core size of the largest program, the number of data files, the organizational structure of those files, and so on.

13. **Interface coordinated (coupling).** An application system that interfaces with other applications affects all of those applications during installation. The introduction of the new system should coordinate potential changes with all other interfaced applications. These should ensure that appropriate notification has been made so that the equivalent versions of all the applications become operational at the same time.

14. **Integration performance monitored.** The cost of installation should be isolated so that it is apparent how many resources are going into the process, and what is the success in using those resources. The establishment of installation goals and budgets, and then monitoring performance during installation, not only helps improve performance, but identifies inefficient and ineffective areas that may be causing application problems after installation.

15. **Operating procedures implemented.** The operations group must be provided with the procedures necessary to execute the new application system. This process must be coordinated with all other aspects of installation. Tests can confirm whether the appropriate documentation has been made available for operator use at the time the application becomes operational.

The installation test process is shown in Work Paper 15.1. A test program is provided for each of the 15 installation phase concerns. Each test program describes the criteria that should be evaluated through testing and the recommended tests, including suggested test techniques and tools. This generalized installation phase test program may need to be customized for a specific installation. The individual responsible for the test should take into account unique application characteristics that may require special testing.

Task 1b: Test Changed Version (of Software)

Information services management establishes both the software maintenance changes for its department and the objectives for making the changes. The establishment of clear-cut objectives helps the software maintenance analyst and operation personnel understand some of the procedures they are asked to follow. This understanding often results in a better controlled operation.

The primary objective in installing the change is to get the right change installed at the right time. Performing the tasks in the previous chapter should have resulted in properly designed and tested changes. In addition, the affected personnel should have received the appropriate training. However, a cautious software maintenance group still guards against undetected potential problems.

The specific objectives of installing the change are as follows:

Put changed application systems into production. Each change should be incorporated through a new version of a program. The production system should have the capability of moving these versions in and out of production on prescribed dates. To do this, it is necessary first to uniquely identify each version of a program, and second to pinpoint the dates when individual program versions are to be placed into and taken out of production.

Assess the efficiency of changes. If a change results in extensive time and effort to do additional checking, or to locate information not provided by the system, additional changes may be desirable.

Monitor the correctness of the change. People should not assume that testing will uncover all of the problems. For example, problems may be encountered in untouched parts of the application. People should be assigned the responsibility to review output immediately following changes. If this is a normal function, then those people should be notified that a change has occurred and should be informed where the change is in the system and what potentially bad outputs might be expected.

Keep systems library up to date. When programs are added to the production and source library, other versions should be deleted. This will not happen unless specific action is taken. The application system project team should ensure that unwanted versions in the source and object code libraries are deleted when they have fulfilled their purposes.

When the change is put into production, information services management can never be sure what type of problems may be encountered shortly thereafter. The concerns during the change process deal with properly and promptly installing the change. It is during the installation that the results of these change activities become known. Thus, many of the concerns culminate during the installation of the change.

Information services management must identify the concerns so that they can establish the proper control mechanisms. The most common concerns during the installation of the change include the following:

Will the change be installed on time? When the testing and training have been completed, an actual installation date can be established. Information services management wants the version to go into production on the date specified.

Is backup data compatible with the changed system? Each time an application system is changed, the backup data required for recovery purposes may also have to be changed. Because this step occurs outside the normal change procedures, it may be overlooked. Backup data includes the new program versions, the job control language associated with those programs, and other documentation procedures involved in making the system operational after a problem occurs.

Are recovery procedures compatible with the changed system? Modifying an application system may also require modifying the recovery procedures. If new files have been established, or if new operating procedures or priorities have been designed, they must be incorporated into the recovery procedures.

Is the source/object library cluttered with obsolete program versions? Large source and object libraries negatively impact operations performance. If these libraries are not regularly reviewed and cleared of obsolete programs, resources will be unnecessarily consumed.

Will errors in the change be detected? Attempt to detect remaining program errors prior to using the new version to conduct business. This may require extra monitoring to ensure that the output data is accurate and complete.

Will errors in the change be corrected? If an error is detected, it should be corrected. A continual concern of all levels of management is that problems will be recognized but not acted upon.

This chapter provides guidance for information services management to address these control concerns. In addition, the chapter recommends gathering data to help monitor these situations. Information services departments installing controls that anticipate problems are normally better-run departments.

Testing the installation of the changes is divided into three tasks, some of which are manual and others heavily automated. Each is explained in detail in upcoming subsections. The three subtasks to install the changes that must be tested are:

1. Develop the restart/recovery plan.

2. Enter the change into production.

3. Delete any unneeded version(s).

1. Test the Adequacy of the Restart/Recovery Plan

Restart and recovery are important stages in application systems processing. Restart means computer operations begin from a point of known integrity. Recovery occurs when the integrity of the system has been compromised. In a recovery process, the systems processing must be backed up to a point of known integrity; thereafter, transactions are rerun to the point at which the problem was detected.

Many aspects of system changes impact the recovery process. Among those to evaluate for their impact on recovery are:

- Addition of a new function
- Change of job control
- Additional use of utility programs
- Change in retention periods
- Change in computer programs
- Change in operating documentations
- Introduction of a new or revised form

The testers should assess each change to determine its impact on the recovery process. If a program is changed, the tester must ensure that those changes are included in backup data. Without the latest version of the program, the tester may not be able to correctly recover computer processing.

If the tester determines that recovery has been impacted by the change, that impact on the recovery plan must be updated. The tester can use Work Paper 15.2 to document the restart/recovery planning process, and forward it to the person responsible for recovery.

2. Verify the Correct Change Has Been Entered into Production

A positive action must be taken to move a changed program from test status to production status. This action should be taken by the owner of the software. When the user department is satisfied with the change, the new program version can be moved into production.

The production environment should be able to control programs according to production date. Each version of a program in production should be labeled according to when it is to go into and be taken out of production. If there is no known replacement, then the date to take that version out of production is the latest date that can be put into that field. When a new version has been selected, that date can be changed to the actual date.

A history of changes should be available for each program, to provide a complete audit trail of everything that has happened to the program since first written. The change history, together with a notification to operations that a change is ready for production, provide the necessary controls during this step.

To verify that the correct change has been placed into production, the tester should answer the following two questions:

1. **Is a change history available?** Changes to an application program should be documented using a Work Paper similar to Work Paper 15.3. The objective of this history-of-change form is to show all of the changes made to a program since its inception. This serves two purposes: First, if problems occur, this audit trail indicates whether the changes have been made; and second, it discourages unauthorized changes. In most organizations, changes to programs/systems are maintained in source code libraries, test libraries, and production libraries. Work Paper 15.3 is a hardcopy format of the type of information that testers should be looking for in software libraries.

2. **Is there a formal notification of production changes?** The procedure to move a version from testing to production should be formalized. Telephone calls and other word-of-mouth procedures are not sufficient. The formal process can be enhanced to prevent the loss of notification forms by using a prenumbered form. The project leader should prepare the notification of production change form, which should then be sent to the computer operations department, which installs the new version. A sample form is illustrated in Work Paper 15.4.

The owner of the software decides when a new version of the software will be placed into production. This approval gives operations the go-ahead to initiate its procedures for notifying the appropriate staff that changes are to be installed. The tester must verify that the appropriate notification has been given, pending the owner's approval, and that the information is correct. The tester can use Work Paper 15.4 for this task.

3. Verify Unneeded Versions
Have Been Deleted

It may or may not be desirable to delete old versions of programs when a new version is entered. The most obvious reason against doing so is to maintain a fallback version in case the new version proves defective. Organizations should establish standards regarding when old versions should be automatically deleted from the library. Some, while not automating this function, periodically notify the project team that older versions will be deleted unless the project team takes specific action to have them retained in the library. Other organizations charge the projects a fee for retaining old versions.

In any case, programs should not be deleted from libraries without authorization. Some type of form should be prepared to authorize computer operations personnel to delete programs from a library. This form also provides a history of additions to the libraries. A source/object library deletions notice form is illustrated in Work Paper 15.5. This form becomes a more effective control if a sequential number is added, so that its loss is more likely to be detected. The form should be filled out by the software maintenance project leader and sent to computer operations for action.

The computer operations department should have a process for deleting unneeded versions of source libraries, test libraries, and production libraries—after receiving authorization to do so, of course. It is recommended that those authorizations be in writing from the owner of the item. The type of information needed for deleting programs from a library is contained in Work Paper 15.5, which also contains instructions for deleting programs.

The objective of the entire correction process is to satisfy the new date need. This is accomplished by incorporating that need into the application system and running it in production status. If all parts of the software change process have been properly performed, the production step is mechanical. The program library automatically calls in the correct version of the program on the proper day. However, if there are special operator instructions, the operator should be alerted to that change on the appropriate day. Most information services organizations have procedures for this purpose.

Task 2: Monitor Production

Application systems are most vulnerable to problems immediately following the introduction of new versions of a program(s). For this reason, many organizations monitor the output immediately following the introduction of a new program version. In organizations that normally monitor output, extra effort or attention may be applied at the time a changed program version is first run.

The following groups may monitor the output of a new program version:

Application system control group. An individual or group that normally monitors the output of an application system.

User personnel. Special user personnel assigned to monitor the output for a limited period of time.

Software maintenance personnel. Selected systems and programming personnel assigned to monitor output for a limited time.

Computer operations personnel. Selected people assigned to monitor the output for a limited period of time.

Regardless of who monitors the output, the software maintenance analyst and user personnel should provide clues about what to look for. User and software maintenance personnel must attempt to identify the specific areas where they believe problems might occur.

The types of clues that could be provided to monitoring personnel include:

Transactions to investigate. Specific types of transactions, such as certain product numbers, that they should monitor.

Customers. Specific customers or other identifiers to help them locate problems on specific pages of reports.

Reports. Specific outputs that should be reviewed.

Tape files. Data records or files that have been changed that they may need to examine by extracting information to determine if data was properly recorded.

Performance. Anticipated improvements in the effectiveness, efficiency, and economy of operations that they should review.

This process is normally more effective if it is formalized. This means documenting the type of clues to look for during the monitoring process. A program change monitor notification form is illustrated in Work Paper 15.6. This form should be completed by the user and/or software maintenance personnel and then given to the people monitoring the transaction. The information contained on the program change monitor notification form is outlined on the form's completion instructions sheet. Both forms are found at the end of the chapter.

Task 3: Document Problems

Individuals detecting problems when they monitor changes in application systems should formally document them. The formal documentation process can be made even more effective if the forms are controlled through a numbering sequence. This enables software maintenance personnel to detect lost problem forms. The individual monitoring the process should keep a duplicate copy of the form on hand, in case the copy sent to the project is lost.

The individual monitoring the process should be asked both to document the problem and to assess the risk associated with that problem. Although this individual may not be the ideal candidate to make a risk assessment, a preliminary assessment is often very helpful in determining the seriousness of the problem. If the initial estimate about the risk is erroneous, it can be corrected at a later time.

The report of a system problem caused by system change, because of the program change monitor notification, enables the individual to associate the problem with a specific problem change. This additional piece of information is usually invaluable in correcting the problem.

A form to record a system problem caused by a system change is illustrated in Work Paper 15.7. This form should be completed by the individual monitoring the application system. The completed form should be given to the software maintenance analyst for correction. The information contained on the system problem caused by system change form is described on the form's completion instructions sheet. Both forms are found at the end of the chapter.

Check Procedures

Work Paper 15.8 is a quality control checklist for this step. It is designed so that Yes responses indicate good test practices; No responses warrant additional investigation. A Comments column is provided to explain No responses and to record results of investigation. The N/A column is used when the checklist item is not applicable to the test situation.

The items in the quality control checklist are written for putting a changed system into operation. This is because most installations will be new versions of systems already in production. However, if a new system is being placed into production the items in the quality control checklist should be viewed from the perspective that the items updated in a change should refer to having that item prepared. For example, Item 1 deals with updating the restart recovery plan. In a new system they will be concerned that the restart recovery plan is prepared.

Output

There are both interim and final outputs to this step. The interim outputs are the various reports that indicate any problems that arise during installation. Problems may relate to installation, deletion of programs from the libraries, or production. Whoever performs these testing tasks should notify the appropriate organization to make adjustments and/or corrections.

The ongoing monitoring process will also identify problems. These problems may deal with both the software and/or the users of the software. For example, problems may occur in the procedures provided users to interact with the software, or it may be that the users are inadequately trained to use this software. All of these problems need to be reported to the appropriate organization.

Guidelines

Feedback enables information services management and users to monitor each phase of the software maintenance process. The feedback information relates to the processes and controls operational during each phase. During the installation of the change, management is able to measure the overall success of the software maintenance process. This gathered data is some of the most valuable. The types of feedback information that have proved most valuable include the following (see Figure 15.3):

Number of changes installed. One of the more meaningful pieces of information is the number of changes actually installed. This piece of feedback data can be mon-

FEEDBACK DATA	SOURCE	PURPOSE
Number of changes installed	Job accounting system	To identify the volume of changes being installed in the operations area.
Number of changes installed by application	Job accounting system	To determine the frequency of change by application in order to evaluate application workload.
Number of problems encountered with installed changes.	System problem encountered due to system change form	To determine the effectiveness of the software maintenance process.
Number of old program versions deleted	Job accounting system	To determine the effectiveness of the software maintenance process.
Number of new program versions installed	Source job accounting system	To determine the magnitude of the change effort as measured by number of new program versions installed.
Number of conditions monitored	Program change monitor notification form	To determine the efforts undertaken to detect problems before they become serious.
Number of changes not installed on time	Departmental job scheduling system	To determine the frequency with which user requirements are not achieved.

Figure 15.3   Common types of feedback.

itored by individuals or by system changes within time spans such as changes per week. This piece of data shows the end result of the change process.

Number of changes installed by application. This piece of feedback information indicates the maintenance activity for each application. It shows information services management the volume of changes occurring from an installation perspective.

Number of problems encountered with installed changes. This piece of data helps measure the success of the software maintenance process. If few problems are encountered after changes are installed, information services management can assume that the software maintenance procedures are effective.

Number of old program versions deleted. This piece of feedback information provides insight into the maintenance being performed on the information services libraries. If more programs are being added than deleted, information services management may wish to take action to reduce the size of the program libraries.

Number of new program versions installed. This is another measure of the size of the change process. A single installed change may involve many new versions of a program. This should take more time and effort than a change involving only a single program.

Number of conditions monitored. Monitoring installed changes is a measure to help reduce the seriousness of problems. The more monitoring that occurs, the greater the assurance to information services management that problems will be detected before they become serious. This type of feedback could be stratified by individual application.

Number of changes not installed on time. It is expected that changes will be installed on schedule. Information services management must monitor conditions where the expected norm is not achieved, such as late implementation of changes. This feedback does not indicate cause, and thus a large number of late installations would warrant investigation to determine the cause.

Summary

Testing software installation is the final step prior to the actual installation. The test involves both the verification of the procedures that place the software into a production status, and the execution of the software by the user(s). Some of the monitoring procedures included in this step may be incorporated by users into their day-to-day procedures for using the software system. Step 10, testing software changes, tests changes to software after it has been installed. However, Step 10 (Chapter 16) can also be used to test changes to the software as it is being developed.

WORK PAPER 15.1 Installation Phase Test Process

#	TEST CRITERIA	ASSESSMENT				RECOMMENDED TEST
		Very Adequate	Adequate	Inadequate	N/A	
1.	Have the accuracy and completeness of the installation been verified?					Examine the completeness of, and the results from, the installation plan.
2.	Have data changes been prohibited during installation?					Compare old and new versions of important data data files.
3.	Has the integrity of the production files been verified?					Confirm their integrity with the users of the production files.
4.	Does an audit trail exist showing installation activity?					Verify the completeness of the audit trail.
5.	Will the integrity of the previous system/version be maintained until the integrity of the new system/version can be verified?					Perform parallel processing.
6.	Assure that a fail-safe installation plan is used for installation?					Determine that the option always exists to revert to the previous system/version.
7.	Assure that adequate security will occur during installation to prevent compromise?					Review the adequacy of the security procedures.
8.	Verify that the defined installation process has been followed?					Confirm compliance on a sampling basis.
9.	Verify that the proper system/version is placed into production on the correct date?					Determine the adequacy of the version control procedures.
10.	Verify that user personnel can understand and use the documentation provided to use the new system/version?					Confirm with users during acceptance testing that their user documentation is adequate.
11.	Verify that all the needed documentation has been prepared in accordance with documentation standards?					Verify on a sampling basis that specified documentation exists and meets standards.
12.	Assure that all involved with the installation are aware of the installation dates and their installation responsibilities?					Confirm with a sample of involved parties their knowledge of installation date(s) and responsibilities.
13.	Assure that the installation performance will be monitored?					Examine the monitoring process.
14.	Assure that the needed operating procedures are complete and installed when needed?					Examine the operating procedures and process for placing those procedures into operation.

541

WORK PAPER 15.2   Restart/Recovery Planning Data

Field Requirements

FIELD	INSTRUCTIONS FOR ENTERING DATA
Application System	The name by which the application is known.
Number	The application numerical identifier.
Change Ident. #.	The sequence number that uniquely identifies the change.
	Note: Restart/recovery planning data, necessary to modify the recovery procedures, comprises the remainder of the form.
Impact on Estimated Total Downtime	If the change affects the downtime, the entire recovery process may have to be reevaluated.
Impact on Estimated Downtime Frequency	The number of times the recovery process will probably have to be executed. An important factor in determining backup data and other procedures. If the change will affect the frequency of downtime, the entire recovery process may have to be reevaluated.
Change in Downtime Risk	The probable loss when a system goes down. May be more important than either the total downtime or downtime frequency. If the loss is potentially very high, management must establish strong controls to lessen the downtime risk. If the change will probably cause a loss, the entire recovery process may have to be reevaluated.
New Program Versions for Recovery	Each new program version must be included in the recovery plan. This action documents the needed changes.
New Files/Data for Recovery	Changes in data normally impact the recovery process. This section documents those changes.
New Recovery Instructions/Procedures	If operating procedures or instructions have to be modified, this section provides space to document those changes.
Date New Version Operational	The date the new programs, files, data, recovery instructions, and procedures must be included in the recovery process.
Comments	Any additional information that may be helpful in modifying the recovery program to better reflect the changed application system.

(Continues)

WORK PAPER 15.2   *(Continued)*

Application   Ident.   Change
System: _____   Number: _____   Ident. # _____

Impact on Estimated Total Downtime

_____

Impact on Estimated Downtime Frequency

_____

Change in Downtime Risk

_____

New Program Versions for Recovery

_____

New Files/Data for Recovery

_____

New Recovery Instructions/Procedures

_____

Date New Version Operational

_____

Comments

_____

WORK PAPER 15.3   Program Change History

Field Requirements

FIELD	INSTRUCTIONS FOR ENTERING DATA
Application System	The name by which the application is known.
Ident. Number	The numerical application identifier.
Program Name	A brief description of the program or its name.
Ident. Number	The program identifier.
Coded by	The programmer who originally coded the program.
Maintained by	The programmer who now maintains the program.
Date Entered into Production	The date on which the program was first used in production.
Version Number	The original version number. *Note:* Program change history provides an audit trail of changes to a program; and is contained in the following fields.
Change ID #	The sequence number that uniquely identifies the change.
New Version Number	The program version number used to code the change.
Coded by	The name of the programmer who coded the change.
Date Entered into Production	The date on which this version went into production.
Comments	Additional information valuable in tracing the history of a change to a program.

(Continues)

WORK PAPER 15.3   *(Continued)*

Application System:_____ Ident. Number _____

_____

Program Name:_____ Ident. Number _____

_____

Coded by: _____

_____

Maintained by: _____

_____

Date Entered into Production: _____ Version # _____

Program Change History

Change Ident. #	New Version #	Coded by	Date Entered into Production	Comments

WORK PAPER 15.4   Production Change Instructions

Field Requirements

FIELD	INSTRUCTIONS FOR ENTERING DATA
Sent to	The name of the person in operations who controls the application system being changed.
Application Control #	A number issued sequentially to control the changes to each application system.
Application Name	The name by which the application is known.
Number	The numerical application identifier.
Change Ident. #	The sequence number that uniquely identifies the change.
	Note: The following production change information includes instructions to computer operations to move programs, job control statements, operator manual procedures, and other items associated with the change to production status. The specific instructions provide both for adding and deleting information.
Resource	The resource that needs to be added to or deleted from the production environment. The most common resources involved in a production change include programs, job statements, and operator manual procedures.
Task	Instructs whether to add or delete the resource from the production status. The Add column indicates that it is to be moved from test status to production status; the Delete column indicates that it is to be removed from production status.
Effective Date	The date on which the tasks are to be performed.
Comments	Additional instructions that help operations personnel perform their assignments. For example, this column might include the location or the source of new pages for the operator's manual.
Prepared by	Usually, the name of the project leader.
Date	The date on which the form was prepared.

(Continues)

WORK PAPER 15.4 *(Continued)*

Sent to: _____

Application
Control #: _____

RE: Application Name
_____ Number: _____

Change
Ident. # : _____

Production Change Instructions

Resource	Task		Effective Dates	Comments
	Add	**Delete**		
Program #				
Program #				
Program #				
Program #				
Job Statements #				
Job Statements #				
Operator Manual procedure #				
Operator Manual procedure #				
Other: _____				
Other: _____				
Other: _____				

Prepared by: _____ Date: _____

WORK PAPER 15.5   Deletion Instructions

Field Requirements

FIELD	INSTRUCTIONS FOR ENTERING DATA
Application Name	The name by which the application is known.
Ident. Number	The numerical application identifier.
Deletion Control Number	A number sequentially issued to control the form.
Sent to	Typically, the person in operations responsible for deleting a program from the application.
Date	The date on which the form was prepared.
From	Usually, the name of the project leader.
Department	The organization or department authorizing the deletion of the program.
	Note: Deletion instructions guide operations personnel to delete unwanted program versions, as follows:
Library	The name or number that identifies the library in which the program resides.
Program version to delete	The program number and version of that program that is to be deleted.
Deletion date	The date on which the program version may be deleted.
Comments	Any additional information helpful to operations staff in performing the required tasks.
Prepared by	The name of the person who prepared the form.
Date	The date on which the form was prepared.

(Continues)

WORK PAPER 15.5   *(Continued)*

Application
Name: _____

Ident.
Number: _____

Deletion
Control #: _____

Sent to: _____   Date: _____

From: _____   Department: _____

Deletion Instructions

Library	Program Version to Delete	Deletion Date	Comments

Prepared by: _____   Date: _____

WORK PAPER 15.6   Form Completion Instructions: Program Change Monitor Notification

Field Requirements

FIELD	INSTRUCTIONS FOR ENTERING DATA
Application System	The name by which the application is known.
Number	The application identifier.
Change Ident. #	The sequence number that uniquely identifies the change.
Description of Change	A description which helps the people monitoring the application gain perspective on the areas impacted.
Date of Change	The date on which the change goes into production. This is the date when the monitoring should commence.
Monitoring	The description of the type of problems to be anticipated. The information should be descriptive enough to tell the monitors both what to look for and what action to take if they find problems. Obviously, those potential problems which are identified are those most likely to occur. However, the monitors should be alert to any type of problem that might occur immediately following introduction of a new program version. The information about the high-probability items is:
	• Area potentially impacted: the report, transactions, or other area in which the individuals monitoring should be looking.
	• Probable impact: this section describes the type of problems that are most likely to occur within the impacted area.
	• Action to take if problem occurs: the people to call, correction to make, or any other action that the individual uncovering the problem should take.
	• Comments: any additional information that might prove helpful to the monitors in attempting to identify problems associated with the program change.
Prepared by	The name of the person who prepared the form, normally the software maintenance analyst.
Date	The date on which the form was prepared.

(Continues)

WORK PAPER 15.6   *(Continued)*

APPLICATION
SYSTEM: _____ NUMBER: _____

CHANGE
IDENT. # _____

<u>DESCRIPTION OF CHANGE</u>

DATE OF CHANGE

_____

MONITORING GUIDELINES

AREA POTENTIALLY IMPACTED	PROBABLE IMPACT	ACTION TO TAKE IF PROBLEM OCCURS	COMMENTS

PREPARED BY: _____   DATE: _____

WORK PAPER 15.7   Form Completion Instructions: System Problem Caused by System Change

Field Requirements

FIELD	INSTRUCTIONS FOR ENTERING DATA
Application name	The name by which the application is known.
Number	The application identifier.
Change Ident. #	The sequence number that uniquely identifies the change.
Problem Date	The date on which the problem was located.
Problem Time	The time within the day the problem was encountered if the time is meaningful.
Problem Control #	A sequential number that controls the form.
Description of Problem	A brief narrative description. Normally, examples of the problem are attached to the form.
Area of Application Affected	This segment is designed to help the software maintenance analyst identify the source of the problem. If it is one of the problems outlined on the program change monitor notification form, the individual completing the form can be very specific regarding the affected area. Otherwise, the individual should attempt to identify areas such as report writing or input validation where the problem seems to originate.
Impact of Problem	The individual identifying the problem should attempt to assess the impact of that problem on the organization. This information is very valuable in determining how fast the problem must be fixed. Ideally this risk would be expressed in quantitative units, such as number of invoices incorrectly processed, dollar loss, number of hours lost because of the problems. It is often helpful to divide the problem into various time periods. This is because some risks are not immediately serious but become serious if they are not corrected by a certain time or date. Some suggested time spans included on the form are: • If not fixed within one hour • If not fixed within one day • If not fixed within one week
Recommendation	The suggestions from the individual uncovering the problem as to what should be done to fix it. This recommendation can either be to correct the errors that have occurred and/or to correct the problems in the application system.
Prepared by	The name of the person who uncovered the system problem caused by the system change.
Date	The date on which the form was prepared.

(Continues)

WORK PAPER 15.7   *(Continued)*

APPLICATION
NAME: _____ NUMBER: _____

CHANGE
IDENT. # _____

PROBLEM DATE _____ PROBLEM TIME _____

PROBLEM
CONTROL # _____

DESCRIPTION OF PROBLEM

AREA OF APPLICATION AFFECTED

IMPACT OF PROBLEM

If not fixed within 1 hour:

If not fixed within 1 day:

If not fixed within 1 week:

RECOMMENDATION

PREPARED BY: _____ DATE: _____

WORK PAPER 15.8   Quality Control Checklist

Field Requirements

FIELD	INSTRUCTIONS FOR ENTERING DATA
Number	A number that sequentially identifies the quality control items, which if positively addressed would indicate that this step has been performed correctly.
Item	The specific quality control item that is used to measure the effectiveness of performing this step.
Response	The testers should indicate in this column whether they have performed the referenced item. The response can be Yes, No, or N/A if it is not appropriate for your organization's testing process.
Comments	This column is used to clarify the Yes, No, or N/A response for the item indicated. Generally the comments column need only be completed for No responses; No responses should be investigated and a determination made as to whether this item needs to be performed before this step can be considered complete.

#	ITEM	RESPONSE			COMMENTS
		YES	NO	N/A	
1.	Is each change reviewed for its impact upon the restart/recovery plan?				
2.	If a change impacts recovery, is the newly estimated downtime calculated?				
3.	If the change impacts recovery, is the new downtime risk estimated?				
4.	Are the changes that need to be made to the recovery process documented?				
5.	Is the notification of changes to the production version of an application documented?				
6.	Are changes to application systems controlled by an application control change number?				
7.	Are there procedures to delete unwanted program versions from the source, test, and object libraries?				
8.	Are program deletion requests documented so that production is authorized to delete programs?				
9.	Are procedures established to ensure that program versions will go into production on the correct day?				
10.	If it affects operating procedures, are operators notified of the date new versions go into production?				
11.	Are procedures established to monitor changed application systems?				

WORK PAPER 15.8   *(Continued)*

#	ITEM	RESPONSE			COMMENTS
		YES	NO	N/A	
12.	Do the individuals monitoring the process receive notification that an application system has been changed?				
13.	Do the people monitoring changes receive clues regarding the areas impacted and the probable problems?				
14.	Do the people monitoring application system changes receive guidance on what actions to take if problems occur?				
15.	Are problems that are detected immediately following changes documented on a special form so they can be traced to a particular change?				
16.	Are the people documenting problems asked to document the impact of the problem on the organization?				
17.	Is software change installation data collected and documented?				
18.	Does information services management review and use the feedback data?				
19.	Does information services management periodically review the effectiveness of installing the software change?				

Step 10: Test Software Changes

Testing and training are as important to software maintenance as they are to new systems development. Frequently, even small changes require extensive testing and training. It is not unusual to spend more time testing a change and training users to operate a new facility than incorporating the change into the application system. This chapter explains the steps that should be performed during testing system changes.

Too frequently, software maintenance has been synonymous with "quick and dirty" programming, which is rarely worth the risk. Frequently, it takes considerable time to correct problems that could have been prevented by adequate testing and training. If testing is properly conducted, it should not take longer to do the job right.

Information technology management has the responsibility for establishing the testing and training procedures for software changes. Many organizations establish change control procedures but do not carry them through testing and training. A checklist is provided for management to review the effectiveness of their testing. See Figure 16.1 for the process for testing changes to software.

Overview

The process outlined in this step is designed to be used two ways. First, it is written as if changes occur after the software has been placed into production. The second and perhaps equally important use will be testing changes during the development of software.

Both of these uses of the process for testing changes require some reiteration of previous steps. For example, the test plan will need to be updated, and the test data will

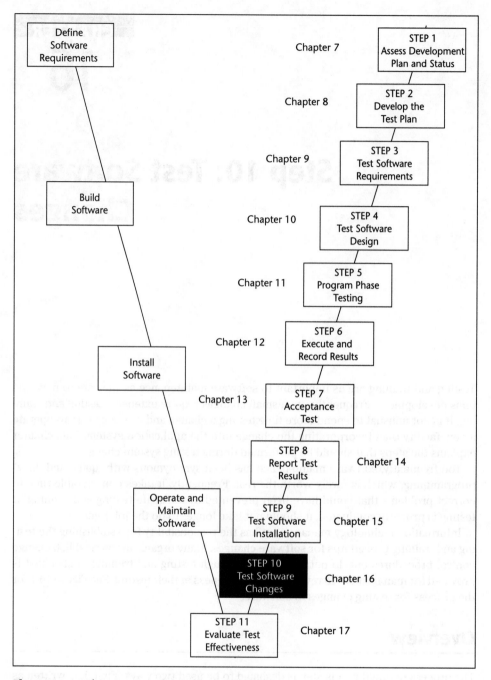

Figure 16.1 The 11-step software testing process.

need to be updated. Since those activities are presented in previous chapters they will not be reiterated in this chapter. Testers are requested to refer back to the appropriate chapter when those topics are addressed. (See Figure 16.1 for chapter reference.)

This process involves three activities. The first is testing a change. The second is testing a change control process. And, the third is testing that training materials and training sessions have been actually prepared and conducted, so that user staff will be adequately prepared to operate the changed software.

Objectives

The overall objective of testing for software changes is to ensure that the changed application will function properly in the operating environment. This includes both the manual and automated segments of the computerized application. The specific objectives of this aspect of testing include:

- Develop tests to detect problems prior to placing the change into production
- Correct problems prior to placing the change in production
- Test the completeness of needed training material
- Involve users in the testing of software changes

Concerns

Information technology management should be concerned about the implementation of the testing and training objectives. These concerns need to be addressed during the development and execution of the testing and training for software changes. The first step in addressing control concerns is identifying the concerns that impact these software changes.

Will the testing process be planned? Inadequate testing is synonymous with unplanned testing. Unless the test is planned, there is no assurance that the results will meet change specifications.

Will the training process be planned? People rarely decide on the spur of the moment to hold a training class or develop training material. What tends to happen is that training is given one-on-one after problems begin to occur. This is a costly method of training.

Will system problems be detected during testing? Even the best training plans rarely uncover all the potential system problems. What is hoped is that the serious problems will be detected during testing.

Will training problems be detected during testing? How people will react to production situations is more difficult to predict than how computerized applications will perform. Thus, the objective in training should be to prepare people for all possible situations.

Will already detected testing and training problems be corrected prior to the implementation of the change? An unforgivable error is to detect a problem and then fail to correct it before serious problems occur. Appropriate records should be maintained and controls implemented so that detected errors will be immediately acted upon.

Workbench

Figure 16.2 illustrates the workbench to test a changed version of the software. The software being changed can be a new version of developing software, or a new version of production software. The testers need to obtain documentation and results from testing a previous version of the software, as well as the documentation of the changes to the software. The workbench shows that the test plan and test data need to be updated or recreated if they are inadequate. Testers must be satisfied that the change control process can adequately control the versions on the program library as well as changes to system documentation. Testers then test both the changed software and the user materials associated with that change.

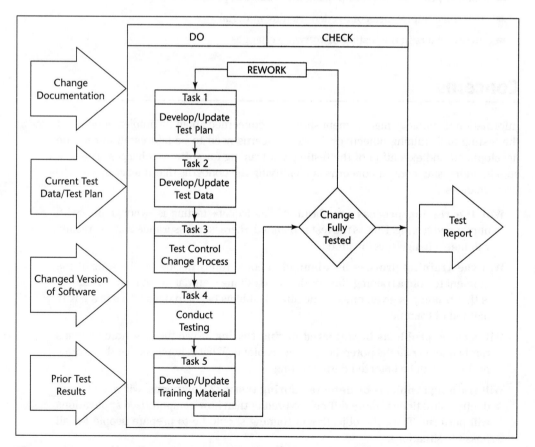

Figure 16.2   Workbench to test changed version of software.

Input

The testers need four inputs to adequately perform testing a changed version of software as follows:

1. **Change documentation.** Full documentation regarding the change, emphasizing which data elements are changed as well as which programs are changed.

2. **Current test data/test plan.** The testers need their documentation and test data used for testing the prior version of the software.

3. **Changed version of software.** The new version of the software on the test library.

4. **Prior test results.** The results produced from testing the prior version. These will be used to determine that the changed portions were corrected, and the unchanged portions still work correctly.

Do Procedures

The following five tasks should be performed to effectively test a changed version of software.

Task 1: Develop/Update the Test Plan

The test plan for software maintenance is a shorter, more directed version of a test plan used for a new application system. While new application testing can take many weeks or months, software maintenance testing often must be done within a single day or a few hours. Because of time constraints, many of the steps that might be performed individually in a new system are combined or condensed into a short time span. This increases the need for planning so that all aspects of the test can be executed within the allotted time.

The types of testing will vary based upon the implemented change. For example, if a report is modified, there is little need to test recovery and backup plans. On the other hand, if new files are created or processing procedures changed, then restart and recovery should be tested.

The preparation of a test plan is a two-part process. The first part is the determination of what types of tests should be conducted, and the second part is the plan for how to conduct them. Both parts are important in software maintenance testing.

Elements to be tested (types of testing) are:

- Changed transactions
- Changed programs
- Operating procedures
- Control group procedures
- User procedures

- Intersystem connections

- Job control language

- Interface to systems software

- Execution of interface to software systems

- Security

- Backup/recovery procedures

The test plan should list the testing objective, the method of testing, and the desired result. In addition, regression testing might be used to verify that unchanged segments have not been unintentionally altered. Intersystem connections should be tested to ensure that all systems are properly modified to handle the change.

An acceptance test plan is included as Work Paper 16.1. This work paper should be completed by the software maintenance analyst and countersigned by the individual responsible for accepting the changed system. The information contained on the work paper is described on the form's completion instructions sheet. Both forms are found at the end of the chapter.

Task 2: Develop/Update the Test Data

Data must be prepared for testing all the areas changed during a software maintenance process. For many applications, the existing test data will be sufficient to test the new change. However, in many situations new test data will need to be prepared.

In some cases, the preparation of test data can be significantly different for software maintenance than for new systems. For example, when the system is operational it may be possible to test the application in a live operational mode, thus eliminating the need for technical test data, and enabling maintenance software analysts to use the same input the users of the application prepare. Special accounts can be established to accumulate test data processed during testing in a production mode. The information in these accounts can then be eliminated after the test, which negates the effect of entering test data into a production environment.

It is important to test both what should be accomplished, as well as what can go wrong. Most tests do a good job of verifying that the specifications have been implemented properly. Where testing frequently is inadequate is in verifying the unanticipated conditions. Included in this category are:

- Transactions with erroneous data

- Unauthorized transactions

- Transactions entered too early

- Transactions entered too late

- Transactions that do not correspond with master data contained in the application

- Grossly erroneous transactions, such as transactions that do not belong to the application being tested

- Transactions with larger values in the fields than anticipated

These types of transactions can be designed by doing a simple risk analysis scenario. The risk analysis scenario involves brainstorming with key people involved in the application, such as users, maintenance systems analysts, and auditors. These people attempt to ask all the questions, such as, "What if this type of error were entered? What would happen if too large a value were entered in this field?"

There are three methods that can be used to develop/update test data as follows:

Method 1: Update Existing Test Data

If test files have been created for a previous version they can be used for testing a change. However, the test data will need to be updated to reflect the changes to the software. Note that testers may wish to use both versions in conducting testing. Version 1 is to test that the unchanged portions perform now as they did in the previous versions. The new version is to test the changes. Updating the test data should follow the same processes used in creating new test data.

Method 2: Create New Test Data

The creation of new test data for maintenance follows the same methods as creating test data for a new software system.

Method 3: Use Production Data for Testing

Tests are performed using some or all of the production data for test purposes (date-modified, of course), particularly when there are no function changes. Using production data for test purposes may result in the following impediments to effective testing:

Missing test transactions. The transaction types on a production data file may be limited. For example, if the tester wants to test an override of a standard price, that transaction may not occur on the production data file.

Multiple tests of the same transaction. Production data usually represents the production environment, in which 80 percent to 90 percent of the transactions are of approximately the same type. This means that some transaction types are not tested at all, while others are tested hundreds of times.

Unknown test results. An important part of testing is to validate that correct results are produced. When testers create test transactions, they have control over the expected results. When production data is used, however, testers must manually calculate the correct processing results, perhaps causing them to misinterpret the intent of the transaction and thereby to misinterpret the results.

Lack of ownership. Production data is owned by the production area, whereas test data created by testers is owned by the testers. Some testers are more involved and interested in test data they created themselves than in test data borrowed from another owner.

Although these potential impediments might cause production data testing to be ineffective, steps can be taken to improve its usefulness. Production data should not be completely excluded as a source of test data.

Production Data Definition

The following categories of production data can be used in testing:

Transaction files. Business transactions entered into business systems (e.g., products to be shipped on a particular day).

Business master files. A collection of semipermanent business data, generally referred to by accountants as ledgers (e.g., a ledger or file of customers, employees for payroll purposes, or vendors in an accounts payable file).

Master files of business data. Files that record processing data used by business software (e.g., lists of products and prices, taxing communities and sales tax rates, and employee pay rates).

Error files. Lists of error transactions or error suspense files (i.e., transactions awaiting correction).

Operations, communications, database, or accounting logs. Files containing information about the operating environment (e.g., the IBM Systems Management Facility (SMF), data, which reports files used, execution time, and invalid attempts to access). These logs can be used to test states and attributes and the processing manipulation of various transaction types.

Manual logs. Maintained by users of the software to record such items as error messages, performance characteristics, results of processing, and questions to be answered.

This production data can be used for test purposes. In some instances, it yields test transactions (e.g., a transaction file); in other cases, it provides information about performance results (e.g., an SMF log or job accounting log). To use production data as test data, testers first must determine the type of production data to use (e.g., a business transaction file). Then they can perform one or more of the following five steps to convert that production file to a test file:

1. Select the First Batch of Records

Production files often are too lengthy to use for test purposes and thus may need to be shortened. One way to do this is to determine the number of records needed and extract that number from the beginning of the file. Some software packages (e.g., audit software) and utility programs can create files using this method. For example, testers who want 500 test records need only type a command such as "SELECT THE FIRST 500 RECORDS" into a data extract software system to create a new test file with that number of records.

2. Protect Production Files from Modification

Many files include protection procedures to prevent them from being modified or changed during testing, particularly when business master files or master files of business data are used. For example, testers processing an accounts receivable file can use the production file; initiating an update or change command to the file does not change the file, but instead creates a memo of that change.

3. Select a Random Sample of Transactions

This method develops a random subset of the production file. The benefit of taking a random sample is that it helps create a test file representative of the various transactions, and in the same type and frequency as on the production file. Although random sampling is typically performed using a statistical software package, audit groups use software that is capable of this type of selection. The selection usually indicates the appropriate type of sampling method (e.g., selecting every nth record or using a random generator facility). These packages also report the number of records that need to be selected, depending on the size of the production file, to obtain an accurate representation of the file.

4. Browse through the Production File

This method combines using a production file and creating individual test conditions. The production file is browsed to determine the type of transactions on the file. Appropriate types of transactions are then copied for test purposes.

Testers do not actually use the production data for test purposes; they copy the data and values in all or part of the records for incorporation into test data. This method is better than creating test data because it uses realistic production values and avoids the trap of using the same condition repeatedly, which is a typical result of the testers' inability to conceptualize the production file's contents.

5. Do Parallel Testing

This method is effective only when minimal changes are made between the current version and the new version of the production system. It uses all production files to compare the test results with previously performed production results.

There are two ways to use this method effectively. The first is to change the production files to permit testers to compare the test results with the production results. This comparison may require adding a few more products or processing conditions to the master tape. The second way is to use regression testing, in which a new function's performance is irrelevant. What is important here is that those areas of processing not affected by the change continue to produce correct results. This method seeks to validate the unchanged rather than the changed portions of the software. Coupled with other methods for using production data to test for regression, this method can also be used to validate the changed portions.

Task 3: Test the Control Change Process

Listed next are three subtasks commonly used to control and record changes. If the staff performing the corrections do not have such a process, the testers can give them these subtasks and then request the work papers when complete. Testers should verify completeness using these three subtasks as a guide:

1. Identify and Control Change

An important aspect of changing a system is identifying which parts of the system will be impacted by that change. The impact may be in any part of the application system, both manual and computerized, as well as in the supporting software system. Regardless of whether impacted areas will require changes, at a minimum there should be an investigation into the extent of the impact.

The types of analytical action helpful in determining the parts impacted include:

- Review system documentation.
- Review program documentation.
- Review undocumented changes.
- Interview user personnel regarding procedures.
- Interview operations personnel regarding procedures.
- Interview job control coordinator regarding changes.
- Interview systems support personnel if the implementation may require deviations from standards and/or IT departmental procedures.

This is a very important step in the systems change process, as it controls the change through a change identification number and through change documentation. The time and effort spent executing this step is usually returned in the form of more effective implementation procedures and fewer problems during and after the implementation of the change. A change control form is presented as Work Paper 16.2. It is used to control and record the change.

2. Document Change Needed on Each Data Element

Whereas changes in processing normally impact only a single program or a small number of interrelated programs, changes to data may impact many applications. Thus, changes that impact data may have a more significant effect on the organization than those that impact processing.

Changes can impact data in any of the following ways:

Length. The data element may be lengthened or shortened.

Value. The value or codes used in data elements may be expanded, modified, or reduced.

Consistency. The value contained in data elements may not be the same in various applications or databases; thus, it is necessary to improve consistency.

Reliability. The accuracy of the data may be changed.

In addition, changes to a data element may require further documentation. Organizations in a database environment need to expend additional effort to ensure that data documentation is consistent, reliable, and understandable. Much of this effort will be translated into data documentation.

A form for documenting data changes is presented as Work Paper 16.3. This form should be used to provide an overview of the data change. In a database environment, a copy of the data definition form should be attached to the data change form as a control vehicle.

3. Document Changes Needed
in Each Program

The implementation of most changes will require some programming alterations. Even a change of data attributes will often necessitate program changes. Some of these will be minor in nature, while others may be extremely difficult and time-consuming to implement.

The change required for each program should be documented on a separate form. This serves several purposes: First, it provides detailed instructions at the individual program level regarding what is required to change the program; second, it helps ensure that changes will be made and not lost—it is difficult to overlook a change that is formally requested; third, and equally important, it provides a detailed audit trail of changes, in the event problems occur.

Work Paper 16.4 is a form for documenting program changes. It should be completed even though doing so may require more time than the implementation of the change itself. The merits of good change documentation have been repeatedly established.

Task 4: Conduct Testing

Software change testing is normally conducted by both the user and software maintenance test team. The testing is designed to provide the user assurance that the change has been properly implemented. Another role of the software maintenance test team is to aid the user in conducting and evaluating the test.

Testing for software maintenance is normally not extensive. In an on-line environment, the features would be installed and the user would test them in a regular production environment. In a batch environment, special computer runs must be set up to run the acceptance testing (because of the cost, these runs are sometimes eliminated).

An effective method for conducting software maintenance testing is to prepare a checklist providing both the administrative and technical data needed to conduct the test. This ensures that everything is ready at the time the test is to be conducted. A checklist for conducting a software maintenance acceptance test is illustrated in Work Paper 16.5. This form should be prepared by the software maintenance analyst as an aid in helping the user conduct the test. The information contained on the conduct acceptance test checklist is described on the form's completion instructions sheet; both forms are found at the end of the chapter.

Task 5: Develop/Update
the Training Material

Updating training material for users, and training users, is not an integral part of many software change processes. Therefore, this task description describes a process for updating training material and performing that training. Where training is not part of software maintenance, the testers can give the software maintenance analyst these materials to use in developing training materials. If training is an integral part of the software maintenance process, the testers can use the material in this task as a guide for evaluating the completion of updating training materials.

Training is an often-overlooked aspect of software maintenance. Many of the changes are small; this fosters the belief that training is not needed. Also, the fact that many changes originate in the user area leads the software maintenance analyst to the conclusion that the users already know what they want and have trained their staff accordingly. All these assumptions may be wrong.

The software maintenance analyst should evaluate each change for its impact on the procedures performed by people. If the change impacts those procedures, then training material should be prepared. However, changes that increase performance and have no impact on users of the system do not require training unless they affect the operation of the system. In that case, computer operations personnel would need training. Training cannot be designed by someone who is unfamiliar with existing training material. The software maintenance change is incorporated into the application system. The training requirements are likewise incorporated into existing training material. Therefore, it behooves the application project personnel to maintain an inventory of training material.

Training Material Inventory Form

Most application systems have limited training materials. The more common types of training materials include:

- Orientation to the project narrative
- User manuals
- Illustrations of completed forms and instructions for completing them
- Explanation and action to take on error listings
- Explanation of reports and how to use them
- Explanation of input data and how to enter it

A form for inventorying training material is included as Work Paper 16.6. This form should be completed and filed with the software maintenance analyst. Whenever a change is made, the form can be duplicated, and at that point the "needs updating" column can be completed to indicate whether training material must be changed as a result of incorporating the maintenance need. The columns to be completed on the form are explained on the form's completion instructions sheet. Both forms are found at the end of the chapter.

Training Plan Work Paper

The training plan work paper is a why, who, what, where, when, and how approach to training. The individual developing the plan must answer those questions about each change in order to determine the scope of training programs. Points to ponder in developing training programs are as follows:

Why conduct training? Do the changes incorporated into the application system necessitate training people?

Who should be trained? If training is needed, then it must be determined which individuals, categories of people, or departments require that training.

What training is required? The training plan must determine the content of the necessary training material.

Where should training be given? The location of the training session, or dissemination of the training material, can impact how and when the material is presented.

When should training be given? Confusion might ensue if people are trained too far in advance of the implementation of new procedures. For example, even training provided a few days prior to the change may cause confusion because people might be uncertain as to whether to follow the new or the old procedure. In addition, it may be necessary to conduct training both immediately before and immediately after the change to reinforce the new procedures and to answer questions immediately after the new procedures are installed.

How should the training material be designed? The objective of training is to provide people with the tools and procedures necessary to do their job. The type of change will frequently determine the type of training material to be developed.

What are the expected training results? The developers of the training plan should have in mind the behavior changes or skills to be obtained through the training sessions. They should also determine whether training is effective.

Work Paper 16.7 documents the training plan by providing space to indicate the above types of information. In addition, the responsible individual and the dates needed for training can also be documented on the form. The information contained on the training plan work paper is described on the form's completion instructions sheet. Both are found at the end of the chapter.

Prepare Training Material

The material judged necessary to the training plan must be prepared. The tasks required to perform this step are similar to those used in making a change to an application system. In most instances, training material will exist, but will need to be modified because of the change. Changes in the program must be accompanied by changes in the training material. Individuals responsible for modifying training should consider the following tasks:

- Identifying the impact of the change on people
- Determining what type of training must be "unlearned" (people must be stopped from doing certain tasks)
- Determining whether "unlearning" is included in the training material
- Making plans to delete outmoded training material
- Determining what new learning is needed (this should come from the training plan)
- Determining where in the training material that new learning should be inserted
- Preparing the training material that will teach people the new skills (this should be specified in the training plan)

- Designing that material
- Determining the best method of training (this should be documented in the training plan)
- Developing procedures so that the new training material will be incorporated into the existing training material on the right date, and that other supportive training will occur at the proper time

An inventory should be maintained of the new/modified training modules. This is in addition to the training material inventory, which is in hardcopy. The training modules are designed to be supportive of that training material. This helps determine what modules need to be altered to achieve the behavior changes/new skills required because of the change.

Work Paper 16.8 is a training module inventory form. This should be completed by the individual responsible for training. The information contained on the form is described on the form's completion instructions, and both are found at the end of the chapter.

Conduct Training

The training task is primarily one of coordination in that it must ensure that everything needed for training has been prepared. The coordination normally involves these steps:

- Scheduling training dates
- Notifying the people who should attend training
- Obtaining training facilities
- Obtaining instructors
- Reproducing the material in sufficient quantity for all those requiring the material
- Training instructors
- Setting up the classroom or meeting room in a desired fashion

Many times training will be provided through manuals or special material delivered to the involved parties. The type of training should be determined when the training plan is developed and the material is prepared.

A training checklist should be prepared. A sample checklist for conducting training is illustrated in Work Paper 16.9. The individual responsible for training should prepare this checklist for use during the training period to ensure all the needed training is provided. The information included on the conduct training checklist is described on the form's completion instructions sheet. Both forms are found at the end of the chapter.

Check Procedures

Work Paper 16.10 is a quality control checklist for this step. It is designed so that Yes responses indicate good test practices; No responses warrant additional investigation. A Comments column is provided to explain No responses and to record results of investigation. The N/A column is used when the checklist item is not applicable to the test situation.

Output

The output will answer these questions and/or provide the following information:

Automated Application Acceptable?

The automated segment of an application is acceptable if it meets the change specification requirements. If it fails to meet those measurable objectives, the system is unacceptable and should be returned for additional modification. This requires setting measurable objectives, preparing test data, and then evaluating the results of those tests.

The responsibility for determining if the application is acceptable belongs to the user. In applications with multiple users, one user may be appointed responsible. In other instances, all users may test their own segments or they may act as a committee to verify whether the system is acceptable. The poorest approach is to delegate this responsibility to the information technology department.

Test results can be verified through manual or automated means. The tediousness and effort required for manual verification has caused many information technology professionals to shortcut the testing process. When automated verification is used, the process is not nearly as time consuming, and tends to be performed more accurately.

A difficult question to answer on acceptability is whether 100 percent correctness is required on the change. For example, if 100 items are checked and 99 prove correct, should the application be rejected because of the one remaining problem? The answer to this question depends upon the importance of that one remaining item.

Users should expect that their systems will operate as specified. However, this may mean that the user may decide to install the application and then correct the error after implementation. The user has two options when installing a change known to have an error. The first is to ignore the problem and live with the results. For example, if a heading is misplaced or misspelled, the user may decide that that type of error, while annoying, does not affect the user of the output results. The second option is to make the adjustments manually. For example, if necessary, final totals could be manually calculated and added to the reports. In either case, the situation should be temporary.

Automated Application Segment Failure Notification

Each failure noted during testing the automated segment of the application system should be documented. If it is known that the change will not be corrected until after the application is placed into production, then a problem identification form should be completed to document the problem. However, if the change is to be corrected during the testing process, then a special form should be used for that purpose.

A form for notifying the software maintenance analyst that a failure has been uncovered in the automated segment of the application is illustrated in Work Paper 16.11. This form is to be used as a correction vehicle within the test phase, and should be prepared by the individual uncovering the failure. It is then sent to the software maintenance analyst in charge of the change for correction. The information contained on the automated application segment test failure notification form is described on the form's completion instructions sheet. Both forms are found at the end of the chapter.

Manual Segment Acceptable?

Users must make the same acceptability decisions on the manual segments of the application system as they make on the automated segments. Many of the manual segments do not come under the control of the maintenance systems analyst. However, this does not mean that the correct processing of the total system is not of concern to the maintenance systems analyst.

The same procedures followed in verifying the automated segment should be followed in verifying the manual segment. The one difference is that there are rarely automated means for verifying manual processing. Verifying manual segments can take as much—if not more—time than verifying the automated segment. The more common techniques to verify the correctness of the manual segment include:

Observation. The individual responsible for verification observes people performing the tasks. That individual usually develops a checklist from the procedures and then determines whether the individual performs all of the required steps.

Examination. The people performing the task need to evaluate whether they can correctly perform the task. For example, in a data entry operation, the data entry operator may be asked to enter that information in a controlled mode.

Verification. The individual responsible for determining that the training is correct examines the results of processing from the trained people to determine whether they comply with the expected processing.

If the training is not acceptable, the user must decide again whether to delay the change. In most instances, the user will not delay the implementation of change if there are only minor problems in training, but instead will attempt to compensate for those problems during processing. On the other hand, if it becomes apparent that the users are ill-equipped to use the application, then the change should be delayed until the individuals are better trained.

The methods that users can incorporate to overcome minor training deficiencies include:

Restricted personnel. The new types of processing are only performed by people who have successfully completed the training. Thus, those who need more skills have time to obtain them before they begin using the new procedures or data.

Supervisory review. Supervisors can spend extra time reviewing the work of people to be assured that the tasks are performed correctly.

Information technology assistance. The software maintenance analysts/programmers can work with user personnel during an interim period to help them process the information correctly.

Overtime. Crash-training sessions can be held in the evening or on weekends to bring the people up to the necessary skill level.

Training Failure Notification Form

Training failures should be documented at the same level of detail as are failures of the computerized segment. However, procedural errors can cause as many serious problems as can incorrect computer code. Unless these failures are documented, people can easily overlook the problem and assume someone else will correct it.

Each failure uncovered in training should be documented on a training failure notification form. This form should be completed by the individual who uncovers the problem, and then presented to the individual responsible for training for necessary action. A form that can be used to document training failures is illustrated in Work Paper 16.12. The information contained on the training failure notification form is described on the form's completion instructions sheet. Both are found at the end of the chapter.

Guidelines

The following should help in performing the step.

Making Test Adjustments

Corrections to problems should be implemented in the application system and then the system should be retested. When a new change is entered to the application system (even a change made during testing), the maintenance software analyst should not assume that previously tested segments will work correctly. It is quite possible that the new change has caused problems to unchanged portions. Unfortunately, it may mean that much of the testing already completed may have to be repeated.

Making Training Adjustments

Identified training adjustments can be made in numerous ways. The methods selected will obviously depend on the type of failure uncovered. In some instances, a single individual may have been overlooked and the training can be presented to that person individually. In other cases, new training material may have to be prepared and taught.

The procedures described in this section for developing training materials apply equally to correcting training materials. In addition, if people have been improperly instructed, steps may have to be taken to inform them of the erroneous training and then to provide them with the proper training.

Software Change Feedback

Without feedback, it is difficult to continually improve the training and testing procedures. The feedback is a byproduct of executing the software change. The incorporation of feedback mechanisms into the training and testing procedures should be specified by information technology management. They should determine the types of feedback they want included to monitor the change and then take the steps necessary to ensure that they get it. The frequency with which information technology management sees feedback information is a function of the effectiveness of the software change.

The types of feedback information that have proved beneficial in monitoring testing and training include:

Number of tests. This category shows the number of acceptance tests conducted for each change. It should also show which changes have not conducted acceptance tests. This will provide information technology management with insight into the effectiveness of acceptance testing and the use of acceptance testing.

Number of problems detected during test. The success of program testing can be determined by the number of problems detected during acceptance testing. However, the number of errors may be attributable to poor user specifications or misunderstanding of user specifications.

Size of changes to training manuals. The number of pages of training material that need to be developed should be monitored. This helps identify the allocation of information technology resources and helps explain the cost of making changes.

Training problems detected during testing. The frequency with which training problems occur indicates the quality of material and training sessions provided. However, it too, can be attributable to making generally poor user specifications.

Testing/training schedules missed. This feedback data indicates when changes fall behind scheduled implementation dates because of the acceptance testing process. Obviously, many of the problems may be attributable to problems in the previous tasks.

Testing/training cost overruns. This feedback data indicates when acceptance testing costs exceed acceptance testing budgets. This can be due to problems in the previous tasks or improperly planned testing/training.

Number of training sessions. This feedback data measures the amount of time and effort that go into conducting training because of system changes. Again, it measures the use of information technology resources.

Summary

This step contains a process for testing changes to a software system. The changes should be incorporated into a new version of the software. The version should be controlled in the software change process. Documentation should also be prepared reflecting the changes. That documentation should update the existing software system documentation.

In this step testers are required to update their test plan, test data, and other test documentation. It is equally important that test documentation be maintained as system documentation. This is because testing is frequently a more costly aspect of change than the process of making the change itself.

Changes occur during both the development and maintenance cycles. The same process can be used for testing both categories of changes. Since much of the 11-step test process incorporates testing changes, testers should have a good familiarity with Steps 1 through 9 before using this step.

The remaining step is designed to evaluate the effectiveness of the test process. This is discussed in Step 11 in the following chapter.

WORK PAPER 16.1   Form Completion Instructions: Acceptance Test Plan

Field Requirements

FIELD	INSTRUCTIONS FOR ENTERING DATA
Application Name	The name by which the application is known.
Number	The application identifier.
Change Ident. #	The sequence number that uniquely identifies the change.
Individual responsible for test	The name of the individual or individuals who will be conducting the test. This normally is the user and the application systems analyst/programmer.
Test Plan	The steps that need to be followed in conducting the test. For the functional, regression, stress, and performance types of testing, these test characteristics need to be defined:
	• Change objective: the description of the objective of the change that was installed. This should be specific so that test planning can be based on the characteristics of the objective.
	• Method of testing: the type of test that will be conducted to verify that the objective is achieved.
	• Desired result: the expected result from conducting the test. If this result is achieved, the implementation can be considered successful, while failure to meet this result means an unsuccessful implementation.
Regression Test Plan	The tests and procedures to be followed to be assured that unchanged segments of the application system have not been inadvertently changed by software maintenance.
Intersystem Test Plan	The tests to be conducted to assure that data flowing from and to other systems will be correctly handled after the change.
Comments	Additional information that might prove helpful in conducting or verifying the test results.
Individual who accepts tested application	The name of the individual who should review this test plan because of the responsibility to accept the change after successful testing.
Date	The date on which the form was completed.

(Continues)

WORK PAPER 16.1   *(Continued)*

APPLICATION
NAME: _____ NUMBER: _____

CHANGE
IDENT. # _____

INDIVIDUAL RESPONSIBLE FOR TEST: _____

TEST PLAN

CHANGE OBJECTIVE	METHOD OF TESTING	DESIRED RESULTS

REGRESSION TEST PLAN

INTERSYSTEM TEST PLAN

COMMENTS

INDIVIDUAL WHO ACCEPTS TESTED APPLICATION	DATE

WORK PAPER 16.2   Change Control Form

Field Requirements

FIELD	INSTRUCTIONS FOR ENTERING DATA
Application System	The name by which the application system is known.
Application Identification #	The identification number of the application system.
Change Identification #	The control number for the change.
Description of Change	The solution and general terms for the change, such as issue a new report, add an input data edit, or utilize a new processing routine.
Changes Required	All impacted areas with instructions for the changes to be made or investigations to be undertaken regarding the impact of the proposed solution. The type of items affected include:

- data elements
- programs
- job control language
- operations manuals
- user training
- user manuals

For each of the affected items, the following information should be provided:

- Item affected: the program, data element, job control or other
- Item identification: the program number or other method of identifying the affected item

FIELD	INSTRUCTIONS FOR ENTERING DATA
Prepared by	The name of the person completing the form.
Date	The date on which the form was completed.

Application
System: _____

Application
Ident. #: _____

Change
Ident. # _____

Description of Change:

_____

Change Overview:

_____

Changes Required

Item	Item Identification	Comments

Prepared by: _____   Date: _____

WORK PAPER 16.3   Data Change Form

Field Requirements

FIELD	INSTRUCTIONS FOR ENTERING DATA
Application System	The name by which the application is known
Application Identification #	The number used to identify the application system.
Change Identification #	The sequential number used to identify the change.
Data Element Name	The name by which the data element is known.
Data Identification #	The number used to uniquely identify the data element. In a data dictionary system, this should be the data dictionary data element number.
Record Name	The record or records in which the data element is contained.
Record Identification #	The number that describes the record or records in which the data element is contained.
File Name	The file or files in which the data element is contained.
File Identification #	The numbers that uniquely describe the file or files in which the data element is contained.
Assigned to	The name of the person, function, or department responsible for making the change to the data element and the associated records and files.
Date Required	The date by which the change should be made (pending user approval).
Data Change	The type of change to be made on the data element. The options on the form include: • Add data element. • Delete data element. • Modify data element attributes. • Modify a data element description.
Description	A detailed narrative description (with examples when applicable) explaining the type of change that must be made to the data element. When a data dictionary is used, the data dictionary form should be attached to the data change form.
Comments	Information helpful in implementing the data change.
Prepared by	The name of the person who completed the form.
Date	The date on which the form was completed.

(Continues)

WORK PAPER 16.3   *(Continued)*

Application System: _____	Application Ident. #: _____	Change Ident. #: _____

Data Element
Name: _____   Data Ident. #: _____

Record
Name: _____   Record Ident. #: _____

File
Name: _____   File Ident. #: _____

Assigned to: _____   Date Required: _____

Date Change

❑ Add element.
❑ Delete element.
❑ Modify element attributes.
❑ Modify element description.

Description of Change

Comments

Prepared by: _____   Date: _____

WORK PAPER 16.4   Program Change Form

Field Requirements

FIELD	INSTRUCTIONS FOR ENTERING DATA
Application System	The name by which the application to be changed is known.
Application Identification #	The identifier that uniquely describes the application system.
Change Identification #	The sequential number used to identify the change.
Program Name	The name by which the program to be changed is known.
Number	The number that uniquely identifies the program.
Version Number	The version number that will be assigned to the altered program.
Date Required	The date on which the change is to be implemented, assuming the user approves the changes.
Assigned to	The name of the person who will make the change in the program.
Description of Change	A narrative description of the change to be made to this specific program. It should provide examples of programs produced before and after the change.
Source Statements	A description of the source statement or statements that should be changed, together with the change to be made. The change may be described in terms of specifications rather than specific source statements.
Comments	Tips and techniques on how best to install the change in the application system.
Prepared by	The name of the person who completed the form.
Date	The date on which the form was completed.

Application
System: _____

Application
Ident. #: _____

Change
Ident. #: _____

Program Name: _____   Number: _____   Version #: _____

New Version #: _____

Date
Required: _____

Assigned
to: _____

Description of Change

Source Statement Affected

Comments

Prepared by: _____   Date: _____

WORK PAPER 16.5 Form Completion Instructions: Acceptance Test Checklist

Field Requirements

FIELD	INSTRUCTIONS FOR ENTERING DATA
Application Name	The name by which the application is known.
Number	The application identifier.
Change Ident. #	The sequence number that uniquely identifies the change.
Administrative Data	The administrative data relates to the management of the test and normally includes the following information:

- Date of test
- Location of test
- Time of test
- Information services person in charge of test
- User person in charge of test
- Computer time
- Other: Any other administrative data needed

Technical Data	The resources needed to conduct the acceptance test and the location of those resources. The information that should be documented about the needed resources includes:

- #: the sequential number of the resources needed
- Resource needed: the exact resource needed
- Location: the physical location of that resource. In many acceptance tests, the resources are marshalled in a common area to await conducting the test.

(Continues)

WORK PAPER 16.5 *(Continued)*

APPLICATION
NAME: _____ NUMBER: _____

CHANGE
IDENT. # _____

ADMINISTRATIVE DATA

Date of test _____

Location of test _____

Time of test _____

Information services person in charge of test _____

User person in charge of test _____

Computer time available _____

TECHNICAL DATA

#	RESOURCE NEEDED	LOCATION	AVAILABLE		
			YES	NO	N/A
1.	Test transactions				
2.	Master files/data base				
3.	Operator instructions				
4.	Special media/forms				
5.	Acceptance criteria				
6.	Input support personnel				
7.	Output support personnel				
8.	Control group				
9.	External control proof				
10.	Backup/recovery plan				
11.	Security plan				
12.	Error message actions				

PREPARED BY: _____ DATE: _____

WORK PAPER 16.6   Form Completion Instructions: Training Material Inventory

Field Requirements

FIELD	INSTRUCTIONS FOR ENTERING DATA
Application Name	The name by which the application is known.
Number	The application identifier.
Change Ident. #	The sequence number that uniquely identifies the change.
Training Material Name	The name or number by which the training material is known.
Training Material Description	A brief narrative description of what is contained in the training material.
Needs Updating	Columns to be completed whenever a change is installed. The columns provide an indication of whether the training material needs updating (Yes column) or does not need updating (No column).
Prepared by	The name of the individual responsible for maintaining the inventory.
Date	The last date on which the inventory was updated.

(Continues)

WORK PAPER 16.6   *(Continued)*

APPLICATION
NAME: _____ NUMBER: _____

CHANGE
IDENT. # _____

AREA NAME	TRAINING MATERIAL DESCRIPTION	NEEDS UPDATING	
		YES	NO

PREPARED BY: _____ DATE: _____

WORK PAPER 16.7   Form Completion Instructions: Training Plan

Field Requirements

FIELD	INSTRUCTIONS FOR ENTERING DATA
Application Name	The name by which the application is known.
Number	The application identifier.
Change Ident. #	The sequence number that uniquely identifies the change.
Individual responsible for training	The individual with the overall responsibility for ensuring that all the training material is prepared, taught, and evaluated prior to the implementation of the change.
Training Plan	The details of why, who, what, where, when, how, and the results to be derived from the training plan. The remainder of the form deals with this plan.
#	A sequential number indicating the number of the group to be trained.
Group needing training	The name of the individual, type of person, or department requiring training. The groups to consider include:

- Transaction origination staff: the people who originate data into the application system.
- Data entry clerk: the person who transcribes data to computer media.
- Control group—information services: the group responsible for ensuring that all input is received and that output is reasonable.
- Control group—user: the group in the user area responsible for the accuracy, completeness, and authorization of data.
- Computer operations: the group responsible for running the application on computer hardware.
- Records retention: the group or groups responsible for saving backup data.
- Third-party customers: people with unsatisfied needs or people who are the ultimate recipients of reports, such as invoices.
- User management and staff: the group responsible for the application.
- Other: any other involved party requiring training.

FIELD	INSTRUCTIONS FOR ENTERING DATA
Training Approach	The why, what, where, when, and how of the training plan.
Desired Results	The expected result, behavior change, or skills to be gained from the training material.
Training Dates	Important dates for implementing the training plan; the most common dates are:

- Date training material prepared
- Date training can commence
- Date training to be completed

FIELD	INSTRUCTIONS FOR ENTERING DATA
Comments	Any material helpful in designing, teaching, or evaluating the training material.
Individual who accepts training as sufficient	The name of the individual or department who must agree if the training is adequate. This individual should also concur with the training plan.
Date	The date the training plan was developed.

(Continues)

WORK PAPER 16.7 *(Continued)*

APPLICATION
NAME: _____ NUMBER: _____

CHANGE
IDENT. # _____

INDIVIDUAL RESPONSIBLE FOR TRAINING _____

TRAINING PLAN

#	GROUP NEEDING TRAINING	TRAINING APPROACH	DESIRED RESULT
1.	Transaction origination staff		
2.	Data entry clerk		
3.	Control group—information services		
4.	Control group—user		
5.	Computer operations		
6.	Records retention		
7.	Third-party customers		
8.	User management and staff		
9.	Other: _____		
10.	Other: _____		

TRAINING DATES

Date training material prepared _____

Date training can commence _____

Date training to be completed _____

COMMENTS

INDIVIDUAL WHO ACCEPTS TESTING AS SUFFICIENT _____   DATE _____

_____   _____

WORK PAPER 16.8   Form Completion Instructions: New/Modified Training Modules

Field Requirements

FIELD	INSTRUCTIONS FOR ENTERING DATA
Application name	The name by which the application is known.
Number	The application identifier.
Change Ident. #	The sequence number that uniquely identifies the change.
Training module inventory	The remainder of the information on the form describes the modules.
Training module description	A brief narrative of the training module. The location of the training material should be identified so that it can be easily obtained.
Description of change	As the training module becomes modified, this column should contain a sequential listing of all the changes made to the training module. In effect, it is a change history for the training module.
Training material	The course material included in the training module.
Who should be trained	The individual(s) to whom the training module is directed.
Method of training	The recommended way in which the training module should be used. The most common methods of training, which are indicated on the form, are:

- Meeting
- Classroom training
- Self-study
- New procedure
- Supervisor given
- Other

Prepared by	The name of the individual who prepared the inventory form.
Date	The date on which it was last updated.

(Continues)

WORK PAPER 16.8 *(Continued)*

APPLICATION
NAME: _____ NUMBER: _____ CHANGE IDENT. # _____

TRAINING MODULE INVENTORY

TRAINING MODULE DESCRIPTION	DESCRIPTION OF CHANGE	TRAINING MATERIAL	WHO SHOULD BE TRAINED	METHOD OF TRAINING					
				Meeting	Class-room	Self-study	New procedure	Super-visor	Other

PREPARED BY: _____ DATE: _____

WORK PAPER 16.9   Form Completion Instructions: Conduct Training Checklist

Field Requirements

FIELD	INSTRUCTIONS FOR ENTERING DATA
Application Name	The name by which the application is known.
Number	The application identifier.
Change Ident. #	The sequence number that uniquely identifies the change.
Training Checklist	The remainder of the form contains the checklist information, which is:

- Name of individual requiring training: whenever possible, actual names should be used, as opposed to groups of people, so records can be maintained as to whether or not the people actually took the training.
- Department: the department/organization with which the individual is affiliated.
- Training required: the training modules and/or material to be given the individual.
- Dates: the dates on which the course is to be given or the training material to be disseminated to the individual. The schedules dates should be listed, as well as the date the individual actually took the course or received the material.
- Location: the location of the course or the location to which the training material should be distributed.
- Instructor: the name of the responsible individual should be listed.
- Comments: any other information that would verify that training took place. In classroom situations where examinations are given, the space could be used to record that grade.

Prepared by	The name of the individual preparing the form who should be the one responsible for ensuring the training is given.
Date	The date on which the form was prepared.

(Continues)

WORK PAPER 16.9   *(Continued)*

APPLICATION
NAME: _____ NUMBER: _____

CHANGE
IDENT. # _____

TRAINING CHECKLIST

NAME OF INDIVIDUAL REQUIRING TRAINING	DEPART-MENT	TRAINING REQUIRED	DATES		LOCATION	INSTRUCTOR	COM-MENTS
			Sched-uled	Taken			

PREPARED BY: _____ DATE: _____

WORK PAPER 16.10   Testing and Training Quality Control Checklist

Field Requirements

FIELD	INSTRUCTIONS FOR ENTERING DATA
Number	A number that sequentially identifies the quality control items, which if positively addressed would indicate that this step has been performed correctly.
Item	The specific quality control item that is used to measure the effectiveness of performing this step.
Response	The testers should indicate in this column whether they have performed the referenced item. The response can be Yes, No, or N/A if it is not appropriate for your organization's testing process.
Comments	This column is used to clarify the Yes, No, or N/A response for the item indicated. Generally the comments column need only be completed for No responses; No responses should be investigated and a determination made as to whether this item needs to be performed before this step can be considered complete.

#	ITEM	YES	NO	N/A	COMMENTS
1.	Are software maintenance analysts required to develop a test plan?				
2.	Must each change be reviewed to determine if it has an impact on training?				
3.	If a change has an impact on training, do procedures require that a training plan be established?				
4.	Is an inventory prepared of training material so that it can be updated?				
5.	Does the training plan make one individual responsible for training?				
6.	Does the training plan identify the results desired from training?				
7.	Does the training plan indicate the who, why, what, where, when, and how of training?				
8.	Does the training plan provide a training schedule, including dates?				
9.	Is an individual responsible for determining if training is acceptable?				
10.	Are all of the training modules inventoried?				
11.	Does each training module have a history of the changes made to the module?				
12.	Is one individual assigned responsibility for testing?				

WORK PAPER 16.10 *(Continued)*

#	ITEM	YES	NO	N/A	COMMENTS
			RESPONSE		
13.	Does the test plan list each measurable change objective and the method of testing that objective?				
14.	Does the training plan list the desired results from testing?				
15.	Does the training plan address regression testing?				
16.	Does the training plan address intersystem testing?				
17.	Is someone responsible for judging whether testing is acceptable?				
18.	Is an acceptance testing checklist prepared to determine the necessary resources are ready for the test?				
19.	Does the acceptance testing checklist include the administrative aspects of the test?				
20.	Is a training checklist prepared which indicates which individuals need training?				
21.	Is a record kept of whether or not individuals receive training?				
22.	Is each test failure documented?				
23.	Is each training failure documented?				
24.	Are test failures corrected before the change goes into production?				
25.	Are training failures corrected before the change goes into production?				
26.	If the change is put into production before testing/training failures have been corrected, are alternative measures taken to assure the identified errors will not cause problems?				
27.	Is feedback data identified?				
28.	Is feedback data collected?				
29.	Is feedback data regularly reviewed?				
30.	Are control concerns identified?				
31.	Does information services management periodically review training and testing software changes?				

WORK PAPER 16.11   Form Completion Instructions: Automated Application Segment Test Failure Notification

Field Requirements

FIELD	INSTRUCTIONS FOR ENTERING DATA
Application Name	The name by which the application is known.
Number	The application identifier.
Change Ident. #	The sequence number that uniquely identifies the change.
Description of Failure	A brief description of the condition that is believed to be unacceptable. In most instances, the detailed information would be presented orally, as would the documentation supporting the failure. The purpose of the form is to record the problem and control the implementation. The information contained in this section includes: • Failure #: a sequentially increasing number used to control the identification and implementation of problems. If a form is lost or mislaid, it will be noticed because a failure number will be missing. • Test date: the date of the test. • System change objective failed: the measurable change objective that was not achieved. • Description of failure: a brief narrative description of what is wrong.
Recommended Correction	Corrections suggested by the individual uncovering the failure or the software maintenance analyst after an analysis of the problem. The type of information included in the recommendation is: • Programs affected: all the programs that contributed to the failure. • Data affected: all the data elements, records, or files that contributed or were involved in the failure. • Description of correction: a brief description of the recommended solution.
Correction Assignments	This section is completed by the software maintenance analyst to assign the correction of the failure to a specific individual. At a minimum, this should include: • Correction assigned to (name of individual) • Date correction needed • Comments (suggestions on how to implement the solution)
Prepared by	The name of the individual who uncovered the failure.
Date	The date on which the form was prepared.

(Continues)

WORK PAPER 16.11   *(Continued)*

APPLICATION
NAME: _____ NUMBER: _____ CHANGE
IDENT. # _____

<u>DESCRIPTION OF FAILURE</u>

TEST DATE _____ FAILURE # _____

SYSTEM CHANGE OBJECTIVE FAILED _____

_____

DESCRIPTION OF FAILURE _____

_____

_____

<u>RECOMMENDED CORRECTION</u>

PROGRAMS AFFECTED _____

_____

DATA AFFECTED _____

_____

DESCRIPTION OF CORRECTION _____

_____

_____

<u>CORRECTION ASSIGNMENTS</u>

CORRECTION ASSIGNED TO _____

DATE CORRECTION NEEDED _____

COMMENTS _____

_____

_____

_____

PREPARED BY: _____ DATE: _____

_____

WORK PAPER 16.12   Form Completion Instructions: Training Failure Notification

Field Requirements

FIELD	INSTRUCTIONS FOR ENTERING DATA
Application Name	The name by which the application is known.
Number	The application identifier.
Change Ident. #	The sequence number that uniquely identifies the change.
Description of Failure	The details of the training failure need to be described. At a minimum, this would include:

- Failure #: a sequentially increasing number used to control the failure form.
- Test date: the date on which the test occurred.
- People not adequately trained: the name of individuals, categories of people or departments who could not adequately perform their tasks.
- Failure caused by lack of training: a description of why the training was inadequate.

Recommended Correction	Suggestions for correcting the failure. This section can be completed either by the individual uncovering the failure and/or by the systems analyst. The type of information helpful in correcting the training failure includes:

- Training material needing revisions: the specific material that should be modified to correct the problem.
- New method of training needed: suggestions for varying the training method, such as going from issuing training bulletins to holding a training class.
- People needing training: all of the people that may need new training.
- Description of (recommended) correction: a brief narrative explanation of the recommended solution.

Correction Assignments	Assignments made by the individual responsible for training. At a minimum, each assignment would include:

- Correction assigned to: name of individual who will make the necessary adjustments to training material.
- Training material corrections needed: the specific training document(s) that need changing.
- Comments: recommendations on how to change the training material.

Prepared by	The name of the individual who uncovered the failure.
Date	The date on which the failure occurred.

(Continues)

WORK PAPER 16.12   *(Continued)*

APPLICATION
NAME: _____ NUMBER: _____ CHANGE IDENT. # _____

DESCRIPTION OF FAILURE

TEST DATE _____ FAILURE # _____

PEOPLE NOT ADEQUATELY TRAINED _____

_____

FAILURE CAUSED BY LACK OF TRAINING _____

_____
_____

RECOMMENDED CORRECTION

TRAINING MATERIAL NEEDING REVISIONS _____

_____

NEW METHOD OF TRAINING NEEDED _____

_____

PEOPLE NEEDING TRAINING _____

_____

DESCRIPTION OF CORRECTION _____

_____
_____

CORRECTION ASSIGNMENTS

CORRECTION ASSIGNED TO _____

_____

TRAINING MATERIAL NEEDING CORRECTION _____

_____

COMMENTS _____

_____
_____
_____

PREPARED BY: _____ DATE: _____

_____

# chapter 17

Step 11: Evaluate Test Effectiveness

A significant portion of information services resources is expended testing application systems. A reasonable question for management to ask is, "Am I getting my money's worth from this testing?" Unfortunately, many information services functions cannot objectively answer that question. Figure 17.1 shows how this step fits into the 11-step testing process.

Overview

The measurement of the effectiveness of testing serves two purposes: First, it evaluates the performance of the individuals conducting the test; and second, and perhaps more important, the results of the evaluation can be used to modify the test process. Identifying the ineffective aspects of testing identifies the areas for improvement. The two evaluation testing objectives of assessing individual performance and improving the test process are closely related. The same evaluation criteria can be used for both purposes. These major evaluation objectives are achieved through the collection of data about more detailed evaluation objectives. The objective of assessment is to identify problems so that corrective action can be taken. Therefore, the evaluation will be looking for the negative aspects of testing. The absence of a negative factor represents a positive evaluation.

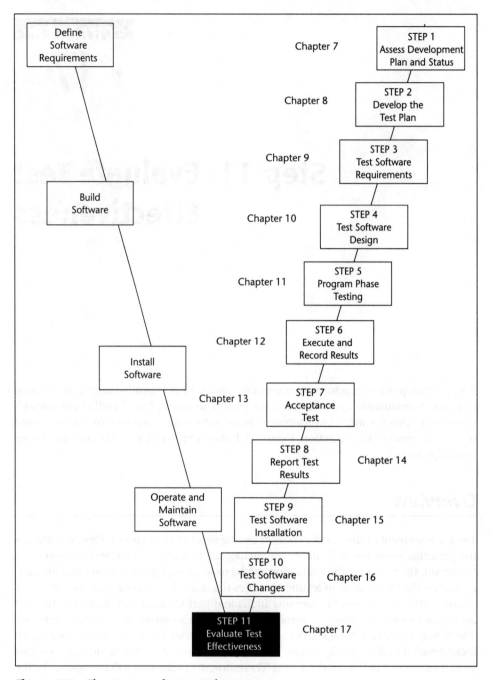

Figure 17.1 The 11-step software testing process.

Objective

This chapter describes the more common objectives for measuring testing, and then recommends criteria for performing those measurements. The chapter explains who should evaluate performance, identifies the common approaches, and then recommends testing metrics for use in a testing assessment process. The concept of metrics is explained, the information needed for the metrics is identified, and the chapter suggests a series of metrics that can be used to mathematically measure the effectiveness of testing.

Concerns

The major concern that testers should have is that their testing processes will not improve. Without improvement, testers will continue to make the same errors and perform testing inefficiently time after time. Experience in many organizations has shown that testers make more errors than developers. Thus, testing is an error-prone process.

To improve the test process the results of testing must be continually evaluated. Unless the results are recorded and retained, the evaluation will not occur. Without a formal process, and management's support for the process, testers need to be concerned that their processes will remain stagnant and not subject to continuous improvement.

Workbench

The workbench for evaluating test effectiveness is illustrated in Figure 17.2. Within this workbench the objective for performing the assessment should be clearly established. Without defining objectives, a measurement process may not be properly directed and thus may not be effective. The categories of information needed to accomplish the measurement objectives should be identified. One group should be made responsible for collecting and assessing testing performance information. Without one individual accountable for measurement, there will be no need for a catalyst to ensure that the data collection and assessment process occurs. Several approaches can be used in performing the assessment process. The one that best matches the managerial style should be selected. The facts necessary to support the approach selected should be identified. Once identified, the evaluation data needs to be collected and reduced to a form suitable for assessment. The raw information must be analyzed to draw conclusions about the effectiveness of systems testing. From this analysis, action can be taken by the appropriate party.

Input

Input to this step should be the results of conducting software tests. The input should be an accumulation of test results over time. The type of information needed as input includes, but is not limited to:

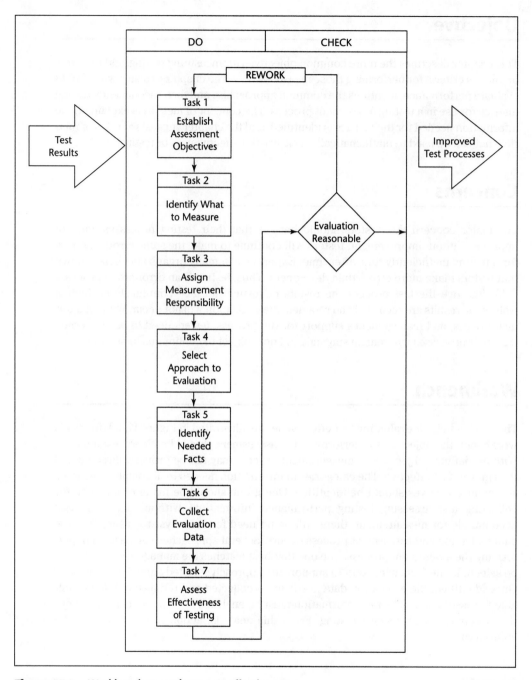

Figure 17.2   Workbench to evaluate test effectiveness.

- Number of tests conducted
- Resources expended in testing
- Test tools used
- Defects uncovered
- Size of software tested
- Days to correct defects
- Defects not corrected
- Defects uncovered during operation that were not uncovered during testing
- Developmental phase in which defects were uncovered
- Names of defects uncovered

Do Procedures

Once a decision has been made to formally assess the effectiveness of testing, an assessment process is needed. A seven-task approach to assessing the effectiveness of systems testing is as follows (see Figure 17.3).

Task 1: Establish Assessment Objectives

The objectives for performing the assessment should be clearly established. If objectives are not defined, the measurement process may not be properly directed and thus may not be effective. These objectives include:

Identify test weaknesses. Identify problems within the test process where the methodology is not effective in identifying system defects.

Identify the need for new test tools. Determine when the existing test tools are not effective or efficient as a basis for acquiring new or improved testing tools.

Assess project testing. Evaluate the effectiveness of the testing performed by a project team to reduce defects from the project at an economical cost.

Identify good test practices. Determine which practices used in the test process are the most effective so that those practices can be used by all projects.

Identify poor test practices. Determine which of the practices used by the project team are ineffective so that other projects can be advised not to use those practices.

Identify economical test practices. Determine what characteristics make testing most economical so that the cost-effectiveness of testing can be improved.

TASK	TASK NAME	DESCRIPTION
1.	Establish assessment objectives	The objectives for performing the assessment should be clearly established. Without defining objectives, a measurement process may not be properly directed and thus may not be effective.
2.	Identify what to measure	The categories of information needed to accomplish the measurement objectives should be identified.
3.	Assign measurement responsibility	One group should be made responsible for collecting and assessing testing performance information. Without one individual accountable for measurement, there will be no need for a catalyst to ensure that the data collection and assessment process occurs.
4.	Select approach to evaluation	Several approaches can be used in performing the assessment process. The one that best matches the managerial style should be selected.
5.	Identify needed facts	The facts necessary to support the approach selected should be identified.
6.	Collect evaluation data	Once identified, the evaluation data needs to be collected and reduced to a form suitable for assessment.
7.	Assess the effectiveness testing	The raw information must be analyzed to draw conclusions about the effectiveness of systems testing. From this analysis, action can be made by the appropriate party.

Figure 17.3   Test assessment steps.

Task 2: Identify What to Measure

The categories of information needed to accomplish the measurement objectives should be identified. Described below are the five characteristics of application system testing that can be measured.

1. **Involvement.** Who is involved in testing and to what extent?

2. **Extent of testing.** What areas are covered by testing and what volume of testing will be performed on those areas?

3. **Resources.** How much information services resources, both people and computer, will be consumed in a test process?

4. **Effectiveness.** How much testing is achieved per unit of resource?

5. **Assessment.** What is the value of the results received from the test process?

Task 3: Assign Measurement Responsibility

One group should be made responsible for collecting and assessing testing performance information. Without a specific accountable individual, there will be no catalyst to ensure that the data collection and assessment process occurs. The responsibility for the use of information services resources resides with IT management. However, they may desire to delegate the responsibility to assess the effectiveness of the test process to a function within the department. If the information services departments have a quality assurance function, that delegation should be made to the quality assurance group. Lacking that function, other candidates for assigning the responsibility include an information services comptroller, manager of standards, manager of software support, or the planning manager.

Task 4: Select Evaluation Approach

Several approaches can be used in performing the assessment process. The one that best matches the managerial style should be selected. The following are the most common approaches to evaluating the effectiveness of testing.

Judgment. In the opinion of the individual doing the assessment, the test process is evaluated. This is normally an arbitrary assessment and one that is difficult to justify. However, if the individual is well respected and the judgments correlate to actual results, the process may work effectively.

Compliance with methodology. If testing standards and guidelines are available, then good testing can be considered to be that which complies with those guidelines and standards, while poor testing is that which does not comply with the test methodology.

Problems after test. The effectiveness of the test process can be measured by the number of problems occurring after the test process is complete. If few problems occur, testing can be considered to be good; if many problems occur, testing can be considered poor.

User reaction. If the user is satisfied with the application system, it can be assumed testing is good; if the user is unhappy with the performance of the application system, testing can be judged poor.

Testing metrics. Criteria are identified that show a high positive correlation to good or bad testing. This correlation or relationship between factors is called a metric. This process is a scientific mathematical approach to the measurement of testing.

The metrics approach is recommended because once established it is easy to use, and can be proven to show a high correlation to effective and ineffective practices. A major advantage to metrics is that the assessment process can be clearly defined, will be known to those people who are being assessed, and is specific enough so that it is easy to determine which testing variables need to be adjusted to improve the effectiveness, efficiency, and/or economy of the test process.

Task 5: Identify Needed Facts

The facts necessary to support the approach selected should be identified. The metrics approach clearly identifies the type of data needed for the assessment process. Using the metrics described later in this chapter, the needed information includes:

Change characteristics. The frequency, size, and type of change occurring in each system.

Magnitude of system. A measure used to equate testing information from system to system, the size being a factor used to relate testing in one application system to another.

Cost of process being tested. The cost to develop a system or install a change, whichever is being tested.

Cost of test. The resources, both people and computer, used to test the new function.

Defects uncovered by testing. The number of defects uncovered as a result of the test.

Defects detected by phase. A breakdown of the previous category for each phase tested to show the effectiveness of the test by system development life cycle (SDLC) phase.

Defects uncovered after test. The number of defects uncovered after the new function is placed into production status.

Cost of testing by function. The amount of resources consumed for testing by each phase of the SDLC in which testing occurs.

System complaints. Complaints of problems by a third party after the system goes operational.

Quantification of defects. The potential dollar loss associated with each defect had it not been detected.

Who conducted the test. The functional unit to which the individuals conducting the test report.

Quantification of correctness of defect. The cost to correct the application system defect.

Task 6: Collect Evaluation Data

Once the data has been identified, a system must be established to collect and store the needed data in a form suitable for assessment. This may require a collection mechanism, a storage mechanism, and a method to select and summarize the information. Wherever possible, utility programs should be used for this purpose.

Task 7: Assess the Effectiveness of Testing

The raw information must be analyzed to draw conclusions about the effectiveness of systems testing. From this analysis, action can be taken by the appropriate party. The summarized results must be output into a form for presentation that provides an assessment of testing. The judgmental approach normally expresses the assessment in terms of an opinion of the assessor. The user reaction provides the same type of assessment, and normally includes examples that illustrate good or poor testing performance. The problems and compliance to standards approaches normally express the assessment in terms of what has or has not happened; for example, there is a known number of problems, or X standards have been violated in a test process. The *metrics approach* provides the assessment in terms that quantitatively show the goodness or badness of the test process.

Use of Testing Metrics

Testing metrics are relationships that show a high positive correlation to that which is being measured. Metrics are used in almost all disciplines as a basis of performing an assessment of the effectiveness of some process. Some of the more common assessments familiar to most people in other disciplines include:

Blood pressure (medicine). Identifies effectiveness of the heart and can be used to assess the probability of heart attack and stroke.

Student aptitude test (education). Test score is a metric measuring a student's achievement in high school studies.

Net profit (accounting). Metric measures the success of the organization in profiting within its field or industry.

Accidents per worker-day (safety). Measures the effectiveness of an organization's safety program.

A metric is a mathematical number that shows a relationship between two variables. The student SAT score used by many colleges to determine whether to accept a student shows the student's mastery of topics asked compared to the total number of topics on the examination. Gross profit is a number showing a relationship between income and the costs associated to produce that income. A testing metric is a number that shows a relationship between two testing variables.

The metric must then be compared to some norm or standard. For example, blood pressure is a number that is compared to a norm for a person's age and sex. The metric by itself is meaningless until it can be compared to some norm. The net profit metric is expressed as a percent, such as 10 percent net profit. This does not take on its true meaning until you know that other companies in that industry are making 20 percent, 10 percent, or 5 percent. Once the norm for the industry is known, then the gross profit metric takes on more meaning.

Briefly explained below, and listed in Figure 17.4, are 30 suggested metrics for evaluating application system testing.

1. **User participation (user participation test time divided by total test time).** Metric identifies the user involvement in testing.

2. **Instructions exercised (number of instructions exercised versus total number of instructions).** Metric shows the number of instructions in the program that were executed during the test process.

3. **Number of tests (number of tests versus size of system tested).** Metric identifies the number of tests required to evaluate a unit of information services work.

METRIC NUMBER	METRIC	USE OF METRIC
1.	User Participation	Involvement in testing
2.	Instructions Exercised	Extent of testing
3.	Number of Tests	Extent of testing
4.	Paths Tested	Extent of testing
5.	Acceptance Criteria Tested	Extent of testing
6.	Test Cost	Resources consumed in testing
7.	Cost to Locate Defect	Resources consumed in testing
8.	Achieving Budget	Resources consumed in testing
9.	Detected Production Errors	Effectiveness of testing
10.	Defects Uncovered in Testing	Effectiveness of testing
11.	Effectiveness of Test to Business	Effectiveness of testing
12.	Asset Value of Test	Effectiveness of testing
13.	Rerun Analysis	Effectiveness of testing
14.	Hang-up Analysis	Effectiveness of testing
15.	Source Code Analysis	Effectiveness of testing
16.	Test Efficiency	Effectiveness of testing
17.	Start-up Failure	Effectiveness of testing
18.	System Complaints	Effectiveness of testing
19.	Test Automation	Effectiveness of testing
20.	Requirements Phase Testing	Effectiveness of testing
21.	Design Phase Testing Effectiveness	Effectiveness of testing
22.	Program Phase Testing Effectiveness	Effectiveness of testing
23.	Test Phase Testing Effectiveness	Effectiveness of testing
24.	Installation Phase Testing Effectiveness	Effectiveness of testing
25.	Maintenance Phase Testing Effectiveness	Effectiveness of testing
26.	Defects Uncovered in Test	Effectiveness of testing
27.	Untested Change Problems	Effectiveness of testing
28.	Testing change Problems	Effectiveness of testing
29.	Loss Value of Test	Assessment of testing
30.	Scale of Ten	Assessment of testing

Figure 17.4   When to use testing metrics.

4. **Paths tested (number of paths tested versus total number of paths).** Metric indicates the number of logical paths that were executed during the test process.

5. **Acceptance criteria tested (acceptance criteria verified versus total acceptance criteria).** Metric identifies the number of user-identified criteria that were evaluated during the test process.

6. **Test cost (test cost versus total system cost).** Metric identifies the amount of resources used in the development or maintenance process allocated to testing.

7. **Cost to locate defect (cost of testing versus the number of defects located in testing).** Metric shows the cost to locate a defect.

8. **Achieving budget (anticipated cost of testing versus the actual cost of testing).** Metric determines the effectiveness of using test dollars.

9. **Detected production errors (number of errors detected in production versus application system size).** Metric determines the effectiveness of system testing in deleting errors from the application prior to it being placed into production.

10. **Defects uncovered in testing (defects located by testing versus total system defects).** Metric shows the percent of defects that were identified as a result of testing.

11. **Effectiveness of test to business (loss due to problems versus total resources processed by the system).** Metric shows the effectiveness of testing in reducing system losses in relationship to the resources controlled by the system being tested.

12. **Asset value of test (test cost versus assets controlled by system).** Metric shows the relationship between what is spent for testing as a percent versus the assets controlled by the system being tested.

13. **Rerun analysis (rerun hours versus production hours).** Metric shows the effectiveness of testing as a relationship to rerun hours associated with undetected defects.

14. **Abnormal termination analysis (installed changes versus number of application system hang-ups).** Metric shows the effectiveness of testing in reducing system abnormal terminations through maintenance changes.

15. **Source code analysis (number of source code statements changed versus the number of tests).** Metrics show the efficiency of testing as a basis of the volume of work being tested.

16. **Test efficiency (number of tests required versus the number of system errors).** Metric shows the efficiency of tests in uncovering errors.

17. **Startup failure (number of program changes versus the number of failures the first time the changed program is run in production).** Metric shows the ability of the test process to eliminate major defects from the application being tested.

18. **System complaints (system complaints versus number of transactions processed).** Metric shows the effectiveness of testing and reducing third-party complaints.

19. **Test automation (cost of manual test effort versus total test cost).** Metric shows the percent of testing performed manually and that performed automatically.

20. **Requirements phase testing effectiveness (requirements test cost versus number of errors detected during requirements phase).** Metric shows the value returned for testing during the requirements phase.

21. **Design phase testing effectiveness (design test cost versus number of errors detected during design phase).** Metric shows the value returned for testing during the design phase.

22. **Program phase testing effectiveness (program test cost versus number of errors detected during program phase).** Metric shows the value returned for testing during the program phase.

23. **Test phase testing effectiveness (test cost versus number of errors detected during test phase).** Metric shows the value returned for testing during the test phase.

24. **Installation phase testing effectiveness (installation test cost versus number of errors detected during installation phase).** Metric shows the value returned for testing during the installation.

25. **Maintenance phase testing effectiveness (maintenance test cost versus number of errors detected during maintenance phase).** Metric shows the value returned for testing during the maintenance phase.

26. **Defects uncovered in test (defects uncovered versus size of systems).** Metric shows the number of defects uncovered through testing based on a unit of work.

27. **Untested change problems (number of tested changes versus problems attributable to those changes).** Metric shows the effect of testing system changes.

28. **Tested change problems (number of tested changes versus problems attributable to those changes).** Metric shows the effect of testing system changes.

29. **Loss value of test (loss due to problems versus total resources processed by system).** Metric shows the result of testing in reducing losses as related to the resources processed by the system.

30. **Scale of ten (assessment of testing rated on a scale of ten).** Metric shows people's assessment of the effectiveness of testing on a scale on which 1 is poor and 10 is outstanding.

Check Procedures

Work Paper 17.1 is a quality control checklist for this step. It is designed so that Yes responses indicate good test practices; No responses warrant additional investigation. A Comments column is provided to explain No responses and to record results of investigation. The N/A column is used when the checklist item is not applicable to the test situation.

Output

The bottom line of assessment is making application system testing more effective. This is performed by a careful analysis of the results of testing, and then taking action to correct identified weaknesses. Facts precede action, and testing in many organizations has suffered from the lack of facts. Once those facts have been determined, action should be taken.

The *measurement first, action second* concept is effective when the measurement process is specific. Measurement must be able to determine the effect of action. For example, the metric approach fulfills this requirement in that it shows very specific relationships. Using this concept, if action is taken by changing one of the metric variables, the result of that action can be quickly measured.

Changing the variable in one metric can normally be measured by the change in another metric. For example, if the number of defects detected after the system goes operational is higher than desirable, then action should be taken. The action taken might be to increase the number of instructions exercised during testing. Obviously, this increases test cost with the hopeful objective of reducing undetected defects prior to operation. If it can be shown that increasing the number of instructions exercised does in fact reduce the number of defects in an operation system, that action can be considered desirable and should be extended. On the other hand, if increasing the number of instructions executed does not reduce the number of defects undetected prior to production, then those resources have not been used effectively and that action should be eliminated and another action tried.

Using the measurement/action approach, the variables can be manipulated until the desired result is achieved. Without the measurement, management can never be sure that intuitive or judgmental actions are effective. The measurement/action approach works and should be followed to improve the test process.

Guidelines

For evaluating test effectiveness to be effective, testers must recognize that they make defects in performing the test processes. Testers need to understand the nature of test defects, and to be able to refer to test defects by name. For example, a test defect might be preparing incorrect test data.

Summary

This step concludes the recommended 11-step testing process. The results of this step will be recommendations to improve the full 11 steps within the testing process. Not only must the 10 testing steps be improved, but the steps taken to improve the effectiveness of testing also require improvement.

The improvement process begins by first adopting the 11-step process; and second by customizing the process to your IT organization's specific needs. The experience gained through usage, if captured, will identify opportunities for improvement. Part Four addresses special testing needs based upon the use of specific technologies and approaches.

WORK PAPER 17.1   Quality Control Checklist

Field Requirements

FIELD	INSTRUCTIONS FOR ENTERING DATA
Number	A number that sequentially identifies the quality control items, which if positively addressed would indicate that this step has been performed correctly.
Item	The specific quality control item that is used to measure the effectiveness of performing this step.
Response	The testers should indicate in this column whether they have performed the referenced item. The response can be Yes, No, or N/A if it is not appropriate for your organization's testing process.
Comments	This column is used to clarify the Yes, No, or N/A response for the item indicated. Generally the comments column need only be completed for No responses; No responses should be investigated and a determination made as to whether this item needs to be performed before this step can be considered complete.

#	ITEM	RESPONSE			COMMENTS
		YES	NO	N/A	
1.	Does management support the concept of continuous improvement to test processes?				
2.	Have resources been allocated to improving the test processes?				
3.	Has a single individual been appointed responsible for overseeing the improvement of test processes?				
4.	Have the results of testing been accumulated over time?				
5.	Do the results of testing include the types of items identified in the input section of this chapter?				
6.	Do testers have adequate tools to summarize, analyze, and report the results of previous testing?				
7.	Do the results of that analysis appear reasonable?				
8.	Is the analysis performed on a regular basis?				
9.	Are the results of the analysis incorporated into improved test processes?				
10.	Is data maintained so there can be a determination as to whether those installed improvements do in fact improve the test processes?				

Testing Specialized Systems and Applications

# CHAPTER 18

Testing Client/Server Systems

The success of a client/server program will depend heavily on the readiness of the organization to use the technology effectively. If the organization is not ready to move to client/server technology, it is far better to work on changing the organization to a ready status than on installing client/server technology. Preparing the organization for client/server technology is an important component of a successful program. This is regardless of whether it is an organizationwide client/server technology or just a small program. If the organization is ready, the client/server approach should be evaluated prior to testing the client systems.

Overview

Figure 18.1 shows a simplified client/server architecture. There are many possible variations of client/server, but for illustration purposes, this is representative.

In this example, application software resides on the client workstations. The application server handles processing requests. The back-end processing (typically a mainframe or super-minicomputer) handles processing such as batch transactions that are accumulated and processed together at one time on a regular basis. The important distinction to note is that application software resides on the client workstation.

Figure 18.1 shows the key distinction between workstations being connected to the mainframe, and the workstations containing the software used for client processing. This distinction represents a major change in processing control. For this reason, client/server testing must first evaluate the organization's readiness to make this control change, and then evaluate the key components of the client/server system prior to conducting tests. This chapter will provide the material on assessing readiness and key components. The actual testing of client/server systems will be achieved using the 11-step testing process described earlier in this book.

Objective

The objective of this test process is to supplement the 11-step process with specific guidance on testing client server systems.

Concerns

The concerns about client/server systems reside in the area of control. The testers need to determine that adequate controls are in place to ensure accurate, complete, timely, and secure processing of client software systems. The testers must address these five concerns:

1. **Organizational readiness.** The culture is adequately prepared to process data using client/server technology. Readiness must be evaluated in the areas of management, client installation, and server support.

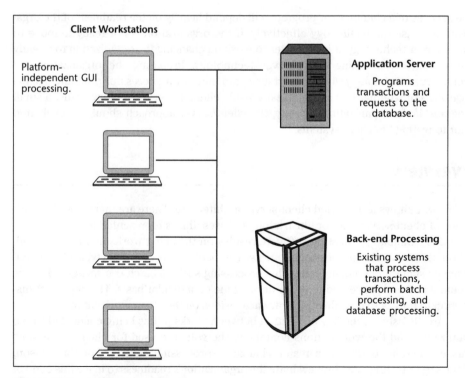

Figure 18.1   Architecture: client/server.

2. **Client installation.** The concern is that the appropriate hardware and software will be in place to enable processing that will meet client needs.

3. **Security.** There is a need for protection of both the hardware, including residence software, and the data that is processed using that hardware and software. Security must address threats from employees, outsiders, and acts of nature.

4. **Client data.** Controls must be in place to ensure that everything is not lost, incorrectly processed, or processed differently on a client workstation than in other areas of the organization.

5. **Client/server standards.** Standards must exist to ensure that all client workstations operate under the same set of rules.

Workbench

Figure 18.2 provides a workbench for testing client/server systems. This workbench can be used in steps as the client/server system is developed, or concurrently after the client/server system has been developed. The workbench shows three steps, as well as the quality control procedures necessary to ensure that those three steps are performed correctly. The output will be any identified weaknesses uncovered during testing.

Input

The input to this test process will be the client/server system. This will include the server technology and capabilities, the communication network, and the client work-

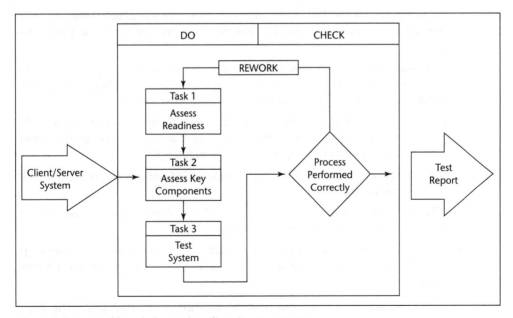

Figure 18.2 Workbench for testing client/server systems.

stations that will be incorporated into the test. Since both the client and the server components will include software capabilities, the materials should provide a description of the client software and any test results on that client software should be input to this test process.

Do Procedures

The testing for client/server software includes the following three tasks.

Task 1: Assess Readiness

Client/server programs should have sponsors. Ideally, these are the directors of information technology and the impacted user management. It is the responsibility of the sponsors to ensure that the organization is ready for client/server technology. However, those charged with installing the new technology should provide the sponsor with a readiness assessment. That assessment is the objective of this chapter.

The readiness assessment proposed in this chapter is a modification of the readiness approach pioneered by Dr. Howard Rubin of Rubin and Associates. There are eight dimensions to the readiness assessment, as follows:

1. **Motivation.** The level of commitment by the organization to using client/server technology to drive improvements in quality, productivity, and customer satisfaction.

2. **Investment.** The amount of monies approved/budgeted for expenditures in the client/server program.

3. **Client/server skills.** The ability of the client/server installation team to incorporate the client/server technology concepts and principles into the users' programs.

4. **User education.** Awareness by the individuals involved in any aspect of the client/server program in principles and concepts. These people need to understand how technology is used in the affected business processes.

5. **Culture.** The willingness of the organization to innovate. In other words, is the organization willing to try new concepts and new approaches, or are they more comfortable using existing approaches and technology?

6. **Client/server support staff.** The adequacy of resources to support the client/server program.

7. **Client/server aids/tools.** The availability of client/server aids and tools to perform and support the client/server program.

8. **Software development process maturity.** The ability of a software development process to produce high-quality (i.e., defect-free) software on a consistent basis.

The following paragraphs address how to measure process maturity. The other dimensions are more organization dependent and require the judgment of a team of knowledgeable people in the organization.

Software Development Process Maturity Levels

The five levels of process maturity are ad hoc, repeatable, consistent, measured, and optimized. They are shown in Figure 18.3 and have the following general characteristics:

1. **Ad hoc.** The software development process is loosely defined, and the project leader can deviate from the process whenever he or she chooses.

2. **Repeatable.** The organization has achieved a stable process with a repeatable level of quality by initiating rigorous requirements, effective project management, cost, schedules, and change control.

3. **Consistent.** The organization has defined the process as a basis for consistent implementation. Developers can depend on the quality of the deliverables.

4. **Measured.** The organization has initiated comprehensive process measurements and analysis. This is when the most significant quality improvements begin.

5. **Optimized.** The organization now has a foundation for continuing improvement and optimization of the process.

These levels have been selected because they:

- Reasonably represent the actual historical phases of evolutionary improvement of real software organizations

- Represent a measure of improvement that is reasonable to achieve from the prior level

- Suggest interim improvement goals and progress measures

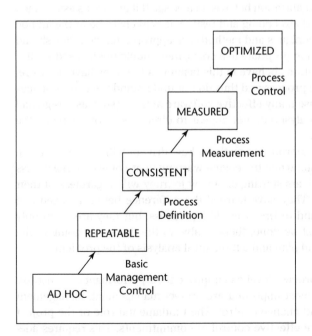

Figure 18.3   Software development process maturity levels.

■ Make obvious a set of immediate improvement priorities once an organization's status in this framework is known

While there are many other elements to these maturity level transitions, the primary objective is to achieve a controlled and measured process as the foundation for continuing improvement.

This software development process maturity structure is intended for use with an assessment methodology and a management system. Assessment helps an organization identify its specific maturity status, and the management system establishes a structure for implementing the priority improvement actions. Once its position in this maturity structure is defined, the organization can concentrate on those items that will help it advance to the next level. When, for example, a software organization does not have an effective project-planning system, it may be difficult or even impossible to introduce advanced methods and technology. Poor project planning generally leads to unrealistic schedules, inadequate resources, and frequent crises. In such circumstances, new methods are usually ignored and priority is given to coding and testing.

The Ad Hoc Process (Level 1)

The ad hoc process level is unpredictable and often very chaotic. At this stage, the organization typically operates without formalized procedures, cost estimates, and project plans. Tools are neither well integrated with the process nor uniformly applied. Change control is lax, and there is little senior management exposure or understanding of the problems and issues. Since many problems are deferred or even forgotten, software installation and maintenance often present serious problems.

While organizations at this level may have formal procedures for planning and tracking their work, there is no management mechanism to ensure that they are used. The best test is to observe how such an organization behaves in a crisis. If it abandons established procedures and essentially reverts to coding and testing, it is likely to be at the ad hoc process level. After all, if the techniques and methods are appropriate, then they should be used in a crisis; if they are not appropriate in a crisis, they should not be used at all.

One key reason why organizations behave in this fashion is that they have not experienced the benefits of a mature process and thus do not understand the consequences of their chaotic behavior. Because many effective software actions (such as design and code inspections or test data analysis) do not appear to directly support shipping the product, they seem expendable.

Driving an automobile is an appropriate analogy. Few drivers with any experience will continue driving for very long when the engine warning light comes on, regardless of their rush. Similarly, most drivers starting on a new journey will, regardless of their hurry, pause to consult a map. They have learned the difference between speed and progress. In software, coding and testing seem like progress, but they are often only wheel spinning. While they must be done, there is always the danger of going in the wrong direction. Without a sound plan and a thoughtful analysis of the problems, there is no way to know.

Organizations at the ad hoc process level can improve their performance by instituting basic project controls. The most important are project management, management oversight, quality assurance, and change control. The fundamental role of the project management system is to ensure effective control of commitments. This requires adequate preparation, clear responsibility, a public declaration, and a dedication to performance. For software, project management starts with an understanding of the job's magnitude. In any but the simplest projects, a plan must then be developed to determine the best schedule and the anticipated resources required. In the absence of such an orderly plan, no commitment can be better than an educated guess.

A suitably disciplined software development organization must have senior management oversight. This includes review and approval of all major development plans prior to their official commitment. Also, a quarterly review should be conducted of facility-wide process compliance, installed quality performance, schedule tracking, cost trends, computing service, and quality and productivity goals by project. The lack of such reviews typically results in uneven and generally inadequate implementation of the process as well as frequent overcommitments and cost surprises.

A quality assurance group is charged with assuring management that software work is done the way it is supposed to be done. To be effective, the assurance organization must have an independent reporting line to senior management and sufficient resources to monitor performance of all key planning, implementation, and verification activities. This generally requires an organization of about 3 percent to 6 percent the size of the software organization.

Change control for software is fundamental to business and financial control as well as to technical stability. To develop quality software on a predictable schedule, requirements must be established and maintained with reasonable stability throughout the development cycle. While requirements changes are often needed, historical evidence demonstrates that many can be deferred and incorporated later. Design and code changes must be made to correct problems found in development and testing, but these must be carefully introduced. If changes are not controlled, then orderly design, implementation, and testing are impossible and no quality plan can be effective.

The Repeatable Process (Level 2)

The repeatable process has one important strength that the ad hoc process does not: It provides control over the way the organization establishes its plans and commitments. This control provides such an improvement over the ad hoc process level that the people in the organization tend to believe they have mastered the software problem. They have achieved a degree of statistical control through learning to make and meet their estimates and plans. This strength, however, stems from their prior experience at doing similar work. Organizations at the repeatable process level thus face major risks when they are presented with new challenges. Examples of the changes that represent the highest risk at this level follow.

- Unless they are introduced with great care, new tools and methods will affect the process, thus destroying the relevance of the intuitive historical base on which the organization relies. Without a consistent process framework in which to address these risks, it is even possible for a new technology to do more harm than good.

- When the organization must develop a new kind of product, it is entering new territory. For example, a software group that has experience developing compilers will likely have design, scheduling, and estimating problems when assigned to write a real-time control program. Similarly, a group that has developed small self-contained programs will not understand the interface and integration issues involved in large-scale projects. These changes again destroy the relevance of the intuitive historical basis for the organization's process.

- Major organizational changes can also be highly disruptive. At the repeatable process level, a new manager has no orderly basis for understanding the organization's operation, and new team members must learn the ropes through word of mouth.

The key actions required to advance from the repeatable process to the next stage, the consistent process, are to establish a process group, establish a development process architecture, and introduce a family of software engineering methods and technologies.

The procedure for establishing a software development process architecture, or development life cycle, that describes the technical and management activities required for proper execution of the development process must be attuned to the specific needs of the organization. It will vary depending on the size and importance of the project as well as the technical nature of the work itself. The architecture is a structural decomposition of the development cycle into tasks, each of which has a defined set of prerequisites, functional descriptions, verification procedures, and task completion specifications. The decomposition continues until each defined task is performed by an individual or single management unit.

If they are not already in place, introduce a family of software engineering methods and technologies. These include design and code inspections, formal design methods, library control systems, and comprehensive testing methods. Prototyping should also be considered, together with the adoption of modern implementation languages.

The Consistent Process (Level 3)

With the consistent process, the organization has achieved the foundation for major and continuing progress. For example, the software teams, when faced with a crisis, will likely continue to use the process that has been defined. The foundation has now been established for examining the process and deciding how to improve it. As powerful as the process is, it is still only qualitative; there is little data to indicate how much was accomplished or how effective the process is. There is considerable debate about the value of software process measurements and the best ones to use. This uncertainty generally stems from a lack of process definition and the consequent confusion about the specific items to be measured. With a consistent process, measurements can be focused on specific tasks. The process architecture is thus an essential prerequisite to effective measurement.

The key steps required to advance from the consistent process to the next level are:

1. Establish a minimum basic set of process measurements to identify the quality and cost parameters of each process step. The objective is to quantify the relative costs and benefits of each major process activity, such as the cost and yield of error detection and correction methods.

2. Establish a process database and the resources to manage and maintain it. Cost and yield data should be maintained centrally to guard against loss, to make it available for all projects, and to facilitate process quality and productivity analysis.

3. Provide sufficient process resources to gather and maintain this process data and to advise project members on its use. Assign skilled professionals to monitor the quality of the data before entry in the database and to provide guidance on analysis methods and interpretation.

4. Assess the relative quality of each product and inform management where quality

targets are not being met. An independent quality assurance group should assess the quality actions of each project and track its progress against its quality plan. When this progress is compared with the historical experience on similar projects, an informed assessment can generally be made.

The Measured Process (Level 4)

In advancing from the ad hoc process through the repeatable and consistent processes to the measured process, software organizations should expect to make substantial quality improvements. The greatest potential problem with the measured process is the cost of gathering data. There are an enormous number of potentially valuable measures of the software process, but such data is expensive to gather and to maintain.

Approach data gathering with care, therefore, and precisely define each piece of data in advance. Productivity data is essentially meaningless unless explicitly defined. For example, the simple measure of lines of source code per expended development month can vary by 100 times or more, depending on the interpretation of the parameters. The code count could include only new and changed code or all shipped instructions. For modified programs, this can cause variations of a factor of 10. Similarly, noncomment nonblank lines, executable instructions, or equivalent assembler instructions can be counted with variations of up to seven times. Management, testing, documentation, and support personnel may or may not be counted when calculating labor months expended. Again, the variations can run at least as high as a factor of seven.

When different groups gather data but do not use identical definitions, the results are not comparable, even if it makes sense to compare them. The tendency with such data is to use it to compare several groups and to criticize those with the lowest ranking. This is an unfortunate misapplication of process data. It is rare that two projects are comparable by any simple measures. The variations in task complexity caused by different product types can exceed five to one. Similarly, the cost per line of code of small modifications is often two to three times that for new programs. The degree of requirements change can make an enormous difference, as can the design status of the base program in the case of enhancements.

Process data must not be used to compare projects or individuals. Its purpose is to illuminate the product being developed and to provide an informed basis for improving the process. When such data is used by management to evaluate individuals or teams, the reliability of the data itself will deteriorate.

The two fundamental requirements for advancing from the measured process to the next level are:

1. Support automatic gathering of process data. All data is subject to error and omission, some data cannot be gathered by hand, and the accuracy of manually gathered data is often poor.

2. Use process data both to analyze and to modify the process to prevent problems and improve efficiency.

The Optimized Process (Level 5)

In varying degrees, process optimization goes on at all levels of process maturity. With the step from the measured to the optimized process, however, there is a paradigm shift. Up to this point, software development managers have largely focused on their products and will typically gather and analyze only data that directly relates to product improvement. In the optimized process, the data is available to tune the process itself. With a little experience, management will soon see that process optimization can produce major quality and productivity benefits.

For example, many types of errors can be identified and fixed far more economically by design or code inspections than by testing. Unfortunately, there is only limited published data available on the costs of finding and fixing defects. However, from experience, I have developed a useful guideline: It takes about one to four working hours to find and fix a bug through inspections, and about 15 to 20 working hours to find and fix a bug in function or system testing. To the extent that organizations find that these numbers apply to their situations, they should consider placing less reliance on testing as their primary way to find and fix bugs.

However, some kinds of errors are either uneconomical to detect or almost impossible to find except by machine. Examples are errors involving spelling and syntax, interfaces, performance, human factors, and error recovery. It would be unwise to eliminate testing completely, since it provides a useful check against human frailties.

The data that is available with the optimized process gives us a new perspective on testing. For most projects, a little analysis shows that there are two distinct activities involved: the removal of defects and the assessment of program quality. To reduce the cost of removing defects, inspections should be emphasized, together with any other cost-effective techniques. The role of functional and system testing should then be changed to one of gathering quality data on the programs. This involves studying each bug to see if it is an isolated problem or if it indicates design problems that require more comprehensive analysis.

With the optimized process, the organization has the means to identify the weakest elements of the process and to fix them. At this point in process improvement, data is available to justify the application of technology to various critical tasks, and numerical evidence is available on the effectiveness with which the process has been applied to any given product. We should then no longer need reams of paper to describe what is happening since simple yield curves and statistical plots could provide clear and concise indicators. It would then be possible to assure the process and hence have confidence in the quality of the resulting products.

Conducting the Client/Server Readiness Assessment

To perform the client/server readiness assessment, you need to evaluate your organization in the eight readiness dimensions, as described in Task 1. You may want to get together a representative group of individuals from your organization to develop the assessment and use Work Paper 18.1 (at the end of the chapter) to assist them in performing the assessment.

Each readiness dimension should be rated in one of the following four categories:

1. **High**—The readiness assessment team is satisfied that the readiness in this dimension will not inhibit, in any way, the successful implementation of client/server technology.

2. **Medium**—The readiness assessment team believes that the readiness in this dimension will not be a significant factor in causing the client/server technology

to fail. While additional readiness would be desirable, it is not considered an inhibitor to installing client/server technology.

3. **Low**—While there is some readiness for client/server technology, there are serious reservations that the readiness in this dimension will have a negative impact on the implementation of client/server technology.

4. **None**—No readiness at all in this area. Without at least low readiness in all eight dimensions, the probability of client/server technology being successful is extremely low.

Work Paper 18.2 can be used to record the results of the client/server technology readiness assessment.

Preparing a Client/Server Readiness Kiviat Chart

A Kiviat chart is a means of graphically illustrating readiness. The end result will be a *footprint* indicating the degree of readiness. The chart is completed by performing the following two steps:

1. Record the point on the dimension line that corresponds to the readiness rating provided on Work Paper 18.2. For example, if the motivation dimension was scored medium, a dot would be put on the medium circle where it intersects with the motivation dimension line.

2. Connect all of the points and color the inside of the readiness lines connecting the eight readiness points.

The shaded area of the Kiviat chart is the client/server readiness footprint. It will graphically show whether your organization is ready for client/server technology. Use Work Paper 18.3 for your client/server readiness Kiviat chart.

Task 2: Assess Key Components

Experience shows that if the key or driving components of technology are in place and working they will provide most of the assurance necessary for effective processing. Four key components are identified for client/server technology:

1. Client installations are done correctly.

2. Adequate security is provided for the client/server system.

3. Client data is adequately protected.

4. Client/server standards are in place and working.

These four key components need to be assessed prior to conducting the detailed testing. Experience has shown that if these key components are not in place and working the correctness and accuracy of ongoing processing may be degraded even though the software works effectively.

A detailed checklist is provided to assist testers in evaluating these four components. The checklists are used most effectively if they are answered after an assessment of the four key areas is completed. The questions are designed to be answered by the testers and not to be asked of the people developing the key component areas.

Task 3: Test the System

The testing of the client/server system should be performed using the 11-step procedure described in Part Three of this book. The 11-step procedure will need to take into account the client/server technology and a communication network in place to support client processing. The testing should be adjusted to take into account the four key components of client/server technology. In addition, the testers may want to use the approach outlined in Chapter 25 for testing a data warehouse to evaluate the data accessible to clients.

Check Procedures

Work Paper 18.4 is a quality control checklist for this client server test process. It is designed so that Yes responses indicate good test practices; No responses warrant additional investigation. A Comments column is provided to explain No responses and to record results of investigation. The N/A column is used when the checklist item is not applicable to the test situation.

Output

The only output from this system is the test report indicating what works and what does not work. The report should also contain recommendations by the test team for improvements where appropriate.

Guidelines

The testing described in this chapter is best performed in two phases. The first phase, Tasks 1 and 2, are best executed during the development of the client/server system. Task 3 can then be used after the client/server system has been developed and is ready for operational testing.

Summary

This chapter provides a test process for testing client/server systems. The materials contained in this chapter are designed to supplement the 11-step process described in Part three of this book. Readiness assessment and key component assessment (Tasks 1 and 2) supplement the 11-step process, specifically in Step 2—test planning. The next chapter is a specialized test process for systems developed using the rapid application development method.

WORK PAPER 18.1   ASSESS CLIENT/SERVER KEY COMPONENTS

Field Requirements

FIELD	INSTRUCTIONS FOR ENTERING DATA
Item	An attribute of the key component that needs to be assessed.
Response	The Yes response is provided to indicate that the item has been successfully incorporated into the key component; a No response indicates that the item has not been incorporated into the key component; N/A (none applicable) indicates that the item is not deemed necessary in the key component of the organization conducting the test.
Comments	This field is used to expand and explain the No response and the type of testing that will be performed to assess the potential impact of a No response.

	ITEM	RESPONSE			COMMENTS
		YES	NO	N/A	
Installing Client System					
1.	Has a personal computer installation package been developed? (If this item has a No response, the remaining items in the checklist can be skipped.)				
2.	Is the installation procedure available to any personal computer user in the organization?				
3.	Does the personal computer installation program provide for locating the personal computer?				
4.	Does the program provide for surge protection for power supplies?				
5.	Does the installation program provide for necessary physical protection?				
6.	Does the installation program identify needed supplies and accessories?				
7.	Does the installation program provide for acquiring needed computer media?				
8.	Does the installation program address storing computer media?				
9.	Does the installation program address storage area for printer supplies, books, and so on?				
10.	Does the installation program address noise from printers, including providing mats and acoustical covers?				
11.	Does the installation program address converting data from paper to computer media?				
12.	Does the installation program arrange for off-site storage area?				
13.	Does the installation program arrange for personal computer servicing?				

WORK PAPER 18.1   *(Continued)*

	ITEM	YES	NO	N/A	COMMENTS
		\ RESPONSE			

	ITEM	YES	NO	N/A	COMMENTS
14.	Does the installation program arrange for a backup processing facility?				
15.	Does the installation program arrange for consulting services if needed?				
16.	Are users taught how to install personal computers through classes or step-by-step procedures?				
17.	Do installation procedures take into account specific organizational requirements, such as accounting for computer usage?				
18.	Is the installation process customized depending on the phase of maturity of personal computer usage?				
19.	Has a means been established to measure the success of the installation process?				
20.	Have potential installation impediments been identified and counterstrategies adopted where appropriate?				
21.	Has the organization determined their strategy in the event that the installation of standard personal computer is unsatisfactory to the user?				
22.	Has the needed client software been supplied?				
23.	Has the needed client software been tested?				

Client/Server Security

	ITEM	YES	NO	N/A	COMMENTS
1.	Has the organization issued a security policy for personal computers?				
2.	Have standards and procedures been developed to ensure effective compliance with that policy?				
3.	Are procedures established to record personal computer violations?				
4.	Have the risks associated with personal computers been identified?				
5.	Has the magnitude of each risk been identified?				
6.	Has the personal security group identified the type of available countermeasures for the personal computer security threats?				
7.	Has an awareness program been developed to encourage support of security in a personal computer environment?				

WORK PAPER 18.1   *(Continued)*

	ITEM	YES	NO	N/A	COMMENTS
			RESPONSE		
8.	Have training programs been developed for personal computer users in security procedures and methods?				
9.	Does the audit function conduct regular audits to evaluate personal computer security and identify potential vulnerabilities in that security?				
10.	Does senior management take an active role in supporting the personal computer security program?				
11.	Have security procedures been developed for operators of personal computers?				
12.	Are the security programs at the central computer site and coordinated?				
13.	Has one individual at the central site been appointed responsible for overseeing security of the personal computer program?				
14.	Have operating managers/personal computer users been made responsible for security over their personal computer facilities?				
15.	Is the effectiveness of the total personal computer security program regularly evaluated?				
16.	Has one individual been appointed responsible for the security of personal computers for the organization?				

Client Data

	ITEM	YES	NO	N/A	COMMENTS
1.	Has a policy been established on sharing data with users?				
2.	Is data recognized as a corporate resource as opposed to the property of a single department or individual?				
3.	Have the requirements for sharing been defined?				
4.	Have profiles been established indicating what user wants which data?				
5.	Have the individuals responsible for that data approved use by the proposed users of the data?				
6.	Has a usage profile been developed that identifies whether data is to be uploaded and downloaded?				

WORK PAPER 18.1   *(Continued)*

	RESPONSE			
ITEM	YES	NO	N/A	COMMENTS
7. Has the user use profile been defined to the appropriate levels to provide the needed security?				
8. Have security standards been established for protecting data at personal computer sites?				
9. Has the personal computer user been made accountable and responsible for the security of the data at the personal computer site?				
10. Does the user's manager share this security responsibility?				
11. Have adequate safeguards at the central site been established to prevent unauthorized access to data?				
12. Have adequate safeguards at the central site been established to prevent unauthorized modification to data?				
13. Are logs maintained that keep records of what data is transferred to and from personal computer sites?				
14. Do the communication programs provide for error handling?				
15. Are the remote users trained in accessing and protecting corporate data?				
16. Have the appropriate facilities been developed to reformat files?				
17. Are appropriate safeguards taken to protect diskettes at remote sites containing corporate data?				
18. Is the security protection required for data at the remote site known to the personal computer user?				
19. Are violations of data security/control procedures recorded?				
20. Is someone in the organization accountable for ensuring that data is made available to those users who need it? (In many organizations this individual is referred to as the data administrator.)				

Client/Server Standards

1. Are standards based on a hierarchy of policies, standards, procedures, and guidelines?				

WORK PAPER 18.1 *(Continued)*

ITEM	YES	NO	N/A	COMMENTS
2. Has the organization issued a personal computer policy?				
3. Have the standards been issued to evaluate compliance with the organization's personal computer policy?				
4. Have policies been developed for users of personal computers that are supportive of the organization's overall personal computer policy?				
5. Have personal computer policies been developed for the following areas:				
a. Continuity of processing				
b. Reconstruction				
c. Accuracy				
d. Security				
e. Compliance				
f. File integrity				
g. Data				
6. Are all standards tied directly to personal computer policies?				
7. Has the concept of ownership been employed in the development of standards?				
8. Can the benefit of each standard be demonstrated to the users of the standards?				
9. Are the standards written in playscript?				
10. Have quality control self-assessment tools been issued to personal computer users to help them comply with the standards?				
11. Has a standards notebook been prepared?				
12. Is the standards notebook divided by area of responsibility?				
13. Are the standards explained to users in the form of a training class or users-group meeting?				
14. Does a representative group of users have an opportunity to review and comment on standards before they are issued?				
15. Are guidelines issued where appropriate?				
16. Is the standards program consistent with the objectives of the phase of maturity of the personal computer in the organization?				

WORK PAPER 18.2   Client/Server Readiness Assessment

	READINESS DIMENSION		READINESS RATING			
#	NAME	DESCRIPTION	HIGH	MEDIUM	LOW	NONE

WORK PAPER 18.3   Kiviat Chart

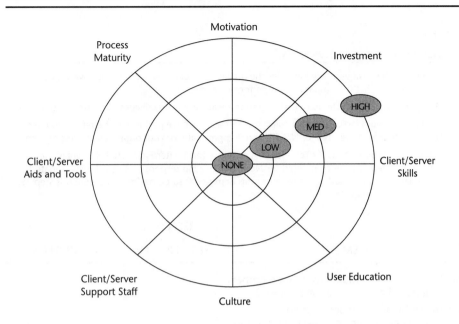

WORK PAPER 18.4   Quality Control Checklist

Field Requirements

FIELD	INSTRUCTIONS FOR ENTERING DATA
Number	A number which sequentially identifies the quality control items, which if positively addressed would indicate that this step has been performed correctly.
Item	The specific quality control item that is used to measure the effectiveness of performing this step.
Response	The testers should indicate in this column whether they have performed the referenced item. The response can be Yes, No, or N/A if it is not appropriate for your organization's testing process.
Comments	This column is used to clarify Yes, No, N/A response for the item indicated. Generally the comments need only be completed for No responses; No responses should be investigated and a determination made as to whether this item needs to be performed before this step can be considered complete.

		RESPONSE			
#	ITEM	YES	NO	N/A	COMMENTS
1.	Does the test team in total have team members who understand client/server technology?				
2.	Have the test team members acquired knowledge of client/server system to be tested?				
3.	Has the readiness of the organization who installs client/server technology been evaluated?				
4.	If the organization is not deemed ready to install client/server technology, have the appropriate steps been taken to achieve a readiness status prior to installing the client/server system?				
5.	Has an adequate plan been developed and implemented to ensure proper installation of client technology?				
6.	Are the communication lines adequate to enable efficient client/server processing?				
7.	Has the server component of the system been developed adequately so that it can support client processing?				
8.	Are security procedures adequate to protect client hardware and software?				
9.	Are security procedures adequate to prevent processing compromise by employees, external personnel, and acts of nature?				
10.	Are procedures in place to adequately protect client data?				
11.	Are procedures in place to ensure that clients can only access data for which they have been authorized?				
12.	Are standards in place for managing client/server systems?				
13.	Does management support and enforce those standards?				

CHAPTER

19

Testing Rapid Application Development

Rapid application development (RAD) is an effective software development paradigm. It provides a systematic and automatable means of developing a software system under circumstances where initial requirements are not well known or where requirements change frequently during development. To provide high software quality assurance requires sufficient software testing. The unique nature of evolutionary iterative developing is not well suited for classical testing methodologies; therefore, the need exists for a testing methodology tailored for this developing paradigm.

Overview

This chapter describes a testing strategy for rapid application development—spiral testing. This document shows key RAD characteristics impinging on testing and the value of spiral testing to support evolutionary iterative rapid developing. This testing strategy assumes the RAD system will have the following characteristics:

- Iterative

- Evolutionary

- Containing RAD language with a defined grammar

- Providing reusable components capability (library and retrieval)

- Using implementation code from reusable components written in a high-level language

- Containing sophisticated support environment

These characteristics will keep the RAD paradigm sufficiently general to discuss testing concerns. Since program verification and validation is the most costly activity in current development, any changes to RAD to simplify testing will accelerate the development process and increase RAD's appeal.

Objective

The RAD testing methodology described in this test process is designed to take maximum advantage of the iterative nature of RAD. It also should focus on the requirements-capturing purpose of developing. Thus, a RAD-based testing technique starts by capturing the testing information resident in the RAD process in a form suitable for thoroughly testing the RAD system. Testers must know both the assumptions and the requirements the designers are trying to meet so that a test oracle and test series can be built to verify the system. Remember, the test personnel are not usually the design personnel, nor should they be; therefore, RAD-based testing must provide tools and methods to analyze system requirements and capture requirement changes.

Concerns

Testers should have four concerns about RAD testing:

1. Test Information from Iteration

The iterative nature of developing implies that the developing system must track revision histories and maintain version control of alternate RAD versions. The user's response to a demonstration may require that the RAD fall back to a previous iteration for change, or the developer might wish to demonstrate several iteration alternatives for user comment (one of which, or portions of several being selected). Requirements may be added (expressed), changed (refined), or deleted. Test goals must easily change to fit modified requirements. Ideally, the developing environment will capture this modification explicitly, along with the accompanying purpose of the modification. Any testing tools developed must take these modifications into account to test the proper version and to appropriately consider the requirements and purpose germane to that version for test development. The tool should also exploit change as a likely source of errors. A tool that helps testers compare changes from one iteration to the next, along with system dependencies potentially affected by changes, will help test development considerably.

2. Test Information about Components

The use of reusable components raises reliability concerns about the reusable component library. Have the components been unit tested, and if so, to what degree? Have they been used in previous implementations before, and if so, which ones? What testing has been conducted on the previous implementations as well as the individual component? The testing methodology must consider how information on past component testing can be recorded and referenced to determine what unit testing might still be needed and what integration testing strategies might best check the components in their instantiated context.

3. Test Information about Performance

One necessary testing component is a set of test conditions. Requirements-based and functional testing base test conditions upon some stated form of behavior or required performance standard such as formal specifications or a requirements document. The developing methodology does not provide a separate performance standard. The testing methodology must establish an objective standard of the intended behavior of the RAD under consideration. Every test involves comparison with an oracle, so every program must have an objective performance standard. The developing system must then, in some fashion, provide the tester and his or her tools with access to a system functionality description and system requirements to allow rapid, complete, and consistent derivation of the test oracle from the RAD. This access to functionality descriptions and requirements has the added benefit of helping develop scripts for demonstrations so that particular iteration changes and enhancements will be highlighted for the user's comments.

4. Record Test Information

The developing environment not only should capture requirements, assumptions, and design decisions, but ideally should map these into the RAD in a way useful to both rapid application development and testing. This mapping automatically provides a trace, documenting the RAD's development. As the size of the system grows, knowing why a particular design decision was made and being able to see where (and how) the RAD implements it will be difficult without automated support. The developing/testing paradigm must capture mappings from design or development decisions to the implementation. These mappings need to be rapidly revisable to quickly make the next RAD iteration.

Workbench

The workbench for testing rapid application developed systems is illustrated in Figure 19.1. This workbench shows the requirements for the RAD system as the input to the workbench. Since rapid application development goes through a series of iterations the tasks in the workbench parallel those iterations. Note that Task 2 may in fact perform multiple times all of the iterations between the planning iteration and the final iteration. The methods for performing the test execution are those that are included in the 11-step testing process, which comprises Part Three of this book.

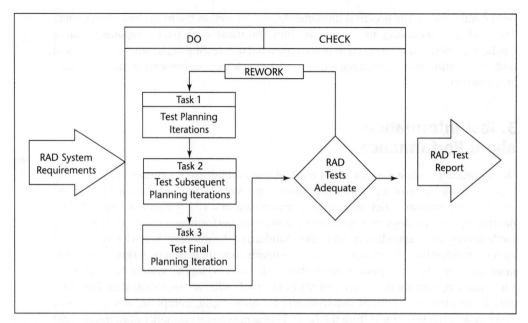

Figure 19.1 Workbench for testing rapid application developed systems.

Input

The only input to this test process is the RAD requirements. Because of the nature of rapid application development, the requirements are normally incomplete when development begins. The requirements will be continually developed throughout various iterations. Thus, the input to each of the three steps in the recommended RAD test process will be different.

Do Procedures

This section presents a process for testing within iterative rapid developing, describes testing-related features that a developing system needs in the light of the developing methodology, and then integrates this into a three-task RAD testing strategy.

Testing within Iterative Rapid Developing

The chapter provides a framework for iterative RAD testing. The most obvious approach to testing during RAD would be to treat each development iteration as one software life cycle. An advantage is that this keeps intact the methodology of testing familiar to most testers. The lack of a conventional specification effectively removes the information basis for test planning. Under current descriptions of the developing process, a specification would need to be generated, at least in part, before conventional techniques could be applied.

The process's complexity is also compounded by the need to conduct a full cycle of testing for each iteration, even though the early iterations will almost never contain detailed or unchanging requirements. This would be inefficient and impractical testing.

An alternative test approach is to iterate test planning in parallel with the developing iterations. This will simplify testing and reduce overall testing costs when compared to the above approach. The initial test plan would only consider the basic system description contained in the initial RAD iteration. As RAD iterations proceed, the test plan would expand to incorporate the latest iteration modifications. One disadvantage is that this approach causes the test plan to follow closely the RAD process. The decisions in the RAD might unduly influence the test plan, causing important test conditions not to be explored. The possible disadvantage suggests that the unit and integration testing might be done iteratively, with acceptance testing occurring entirely on the final iteration of the development cycle.

By considering how the developing process closely follows the spiral process model, that leads to a spiral iterative test planning process. Figure 19.2 illustrates this process.

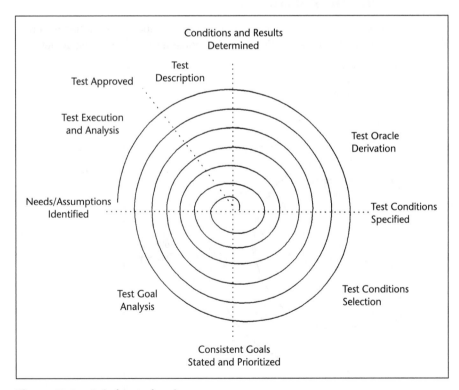

Figure 19.2   Spiral test planning process.

Spiral Testing

The proposed RAD testing strategy, termed "spiral testing," remains iterative and parallels the RAD process. Spiral testing characterizes the varying types of RAD iterations by tailoring the testing process to account for these differences. Spiral testing distinguishes between the initial few RAD testing iterations, subsequent iterations, and the final few iterations. The major distinction between the first few testing iterations and the subsequent ones is that the first iterations, for any but the smallest of systems, probably will have only test planning and structuring activities that establish priorities and areas of test emphasis.

The framework for intermediate testing activity and final acceptance testing, to include test oracle derivation, is laid in the initial iterations. Test oracle derivation and unit and integration testing will likely be confined to subsequent and final testing iterations. Subsequent testing iterations will have less framework-related activity and more acceptance test oracle derivation activity. The major distinction between the subsequent and final iterations is that the final iterations are where developers return to their RAD to fix identified errors and testers conduct final integration and acceptance and regression testing. Figure 19.3 shows the separation of the groups of iterations for either the development or testing spiral. The following sections cover spiral testing in detail.

Task 1: Test Planning Iterations

The first few iterations of the RAD serve varying purposes, depending on the particular software under design. When feasibility is not a consideration or when a detailed

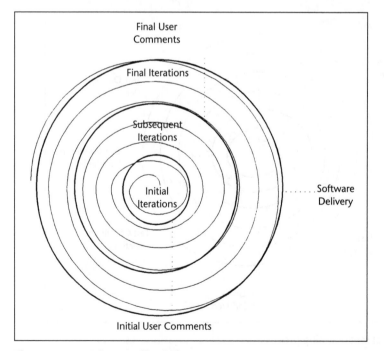

Figure 19.3   A "targeted" spiral.

requirements document exists, the first development iterations establish the product's design framework as a base upon which to RAD the remainder of the system. When feasibility must be investigated and/or when requirements are unknown, the first several development iterations seek to construct abstract RADs to see if an acceptable system can be designed. If the RAD is feasible, developers establish the major software requirements and design a development plan upon which to build the system during successive iterations, as in the first case above. The first few development iterations will usually be devoted to establishing an overall RAD structural framework.

To mirror this process for test planning purposes, the initial test planning iterations consider the developing results and frame the testing process for the remainder of the project. This is the logical point for testers to determine the major critical portions of the RAD, and establish test priorities. As RADs establish major requirements, the test team begins to break these down into test goals, determining derived goals as well. As development continues, the testers can define the testing emphasis in greater detail, make needed test plan adjustments, and record test justifications.

It appears prudent (though not essential) throughout the development process for the test team to review user input and generate goals independently from the RAD team, so as to identify misstated requirements and to find missing requirements. This increases the quality of the RAD versions, decreasing the number of iterations needed.

The initial iterations are where the test team will forecast the most important portions of the system to test. As the implementation hierarchy of the system takes shape, the testers establish test sections for path and integration testing. The long-term testing purpose is to build the framework for constructing the final acceptance-test oracle and to fit the intermediate testing activities into the overall development plan. The process will be manual for the most part, and this would be where initial testing tools and their databases/instrumentation would be initialized. The initial iteration phase would end at the RAD iteration in which the top-level requirements specification is established.

It is recommended that the documentation for each iteration of the RAD process be subject to the inspection process. You should use the inspection process that is outlined in Part Three of this book for that purpose. Work Paper 19.1 contains a series of inspection questions to be used during Task 1.

Task 2: Test Subsequent Planning Iterations

Once the basic RAD framework is established, subsequent iterations commence in which developers enhance the RAD's functionality and demonstrate it for user/designer review. In the typical case, additional requirements are identified and the design matures in parallel over multiple iterations. Both are validated in the review process. At some point, sufficient requirements are identified to establish the overall system design.

The subsequent testing iterations will be characterized by unit testing, integration testing, and continued requirements review to determine if there are missing requirements. To complement the design process, the test team concurrently develops integration test plans as designers complete subsections of the system design. In addition, as reusable components are instantiated to provide required functionality, the test team or design team unit tests these modules (both approaches are acceptable in current practice) by consulting the test history of the instantiated modules and conducting additional unit testing appropriate to the developing system.

Should this additional testing be necessary, the test team updates the test history to reflect the additional testing and its results. This update could be as simple as appending a test script (though this could eventually cost a large amount of storage for a large components test library) or as complex as completely revising the test history to incorporate new test sets, assumptions tested, test case justifications, and additional test history details. The complex update may be needed to reduce a series of simple updates into a consistent and usefully compact synthesis. As performance aberrations are found during a given iteration's tests, they are readdressed to the design team for correction prior to the next iteration demonstration.

As the design team RADs system components, the test team can commence integration test planning for those components. The integration testing process is the same at any hierarchical system level for integration testing. The test team needs to keep integration testing at various levels coordinated to maximize test efficiency. If a standard structure for integration test sets could be constructed, then it might be possible to develop tools to manipulate these to conduct increasing levels of integration testing as more components and system subsections are implemented. Currently, most of this process would be manual. Final integration testing cannot commence until the RAD implementation is complete.

Throughout testing, testers consult the RAD specification and all requirements to determine the correct responses to test data. Considerable information needed for test data selection will likely be found in the RAD specification language. Automated support to extract this information would be very helpful, but will depend on the developing language in question and in possessing the capability automatically to relate the criteria to selected test data and execute the test.

Throughout the iterations, the test methodology must remain responsive to change. Existing components and specifications may change or disappear between iterations, contingent with user/developer/tester input. Additionally, each new iteration will add increased functionality or further the completion of existing incomplete implementations. The test development process must capture all effects of change because additional testing or retesting of previously tested code may be required. This retesting raises the issue of "phase agreement" between the RAD spiral and the test-planning spiral.

An "in-phase" agreement would have formal iteration testing proceed at the completion of a development iteration and prior to iteration demonstration to the user. The advantage here is that the test team will have tested the system and the developers are not as likely to demonstrate a system that contains undiscovered or obvious bugs. Any problems encountered in testing are corrected prior to user review. User confidence is not enhanced when bugs are discovered during the demonstration that are not related to design issues. On the other hand, many iterations will usually be demonstrating requirements not yet validated and it is wasteful to test requirements that have not been validated.

An "out-of-phase" testing approach would rely on the designers to test their RAD iteration sufficiently prior to demonstration (for their reputation, not for formal testing). The test team would conduct formal testing for an iteration at the conclusion of the user demonstration. They would modify the formal test plan, developed during the development iteration, by removing any planned testing of eliminated, changed, or superseded requirements and by adding additional testing of corrections and modifications resulting from the user's review. Test planning would proceed in tandem with iterations development, but actual testing would wait for the results of the user's review. Once the testers obtain user comments, they may assume that the stated requirements at that point represent solid requirements for the purpose of testing. This assumption continues until a requirement is explicitly or implicitly changed or eliminated. The advantages of out-of-phase testing are a savings in testing conducted (due to testing only reviewed requirements) and increased test responsiveness to user review. The disadvantages are the increased likelihood of missed requirements and the possibility of bugs in the demonstrated systems. Work Paper 19.2 should be used when subsequent iterations are inspected.

Task 3: Test Final Planning Iteration

Once developers establish all requirements (usually in the latter iterations), the final few iterations of development are devoted to implementing the remaining functionality, followed by error correction. Therefore, the testers can devote their work to completing the test oracle for acceptance testing, and to remaining unit testing and subsection integration testing.

The final test planning iterations commence with the completion of the operational RAD and prior to final user acceptance. As any final requirements are implemented or as system components are fine-tuned, tests are developed and conducted to cover these changes. Most importantly, the test team completes the acceptance test plan. Once the system is completely implemented and the acceptance test design, including the test oracle, is complete, the test team conducts the acceptance test. The test team checks differences in actual results from expected results and corrects the tests as appropriate while the design team corrects system faults. The cycle continues until the system successfully completes testing. If the design team is busier than the test team, then the test team can use the available time to conduct additional testing or priority-superseded testing previously skipped. The result should be a sufficiently tested software system. Work Paper 19.3 should be used when the final iteration is inspected.

Check Procedures

Work Paper 19.4 is a quality control checklist for testing Rapid Application Developed systems. It is designed so that Yes responses indicate good test practices; No responses warrant additional investigation. A Comments column is provided to explain No responses and to record results of investigation. The N/A column is used when the checklist item is not applicable to the test situation.

Output

This testing process will have multiple outputs of approximately the same composition. These outputs are test reports indicating findings at the end of the testing of each iteration of the RAD development. Those reports should indicate what works and what does not work. It should also contain testers' recommendations for improvement. Note that if there are many iterations of the system being developed, the reports maybe less formal, so that they can be more quickly provided to the development team.

Guidelines

Spiral testing has the advantages of being flexible and maximizing the amount of testing conducted during the RAD process. It allows for the steady development of an acceptance test in the face of continual system change and facilitates lower-level testing as soon as implementation code is instantiated. The spiral testing approach particularly suits the methodology for use with evolutionary iterative rapid developing that is itself spiral. Using test histories for reusable components should speed the testing process by reducing the amount of unit testing required. A further benefit of the test history feature is the compounding of unit testing for reusable components with use, either increasing our component confidence factor or at least delineating the bounds within which it may be successfully used.

The spiral testing approach also results in thorough documentation of the testing conducted and a formal, written test plan that can be viewed with the user for approval. The extended time for test development (considerably more than in conventional life cycle models) also should provide for a more thorough test.

The major disadvantage to the approach is that the final acceptance test remains a moving target until the completion of implementation coding. Additionally, the test team must remain vigilant against following the development process so closely that they fail to view the system objectively from the outside. The first disadvantage is inherent to the development process; therefore, our goal is to minimize its effect. Spiral testing is likely to do this. The second disadvantage may be reduced with experience, but will likely require separate test teams to conduct critical acceptance tests. One should note that the spiral testing strategy remains a theory at this point. Further research will be required to determine its feasibility and practicality.

Summary

This chapter provides a testing process for systems developed using the rapid application development methodology. Testers need to be familiar with the rapid application development methodology in use in their organization. The materials contained in this chapter are focused more on the inspection process because it is more effective in uncovering defects than is dynamic testing. Dynamic testing is more effective when used in the later iterations of the RAD process. This chapter is designed to be used in conjunction with the 11-step process outlined in Part Three of this book.

WORK PAPER 19.1   RAD Inspection Checklist for Task 1

Field Requirements

FIELD	INSTRUCTIONS FOR ENTERING DATA
Number	A number that sequentially identifies the inspection items, which if positively addressed would indicate that the inspection has incorporated the most significant items.
Inspection Item	For specific inspection question/item to be evaluated during the inspection process.
Inspection Results	Tester's indication as to the results of performing the inspection. Pass means that the RAD system met the intent of the inspection item, fail means that it did not, and N/A indicates that the specific inspection item is not applicable for the RAD system being tested.
Description/Location of Noted Defect	Enter the type and location of a defect uncovered in the inspection process related to this specific inspection item.

#	INSPECTION ITEM	PASS	FAIL	N/A	DESCRIPTION/LOCATION OF NOTED DEFECT
	Define Purpose and Scope of System				
1.	Is the defined system within the context of the organization's goals?				
2.	Is the defined system within the context of the organization's information requirements?				
3.	Have the objectives that are critical to the success of the organization been identified in the RAD purpose and scope?				
4.	Does the system scope identify the user environment?				
5.	Does the system scope identify the hardware environment?				
6.	Does the system scope identify the other systems that interact with this system (e.g., regarding input and output)?				
7.	Does the RAD system scope define available funding?				
8.	Does the RAD system scope identify time constraints?				
9.	Does the RAD system scope identify the available resources to build the system?				
10.	Does the RAD system scope state the security needs for the data and software?				

WORK PAPER 19.1 *(Continued)*

#	INSPECTION ITEM	INSPECTION RESULT			DESCRIPTION/LOCATION OF NOTED DEFECT
		PASS	FAIL	N/A	
11.	Has the RAD team been established?				
12.	Is the RAD team trained in the techniques of RAD and the use of specific fourth-generation language for implementing RAD?				
13.	Is the RAD software development group enthusiastic about the RAD concept?				
14.	Does the RAD team know how to control RAD?				

Develop System Conceptual Model

#	INSPECTION ITEM	PASS	FAIL	N/A	DESCRIPTION
1.	Does the RAD team use a graphic method (e.g., a data flow diagram) to construct a model of the system to be developed?				
2.	Are the data definitions used for the RAD included in the data dictionary?				
3.	Are the critical system objectives defined in the project scope related to specific components of the conceptual model?				
4.	Has the major business input been defined?				
5.	Has the major business output been defined?				
6.	Has the cost to implement the system using traditional systems development processes been estimated?				
7.	Has the cost of the RAD been estimated? (The RAD should cost no more than 6% to 10% of the full-scale development effort.)				
8.	Have the benefits of the RAD system been developed?				
9.	Have the risks associated with developing this system when it goes into production been identified?				
10.	Have the files needed to support the RAD system when it goes into production been identified?				
11.	Has a database administrator been consulted to determine whether the needed data will be available?				

WORK PAPER 19.1   *(Continued)*

#	INSPECTION ITEM	INSPECTION RESULT			DESCRIPTION/LOCATION OF NOTED DEFECT
		PASS	FAIL	N/A	
12.	Has the computer operations department been consulted to determine whether it could run the system if it were implemented?				
13.	Are there sufficient communications lines to support the system?				

Develop Logical Data Model

#	INSPECTION ITEM	INSPECTION RESULT			DESCRIPTION/LOCATION OF NOTED DEFECT
1.	Has a model of the local information flow for individual subsystems been designed?				
2.	Has a model for the global information flow for collections of subsystems been designed?				
3.	Have the conceptual schemas for the RAD system been defined?				
4.	Does the conceptual schema define the attributes of each entity in the subschema?				
5.	Has a model been developed for each physical external schema?				
6.	Has the physical database been designed to provide optimum access for the prototype transactions?				
7.	Does the physical database design provide efficiency in operation?				
8.	Is the RAD design restricted to accessing the database at the logical level?				
9.	Have the functions to be performed by the RAD system been defined?				
10.	Has the sequence of performing the functions been defined?				
11.	Has the potential source of input transactions and data been defined?				
12.	Has a determination been made that the needed data can be prepared in time to meet RAD processing schedules?				

WORK PAPER 19.2   RAD Inspection Checklist for Task 2

Field Requirements

FIELD	INSTRUCTIONS FOR ENTERING DATA
Number	A number that sequentially identifies the inspection items, which if positively addressed would indicate that the inspection has incorporated the most significant items.
Inspection Item	For specific inspection item to be evaluated during the inspection process.
Inspection Results	Tester's indication as to the results of performing the inspection. Pass means that the RAD system met the intent of the inspection item, fail means that it did not, and N/A indicates that the specific inspection item is not applicable for the RAD system being tested.
Description/Location of noted defect	Enter the type and location of a defect uncovered in the inspection process related to this specific inspection item.

#	INSPECTION ITEM	INSPECTION RESULT			DESCRIPTION/LOCATION OF NOTED DEFECT
		PASS	FAIL	N/A	
	Develop and Demonstrate RAD System				
1.	Have the basic database structures derived from the logical data modeling been defined?				
2.	Have the report formats been defined?				
3.	Have the interactive data entry screens been defined?				
4.	Have the external file routines to process data been defined?				
5.	Have the algorithms and procedures to be implemented by the RAD been defined?				
6.	Have the procedure selection menus been defined?				
7.	Have the test cases to ascertain that data entry validation is correct been defined?				
8.	Have report and screen formatting options been defined?				
9.	Has a RAD system been developed using a fourth-generation language?				
10.	Has the RAD been demonstrated to management?				
11.	Has management made strategic decisions about the application based on RAD appearance and objectives?				
12.	Has the RAD been demonstrated to the users?				

WORK PAPER 19.2   *(Continued)*

#	INSPECTION ITEM	INSPECTION RESULT			DESCRIPTION/LOCATION OF NOTED DEFECT
		PASS	FAIL	N/A	
13.	Have the users been given the opportunity to identify problems and point out unacceptable procedures?				
14.	Has the prototype been demonstrated before a representative group of users?				
15.	If the RAD is unacceptable to management or users, have requests for changes or corrections been documented?				
16.	Has a decision been made concerning whether to develop another RAD iteration?				

WORK PAPER 19.3   RAD Inspection Checklist for Task 3

Field Requirements

FIELD	INSTRUCTIONS FOR ENTERING DATA
Number	A number that sequentially identifies the inspection items, which if positively addressed would indicate that the inspection has incorporated the most significant items.
Inspection Item	For specific inspection item to be evaluated during the inspection process.
Inspection Results	Tester's indication as to the results of performing the inspection. Pass means that the RAD system met the intent of the inspection item, fail means that it did not, and N/A indicates that the specific inspection item is not applicable for the RAD system being tested.
Description/Location of noted defect	Enter the type and location of a defect uncovered in the inspection process related to this specific inspection item.

#	INSPECTION ITEM	INSPECTION RESULT			DESCRIPTION/LOCATION OF NOTED DEFECT
		PASS	FAIL	N/A	
	Revise and Finalize Specifications				
1.	Is someone on the RAD team responsible for reviewing each component for inconsistencies, ambiguities, and omissions?				
2.	Has the statement of goals and objectives been reviewed to ensure that all elements are present, that all components have been defined, and that there are no conflicts?				
3.	Has the definition of system scope been reviewed to ensure that all elements are present, that all components have been defined, and that there are no conflicts?				
4.	Have the system diagrams been reviewed to ensure that all elements are present, that all components have been defined, and that there are no conflicts?				
5.	Has the data dictionary report been reviewed to ensure that all elements are present, that all components have been defined, and that there are no conflicts?				
6.	Has the risk analysis been reviewed to ensure that all elements are present, that all components have been defined, and that there are no conflicts?				
7.	Has the logical data model been reviewed to ensure that all elements are present, that all components have been defined, and that there are no conflicts?				

WORK PAPER 19.3 *(Continued)*

#	INSPECTION ITEM	INSPECTION RESULT			DESCRIPTION/LOCATION OF NOTED DEFECT
		PASS	FAIL	N/A	
8.	Have the data entry screens been reviewed to ensure that all elements are present, that all components have been defined, and that there are no conflicts?				
9.	Have the report layouts been reviewed to ensure that all elements are present, that all components have been defined, and that there are no conflicts?				
10.	Have the selection menus and operational flow been reviewed to ensure that all elements are present, that all components have been defined, and that there are no conflicts?				
11.	Has the physical database structure been reviewed to ensure that all elements are present, that all components have been defined, and that there are no conflicts?				
12.	Has the draft user manual been reviewed to ensure that all elements are present, that all components have been defined, and that there are no conflicts?				
13.	Have all of the RAD elements been indexed?				
14.	Have all of the RAD elements been cross-referenced by subject and component?				
15.	Does the RAD documentation contain sample reports?				
16.	Does the RAD documentation contain sample data entry screens?				
17.	Does the RAD documentation contain a listing of the fourth-generation commands for each programmed function?				

Develop Production System

#	INSPECTION ITEM	PASS	FAIL	N/A	DESCRIPTION/LOCATION OF NOTED DEFECT
1.	Has a decision been made by the end user regarding putting the system in production?				
2.	If so, have all the significant system problems been resolved?				
3.	If the RAD is very inefficient, is it discarded in place of a production system built using traditional methods?				
4.	If the RAD does not have adequate controls, is it thrown away and a new system developed using traditional methods?				
5.	If the RAD is placed into production, does it have adequate data validation?				

WORK PAPER 19.3   *(Continued)*

#	INSPECTION ITEM	INSPECTION RESULT			DESCRIPTION/LOCATION OF NOTED DEFECT
		PASS	FAIL	N/A	
6.	If the RAD is placed into production, does it have adequate system controls?				
7.	If the RAD is placed into production, does it have adequate documentation for maintenance purposes?				
8.	If the system is rebuilt using traditional methods, does the developmental project team believe that the RAD documentation is adequate for developing a production system?				

Release Test System

#	INSPECTION ITEM	PASS	FAIL	N/A	
1.	Has the system been approved by the test team before being released for test?				
2.	Has the system design been documented in detail?				
3.	Have the user manuals been revised?				
4.	Has a training plan been developed?				
5.	Are the users involved in the testing?				
6.	Is the system put under full production conditions during testing?				
7.	Does the existing system remain in place until the new system has passed testing?				
8.	Have all end users been trained in the operation of the system?				
9.	If the output is crucial to the organization, has a parallel operation test been performed?				
10.	Are errors noted during testing documented?				
11.	Are needed changes noted during testing documented?				
12.	Has a formal decision procedure been developed to determine when to move the system out of testing?				

Release Production System

#	INSPECTION ITEM	PASS	FAIL	N/A	
1.	Have the users accepted the system before it is placed into production?				
2.	Have the final user manuals been prepared?				
3.	Have the final user manuals been distributed to the end users?				
4.	Have the end users been trained in any changes occurring between testing and placement of the system into production?				

WORK PAPER 19.4   Quality Control Checklist

Field Requirements

FIELD	INSTRUCTIONS FOR ENTERING DATA
Number	A number that sequentially identifies the quality control items, which if positively addressed would indicate that this step has been performed correctly.
Item	The specific quality control item that is used to measure the effectiveness of performing this step.
Response	The testers should indicate in this column whether they have performed the referenced item. The response can be Yes, No, or N/A if it is not appropriate for your organization's testing process.
Comments	This column is used to clarify the Yes, No, or N/A response for the item indicated. Generally the comments column need only be completed for No responses; No responses should be investigated and a determination made as to whether this item needs to be performed before this step can be considered complete.

#	ITEM	RESPONSE			COMMENTS
		YES	NO	N/A	
1.	Does the test team contain a collective knowledge and insight into how RAD systems are developed?				
2.	Does the test team collectively understand the tool that is used in RAD?				
3.	Do the testers understand that the RAD's requirements will be continually changing as development progresses?				
4.	Does the test team collectively understand how to use the inspection tools?				
5.	Is the inspection process used at the end of each iteration of RAD?				
6.	Are new requirements documented prior to developing each RAD iteration?				
7.	Did the testers test each RAD iteration?				
8.	Is the tester's input incorporated into the process of updating requirements for the next iteration of a RAD?				

Testing the Adequacy of System Documentation

Approximately 10 to 25 percent of a system's development and maintenance effort is put toward developing and maintaining documentation. The real cost of documentation, however, should include the extra expenses that result from lack of documentation. Although documentation testing should be performed along with other testing, it is treated as a separate chapter because it requires special attention.

Overview

It is important to ensure that the right documentation has been prepared, is complete and current, reflects the criticality of the system, and contains all necessary elements. If any part of the documentation is not current, the user must assume that none of it may be current and look for other sources to substantiate what has been developed and how it works.

Objective

The testing of documentation should conform to other aspects of systems and program testing. Documentation is as prone to error as computer programs. The difference is that defective programs usually lead to defective results, whereas defective documentation may not. Defective documentation, however, is a time bomb; it can cause systems to be improperly changed or system output to be improperly used. Both of these errors can lead to incorrect system results.

The proposed test method for documentation is a generalized approach that must be customized for each organization. Customization involves the following tasks:

Customizing vocabulary. The terms used in the test methodology should be the ones used in the organization for describing various system components and documents. For example, the test methodology discusses a feasibility study document, but an organization might refer to this as a project justification document. The vocabulary used in testing should be the same vocabulary used in development.

Expanding or contracting the approach to be consistent with the organization's documentation standards. The test methodology identifies 14 documents needed for system development, maintenance, and operations. An organization's documentation standard may have more or fewer documents or may combine two or three documents. The test team should identify or change the documents used in this approach so that they relate to the specific documents used in the organization.

Continually modifying the documentation test approach to make it more effective. Experience gained in testing documentation can help refine the documentation test method.

Concerns

The concerns regarding computer systems documentation are that the documentation process will fail to:

- Bring discipline to the performance of an IT function.
- Assist in planning and managing resources.
- Help in planning and implementing security procedures.
- Assist auditors in evaluating applications systems.
- Help transfer knowledge of software development throughout the life cycle.
- Promote common understanding and expectation about the system, within the organization and—if the software is purchased—between the buyer and seller.
- Define what is expected and verify that that is what is delivered.
- Provide flexibility within an organization by enabling personnel to move from one job to another.
- Provide the basis for training individuals in how to maintain software.
- Provide managers with technical documents to review at the significant development milestones, to determine that requirements have been met and that resources should continue to be expended.

Workbench

Figure 20.1 illustrates the workbench for testing the adequacy of system documentation. This workbench outlines a test method for documentation, consisting of the following four tasks:

1. **Measure project documentation needs.** This task helps underscore the importance of documentation to the success of the system.

2. **Determine what documents must be produced.** This task uses the measure of documentation developed in Task 1 to select the list of documents that should be produced for the project.

3. **Determine the completeness of individual documents.** This task determines whether all the elements for each document defined in Task 2 have been prepared.

4. **Determine how current project documents are.** This task determines whether the information contained within the documents is still relevant to the system as it is being run.

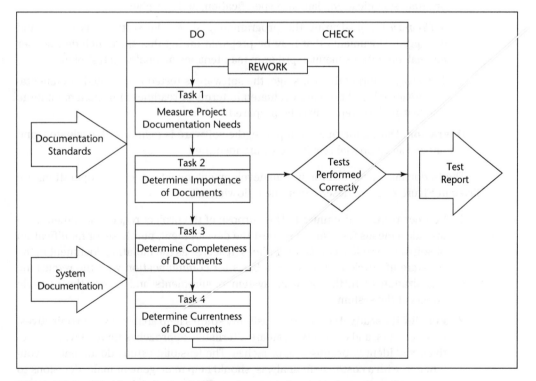

Figure 20.1   Workbench for testing the adequacy of system documentation.

Input

Programs and systems are developed in phases, from the time the idea for a system occurs to the time the system produces the desired output. The terminology used to identify these inputs, phases, and the stages within these phases is defined in the following list:

Initiation. The objectives and general definition of the software requirements are established during the initiation phase. Feasibility studies, cost/benefit analyses, and the documentation prepared in this phase are determined by the organization's procedures and practices.

Development. During the development phase, the requirements for the software are determined and the software is then defined, specified, programmed, and tested. The following documentation is prepared during the four stages of this phase:

1. *Definition*—During the definition stage, the requirements for the software and documentation are determined. The functional requirements document and the data requirements document may be prepared.

2. *Design*—During the design stage, the design alternatives, specific requirements, and functions to be performed are analyzed and a design is specified. Documents that may be prepared include the system/subsystem specification, program specification, database specification, and test plan.

3. *Programming*—During the programming stage, the software is coded and debugged. Documents that may be prepared during this stage include the user manual, operations manual, program maintenance manual, and test plan.

4. *Testing*—During the test stage, the software is tested and related documentation reviewed, and both are evaluated in terms of readiness for implementation. The test analysis report may be prepared.

Operation. During the operation phase, the software is maintained, evaluated, and changed as additional requirements are identified.

The 14 documents needed for system development, maintenance, and operations are listed in Figure 20.2 and described in the following list:

1. **Project request document.** The purpose of the project request document is to provide a means for users to request the development, purchase, or modification of software or other IT-related services. It serves as the initiating document in the software life cycle and provides a basis for communication with the requesting organization to further analyze system requirements and assess the possible effects of the system.

2. **Feasibility study document.** Feasibility studies help analyze system objectives, requirements, and concepts; evaluate alternative approaches for achieving objectives; and identify proposed approaches. The feasibility study document, in conjunction with a cost/benefit analysis, should help management make decisions to initiate or continue an IT project or service. The study can be supplemented with an appendix containing details of a cost/benefit analysis or considered with a separate cost/benefit analysis document.

INITIATION PHASE	DEVELOPMENT PHASE				OPERATION PHASE
	Definition Stage	**Design Stage**	**Programming Stage**	**Test Stage**	
SOFTWARE SUMMARY					
Project Request Document	Functional Requirements Document	System/ Subsystem Specification	User Manual		(Uses and updates many of the initiation and development phase documents.)
Feasibility Study Document		Program Specification	Operations Manual		
Cost/Benefit Analysis Document	Data Requirements Document	Database Specification	Program Maintenance Manual		
TEST PLAN					
				Test Analysis Report	

Figure 20.2   Documentation within the software life cycle.

3. **Cost/benefit analysis document.** Such analyses can help managers, users, designers, and auditors evaluate alternative approaches. The analysis document, in conjunction with the feasibility study document, should help management decide to initiate or continue an IT project or service.

4. **Software summary document.** This document is used for very small projects to substitute for other development-phase documentation when only a minimal level of documentation is needed.

5. **Functional requirements document.** The purpose of the functional requirements document is to provide a basis for users and designers to mutually develop an initial definition of the software, including the requirements, operating environment, and development plan.

6. **Data requirements document.** During the definition stage, the data requirements document provides data descriptions and technical information about data collection requirements.

7. **System/subsystem specification.** Designed for analysts and programmers, this document specifies requirements, operating environment, design characteristics, and program specifications.

8. **Program specification.** The purpose of the program specification is to specify program requirements, operating environment, and design characteristics.

9. **Database specifications.** This document specifies the logical and physical characteristics of a particular database.

10. **User manual.** Written in nontechnical terminology, this manual describes system functions so that user organizations can determine their applicability and when and how to use them. It should serve as a reference document for preparation of input data and parameters and for interpretation of results.

11. **Operations manual.** The purpose of this manual is to provide computer operation personnel with a description of the software and its required operational environment.

12. **Program maintenance manual.** This manual provides the information necessary to understand the programs, their operating environment, and their maintenance procedures.

13. **Test plan.** This document provides detailed specifications, descriptions, and procedures for all tests and test data reduction and evaluation criteria.

14. **Test analysis report.** The purpose of the test analysis report is to document test results and findings, present the proven capabilities and deficiencies for review, and provide a basis for preparing a statement of software readiness for implementation.

The standards for preparing documentation, as developed by your IT organization, is the second input to this test process.

Do Procedures

The four tasks for testing the adequacy of systems documentation are as follows.

Task 1: Measure Project Documentation Needs

The formality, extent, and level of detail of the documentation to be prepared depends on the organization's IT management practices and the project's size, complexity, and risk. What is adequate for one project may be inadequate for another. The first task in testing documentation is to test the sufficiency or adequacy of the documentation produced.

Too much documentation can also be wasteful. An important part of testing documentation is to determine first that the right documentation is prepared; there is little value in confirming that unneeded documentation is adequately prepared.

This task attempts to quantitatively measure the need for documentation by evaluating the criteria that establish such a need and determining the extent and level of documentation required.

The testing methodology uses 12 criteria to establish the need for required documentation:

1. **Originality required.** The uniqueness of the application within the organization.

2. **Degree of generality.** The amount of rigidity associated with the application and the need to handle a variety of situations during processing.

3. **Span of operation.** The percentage of total corporate activities affected by the system.

4. **Change in scope and objective.** The frequency of expected change in requirements during the life of the system.

5. **Equipment complexity.** The sophistication of the hardware and communications lines needed to support the application.

6. **Personnel assigned.** The number of people involved in development and maintenance of the application system.

7. **Developmental cost.** The total dollars required to develop the application.

8. **Criticality.** The importance of the application system to the organization.

9. **Average response time to program change.** The average amount of time available to install a change to the application system.

10. **Average response time to data input.** The average amount of time available to process an application transaction.

11. **Programming languages.** The language used to develop the application.

12. **Concurrent software development.** Other applications and support systems that need to be developed concurrently with this project to fulfill the total mission.

A five-point weighting system is used for each of the 12 criteria; Figure 20.3 provides the basis for determining the weight to be assigned to each. For example, if two people have been assigned to the project, a weight of 1 is allocated for criterion 6, but if seven people were assigned, a weight of 3 would be used.

Work Paper 20.1 should be used in developing the total weighted documentation score as follows:

Determine the weight for each of the 12 criteria. This is done by determining which weights for each criterion are appropriate for the application being tested. The descriptive information in the five weight columns should be the basis of this determination.

Enter the weight number on Work Paper 20.1 for each of the 12 criteria. For example, if under the originality criterion weight 5 is most applicable, a 5 should be placed in the weight column.

Total the weights for the 12 criteria. The minimum score is 12; the maximum is 60.

The weighted score is used in determining what specific documents should be prepared for the software system being tested.

CRITERIA	WEIGHTS				
	1	2	3	4	5
1. Originality required	None–reprogram on different equipment	Minimum–more stringent requirements	Limited–new interfaces	Considerable–apply existing state of the art to environment	Extensive–requires advance in state of the art
2. Degree of generality	Highly restricted–single purpose	Restricted–parameterized for a range of capacities	Limited flexibility–allows some change in format	Multipurpose–flexible format, range of subjects	Very flexible–able to handle a broad range of subject matter on different equipment
3. Span of operation	Local or utility	Small group	Department	Division	Entire corporation
4. Change in scope and objective	None	Infrequent	Occasional	Frequent	Continuous
5. Equipment complexity	Single machine–routine processing	Single machine–routine processing, extended peripheral system	Multicomputer–standard peripheral system	Multicomputer–advanced programming, complex peripheral system	Master control system–multicomputer, auto input/output, and display equipment
6. Personnel assigned	1 to 2	3 to 5	6 to 10	11 to 18	More than 18
7. Developmental cost ($)	1K to 10K	10K to 50K	50K to 200K	200K to 500K	More than 500K
8. Criticality	Limited to data processing	Routine corporate operations	Important corporate operations	Area/product survival	Corporate survival
9. Average response time to program change	2 or more weeks	1 to 2 weeks	3 to 7 days	1 to 3 days	1 to 24 hours
10. Average response time to data input	2 or more weeks	1 to 2 weeks	1 to 7 days	1 to 24 hours	0 to 60 minutes
11. Programming languages	High-level language	High-level and limited assembly language	High-level and extensive assembly language	Assembly language	Machine language
12. Concurrent software development	None	Limited	Moderate	Extensive	Exhaustive

Figure 20.3 Example of weighting criteria.

Task 2: Determine What Documents Must Be Produced

The specific documents that are needed can be determined through the use of the total weighted criteria score calculated in Task 1. Figure 20.4 relates the total weighted criteria score to the 14 previously described software documents and recommends which document should be prepared based on the total weighted criteria. The need for several of the documents depends on the situation (e.g., database specifications and data requirement documents are usually required for systems using database technology). A project request document is needed in organizations that require formal approvals before conducting a feasibility study. Cost/benefit analysis documents are needed in organizations requiring that such analyses be performed before a project is put into development.

With the total weighted criteria score developed in Task 1, Figure 20.4 can be used as follows:

- The appropriate row for selecting documents is determined through the cross-referencing of the score developed in Task 1 to the score in the total weighted criteria column. Some of the scores in this column overlap to accommodate highly critical projects, regardless of their scores.

- For the row selected, the columns indicate which documents are needed.

If the project did not generate these documents, the test team should question the documentation. If unneeded documents were prepared, the test team should challenge the need for maintaining them.

Another, simpler, method can be used to determine the level of documentation needed. The alternate method for determining documentation is illustrated in Figure 20.5. The four levels of documentation are:

1. Minimal
2. Internal
3. Working document
4. Formal publication

The criteria determining these levels of documentation are summarized in Figure 20.5. Additional criteria peculiar to an installation regarding program-sharing potential, life expectancy, and use frequency should also be considered when determining documentation levels.

Level 1 (minimal) documentation guidelines are applicable to single-use programs of minimal complexity. This documentation should include the type of work being produced and a description of what the program really does. Therefore, the documentation that results from the development of the programs (i.e., program abstract, compile listing, test cases) should be retained as well. The criteria for categorizing a program as level 1 can be its expected use or its cost to develop (in hours or dollars) and may be modified for the particular requirements of the installation. Suggested cost criteria are programs requiring less than one worker-month of effort or less than $1,000 (these are not assumed to be equal).

TOTAL WEIGHTED CRITERIA	SOFTWARE SUMMARY	USER MANUAL	OPERATIONS MANUAL	PROGRAM MAINTENANCE MANUAL	TEST PLAN	FEASIBILITY STUDY DOCUMENT	FUNCTIONAL REQUIREMENTS DOCUMENT	SYSTEM/SUBSYSTEM SPECIFICATION	TEST ANALYSIS REPORT	PROGRAM SPECIFICATION	DATA REQUIREMENTS DOCUMENT	DATABASE SPECIFICATION	PROJECT REQUEST DOCUMENT	COST/BENEFIT ANALYSIS DOCUMENT
0 to 12*	X													
12 to 15*	X	X												
16 to 26	X	X	X	X	X	X			**		***	***	***	***
24 to 38	X	X	X	X	X	X	X		**		***	***	***	***
36 to 50	X	X	X	X	X	X	X	X	X		***	***	***	***
48 to 60	X	X	X	X	X	X	X	X	X	X	***	***	***	***

Notes:

*Additional document types may be required at lower-weighted criteria totals to satisfy local requirements.

**The test analysis report logically should be prepared, but may be informal.

***Preparation of the project request document, cost/benefit analysis document, data requirements document, and database specification is situationally dependent.

Figure 20.4 Total weighted documentation criteria versus required document types.

Level 2 (internal) documentation applies to special-purpose programs that, after careful consideration, appear to have no sharing potential and to be designed for use only by the requesting department. Large programs with a short life expectancy also fall into this category. The documentation required (other than level 1) includes input/output formats, setup instructions, and sufficient comments in the source code to provide clarification in the compile listing. The effort spent toward formal documentation for level 2 programs should be minimal.

Level 3 (working document) documentation applies to programs that are expected to be used by several people in the same organization or that may be transmitted on request to other organizations, contractors, or grantees. This level should include all documentation types. The documentation should be typed but need not be in a finished format suitable for publication. Usually, it is not formally reviewed or edited; however, certain programs that are important to the using organization but not considered appropriate for publication should undergo a more stringent documentation review.

LEVEL	USE	DOCUMENTATION ELEMENTS	EXTENT OF EFFORT
1	Single Use	Software summary plus any incidentally produced documentation.	No special effort, general good practice.
2	Special or Limited Purpose or Application	Level 1 plus user manual and operations manual.	Minimal documentation effort spent on informal documentation. No formal documentation effort.
3	Multipurpose or Multiuser	Level 2 plus functional requirements document, program specification, program maintenance manual, test plan, test analysis report, system/subsystem specification, and feasibility study document.*	All basic elements of documentation should be typewritten, but need not be prepared in finished format for publication or require external edit or review.
4	Publicly Announced or Critical to Operations	Level 3 produced in a form suitable for publication.*	At a minimum, all basic elements prepared for formal publication, including external review and edit.

*In addition, the following documents should be prepared, depending on the situation: data requirements document, database specification document, project report document, and cost/benefit analysis document.

Figure 20.5   Alternate method for determining documentation.

Level 4 (formal publication) documentation applies to programs that are of sufficient general interest and value to be announced outside the originating installation. This level of documentation is also desirable if the program is to be referenced by a technical publication or paper.

Programs critical to the activities of the installation should be included in this level and should be formally documented, reviewed in depth, and subjected to configuration control procedures. Recurring applications (e.g., payroll) should also be considered for inclusion in this level to maintain an accurate history of conformation to changing laws, rules, and regulations.

Using the Alternate Method

Determining which of the four levels of documentation is appropriate can be done:

- As an alternate to the total weighted criteria score method.
- As a means of validating the correctness of the total weighted score to the application system. If the same types of documentation are indicated by both methods, there is greater assurance that the documentation indicated is the correct one.

Task 3: Determine the Completeness of Individual Documents

Thirteen criteria can be used in evaluating the completeness of each document. Work Paper 20.2 can be used for documenting the results of the completeness test. The tester must determine whether each document is adequate for each criterion. If the documentation does not meet a criterion, the comments column should be used to explain the deficiency. This column becomes the test report on the completeness of the documentation.

The 13 criteria used to evaluate the completeness of a document are discussed in the following list:

1. **Documentation content.** The suggested content for all the documents (except the software summary) is included in a later section. A table of contents for each document is followed by a brief description of each element within the document.

   These document content guidelines should be used to determine whether the document contains all the needed information. If elements are missing, there is a potential documentation completeness defect, which should be noted in the comments column of Work Paper 20.2.

2. **Document audience.** Each document type is written for a particular audience, which may be an individual or a group expected to use the document to perform a function (e.g., operation, maintenance, design, and programming). The information should be presented with the terminology and level of detail appropriate to the audience.

3. **Redundancy.** The 14 document types in this section have some redundancy. Introductory material has been included in each document type to provide the reader with a frame of reference, facilitating an understanding of the document with a minimum need for cross-referencing to parts of other documents. In addition, most document types are specific (e.g., descriptions of input, output, or equipment). Information that should be included in each of the document types differs in context and sometimes in terminology and level of detail, because it is intended to be read by different audiences at different points in the software life cycle.

4. **Flexibility.** Flexibility in the use of the document results from the organization of its contents.

5. **"Sizing" document types.** Each document-type outline can be used to prepare documents that range in size from a few to several hundred pages. Length depends on the size and complexity of the project and the project manager's judgment as to the level of detail necessary for the environment in which the software will be developed or run.

6. **Combining and expanding document types.** It is occasionally necessary to combine several document types under one cover or to produce several volumes of the same document type. Document types that can be combined are manuals for users, operations, and program maintenance. The contents of each document type should then be presented with the outline (e.g., Part I—Users, Part II—Operations, and Part III—Program Maintenance).

For large systems, a document can be prepared for each module. Sometimes, the size of a document may require it to be issued in multiple volumes to allow ease of use. In such cases, the document should be separated at a section division (e.g., the contents of the test plan may be divided into sections of plan, specifications and evaluation, and specific test descriptions).

7. **Format.** The content guidelines have been prepared in a generally consistent format. This particular format has been tested, and its use is encouraged.

8. **Sequencing of contents.** In general, the order of the sections and paragraphs in a particular document type should be the same as shown in the content guidelines. The order may be changed if it significantly enhances the presentation.

9. **Documenting multiple programs or multiple files.** Many of the document content outlines anticipate and are adaptable to documenting a system and its subsystems, multiple programs, or multiple files. All of these outlines can, of course, be used for a single system, subsystem, program, database, or file.

10. **Section/paragraph titles.** These titles are generally the same as those shown in the content guidelines. They may be modified to reflect terminology unique to the software being documented if the change significantly enhances the presentation. Sections or paragraphs may be added or deleted as local requirements dictate.

11. **Expansion of paragraphs.** Many of the document types have paragraphs with a general title and a list of factors that might be discussed within that paragraph. The intent of the content guidelines is not to prescribe a discussion of each of these items but to suggest that these items be considered during the writing of that paragraph. These and all other paragraphs may be expanded and further subdivided to enhance the presentation.

12. **Flowcharts and decision tables.** The graphic representations of some problem solutions in the form of flowcharts or decision tables may be included in or appended to the documents produced.

13. **Forms.** The use of specific forms depends on organizational practices. Some of the information specified in a paragraph in the content guidelines may be recorded on such forms. If so, the form can be referenced from the appropriate paragraph. The use of standard forms is encouraged.

Testing the Completeness of Documentation

If time and resources permit, it is advisable to conduct one or more tests of the adequacy of documentation. Such tests require that a skilled individual not associated with the project make a simulated change to the system based on the current documentation and the change request. (No actual documentation or program should be changed.) After this individual has made the change, someone familiar with the project must assess whether it has been performed correctly.

This test will reveal whether:

- The documentation is understandable to an independent person.

- An independent person can use the documentation to correctly make a change, and can do so in an efficient, effective manner.

NOTE It is recommended that the testers use the inspection process to determine the completeness of systems documentation.

Task 4: Determine the Currentness of Project Documents

Documentation that is not current is worthless. Most MIS professionals believe that if one part of the documentation is incorrect, other parts are probably incorrect, and they are reluctant to use it.

The documentation test team can use any or all of the following four tests to validate the currentness of documentation. (These tests can be done on complete documents or parts of documents. Testers familiar with statistics can perform sampling and validate the currentness of that sample. Testers should strive for a 95 percent confidence level that the documentation is current.)

Test 1: Use the Documentation to Change the Application

Currentness can be validated with the same test process described in Task 3. The currentness test enables the tester to search for and confirm consistency between the various documents (e.g., that specifications in the program design documents are the same as they are in the actual code) and to determine whether the documentation supports the operational system.

Test 2: Compare the Code with the Documentation

This test uses the current version of the programs as the correct basis for documentation. This test is usually done on a sampling basis; the tester randomly selects several parts of the program and traces them to the appropriate levels of documentation. The objective is to determine whether the code is properly represented in the documentation. Because this test is done statistically, a few variations might imply extensive segments of obsolete documentation.

Test 3: Confirm Documentation Currentness with Documentation Preparers

The individuals who prepare the documentation should be asked whether it is current. Specific questions should be asked, including:

- Is this documentation 100 percent representative of the application in operation?
- Is the documentation changed every time that a system change is made?
- Do the individuals who change the system rely on the documentation as correct?

Test 4: Confirm the Currentness of Documentation with End Users

End users should be asked whether the documentation for the system is current. Because end users might not be familiar with the documentation, they may need to be selected on a sampling basis and asked about specific pieces of documentation. Selected documentation should be familiar to end users so that they can be given several representative pieces of documentation and asked to validate that they are current and correct. Again, because sampling is used, a few variances may mean extensive amounts of obsolete documentation.

Check Procedures

Work Paper 20.3 is a quality control checklist for testing the adequacy of system documentation. It is designed so that Yes responses indicate good test practices; No responses warrant additional investigation. A Comments column is provided to explain No responses and to record results of investigation. The N/A column is used when the checklist item is not applicable to the test situation.

Output

The only output from this system is the report outlining deficiencies within systems documentation. The deficiencies should be based first on variance from standards, and second on failure to meet the intent of the standards. The report should be documented and delivered to the individual responsible for documentation. The testers should determine that the items in the report are acted upon.

Guidelines

There are only two courses of action to take when documentation is insufficient, incomplete, or not current:

1. **Bring the documentation up to current standards.** This involves adding missing documents, completing documents, and ensuring that the documentation is current.
2. **Dispose of the documentation.** Money should not be spent on documentation that is extremely incomplete or obsolete. If management is unwilling to spend the money to bring it up to current standards, the documentation should be disposed of.

Summary

This chapter has provided a four-task process for testers to determine the adequacy of system documentation. It is included as a separate test process because documentation is prepared through the development and test cycles. Therefore, this process will be used periodically during the 11-step test process. For example, the requirements documentation would be tested for adequacy during the testing of the requirements to the system of the 11-step process (note: requirement test is the third step of the 11-step process).

WORK PAPER 20.1 Calculation of Total Weighted Documentation Criteria Score

Field Requirements

FIELD	INSTRUCTIONS
Number	The sequential number identifying the twelve criteria used in calculating weight.
Criterion	The name of the criterion used in calculating weight.
Weight	The weight assigned to this criterion as calculated in accordance with the instructions included in this step.
Explanation of Weight	A discussion of the considerations that were included in determining the weight for this criterion.
Total Weighted Criteria Score	This is the total of the weight for the twelve criteria.

#	CRITERION	WEIGHT	EXPLANATION OF WEIGHT (IF NECESSARY)
1.	Originality required		
2.	Degree of generality		
3.	Span of operation		
4.	Change in scope and objective		
5.	Equipment complexity		
6.	Personnel assigned		
7.	Developmental cost		
8.	Criticality		
9.	Average response time to program change		
10.	Average response time to data input		
11.	Programming languages		
12.	Concurrent software development		

Total Weighted Criteria Score:

WORK PAPER 20.2 Testing Documentation Completeness

Field Requirements

FIELD	INSTRUCTIONS
Number	The sequential number identifying one of the 13 completeness criteria.
Completeness Criterion	The name of the completeness criterion.
Adequacy	This field should indicate that the testers have determined that the documentation is either adequate or inadequate for this specific completion criterion. The method for determining adequacy is outlined in this step.
Explanation of Inadequacies	This field should indicate the reasons why the testers determined this specific completeness criterion was inadequate.

#	COMPLETENESS CRITERION	ADEQUACY		EXPLANATION OF INADEQUACIES
		ADEQUATE	INADEQUATE	
1.	Documentation content			
2.	Document audience			
3.	Redundancy			
4.	Flexibility			
5.	"Sizing" of document types			
6.	Combining and expanding of document types			
7.	Format			
8.	Sequencing of contents			
9.	Documenting of multiple programs or multiple files			
10.	Section/paragraph titles			
11.	Expansion of paragraphs			
12.	Flowcharts and decision tables			
13.	Forms			

WORK PAPER 20.3   Quality Control Checklist

Field Requirements

FIELD	INSTRUCTIONS FOR ENTERING DATA
Number	A number that sequentially identifies the quality control items, which if positively addressed would indicate that this step has been performed correctly.
Item	The specific quality control item that is used to measure the effectiveness of performing this step.
Response	The testers should indicate in this column whether they have performed the referenced item. The response can be Yes, No, or N/A if it is not appropriate for your organization's testing process.
Comments	This column is used to clarify the Yes, No, or N/A response for the item indicated. Generally the comments column need only be completed for No responses; No responses should be investigated and a determination made as to whether this item needs to be performed before this step can be considered complete.

#	ITEM	RESPONSE			COMMENTS
		YES	NO	N/A	
1.	Are there standards for system documentation?				
2.	Are the members of the test team in total knowledgeable of the intent and content of those standards?				
3.	Are the standards customizable for systems of various sizes, so that small projects may not need as extensive documentation as large projects?				
4.	Are the testers provided a complete copy of system documentation current to the point where the tests occur?				
5.	Have the testers measured the documentation needs for the project based on the twelve criteria included in this chapter?				
6.	Have the testers determined what documents must be produced?				
7.	Do the project personnel agree with the testers' assessment as to what documents are needed?				
8.	Have the testers determined the completeness of individual documents using the 13 criteria outlined in Task 3?				
9.	Have the testers used the inspection process to determine the completeness of system documentation?				
10.	Have the testers determined the currentness of the project documentation at the point of test?				

WORK PAPER 20.3   *(Continued)*

#	ITEM	RESPONSE			COMMENTS
		YES	NO	N/A	
11.	Have the testers prepared a report that outlines documentation deficiency?				
12.	Do the testers ensure that the documentations deficiency outlined in their report is acted upon?				

Testing Web-based Systems

Web-based systems are those systems using the Internet, intranets, and extranets. The Internet is a worldwide collection of interconnected networks. An intranet is a private network inside a company using web-based applications, but for use only within an organization. An extranet is a private network that allows external access to customers and suppliers using web-based applications.

> **NOTE** This chapter's materials are from the Quality Assurance Institute's *Web-Based Testing* Seminar, authored by Randall Rice.

Overview

This chapter focuses on the unique characteristics of web-based testing. Test execution can use the same 11-step process described in Part Three of this book. This chapter focuses on determining whether web-based risk should be included in the test plan; which types of web-based testing should be used; and selecting the appropriate web-based test tools for the test execution phase.

Web-based architecture is an extension of client/server architecture. The difference between client/server architecture and web-based architecture is described below.

Client/Server Architecture

In the diagram, a simplified client/server architecture is shown. There are many possible variations of client/server, but for illustration purposes, this is representative.

In the example shown in Figure 18.1, application software resides on the client work-stations. The application server handles processing requests. The back-end processing (typically a mainframe or super-minicomputer) handles processing such as batch trans-actions that are accumulated and processed together at one time on a regular basis.

The important distinction to note is that application software resides on the client workstation.

Web-based Architecture

In the example shown in Figure 18.1, browsers reside on client workstations. These client workstations are networked to a web server, either through a remote dial-in con-nection or through a network such as a local area network (LAN) or wide area network (WAN).

As the web server receives and processes requests from the client workstation, requests may be sent to the application server to perform actions such as data queries, electronic commerce transactions, and so forth.

The back-end processing works in the background to perform batch processing and handle high-volume transactions. The back-end processing can also interface with transactions to other systems in the organization. For example, when an on-line bank-ing transaction is processed over the Internet, the transaction will eventually be updated to the customer's account and shown on a statement in a back-end process.

Objective

The objective of this test program is to assess the adequacy of the web components of software applications. Web-based testing generally only needs to be done once for any applications using the web.

Concerns

The concerns that the tester should have when conducting web-based testing are as follows:

- **Browser compatibility.** These tests validate consistent application performance on a variety of browser types and configurations.
- **Functional correctness.** These tests validate that the application functions cor-rectly. This includes validating links, calculations, displays of information, and navigation.
- **Integration.** This tests the integration between browsers and servers, applica-tions and data, hardware and software.
- **Usability.** This tests the overall usability of a web page or a web application, including appearance, clarity, and navigation.
- **Security.** This tests the adequacy and correctness of security controls including access control and authorizations.

- **Performance.** This tests the performance of the web application under load.

- **Verification of code.** This validates that the code used in building the web application (HTML, Java, etc.) has been used in a correct manner. For example, no nonstandard coding practices should be used that would cause an application to function incorrectly in some environments.

An additional concern is that web terminology will not be understood by the web-based testers. The following are the common web terms:

Browser. Client software that is used to view various kinds of Internet resources.

HyperText Markup Language (HTML). The coding language used to create Hypertext documents on the web to be viewed using a browser.

Platform. A combination of hardware and operating system upon which browser software operates. Examples include a PC using Windows 98 and Internet Explorer, or an Apple Macintosh using the Mac operating system and Netscape. Basically, the platform is the basis of the user interface for accessing web-based applications.

Java. A network-oriented programming language developed by Sun Microsystems that is designed for writing programs that can be safely downloaded to a computer via the Internet and immediately run without fear of viruses or other harm to the computer or files. Small Java programs are called "applets."

Web server. A computer dedicated to providing web access.

Application server. A computer dedicated to hosting application software and the execution of such software.

Back end. Processing performed in a separate, centralized environment, such as a mainframe.

Firewall. A combination of hardware and software that separates a LAN into multiple components to prevent unauthorized access.

Uniform Resource Locator (URL). The standard way to address resources on the Internet that are part of the World Wide Web (WWW).

Electronic commerce (e-commerce). Conducting financial transactions via web-based technologies. (Also becoming known as "I-Commerce" to distinguish specifically as "Internet commerce.")

Component. A physical and replaceable part of a system.

Common Gateway Interface (CGI). A set of rules that describe how a web server communicates with another piece of software on the same machine, and how the other piece of software (the "CGI program") talks to the web server. Any piece of software can be a CGI program if it handles input and output according to the CGI standard.

Bandwidth. The amount of information that can be transmitted through a connection. Usually measured in bits-per-second.

Secure Socket Layer (SSL). A protocol designed by Netscape Communications to enable encrypted, authenticated communications across the Internet.

File Transfer Protocol (FTP). A common method of transferring files between two Internet sites.

Workbench

Figure 21.1 illustrates the workbench for web-based testing. The input to the workbench is the hardware and software that will be incorporated in the web-based system to be tested. The first three tasks of the workbench are primarily involved in web-based test planning. The main difference between web-based testing and other types of testing is addressing the unique concerns and risks associated with web-based technology. The fourth task is traditional software testing. The output from the workbench is to report what works and what does not work, as well as any concerns over the use of web technology.

Input

The input to this test process is the description of web-based technology used in the systems being tested. The following list shows how web-based systems differ from other

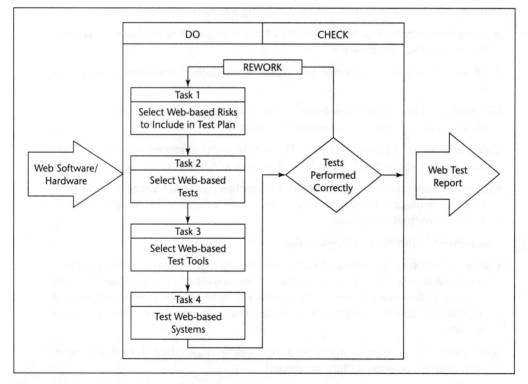

Figure 21.1 Workbench for web-based testing.

technologies. The description of the web-based systems under testing should address these differences:

Uncontrolled user interfaces (Browsers). Because of the variety of web browsers that are available, a web page must be functional on those browsers that you expect to be used in accessing your web applications. Furthermore, as new releases of browsers emerge, your web applications will need to keep up with compatibility issues.

Complex distributed systems. In addition to being complex and distributed, web-based applications are also remotely accessed, which adds even more concerns to the testing effort. While some applications may be less complex than others, it is safe to say that the trend in web applications is to become more complex rather than less.

Security issues. Protection is needed from unauthorized access that can corrupt applications and/or data. Another security risk is that of access to confidential information.

Multiple layers in architecture. These layers of architecture include application servers, web servers, back-end processing, data warehouses, and secure servers for electronic commerce.

New terminology and skill sets. Just as in making the transition to client/server, new skills are needed to develop, test, and use web-based technology effectively.

Object-oriented. Object-oriented languages such as Java are becoming the mainstay of web development.

Nonstandardized. Because Internet technology is still maturing, there are few, if any, standards. Some standards, such as Java language standards, are competing for position.

Do Procedures

Testing of a web-based system involves performing the following four tasks.

Task 1: Select Web-Based Risks to Include in the Test Plan

Risks are important to understand because they reveal what to test. Each risk points to an entire area of potential tests. In addition, the degree of testing should be based on risk. The risks are briefly listed below followed by a more detailed description of the concerns associated with each risk.

Security. As we have already seen, one of the major risks of Internet applications is security. It is very important to validate that the application and data are protected from outside intrusion or unauthorized access.

Performance. An Internet application with poor performance will be judged hard to use. Web sites that are slow in response will not retain the visitors they attract and will be frustrating to the people who try to use them.

Correctness. Obviously, correctness is a very important area of risk. It is essential that the functionality and information obtained from web-based applications is correct.

Compatibility (configuration). A web-based application must be able to work correctly on a wide variety of system configurations including browsers, operating systems, hardware systems. All of these are out of the control of the developer of the application.

Reliability. An Internet application must have a high level of availability and the information provided from the application must be consistent and reliable to the user.

Data integrity. The data entered into an Internet application must be validated to ensure its correctness. In addition, measures must be taken to insure the data stays correct after it is entered into the application.

Usability. The application must be easy to use. This includes things like navigation, clarity, and understandability of the information provided by the application.

Recoverability. In the event of an outage, the system must be recoverable. This includes recovering lost transactions, recovering from loss of communications, and ensuring that proper backups are made as a part of regular systems maintenance.

Key Areas of Concern: Security Risk

In this area of concern, we will explore some of the detailed security risks that need to be addressed in an Internet application test plan.

External intrusion. Perhaps the most obvious security concern is that of protecting the system from external intrusion. This can include intrusion from people who are trying to gain access to sensitive information, people who are trying to intentionally sabotage information, and people who are trying to intentionally sabotage applications.

Protection of secured transactions. Another major area of concern is that of protecting transactions over the Internet. This is especially true in dealing with electronic commerce transactions. Many consumers are reluctant to give credit card information over the Internet for fear that information will be intercepted and used for fraudulent purposes.

Viruses. The Internet has become a vehicle for propagating tens of thousands of new viruses. These viruses are contained in downloaded files that can be distributed from web sites and e-mail.

Access control. Access control means that only authorized users have security access to a particular application or portion of an application. This access is typically granted with a user ID and password.

Authorization levels. Authorization levels refer to the ability of the application to restrict certain transactions only to those users who have a certain level of authorization.

Key Areas of Concern: Performance

System performance can make or break an Internet application. There are several types of performance testing that can be done to validate the performance levels of an application. Performance testing is a very precise kind of testing and requires the use of automated tools to be achieved with any level of accuracy and efficiency. Unfortunately, manual approaches to performance testing fall short of the accuracy needed to correctly gauge an application's performance and may lead to a false level of confidence in the test.

Typically, the most common kind of performance testing for Internet applications is load testing. Load testing seeks to determine how the application performs under expected and greater-than-expected levels of activity. Application load can be assessed in a variety of ways:

Concurrency. Concurrency testing seeks to validate the performance of an application with a given number of concurrent interactive users.

Stress. Stress testing seeks to validate the performance of an application when certain aspects of the application are stretched to their maximum limits. This can include maximum number of users, and can also include maximizing table values and data values.

Throughput. Throughput testing seeks to validate the number of transactions to be processed by an application during a given period of time. For example, one type of throughput test might be to attempt to process 100,000 transactions in one hour.

Key Areas of Concern: Correctness

Of course, one of the most important areas of concern is that the application functions correctly. This can include not only the functionality of buttons and "behind the scenes" instructions, but also calculations and navigation of the application.

Functionality. Functional correctness means that the application performs its intended tasks as defined by a stated set of specifications. The specifications of an application are the benchmark of what the application should do. Functional correctness is determined by performing a functional test. A functional test is performed in a cause-effect manner. In other words, if a particular action is taken, a particular result should be seen.

Calculations. Many web-based applications include calculations. These calculations must be tested to insure correctness and to find defects.

Navigation. Navigation correctness can include testing links, buttons, and general navigation through a web site or web-based application.

Key Areas of Concern: Compatibility

Compatibility is the ability of the application to perform correctly in a variety of expected environments. Two of the major variables that affect web-based applications are the operating systems and browsers.

Currently, operating systems (or platforms) and how they support the browser of your choice will affect the appearance and functionality of a web application. This requires testing your web-based applications as accessed on a variety of common platforms and browsers. You should be able to define the most commonly used platforms by reviewing the access statistics of your web site.

Specifically, the following concerns address the compatibility issues of a web-based application. Common operating systems include:

- DOS/Windows
- Mac OS
- UNIX
- VMS
- Sun and SGI (Silicon Graphics Inc.)
- Linux

Popular browsers include:

- Microsoft Internet Explorer
- Netscape Communicator
- Mosaic

There are many other lesser-known browsers. You can find information on all different types of browsers at www.browserwatch.com.

Browser Configuration

Each browser has configuration options that affect how it displays information. These options vary from browser to browser and are too diverse to address in this text. The most reasonable testing strategy is to define optimal configurations on the most standard kinds of browsers and test based on those configurations.

Some of the main things to consider from a hardware compatibility standpoint are:

Monitors, video cards, and video RAM. If you have a web site that requires a high standard of video capability, some users will not be able to view your site, or will not get a positive experience at your site. You may need to consider alternate forms of viewing your site, such as text-only pages.

Audio, video, and multimedia support. Once again, you need to verify that a web application is designed to provide a level of multimedia support that a typical end-user will need to be able to access your site. If software plug-ins are required, there should be links on your page to facilitate the user downloading the plug-in.

Memory (RAM) and hard drive space. RAM is very important for increasing the performance of a browser on a particular platform. Browsers also make heavy use of caching, which is how a browser stores graphics and other information on a user's hard drive. This helps speed the display of web pages the next time the user visits a web site.

Bandwidth access. Many corporate users have high-speed Internet access based on T-1 or T-3 networks, or ISDN telephone lines. Most home users still rely on standard telephone lines to connect to the Internet at speeds ranging from 14.4 Kbps to 56 Kbps. The advent of cable modems and ASDL telephone access is providing more and more home users with high-speed Internet access. The bottom line is that if users can't access the information from your web site in a reasonable amount time, they will likely move on to the next available sites to get the information they need.

Browser differences can make a web application appear differently to different people. These differences may appear in any of the following areas (this is not intended to be an exhaustive list; these are merely the more common areas of browser differences):

Print handling. To make printing faster and easier, some pages add a link or button to print a browser-friendly version of the page being viewed.

Reload. Some browser configurations will not automatically display updated pages if a version of the page still exists in the cache. Some pages indicate if the user should reload the page.

Navigation. Browsers vary in the ease of navigation, especially when it comes to visiting pages previously visited during a session. A web application developer may need to add navigational aides to the web pages to facilitate ease of navigation.

Graphics filters. Browsers may handle images differently, depending on the graphic filters supported by the browser. In fact, some browsers may not show an image at all. By standardizing on JPG and GIF images you should be able to eliminate this concern.

Caching. How the cache is configured (size, etc.) will have an impact on the performance of a browser to view information.

Dynamic page generation. This includes how a user receives information from pages that change based on input. Examples of dynamic page generation include:

- Shopping cart applications
- Data search applications
- Calculation forms

File downloads. Movement of data from a remote data storage for user processing.

E-mail functions. The functions associated with e-mail activities.

Each browser has its own interface and functionality for e-mail. Many people use separate e-mail applications outside of a browser, but for those who don't, this can be a concern for users when it comes to compatibility.

Key Areas of Concern: Reliability

Because of the continuous uptime requirements for most Internet applications, reliability is a key concern. However, reliability can be considered in more than system availability; it can also be expressed in terms of the reliability of the information obtained from the application:

- Consistently correct results
- Server and system availability

Key Areas of Concern: Data Integrity

Not only must the data be validated when it is entered into the web application, but it must also be safeguarded to ensure the data stays correct:

Ensuring only correct data is accepted. This can be achieved by validating the data at the page level when it is entered by a user.

Ensuring data stays in a correct state. This can be achieved by procedures to back up data and ensure that controlled methods are used to update data.

Key Areas of Concern: Usability

If users or customers find an Internet application hard to use, they will likely go to a competitor's site. Usability can be validated and usually involves the following:

- Ensuring the application is easy to use and understand
- Ensuring that users know how to interpret and use the information delivered from the application
- Ensuring that navigation is clear and correct

Key Areas of Concern: Recoverability

Internet applications are more prone to outages than systems that are more centralized or located on reliable, controlled networks. The remote accessibility of Internet applications make the following recoverability concerns important:

- Lost connections
  - Timeouts
  - Dropped lines
- Client system crashes
- Server system crashes or other application problems

Work Paper 21.1 is designed to determine which web-based risks need to be addressed in the test plan, and how those risks will be included in the test plan. The use of this work paper should be associated with a "brainstorming session" by the web-based test team. The work paper should be completed once the web-based test team has reached consensus regarding inclusion of risks in the test plan.

Task 2: Select Web-based Tests

Now that we have selected the risks to be addressed in the web-based applications, let's examine the types and phases of testing needed to validate them.

Unit or Component

This includes testing at the object, component, page, or applet level. Unit testing is the lowest level of testing in terms of detail. During unit testing, the structure of languages, such as HTML and Java, can be verified. Edits and calculations can also be tested at the unit level.

Integration

Integration is the passing of data and/or control between units or components, which includes testing navigation (i.e., the paths the test data will follow). In web-based applications, this includes testing links, data exchanges, and flow of control in an application.

System

System testing examines the web application as a whole and with other systems. The classic definition of system testing is to validate that a computing system functions according to written requirements and specifications. This is also true in web-based applications. The differences apply in how the system is defined. System testing typically includes hardware, software, data, procedures, and people.

In corporate web-based applications, a system might interface with Internet web pages, data warehouses, back-end processing systems, and reporting systems.

User Acceptance (Business Process Validation)

This includes testing that the web application supports business needs and processes. The main idea in user acceptance testing (or business process validation) is to ensure that the end product will support the users' needs. For business applications, this means testing that the system will allow the user to conduct business correctly and efficiently. For personal applications, this means that users will be able to get the information or service they need efficiently from a web site.

In a corporate web page, the end-user testers may be from end-user groups, management, or an independent test team that takes the role of end-users. In public web applications, the end-user testers may be beta testers, who receive a prototype or early release of the new web application, or independent testers who take the role of public web users.

Performance

This includes testing that the system will perform as specified at predetermined levels, including wait times, static processes, dynamic processes, transaction processes. Performance is also tested at the client/browser and server levels.

Load/Stress

This type of testing checks to see that the server will perform as specified at peak concurrent loads or transaction throughput. It includes stressing servers, networks, and databases.

Regression

Regression testing checks that unchanged parts of the application work correctly after a change has been made. Many people mistakenly believe that regression testing means testing everything you ever tested in an application every time you perform a test. However, depending upon the relative risk of the application you are testing, regression testing may not need to be that intense. The main idea is to test a set of specified critical test cases each time you perform the test. Regression testing is an ideal candidate for test automation, due to its repetitive nature.

Usability

This type of testing assesses the ease of use of an application. Usability testing may be accomplished in a variety of ways, including direct observation of people using web applications, usability surveys, and beta tests. The main objective of usability testing is to assure that an application is easy to understand and navigate.

Compatibility

Compatibility testing insures that the application functions correctly on multiple browsers and system configurations. Compatibility testing may be performed in a test lab that contains a variety of platforms, or may be performed by beta testers. The downside with beta testing is the increased risk of bad publicity, the lack of control, and the lack of good data coming back from the beta testers.

Work Paper 21.2 is designed to assist testers in selecting testing types. The type of testing to be performed should be focused on the web-based risks addressed by the test plan. The test team should determine how the various types of web-based testing selected should be used to assess the various risks. This work paper, like Work Paper 21.1, should be developed through brainstorming and consensus by the web-based test team.

Task 3: Select Web-based Test Tools

Effective web-based testing necessitates the use of web-based test tools. A brief description of the more common web-based test tools follows.

HTML Test Tools

Although many web development packages include an HTML checker, there are ways to perform a verification of HTML if you do not use/have such a feature. An example of a standalone tool is Doctor HTML by Imagineware (http://drhtml.imagiware.com/).

Site Validation

Site validation tools check your web applications to identify inconsistencies and errors such as:

- Moved pages
- Orphaned pages
- Broken links

An example of a site validation tool is SQA Site Check by Rational Software.

Java Test Tools

Java test tools are specifically designed for testing Java applications. Examples include:

NuMega TrueTime Java Edition. A performance analysis tool for Java. Automatically locates performance problems in Java applications and components.

Sun Test Suite by Sun Microsystems. JavaStar for testing GUIs, JavaSpec, and API test tool, and JavaScope to measure coverage.

SilkTest by Segue Software. Capture/playback geared specifically for web-based applications.

SilkScope by Segue Software. Code coverage for Java applications.

Silk Spec by Segue Software. Tests the non-GUI code of applications and applets.

Load/Stress Testing Tools

Load/stress tools evaluate web-based systems when subjected to large volumes of data or transactions. Examples of tools that can simulate numerous virtual users and vary transaction rates include:

- Astra Site Test by Mercury Interactive
- Silk Performer by Segue Software

These tools enable organizations to stress test a web site from a single Windows 95 or Windows NT workstation.

Test Case Generators

Test case generators create transactions for use in testing. This tool can tell you what to test, as well as create test cases that can be used in other test tools. An example of a test case generator is the Astra Quick Test by Mercury Interactive. This tool captures business processes into a visual map to generate data-driven tests automatically. Test scripts can be imported to Mercury's Load Runner and managed by Test Director.

Work Paper 21.3 is designed to document the web-based test tools selected by the test team, as well as how those tools will be used. The work paper should contain all of the specific test tools available to the web-based testing team.

Task 4: Test Web-based Systems

The tests to be performed for web-based testing will be the types of testing described in the 11-step testing process, which is Part Three of this book. The 11-step process may have to be modified based on the risks associated with web-based testing.

Check Procedures

At the conclusion of web-based testing, after Tasks 1 through 3 have been performed, the web-based test team should verify that the web-based test planning has been conducted effectively. The Quality Control Checklist for conducting a web-based testing review is included as Work Paper 21.4. It is designed for Yes/No responses. Yes indicates a positive response; No responses should be investigated. The Comments column is provided to clarify No responses. The N/A column is provided for items that are not applicable to this specific web-based test plan.

Output

The only output from this test process is a report on the web-based system. At a minimum this report should contain:

- Brief description of the web-based system
- Risks addressed and not addressed by the web-based test team
- Types of testing performed, and types of testing not performed
- Test tools used
- Web-based functionality and structure tested that performed correctly
- Web-based structure and functionality tested that did not perform correctly
- Web-based test team's opinion regarding the adequacy of the web-based system to be placed into a production status.

Guidelines

Successful web-based testing necessitates a portfolio of web-based testing tools. It is important that these test tools are used effectively. These are some common critical success factors for buying, integrating, and using test tools:

Get senior management support for buying and integrating test tools. Top-down support is critical. Management must understand the need for test tools and the risks of not using test tools.

Know your requirements. This will help you avoid costly mistakes. You may not be able to meet all your requirements, but you should be able to find the best fit.

Be reasonable in your expectations—start small and grow. Your first project using any kind of tool is your learning project. Expect to make some mistakes. You can hedge your risk by applying the test tool(s) to simple tasks with high payback.

Have a strong testing process that includes tools. Until this is in place, test tool usage will be seen as optional and the tool may die due to lack of interest. In addition, people need to know how to define what to test.

Don't cut the training corner. People must understand how to use the test tool. Most people will naturally use about 20 to 25 percent of the tool's functionality. If training is not obtained and the tool is not effective, don't blame the tool.

Summary

This chapter provides guidelines on how to properly plan for web-based testing. Like other aspects of testing, web-based testing should be risk oriented. The chapter describes the risks, presents the types of testing that can be used to address those risks in testing, and provides guidance in using web-based test tools. The approach for testing web-based systems should be incorporated into a test plan and that plan should be followed during test execution. This chapter does not address the test execution part of web-based testing. Testers should follow the execution components of the 11-step testing process described in Part Three of this book.

WORK PAPER 21.1   Web-Based Risks to Include in the Test Plan

Field Requirements

FIELD	INSTRUCTIONS FOR ENTERING DATA
#	The sequential numbering of the eight web-based risks.
Web-based Risks	This field lists the eight web-based risks described in this chapter. The description implies that "lack of" is associated with the risk.
Include in Test	The web-based testing should determine whether any or all of the eight identified web-based risks need to be addressed in the test plan. A check in the Yes column indicates that it should be included in the plan, and a check in the No column indicates it is not needed in the plan.
How risk will be included in the web-based test plan	This column is designed to be used in two ways. If the risk is not to be included in test plan, a justification as to why not could be included in this column. The second use is the test team's preliminary thoughts on how this risk will be included in the test plan. The description might involve the types of tests, the types of tools, and/or the approach to be used in testing.

# WEB-BASED RISKS (LACK OF)	INCLUDE IN TEST		HOW RISK WILL BE INCLUDED IN WEB-BASED TEST PLAN
	YES	NO	
1. Security			
2. Performance			
3. Correctness			
4. Compatibility (Configuration)			
5. Reliability			
6. Data Integrity			
7. Usability			
8. Recoverability			

WORK PAPER 21.2   Types of Web-Based Testing to Perform

Field Requirements

FIELD	INSTRUCTIONS FOR ENTERING DATA
#	The sequential numbering of the eight web-based risks.
Types of Web-based Testing	This column contains the more common types of web-based testing. The names may need to be modified for your culture. Additional types of testing performed by your test group may need to be added to this column.
Perform	This field is used for the web-based test team to indicate which types of testing will be used during web-based testing. A check mark in the Yes column indicates the type of testing that will be performed, and check mark in the No column indicates that type of testing will not be performed.
Risk Focus	The web-based test team should indicate the risk that this test type will be used to address. The type of risk to be incorporated into the test plan has been identified on Work Paper 21.1. In addition, the column can be used to indicate the justification for not using various types of web-based testing, if appropriate.
How to Be Used	The web-based test team should write a brief narrative description of how they plan to use this test type to address the risks that will be incorporated into the test plan.

#		PERFORM			
	TYPES OF WEB-BASED TESTING	YES	NO	RISK FOCUS	HOW TO BE USED
1.	Unit/Component				
2.	Integration				
3.	System				
4.	User Acceptance				
5.	Performance				
6.	Load/Stress				
7.	Regression				
8.	Usability				
9.	Compatibility				

WORK PAPER 21.3   Select Web-Based Test Tools

Field Requirements

FIELD	INSTRUCTIONS FOR ENTERING DATA
#	The sequential numbering of the eight web-based risks.
Web-based Test Tool	All of the test tools available to your web-based test team should be listed in this column. The column contains generic types of test tools, but they should be replaced by specific test tools.
Perform	The web-based test team should identify which web-based test tool will be used during testing. A check in the Yes column indicates that the tool is to be used, and check in the No column indicates that the tool is not to be used.
Test Type Focus	The test team should indicate in this column which type of testing will be performed using this test tool. The test types are those indicated by the check mark in the Yes column on Work Paper 21.3. All of the test types with a Yes check mark on Work Paper 21.2 should be addressed in this column. Note that a single test tool may be used for multiple test types.
How to Be Used	The web-based test team should indicate in this test column how they plan to use a specific test tool during web-based testing. The testers should be as specific as possible in completing this column.

#	WEB-BASED TEST TOOLS	PERFORM		TEST TYPE FOCUS	HOW TO BE USED
		YES	NO		
1.	HTML text tool				
2.	Site validation test tool				
3.	Java test tool				
4.	Load/stress test tool				
5.	Test case generator				
6.	Other (list tools)				

WORK PAPER 21.4   Web-Based Test Quality Control Checklist

Field Requirements

FIELD	INSTRUCTIONS FOR ENTERING DATA
Number	A sequential number that identifies items to be incorporated in the review.
Specific items that need to be incorporated in the review	Whether or not the web-based test team has specifically addressed an item. A Yes response means that it has, a No response means it has not, an N/A response means the item was not applicable to this specific web-based test.
Comments	Used to explain No responses. Comments should indicate why there is a No response, and eventually, the disposition of that concern.

		RESPONSE			
#	ITEM	YES	NO	N/A	COMMENTS
1.	Has a web-based test team been organized?				
2.	Does the web-based test team understand the differences between client/server and web-based technology?				
3.	Does the web-based test team understand web terminology?				
4.	Does the web-based test team understand the risk associated with web technology?				
5.	Has the web-based test team reached consensus on which risks are applicable to this specific web-based system?				
6.	Has a determination been made as to how the identified risks will be incorporated in the test plan?				
7.	Is there a consensus that the web-based risks not included in the test plan are of minimal concern to this web-based system?				
8.	Has the web-based test team identified the types of testing required for this system?				
9.	If so, how have those testing types been correlated to the web-based risks?				
10.	Has the web-based test team reached consensus on how the web-based types of testing will be used for test purposes?				
11.	Is there a portfolio of web-based test tools available in the organization?				
12.	Are the available test tools adequate for the web-based system being tested?				
13.	Have the appropriate test tools been selected?				
14.	Has each type of testing that will be included in the test plan been supported by a specific web-based test tool?				

WORK PAPER 21.4   *(Continued)*

#	ITEM	RESPONSE			COMMENTS
		YES	NO	N/A	
15.	Has the test team reached consensus on how the test tools will be used during testing?				
16.	Have all of the web-based testing decisions made by the test team been incorporated into the test plan?				

# CHAPTER 22

Testing Off-the-Shelf Software

A growing source of software is software sold in stores. It is sometimes referred to as "shrink wrap" software or off-the-shelf software. The fact that it is commercially available does not mean that it is defect free, or that it will meet the needs of the user. Off-the-shelf software needs to be tested.

Overview

Off-the-shelf software must be made to look attractive if it is to be sold. Thus, the developer of off-the-shelf software (OTSS) will emphasize the benefits of the software. Unfortunately, there is often a difference between what the user believes the software can accomplish and what it actually does accomplish. The chapter recommends both static and dynamic testing. The static testing will concentrate on the user manual and other documentation, while the dynamic testing will examine the software in operation. Note that in some cases you may have to purchase the software to perform these tests, but that cost is usually insignificant compared to the problems that can be caused by software that does not meet needs. The cost of testing is always less than the cost of improper processing.

Objective

The objective of this off-the-shelf testing process is to provide the highest possible assurance of correct processing with a minimal effort. However, the process should be used for noncritical off-the-shelf software. If the software is critical to the ongoing operations of the organization, the software should be subject to a full scale of system testing, which is described in Part Three of this book. The testing in the process might be called "80-20" testing because it will attempt with 20 percent of the testing effort to catch 80 percent of the problems. That 80 percent should include almost all of the significant problems if they exist.

Concerns

The user of off-the-shelf software should be concerned with these areas:

Task/items missing. A variance between what is advertised or included in the manual versus what is actually in the software.

Software fails to perform. The software does not correctly perform the tasks/items it was designed to perform.

Extra features. Features may be included in the software that were not specified or included in the instruction manual. This poses two problems. First, the extra tasks may cause problems during processing; and second, if you discover the extra task and rely on it, it may not be included in future versions.

Does not meet business needs. The software does not fit with the user's business need.

Does not meet operational needs. The system does not operate in the manner, or on the hardware configuration, that is expected by the user.

Does not meet people needs. The software does not fit with the skill sets of the users.

Workbench

A workbench for testing off-the-shelf software is illustrated in Figure 22.1. The workbench shows three static tasks, which are to (1) test business fit, (2) test system fit, and (3) test people fit. Task 4 is the dynamic test when the software is in a executable mode and the processing is validated. As stated earlier, the tests are designed to identify the more significant problems because a tester cannot know all of the ways in which off-the-shelf software might be used. It is particularly true if the software is disseminated to many users within the organization.

It is generally advisable with off-the-shelf software to have a repository for user-reported problems. This can be accomplished by having a single individual appointed manager for a specific off-the-shelf software package. All problems are reported to that individual. The individual will determine what action needs to be taken, and then notify all of the users of the software.

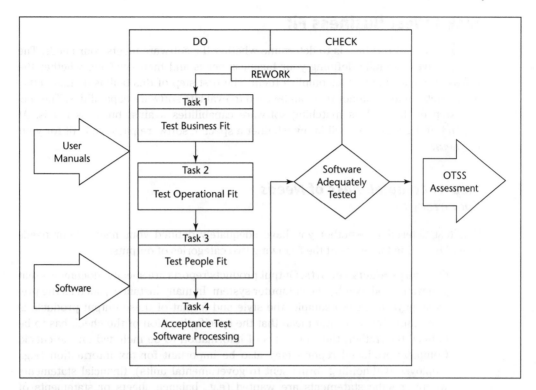

Figure 22.1   Workbench for testing off-the-shelf software (OTSS).

Input

There are two inputs to this step. The first input is the manuals that accompany the OTSS. These normally include installation and operation manuals. The manuals describe what the software is designed to accomplish, and how to perform the tasks necessary to accomplish the software functions. The second input is the software itself. Note that in some instances the user instructions will be contained within the software. Thus, the first few screens of the software may explain how to use the software.

Do Procedures

The execution of this process involves four tasks plus the check procedures. The process assumes that the individual(s) performing the test has knowledge of how the software will be used in the organization. If the tester does not know how it will be used, an additional step is required for the tester to identify the functionality that will be needed by the users of the software. The four tasks are described as follows:

Task 1: Test Business Fit

The objective of this task is to determine whether the software meets your needs. The task involves carefully defining your business needs and then verifying whether the software in question will accomplish them. The first step of this task is defining business functions in a manner that can be used to evaluate software capabilities. The second step of this task is matching software capabilities against business needs. At the end of this task, you will know whether a specific software package is fit for your business.

Step 1: Completeness of Needs Specification

This test determines whether you have adequately defined your needs. Your needs should be defined in terms of the following two categories of outputs:

1. **Output products/reports.** Output products/reports are specific documents that you want produced by the computer system. In many instances, such as the previous payroll check example, the style and format of these output products is important. This does not mean that the specific location of the check has to be defined but, rather, the categories of information to be included on the check. Computer-produced reports may also be important for tax information (e.g., employee withholding forms sent to governmental units), financial statements where specific statements are wanted (e.g., balance sheets or statements of income and expense), or customer invoice and billing forms which you might want preprinted to include your logo and conditions of payment.

2. **Management decision information.** This category tries to define the information needed for decision-making purposes. In the computer product/report category you were looking for a document; in this case you are looking for information. How that information is provided is unimportant. Thus, the structure of the document, what the documents are, or their size, frequency, or volume are not significant. All you need is information.

No form is provided for documenting these needs, because the method of documentation is unimportant. Writing them in pencil on a yellow pad is sufficient. However, it is important to define, document, and have those needs available when you begin your software selection process.

Testing the Completeness of Needs

The first test to be performed for computer software is a test of completeness of needs. This has proved to be one of the major causes of problems in OTSS.

The objective of this first test is to help you determine how completely your needs are defined. The test is based on the criteria learned by the large corporations.

The first test is a cause-effect test that attempts to identify the potential causes of poor needs definition. This test indicates the probability of completeness of needs documentation. For example, the fact that you smoke does not indicate that you will get lung cancer, but it does increase the probability of lung cancer.

After your needs are documented, they should be evaluated using the 10-factor test of completeness of business requirements illustrated in Work Paper 22.1. To use this test you need to do the following:

1. Familiarize yourself with the documented business needs.

2. Consider each of the 10 items in Work Paper 22.1 one at a time as they relate to the documented business needs. This review challenges the adequacy of your business needs based on your personal knowledge of the business. Thus, this test must be done by someone knowledgeable in the business. (Note: It can be done by two or more people, if appropriate. In such cases, a consensus can be arrived at by either averaging the assessments or negotiating a common assessment.)

3. Indicate your agreement or disagreement with the statement based on your understanding of each item. Consider, for example, the first item in Work Paper 22.1 (i.e., that the system will experience very few changes over time). For each item assessed in regard to that statement, indicate whether you:

   - Strongly agree with the statement **(SA)**
   - Agree with the statement **(A)**
   - Neither agree nor disagree with the statement (i.e., are basically neutral and are not sure whether the statement is applicable or inapplicable) **(N)**
   - Disagree with the statement **(D)**
   - Strongly disagree with the statement **(SD)**

   Check the appropriate assessment column for each of the 10 statements.

4. Calculate an assessment score for each of the 10 statements as follows: For each item checked SA, score 5 points; for each S, score 4 points; for each N, score 3 points; for each D, score 2 points; for each SD, score 1 point. Your final score will range between 10 and 50.

   The score can be assessed as follows:

   - **10–25 points: Poorly defined requirements.** You are not ready to consider buying a software package; do some additional thinking and discussion about this need.
   - **26–37 points: The needs are barely acceptable, particularly at the low end of the range.** While you have a good start, you may want to do some clarification of the reports or decision-making information.
   - **38–50 points: Good requirements.** In this range, you are ready to continue the software testing process.

At the conclusion of this test you will either go on to the next test or further clarify your needs. The experience of the "big boys" in computing indicates that it is a mistake to pass this point without well-defined needs.

Step 2: Critical Success Factor Test

This test tells whether the software package will be successful in meeting your business needs.

Critical success factors (CSFs) are those criteria or factors that must be present in the acquired software for it to be successful. You might ask whether the needs are the same as the critical success factors. They are, but they are not defined in a manner that makes them testable, and they may be incomplete. Often the needs do not take into account some of the intangible criteria that make the difference between success and failure. In other words, the needs define what we are looking for, and the critical success factors tell us how we will evaluate that product after we get it. They are closely related and complementary, but different in scope and purpose.

The following list indicates the needs/requirements for the automobile, and is then followed by the CSFs on which the automobile will be evaluated:

- Automobile requirements/needs:
  - Seats six people
  - Four doors
  - Five-year guarantee on motor
  - Gets 20 miles per gallon or greater
  - Costs under $12,000
- Critical success factors:
  - Operates at 20.5 cents or less per mile
  - Experiences no more than one failure per year
  - Maintains its appearance without showing signs of wear for two years

Some of the more common critical success factors for OTSS you may want to use are:

Ease of use. The software is understandable and usable by the average person.

Expandability. The vendor plans to add additional features in the future.

Maintainability. The vendor will provide support/assistance to help utilize the package in the event of problems.

Cost-effectiveness. The software package makes money for your business by reducing costs, and so on.

Transferability. If you change your computer equipment the vendor indicates that they will support new models or hardware.

Reliability. In computer language, the system is friendly, meaning that it will help you get your transactions entered into the system so that you can produce your results readily.

Security. The system has adequate safeguards to protect the data against damage (for example, power failures, operator errors, or other goofs that could cause you to lose your data).

The CSFs should be listed for each business application under consideration. Work Paper 22.2, which is a test of fit, provides space to list those factors. Note that in most applications there are eight or fewer critical success factors. Thus, this test is not as time consuming as it might appear.

Once Work Paper 22.2 has been considered, it can be used to test the applicability of the software package being evaluated. Work Paper 22.2 provides space to indicate the software package that is being tested.

In making the evaluation, the following factors must be considered:

- Thorough understanding of the business application.
- Knowledge of the features of the software package.
- Ability to conceptualize how the software package will function on a day-to-day basis.
- Use of CSFs to indicate whether you believe:
    - There is a high probability that the software package will meet the CSF (put an X in the Yes column).
    - The software package does not have a high probability of meeting the CSF (put an X in the No column).
    - There is more or less than a 50–50 probability of the software package's success (put an X in the appropriate column and then clarify your assessment in the comments column).

At the conclusion of this test, you will have matched your business needs against the software capabilities, and assessed the probability of its success. If the probability of success is low (i.e., there are several No responses or highly qualified Yes responses), you should probably not adopt this software package. Clearly, additional study and analysis is warranted before you move forward and expend the resources to implement a potentially unsuccessful system.

Task 2: Test Operational Fit

The objective of this task is to determine whether the software will work in your business. Within your business there are several constraints that must be satisfied before you acquire the software, including:

- Computer hardware constraints
- Data preparation constraints
- Data entry constraints

Other automated processing constraints (e.g., if data from this software package must be fed into another software package, or receive data from another software package, those interface requirements must be defined).

At the end of this task, you will know whether the software fits into the way you do business, and will operate on your computer hardware.

This task includes three steps that need to be performed to ensure an appropriate fit between the software being evaluated and your in-house systems:

Step 1: Compatibility with Your Hardware, Operating System, and Other Software Packages

This is not a complex test. It involves a simple matching between your processing capabilities and limitations, and what the vendor of the software says is necessary to run the software package. The most difficult part of this evaluation is ensuring the multiple software packages can properly interface.

This test is best performed by preparing a checklist defining your compatibility needs. Software vendors are generally good about identifying the needed hardware and operating system compatibility. They are generally not good in identifying compatibility with other software packages.

In addition to the hardware on which the software runs, and the operating system with which it must interact to run, there are two other important compatibilities: (1) compatibility with other software packages and (2) compatibility with available data. If you have no other software packages that you want to have interact with this one, or no data on computer-readable media, you need not worry about these aspects of compatibility. However, as you do more with your computer these aspects of compatibility will become more important, and the hardware and operating compatibility will become routine and easy to verify.

Systems compatibility is defined in data processing jargon as "interoperability." This term refers to the amount of effort required to intercouple or interconnect computer systems. In other words, how do you tie two or more programs together so that they will work and pass data between them? For example, if you have a payroll system it may be desirable to pass that payroll summary information to your general-ledger system. The ability to pass information from system to system is an extremely important part of data processing. Much of the success of the Lotus Corporation was based in its ability to intercouple five office software functions so that information could be readily passed from one to another.

If you cannot pass information easily (i.e., worksheet, word processing, database, graphics, and communications), information transfer will by definition be difficult. Difficulty means that you may have to print information out of one program, and then manually reenter it at the keyboard into another program. Let us assume, for example, you used word processor A and over a period of months created entire files of form letters and parts of letters. You decided to acquire word processor B to meet a new business need. If word processor B cannot retrieve all of the data prepared for word processor A, each of those thousands of keystrokes will have to be reentered. This is an unnecessary waste of time, which you will quickly recognize the first time you have to do it.

Commercial data processing installations estimate that they spend about one-half of their total computer effort entering, validating, and correcting data. In other words, when the input data is entered correctly they are halfway home. To lose their data means that they have lost half of their total data processing effort to date.

Finding someone who can tell you whether you have program and/or data compatibility is difficult. That someone must understand data formats, know what data formats programs use, and know that those programs or data will work when they are interconnected. In many instances, trial and error is the only method of determination. However, the fact that one program cannot read the data created by another program does not mean that the original data cannot be reused. For example, there are utility programs that can convert data from one format to another. It may be significantly cheaper to hire someone to make this conversion rather than rekeying the data. This is particularly true if the data has been entered correctly and can be relied on. Reentering it will invariably introduce defects into your data, which will either cause subsequent problems or require analysis and correction.

To help you prepare a compatibility list for the purpose of testing, the information that needs to be included is described below. The list is divided into hardware, operating systems, programs, and data.

Hardware compatibility. List the following characteristics for your computer hardware:

- Hardware vendor
- Amount of main storage
- Disk storage unit identifier
- Disk storage unit capacity
- Type of printer
- Number of print columns
- Type of terminal
- Maximum terminal display size
- Keyboard restrictions

Operating systems compatibility. For the operating system used by your computer hardware, list:

- Name of operating system (e.g., UNIX or Windows)
- Version of operating system in use

Program compatibility. List all of the programs with which you expect or would like this specific application to interact. Be sure that you have the name of the vendor and, if applicable, the version of the program. Note that as discussed earlier this linkage may only be verifiable by actually attempting to interact two or more systems using common data.

Data compatibility. In many cases, program compatibility will answer the questions on data compatibility. However, if you created special files you may need descriptions of the individual data elements and files. Again, as with program compatibility, you may have to actually verify through trial whether the data can be read and used by other programs. Note that in step 3 (demonstration) you will have the opportunity to try using your own data or programs to see if you can utilize common data and pass parameters from program to program.

Step 2: Integrating the Software into Your Business System Work Flow

Each computer system makes certain assumptions. Unfortunately, these assumptions are rarely stated in the vendor literature. The danger is that you may be required to do some manual processing functions that you may not want to do in order to utilize the software.

The objective of this test is to determine whether you can plug the OTSS into your existing manual system without disrupting your entire operation. Remember that:

- Your manual system is based on a certain set of assumptions.
- Your manual system uses existing forms, existing data, and existing procedures.
- The computer system is based on a set of assumptions.
- The computer system uses a predetermined set of forms and procedures.
- Your current manual system and the new computer system may be incompatible.

- If they are incompatible, the computer system is not going to change—you will have to.

- You may not want to change—then what?

The process for test of fit of the computer system into your existing manual system requires you to prepare a document flow diagram or narrative description. A document flow diagram is a pictorial or narrative description of how your process is performed. That is, you plug the computer system into your existing system and then determine if you like what you see. If you do, your computer system has passed this test. If not, you will either have to change your existing method of doing work, or search for another computer system.

Performing the Data Flow Diagram Test

The data flow diagram is really more than a test. At the same time that it tests whether you can integrate the computer system into your business system, it shows you how to do it. It is both a system test and a system design methodology incorporated into a single process. So, to prepare the document flow narrative or document flow description, these three tasks must be performed:

1. **Prepare a document flow of your existing system.** Through personal experience or inquiry, quickly put down in document flow format the steps required to complete the process as it is now performed. Since there will be 15 or fewer steps in most instances, this should only take a few minutes.

2. **Add the computer responsibility to the data flow diagram.** Use a colored pencil to cross out each of the tasks now being performed manually that will be performed by the computer. Indicate the tasks you will continue to perform manually in a different color pencil. If the computer is going to perform tasks that were not performed before, those should be indicated by using a third color. At the end of this exercise, you will have a clearly marked list of which manual tasks were replaced by the computer, which manual tasks will remain as such, and which new tasks have been added.

3. **Modify the manual tasks as necessary.** Some of the manual tasks can stay as is, others will need to be added or modified. Again do this in a different color. The reason for the different color pencils is to highlight and illustrate these changes.

The objective of this process is to illustrate the type and frequency of work flow changes that will be occurring. You can see graphically illustrated what will happen when the computer system is brought into your organization. For example, there might be tasks performed now that weren't performed before, or tasks that were previously performed but are no longer necessary, or tasks which had been performed by people which will now be performed by the computer. Having the computer perform those tasks might mean that the oversight that people had been giving will not be available any more.

At the end of this test, you will need to decide whether you are pleased with the revised work flow. If you feel the changes can be effectively integrated into your work flow, the potential computer system has passed the test. If you feel the changes in work flow will be disruptive, you may want to fail the software in this test and either look for other software or continue manual processing.

If the testing is to continue, you should prepare a clean data flow diagram indicating what actions need to be taken to integrate the computer system into your organization's work flow. This new data flow diagram becomes your installation plan of action. It will tell you what changes need to be made, who is involved in them, what training might be necessary, and areas of potential work flow problems.

Step 3: Demonstrating the Software in Operation

This test analyzes the many facets of software. Software developers are always excited when their program goes to what they call "end of job." This means that it executes and concludes without abnormally terminating (i.e., stops after doing all the desired tasks). While this is one aspect of the demonstration, observing the functioning of software is like taking an automobile for a test drive. The more rigorous the test, the greater the assurance you are getting what you expect.

Demonstrations can be performed in either of the following ways:

1. **Computer store–controlled demonstration**—In this mode, the demonstration is conducted at the computer store, by computer store personnel, using their data. The objective is to show you various aspects of the computer software, but not to let you get too involved in the process. This is done primarily to limit the time involved in the demonstration.

2. **Customer site demonstration**—In this mode, the demonstration takes place at your site, under your control, by your personnel, using your information. It is by far the most desirable of all demonstrations, but many software OTSS computer stores may not permit it unless you purchase the OTSS.

These aspects of computer software should be observed during the demonstration:

Understandability. As you watch and listen to the demonstration, you need to evaluate the ease with which the operating process can be learned. If the commands and processes appear more like magic than logical steps, you should be concerned about implementing the concept in your organization. If you have trouble figuring out how to do it, think about how difficult it may be for some of your clerical personnel who understand neither the business application nor the computer.

Clarity of communication. Much of the computer process is communication between man and machine. That is, you must learn the language of the computer software programs in order to communicate with the computer. Communication occurs through a series of questions and responses. If you do not understand the communications, you will have difficulty using the routine.

East of use of instruction manual. While monitoring the use of the equipment, the tasks being demonstrated should be cross-referenced to the instruction manual. Can you identify the steps performed during the demonstration with the same steps included in the manual? In other words, does the operator have to know more than is included in the manual, or are the steps to use the process laid out so clearly in the manual that they appear easy to follow?

Functionality of the software. Ask to observe the more common functions included in the software: Are these functions described in the manual? Are these the functions that the salesperson described to you? Are they the functions that you expected? Concentrate extensively on the applicability of those functions to your business problem.

Knowledge to execute. An earlier test has already determined the extent of the salesperson's knowledge. During the demonstration, you should evaluate whether a lesser-skilled person could as easily operate the system with some minimal training. Probe the demonstrator about how frequently they run the demonstration and how knowledgeable they are about the software.

Effectiveness of help routines. Help routines are designed to get you out of trouble when you get into it. For example, if you are not sure how something works you can type the word "help" or an equivalent and the screen should provide you additional information. Even without typing "help" it should be easy to work through the routines from the information displayed on the screen. Examine the instructions and evaluate whether you believe you could have operated the system based on the normal instructions. Then ask the operator periodically to call the help routines to determine their clarity.

Evaluate program compatibility. If you have programs you need to interact with, attempt to have that interaction demonstrated. If you purchased other software from the same store where you are now getting the demonstration, they should be able to show you how data is passed between the programs.

Data compatibility. Take one of your data files with you. Ask the demonstrator to use your file as part of the software demonstration. This will determine the ease with which existing business data can be used with the new software.

Smell test. While watching the demonstration, let part of your mind be a casual overseer of the entire process. Attempt to get a feel for what is happening and how that might impact your business. You want to end up being able to assess whether you feel good about the software. If you have concerns, attempt to articulate them to the demonstrator as well as possible to determine how the demonstrator responds and addresses those concerns.

To determine whether an individual has the appropriate skill level to use the OTSS it is recommended to involve one or more typical users of the OTSS in software demonstrations (i.e., Task 3) and in the validation of the software processing (i.e., Task 4). If the selected users are able to perform those dynamic tests with minimal support, it is reasonable to assume that the average user will possess the number of skills necessary to master the use of the OTSS. If, on the other hand, the selected user appears unable to operate the software in a dynamic mode, it is logical to assume that significant training and/or support will be required for effectively using this OTSS.

Task 3: Test People Fit

The objective of this task is to determine whether your employees can use the software. This testing consists of ensuring that your employees have or can be taught the necessary skills.

This test evaluates whether people possess the skills necessary to effectively use computers in their day-to-day work. The evaluation can be of current skills, or the program that will be put into place to teach individuals the necessary skills. Note that this includes the owner-president of the organization as well as the lowest-level employee in the organization.

The test is performed by selecting a representative sample of the people who will use the software. The sample need not be large. This group is given training that may only involve handing someone the manuals and software. The users will then attempt to use the software for the purpose for which it was intended. The results of this test will show:

1. The software can be used as is.

2. Additional training/support is necessary.

3. The software is not usable with the skill sets of the proposed users.

Task 4: Validate Acceptance Test Software Process

The objective of this task is to validate that the off-the-shelf software will in fact meet the functional and structural needs of the user of the software.

We have divided testing into functional and structural testing, which also could be called correctness and reliability testing. "Correctness" means that the functions produce the desired results. "Reliability" means that the correct results will be produced under actual business conditions.

Step 1: Create Functional Test Conditions

It is important to understand the difference between correctness and reliability because it impacts both testing and operation. Let's look at a test example to verify that gross pay was properly calculated. This could be done by entering a test condition showing 30 hours of work and $6 per hour pay, so that if the program worked correctly it would produce $180 gross pay. If this happens, we can say that the program is functionally correct. These are the types of tests that should be prepared under this category.

The types of test conditions that are needed to verify the functional accuracy and completeness of computer processing include:

- All transaction types to ensure they are properly processed

- Verification of all totals

- Assurance that all outputs are produced

- Assurance that all processing is complete

- Assurance that controls work (e.g., input can be balanced to an independent control total)

- Reports that are printed on the proper paper, and in the proper number of copies

- Correct field editing (e.g., decimal points are in the appropriate places)

- Logic paths in the system that direct the inputs to the appropriate processing routines

- Employees that can input properly
- Employees that understand the meaning and makeup of the computer outputs they generate

The functional test conditions should be those defined in the test plan. However, since some of the test methods and business functions may be general in nature, the interpretation and creation of specific test conditions may require an explosion of the test conditions. To help in this effort, a checklist of typical functional test conditions is provided as Work Paper 22.3.

The objective of this checklist is to help ensure that sufficient functional test conditions are used. As test conditions for the types listed on Work Paper 22.3 are completed, that line should be checked. At the completion of the test conditions, those types of functional test conditions that have not been checked should be evaluated to determine whether they are needed. The checklist is designed to help ensure the completeness of functional test conditions.

Step 2: Create Structural Test Conditions

Structural, or reliability, test conditions are challenging to create and execute. Novices to the computer field should not expect to do extensive structural testing. They should limit their structural testing to conditions closely related to functional testing. However, structural testing is easier to perform as computer proficiency increases. This type of testing is quite valuable.

Some of the easier-to-perform structural testing relates to erroneous input. In some definitions of testing, this reliability testing is included in functional testing. It is included here because if the input was correct the system would perform in a functionally correct way; therefore, incorrect input is not a purely functional problem.

Most of the problems that are encountered with computer systems are directly associated with inaccurate or incomplete data. This does not necessarily mean that the data is invalid for the computer system. Let's look at an example:

A photographic wholesaler only sells film by the gross. The manufacturer shrink-wrapped film in lots of 144, and the wholesaler limited sales to those quantities. If a store wanted less film, they would have to go to a jobber and buy it at a higher price. A small chain of photo processing stores ordered film from this manufacturer. Unfortunately, the clerks did not really understand the ordering process. They only knew that they would get 144 rolls of film when they ordered. On the order form submitted to the manufacturer, the clerks indicated a quantity of 144. This resulted in 144 gross of film being loaded onto a truck and shipped to the shopping center. The small photo shop could not store that much film, and 143 gross were returned to the wholesaler. The new result was lost money for the manufacturer. In this case, 14 was a valid quantity, but incorrect for the desired order. This is a structural problem that needs to be addressed in the same manner that entering 144 on the computer when you meant to enter 14 must be addressed.

The second part of structural testing deals with the architecture of the system. Architecture is a data processing term that describes how the system is put together. It is used in the same context that an architect designs a building. Some of the architectural problems that could affect computer processing include:

- Internal limits on number of events that can occur in a transaction (e.g., number of products that can be included on an invoice)
- Maximum size of fields (e.g., quantity is only two positions in length, making it impossible to enter an order for over 99 items)
- Disk storage limitations (e.g., you are only permitted to have X customers)
- Performance limitations (e.g., the time to process transactions jumps significantly when you enter over X transactions)

These are but a few of the potential architectural limitations placed on computer software. You must remember that each software system is finite and has built-in limitations. Sometimes the vendor tells you that you can from time to time find these limitations if you search through the documentation, and occasionally you won't know them until they occur. However, all limits can be determined through structural testing. The questions at hand are: Do you feel competent to do it? and Is it worth doing? The answers to these questions depend on the critical nature of the software and what would happen if your business was unable to continue computer processing because you reached the program limitation.

A final category of potential structural problems relates to file-handling problems. While these do appear to be a problem, they are frequently found in computer software. Typical problems that occur are incorrect processing when the last record on a file is updated, or adding a record that will become the first record on a file. These types of problems have haunted the computer programming profession for years. In the personal computer software market there are literally thousands of people writing software. Some have good ideas but are not experienced programmers; thus, they fall into the age-old traps of file manipulation problems.

As an aid in developing structural test conditions, Work Paper 22.4 lists the more common structural problem areas. You can use this checklist either to determine which types of structural test conditions you want to prepare or to check the completeness of the structural conditions included in your test matrix. Either way, it may spark you to add some additional test conditions to verify that the structure of your software performs correctly.

Check Procedures

At the conclusion of this testing process, the tester should verify that the OTSS test process has been conducted effectively. The quality control checklist for conducting the OTSS review is included as Work Paper 22.5. It is designed for Yes/No responses. Yes indicates a positive response; No responses should be investigated. The Comments column is provided to clarify No responses. The N/A column is provided for items that are not applicable to a specific OTSS test process.

Output

There are three potential outputs as a result of executing the OTSS test process:

1. **Fully acceptable.** The software meets the full needs of the organization and is acceptable for use.

2. **Unacceptable.** The OTSS package has sufficient deficiencies that it is not acceptable for use.

3. **Acceptable with conditions.** The OTSS package does not fully meet the needs of the organization, but either lowering those expectations or taking alternate procedures to compensate for deficiencies makes the package usable, and thus it will be disseminated for use.

Guidelines

The following guidelines are given to aid in testing off-the-shelf software:

- Spend one day of your time learning and evaluating software, and you will gain problem-free use of that software.

- Only acquire computer software after you have established the need for that software and can demonstrate how it will be used in your day-to-day work.

- Instinct regarding goodness and badness should be used to help you select software.

- Testing is not done to complicate your life, but rather to simplify it. After testing, you will operate your software from a position of strength. You will know what works, what doesn't work, and how it works. After testing, you will not be intimidated by the unknown.

- The cost of throwing away bad software will be significantly less than the cost of keeping it. In addition to saving you time and money, it will also save frustration.

- The best testing is that done by the individuals who have a stake in the correct functioning of the software. These stakeholders should both prepare the test and evaluate the results of testing.

- If your users can run the acceptance tests successfully from their procedures and training courses, they will be able to run their software successfully in conjunction with their business function.

Summary

The process outlined in this chapter is designed for testing off-the-shelf software. It assumes that the testers will not have access to the program code; therefore, the test emphasizes usability. The test is similar in approach to acceptance testing.

WORK PAPER 22.1   Test of Completeness of Business Requirements

Field Requirements

FIELD	INSTRUCTIONS FOR ENTERING DATA
Number (#)	A number that sequentially identifies the quality control items, which if positively addressed would indicate that this step has been performed correctly.
Item to consider	A characteristic of the process of collecting and documenting business requirements that contribute to good requirement gathering.
Assessment	For each item assessed in regard to that statement, indicate whether you: Strongly agree with the statement **(SA)** Agree with the statement **(A)** Neither agree nor disagree with the statement (i.e., are basically neutral and are not sure whether the statement is applicable or inapplicable) **(N)** Disagree with the statement **(D)** Strongly disagree with the statement **(SD)**
Comments	This column is used to clarify the Yes, No, or N/A response for the item indicated. Generally the comments column need only be completed for No responses; No responses should be investigated and a determination made as to whether this item needs to be performed before this step can be considered complete.

		ASSESSMENT					
#	ITEM TO CONSIDER	SA (5)	A (4)	N (3)	D (2)	SD (1)	COMMENTS
1.	The system will experience few changes over time.						
2.	All involved parties agree the needs are well defined.						
3.	The use of the results of the application will require very little judgment on the part of the users of the computer outputs.						
4.	The input to the system is well defined.						
5.	The outputs from the system and the decision material are well defined.						
6.	The users of the system are anxious to have the area automated.						
7.	The users want to participate in the selection and implementation of the software.						
8.	The users understand data processing principles.						

WORK PAPER 22.1   *(Continued)*

#	ITEM TO CONSIDER	SA (5)	A (4)	N (3)	D (2)	SD (1)	COMMENTS
		__ ASSESSMENT __					
9.	The application does not involve any novel business approach (i.e., an approach that is not currently being used in your business).						
10.	The users do not expect to find other good business ideas in the selected software.						

Assessment Score = _____

Legend:

SA = Strongly agree

A = Agree

N = Neither agree nor disagree

D = Disagree

SD = Strongly disagree

WORK PAPER 22.2   Test of Fit

Field Requirements

FIELD	INSTRUCTIONS FOR ENTERING DATA
Business Application	Name of business application being tested.
Number	A number which sequentially identifies a CSF.
Critical Success Factor (CSF)	A factor which those responsible for the success of the business application must meet in order for the business application to be successful.
Meets CSF	An assessment as to whether a specific CSF has been met, with a comments column to explain how the assessment was determined.

Business Application

		MEETS CSF		
NUMBER	CRITICAL SUCCESS FACTORS	YES	NO	COMMENTS

WORK PAPER 22.3   Functional Test Condition Checklist

Field Requirements

FIELD	INSTRUCTIONS FOR ENTERING DATA
Number	A number that sequentially identifies the quality control items, which if positively addressed would indicate that this step has been performed correctly.
Item	The specific quality control item that is used to measure the effectiveness of performing this step.
Response	The testers should indicate in this column whether they have performed the referenced item. The response can be Yes, No, or N/A if it is not appropriate for your organization's testing process.
Comments	This column is used to clarify the Yes, No, or N/A response for the item indicated. Generally the comments column need only be completed for No responses; No responses should be investigated and a determination made as to whether this item needs to be performed before this step can be considered complete.

#	ITEM	RESPONSE YES	NO	N/A	COMMENTS
	Have tests for these conditions been prepared:				
1.	Test conditions for each input transaction				
2.	Variations of each input transaction for each special processing case				
3.	Test conditions which will flow through each logical processing path				
4.	Each internal mathematical computation				
5.	Each total on an output verified				
6.	Each functional control (e.g., reconciliation of computer controls to independent control totals)				
7.	All the different computer codes				
8.	The production of each expected output				
9.	Each report/screen heading and column heading				
10.	All control breaks				
11.	All mathematical punctuation and other editing				
12.	Each user's preparation of input				
13.	Completeness of prepared input				
14.	User's use of output, including the understanding and purpose for each output				
15.	A parallel test run to verify computer results against those which were produced manually				
16.	Matching of two records				
17.	Nonmatch of two records				

WORK PAPER 22.4   Structural Test Condition Checklist

Field Requirements

FIELD	INSTRUCTIONS FOR ENTERING DATA
Number	A number that sequentially identifies the quality control items, which if positively addressed would indicate that this step has been performed correctly.
Item	The specific quality control item that is used to measure the effectiveness of performing this step.
Response	The testers should indicate in this column whether they have performed the referenced item. The response can be Yes, No, or N/A if it is not appropriatefor your organization's testing process.
Comments	This column is used to clarify the Yes, No, or N/A response for the item indicated. Generally the comments column need only be completed for No responses; No responses should be investigated and a determination made as to whether this item needs to be performed before this step can be considered complete.

#	ITEM	RESPONSE			COMMENTS
		YES	NO	N/A	
	Have test conditions for each of these conditions been prepared:				
1.	Addition of a record before the first record on a file				
2.	Addition of a record after the last record on a file				
3.	Deletion of the first record on a file				
4.	Deletion of the last record on a file				
5.	Change information on the first record on a file				
6.	Change information on the last record on a file				
7.	Cause the program to terminate by predetermined conditions				
8.	Accumulate a field larger than the mathematical accumulators can hold				
9.	Verify that page counters work				
10.	Verify that page spacing works				
11.	Enter invalid transaction types				
12.	Enter invalid values in fields (e.g., put alphabetic characters in a numeric field)				
13.	Process unusual conditions (of all types)				
14.	Test principle error conditions				
15.	Test for out-of-control conditions (e.g., the value of records in the batch does not equal the entered batch total)				
16.	Simulate a hardware failure forcing recovery procedures to be used				
17.	Demonstrate recovery procedures				
18.	Enter more records than disk storage can hold				
19.	Enter more values than internal tables can hold				
20.	Enter incorrect codes and transaction types				
21.	Enter unreasonable values for transaction processing				
22.	Violate software rules not violated by above structural test conditions				

WORK PAPER 22.5   Off-the-Shelf Software Testing Quality Control Checklist

Field Requirements

FIELD	INSTRUCTIONS FOR ENTERING DATA
Number	A number that sequentially identifies the quality control items, which if positively addressed would indicate that this step has been performed correctly.
Item	The specific quality control item that is used to measure the effectiveness of performing this step.
Response	The testers should indicate in this column whether they have performed the referenced item. The response can be Yes, No, or N/A if it is not appropriate for your organization's testing process.
Comments	This column is used to clarify the Yes, No, or N/A response for the item indicated. Generally the comments column need only be completed for No responses; No responses should be investigated and a determination made as to whether this item needs to be performed before this step can be considered complete.

#	ITEM	RESPONSE			COMMENTS
		YES	NO	N/A	
	Have test conditions for each of these conditions been prepared:				
1.	Addition of a record before the first record on a file				
2.	Addition of a record after the last record on a file				
3.	Deletion of the first record on a file				
4.	Deletion of the last record on a file				
5.	Change information on the first record on a file				
6.	Change information on the last record on a file				
7.	Cause the program to terminate by predetermined conditions				
8.	Accumulate a field larger than the mathematical accumulators can hold				
9.	Verify that page counters work				
10.	Verify that page spacing works				
11.	Enter invalid transaction types				
12.	Enter invalid values in fields (e.g., put alphabetic characters in a numeric field)				
13.	Process unusual conditions (of all types)				
14.	Test principle error conditions				
15.	Test for out-of-control conditions (e.g., the value of records in the batch does not equal the entered batch total)				
16.	Simulate a hardware failure forcing recovery procedures to be used				
17.	Demonstrate recovery procedures				

WORK PAPER 22.5   *(Continued)*

#	ITEM	YES	NO	N/A	COMMENTS
		RESPONSE			
18.	Enter more records than disk storage can hold				
19.	Enter more values than internal tables can hold				
20.	Enter incorrect codes and transaction types				
21.	Enter unreasonable values for transaction processing				
22.	Violate software rules not violated by above structural test conditions				

Task 1: Test Business Fit

#	ITEM	YES	NO	N/A	COMMENTS
1.	Have the business needs been adequately defined?				
2.	Does the selected software package meet those needs?				
3.	Have the critical success factors for the business application been defined?				
4.	Is there a high probability that the software package under consideration will satisfy the critical success factors?				
5.	Is the software being evaluated designed to meet this specific business need?				
6.	Does the software under consideration push the critical success factors to their limit?				
7.	Do you personally believe the software under consideration is the right software for you?				
8.	Do you believe this software package will provide your business with one of the four benefits attributable to software (i.e., perform work cheaper, perform work faster, perform work more reliably, or perform tasks not currently being performed)?				
9.	Does the business approach, and the software package, fit into your business' long-range business plan?				
10.	Is your business system that is being considered for computerization relatively stable in terms of requirements?				

Task 2: Testing System Fit

#	ITEM	YES	NO	N/A	COMMENTS
1.	Will the selected software package operate on your computer hardware?				
2.	Will the selected software package operate on your equipment's operating system?				

WORK PAPER 22.5   *(Continued)*

#	ITEM	RESPONSE			COMMENTS
		YES	NO	N/A	
3.	Is the proposed software package compatible with your other computer programs (applicable programs only)?				
4.	Can the proposed software package utilize applicable existing data files?				
5.	Is the method in which the software operates consistent with your business cycle?				
6.	Are you willing to have you and your personnel perform the business steps needed to make the software function correctly?				
7.	Is the computer work flow for this area consistent with the general work flow in your business?				
8.	Were the software demonstrations satisfactory?				
9.	Do you believe that the software has staying power (i.e., the vendor will continue to support it as technological and business conditions change)?				
10.	Are you pleased with the fit of this software package into your computer and systems environment?				

Task 3: Testing People Fit

#	ITEM	YES	NO	N/A	COMMENTS
1.	Were the workers exposed to or involved in the decision to acquire a computer, and specifically the applications that affect their day-to-day job responsibilities?				
2.	Have your and your staff's jobs been adequately restructured after the introduction of the computer?				
3.	Have the people involved with the computer been trained (or will they be trained) in the skills needed to perform their new job function?				
4.	Has each worker been involved in the establishment of the procedures that he or she will use in performing day-to-day job tasks?				
5.	Have the workers been charged with the responsibility for identifying defects in computer processing?				
6.	Does each worker have appropriate feedback channels to all of the people involved with his or her work tasks?				
7.	Are your people enthusiastic over the prospects of involving a computer in their work?				

WORK PAPER 22.5   *(Continued)*

#	ITEM	YES	NO	N/A	COMMENTS
		RESPONSE			
8.	Have supervisors been properly instructed in how to supervise computer staff?				
9.	Have adequate controls been included within computer processing?				
10.	Do you believe your people have a positive attitude about the computer and will work diligently to make it successful?				

Task 4: Validate Acceptance Test Software Process

#	ITEM	YES	NO	N/A	COMMENTS
1.	Were test conditions created for all of the test methods included in the test matrix?				
2.	Were both static and dynamic tests used as test methods?				
3.	Have functional test conditions been prepared which are consistent with the functional requirements and critical success factors?				
4.	Have you prepared structural test conditions which address the more common computer architectural problems and incorrect data entry?				
5.	Has the sequence in which test conditions will be executed been determined?				
6.	Are the test conditions prepared using the most economical source of data?				
7.	Have the test conditions been prepared by the appropriate "stakeholder"?				
8.	Have the test conditions been prepared in an easy-to-use format?				
9.	Has the validity of the test process been adequately challenged?				
10.	Do you believe that the test conditions when executed will adequately verify the functioning of the software?				

Testing in a Multiplatform Environment

Software that is designed to run on more than one platform must undergo two tests. The first is to validate that the software performs its intended functions. This testing involves the 11-step testing process described in Part Three of this book. The second test is that the software will perform in the same manner regardless of the platform on which it is executed. This chapter focuses on the second test process.

Overview

Each platform on which software is designed to execute operationally may have slightly different characteristics. These distinct characteristics include various operating systems, hardware configurations, operating instructions, and supporting software, such as database management systems. These different characteristics may or may not cause the software to perform its intended functions differently. The objective of testing is to determine whether the software will produce the correct results on various platforms.

This chapter provides a six-task process for testing in a multiplatform environment. The test process preassumes that the platforms for which the software must execute are known. The process also preassumes that the software has already been tested, and the testers have validated that it performs its intended functions correctly.

Objective

The objective of this six-task process is to validate that a single software package executed on different platforms will produce the same results. The test process is basically the same that was used in parallel testing. Software must operate on multiple platforms with the individual results being compared to assure consistency in output. The testing normally requires a test lab that includes the predetermined platforms.

Concerns

There are three major concerns in multiplatform testing:

1. **The platforms in the test lab will not be representative of the platforms in the real world.** This can happen because the platform in the test lab may not be upgraded to current specifications, or may be configured in a manner that is not representative of the typical configuration for that platform.

2. **The software will be expected to work on platforms not included in the test labs.** By implication, users may expect the software to work on a platform that has not been included in testing.

3. **The supporting software on various platforms is not comprehensive.** User platforms may contain software that is not the same as that used on the platform in the test lab, for example, a different database management system and so forth.

Workbench

The workbench for testing in a multiplatform environment is illustrated in Figure 23.1. This figure shows that six tasks are needed to effectively test in a multiplatform environment. Most tasks assume that the platforms will be identified in detail, and that the software to run on the different platforms has been previously validated as being correct. Five of the six tasks are designed to determine what tests are needed to validate the correct functioning of the identified platforms, and the sixth task executes those tests.

Input

The two inputs needed for testing in a multiplatform environment are as follows:

1. **List of platforms on which software must execute.** The main requirement for multiplatform testing is a list of the platforms. These platforms must be described in detail as input to testing, or described in detail prior to commencing testing.

2. **Software to be tested.** The software package(s) to be tested is input to the test process. This software must be validated that it performs its functions correctly prior to multiplatform testing. If this has not been done, then the software should

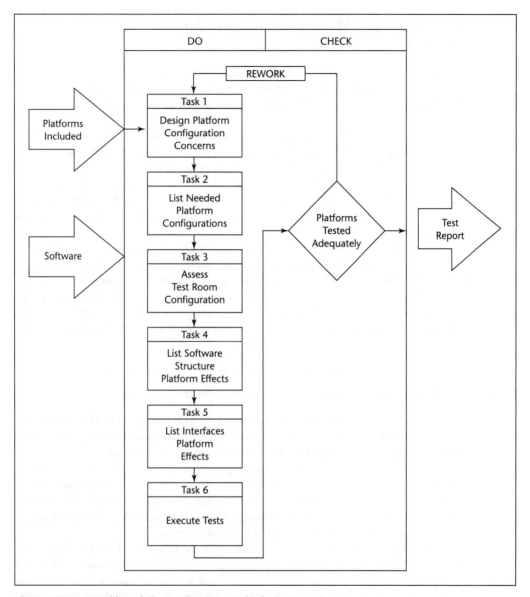

Figure 23.1   Workbench for testing in a multiplatform environment.

be subject to the 11-step testing process, described in Part Three of this book, prior to commencing multiplatform testing.

Do Procedures

The following six tasks should be performed to validate that software performs consistently in a multiplatform environment.

Task 1: Define Platform Configuration Concerns

The first task in testing a multiplatform environment is to develop a list of potential concerns about that environment. The testing that follows will then determine the validity of those concerns. The recommended process for identifying concerns is error guessing.

Error guessing attempts to anticipate problems within the software package and its operation. The proverb "an ounce of prevention is worth a pound of cure" speaks to the error-guessing process. Studies by the IBM Corporation indicate that the same types of software defects occur with the same frequency from project to project. Just as medicine can predict that X percent of the 55-year-old age group that will die of a heart attack during the year, so the software test experts can predict the types of defects that will occur in software.

This means that the types of problems that you encounter in one will occur in most other similar tests. The problem may surface in a slightly different way, but it will be the same basic problem. For example, the problem of data exceeding its allocated field size is a type of problem that will appear sooner or later in almost all software applications. If you anticipate it and decide (1) what you will do when it happens and (2) how the software will react to the situation, successful use of the software will not be threatened.

Error guessing requires two prerequisites:

1. The error-guessing group understands how the platform works.

2. The error-guessing group knows how the software functions.

If the group that tested the software function is the same group doing the error guessing, they will know how the software works. Knowing the platforms may require the addition of platform-knowledgeable people to the error-guessing team.

While it is possible to perform error guessing with one person, it is basically a brainstorming process. Thus, it is always better when two or more people participate. This is because of the powerful synergistic effect of a group. Synergism means that one individual's comments spark another individual to think about something he or she might not have thought about without the other individual present.

Error guessing requires a recorder to write down the ideas developed by the group. Each member of the group is allowed time to express what he or she believes might go wrong with the software. Until every individual has had an initial opportunity to list problems, there can be no criticism or comment on what other individuals have stated. After the initial go-round, the recorder reads back these items one by one. At this point, open discussion—that is, interactive discussion—commences. One group rule of this discussion is that there can be no criticism of errors raised or the individual who raised them. All comments must be stated positively. If an individual believes that the type of error or condition raised is not realistic, the ensuing discussion should be based on the probability of occurrence rather than the point's validity. If criticism is permitted during brainstorming, communication will cease and much of the value of the process will be lost.

The error-guessing process is normally very brief. In some instances, it lasts no longer than 15 minutes, and only rarely would it exceed one hour. However, the process does require total concentration. Therefore, the group should be removed from normal business interruptions during this exercise.

The end product of error guessing is a list of potential error conditions for additional investigation and test. It is not up to the error-guessing team to determine what happens when these error conditions occur. They need to be familiar enough with the software to know whether there may be a problem, but they do not need to know all of the solutions. This will be done in future testing steps.

Error guessing is meant to be a relatively unstructured, unorganized process. Generally, sufficient ideas are generated to prepare a reasonably comprehensive list of potential problems—particularly when performed by two or more people. The following is a short list of questions to brainstorm during error guessing:

- Does your software have any unusual transactions?
- What are the most common errors that you are now making?
- What would happen to processing if you forgot to perform one of the steps?
- What would happen if you did not enter all of the data in an input transaction?
- Will you be able to determine who performed what computer operation in case questions arise regarding the correctness of operations?
- If a diagnostic message is produced by the computer, how will you know it has been properly corrected?
- How will you know the person operating the computer knows how to operate it correctly?

These questions are designed to spark ideas about what might go wrong within a platform. The questions are not intended to be complete, nor do they need to be answered precisely. Their sole purpose is to steer you into areas for further exploration regarding potential errors.

The concerns should be listed on Work Paper 23.1. Part 1 of that work paper provides space for listing multiplatform testing concerns, as well as any recommended test to address those concerns to determine whether they are valid or have already been handled by the software and/or platform.

Task 2: List Needed Platform Configurations

The test must identify the platforms that must be tested. Ideally this list of platforms and detailed description of the platforms would be input to the test process. If so, this step need only determine if those platforms are available in the test lab.

The needed platforms are either those that will be advertised as acceptable for using the software, or platforms within an organization on which the software will be executed. The platforms need to be described in detail. This information should be recorded on part 2 of Work Paper 23.1. Note that the description of the work paper will list some of the items needed about each platform.

Testers must then determine whether those platforms are available for testing. If the exact platform is not available, the testers need to determine whether an existing platform is acceptable. For example, if an available platform did not contain some feature or configuration, would the existing platform provide a reasonable test? If so, that platform can be used for testing. If the needed platform is not available the testers must make a determination of whether to obtain such a platform or accept the risk that the software will be released without testing that specific platform.

The determination of whether an available test platform meets the needed test platform should be recorded on part 2 Work Paper 23.1. If the needed test platform is not available, then the testers should record on part 2 of Work Paper 23.1 the action they will take based on the availability of the needed test platform.

Task 3: Assess Test Room Configurations

The testers need to make a determination as to whether the platforms available in the test room are acceptable for testing. This involves two steps:

1. For each needed platform listed on Work Paper 23.1, document the platform to be used for testing, if any is available, on the work paper.

2. Make a determination as to whether the available platform is acceptable for testing. Indicate your decision on Work Paper 23.1. If not acceptable, note any actions to be taken on the work paper.

Task 4: List Structural Components Affected by the Platform(s)

Structural testing deals with the architecture of the system. Architecture describes how the system is put together. It is used in the same context that an architect designs a building. Some of the architectural problems that could affect computer processing include:

- Internal limits on number of events that can occur in a transaction (e.g., number of products that can be included on an invoice).

- Maximum size of fields (e.g., quantity is only two positions in length, making it impossible to enter an order for over 99 items).

- Disk storage limitations (e.g., you are only permitted to have X customers).

- Performance limitations (e.g., the time to process transactions jumps significantly when you enter over X transactions).

These are but a few of the potential architectural limitations placed on computer software. You must remember that each software system is finite and has built-in limitations. Sometimes the vendor tells you these limitations, sometimes you can find them if you search through the documentation, and sometimes you won't know them until they occur. However, all limits can be determined through structural testing. The questions at hand are Do you feel competent to do it? and Is it worth doing? The answers to these questions depend on the critical nature of the software and what would happen if your business was unable to continue computer processing because you reached the program limitation.

Structural testing also relates to file-handling problems. Typical of the types of file problems that occur are incorrect processing when the last record on file is updated or adding a record that will become the first record on a file. In the personal computer software market there are literally thousands of people writing software. Some have good ideas but are not experienced programmers—thus, they fall into the age-old traps of file manipulation problems.

As an aid in developing structural test conditions, the more common structural problem areas are listed below. You can use this checklist either to determine which types of structural test conditions you want to prepare or to check the completeness of the structural conditions. Either way, it may spark you to add some additional test conditions to verify that the structure of your software performs correctly.

Have test conditions for each of the following conditions been prepared:

- Addition of a record before the first record on a file.
- Addition of a record after the last record on a file.
- Deletion of the first record on a file.
- Deletion of the last record on a file.
- Change information on the first record on a file.
- Change information on the last record on a file.
- Cause the program to terminate by predetermined conditions.
- Accumulate a field larger than the mathematical accumulators can hold.
- Verify that page counters work.
- Verify that page spacing works.
- Enter invalid transaction types.
- Enter invalid values in fields (e.g., put alphabetic characters in a numeric field).
- Process unusual conditions (of all types).
- Test major error conditions.
- Test for out-of-control conditions (e.g., the value of records in the batch do not equal the entered batch total).
- Simulate a hardware failure that forces recovery procedures to be used.
- Demonstrate recovery procedures.
- Enter more records than disk storage can hold.
- Enter more values than internal tables can hold.
- Enter incorrect codes and transaction types.
- Enter unreasonable values for transaction processing.
- Violate software rules not violated by above structural test conditions.

While some functional processing maybe impacted by various platforms, it is normally the structural component of the function that is affected. The test team needs to identify the structural components of functions that will be impacted by the platform. They may want to use the "error guessing" technique described in Task 1 for identifying these structural components.

The potentially impacted structural component should be documented on Work Paper 23.2. The work paper lists the structural component, then each platform that may affect that structural component, as well as how the structural component may be affected by the platform. The testers should then determine which tests are needed to validate that the structural component will or will not be impacted by a platform.

Task 5: List Interface-Platform Effects

Systems tend to fail at interface points, an interface being when control is passed from one processing component to another as, for example, when data is retrieved from a database, output reports are printed or transmitted, or a person interrupts processing to make a correction.

These interface points are where most failures will occur. Thus, the purpose of this task is to identify those interfaces so that they can be tested. Note that some of these interfaces will also overlap the software structural components affected by the platform. If the test has been included in the structural component task Work Paper, it need not be duplicated in the test recommended in this task.

This is a two-part task. Part one is to identify the interfaces within the software systems. These interfaces should be readily identifiable in the user manual for the software. The second part is to determine whether those interfaces could be impacted by the specific platform on which the software executes. This is a judgmental exercise. However, if there is a doubt in the tester's mind, he or she should test that interface on all of the platforms that might impact that interface. The work paper should identify the platform on which the interface may be impacted, the interface itself, the interface both to and from the potential effect of the platform, and the test(s) that should be undertaken to validate whether the interface is impacted by the platform. Note that this same test for a single interface may have to be performed on multiple platforms. Document the results of this task on Work Paper 23.3.

At the conclusion of this task the tests that will be needed to validate multiplatform operations will have been determined. The remaining task will be to execute those tests.

Task 6: Execute the Tests

The platform test should be executed in the same manner as other tests are executed in the 11-step software testing process described in Part Three of this book. The only difference may be that the same test would be performed on multiple platforms to determine that consistent processing occurs.

Check Procedures

Prior to completing multiplatform testing a determination should be made that testing was performed correctly. Work Paper 23.4 provides a series of questions to challenge correctness of multiplatform testing. A Yes response to those items indicates that multiplatform testing was performed correctly; a No response indicates that it may or may not have been done correctly. Each No response should be clarified in the Comments column. The N/A column is for items that are not applicable to this specific platform test.

Output

The output from this test process is a report indicating:

- Structural components that work or don't work by platform
- Interfaces that work or don't work by platform
- Multiplatform operational concerns that have been eliminated or substantiated
- Platforms on which the software should operate, but that have not been tested

The report will be used to clarify user operation instructions and/or make changes to the software.

Guidelines

Multiplatform testing is a costly, time-consuming, and extensive component of testing. The resources expended on multiplatform testing can be significantly reduced if that testing focuses on predefined multiplatform concerns. Identified structural components that might be impacted by the software and interfaces that might be impacted by multiple platforms should comprise most of the testing. This will focus the testing on what should be the major risks faced in operating a single software package on many different platforms.

Summary

This multiplatform testing process is designed to be used in conjunction with the 11-step testing process in Part Three. It is essential that the software that is to be tested on multiple platforms be validated as correct prior to multiplatform testing. Combining software validation testing with multiplatform testing normally will slow the test process and increase the cost.

WORK PAPER 23.1 Multiplatform Concerns and Configurations

Field Requirements

FIELD	INSTRUCTIONS FOR ENTERING DATA
Concerns	A narrative description of the concerns that need to be addressed in multi-platform testing.
Recommended Test to Address Concerns	This field should include any tests that the group developing the concerns believes could be made to determine the validity of that concern.
Needed Test Platform	Detailed description of the platform on which the software will be executed. The description should include at a minimum: Hardware vendor Memory size Hard disk size Peripheral equipment Operating system Needed supporting software (i.e., database management systems)
Available Test Platform	This column should indicate whether the needed test platform is available, and if not, what actions will be taken for test purposes.

Part 1 Multiplatform Testing Concerns

Concern	Recommended Test to Address Concern

Part 2 Needed versus Available Platform Configurations

Needed Test Platform	Available Test Platform	Acceptable	
		Yes	**No**

WORK PAPER 23.2   Test to Validate Platform-Affected Software Structure

Field Requirements

FIELD	INSTRUCTIONS FOR ENTERING DATA
Structural Component	The name or identifier of the structural component affected by a platform.
Platform	The specific platform or platforms that may affect the correct processing of the identified structural component.
How Affected	A narrative explanation of how the platform may affect the structural component should be documented.
Test(s) to Validate Structural Component	The test group should recommend one or more tests to validate whether the platform affects the structural component. Note that these tests may be different for different platforms.

Software Structure Affected by Platform			Test(s) to Validate Structural Component
Structural Component	**Platform**	**How affected**	

WORK PAPER 23.3   Test(s) to Validate Platform-Affected Interfaces

Field Requirements

FIELD	INSTRUCTIONS FOR ENTERING DATA
Software to Be Tested	The name of the software package that is being tested.
Platform	Description of the platform that may affect an interface.
Interface Affected	A brief narrative name or description of the interface affected, such as "retrieving a product price from the pricing database."
Interface	The interface should be described to indicate the movement of data or processing from one point to another. For example, a product price will be moved from the product price database to the invoice pricing software package.
Effect	This field should explain the potential risk or effect that could be caused by a specific platform. For example, platform X may not have adequate space for over 1,000 product prices.
Test(s) to Validate Interface	This column should describe in detail each task that should be performed to validate interface processing. For example, put 1,001 product prices into the pricing database to validate that the platform can support a pricing database that contains over 999 product prices.

Interfaces Affected by Platform					Test(s) to Validate Interface
Platform	**Interface Affected**	**Interface**			
		From	**To**	**Effect**	

WORK PAPER 23.4   Multiplatform Quality Control Checklist

Field Requirements

FIELD	INSTRUCTIONS FOR ENTERING DATA
Number	A number that sequentially identifies the quality control items, which if positively addressed would indicate that this step has been performed correctly.
Item	The specific quality control item that is used to measure the effectiveness of performing this step.
Response	The testers should indicate in this column whether they have performed the referenced item. The response can be Yes, No, or N/A if it is not appropriate for your organization's testing process.
Comments	This column is used to clarify the Yes, No, or N/A response for the item indicated. Generally the comments column need only be completed for No responses; No responses should be investigated and a determination made as to whether this item needs to be performed before this step can be considered complete.

#	ITEM	YES	NO	N/A	COMMENTS
1.	Have all of the platforms in which the software is intended to be run been identified?				
2.	Has each platform configuration been described?				
3.	Have the concerns for correct multiplatform processing been identified?				
4.	If so, are those concerns reasonable and complete?				
5.	Has a determination been made that the identified platforms will be available for test?				
6.	If not, has a decision been made on how to handle the potential risk associated with platforms not being tested?				
7.	Have the structural components of the software to be tested been identified?				
8.	Are those structural components complete?				
9.	Has a determination been made as to how each of the identified platforms may impact those structural components?				
10.	Have the interfaces for the software package been identified and documented?				
11.	Has a determination been made as to whether any or all of the platforms may affect those interfaces?				
12.	Was multiplatform testing conducted under real-world conditions?				

WORK PAPER 23.4 *(Continued)*

#	ITEM	RESPONSE			COMMENTS
		YES	NO	N/A	
13.	Did acceptance testing prove that the procedures were correct and usable?				
14.	Did the acceptance test process verify that people are adequately trained to perform their job tasks on multiple platforms?				
15.	Did acceptance testing verify that the software performs the functional and structural tasks correctly (i.e., those tested)?				
16.	Did acceptance testing verify that the products produced by the computer system are correct and usable?				
17.	Did acceptance testing verify that the operations personnel could correctly and effectively operate the software on the multiple platforms?				
18.	Did the acceptance test process verify that the operational software system satisfied the predefined critical success factors for the software?				
19.	Did the acceptance test process verify that the users/operators of the system can identify problems when they occur, and then correctly and on a timely basis correct and reenter those transactions?				
20.	Have all the problems identified during acceptance testing been adequately resolved?				

Testing Security

In today's environment security is becoming an important strategy of organizations. The features for physical security have been proven to be effective. However, one of the greatest risks organizations now face is computer software security. This occurs both internally, through employees, and externally through communication lines and Internet processing.

Testing security is a very complex and costly activity. Performing comprehensive security testing is generally not practical.

Effectiveness of security testing can be improved by focusing on the points where security has the highest probability of being compromised. A testing tool that has proved effective in identifying these points is the penetration point matrix. The security testing process described in this chapter focuses primarily on developing the penetration point matrix, as opposed to the detailed testing of those identified points.

Overview

This test process provides a tool to assist in identifying points in a physical location or information system that have high risks of being penetrated. The technique is not statistically accurate, but has proven to be highly reliable when used by individuals knowledgeable in the area that may be penetrated.

The technique involves building a matrix. In one dimension are the potential perpetrators; in the other dimension are potential points of penetration. The developers of the matrix assess the probability of penetration by the perpetrators at the points of intersection. By identifying the points with the highest probability of penetration, organizations are given insight into where physical locations/information systems are most likely to be penetrated.

Objective

The object of the penetration point matrix is to enable organizations to focus security measures on the points of highest risk. While no location/information system can be penetration proof, focusing the majority of security resources on the high-risk points increases the probability of preventing or detecting penetration.

Concerns

There are two major security concerns. The first is that the security risks will be identified, the second is that adequate controls are installed to minimize these risks.

Workbench

This workbench assumes that there is a team of individuals knowledgeable about the location/information system to be secured.

It is important that this team of individuals possess the following knowledge/skills:

- Communication network in use
- Individuals having access to those communication networks
- Software systems containing data or processes requiring protection
- Value of information or processes requiring protection
- Processing flow of software systems so that points of data movement can be identified
- Knowledge of security systems and concepts
- Knowledge of security penetration methods and techniques

The workbench provides five tasks for building and using a penetration point matrix (see Figure 24.1). The tool that is used in this workbench is the penetration point matrix. The prime purpose of the matrix is to focus discussion on high-risk points of potential penetration and to assist in determining which points require the most attention. The tool can be used by project teams, special teams convened to identify its security, or by quality assurance/quality control personnel to assess the adequacy of security systems.

Input

The input to this test process is a team that is knowledgeable about the location/information system to be protected. The reliability of the results will be heavily dependent

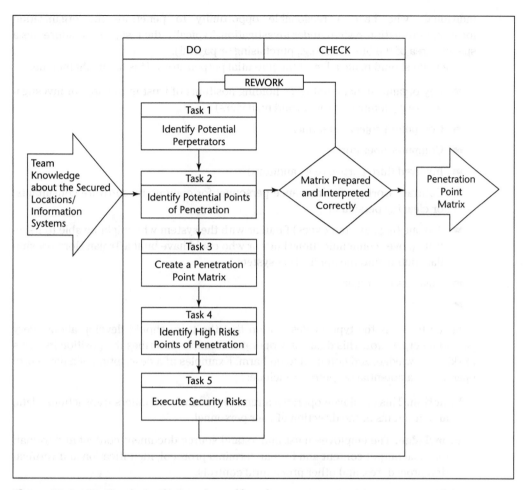

Figure 24.1 Penetration point matrix workbench.

upon the knowledge of the individuals involved with the location/information system and the specific types of individuals that are likely to penetrate the system at those points. The technique is simplistic enough that the team would not require prior training in the use of the test process.

Do Procedures

This test process involves performing the following five tasks, explained below:

Task 1: Identify Potential Perpetrators

In conducting this test process, the team should narrow down the list of potential suspects and points of possible penetration. The list of likely perpetrators includes all the individuals who have a reasonable opportunity to penetrate the organization location/information system under investigation. Typically, the test process addresses a specific area of the business (e.g., purchasing or payroll).

The team should make a list of the potential perpetrators. This list might include:

- Key organizational employees holding positions of trust in the area of investigation (e.g., company officers and managers)
- Computer project personnel
- Computer operators
- Involved third parties (e.g., auditors)
- Contract workers: maintenance personnel for computers, software consultants, or cleaning personnel
- Anyone (e.g., ex-employees) familiar with the system who might be able to penetrate it over communications lines or who could have built a Trojan Horse or similar routine into the application system
- Business customers
- Others

Listed below is the type of description that the team should develop about every potential perpetrator. This data entry operator example describes the position in terms of skill, knowledge, and potential to do harm. Examples of a description of a data entry operator as a potential perpetrator include:

Function. This employee operates a remote terminal and enters transactions, data, and programs at the direction of user personnel.

Knowledge. The employee must understand source document content and format; terminal output content and format; terminal protocol, identification and verification procedures; and other procedural controls.

Skills. Typing and keyboard operation, manual dexterity for equipment operation, and basic reading skills are all required.

Access. This operator has access to the terminal area, source documents, terminal output, terminal operation instructions, and identification and verification materials.

Vulnerability. The system is vulnerable to both physical and operational violations by this individual. The principal area of vulnerability involves the modification, destruction, or disclosure of data belonging to the individual's immediate user organization (either internal or external to the system). Two secondary areas of vulnerability are the destruction or disclosure of the user organization's application programs and the physical destruction or taking of terminal equipment.

Conclusions. This individual is in a key position relative to the immediate user organization's data and programs entering the system and results (i.e., output) exiting the system. Data modification is more of a threat than program modification because this individual is not apt to understand enough about the programs to do significant damage. A serious danger is the destruction of data or programs, particularly when source documents have no backup. Individual operators, however, can manipulate data and programs only for the application areas that they service.

Task 2: Identify Potential Points of Penetration

Penetration points are points within the computerized business environment at which penetration could occur. Penetration points are typically the least-controlled areas and thus the most vulnerable to unauthorized manipulation.

The objective of this task is to develop a list of points in application processing at which a reasonable possibility of penetration exists. Generally, penetration occurs at such points in the system as when the transaction is originated, entered into a system, stored, retrieved, processed, outputted, or used. In Task 4, the team determines the probability of penetration occurring at these points; at this task, however, only those points at which the team believes a reasonable opportunity for penetration exists should be listed.

The following sections describe the areas of greatest vulnerabilities in security, the primary locations of those vulnerabilities, distinctions between accidental and intentional losses, and natural forces that increase system vulnerability.

Functional Vulnerabilities

The eight primary functional vulnerabilities to computer abuse are listed and summarized below in order of frequency of occurrence.

1. **Poor controls over manual handling of input/output data.** The greatest vulnerability here occurs whenever access is most open. Historically, access has been most easy and subject to human acts before data is entered into and after data is outputted from the computer. Data access is easier when manipulating manual controls, than when programs must be manipulated to achieve unauthorized access. Controls that are often absent or weak include separation of data handling and conversion tasks, dual control of tasks, document counts, batch total checking, audit trails, protective storage, access restrictions, and labeling.

2. **Weak or nonexistent physical access controls.** When physical access is the primary vulnerability, nonemployees have gained access to computer facilities, and employees have gained access at unauthorized times and in unauthorized areas. Perpetrators' motivations include political, competitive, and financial gain. Financial gain can occur through the unauthorized selling of computer services, burglary, and larceny. In some cases, a disgruntled employee is the motivating factor. In the cases reported, some of these employees had become frustrated with various aspects of automated society. Controls that were found to be weak or nonexistent involved door access, intrusion alarms, low visibility of access, identification and establishment of secure perimeters, badge systems, guard and automated monitoring functions (e.g., closed-circuit television), inspection of transported equipment and supplies, and staff sensitivity to intrusion. Some of the violations occurred during nonworking hours when safeguards and staff were not present.

3. **Computer and terminal operational procedures.** Here, losses have resulted from sabotage, espionage, sale of services and data extracted from computer systems, unauthorized use of facilities for personal advantage, and direct financial

gain from negotiable instruments in IT areas. The controls whose weakness or absence facilitates these kinds of acts include: separation of operational staff tasks, dual control over sensitive functions, staff accountability, accounting of resources and services, threat monitoring, close supervision of operating staff, sensitivity briefings of staff, documentation of operational procedures, backup capabilities and resources, and recovery and contingency plans. The most common abuse problem is the unauthorized use or sale of services and data. The next most common problem is sabotage perpetrated by disgruntled IT operations staff.

4. **Weaknesses in the business test process.** A weakness or breakdown in the business test process can result in computer abuse perpetrated in the name of a business or government organization. The principal act is related more to corporate test processes or management decisions rather than to identifiable unauthorized acts of individuals using computers. These test processes and decisions result in deception, intimidation, unauthorized use of services or products, financial fraud, espionage, and sabotage in competitive situations. Controls include review of business test processes by company board of directors or other senior-level management, audits, and effective regulatory and law enforcement.

5. **Weaknesses in the control of computer programs.** These are programs that are subject to abuse. They can also be used as tools in the perpetration of abuse and are subject to unauthorized changes to perpetrate abusive acts. The abuses from unauthorized changes are the most common. Controls found lacking include: labeling programs to identify ownership, formal development methods (including testing and quality assurance), separation of programming responsibilities in large program developments, dual control over sensitive parts of programs, accountability of programmers for the programs they produce, safe storage of programs and documentation, audit comparisons of operational programs with master copies, formal update and maintenance procedures, and establishment of program ownership.

6. **Weaknesses in operating system access and integrity.** These abuses involve the use of time-sharing services. Frauds can occur as a result of discovering design weaknesses or by taking advantage of bugs or shortcuts introduced by programmers in the implementation of operating systems. The acts involve intentional searches for weaknesses in operating systems, unauthorized exploitation of weaknesses in operating systems, or the unauthorized exploitation of weaknesses discovered accidentally. Students committing vandalism, malicious mischief, or attempting to obtain free computer time have perpetrated most of the acts in university-run time-sharing services. Controls to eliminate weaknesses in operating system access include: ensuring the integrity and security of the design of operating systems, imposing sufficient implementation methods and discipline, proving the integrity of implemented systems relative to complete and consistent specifications, and adopting rigorous maintenance procedures.

7. **Poor controls over access through impersonation.** Unauthorized access to time-sharing services through impersonation can most easily be gained by obtaining secret passwords. Perpetrators learn passwords that are exposed accidentally through carelessness, administrative error, and conning people into revealing their passwords, or by guessing obvious combinations of characters and digits. It is sus-

pected that this type of abuse is so common that few victims bother to report cases. Control failures include poor administration of passwords, failure to change passwords periodically, failure of users to protect their passwords, poor choices of passwords, absence of threat monitoring or password-use analysis in time-sharing systems, and failure to suppress the printing or display of passwords.

8. **Weaknesses in media control.** Theft and destruction of magnetic data are acts attributed to weaknesses in the control of magnetic media. Many other cases, identified as operational procedure problems, involved the manipulation or copying of data. Controls found lacking include limited access to data libraries, safe storage of magnetic media, labeling data, location, number accounting, controls of degausser equipment, and backup capabilities.

Locations of Vulnerabilities

Data and report preparation areas and computer operation facilities with the highest concentration of manual functions were found to be the most vulnerable locations. Nine primary functional locations are listed, described, and ranked in Figure 24.2, according to vulnerability. They are also discussed below in detail.

1. **Computer data and report preparation facilities.** Vulnerable areas include key-to-disk; computer job setup; output control and distribution; data collection; and data transportation. Input and output areas associated with on-line remote terminals are excluded here.

2. **Computer operations.** All functional locations concerned with operating computers in the immediate area or rooms housing central computer systems are included in this category. Detached areas containing peripheral equipment connected to computers by cable and computer hardware maintenance areas or offices are also included. On-line remote terminals (connected by telephone circuits to computers) are excluded here.

3. **Non-IT areas.** Many of these cases involve business decisions in which the primary abusive act occurs in such non-IT areas as management, marketing, sales, and business offices.

4. **Central processors.** These functional areas are within computer systems where acts occur in the computer operating system (not inducted from terminals).

5. **Programming offices.** This area includes office areas in which programmers produce and store program listings and documentation.

6. **Magnetic media storage facilities.** This area includes data libraries and any storage place containing usable data.

7. **On-line terminal systems.** The vulnerable functional areas are within on-line systems where acts occur by execution of such programmed instructions as are generated by terminal commands.

8. **On-line data preparation and output report handling areas.** This category includes the same functions described in Chapter 12 for preparing on-line scripts.

9. **On-line operations.** This category is the equivalent of the computer operations discussed previously, but involves the on-line terminal areas.

LOCATIONS	RANK
Data preparation and report preparation	1
Computer operations	2
Non-IT areas	3
Central processors	9
Programming offices	5
Magnetic media storage	7 (tie)
On-line terminal storage	4
On-line data preparation and report generation	6
On-line operations	7 (tie)

Figure 24.2 Vulnerabilities to computer security according to functional location.

Accidental versus Intentional Losses

Errors and omissions generally occur in labor-intensive functions in which people are involved in detail work. The vulnerabilities occur when detailed, meticulous, and intense activity requires close concentration. They are usually manifested in data errors, computer program errors (bugs), and damage to equipment or supplies. This requires frequent rerunning of a job, error correction, and replacement and repair of equipment or supplies.

Nevertheless, it is often difficult to distinguish between accidental loss and intentional loss. In fact, some reported intentional loss comes from perpetrators discovering and making use of errors that result in their favor. When loss occurs, employees and managers tend to blame the computer hardware first because this would absolve them from blame, and the problem becomes one for the vendor to solve. The problem is rarely a hardware error, but proof of this is usually required before the source of the loss is searched for elsewhere. The next most common area of suspicion is the user department or the source of data generation because, again, the IT department can blame another organization. Blame is usually next placed on the computer programming staff. Finally, when all other targets of blame have been exonerated, IT employees will suspect their own work.

It is not uncommon to see informal meetings between computer operators, programmers, maintenance engineers, and users arguing over who should start looking for the cause of a loss. The thought that the loss was intentional is remote because they generally assume they function in a benign environment.

In many computer centers, employees do not understand the significant difference between accidental loss from errors and omissions and intentionally caused losses.

Organizations using computers have been fighting accidental loss for 40 years, since the beginning of automated data processing. Solutions are well known and usually well applied relative to the degree of motivation and cost-effectiveness of controls. They anticipate, however, that the same controls used in similar ways also have an effect on people engaged in intentional acts that result in losses. They frequently fail to understand that they are dealing with an intelligent enemy who is using every skill, experience, and access capability to solve the problem or reach a goal. This presents a different kind of vulnerability, one that is much more challenging and that requires adequate safeguards and controls not yet fully developed or realized, let alone adequately applied.

Vulnerabilities Caused by Natural Forces

Computer systems clearly are vulnerable to a wide range of natural as well as manufactured forces. Computer systems and facilities are fragile, and intruders can use simple methods to engage in malicious mischief, arson, vandalism, sabotage, and extortion with threats of damage. Natural events such as extreme weather and earth movements can also be used by an intruder to achieve destructive purposes.

Most computer centers possess a degaussing (demagnetizing) device for the purpose of erasing magnetic tapes. It is about the size of a portable electric hot plate. Degaussers should be kept under lock and key or at least located in a different room or area from the one used to store magnetic tapes.

Task 3: Create a Penetration Point Matrix

To build a penetration point matrix, the vertical and horizontal axis of a matrix are completed. The vertical axis of the penetration point matrix is the list of potential perpetrators identified in Task 1; the horizontal axis is the list of points of penetration identified in Task 2. The completion of the penetration point matrix involves two parts. (See Table 24.1 for an example.)

Part 1: Identify Probability of Penetration of Each Point

The team must examine each point in the matrix. In the penetration point matrix example (Table 24.1), the team would determine the probability of a perpetrator penetrating at point 1. This estimation should be based on the team's experience and judgment in this and other similar applications. The probability should be scored as follows:

3 A high probability of the individual penetrating at this point.

2 An average probability of the individual penetrating at this point.

1 Some probability of the individual penetrating at this point.

0 Minimal or no probability of penetration at this point.

Table 24.1   Penetration Point Matrix Example

PENETRATION POINTS								PERPETRATOR
POTENTIAL PERPETRATORS	1	2	3	4	5	6	7	TOTALS
A	1	2	3	-	-	-	-	6
B	1	2	1	3	1	1	1	10
C	-	-	3	2	1	1	-	7
D	1	1	1	1	-	-	-	4
E	-	-	-	-	1	2	3	6
F	-	-	1	1	1	2	-	5
G	3	1	1	-	-	-	-	5
H	-	-	2	2	2	-	-	6
I	1	1	2	-	-	-	-	4
J	3	2	③	1	2	2	-	⑬
K	-	-	-	-	1	2	1	4
L	3	2	3	1	-	-	-	9
M	-	-	1	-	2	1	1	5
Point Totals	13	11	㉑	11	11	11	6	

Part 2: Add Vertical and Horizontal Axes

The probability scores should be added both vertically and horizontally. In the penetration point matrix example, potential penetrator "A" scores 6 points in the perpetrator total column; penetration point "1" scores a total of 13. All of the rows and columns should be totaled. Although it is not statistically accurate to add probabilities, the objective of this task is to identify the person and points with the greatest probability, and experience has shown that this partial violation of statistics is still a very helpful tool in improving security.

Work Paper 24.1 should be used to create the matrix. The penetration point matrix indicates the potential perpetrators, the points at which penetration may occur, and the probability of penetration at those points. Task 4 will use the information in the matrix to calculate the most probable points of penetration.

Task 4: Identify High-Risk Points of Penetration

The penetration point matrix can be used to identify the point of probable penetration and the most likely individual to commit that violation. The penetration point is based on the following two assumptions:

■ The individual with the greatest opportunity would commit fraud most frequently.

■ The system would be defrauded at its most vulnerable point.

These assumptions have held true in numerous computer crime cases. It is important to understand them because the fraud methodology discussed here is based on probability.

The objective of Task 4 is to select the point or points requiring investigation. In the example, only one point has been selected, but in the actual test process many points can be selected. The method for selecting points is to identify the highest perpetrator totals and highest point totals. In most instances, the team would select three to five of the highest perpetrator totals and three to five of the highest point totals. After the high totals have been circled, the intersection between the circled totals should be identified.

The team should look for those intersections that have a probability of 3 or 2. The number 3 probabilities are the points with the greatest potential for penetration.

At the end of this task, the team has identified the most probable points for penetration and the sequence in which they should be investigated or controlled. The sequence starts with the high-number totals. For example, on the penetration point matrix, the circled area has a total point value of 34 (i.e., 21 plus 13). Because it has a number 3 probability and a point total of 34, it can be used as a starting point to develop a list for investigation or control.

Task 5: Execute Security Test

One or all of the following three tests should be executed for the points with the highest probability of penetration. Assuming that those points will be penetrated by the perpetrators with the highest probability of penetrating will limit security testing. Fraud studies indicate that those points with the highest potential to penetrate are the ones where penetration is most likely to occur. The three tests that can be performed are as follows:

1. **Evaluate the adequacy of security controls at identified points.** The objective of this test is to evaluate whether the security controls in place are adequate to prevent or significantly deter penetration. The process is one of evaluating the magnitude of the risk and strength of controls. If the controls are perceived to be stronger than the magnitude of the risk, the probability of penetration at that point would be significantly reduced. On the other hand, if the controls appear inadequate the testers could conclude that the identified point is of high risk.

2. **Determine if penetration can occur at identified point(s).** In this test, the testers actually try to penetrate the system at the identified point. For example, if it was the payroll system and the determination was trying to be made whether invalid overtime can be entered into the payroll system, the testers would attempt to do this. In fact, the testers would attempt to break security by actually doing it.

   This type of test requires preapproval by management. The testers must protect themselves so that they are not improperly accused of actually trying to penetrate the system. Also, if the system is actually penetrated at that point by the technique used by the testers, they stand to be among the potential perpetrators that might be investigated.

3. **Determine if penetration has actually occurred at this point.** This test would involve conducting such investigation as to determine whether the system has actually been penetrated. For example, if improper overtime was the area of concern and the payroll clerks were the most likely perpetrators then the testers investigate paid overtime to determine that it was in fact properly authorized overtime.

> **NOTE** The creation of the penetration point matrix can be effectively developed by software testers. However, the three tests identified in Task 5 are normally best performed by internal auditors/external auditors as opposed to software testers. However, the testers may wish to work in conjunction with internal/external auditors in performing any or all of the three tests. The software testers can be helpful in this process, and also learn how auditors perform these types of tests.

Check Procedures

The check procedures for this test process should focus on the completeness and competency of the team using the penetration point matrix, as well as the completeness of the list of potential perpetrators and potential points of penetration. The analysis should also be challenged.

Work Paper 24.2 contains questions that are designed to aid in checking the completeness and correctness of the prepared penetration point matrix. The questions are designed so that Yes responses are indicative of good control, while No responses to the questions should result in challenging the completeness and correctness of the conclusions drawn from the matrix.

Output

The output from this test process is the penetration point matrix identifying the high-risk points of penetration. If Task 5 is performed, the output will expand on the high-risk points identified in the matrix.

Guidelines

The penetration point matrix can be used in one of two ways:

1. It can be used to identify the people and the potential points of penetration so that an investigation can undertake to determine whether a particular location/information system has been penetrated.

2. It can be used to evaluate/build/improve the system of security to minimize the risk of penetration at the high-risk point.

Summary

This test process is designed to help software testers conduct tests on the adequacy of computer security. The process is built on two premises: First, extensive security testing is impractical. Practical security testing involves focusing on specific points of vulnerability. Second, software testers are most effective in identifying points of potential security weakness, while auditors are more effective in performing the actual test.

This test process has described how to complete a penetration point matrix. The matrix identifies the points most likely to be penetrated. Given this information, tests can be performed to (1) determine probability of penetration occurring based on the adequacy of controls; (2) test the probability of penetration; and (3) test whether penetration has occurred.

WORK PAPER 24.1   Security Penetration Point Matrix

Field Requirements

FIELD	INSTRUCTIONS FOR ENTERING DATA
Area Under Security Test	The area can be a single software system, multiple software systems, a processing capability such as agents interacting with the home office, or processing technology such as Internet.
Potential Perpetrators	The name of specific individuals or categories of individuals that have the potential for breaking security. All individuals or groups of individuals that may have potential should be listed, not just those the team believes have a desire to penetrate security.
Penetration Points	A specific identification of a point within an information system(s) or technology at which security can be penetrated. These are normally points where information is transferred from one unit to another, or passing of information to another processing entity.
Probability of Penetration	These are the intersection points for the probability of penetration that is described in part 1 of Task 3.
Point Totals	This is the accumulation of the probability numbers both horizontally and vertically. Horizontal equals the probability that a specific perpetrator can penetrate security. Vertical totals indicate the point at which penetration is most likely to occur.

3   A high probability of the individual penetrating at this point.

2   An average probability of the individual penetrating at this point.

1   Some probability of the individual penetrating at this point.

0   Minimal or no probability of penetration at this point.

(Continues)

WORK PAPER 24.1 *(Continued)*

Penetration Points Potential Perpetrators	1	2	3	4	5	6	7	Perpetrator Total
Point Totals								

WORK PAPER 24.2   Test Security Quality Control Checklist

Field Requirements

FIELD	INSTRUCTIONS FOR ENTERING DATA
Number	A number that sequentially identifies the quality control items, which if positively addressed would indicate that this step has been performed correctly.
Item	The specific quality control item that is used to measure the effectiveness of performing this step.
Response	The testers should indicate in this column whether they have performed the referenced item. The response can be Yes, No, or N/A if it is not appropriate for your organization's testing process.
Comments	This column is used to clarify the Yes, No, or N/A response for the item indicated. Generally the comments column need only be completed for No responses. No responses should be investigated and a determination made as to whether this item needs to be performed before this step can be considered complete.

#	ITEM	RESPONSE			COMMENTS
		YES	NO	N/A	
1.	Has a team of three or more people been put together to prepare and use the penetration point matrix?				
2.	Is there a reasonable possibility that the team members can identify all of the major potential perpetrators?				
3.	Do the team members have knowledge of the location/information system under investigation?				
4.	Is there a high probability that the team will identify all of the major potential points of penetration?				
5.	Will the team use a synergistic tool to facilitate brainstorming/discussion to identify potential perpetrators/penetration points?				
6.	Does the prepared penetration point matrix include the identified potential perpetrators and the identified potential points of penetration?				
7.	Has the team used appropriate synergistic tools (i.e., risk ranking) to rate the probability that a given perpetrator will penetrate a specific point?				
8.	Has every perpetrator and every point been analyzed?				
9.	Has the accumulation of points been performed correctly?				

WORK PAPER 24.2   *(Continued)*

#	ITEM	YES	NO	N/A	COMMENTS
		RESPONSE			
10.	Have the high-risk points been identified?				
11.	Has there been a reasonable challenge that the identified high-risk points are in fact the high-risk points of penetration?				

Testing a Data Warehouse

A data warehouse is a central repository of data made available to users. The centralized storage of data provides significant processing advantages to users, but at the same time raises concerns of the security, accessibility, and integrity of data. This chapter focuses on where testing would be most effective in determining the risks associated with those concerns.

Overview

This testing process lists the more common concerns associated with the data warehouse concept. It also explains the more common activities performed as part of a data warehouse. Testing begins by determining the appropriateness of those concerns to the data warehouse process under test. If appropriate, then the severity of those concerns must be determined. This is accomplished by relating those high-severity concerns to the data warehouse activity controls. If in place and working, the controls should minimize the concerns.

Objective

The objectives of this test are to determine whether the data warehouse activities have adequately addressed the concerns associated with the operation of the data warehouse. Those activities should address installation of the appropriate infrastructure and data controls to ensure that the concerns do not turn into data warehouse failures.

Concerns

The 14 concerns most commonly associated with a data warehouse activity are described below:

1. **Inadequate assignment of responsibilities.** There is inappropriate segregation of duties or failure to recognize placement of responsibility.

2. **Inaccurate or incomplete data in a data warehouse.** The integrity of data entered in the data warehouse is lost due to inadvertent or intentional acts.

3. **Losing an update to a single data item.** One or more updates to a single data item can be lost due to inadequate concurrent update procedures.

4. **Inadequate audit trail to reconstruct transactions.** The use of data by multiple applications may split the audit trail among those applications and the data warehouse software audit trail.

5. **Unauthorized access to data in a data warehouse.** The concentration of data may make sensitive data available to anyone gaining access to a data warehouse.

6. **Inadequate service level.** Multiple users contesting for the same resources may degrade the service to all due to excessive demand or inadequate resources.

7. **Placing data in the wrong calendar period.** Identifying transactions with the proper calendar period is more difficult in some on-line data warehouse environments than in others.

8. **Failure of data warehouse software to function as specified.** Most data warehouse software is provided by vendors, making the data warehouse administrator dependent on the vendor to assure the proper functioning of the software.

9. **Improper use of data.** Systems that control resources are always subject to misuse and abuse.

10. **Lack of skilled independent data warehouse reviewers.** Most reviewers are not skilled in data warehouse technology and thus have not evaluated data warehouse installations.

11. **Inadequate documentation.** Documentation of data warehouse technology is needed to ensure consistency of understanding and use by multiple users.

12. **Loss of continuity of processing.** Many organizations rely heavily on data warehouse technology for the performance of their day-to-day processing.

13. **Lack of criteria to evaluate.** Without established performance criteria, an organization cannot be assured that it is achieving data warehouse goals.

14. **Lack of management support.** Without adequate resources and "clout," the advantages of data warehouse technology may not be achieved.

Workbench

The workbench for testing the adequacy of the data warehouse activity is listed in Figure 25.1. The workbench is a three-task process which measures the magnitude of the

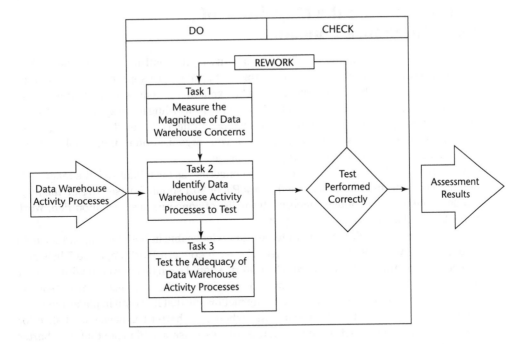

Figure 25.1 Workbench for testing a data warehouse.

concerns, identifies the data warehouse activity processes, and then determines the tests necessary to determine whether the high-magnitude concerns have been adequately addressed. Those performing the test must be familiar with the data warehouse activity processes. The end result of the test is an assessment of the adequacy of those processes to minimize the high-magnitude concerns.

Input

Organizations implementing the data warehouse activity need to establish processes to manage, operate, and control that activity. The input to this test process is a knowledge of those data warehouse activity processes. If the test team does not have that knowledge, they should be supplemented with an individual(s) possessing a detailed knowledge of the data warehouse activity processes.

Do Procedures

The three tasks included in this test process are as follows.

Task 1: Measure the Magnitude of Data Warehouse Concerns

This task involves two activities. The first activity is the confirmation that the 14 data warehouse concerns described earlier in this test process are appropriate for the organization under test. The list of concerns can be expanded or reduced. In addition, it may be advisable to change the wording of the concerns to wording more appropriate for the culture of the organization under test. For example, Concern 1 is inadequate assignment of responsibilities. If it is more appropriate in your organization to talk of job description responsibilities, make the appropriate change.

Once the list of potential data warehouse concerns has been finalized, the magnitude of those concerns must be determined. Work Paper 25.1 should be used to rate the magnitude of the data warehouse concerns. If the list of concerns has been modified, Work Paper 25.1 will also have to be modified.

To use Work Paper 25.1, a team of testers knowledgeable in both testing and the data warehouse activity should be assembled. For each concern Work Paper 25.1 lists several criteria relating to that concern. The criteria should each be answered with a Yes or No response. The test team should have a consensus on the response. A Yes response means that the criterion has been met. Being met means that it is both in place and used. For example, Criterion 1 for Concern 1 asks whether a charter has been established for a data warehouse administration function. A Yes response would mean that the charter has been established and is in fact in place and used. A No response means that either the criterion has not been established or it is not being used. The Comments column is available to clarify the Yes and No responses.

At the conclusion of rating the criteria for each concern, the percent of No responses should be calculated. For example, in Concern 1 there are seven criteria. If three of the seven criteria have a No response, then approximately 43 percent would have received a No response.

When Work Paper 25.1 has been completed, the results should be posted to Work Paper 25.2. The percent of No responses should be posted for each of the 14 concerns. The data warehouse concerns column of Work Paper 25.1 shows the percent of No responses from 0 to 100 percent. If Concern 1 received 43 percent of No responses, the bar would be completed vertically above Concern 1 on Work Paper 25.2 to 43 percent. This would put that concern in the "medium" category. At the conclusion of this task, Work Paper 25.2 will show the magnitude of the identified data warehouse concerns.

Task 2: Identify Data Warehouse Activity Processes to Test

There are many ways organizations can establish a data warehouse activity. Associated with the data warehouse are a variety of processes. The more common processes associated with the data warehouse activity are described below:

Organizational Process

The data warehouse introduces a new function into the organization. With that function comes a shifting of responsibilities. Much of this shifting involves a transfer of responsibilities from the application system development areas and the user areas to a centralized data warehouse administration function.

The introduction of the data warehouse is normally associated with the organization of a formal data warehouse administration group. This group usually reports within the data processing function, and frequently directly to the data processing manager. The objective of the data warehouse administration function is to oversee and direct the installation and operation of the data warehouse.

The data warehouse administration function normally has line responsibilities for data documentation, system development procedures, and standards for those applications using data warehouse technology. The database administrator (DBA) function also has indirect or dotted-line responsibilities to computer operations and users of data warehouse technology through providing advice and direction. In addition, the data warehouse administrator should be alert to potential problems and actively involved in offering solutions.

Studies on the success of data warehouse technology strongly indicate the need for planning. A key part of this planning is the integration of the data warehouse into the organizational structure. This integration requires some reorganization within both the data processing and user areas.

Data Documentation Process

The transition to data warehouse technology involves the switching of information technology emphasis from processing to data. Many existing systems are process driven, while data warehouse technology involves data-driven systems. This change in emphasis necessitates better data documentation.

If multiple users are using the same data, there is a need for easy-to-use and complete documentation. If there are misunderstandings regarding the data's content, reliability, consistency, and so on, this will lead to problems in the interpretation and use of data. Clear, distinct documentation helps reduce this risk.

Many organizations use standardized methods of data documentation. The simplest method is to use forms and written procedures governing the method of defining data. More sophisticated installations use data dictionaries. The data dictionary can be used as a standalone automated documentation tool or can be integrated into the processing environment. It is through this integration that adherence to data definition is assured.

The data warehouse administrator normally oversees the use of the data dictionary. This involves determining what data elements will be documented, the type and extent of documentation requested, and assurance that the documentation is up to date and in compliance with the documentation quality standards.

The documentation requirement for data is a threefold responsibility. First, individuals must be educated into the type of documentation required and provide that documentation. Second, the documentation must be maintained to ensure its accuracy and completeness. Third, the data used in the operating environment must conform to the documentation. If the data in operation is different from the documentation specifications, the entire process will collapse.

System Development Process

Data warehouse technology is designed to make system development easier; however, this occurs only when the application system fits into the existing data hierarchy. If the system requirements are outside the data warehouse structure, it may be more difficult and costly to develop that system by using the data warehouse than by using non–data warehouse methods.

The method to ensure that the applications effectively use data warehouse technology is to have data warehouse administration personnel involved in the development process. In other words, more front-end planning and assessment are required to ensure the effective use of data warehouse technology than when data warehouse is not used. This front-end effort also ensures that the application project team understands the resources available through data warehouse technology.

The data warehouse is a continually changing grouping of data. Part of the data warehouse involvement in system development is to adjust and modify the structure continually to meet the changing needs of application systems. Thus, the development process for the data warehouse is twofold: first, to ensure that the applications effectively use the data warehouse; and second, to establish new data warehouse directions in order to keep the data warehouse in step with application needs.

The system development process in the data warehouse technology has the following three objectives:

1. To familiarize the system's development people with the resources and capabilities available for their use

2. To ensure that the proposed application system can be integrated into the existing data warehouse structure, and if not, to modify the application and/or the data warehouse structure

3. To ensure that application processing will preserve the consistency, reliability, and integrity of data in the data warehouse

A problem that often surfaces in the use of data warehouse technology is how to charge for data warehouse usage. Some applications operate more effectively using the data warehouse than others. Experience has shown that moving some applications from non–data warehouse to data warehouse technology substantially reduces the cost of processing, while in other instances the cost increases. The reason for this is that the data warehouse must be optimized toward a specific data usage. Obviously, the data warehouse administrator must attempt to optimize the data warehouse toward the high-usage applications and let the usage be less efficient in the small-volume applications. Data warehouse costs should not be allowed to discourage the use of the data warehouse.

Access Control Process

One of the major concerns to management about the data warehouse is the ready accessibility of information. As more data is placed into a single repository, that repository becomes more valuable to perpetrators.

The access control function has two primary purposes. The first is to identify the resources requiring control and determine who should be authorized access to those resources. The second is to define and enforce the control specifications identified in the previous responsibility in the operating environment.

The access control function can be performed by the data warehouse administration function or an independent security officer. Obviously, an independent function is stronger than the same function that administers the data warehouse. The method selected will be dependent on the value of the information in the data warehouse and the size of the organization. The more valuable the data, or the larger the organization, the more likely it is that the function will be implemented through an independent security officer.

The enforcement of the security profile for the data warehouse in on-line systems is performed by security software. Some data warehouse management systems have security features incorporated in the data warehouse software, while others need to be supplemented by security packages. Many of the major hardware vendors, such as IBM, provide security software. However, there are several independent vendors providing general-purpose security software that interfaces with many data warehouse software systems.

The access control function has the additional responsibility of monitoring the effectiveness of security. Detecting and investigating potential access violations are important aspects of data warehouse access control. First, unless the access control procedures are monitored, violators will not be detected; and second, if violators are not reprimanded or prosecuted, there will be little incentive for other involved parties to comply with access control rules.

Data Integrity Process

The integrity of the contents of the data warehouse is the joint responsibility of the users and the data warehouse administrator. The data warehouse administrator is concerned more about the integrity of the structure and the physical records, while the users are concerned about the contents or values contained in the data warehouse.

In dedicated files, the integrity of the file is primarily the responsibility of the user. The data processing department has a responsibility to use the correct version of the file and to add those features that protect the physical integrity of the records on the file. However, the ultimate responsibility for the integrity resides with the user, and the application systems need to be constructed to ensure that integrity. This is usually accomplished by accumulating the values in one or more control fields and developing an independent control total which can be checked each time the file is used.

In a data warehouse environment, the traditional integrity responsibilities change. No longer does a single user have control over all the uses of data in a data warehouse. For example, several different application systems may be able to add, delete, or modify any single data element in the data warehouse. In an airline reservation system, any authorized agent can commit or delete a reserved seat for a flight. On the other hand, the data warehouse administrator doesn't have control over the uses of the data in the data warehouse. This means that the data integrity must be assured through new procedures.

The data integrity process may involve many different groups within an organization. These groups, such as various users and the data warehouse administration function, will share parts of this data integrity responsibility. In fulfilling data integrity responsibility, the following tasks need to be performed:

1. Identify the method of ensuring the completeness of the physical records in the data warehouse.

2. Determine the method of ensuring the completeness of the logical structure of the data warehouse (i.e., schema).

3. Determine which users have responsibility for the integrity of which segments of the data warehouse.

4. Develop methods to enable those users to perform their data integrity responsibilities.

5. Determine at what times the integrity of the data warehouse will be verified, and assure there is adequate backup data between the periods of proven data integrity.

Operations Process

The normal evolution of data warehouse operations is from the data warehouse administration function to specialized operations personnel and then to regular computer operators. This evolution is necessary so that an organization can develop the appropriate skills and methods needed for training and monitoring regular computer operators. Without taking the appropriate time to develop skills, operators may be placed into a position where their probability of success is minimal.

Data warehouse technology is more complex than non–data warehouse technology. Normally, the data warehouse is coupled with communication technology. This means that two highly technical procedures are coupled, making the resulting technology more complex than either of the contributing technologies.

Most of the day-to-day operations are performed by users. The data warehouse provides the basis for a user-operated technology. One of the advantages of the data warehouse is the powerful utilities associated with the technology that are available to the users. One of the more powerful utilities is the query languages, which provide almost unlimited capabilities for users to prepare analyses and reports using the data within the data warehouse.

Operating data warehouse technology poses the following challenges to computer operators:

- Monitoring space allocation to ensure minimal disruptions due to space management problems

- Understanding and using data warehouse software operating procedures and messages

- Monitoring service levels to ensure adequate resources for users

- Maintaining operating statistics so that the data warehouse performance can be monitored

- Reorganizing the data warehouse as necessary (usually under the direction of the data warehouse administrator) to improve performance and add capabilities where necessary

Backup/Recovery Process

One of the most technically complex aspects of data processing is recovering a crashed data warehouse. This procedure involves the following four major challenges:

1. Identifying that the integrity of the data warehouse has been lost

2. Notifying users that the data warehouse is inoperable and providing them with alternate processing means. (Note: These means should be predetermined and may be manual.)

3. Ensuring and having ready adequate backup data.

4. Performing those procedures necessary to recover the integrity of the data warehouse.

Many data warehouses are operational around the clock during business days, and some, seven days a week. It is not uncommon for many thousands of transactions to occur in a single day. Thus, unless recovery operations are well planned, it may take many hours or even days to recover the integrity of the data warehouse. The complexity and planning that must go into data warehouse contingency planning cannot be overemphasized.

The responsibility for data warehouse recovery is normally that of computer operations. However, the users and data warehouse administrators must provide input into the recovery process. The data warehouse administrator usually develops the procedures and acquires the recovery tools and techniques. The user provides the specifications on time span for recovery and determines what alternate procedures are acceptable during this period.

One of the problems encountered is notifying users that the data warehouse is no longer operational. In larger organizations, there may be many users, even hundreds of users, connected to a single data warehouse. It may take longer to notify the users that the data warehouse is not operational than it will take to get the data warehouse back on-line. The group involved in the recovery may not have adequate resources to inform all of the users. Some of the alternate procedures include:

- Messages to terminals if facilities to transmit are available
- User call-in to a recorded message indicating the data warehouse is down
- Education of users to desired service expectations, and procedures established if those expectations are not met

The backup/recovery process begins with determining what operations must be recovered and in what time frame. This provides the recovery specifications. From these specifications, the procedures are developed and implemented to meet the recovery expectations. Much of the process involves collecting and storing backup data. Backup data is defined rather than for day-to-day operational purposes. One type of data needed for recovery of the major files is the data warehouse software log. This provides sequencing and content of data warehouse transactions.

Performing Task 2

There are two events associated with performing Task 2. The first is to determine whether the above activities are appropriate to your data warehouse activity. Work Paper 25.3 can be used for that purpose. The work paper lists the seven data warehouse activity processes described above. This list can be supplemented or reduced. In addition, the process name should be changed to the specific vocabulary of the organizational culture. At the end of this task, Work Paper 25.3 will indicate which processes are appropriate for your data warehouse activity.

Task 3: Test the Adequacy of Data Warehouse Activity Processes

This task is to evaluate that each of the seven identified processes contains controls that are adequate to reduce the concerns identified earlier in this chapter. A control is any means used to reduce the probability of a failure occurring. The determination of whether the individual applications enter, store, and use the correct data will be performed using the 11-step process included in Part Three of this book.

Figure 25.2 indicates which activity processes should be tested. This figure is used by first identifying the significant data warehouse concerns. This was determined in Task 1. The check marks in the data warehouse activity process columns indicate which processes should reduce the concerns so that the probability of failure is minimized. For example, if a significant data warehouse concern is that "there is an inadequate assignment of responsibility," then the three data activity processes of organization, system development, and access control should be tested.

Figure 25.3 recommends the types of test that should be undertaken for each data warehouse activity process for the identified concerns. This figure lists the concerns and tests. The tests are those focused on determining that specific controls exist. If those controls exist, then the testers can assume that the process is adequately controlled so that the probability of failure is minimized.

Check Procedures

Work Paper 25.4 is a quality control checklist for this step. It is designed so that Yes responses indicate good test practices; No responses warrant additional investigation. A Comments column is provided to explain No responses and to record results of investigation. The N/A response is used when the checklist item is not applicable to the test situation.

Output

The output from this data warehouse test process is an assessment of the adequacy of the data warehouse activity processes to assure the activity is effectively operated. The assessment report should indicate the concerns that the test team addressed, the processes in place in the data warehouse activity, and the adequacy of those processes to insure that the concerns do not result in data warehouse failures.

Guidelines

The testing of the data warehouse activity as proposed in this chapter is one of risk assessments. It is not designed to ensure that the data warehouse will function properly for each use, but rather to appraise management of the probability that failures will be minimized or that additional management action should be taken to minimize those concerns. The actual determination of the correct processing of the warehouse should be done in conjunction with the application software that uses the data warehouse.

Data Warehouse Activity Processes / Data Warehouse Concerns	Organization	Data Documentation	System Development	Access Control	Data Integrity	Operation	Backup/Recovery
Inadequate assignment of responsibility	√		√	√			
Inaccurate or incomplete data in a database	√		√		√	√	√
Losing an update to a single data item			√		√		
Inadequate audit trail	√	√			√	√	
Unauthorized access to a database					√	√	
Inadequate service level		√			√	√	
Placing data in the wrong calendar period		√	√		√		
Failure of data warehouse software to function as specified	√	√	√		√	√	√
Fraud/embezzlement	√		√	√			
Lack of independent database reviews	√		√				
Inadequate documentation	√	√	√		√	√	√
Continuity of processing			√		√	√	
Lack of performance criteria	√		√			√	
Lack of management support	√		√	√			

√ = should be tested

Figure 25.2 Which data warehouse activities should be tested?

ORGANIZATIONAL CONTROL OBJECTIVES		
Concern Number	**Concern**	**Test should determine that a control exists**
1.	Inadequate assignment of responsibilities	1. To assign data warehouse responsibilities to individuals 2. To see that user retains organizational responsibility for the accuracy, completeness, and security of data 3. To perform independent reviews to ensure the adequate assignment of responsibilities
2.	Inaccurate or incomplete data in a data warehouse.	1. To see that the organizational structure is designed to ensure the adequate assignment of responsibilities

Figure 25.3 Organizational control objectives.   (*Continues*)

ORGANIZATIONAL CONTROL OBJECTIVES		
Concern Number	**Concern**	**Test should determine that a control exists**
8.	Failure of the data warehouse software to function as specified	1. To see that the organizational structure is designed to ensure prompt detection and correction of data warehouse software errors 2. To document data warehouse expectations
9.	Fraud/embezzlement	1. To divide responsibilities so that an individual cannot perform *and* conceal a single event
10.	Lack of independent data warehouse reviews	1. To see that a data warehouse review group is established that is independent of the data warehouse function 2. To define review responsibilities
11.	Inadequate documentation	1. To document departmental data warehouse organizational responsibilities in the department charter 2. To document individual data warehouse responsibilities in their job description
13.	Lack of performance criteria	1. To define data warehouse expectations in measurable terms
14.	Lack of management support	1. To ensure that senior management defines and enforces data policy 2. To ensure that senior management participates in data warehouse decision making 3. To ensure that senior management supports independent data warehouse review groups
DATA DOCUMENTATION CONTROL OBJECTIVES		
4.	Inadequate audit trail	1. To define data warehouse audit trail requirements 2. To divide requirements between the user and the DBA function 3. To document data warehouse deletions
7.	Placing data in the wrong calendar period	1. To define data accounting requirements
8.	Failure of data warehouse software to function as specified	1. To assign centralized control of external schema 2. To define data independently of the applications that use the data
11.	Inadequate documentation	1. To develop an inventory of data elements 2. To document data in accordance with documentation standards 3. To enforce the use of data as documented

Figure 25.3   *(Continued)*

(Continues)

SECURITY/ACCESS CONTROL OBJECTIVES		
Concern Number	**Concern**	**Test should determine that a control exists**
1.	Inadequate assignment of responsibilities	1. To assign responsibility for security to a function independent of the one requiring security
5.	Unauthorized access in the data warehouse	1. To define access to each data warehouse resource 2. To include all individuals involved in data warehouse in the access control process 3. To ensure prompt punishment of violators 4. To create logs of security-related activities
9.	Fraud/embezzlement	1. To see that security measures address the common methods of fraud
12.	Continuity of processing	1. To ensure that visitors and service personnel are escorted 2. To assess the risks of security problems on disruptions to processing
14.	Lack of management support	1. To see that management establishes the desired level of security 2. To see that management supports punishment for security violations
COMPUTER OPERATIONS ACTIVITY CONTROL OBJECTIVES		
2.	Inaccurate or incomplete data in a data warehouse	1. To ensure that data is not lost or changed due to improper operations
5.	Unauthorized access in a data warehouse	1. To physically protect the data warehouse from unauthorized access
6.	Inadequate service level	1. To minimize both the frequency and the impact of inadequate service level 2. To monitor service-level performance
8.	Failure of the data warehouse software to function as specified	1. To monitor data warehouse software failures to determine responsibility and implement fixes as appropriate
11.	Inadequate documentation	1. To document data warehouse software operating procedures and controls
12.	Continuity of processing	1. To plan for expected capacity requirements 2. To minimize data warehouse software downtime
13.	Lack of performance criteria	1. To establish data warehouse software expectations

Figure 25.3 *(Continued)*   *(Continues)*

DATA WAREHOUSE BACKUP/RECOVERY CONTROL OBJECTIVES		
Concern Number	**Concern**	**Test should determine that a control exists**
2.	Inaccurate or incomplete	1. To verify controls after recovery to ensure the integrity of the recovered data warehouse
4.	Inadequate audit trail	1. To maintain records on the recovery process
6.	Inadequate service level	1. To include segments of the application in the recovery process 2. To specify assignments 3. To retain adequate backup data
8.	Failure of the data warehouse software to function as specified	1. To test the recovery process
11.	Inadequate documentation	1. To document recovery procedures
12.	Continuity of processing	1. To determine expected failure rates 2. To specify recovery requirements 3. To define alternate processing procedures 4. To inform users about service interruptions
DATA WAREHOUSE INTEGRITY CONTROL OBJECTIVES		
2.	Inaccurate or incomplete data in a data warehouse	1. To verify the integrity of the initial population of the data warehouse 2. To validate conformance to data definition 3. To control access for data modification 4. To provide adequate backup and recovery methods 5. To preserve the integrity of the data warehouse 6. To preserve the consistency of data redundancy 7. To control the placement of data warehouse data on media and devices 8. To maintain independent data warehouse controls 9. To maintain data warehouse segment counts
3.	Losing an update to a single data item	1. To utilize concurrency and lockout controls
4.	Inadequate audit trail	1. To maintain adequate audit trails to permit reconstruction of processing

Figure 25.3   *(Continued)*

(Continues)

DATA WAREHOUSE INTEGRITY CONTROL OBJECTIVES		
Concern Number	**Concern**	**Test should determine that a control exists**
7.	Placing data in the wrong calendar period	1. To establish accounting controls to ensure that data is recorded in the proper calendar period
8.	Failure of data warehouse software to function as specified	1. To verify the proper functioning of the data warehouse software 2. To verify the correctness of the interface to the data warehouse software
11.	Inadequate documentation	1. To document the data definitions for creation of the data warehouse

SYSTEM DEVELOPMENT CONTROL OBJECTIVES			
1.	Inadequate assignment of responsibilities	Requirements	1. To divide system development responsibilities among the DBA function, the application project team, and the user
14.	Lack of management support	Requirements	1. To ensure that senior management participates in data warehouse application system planning 2. To ensure that senior management approves data warehouse application proposals
13.	Lack of performance criteria	Requirements	1. To establish performance criteria for all data warehouse applications
4.	Inadequate audit trail	Design	1. To include the audit trail in the design specifications
2.	Inaccurate or incomplete data in the data warehouse	Design	1. To include the methods of ensuring accurate and complete data in the design specifications
7.	Placing data in the wrong calendar period	Design	1. To include the accounting requirements in the design specifications

Figure 25.3   *(Continued)*   *(Continues)*

SYSTEM DEVELOPMENT CONTROL OBJECTIVES		
Concern Number / **Concern**		**Test should determine that a control exists**
11. Inadequate documentation	Program	1. To ensure that documentation conforms to data warehouse documentation standards 2. To ensure that documentation is up to date
3. Losing an update to a single data item	Program	1. To implement controls to ensure the proper sequencing of updates
10. Lack of independent data warehouse reviews group	Test	1. To establish a test plan 2. To have the test plan implemented or monitored by an independent group
9. Fraud/embezzlement	Test	1. To test the adequacy of of controls
8. Failure of the data warehouse software to function as specified	Test	1. To test to ensure that the system achieves specified performance criteria
6. Inadequate service	Installation	1. To monitor the installed application to ensure that specified performance criteria are achieved

Figure 25.3   *(Continued)*

Summary

The test process presented in this chapter is designed to assist testers in evaluating the work processes associated with a data warehouse activity. It is designed to be used in conjunction with the test of application software that uses the data warehouse. The actual processing of data from the data warehouse should be tested using the 11-step process included in Part Three of this book. However, unless adequate control procedures are in place and working, the testers cannot rely on results of the one application software test to be applicable to other data warehouse applications.

If the data warehouse activity processes are adequate to address the concerns, the testers can assume that the results of testing one application will be similar to testing other applications using the data warehouse. On the other hand, if the processes do not adequately minimize the probability of failure in the data warehouse, more extensive testing may be required of all the individual applications using the data warehouse.

Field Requirements

FIELD	INSTRUCTIONS FOR ENTERING DATA
Data Warehouse Concerns	This field contains the name of the 14 data warehouse concerns described in this chapter.
Description of Concern	This field contains the description for the 14 concerns described earlier in this chapter.
Number	This is the sequential number of the criterion for each of the concerns.
Criterion	This is the description of the criterion that must be responded to in determining the potential magnitude of the concern.
Response	This file indicates whether the criterion is adequately addressed (a Yes response) or has not been adequately addressed (a No response).
Comments	This field provides an opportunity for the test team to clarify why they made a Yes or No response to a specific criterion.
Percent of No Responses	This is a calculation of the number of No responses in relationship to the total number of responses for the criteria for a specific concern.

Data Warehouse Concern Rating

Worksheet Concern #1:   Inadequate Assignment of Responsibilities

Description of Concern:

There is inappropriate segregation of duties or failure to recognize placement of responsibility.

#	CRITERION	RESPONSE YES	RESPONSE NO	COMMENTS
1.	Has a charter been established for the database administration function outlining the role and responsibilities for the function?			
2.	Have the user responsibilities regarding the integrity of the data warehouse been defined?			
3.	Have job descriptions been modified for all individuals interfacing with the data warehouse to define their data warehouse responsibilities?			
4.	Have job descriptions been developed for full-time data warehouse administration personnel?			
5.	Has a formal method of resolving data warehouse disputes been established?			
6.	Does the organization have a data policy which outlines organizational data responsibility?			
7.	Are the functions being performed by data warehouse administration within that administration's formal role and responsibility?			
	Percent of No responses		%	

WORK PAPER 25.1   *(Continued)*

Data Warehouse Concern Rating

Worksheet Concern #2:   **Inaccurate or Incomplete Data in a Data Warehouse**

Description of Concern:

The integrity of data entered in the data warehouse is lost due to inadvertent or intentional acts.

#	CRITERION	RESPONSE		COMMENTS
		YES	NO	
1.	Has each element of data in the data warehouse been identified?			
2.	Have the data validation rules for each data element been documented?			
3.	Have the data validation rules for each data element been implemented?			
4.	Are the data validation rules adequate to ensure the accuracy of data?			
5.	Have procedures been established to ensure the consistence of redundant data elements?			
6.	Have procedures been established for the timely correction of data entry errors?			
7.	Are procedures established to promptly notify all users of the data warehouse when an inaccuracy or incomplete data condition has been identified?			
8.	Are the data warehouse administration tools and techniques adequate to ensure the consistency of redundant data elements?			
	Percent of No responses		%	

WORK PAPER 25.1   *(Continued)*

Data Warehouse Concern Rating

Worksheet Concern #3:   **Losing an Update to a Single Data Item**

Description of Concern:

One or more updates to a single data item can be lost due to inadequate concurrent update procedures.

#	CRITERION	RESPONSE YES	RESPONSE NO	COMMENTS
1.	Does the data warehouse software in use have a lockout feature to prevent concurrent updates to a single data item?			
2.	Does the data warehouse software have a feature to resolve deadlock in accessing data (for example, user A has item 1 and wants item 2, while user B has item 2 and wants item 1)?			
3	Has the sequencing of updates to the data warehouse been defined?			
4.	Are there controls in the data warehouse software to ensure that events can only be recorded in the predetermined sequence?			
5.	Have the parties that can create, update, or delete a data element been identified?			
	Percent of No responses		%	

WORK PAPER 25.1   *(Continued)*

Data Warehouse Concern Rating

Worksheet Concern #4:   Inadequate Audit Trail

Description of Concern:

The use of data by multiple applications may split the audit trail among those applications and the data warehouse software audit trail.

#	CRITERION	RESPONSE YES	RESPONSE NO	COMMENTS
1.	Has the audit trail for data warehouse applications been identified and documented?			
2.	Has the retention period for each part of the data warehouse audit trail been determined?			
3.	Is a data warehouse software log maintained?			
4.	Does management determine what information will be maintained in the data warehouse software log?			
5.	Can the audit trail trace source transactions to control totals and trace control totals back to the initiating transactions?			
6.	Can the audit trail provide the evidence needed to reconstruct transaction processing?			
7.	Is the audit trail in operation whenever the data warehouse is in operation?			
8.	Are all overrides of normal data warehouse software procedures recorded on the data warehouse software log?			
9.	Can the application audit trail records be cross-referenced to the data warehouse software log audit trail records?			
	Percent of No responses		%	

WORK PAPER 25.1   *(Continued)*

Data Warehouse Concern Rating

Worksheet Concern #5:   Unauthorized Access to Data in a Data Warehouse

---

Description of Concern:
The concentration of sensitive data may make it available to anyone gaining access to a data warehouse.

#	CRITERION	RESPONSE YES	RESPONSE NO	COMMENTS
1.	Have all of the data elements requiring security procedures been identified?			
2.	Have all of the data warehouse users been identified?			
3.	Has a user profile been established indicating which resources can be accessed by which users?			
4.	Has the enforcement of the user profile been automated?			
5.	Is the access mechanism, such as passwords, protected from unauthorized manipulation?			
6.	Has the organization established a data warehouse security officer function (note that this need not be a full-time function)?			
7.	Are security violators promptly punished?			
8.	Are formal records maintained on security violations?			
9.	Are security violation summaries presented to management in regular reports?			
	Percent of No responses		%	

WORK PAPER 25.1   *(Continued)*

Data Warehouse Concern Rating

Worksheet Concern #6: __Inadequate Service Level__

Description of Concern:

Multiple users contesting for the same resources may degrade the service to all due to excessive demand or inadequate resources.

#	CRITERION	YES	NO	COMMENTS
		RESPONSE		
1.	Has the level of service that is desired been documented?			
2.	Are procedures established to monitor the desired level of service to users?			
3.	Are users encouraged, by the use of such techniques as varying chargeout rates, to spread out their nonurgent processing?			
4.	Have the identified options to improve service when it degrades been identified?			
5.	Does the data warehouse administrator continually monitor the service level and make adjustments where appropriate?			
6.	Are steps to take established at points where service level degrades?			
7.	Do procedures identify the cause of degradation in service, such as a single user consuming exorbitant amounts of resources, so that action can be taken to eliminate those causes where appropriate?			
	Percent of No responses		%	

WORK PAPER 25.1   *(Continued)*

Data Warehouse Concern Rating

Worksheet Concern #7:   **Placing Data in the Wrong Calendar Period**

Description of Concern:
Identifying transactions with the proper calendar period is more difficult in some on-line data warehouse environments than in others.

#	CRITERION	RESPONSE YES	RESPONSE NO	COMMENTS
1.	Do procedures identify the criteria for determining into which accounting period transactions are placed?			
2.	Are all postdated transactions date-stamped to identify the accounting period in which they belong?			
3.	Are procedures established to cut off processing at the end of significant accounting periods, such as at year-end?			
4.	For applications where data must be segregated into accounting periods, are significant transactions entered both immediately before and immediately after the accounting cutoff period manually reviewed to ensure they are in the appropriate accounting period?			
5.	Are formal procedures established to move data from one accounting period to another if appropriate?			
	Percent of No responses		%	

WORK PAPER 25.1   *(Continued)*

Data Warehouse Concern Rating

Worksheet Concern #8:   **Failure of Data Warehouse Software to Function as Specified**

Description of Concern:

Most data warehouse software is provided by vendors, making the data administrator dependent on the vendor to assure the proper functioning of the software.

#	CRITERION	RESPONSE YES	RESPONSE NO	COMMENTS
1.	Have the processing expectations been determined?			
2.	Is the data warehouse software evaluated to determine that it performs in accordance with the predetermined requirements?			
3.	Is each new release of data warehouse software thoroughly tested?			
4.	Has a maintenance contract for the data warehouse software been established?			
5.	Are procedures established to identify data warehouse software problems?			
6.	Are operations personnel trained to identify and report data warehouse software problems?			
7.	Have backup procedures been developed for use in the event of a data warehouse software failure?			
8.	Are data warehouse software failures recorded and regularly reported to the data warehouse administrator?			
9.	Are the vendors promptly notified in the event of a data warehouse software problem so that they can take appropriate action?			
	Percent of No responses		%	

WORK PAPER 25.1   *(Continued)*

Data Warehouse Concern Rating

Worksheet Concern #9:   Fraud/Embezzlement

Description of Concern:
Systems that control resources are always subject to fraud and embezzlement.

#	CRITERION	RESPONSE		COMMENTS
		YES	NO	
1.	Do data warehouse administration personnel have access to the data in the data warehouse?			
2.	Has methodology been established for designing data warehouse controls?			
3.	Has the data warehouse been reviewed within the last year by an independent reviewer?			
4.	Have procedures been established to identify and report errors, omissions, and frauds to senior management?			
5.	Are all data warehouse resources access controlled?			
6.	Are passwords or other access control procedures changed at least every six months?			
7.	Are all error messages acted upon in a timely fashion?			
8.	Are deviations from normal processing investigated?			
9.	Do data validation routines anticipate and report on unusual processing?			
	Percent of No responses		%	

WORK PAPER 25.1 *(Continued)*

Data Warehouse Concern Rating

Worksheet Concern #10: <u>**Lack of Independent Data Warehouse Reviews**</u>

Description of Concern:

Most reviewers are not skilled in data warehouse technology and thus have not evaluated data warehouse installations; in addition, many auditor software packages cannot access data warehouse software.

#	CRITERION	RESPONSE YES	RESPONSE NO	COMMENTS
1.	Is there an internal audit function having jurisdiction over reviewing data warehouse technology?			
2.	Is there an EDP quality assurance group having jurisdiction over reviewing data warehouse technology?			
3.	Does either of these groups have adequate skills to perform such a review?			
4.	Has an independent review of data warehouse technology been performed within the last 12 months?			
5.	Was a report issued describing the findings and recommendations from that review?			
6.	Were the findings and recommendations reasonable based upon the current use of data warehouse technology?			
7.	Is an independent review of data warehouse technology planned during the next 12 months?			
	Percent of No responses		%	

WORK PAPER 25.1   *(Continued)*

Data Warehouse Concern Rating

Worksheet Concern #11:   Inadequate Documentation

Description of Concern:

Documentation of data warehouse technology is needed to ensure consistency of understanding and use by multiple users.

#	CRITERION	YES	NO	COMMENTS
		RESPONSE		
1.	Do data documentation standards exist?			
2.	Are data documentation standards enforced?			
3.	Is a data dictionary used to document the attributes of data elements?			
4.	Is a data dictionary integrated into the data warehouse software operation, so that the only entry into data warehouse software-controlled data is through the data dictionary?			
5.	Does the data warehouse administration group provide counsel in documenting and using data?			
6.	Does the data documentation contain the data validation rules?			
	Percent of No responses		%	

WORK PAPER 25.1 *(Continued)*

Data Warehouse Concern Rating

Worksheet Concern #12: <u>Continuity of Processing</u>

Description of Concern:

Many organizations rely heavily on data warehouse technology for the performance of their day-to-day processing.

#	CRITERION	RESPONSE YES	RESPONSE NO	COMMENTS
1.	Have the potential causes of data warehouse failure been identified?			
2.	Has the impact of each of those failures on the organization been assessed?			
3.	Have procedures been developed to continue processing during a data warehouse failure?			
4.	Are procedures established to ensure that the integrity of the data warehouse can be restored after data warehouse failure?			
5.	Has the sequence of actions necessary to restore applications after a data warehouse failure been documented?			
6.	Have computer operations personnel been trained to data warehouse recovery procedures?			
7.	Is sufficient backup data stored off-site to permit reconstruction of processing in the event of a disaster?			
8.	Are records maintained on data warehouse failures so that specific analysis can be performed?			
	Percent of No responses		%	

WORK PAPER 25.1   *(Continued)*

Data Warehouse Concern Rating

Worksheet Concern #13:   Lack of Performance Criteria

Description of Concern:
Without established performance criteria, an organization cannot be assured that it is achieving data warehouse goals.

#	CRITERION	RESPONSE YES	RESPONSE NO	COMMENTS
1.	Have measurable objectives for data warehouse technology been established?			
2.	Are those objectives monitored to determine whether they are achieved?			
3.	Can the cost associated with data warehouse technology be identified?			
4.	Can the benefits associated with data warehouse technology be identified?			
5.	Was a cost/benefit analysis prepared for the installation and operation of data warehouse technology?			
6.	Has the cost/benefit projection been monitored to measure whether those projections have been achieved?			
7.	Is the achievement of the performance criteria evaluated by an independent group, such as EDP quality assurance?			
	Percent of No responses		%	

WORK PAPER 25.1   *(Continued)*

Data Warehouse Concern Rating

Worksheet Concern #14:   <u>**Lack of Management Support**</u>

Description of Concern:

Without adequate resources and "clout," the advantages of data warehouse technology may not be achieved.

#	CRITERION	RESPONSE YES	RESPONSE NO	COMMENTS
1.	Has a member of senior management been appointed responsible for managing data for the organization?			
2.	Was senior management involved in the selection of the organization's data warehouse technology approach?			
3.	Has a review board been established comprising users, EDP personnel, and senior managers to oversee the use of data warehouse technology?			
4.	Has data processing management attended courses on the use of data warehouse technology?			
5.	Has senior management requested regular briefing and/or reports on the implementation and use of data warehouse technology?			
6.	Has senior management been involved in the preparation of a long-range plan for use of information in the organization?			
7.	Is senior management involved in the settlement of disputes over the attributes or use of information in the organization?			
	Percent of No responses		%	

WORK PAPER 25.2   Magnitude of Data Warehouse Concerns

Field Requirements

FIELD	INSTRUCTIONS FOR ENTERING DATA
% of No Responses	This column divides the percentage of No responses into three categories: low, medium, and high.
Concern Rating	The rating for the concerns listed on this work paper represents the percentages of No responses calculated for those concerns on Work Paper 25.1.
Data Warehouse Concerns	These are the 14 data warehouse concerns described earlier in this chapter.

	1.	2.	3.	4.	5.	6.	7.	8.	9.	10.	11.	12.	13.	14.
% OF NO RESPONSES CONCERN RATINGS	Inadequate assignment of responsibilities	Inaccurate or incomplete data in a database	Losing an update to a single database	Inadequate audit trail	Unauthorized access in a database	Inadequate service level	Placing data in the wrong calendar period	Failure of DBMS to function as specified	Fraud/embezzlement	Lack of independent database reviews	Inadequate documentation	Continuity of processing	Lack of performance criteria	Lack of management support

(Continues)

WORK PAPER 25.2 (Continued)

% OF NO RESPONSES	CONCERN RATINGS
100%	High
68% 67%	Medium
34% 33%	Low
0%	

WORK PAPER 25.3   Data Warehouse Activity Process

Field Requirements

FIELD	INSTRUCTIONS FOR ENTERING DATA
Item	These are each of the seven data warehouse activity processes described in this chapter, or a revised list of processes in place in your organization.
Appropriate	This indicates whether the seven generic data warehouse activity processes described in this chapter are appropriate (i.e., Yes) or not appropriate (i.e., No).
Comments	This field provides an opportunity to describe new processes and to modify descriptions of existing processes.

ITEM	APPROPRIATE			COMMENTS
	YES	NO	N/A	
1. Organizational Process				
2. Data Documentation Process				
3. System Development Process				
4. Access Control Process				
5. Data Integrity Process				
6. Operations Process				
7. Backup/Recovery Process				

WORK PAPER 25.4   Data Warehouse Quality Control Checklist

Field Requirements

FIELD	INSTRUCTIONS FOR ENTERING DATA
Number	A number that sequentially identifies the quality control items, which if positively addressed would indicate that this step has been performed correctly.
Item	The specific quality control item that is used to measure the effectiveness of performing this step.
Response	The testers should indicate in this column whether they have performed the referenced item. The response can be Yes, No, or N/A if it is not appropriate for your organization's testing process.
Comments	This column is used by to clarify the Yes, No, or N/A response for the item indicated. Generally the comments column need only be completed for No responses; No responses should be investigated and a determination made as to whether this item needs to be performed before this step can be considered complete.

#	ITEM	RESPONSE			COMMENTS
		YES	NO	N/A	
1.	Does someone assigned to the test team have data warehouse skills?				
2.	Does the tester understand the generic data warehouse concerns?				
3.	Does the final list of data warehouse concerns represent the true concerns of your organization?				
4.	Has the vocabulary in all of the work papers and figures been adjusted to the vocabulary in use in your organization?				
5.	Does the test team understand the criteria that are used to determine the magnitude of the data warehouse concerns?				
6.	Do the ratings of the magnitude of the concerns seem reasonable?				
7.	Have the data warehouse activity processes been identified?				
8.	Do the identified processes appear to represent the actual processes in use in the data warehouse activity?				
9.	Does the test team understand the controls that are needed to minimize failure in each of the data warehouse activities processes?				
10.	Does the final assessment of the test team regarding the data warehouse appear reasonable to the test team?				
11.	Does the assessment report issued by the test team appear to represent the results of the test?				

Building Test Documentation

# CHAPTER 26

Creating Test Documentation

This chapter provides guidance on preparing test documentation for the major test documents and on using that documentation. Documentation of the test process records both the tests to be performed and the results of those tests. Computer testing is too complex not to formalize the process. Documentation is an integral part of the formalization of testing. Test documentation is important for conducting the test and for the reuse of the test program during maintenance. Test documentation should be continually updated. Testing should be covered by the same documentation standards as are other types of system documentation. The more structured the documentation, the easier it is to update and reuse. This chapter provides the recommended documentation for the test plan and the report explaining the analysis of the test. Recommended tables of contents for both types of test documentation are presented together with an explanation of each component of the table of contents.

Uses

The test documentation should be an integral part of the documentation of application systems. Information services documentation standards should specify the type and extent of test documentation to be prepared and maintained. The type and extent of documentation needed will depend on its usefulness. Test documentation should commence in the requirements phase and continue through the life of the project. The test process that has been outlined in each phase of the life cycle should be documented. The uses for that documentation include:

Verify correctness of requirements. Test documentation defines test conditions to verify the correctness of the requirements. An evaluation of those test conditions by the project team is frequently helpful in clarifying the intent of user requirements.

Improve user understanding of information services. Involving users in the test process provides them with an appreciation of the complexity and detail required to develop and operate an automated application. As users prepare test documentation, they develop an appreciation for the systems development process.

Improve user understanding of application systems. If the users can prepare test conditions, and document those conditions, they will gain an understanding of the application system in the process. It is impossible to create the test conditions and produce the expected results from those conditions without understanding in detail how the application system works. This also helps the users clarify what they want from the system.

Justify test resources. Documenting the test plan specifies the tasks that need to be performed in the test process. The same documentation can be used to identify the resources needed for testing, and thus justify the use of those resources. If an effective test plan is developed, and resources are not made available for testing, it will be known in advance.

Determine test risk. The completeness of the test plan, and the allocation of resources to accomplish that plan, will provide the user with an understanding of what testing can and cannot do. Understanding the test risk will help the user either prepare for potential problems or authorize additional test resources.

Create test transactions. The documentation should become the basis for creating the transactions that will test the application system. The documentation can include the test transactions on a character-by-character basis, or explain the information needed to test the identified conditions.

Evaluate test results. The documentation should contain the expected results from each test transaction. This analysis may be manual or the results may be converted to machine-readable media and the verification process automated.

Retest the system. The test plan and selected test conditions provide the basis for retesting the application throughout the maintenance phase.

Analyze the effectiveness of the test. Documenting the test results provides a basis for analysis of the soundness of the application system and to substantiate that opinion to concerned parties.

Types

The two general categories of test documentation are:

1. **Test plan.** The plan for the testing of the application system, including detailed specifications, descriptions, and procedures for all tests, and test data reduction and evaluation criteria.

2. **Test analysis documentation.** Documentation that covers the test analysis results and findings; presents the demonstrated capabilities and deficiencies for review; and provides a basis for preparing a statement of the application system readiness for implementation.

The documentation may be manual or automated. Generally, automating the documentation increases its usefulness. It is particularly valuable to have test transactions and the expected results of those transactions on a machine that can read the specific data. Experience has shown that documentation on machine-readable media is updated more frequently and more effectively than manually written documentation.

Responsibility

The responsibility for the preparation of test documentation will depend on the group assigned test responsibility. For example, if the project team is responsible for testing, they should prepare and maintain the test documentation; if an independent test team is established, they should be assigned that responsibility. Test documentation is prepared over an extended period of time. Numerous parties will be involved in this process, as has been described in the chapters of this book outlining the test process for each phase of the life cycle. These parties include information services personnel, users, and professional testers. Each of these will contribute to the test documentation, but one individual or group should be assigned responsibility for that documentation. The recommended approach to testing an application system is the establishment of a test team. This team should be given responsibility for testing throughout the life cycle and during maintenance. When such a team is established, the team should have responsibility for maintenance of the test documentation.

Storage

The test documentation is a part of the systems documentation; therefore, it should be stored with the system documentation. However, it should be clearly identified as test documentation and not intermixed with the other documentation. It is recommended that documentation be stored by type. The test plan documentation should be stored in one container, and the results in another. Each should include a table of contents outlining each piece of information in the documentation and where that information is located. For example, information contained on computer media may be stored in the data library. Computer-maintained documentation may be in a documentation library, while other documentation could be stored in a test notebook.

Test Plan Documentation

The test plan outlines the process to be followed in testing the application system. It includes the plan, the specifications for the test and how those tests will be evaluated, plus the description of the tests themselves. The information in the test plan may be minimal during the requirements phase, but will continue to grow throughout the developmental life cycle.

A recommended table of contents for the test plan documentation is illustrated in Figure 26.1. The table of contents divides the documentation into four sections: Section 1 contains general information; section 2 contains the test plan itself; section 3 describes the test specifications, the methods and constraints for conducting the test, and the evaluation process; and section 4 contains the test descriptions (i.e., test conditions). Each item in the table of contents is individually described below.

Section 1: General Information

1.1   *Summary.* This item summarizes the functions of the application system and the tests to be performed.

1.2   *Environment and Pretest Background.* This item summarizes the history of the project. It is used to identify the user organization and the computer center where the testing will be performed. It also describes any prior testing and notes results that may affect this testing. This pretest background is particularly helpful in later phases of the life cycle.

1.3   *References.* References that are helpful in preparing for the test or conducting the test should be listed, such as:

a.   Project request (authorization)

b.   Previously published documents on the project (project deliverables)

c.   Documentation concerning related projects

d.   Testing policies, standards, and procedures

e.   Books and articles describing test processes, techniques, and tools

Section 2: Plan

2.1   *Software Description.* At a minimum, this section should contain the flowchart of the application system and a brief description of the inputs, outputs, and functions of the application system that are being tested. This description will provide a frame of reference for the test conditions. It is frequently advisable to cross-reference to application system documentation that provides this type of information.

2.2   *Milestones.* Identifies the milestone events, where they will occur, and the dates on which the milestones should be achieved. Responsibility for accomplishing the milestone events may also be listed.

2.3   *Testing (Identify Location).* This section identifies the participating organizations in the test process and the locations where the software will be tested. This section will be repeated for each test that will be performed during the testing of the application system. A generalized test plan may be prepared for systems maintenance, rather than providing a different section for each appropriate test.

RECOMMENDED TABLE OF CONTENTS

SECTION 1. GENERAL INFORMATION
1.1   Summary
1.2   Environment and Pretest Background
1.3   References

SECTION 2. PLAN
2.1   Software Description
2.2   Milestones
2.3   Testing (Identify Location)
    2.3.1   Schedule
    2.3.2   Requirements
    2.3.3   Testing Materials
    2.3.4   Test Training
2.4   Testing (Identify Location)

SECTION 3. SPECIFICATIONS AND EVALUATION
3.1   Specifications
    3.1.1   Requirements
    3.1.2   Software Functions
    3.1.3   Test/Function Relationships
    3.1.4   Test Progression
3.2   Methods and Constraints
    3.2.1   Methodology
    3.2.2   Conditions
    3.2.3   Extent
    3.2.4   Data Recording
    3.2.5   Constraints
3.3   Evaluation
    3.3.1   Criteria
    3.3.2   Data Reduction

SECTION 4. TEST DESCRIPTIONS
4.1   Test (Identify)
    4.1.1   Control
    4.1.2   Inputs
    4.1.3   Outputs
    4.1.4   Procedures
4.2   Test (Identify)

TEST PLAN

1.   GENERAL INFORMATION
    1.1   Summary. Summarize the functions of the software and the tests to be performed.
    1.2   Environment and Pretest Background. Summarize the history of the project. Identify the user organization and computer center where the testing will be performed. Describe any prior testing and note results that may affect this testing.
    1.3   References. List applicable references, such as:

Figure 26.1   Test plan documentation.   *(Continues)*

a) Project request (authorization)
b) Previously published documents on the project
c) Documentation concerning related projects
d) Testing policies, standards, and procedures
e) Books and articles describing test processes, techniques, and tools

2. PLAN
   2.1 Software Description. Provide a chart and briefly describe the inputs, outputs, and functions of the software being tested as a frame of reference for the test descriptions.
   2.2 Milestones. List the locations, milestone events, and dates for the testing.
   2.3 Testing (Identify Location). Identify the participating organizations and the location where the software will be tested.
      2.3.1 Schedule. Show the detailed schedule of dates and events for the testing at this location. Such events may include familiarization, training, data, as well as the volume and frequency of the input.
      2.3.2 Requirements. State the resource requirements, including:
         a) Equipment. Show the expected period of use, types, and quantities of the equipment needed.
         b) Software. List other software that will be needed to support the testing that is not part of the software to be tested.
         c) Personnel. List the numbers and skill types of personnel that are expected to be available during the test from both the user and the development groups. Include any special requirements such as multishift operation or key personnel.
      2.3.3 Testing Materials. List the materials needed for the test, such as:
         a) Documentation
         b) Software to be tested and its medium
         c) Test inputs and sample outputs
         d) Test control software and worksheets
      2.3.4 Test Training. Describe or reference the plan for providing training in the use of the software being tested. Specify the types of training, personnel to be trained, and the training staff.
   2.4 Testing (Identify Location). Describe the plan for the second and subsequent locations where the software will be tested in a manner similar to paragraph 2.3.

3. SPECIFICATIONS AND EVALUATION
   3.1 Specifications.
      3.1.1 Requirements. List the functional requirements by earlier documentation.
      3.1.2 Application Functions. List the detailed application functions to be exercised during the overall test. Consider including a test matrix in this section.
      3.1.3 Test/Function Relationships. List the tests to be performed on the software and relate them to the functions in paragraph 3.1.2.
      3.1.4 Test Progression. Describe the manner in which progression is made from one test to another so that the entire test cycle is completed.

Figure 26.1   *(Continued)*   *(Continues)*

3.2 Methods and Constraints
    3.2.1 Methodology. Describe the general method or strategy of the testing.
    3.2.2 Conditions. Specify the type of input to be used, such as live or test data, as well as the volume and frequency of the input.
    3.2.3 Extent. Indicate the extent of the testing, such as total or partial. Include any rationale for partial testing.
    3.2.4 Data Recording. Discuss the method to be used for recording the test results and other information about the testing.
    3.2.5 Constraints. Indicate anticipated limitations on the test due to test conditions, such as interfaces, equipment, personnel, data bases.
3.3 Evaluation.
    3.3.1 Criteria. Describe the rules to be used to evaluate test results, such as range of data values used, combinations of input types used, maximum number of allowable interrupts or halts.
    3.3.2 Data Reduction. Describe the techniques to be used for manipulating the test data into a form suitable for evaluation, such as manual or automated methods, to allow comparison of the results that should be produced to those that are produced.

4. TEST DESCRIPTIONS
  4.1 Test (Identify). Describe the test to be performed.
    4.1.1 Methods to Control the Test Process. Describe the test control, such as manual, semiautomatic, or automatic insertion of inputs, sequencing of operations, and recording of results.
    4.1.2 Inputs. Describe the input data and input commands used during the test.
    4.1.3 Outputs. Describe the output data expected as a result of the test and any intermediate messages that may be produced.
    4.1.4 Procedures. Specify the step-by-step procedures to accomplish the tests. Include test setup, initialization, steps, and termination.
  4.2 Test (Identify). Describe the second and subsequent tests in a manner similar to that used in paragraph 4.1.

Figure 26.1 *(Continued)*

2.3.1 *Schedule.* Shows the detailed schedule of dates and events for the testing at this location. Such events may include familiarization, training, data, as well as the volume and frequency of the input.

2.3.2 *Requirements.* States the resource requirements, including:

    a. *Equipment.* Show the expected period of use, types, and quantities of the equipment needed.

    b. *Software.* List other software that will be needed to support the testing that is not part of the software to be tested.

    c. *Personnel.* List the numbers and skill types of personnel that are expected to be available during the test from both the user and development groups. Include any special requirements such as multishift operation or key personnel.

    2.3.3 *Testing Materials.* List the materials needed for the test, such as:

       a. Documentation

       b. Software to be tested and its medium

       c. Test inputs and sample outputs

       d. Test control software and work papers

    2.3.4 *Test Training.* Describe or reference the plan for providing training in the use of the software being tested. Specify the types of training, personnel to be trained, and the training staff.

  2.4 *Testing (Identify Location).* Describe the plan for the second and subsequent locations where the application system will be tested in a manner similar to paragraph 2.3.

Section 3: Specifications and Evaluation

  3.1 *Specifications.* This section describes the test conditions to be evaluated during the test process. Test matrices are an effective means of documenting test specifications. At a minimum, the test specification documentation should include:

    3.1.1 *Requirements.* List the functional requirements established by earlier documentation.

    3.1.2 *Software Functions.* List the detailed application functions to be exercised during the overall test. Consider including a test matrix in this section.

    3.1.3 *Test/Function Relationships.* List the tests to be performed on the software and relate them to the functions in paragraph 3.1.2.

    3.1.4 *Test Progression.* Describe the manner in which progression is made from one test to another so that the entire test cycle is completed.

  3.2 *Methods and Constraints.* This section should outline the test process. Organizations that have a well-established test structure, standards, guidelines, and procedures may only need minimal documentation for this section. Where well-established test standards exist, one of the main objectives of this section will be to identify standards that are not applicable to the testing of this application system. The information that can be included in this section is:

    3.2.1 *Methodology.* Describe the general method or strategy of the testing.

    3.2.2 *Conditions.* Specify the type of input to be used, such as live or test data, as well as the volume and frequency of the input.

    3.2.3 *Extent.* Indicate the extent of the testing, such as total or partial. Include any rationale for partial testing.

    3.2.4 *Data Recording.* Discuss the method to be used for recording the test results and other information about the testing.

3.2.5   *Constraints*. Indicate anticipated limitations on the test due to test conditions, such as interfaces, equipment, personnel, databases.

3.3   *Evaluation*. Explain the process that will be used to evaluate the test results. If the test verifies that the application conforms to the criteria described in this section of the test plan, the application should be considered ready to be placed in a production status, and the test process complete. Specifically, this section should include:

3.3.1   *Criteria*. Describe the rules to be used to evaluate test results, such as range of data values used, combinations of input types used, maximum number of allowable interrupts or halts.

3.3.2   *Data Reduction*. Describe the technique to be used for manipulating the test data into a form suitable for evaluation, such as manual or automated methods, to allow comparison of the results that should be produced to those that are produced.

Section 4: Test Descriptions

4.1   *Test (Identify)*. This section describes the test to be performed. Section 2.3 described the location and administrative aspects of each test to be conducted. A corresponding section for each test will describe in detail the test to be performed. These sections may be very lengthy, and some of the information may be included on computer media. At a minimum this section should include:

4.1.1   *Control*. Describe the test control, such as manual, semiautomatic, or automatic insertion of inputs, sequencing of operations, and recording of results.

4.1.2   *Inputs*. Describe the input data expected as a result of the test and any intermediate messages that may be produced.

4.1.3   *Outputs*. Describe the output data expected as a result of the test and any intermediate messages that may be produced.

4.1.4   *Procedures*. Specify the step-by-step procedures to accomplish the test. Include test set-up, initialization, steps, and termination.

4.2   *Test (Identify)*. Describe the second and subsequent tests in a manner similar to that used in paragraph 4.1.

Test Analysis Report Documentation

The test analysis report documents the results of the test. It serves the dual purposes of recording the results for analysis, and a means to report those analyses to involved parties. The information contained in this document can be used to evaluate the effectiveness of the department's test process. An analysis of the results of the testing of multiple applications will indicate which processes are effective and which are not. This information can be used to modify and approve the test methods used by information services organizations.

A recommended table of contents for the test analysis report documentation is illustrated in Figure 26.2. The proposed table of contents contains four sections. Section 1 provides general information about the test; section 2 documents the test results and findings; section 3 documents the application findings; and section 4 summarizes the analysis of the tests of the application system. Each of the items contained in the recommended table of contents are individually described below.

RECOMMENDED TABLE OF CONTENTS

SECTION 1. GENERAL INFORMATION
1.1   Summary
1.2   Environment
1.3   References

SECTION 2. TEST RESULTS AND FINDINGS
2.1   Test (Identify)
      2.1.1   Dynamic Data Performance
      2.1.2   Static Data Performance
2N   Test (Identify)

SECTION 3. SOFTWARE FUNCTION FINDINGS
3.1   Function (Identify)
      3.1.1   Performance
      3.1.2   Limits
3N   Function (Identify)

SECTION 4. ANALYSIS SUMMARY
4.1   Capabilities
4.2   Deficiencies
4.3   Recommendations and Estimates
4.4   Opinion

TEST ANALYSIS REPORT

1.   GENERAL INFORMATION
    1.1   Summary. Summarize both the general functions of the software tested and the test analysis performed.
    1.2   Environment. Identify the application developer, user organization, and the computer center where the software is to be installed. Assess the manner in which the test environment may be different from the operational environment and the effects of this difference on the tests.
    1.3   References. List applicable references, such as:
        a)   Project request (authorization)
        b)   Previously published documents on the project
        c)   Documentation concerning related projects

Figure 26.2   Test analysis report documentation.   *(Continues)*

2. TEST RESULTS AND FINDINGS
    2.1   Test (Identify)
        2.1.1   Dynamic Data Performance. Compare the dynamic data input and output results, including the output of internally generated data, of this test with the dynamic data input and output requirements. State the findings.
        2.1.2   Static Data Performance. Compare the static data input and output results, including the output of internally generated data, of this test with the static data input and output requirements. State the findings.
    2N   Test (Identify). Present the results and findings of the second and succeeding tests in a manner similar to that of paragraph 2.1.

3. SOFTWARE FUNCTION FINDINGS
    Identify and describe the findings on each function separately in paragraphs 3.1 through 3N.
    3.1   Function (Identify)
        3.1.1   Performance. Describe briefly the function. Describe the software capabilities that were designed to satisfy this function. State the findings as to the demonstrated capabilities from one or more tests.
        3.1.2   Limits. Describe the range of data values tested, including both dynamic and static data. Identify the deficiencies, limitations, and constraints detected in the software during the testing with respect to this function.
    3N   Function (Identify). Present the findings on the second and succeeding functions in a manner similar to that of paragraph 3.1.

4. ANALYSIS SUMMARY
    4.1   Capabilities. Describe the capabilities of the application system as demonstrated by the tests. Where tests were to demonstrate fulfillment of one or more specific performance requirements, prepare findings showing the comparison of the results with these requirements. Assess the effects of any differences in the test environment as compared to those the operational environment may have had on this test demonstration of capabilities.
    4.2   Deficiencies. Describe the deficiencies of the application system as demonstrated by the tests. Describe the impact of each deficiency on the performance of the application. Describe the cumulative or overall impact on performance of all detected deficiencies.
    4.3   Recommendations and Estimates. For each deficiency provide any estimates to time and effort required for its correction and any recommendations as to:
        a)   The urgency of each correction
        b)   Parties responsible for corrections
        c)   How the corrections should be made
    4.4   Opinion. State the readiness for implementation of the application to be placed into production or proceed to the next phase of the SDLC.

Figure 26.2 *(Continued)*

Section 1: General Information

This is an overview of the application being tested and the test process. The information that could be included in this section is:

1.1 *Summary.* Summarize both the general function of the application system tested and the test analysis performed on the results of those tests.

1.2 *Environment.* Identify the application, developer, user organization, and the computer center where the software is to be installed. Asses the manner in which the test environment may be different from the operational environment and the effects of this difference on the tests.

1.3 *References.* List applicable references, such as:

    a. Project request (authorization)

    b. Previously published documents on the project

    c. Documentation concerning related projects

Section 2: Test Results and Findings

This section should identify and present the results and findings of each test separately as described in paragraph 2.1. The results of subsequent tests would be identified in future sections following the same format as outlined in paragraph 2.1.

2.1 *Test (Identify).* For each test performed one or both of the following analyses should be included:

    2.1.1 *Dynamic Data Performance.* Compare the dynamic data input and output results, including the output of internally generated data, of this test with the dynamic data input and output requirements. State the findings.

    2.1.2 *Static Data Performance.* Compare the static data input and output results, including the output of internally generated data, of this test with the static data input and output requirements. State the findings.

2.3 *Test (Identify).* Present the results and findings of the second and succeeding tests in a manner similar to that of paragraph 2.1.

Section 3: Software Function Findings

This section identifies and describes the findings of each function identified for test purposes. Each finding should be described individually using the format outlined in paragraph 3.1.

3.1 *Function (Identify)*

    3.1.1 *Performance.* Describe briefly the function. Describe the software capabilities that were designed to satisfy this function. State the findings as to the demonstrated capabilities from one or more tests.

    3.1.2 *Limits.* Describe the range of data values tested, including both dynamic and static data. Identify the deficiencies, limitations, and constraints detected in the software during the testing with respect to this function.

3.2   *Function (Identify)*. Present the findings on the second and succeeding functions in a manner similar to that of paragraph 3.1.

Section 4: Analysis Summary

This section summarizes the results of conducting the test. At a minimum it should include:

4.1   *Capabilities*. Describe the capabilities of the application system as demonstrated by the tests. Where tests were to demonstrate fulfillment of one or more specific performance requirements, prepare findings showing the comparison of the results with these requirements. Assess the effects of any differences in the test environment as compared to those the operational environment may have had on this test demonstration of capabilities.

4.2   *Deficiencies*. Describe the deficiencies of the application system as demonstrated by the tests. Describe the impact of each deficiency on the performance of the application. Describe the cumulative or overall impact on performance of all detected deficiencies.

4.3   *Recommendations and Estimates*. For each deficiency provide any estimates of time and effort required for its correction and any recommendations concerning:

   a.   The urgency of each correction

   b.   Parties responsible for corrections

   c.   How the corrections should be made

4.4   *Opinion*. State the readiness for implementation of the application to be placed into production or to proceed to the next phase of the SDLC.

Summary

Test documentation is needed for three purposes:

1. To record the planning and results of testing

2. To use when the software is changed and will be retested

3. As evidence in any lawsuit challenging the adequacy of software testing

This chapter describes the basic documentation that software testers should prepare. This documentation should be a by-product of the 11-step testing process. The documentation has two purposes. First, to aid in initial system testing, and secondly, to aid testers in testing the software after it has been changed. Retesting involves most of the same testing steps described in this book.

Bibliography

Beizer, Boris, *Software Testing Techniques*, Second Edition. New York: Van Nostrand Reinhold Co., 1990.

Boehm, Barry, *Software Risk Management*. New York: IEEE Computer Society, 1990.

DeMarco, Tom, *Controlling Software Projects: Management, Measurement, and Estimation*. Englewood Cliffs, NJ: Prentice-Hall, 1986.

Gilb, Tom, et al., *Software Inspection*. Reading, MA: Addison-Wesley Publishing Co., 1993.

Humphrey, Watts S., *A Discipline for Software Engineering*. Reading, MA: Addison-Wesley Publishing Co., 1995.

Jones, Capers, *Assessment and Control of Software Risks*. Englewood Cliffs, NJ: Yourdon Press Computing Services, 1993.

Jones, Capers, *Critical Problems in Software Measurement*. Carlsbad, CA: Infosystems Management, 1993.

Lewis, Robert O., *Independent Verification & Validation: A Life Cycle Engineering Process for Quality Software*. New York: John Wiley & Sons, 1992.

McConnell, Steve, *Software Project Survival Guide*. Redmond, WA: Microsoft Press, 1998.

Musa, John D., *Software Reliability: Professional Edition*. New York: McGraw-Hill Book Co., 1990.

Perry, William E., *Year 2000 Software Testing*. New York: John Wiley & Sons, 1999.

Rice, Randall and Perry, William E., *Surviving the Top Ten Challenges of Software Testing*. New York: Dorset House, 1997.

Schulmeyer, W. Gordon and McManus, James, *Total Quality Management for Software*. New York; Van Nostrand Reinhold Co., 1992.

Index

Acceptance criteria, 136
  defining, 467–469
Acceptance decisions,
  481–482
Acceptance issues, examples
  of, 468–469
Acceptance plan
  developing, 470–471
  executing, 471–481
Acceptance testing, 461–482
  check procedures for, 482
  do procedures for, 467–482
  guidelines for, 482
  objectives in, 463–464
  tester concerns for, 464–465
Acceptance test report, 514
Acceptance test software
  process validation, for off-
  the-shelf software, 707–709
Acceptance tests/reviews,
  conducting, 471–481
Access control, data warehousing, 759. *See also*
  Security testing
Access procedures, 321
Algebraic specification, 126
Analysis, 123
  data flow, 127
  functional, 124
  structural, 127–129
Analysis errors, 45
Application fit concept,
  99–100

Application functioning, Web-
  based systems, 681
Application risks, general,
  281–286
Applications
  automated segments of,
  571–572
  manual segments of,
  572–573
Application systems, docu-
  menting problems with,
  537–538
Assessment check proce-
  dures, 14–15
Assessment objectives, 603
Assessment questionnaires,
  11–12
Assessment team, 10–11
Assistant tool manager,
  154–155
ATM system use case defini-
  tion, 475
ATM Test Case Worksheet,
  477–481
Audit trail, 320, 376, 432
Authorization rules, 320, 375
Authorization testing, 432
Automated testing, 102–103
Axiomatic specifications,
  126

Backup/recovery control, in
  data warehousing, 765

Backup/recovery process,
  data warehousing, 761–762
Batch testing, 228, 229
Black box testing, 67
Boundary value analysis,
  136
Branch testing, 128
Browser configuration,
  682–683
Business fit, of off-the-shelf
  software, 698–701
Business process validation,
  685
Business risks, 52
Business system work flow,
  off-the-shelf software and,
  703–705

Cascading effect, 115
Cause-effect graphing, 136
Causes, documentation of,
  437
Checklists, 136
Checkpoint administration,
  defining, 232
Check procedures, 165, 204
  acceptance testing, 482
  client/server system testing,
  626
  data warehouse testing, 768
  design phase testing, 325
  multiplatform environment
  testing, 728–729